Views on U.S. Economic and Business History

Molding the Mixed Enterprise Economy

Edited by
Jack Blicksilver

Department of Economics
Georgia State University

Research Monograph No. 95
1985

Business Publishing Division
COLLEGE OF BUSINESS ADMINISTRATION
GEORGIA STATE UNIVERSITY
Atlanta, Georgia 30303-3093

Library of Congress Cataloging in Publication Data

Main entry under title:

Views on U.S. economic and business history.

   1. United States—Economic conditions—Addresses, essays,
lectures. 2. United States—Industries—History—Addresses, essays,
lectures. I. Blicksilver, Jack. II. Title: Views on United States economic and
business history.
HC103.V52   1984   330.973   83-25404
ISBN 0-88406-165-5

Published by:
Business Publishing Division
College of Business Administration
Georgia State University
University Plaza
Atlanta, Georgia 30303-3093
Telephone: 404/658-4253

88 87 86 85   4 3 2 1

Georgia State University, a unit of the University System of Georgia, is an
equal educational opportunity institution and an equal opportunity/
affirmative action employer.

Printed in the United States of America

Cover design by Marcia Lampe

To the authors whose contributions spanning three and one-half centuries illuminate significant facets of the nation's evolving economy; and to the readers who will shape the economy's pace and performance into the twenty-first century.

Contents

PART IV

**The Shaping of the National Economy:
1860 to the Turn of the Century**

PART V

**Large-scale Enterprise, Finance Capitalism,
and the Roller-coaster Economy, 1900-1945**

PART VI

The Mixed Enterprise Economy in Transition, 1945-Present

Preface

The compiler of an anthology has an obligation to both contributors and potential readers to explain its purpose and the criteria for the selections used. This collection of readings is designed primarily to make a broad range of scholarly articles and contemporary points of view accessible to students of United States economic and business history. The rationale for its particular approach to the subject is rooted in the conviction that a vital interaction exists between the pace and performance of the aggregate economy and the economic behavior of the units—entrepreneurs, business firms, consumers—that are its prime participants. Additionally, in the evolution of the American mixed enterprise system, government at all levels historically has played a prime role.

The readings included in this collection focus on major facets of the changing fortune of the U.S. economy as well as on the contributions of significant businessmen and firms dating from the economy's emergence within the mercantilistic environment of the seventeenth century until its post-1976 entry into the third century of national existence. The specific readings were selected with several criteria in mind. These include: (1) to make students aware of the contributions of major scholars in the subject matter discipline; (2) to convey the inherent complexity in a range of controversial issues punctuating the historical transition of the U.S. economy; and (3) to illustrate through the inclusion of case studies of business leaders and significant firms the constant interaction between the micro units and the macro performance of the economy.

The readings are diverse in length and scope, befitting the richness of the literature. They reflect the belief of the compiler that the study of economic and business history is a stimulating, highly relevant subject, well deserving a place in the curriculum not only of students majoring in Economics and History, but of all students who wish to gain more insight into the range of forces molding the current status and future direction of the economic system within which they will participate both as producers and consumers. If the readings that follow succeed in arousing student interest, serve as a basis for stimulating class discussion and subsequent individual reflection, and at least in some few instances entice readers to stalk the stacks of their libraries in search of related materials on the range of issues explored, the purpose of the compiler will be richly fulfilled.

In the preparation of such a volume of readings numerous obligations are incurred. R. Cary Bynum, director of the Business Publishing Division of Georgia State University's College of Business Administration, perceived the potential of such an anthology and consistently extended encouragement as the project evolved. A number of anonymous reviewers of earlier drafts of the proposal provided sound advice that helped shape the subsequent choice of selections. Members of the staff of the Business Publishing Division, and especially Elizabeth C. Brooks, Margaret F. Stanley, and Michal N. Yanson, were unvaryingly helpful and encouraging during the early, vital stages of the project. The chairman of the Department of Economics at Georgia State University, Dr. Francis W. Rushing, provided needed support in making available members of the staff and departmental facilities. I am much indebted to research assistants Chen-Der Chou, Cheng Hwa Lee, and Robert E. Johnson for help in locating materials and to the excellent reference staff of the university's main library. In such a project as mine, the time and talents of the immediate family are inevitably tapped, and exploited. Mine was enormously supportive and helpful. The experiences of Professor Edith Blicksilver in assembling her award-winning anthology, *The Ethnic American Woman* (Kendall/Hunt, 1981), enabled me to avoid many pitfalls. Robert Blicksilver located a hard-to-find selection in the University of North Carolina at Chapel Hill library and duplicated it for me. Diane Blicksilver, from her present base in Boston, offered assistance in tracking down the copyright holder of a key selection. The extensive social science collection in Paul Blicksilver's Aspen Book Shop contained a considerable number of anthologies that served as useful guides. Finally, my greatest debt of gratitude goes to Mrs. Helen Gatlin and Ms. Mary Ann Maguire of the Economics Department, who typed the heavily edited manuscript with exceptional competence and unfailing good humor.

PART ONE

CONCEPTS AND INSTITUTIONS: GOALS AND FORCES SHAPING THE AMERICAN ECONOMY

1

The Relation of Economic History to Economic Theory

T. S. ASHTON

. . . By training I am more of an economist than a historian. In the first decade of this century I was one of a small group of students at Manchester who took draughts of Marshallian theory at the hands of Sydney Chapman. . . . Chapman, like Marshall himself, always insisted that high theory must be supplemented by realistic and historical investigation; it was under his direction that I made a few halting enquiries into the growth of businesses in the textile industries. Some years later, as lecturer in Economics at Manchester, I had the supreme fortune to be the colleague of one whom Eileen Power spoke as the most original of English economic historians—a man in whom faith and scepticism, tenderness and irony, daring speculation and austere scholarship were combined in a way that only a biographer of exceptional insight and skill could possibly convey to those who had not been in daily contact with him. . . . The personality of George Unwin was magnetic. One by one, the young theorists ceased to

T.S. Ashton, "The Relation of Economic History to Economic Theory," *Economica,* New Series, Vol. XIII (May, 1946), pp. 81-95, initially an Inaugural Lecture delivered at the London School of Economics and Political Science, University of London, on 7 February 1946. Excerpted and reprinted by permission of Tieto, Ltd., on behalf of *Economica.*

twitter in their nests of indifference curves and fluttered down to earth. If only the first World War had not deflected Chapman's abilities from academic life to government service, if only it had not broken Unwin's constitution, Manchester might have effected that synthesis of theory and history about which, at a later stage, I propose to offer a few remarks.

These autobiographical details have been mentioned, not out of egotism, but simply in order to explain how it has come about that one who until recently made a living by teaching Currency and Public Finance now appears in the robe of the historian. When I think of the superb equipment of my predecessor in this Chair, of the learning that she bore so lightly, of her gifts of speech, of her literary grace and wit, of her personal charm, I can only say that the early death of Eileen Power was a catastrophe to historical studies comparable to that occasioned by the death of Unwin. ...

One thing at least, however, I have in common with Eileen Power—there is her own word for it—a constitutional inaptitude for philosophic speculation. That is why I shall not attempt this afternoon to discuss at any length the ultimate purposes of the study of economic history. I will say only this. Interest in history, so it seems to me, arises out of the simple delight we all take in watching things grow—whether it be babies, or puppies, or delphiniums, or social institutions. That in itself would make the study worthwhile. But the adult mind asks for something more than narrative. ... It is not satisfied with the book that is "all story and no reflection." It seeks not only to see things grow, but also to know how things grow, and what circumstances are favourable, and what hostile, to growth. Now historians, political, constitutional, and economic alike, are doing their best to satisfy that demand. They are increasingly preoccupied less with the configuration and more with the geological structure of their territories. Or, to change the metaphor, they are looking less to the physiognomy, and more to the bony framework and organic processes, of the societies with which they are concerned. ... It is, of course, true that every historical fact is unique, just as it is true that every individual body and soul is unique. But the uniqueness of the individual does not preclude the possibility of statistical generalisation where large groups are concerned. Economic history—whatever may or may not be true of political history—is concerned with large groups: with the general, rather than with the particular; with processes, rather than with events; with the typical, representative, or statistical fact, rather than with the unique, individual fact. And it is about such groups, such processes, such facts, that the modern mind seeks to satisfy its curiosity.

But it is not curiosity alone that draws men and women to the study of history. Interest in the past arises as often as not out of the urgencies of the present, and it is because of a belief that history has some meaning and message that so many people, especially of our own unhappy day, turn to it for both guidance and solace. Even if some who seek fail to find in it direct answers to the questions they ask, this does not mean that the search has been in vain. For the fruits of history, like those of all humane studies, are things not only of the mind but also of the spirit. . . .

II

Economic history is but one country in a great hemisphere of scholarship. Its position between History on the one hand and Economics on the other reminds me of that in which the diminutive Boswell found himself when acting as interpreter between Dr. Johnson and the Corsican General. "I compared myself," he said, "to an isthmus which joins two great continents." Now, an isthmus may either connect or separate. Those who inhabit it may build up an independent life and character of their own or, as more often happens, they may fall under the tutelage of one or other of the neighbouring powers. For long, economic history remained under the domination of the politically minded historians. Like the British in Egypt, or the Americans in Panama, these brought with them a developed technique; they raised the subject to academic status; and, on the whole, they exercised a civilising influence. But their work is now done, and labour is required to clear away some of the traces of their occupation. The very periods into which economic historians divide, one from another, their varied specialisms, are still described in terms drawn from the vocabulary of politics or political history. "The Feudal System," "Mercantilism," "Laissez-faire," "Collectivism": the ideas behind words such as these are associated with the policies of government rather than with the postulates of economic science. . . . One widely read textbook announces that Napoleon I restarted the Industrial Revolution in France—as though that series of inter-related technical, economic, and social changes was a mechanism to be stopped or started at the bidding of a dictator. There are still writers who believe that some Colbert or Frederick or Bismarck, some Marx or Lenin, was really "the obstetrician of a new age." . . .

In face of such crude interpretations it is the duty of economic historians to point to those spontaneous forces of growth in society that arise from ordinary men and women and find expression in voluntary association, as well as in the state. "Society," Unwin once said, in one of those *obiter dicta* which every good teacher uses to arouse his students from their habitual torpor—"Society cannot direct its destiny by policy." As it stands, that is perhaps an overstatement. But it sprang not from any spirit of negation, but from exasperation with those so obtuse that they fail to see in History any territory in which the writ of the sovereign state does not run.

It is not, however, only the political historians and political theorists that have occupied the isthmus. At a later stage there appeared a swarm of sociologists and economists of the so-called Historical School, bringing with them an avidity for classification that might well have done credit to a contemporary academy of botany or zoology. With great ingenuity they traced out stages of economic development through which all societies were supposed to travel: from barter, through money, to credit; from a subsistence economy through a village, town and national to an international economy; from an eotechnic, through a paleotechnic, to a neotechnic phase; from household production, through a gild and a domestic, to a factory system; from pre-capitalism, through mercantile capitalism, industrial capitalism, finance capitalism, monopoly capitalism, and several other forms of capitalism to wherever you will. Those who constructed them hoped that in time their schematic presentations might come to be regarded as a body of doctrine, parallel to, and perhaps in the end destined to supersede, what used to be called the laws of Political Economy. That hope was a fond one. Take only the first of the series: Hildebrand's master-generalisation about the development from barter, through money, to credit. Professor Postan has pointed out that when documented history began money was already in use; that though there have been many periods of advance towards, there have also been others of retreat from, a greater money economy; and that in times of which it was assumed that men exchanged their goods and services only through the medium of the precious metals there was, in fact, a highly developed system of credit. There is no need to proceed with the other pedigrees of economic institutions. "Everything we know about economic history warns us against belief in steady advances and unbroken lines of progress." The quotation is from Eileen Power's posthumously published work and expresses her mature judgment on this matter.

It is not to be denied that the effort to discover stages of development has yielded some useful results. It has at least presented us with a set of labels which we can attach, if we are so minded, to the files in which we assemble our facts. But facts are stubborn, willful things. You can arrange them in either logical or chronological order, but very seldom at the same time in both. Therein lie at once the difficulty and the fascination of historical composition.

It is not only the systematisers who have, as I think, on balance done harm to the subject. The whole practice of coining phrases and attaching them to particular periods of time has tended to cloud, rather than illumine, our vision of the past. The attribution to the years 1760-1830 of the epithet "The Industrial Revolution" is the outstanding case in point....

It is now too late to alter this particular superscription, for the words have entered the currency of common speech from which there is no recall. But for other periods something may yet be done. Take, for example, the years 1873-96, to the whole series of which the term "The Great Depression" has come to be attached. Thanks to the work of Lord Keynes, Mr. Beales, and Mr. Rostow, we now have a clearer view of what was really going on than was open to the members of the *Royal Commission on the Depression of Trade and Industry* which issued its final report in the middle of the period. We know that in the technical sense of a fall in the marginal efficiency of capital there *was* depression. But we also know that, alongside the dwindling of profits, there took place a great expansion of the national income, an increase in the proportion of that income that went into the pockets of the workers, and a substantial rise of average real wages. These are not movements of the kind that the plain man normally associates with depression. . . .

Economic history is concerned primarily with processes that persist over long stretches of time. It is preoccupation with these that binds economic historians together and differentiates them from other kinds of historians. Some specialisation by periods there must be, since to elicit information from a Charter or Pipe Roll requires skill of a different order from that needed to draw out the meaning hidden behind the magisterial pronouncements of a Royal Commission, or submerged in the detail of a nineteenth-century business ledger. But the centuries and years of the calendar should supply all the palings we need: it is unnecessary to plaster these over with signs. "Stick no bills," and "Leave no litter," are maxims of conduct for the historian as for the citizen.

III

Understanding of the processes which it is the business of economic historians to trace through the centuries does not come by the light of nature. The data do not wear their hearts on their sleeves: it is only by selecting and grouping them that they can be made to yield a meaning. But (as others have said) as soon as the historian begins to select his facts from the myriads available to him he becomes a theorist of sorts. The poorer type of historian is one who allows the stray reflections that pass through the mind to serve as a substitute for the thought that the processes of selection and grouping demand. And even the historian of disciplined intellect requires some more or less systematic body of principles to which he can relate his facts. . . . The economic historian, like the fisherman, needs a net to help to separate those fish that may be marketable from those that may as well be left in the sea. But it must be a net made by skilled hands and not just a reticulation of odd ideas. The men who make the special nets for the craft are the economists.

This somewhat blunt statement will appear as a platitude to some, but as a rock of offence to others. Is it not, these latter will ask, an attempt to justify yet one more of the long series of efforts to interpret the human story in the light of a doctrine? Even if that were so it would not dispose of the matter. For the question might be answered by asking for the alternative. "Don't forget," wrote James Wilson in an early page of that great journal of which he was founder and first editor, "the people who attack Political Economy have a Political Economy of their own; and what is it?" But the real answer to those who shrink from the suggestion that modern economic theory should be applied to the study of earlier forms of society is that they misunderstand the nature of Economics. For, whatever may have been its origin, the subject has ceased (or almost ceased) to be a set of conclusions and has become an apparatus of thought: no longer a doctrine, it has become a method. The only question is whether this method is appropriate to the study of history.

Until recent years the answer might have been in the negative. For though Adam Smith had provided a nursery in which it was possible for theory and history to play happily side by side, as theory grew up it became cold and abstracted; and a later preoccupation with margins completed the rift. The static analysis on which most of us were reared had its uses, but it had little or no bearing on the problems of change over periods of time. Professor Robbins put the correct relation between the two disciplines neatly when he said that economics is concerned with the form, economic history with the substance. Most of what I have to say this afternoon is a variation on that theme. But it can hardly be said that at the time when he coined the aphorism the form was really appropriate to the medium: economic historians were offered a set of implements devised for other jobs than theirs—tools that would cut only *across* the grain, and not, as they required, *along* the grain. It is true that about the same time, in one brief article, Allyn Young pointed the way to that theory of economic development which is what is needed: had historians taken more heed of this we should have been spared some barren disputation as to whether expansion of trade precedes or follows expansion of industry, and so on. But economists as a whole were beset with so many problems of current concern that they had little time for sustained thought on these wider questions. If, in the event, they have shaped an instrument that may be of use to historians it is by accident rather than design.

It was during and immediately after the first world war that there took place the first of those developments in thought that have made possible a closer intimacy between economists and historians. Under the pressure of events, economists became increasingly less theoretical and more statistical in their approach. It would be too much to attribute to contagion the tendency of economic historians to concern themselves with the statistical aggregate or average, rather than with the outstanding or picturesque incident. For that tendency had long been at work. The senior British economic historian, Sir John Clapham, certainly did not wait for the impetus to a quantitative treatment to come from the professional statisticians, though he would, one imagines, be among the first to recognise the great service that Professor Bowley has rendered to our subject. The work of Bowley and those he has trained and stimulated is certain to have a profound effect on the future of historical studies. It has made us all less tolerant of the loose, unsupported generalisation. . . .

The violent movement of prices during and after the war turned attention to the causes and social consequences of changes in the value of money. Here was a field which required the skills of economists, statisticians, and historians alike. Where so much valuable work has been done by so many students it is invidious to mention individuals, but I cannot refrain from reference to the light thrown on the social history of the sixteenth and seventeenth centuries by Professor Hamilton's study of the effects of Spanish Treasure; to the clearer understanding of the economic background to the French Revolution that has come from the brilliant and scholarly work of M. Labrousse; and to the enormous debt that every student of the last quarter of the eighteenth, and the first half of the nineteenth, centuries owes to the statistical labours of Professor Silberling. More recently, the assembly of material on prices by Sir William Beveridge and his colleagues for England, and of Posthumus for Holland, opens possibilities of new interpretations of large tracts of the past. . . .

Out of the exigencies connected with the growth of the national debt between 1914 and 1920 came a revival of concern with the theory of interest; and this, in turn, led to a study of the effects of changes of both long- and short-term rates on investment and activity. I wish it could be said that here too there had been enquiries by historians parallel to those of the theorists. . . .

Chronological tables of rates of interest, similar to those of the price series, would be valuable in a variety of ways. Changes in short-term rates, as Wicksell pointed out, have important effects in determining the nature of the medium of circulation. The high rates of interest between 1797 and 1815 stimulated the substitution of small bills of exchange for notes and even for coin; and the fall in the rates that followed the Napoleonic war was accompanied by a reversal of the process. It may be that if we knew more of these things we should find that those earlier oscillations from money to credit or from credit to money, to which I have referred, were susceptible of similar explanation. Changes in the long-term rates of interest, it may be supposed, had even more potent effects. Long ago Philip Wicksteed made the interesting observation that the substantial quality of the houses in many Dutch cities might be attributed to the fact that, at the close of the eighteenth century, interest on good security in Holland was as low as two per cent. I have often wondered whether the first country textile factories of the north of England (so different, at least in outward appearance, from the satanic mills of textbook imagination) do not owe their permanence and their beauty to the accident, if accident it was, that they were constructed during the period of low rates of interest between 1783 and 1797. And these low rates may also have had an effect on such things as the depth to which mines were sunk, the size and type of the dwellings of the workers, the state of the highroads, and the development of canals. . . .

The reconsideration by the economists of the nature and effects of national debt had results in other spheres. There is need for historians to rewrite their essays on the financial policies of, for example, Peel and Gladstone in the light of new ideas. If it were possible to extend to earlier periods those methods of estimating national income and capital that have been devised by economists and statisticians of this generation, we should be able to speak with more assurance about the wider social effects of these policies. We might also be able to answer with less hesitation the question as to how far what seem to us the miserably low standards of comfort of the labouring classes in earlier times were the inevitable consequences of low productivity and how far they resulted from avarice or want of social sympathy on the part of employers and landowners.

Again, in the nineteen twenties the problems of external debts and reparations led to reexamination of theories of international trade and the foreign exchanges. The principles laid bare by Taussig, Angell, Ohlin, Viner, Whale, and others are now beginning to inform the work of historians. The concept of the terms of trade, essentially a historical concept, might be used to enlighten discussion on the economic relations between nations in earlier centuries, and, applied internally, on those of the relative rates of growth of agriculture and manufactures.

Yet again, the development in the twenties of monopolistic forms of organisation led other economists to refine that theory of value which had hitherto seemed to serve their purposes. Studies in imperfect or mono-polistic competition provide tools better shaped for work on the past, no less than on the present, than those in perfect competition or pure monopoly on which most of us were brought up. . . .

Unemployment and labour disputes in the same period drew the attention of other economists to the unsatisfactory state of the theory of wages, and new formulations resulted. Mr. Rostow has applied Professor Hicks' analysis to one period, at least, of the nineteenth century. But it can hardly be said that the second thoughts of economists in this field have yet been reflected in the works of economic historians in general. Thanks to Professor Bowley, we know something about the course of real wages in the nineteenth century, and others, like Knoop and Jones, and Mrs. Gilboy have provided valuable material for earlier times. There are excellent histories of trade unionism, detailed studies of labor movements such as Chartism, monographs on factory reformers, and chronological accounts of industrial and social legislation. But we know very little about the gradual changes in the status of the workers, and in their personal relations with the employers. Let me give one example of the kind of relation I have in mind. No one who glances through the records of industrial concerns of the period we call the Industrial Revolution can fail to be struck by the almost universal tendency of the workers to borrow from their employers on the security of future earnings. The effects on the mobility and bargaining strength of labour are obvious. To-day, as John Hilton has reminded us, debt is the key to all working-class life; but the debt is no longer owed to the employer, but to agencies outside the factory—money-lenders, pawnbrokers, above all instalment-selling concerns. Where and how was the change effected? I know of no economic historian who has investigated this or similar matters. Or, to mention a wider problem: we are almost entirely ignorant of the changes in the relative scarcities of different kinds of skill and of the elasticities of substitution between labour and capital at particular periods of time. Yet these are matters which may in the end prove to have been of at least as much account as the self-sacrifice of Lord Shaftesbury or the devoted energy of Ben Tillett. Labour, in the sense in which the word is used by the economist, still awaits its historian.

It was in the decade before the recent war, however, that there occurred the most spectacular of those developments in thought which make possible a closer co-operation of economists and historians. In this many played a part, but the work of Lord Keynes is outstanding. The introduction of an income-and-expenditure approach to the problem of money and prices and the analysis in terms of aggregates, rather than of marginal differences, were of some consequence. But what is even more important than these is that, at last, the theorists have provided an organon that can be applied to explain those alternations of activity and depression that have characterised the last two centuries or more of economic society. If we accept Lord Keynes teaching that (except in conditions of full employment) the growth of capital is retarded, rather than advanced, by a low propensity to consume, we must seek the causes of that growth, no longer in the parsimony of the early factory employers, but in the relatively high expenditure of others (including the government) during the formative years of the Industrial Revolution. Already the economic outlines of the nineteenth century are seen in a new light. . . .

The effect on the study of the development of particular institutions is likely to be profound. For to write of these, as some have done, without reference to the periodic variations of activity is like writing the life-history of a tree without reference to the climate or the seasons. The fluctuations of interest, investment, incomes, employment, and prices are not just incidents to be mentioned in passing; they are an essential part of the environment in which social and political institutions flourish and decay. . . .

What has been said so far may be read by some as an invitation to theorists to occupy the isthmus. That is not the intention. The interest of the economist in the past arises, as often as not, out of a wish to test his conclusions in a series of different environments: the interest of the historian is wider than that. The theorist has taught us that economic phenomena are bound together in ways that the uninstructed would not suspect. He has created an apparatus which explains any given economic situation in terms of profit expectations, the propensity to consume, and so on. But beyond that he cannot go. It rests with the historian to trace the causes, or as he would prefer to say, the antecedents and predisposing circumstances of these expectations and propensities: to say how it came about that at one time men were inclined to spend freely, and at another to hoard their resources, how it was that men were enterprising and optimistic in this year or this decade, cautious and penurious in that. Sir William Beveridge tells us that in his pursuit of prices and wages through the centuries he was like one driving a car by night through unfamiliar country, with the glare of headlamps lighting up a narrow strip of road, and giving only occasional glimpses of the surrounding countryside. The historian can be no mere tourist: he must be a native who knows the fields and hedges and hidden valleys, as well as the highroads. All that is urged is that, when moving along some more or less defined route he should trust less to unaided vision or native wit and more to the process of systematic thought: that he should make some use of imported headlamps. Not all the gadgets that the economist carries in his toolbag will be of direct use to the historian; some are whetstones for the sharpening of other implements; others, one suspects, are little more than ingenious toys. But that some of those I have mentioned can be used to make a cleaner job of our work on the past seems to me already to have been set beyond doubt.

I have said something about what the historian may learn from the economist, but little or nothing of what the economist may gain from a closer contact with historians. It is often urged that some acquaintance with history may save him from the hasty conclusion, the easy generalisation, the belief that because an idea is new it is true, the tendency to dogmatism. I would not lay stress on this, for, in my experience, economists are no more prone to these weaknesses than other specialists. . . . Nor is the gain merely that of being able to try out theoretic models at different altitudes, though there is something in that. It lies in the reminder that the institutions or factors about which economists generalise are concrete realities, with a past without knowledge of which they cannot be apprehended: in that widening of experience in time which history offers to us all. . . .

To sum up: the historian is increasingly feeling for the structure that underlies the surface of events, for explanation and interpretation. The economist is increasingly concerned not with static equilibrium, but with the transition from one equilibrium to another, with problems in which *time* is one of the dimensions. If they will take counsel together they may move towards that ideal in which no longer will the one look at his facts in the hope of inducing from them a theory, and the other deduce from first principles a theory in the hope that it may be found to fit the facts, but in which the two cooperate so that, in the words of Croce, the facts and the theory demonstrate each other. . . .

IV

Economic history, though an isthmus, is a wide territory. In this lecture I have said nothing of many of its outlying provinces: nothing of that area in which the demographers are sinking their shafts to strata deeper than the economic; nothing of that terrain, explored by Mr. Beales, where industrial and social streams of development mingle their waters; nothing of that region of battles between old privilege and new aspiration which the Hammonds have observed with their clear eyes and described in their sensitive speech; nothing of that coast, known to few as to Professor Tawney, where the waves of economic impulse beat on the eternal verities. That is not because I count these provinces as of small importance. It is, in fact, precisely in them that the moving frontier of the subject is likely to be pushed forward with most benefit. But, even in these, no economic historian is likely to add much to the work of the pioneers unless he brings with him some, at least, of the appliances of modern thought.

There is a group of historians who are disposed to argue that the course of events of each age expresses, in some way not very clearly defined, the spirit of that age. In the writings of some that spirit or *Zeitgeist* ceases to be merely an habitual character and becomes a daemon, sometimes almost a malicious personal devil. There are others, less apocalyptic in outlook, who write of some abstract idea, such as Capitalism, as though it had the attributes of a living human being. It would be foolish to deny the existence of the phenomenon of Capitalism—the whole set of influences of which I have been speaking this afternoon may, indeed, be usefully described as manifestations of it. But what is to be resisted is the tendency of some who make much use of the word to a teleological interpretation of events: Capitalism required this, demanded that, necessitated everything. . . . If, by the grace of God, we managed to cast out the devil of Teutonic mysticism from the house, of what profit would it be if we let in seven more demons under the name of Economic Determinants?

The best antidote I can think of to all this is detailed work on the records of some one merchant, manufacturing concern, banking house, trade union, or other organisation. The sense of the individual or group overcoming obstacles and building some fragment into the social fabric is heartening. And since, until within the last hundred years, life had not become departmentalised, the ledgers and letters and pay books tell us much, not only about prices and terms of credit and wages, but also about the people of whose work they are the record. The student will learn from them, it may be, little about the Spirit of the Age, but he will come to know more about the spirit of men. And in the light of that knowledge some of what pass as works of history will come to appear as shabby caricatures, often little better than crude libels on the dead.

The study of what by yet another misfortune of terminology has come to be called business history should be pursued alongside the interpretation of the past with the aid of the apparatus of economic thought. For it is in the business unit that economic forces can be seen in operation, as it were in the front line. Business history may serve as a reminder that demand and supply, the various elasticities and multipliers, the determinants and stabilisers, are all generalisations, useful indeed, but causal factors at one remove; and that it is the wills and choices and acts of men and women that are the ultimate data for economists and historians alike.

2

The American Economic System

DAVID M. POTTER

. . . Capitalism in the United States has been only an economic means to the attainment of certain basic social goals, and these broader goals have done more than our economic beliefs to control our economic practices. If we try to search out what the essential goals have been, we can define at least two which have had a fundamental bearing on the American economy. One of these is the goal of maximum opportunity for the individual arising from the strong American belief in the dignity and worth of man. The other is the goal of a high and steadily improving standard of living. . . .

Historically, what have the American people expected of their economy? They have not cared very much for maximum efficiency. . . . In fact, they have tolerated immense waste in the use of natural resources. They have not sought the elimination of inefficient . . . producers . . . but have often gone to the aid of marginal producers. . . . The only economic policy that the American people have always insisted upon and consistently applied is that the system should operate in such a way as to give the bulk of the population access to the sources of wealth. These sources have changed

Excerpted from David M. Potter, "The American Economic System," in *An Outline of Man's Knowledge of the Modern World*, ed. Lyman Bryson (New York: McGraw Hill) © 1960 by Catherine McGrattan Bryson. Reprinted by permission of Doubleday & Company, Inc.

during our historical experience, but the policy of giving access to them has not. . . .

The American economy today is as far from Ricardo as it is from Marx. . . . It has been based, from the beginning, upon a rejection of their idea that the exploitation of labor was inevitable. America began with an abundance of physical resources, with more land than men could use. During our history, technological progress has steadily increased our supply of energy. . . . When Franklin Roosevelt proclaimed that one-third of our nation was ill-housed, ill-fed, and ill-clothed, the statement was not . . . a mere observation—it was a reproach. . . .

. . . The American economy is a unique system which uses the capitalistic devices of private property, financial incentives, and the free market but combines these with heavy infusions of governmental regulation and of control of the distribution of wealth through taxation—all as devices to achieve the goals of material abundance democratically shared.

. . . The defects of the American economic system are peculiarly characteristic of its qualities. . . . Such an economy will escape the problems and the evils of excessive rigidity, of overcentralized control, of static conditions, of bureaucratic paralysis, and lack of initiative. But it will face the problems inherent in a situation where there is no central directing authority and many uncontrolled factors are at work.

. . . Our dangers are . . . that our production will outrun our natural resources, that inflation rather than deflation will overtake us, that population is increasing at too rapid a rate, that our technological knowledge will outrun the supply of investment capital necessary to make use of it. In short, the problems of the American economic system are distinctively the problems of a democratic economy of abundance, of a dynamic economy, and of a free economy.

3

Capitalism, Socialism and Democracy

JOSEPH A. SCHUMPETER

The essential point to grasp is that in dealing with capitalism we are dealing with an evolutionary process. It may seem strange that anyone can fail to see so obvious a fact which moreover was long ago emphasized by Karl Marx. Yet that fragmentary analysis which yields the bulk of our propositions about the functioning of modern capitalism persistently neglects it. Let us restate the point and see how it bears upon our problem.

Capitalism, then, is by nature a form or method of economic change and not only never is but never can be stationary. And this evolutionary character of the capitalist process is not merely due to the fact that economic life goes on in a social and natural environment that changes and by its change alters the data of economic action; this fact is important and these changes (wars, revolutions, and so on) often condition industrial change, but they are not its prime movers. Nor is this evolutionary character due to a quasi-automatic increase in population and capital or to the vagaries of monetary systems of which exactly the same thing holds true. The fundamental impulse that sets and keeps the capitalist engine in

Joseph A. Schumpeter, *Capitalism, Socialism and Democracy*, Third edition (Harper Torchbooks: 1962) pp. 82-86. Reprinted by permission from Harper & Row Publishers, Inc.

motion comes from the new consumers' goods, the new methods of production or transportation, the new markets, the new forms of industrial organization that capitalist enterprise creates.

. . . The contents of the laborer's budget, say from 1760 to 1940, did not simply grow on unchanging lines but they underwent a process of qualitative change. Similarly, the history of the productive apparatus of a typical farm, from the beginnings of the rationalization of crop rotation, plowing, and fattening to the mechanized thing of today—linking up with elevators and railroads—is a history of revolutions. So is the history of the productive apparatus of the iron and steel industry from the charcoal furnace to our own type of furnace, or the history of the apparatus of power production from the overshot water wheel to the modern power plant, or the history of transportation from the mailcoach to the airplane. The opening up of new markets, foreign or domestic, and the organizational development from the craft shop and factory to such concerns as U.S. Steel illustrate the same process of industrial mutation—if I may use that biological term—that incessantly revolutionizes[1] the economic structure *from within*, incessantly destroying the old one, incessantly creating a new one. This process of Creative Destruction is the essential fact about capitalism. It is what capitalism consists in and what every capitalist concern has got to live in. This fact bears upon our problem in two ways.

First, since we are dealing with a process whose every element takes considerable time in revealing its true features and ultimate effects, there is no point in appraising the performance of that process *ex visu* of a given point of time; we must judge its performance over time, as it unfolds through decades or centuries. A system—any system, economic or other—that at *every* given point of time fully utilizes its possibilities to the best advantage may yet in the long run be inferior to a system that does so at *no* given point of time, because the latter's failure to do so may be a condition for the level or speed of long-run performance.

Second, since we are dealing with an organic process, analysis of what happens in any particular part of it—say, in an individual concern or industry—may indeed clarify details of mechanism but is inconclusive beyond that. Every piece of business strategy acquires its true significance only against the background of that process and within the situation created by it. It must be seen in its role in the perennial gale of creative destruction; it cannot be understood irrespective of it or, in fact, on the hypothesis that there is a perennial lull.

But economists who, *ex visu* of a point of time, look for example at the behavior of an oligopolist industry—an industry which consists of a few big firms—and observe the well-known moves and countermoves within it that seem to aim at nothing but high prices and restrictions of output are making precisely that hypothesis. They accept the data of the momentary situation as if there were no past or future to it and think that they have understood what there is to understand if they interpret the behavior of those firms by means of the principle of maximizing profits with reference to those data. The usual theorist's paper and the usual government commission's report practically never try to see that behavior, on the one hand, as a result of a piece of past history and, on the other hand, as an attempt to deal with a situation that is sure to change presently—as an attempt by those firms to keep on their feet, on ground that is slipping away from under them. In other words, the problem that is usually being visualized is how capitalism administers existing structures, whereas the relevant problem is how it creates and destroys them. As long as this is not recognized, the investigator does a meaningless job. As soon as it is recognized, his outlook on capitalist practice and its social results changes considerably.[2]

The first thing to go is the traditional conception of the *modus operandi* of competition. Economists are at long last emerging from the stage in which price competition was all they saw. As soon as quality competition and sales effort are admitted into the sacred precincts of theory, the price variable is ousted from its dominant position. However, it is still competition within a rigid pattern of invariant conditions, methods of production, and forms of industrial organization in particular, that practically monopolizes attention. But in capitalist reality as distinguished from its textbook picture, it is not that kind of competition which counts but the competition from the new commodity, the new technology, the new source of supply, the new type of organization (the largest-scale unit of control for instance)—competition which commands a decisive cost or quality advantage and which strikes not at the margins of the profits and the outputs of the existing firms but at their foundations and their very lives. This kind of competition is as much more effective than the other as a bombardment is in comparison with forcing a door, and so much more important that it becomes a matter of comparative indifference whether competition in the ordinary sense functions more or less promptly; the powerful lever that in the long run expands output and brings down prices is in any case made of other stuff.

It is hardly necessary to point out that competition of the kind we now have in mind acts not only when in being but also when it is merely an ever-present threat. It disciplines before it attacks. The businessman feels himself to be in a competitive situation even if he is alone in his field or if, though not alone, he holds a position such that investigating government experts fail to see any effective competition between him and any other firms in the same or a neighboring field and in consequence conclude that his talk, under examination, about his competitive sorrows is all make-believe. In many cases, though not in all, this will in the long run enforce behavior very similar to the perfectly competitive pattern.

Many theorists take the opposite view which is best conveyed by an example. Let us assume that there is a certain number of retailers in a neighborhood who try to improve their relative position by service and "atmosphere" but avoid price competition and stick as to methods to the local tradition—a picture of stagnating routine. As others drift into the trade that quasi-equilibrium is indeed upset, but in a manner that does not benefit their customers. The economic space around each of the shops having been narrowed, their owners will no longer be able to make a living and they will try to mend the case by raising prices in tacit agreement. This will further reduce their sales and so, by successive pyramiding, a situation will evolve in which increasing potential supply will be attended by increasing instead of decreasing prices and by decreasing instead of increasing sales.

Such cases do occur, and it is right and proper to work them out. But as the practical instances usually given show, they are fringe-end cases to be found mainly in the sectors furthest removed from all that is most characteristic of capitalist activity.[3] Moreover, they are transient by nature. In the case of retail trade the competition that matters arises not from additional shops of the same type, but from the department store, the chain store, the mail-order house and the super-market which are bound to destroy those pyramids sooner or later.[4] Now a theoretical construction which neglects this essential element of the case neglects all that is more typically capitalist about it; even if correct in logic as well as in fact, it is like *Hamlet* without the Danish prince.

Endnotes

1. Those revolutions are not strictly incessant; they occur in discrete rushes that are separated from each other by spans of comparative quiet. The process as a whole works incessantly, however, in the sense that there always is either revolution or absorption of the results of revolution, both together forming what are known as business cycles.

2. It should be understood that it is only our appraisal of economic performance and not our moral judgment that can be so changed. Owing to its autonomy, moral approval or disapproval is entirely independent of our appraisal of social (or any other) results, unless we happen to adopt a moral system such as utilitarianism which makes moral approval and disappproval turn on them *ex definitione*.

3. This is also shown by a theorem we frequently meet with in expositions of the theory of imperfect competition, viz., the theorem that, under conditions of imperfect competition, producing or trading businesses tend to be irrationally small. Since imperfect competition is

at the same time held to be an outstanding characteristic of modern industry we are set to wondering what world these theorists live in, unless, as stated above, fringe-end cases are all they have in mind.

4. The mere threat of their attack cannot, in the particular conditions, environmental and personal, of small-scale retail trade, have its usual disciplining influence, for the small man is too much hampered by his cost structure and, however well he may manage within his inescapable imitations, he can never adapt himself to the methods of competitors who can afford to sell at the price at which he buys.

4

England and America; The Ties that Bind

LOUIS M. HACKER

... Now, more than ever, Englishmen and Americans are called upon to know the ties that bind them together: to be familiar with those grand conceptions that represent their joint contributions and commitments to Western civilization. ...

This is a curious thing for an American historian to say: for the whole tendency of American historical scholarship, over the past fifty years broadly conceived, has been—it seems—to stress the uniqueness of the American experience. Settled by the unwanted and humble men and women of Europe—the landless, the dispossessed, the victims of political prescription, economic privilege, and ecclesiastical authoritarianism—and concerned with the conquest of a vast continent, America turned its back on Europe for more than a century. This epoch began with the appearance of the young War Hawks who forced the United States into the second war with England in 1812; it really ended with our entry into World War I a little more than one hundred years later. Between these two terminal dates,

"England and America; The Ties that Bind," an Inaugural Lecture delivered before the University of Oxford on 8 November 1948, by Louis M. Hacker (Oxford, 1948). Excerpted and reprinted by permission of Dr. Hacker.

by purchase, negotiation, and war, the United States acquired sovereignty over its continental domain. Within that same one hundred years waves of pioneers—coming from Europe and the farms of eastern United States— conquered the successive frontiers of densely settled forests, long-grass prairies, short-grass plains, and arid deserts to emerge in settled communities on the Pacific coast. By 1890 the final frontier was gone; the same decade was to see the formulation of a nationalistic philosophy of history that explained America entirely in terms of these frontier experiences.

Frederick J. Turner was thirty-two years old in 1893 when he read his paper "The Significance of the Frontier in American History" before the American Historical Association.[1] Turner taught altogether for some thirty-four years at Wisconsin and Harvard and his impact on teaching and research was immense. In consequence, a large body of disciples— teachers and scholars—filled the land, not only leaving their impress on the texts of the schools but affecting the attitudes of the American people. There can be no doubt that, in part, the isolationism of America during the next two generations was due to the influence of the frontier interpretation of American history.

The intellectual and emotional origins of the Turner, or frontier, thesis have not been adequately examined. He himself had been brought up in Wisconsin and had spent his boyhood in a region newly wrested from the wilderness: as an undergraduate at the University of Wisconsin he had been profoundly influenced by a teacher who had studied in Germany and who was devoted to German scholarship. Perhaps from him he had learned of Ratzel's ideas concerning anthropogeography at that time being eagerly received in Germany. These must have left their mark on Turner: on the other hand, Turner always showed little if any familiarity with the economic and political thinking of the Enlightenment. One may point out that a religious emotionalism is not alien to the ways of frontier peoples— and this despite the hard, matter-of-fact living to which they are subjected. The anthropogeography of Ratzel and Semple and Turner . . . had also mystical strains in it: for it assumed (in Turner's hands, at any rate) that each generation of frontiersmen repeated the same cycle of cultural youth and maturity.[2]

American development, in other words, was unique in historical annals in that it was constantly being affected by the frontiers which had to be conquered until the last one was gone in 1890; and what made the frontier an ever-present force in American history was the existence of the public domain of usable and largely free lands. Into these successions of Wests poured waves of pioneers to influence subtly but pervasively all forms of American living. These were the outstanding effects of the frontier experiences: out of the common habits of Western life emerged a distinctly American people; under the cruel conditions of frontier pioneering, where only the hardy individual could survive, was born the doctrine of democracy; because the frontier areas were, in effect, creations of the American Government and because the frontiersmen looked to Washington for comfort and relief, loyalty was to the nation and not to the individual states—hence the American nationalistic spirit; and finally, because the westerners regarded their governments not as sovereign controllers but as agencies for the performance of delegated public functions, the frontier states were turned into so many social laboratories where experiments in the extension of public activities were continually going on.

A corollary of the frontier doctrine was the "safety-valve" theory which argued that because the propertyless—whether European peasants or American workers—could become free-holders, class hostilities, economic privilege, and the unequal distribution of wealth could not occur in America. One went West (Turner always disregarded the realities of capital requirements), girdled trees or ploughed up the tough prairie sod, and immediately became a self-sufficing agricultural producer. Thus, availability of land was the great social and economic leveller in America. . . .

Thus America during its dynamic, expansive period. But what was to be its subsequent development? With the final frontier gone, Turner went on to predict, the United States was destined to become a settled nation and reach "a more stable equilibrium" in which the chief influence at work—again differentiating American civilization from all others—would be the existence of regional sections. In these sections—the New England and North Atlantic States, the Old South, the Middle West, the South-west, the North-west, the Pacific area—formed by "physiographic conditions, economic interests and constituent stocks of settled societies," where denser populations would be pressing upon the means of subsistence, "would spring up groups of peoples as unlike each other as the different nations of Europe." In 1925 Turner therefore wrote: "The significant fact is that sectional self-consciousness and sensitiveness is likely to be increased as time goes on and crystallized sections feel the full influence of their geographic peculiarities, their special interests, and their developed ideals, in a closed and static nation."

Why so? Because the various sections were settled at different times; because each went through its own life-cycle of growth and maturity so that there existed side by side sections at lower and higher economic and cultural stages of development; and because sectional peculiarities were accentuated and perpetuated by physiographic and demographic differences. Conflict thus was inevitable; it was the role of politics to reconcile antagonisms and discover ways of accommodation. True, once in American history "party ties, working nationally, like elastic bands, to hold the sections together" broke under "especial strain," and the Civil War followed. By this reading, then, the Civil War was a war between two different nations: their moral values and psychological drives profoundly affected by their sectional dissimilarities.

This is the Turner interpretation and it has been followed by literally hundreds of American historians with slight deviation from the original text. There is no doubt that such an entirely nationalistic preoccupation filled with exciting pages the American story; there is no doubt that an understanding of it helped to explain in part the national character. Americans *are* different from Europeans—as Englishmen are different from the Scotsmen and the Frenchmen from Germans. But because it helped to explain differences it also accentuated them. Turner and his disciples lost sight of this important fact: that Americans were also the inheritors of the Western tradition and that (unconsciously, it is true, for the most part; that is to say, through the educational process) they were as much the descendants of Aristotle, Descartes, Locke, and Bentham as they were of Daniel Boone and Davy Crockett. . . .

Nor am I seeking to deny that there were important elements of uniqueness in the American experience. But a more subtle analysis is required than one based on the dubious science of anthropogeography alone. We can come closer to the heart of the matter, I think, if we talk in terms of rejection and reception.

I myself, elsewhere and in some detail, have tried to account for aspects of uniqueness in American institutions by describing the role of rejection.[3] The European emigrants who left for America in the seventeenth, eighteenth, nineteeth and twentieth centuries were largely the unwanted simple (rather than gentle) folk of the countryside and the smaller communities. Many departed voluntarily; some were forced; a few were assisted. They came—when they could pay their passage in the seventeenth and eighteenth centuries—as freemen; the larger number, certainly in the one hundred years 1650-1750, came as bond servants. They came, for the most part, as young men and women who had been the victims of war and famine (as in the case of the Palatinate Germans in the eighteenth century and the Irish in the nineteenth century); religious persecution (as in the case of the English Pilgrims, Puritans, and Quakers in the seventeenth century), ecclesiastical and economic oppression (as in the case of Scotch-Irish in the eighteenth century), unequal land systems and guild restrictions (as in the case of the Germans, Czechs, and Scandinavians in the nineteenth century), racial discrimination (as in the case of the eastern European Jews in the twentieth century).

The settlers of America came lightly burdened—with this world's goods and as regards their loyalties. It is interesting to note what they left behind—and how, therefore, the ways of life and attitudes they created were sharply opposed to those with which they had been familiar.

They left behind the medieval land system of tenure and organization. True, in England, that system had been in process of dissolution since the fourteenth century; but there were many hangovers that continued to survive, all of which made for concentrated land ownership and backward agricultural practices. . . . Because, in Europe, for the little men, the possession of a freehold was next to impossible; because the common lands continued to exist (with their harmful effect on animal husbandry); because landlords continued to exact their dues and obligations and were resuming their raids on the common lands—thus making the plight of the cottagers even more desperate; and because the village still dominated planting programmes—the new-comers to America left all these practices behind. Land tenure in America, in consequence, was revolutionized: for the first time men of little or no means could hope to become freeholders. And they did so—as purchasers, preemptioners, and homesteaders. This was the hope of America; this was its most significant and magical attraction which drew millions of Europeans out of the British Isles, Germany and central Europe, and Scandinavia for 250 years.

The possession of a freehold in fee simple made it possible to disregard the ancient manorial and communal rights which continued to encumber and retard European agriculture. In consequence, the American did not have to settle in a village, observe the village planting program, pay dues—whether in work or cash—to the landlord or use his public utilities. He could live where he pleased—and he chose to live in the centre of his farm away from his neighbours; he could plant what he pleased, and more and more he chose to grow staples: he had water rights, subsoil rights, and the rights to bequeath and devise his property as he willed. The right to possessions was free; and because there were so many freeholders there were so many freemen in America.

The new-comers left behind them Europe's corporate organization—in industry, trade, the churches, the state. And with their rejection of corporativism they rejected authoritarianism. . . . The medieval world had been founded on corporate authority—whether of manor, guild, or church. Even as if dissolved, hangovers persisted into early modern Europe. The corporate guilds survived—although in England many became privileged trading companies; new corporations made their appearance—as regulated companies and joint-stock companies; monopolies flourished.

The guild system, with its controls over wages, apprentices, production, and new capital investments, was not transplanted into the New World. Whether as enterpriser or worker the American again was a free man: to open his own establishment, move where he pleased, trade where and when and under whatever conditions he chose. . . . Corporate charters—except in banking and transportation—were granted only with the utmost caution in early America. Indeed, it was not until the mid-nineteenth century that legislatures were ready to enact general enabling statutes which permitted corporations to arise, without legislative restrictions, in industry and commerce. And the hostility to corporate power led Congress, beginning with the Sherman Anti-Trust act in 1890, to pass a series of laws whose intention was the curbing of monopoly and the maintenance of fair competition. The laws, it is true, work imperfectly; but what is important is that Americans continue committed to the basic principles responsible for their enactment. . . .

Up to this point I have talked of institutions which were rejected; I wish to speak now of an attitude. The dignity of human labour has, of course, been at the heart of the Christian system of ethics; notably Protestantism, because it linked the idea of the calling with salvation, did much to ennoble man in his humble pursuits. But practices and professions did not always go hand in hand. The medieval serf was despised by his lord; he repaid ill will with the treachery and violence that have so darkened the pages of medieval life. The seventeenth and eighteenth centuries also saw the same wide gulf existing. The theory of mercantilism—which expressed the concept of authority in the early modern world—was founded, ironically, on the debasement of labour. . . .

Mercantilism held that the wealth of the world was fixed; and that the wealth of each nation was derived from its foreign trade. A nation's foreign trade could expand—at the expense of its rivals—only as it kept its domestic costs of production down. The wealth of the nation, therefore, was in its labour supply engaged in the production of goods and services for export; and the size, docility, and poverty of its workers made possible the riches of the whole body politic.

Who were these workers? Collectively England called them "The Poor." One may observe in passing that right into the last quarter of the nineteenth century the term "The Poor" still designated the English working class.

The moral and social consequences of this conception were immense. "The Poor" were needed and they were assured the right to work—by apprenticeship laws, labour contracts, guild restrictions—but they also had the duty to labour. Public authority used persuasion and discipline; in the last resort—through the institution of the workhouse, established in England at the end of the seventeenth century—it used coercion and punishment. The rights of "The Poor" were set forth in the great Elizabethan Statute of Artificers. The medieval apprenticeship period of seven years was extended to most of the highly skilled industries; labour contracts were to run for at least a year; and the local justices of the peace were given the power to fix minimum—and also maximum—wages.

Work was demanded; but the worker was held in contempt. He was kept badly fed, ill clad, and wretchedly housed, while lay and ecclesiastical moralists constantly called attention to his improvidence and want of industry. . . .

II

So much for rejection. But the other side of the shield is reception. Here I wish to talk of three notions—ideas and institutions—which Americans received from England and which constitute, among others, the ties that bind the two peoples together. The first is the conception of the nature of man. The second is the founding of political institutions upon the Rule of Law and the preservation of individual right. The third is the acceptance, among the functions of capital, of its ability—nay, duty—to move freely across international borders as an instrumentality of welfare.

The American conception of the nature of man is largely English in its origins rather than French or German or Italian. For we have tended to follow Locke and Bentham rather than Rousseau; Mill rather than Hegel or Pareto. For the belief that man could shape his own destiny and achieve welfare through his own striving; the assumption that freedom could be maintained—whether because of natural right or beneficent law—not in a social order so much as through it; the hope that equality of opportunity was realizable only through the creation of democratic institutions: this optimistic faith of Americans is part of their English heritage.

The early settlers brought to the American continent Protestantism, which clothed with dignity the individual and his rationality and made his personal conduct the basis of a Christian life. Locke's ideas—in religion, psychology, education, politics, and economics—buttressed at every point this hopeful view that man could order his existence successfully. As a consequence, Locke powerfully influenced not only the founders of the American republic but the first two generations of American thinkers as well. And Locke was replaced, in very considerable measure, by Mill who, starting with utility instead of natural right, nevertheless came out at the same place.

We are what our experiences make us, taught Locke. What better justification had Americans for their confident belief that a broad educational system was the means of guaranteeing the continuance of the democratic way of life and the assurance of equality of opportunity? Men have certain inalienable rights. Was not this the basis for the necessity to uphold the individual's right to dissent against an oppressive Church and an authoritarian State? Political power must be widely dispersed. What better support could one find for the whole theory of the separation of powers and popular sovereignty? The universe is orderly; it is ruled by law. Was not the Rule of Law the shield men had against prescription and tyranny? The Rule of Law—again whether based on natural right as Locke had it or a constitution as Bentham insisted—protected the citizen against the coercive conduct of his fellows and the State.

Man was egoistic; man was selfish; man sought his personal happiness. But, at the same time, man was rational, and because this was so he was capable of self-improvement. Reason curbed egoism, prudence tempered selfishness, self-improvement and social well-being became inextricably linked. This belief in rational behavior, this determination to defend man's individuality, and this devotion to welfare are the roots of the Anglo-American ideal. . . .

If our conception of man's nature Englishmen and Americans hold in common, the same is true of the legal and political institutions they have set up for its maintenance.

Englishmen and Americans believe in the Rule of Law, which, as Dicey put it, "excludes the existence of arbitrariness, of prerogative, or even of wide discretionary authority on the part of government."[4] . . .

Englishmen and Americans believe in safeguarding the rights of the individual through exact procedural guarantees. What Englishmen have written into the Magna Carta, the Petition of Rights, the Habeas Corpus Act, the Bill of Rights, the Act of Succession, we have written into the first Ten Amendments of the American Constitution. Free men have the rights of conscience, speech, the press, association; they have the rights of jury trial and a hearing according to the law of the land. They have the right to continue to dissent until such point when action may jeopardize the lives and properties of others.

Guided by such precepts and because they have had a long training in citizenship, Englishmen and Americans have learned political responsibility. . . . An acceptance of this obligation of citizenship is a uniquely Anglo-American idea; it is one of the important ties that bind us together.

There is a third category of relations I wish to mention; these have also been binding ties and they constitute commitments which we—Englishmen and Americans—must assume in our intercourse with other peoples. I refer to the role of capital movements in our modern world.

The flow of capital across national boundaries—for portfolio investments, for the creation of internal improvements and the erection of factories, for the financing of trade—in recent years has been submitted to a strange examination. Such international transfers, instead of being regarded as one of the really cementing influences in our world, are considered disruptive and aggressive. . . .

What I am trying to say as simple and as emphatically as I can is this: that colonial expansion and capital movements have not necessarily been parts of the same process. Indeed, in the cases of Britain and the United States, capital has flowed in far greater measure into regions where political domination and, therefore, exploitation have been impossible. In the process investors have taken risks—and frequently the consequences have been unhappy and without recourse.

A final observation: Capital movements, instead of constituting a malevolent force—as Lenin had it—are one of the great civilizing agencies of the modern world. If used to effect the change-over from primary to secondary and tertiary production—to convert primitive agricultural societies into manufacturing economies; to inaugurate hydro-electric projects, erect steel furnaces, build railways, improve harbours, establish branch banks—capital movements in the process raise standards of living and make welfare realizable. The misery of the East is not due to the foreign capital that shattered its idyllic content; its misery continues because the West never had enough surplus funds to invest in this area where such a large part of the world's population is to be found.

The whole theory of imperialistic exploitation can be disposed of easily enough by an examination of the experiences of Great Britain and the United States. In 1914 the long-term British investments overseas came to about four billions of pounds; all but three hundred millions were publicly issued securities, or portfolio investments. We have available a statistical breakdown for this latter group. How much of these holdings were to be found in regions of the earth where the exploitation of native peoples— because of political domination or interference—was possible? Actually, not much more than 30 per cent. That is to say, nearly 70 per cent of British portfolio investments were to be found in politically independent lands— where the investor entered at his own risk, and where standards of living were high rather than low. British capital had helped raise those standards; interestingly enough in some of those countries—in the United States, Canada, Australia, New Zealand—*per capita* national income per worker and *per capita* real wages were higher than those existing in England itself.

The record of the United States has been similar. In 1930 America had sixteen billions of dollars invested overseas divided equally between portfolio and direct investments. Where were these funds to be found? In the Caribbean, in China, in the Middle East? Not at all. Four billions were invested in Canada, five billions in Europe, three billions in Mexico, Argentina, Brazil, and Chile. In all, almost 75 per cent of American investments were in politically mature countries whose standards of living were already high or were rising because American funds were helping to improve the levels of production.

The English investor returned to America at the conclusion of the Civil War, in this case helping to lay down the great American railway net. The rails opened up the West and made America's agricultural surpluses available to Europe, thus for the first time changing the balance of trade in our favour. The rails were built of American iron and steel and made possible the appearance of her great steel industry, so that America's steel capacity was greater than England's by 1900. In short, English—and to a much lesser extent German and Dutch—capital helped to convert America into an industrial nation and to change its production from the primary to the secondary and tertiary stages. It was no accident that from 1850 to 1900 the real wages of American workers increased 100 per cent.

By 1899 foreign long-term capital invested in the United States stood at $3,300,000,000, of which $2,500,000,000 was British. Most of these funds were in American rails. By 1914—the last year that America was a debtor nation—foreign long-term investments in the United States totaled $7,090,000,000, of which $4,250,000,000 was British. In the depressions of 1873-9 and 1893-7 these investors lost heavily as many of the American railway companies were thrown into receivership.

In opening up these little-read chapters in English-American relations my intention is more than a sentimental one. If, by a common tradition, the two peoples are committed to an optimistic conception of human nature: to man's ability to rise through his personal striving because he is moral, rational and educable; if they are committed to the theory that through the Rule of Law and the maintenance of free political institutions, the indefeasible worth of every individual soul can be preserved; if they are committed to the idea of welfare—then how can we fail to agree on the programme to be carried out? . . .

Capital formation—in the nineteenth and a part of the twentieth centuries—in still under-developed countries was helped through capital movements. That was one of the great roles England performed for more than one hundred years; the United States, since World War I, has been seeking to follow in England's footsteps. Capital movements took place as a result of private initiative and the willingness to assume risks. With capital went engineers and chemists, physicians and teachers, periodicals and books: and the values of a civilization dedicated to the preservation of human freedom and individual integrity. These values Americans cherish and many know that they came to flower in England.

The relations between Britain and the United States prove the point I am trying to make. English capital—poured into America with a generous hand; frequently to the accompaniment of real risk; often with unfortunate results as investors were able to testify—helped to put the young republic on its feet and, in time, to make it one of the great producing nations of the world. . . .

The wisdom of Alexander Hamilton established the public and the private credit of the United States; the revolutionary foreign debt was to be paid; new public debt was to be secured by a sinking fund; the pre-war commercial claims of English merchants were to be met. In consequence, long-term foreign funds flowed into the United States to finance the American Government, to provide capital for the Bank of the United States, to start all kinds of private ventures in the new country. By 1803, according to the estimates of Samuel Blodget,[5] almost one-half of American public and private securities were to be found in foreign portfolios. Total security issues came to $129,700,000 of which $59,250,000 were in foreign hands and $34,700,000 were by British investors. The federal debt stood at $81,000,000; foreign ownership accounted for $43,000,000 of this. The Bank of the United States stock was $10,000,000; foreigners held $6,200,000. The stock of state-chartered banks totalled $26,000,000; foreign ownership came to $9,000,000. Lesser amounts had been invested by the British and the Dutch in American insurance and turnpike companies. Amusingly enough, even the purchase of Louisiana by the United States in the same year was made possible only because the actual cash payments Napoleon demanded were raised largely in London. The Louisiana bond issue was $11,250,000; $9,250,000 was taken by the English.

What was true—in the early years of the American republic—of dependence upon foreign capital for long-term requirements was even truer in the case of short-term financing. Up to the 1830s it was British funds that made possible the expansion of the American foreign trade—and the building up of America. American exports were paid for in cash through the English bill market; American imports—from Britain and from all parts of the world as well—were financed by English credits. In effect, an English private revolving fund was set up which protected the American dollar despite the fact that the balance of trade continued against the United States until long after the Civil War. . . .

Endnotes

1. Frederick J. Turner, *The Frontier in American History* (New York, 1920); *The Significance of Sections in American History* (New York, 1932).

2. Friedrich Ratzel, *Anthropogeographie*, 2 v. (Stuttgart, 1882-91). See also Ellen Churchill Semple, *Influences of Geographic Environment, on the Basis of Ratzel's System of Anthropogeography* (New York, 1911).

3. Louis M. Hacker, *The Shaping of the American Tradition*, 2 v. (New York, 1947). Cf. pp. xiv-xxiii, 3-28.

4. A. V. Dicey, *Introduction to the Study of the Law of the Constitution* (London, 1885).

5. Samuel Blodget, Jun., *Economica: A Statistical Manual for the United States of America* (Washington, 1806).

5

America's Frontier Heritage

RAY ALLEN BILLINGTON

Just as the political and social behavior of the American people was slightly altered by their frontiering experience, so were their habits as breadwinners. This is not to suggest that either today's industrial complexes or the country's economic might are the product of the pioneering past; the economy of the modern United States is primarily based upon the marketing and production revolutions that reshaped the entire Western world in the eighteenth and nineteenth centuries. Techniques utilizing machines rather than men originated largely in Europe, and on these the nation's production system rests. Yet three centuries of expansion gave the economy a new direction, endowed it with unusual vitality, and helped create a social environment in which it could thrive. Without a frontier the courses of the country's economic evolution would have been different; without an industrial revolution in Europe the differences would have been far greater.

These differences can be understood only if we think in terms of a major area of economic change lying adjacent to and immediately behind the spatial frontier, and steadily advancing westward with it. On the spatial

Ray Allen Billington, *America's Frontier Heritage* (New York: Holt, Rinehart and Winston,), pp. 159-179, 273-277. Copyright 1966 by Ray Allen Billington. Reprinted by permission of Mrs. Ray Allen Billington.

frontier itself, unusually abundant natural resources were exploited without substantially changing the national technology or marketing procedures. The merchants, speculators, millers, artisans, railroad builders, and others who catered to the needs of pioneer farmers or ranchers followed business customs perfected in the East with relatively few innovations. Nor did the frontier zone contribute markedly to the nation's economic growth, save during periods of spectacular mineral production such as that occurring between 1849 and 1876. During the pioneering period, speculative wealth flowed westward, in the pockets of frontiersmen who purchased excess lands against resale or from the pockets of Eastern and European investors who were willing to gamble for the high returns in an undeveloped region. The capital generated in the West by this flow was often plowed back into local business enterprises, for as long as a community was growing, merchants and shopkeepers wanted to grow with it. While the national economy benefited from the expansion of credit needed to sustain a pioneer economy—the proprietor of a frontier trading post or store usually obtained goods on credit from a wholesaler in a nearby city, who in turn purchased from an Eastern supplier, who often was financed by a New York or London bank—the volume of capital flow was too small to have a major influence on the pattern of economic growth nationally.

The area lying immediately behind the spatial frontier contributed far more substantially to the growth of the country's economy. There production could be stimulated only by technological improvements and expansion of markets, as abundant resources scarcely scratched by the pioneering generation were gradually brought into full use. There a concentration of capital attracted by the prospect of large return, a thickening population promising expanding markets, a more abundant labor pool than that provided on the frontier where cheaper lands were available, and improved transportation outlets connecting with both the populated East and the growing West, attracted business enterprise and men with inventive skills. Within this post-frontier zone occurred the full exploitation of natural resources that had been discovered on the spatial frontier.[1]

The exploitation that went on within this area must be conceived as constantly recurring; the process can best be visualized as the gradual peeling away of successive layers of resources, with each layer thicker than the last as techniques for its removal were more highly refined and manpower made available.[2] The rate of exploitation was determined by conditions behind this zone, where shifts or changes in population, improvements in technology, and fluctuations in demand made certain resources valuable and so worth producing in quantity. The spatial frontier also played a part, for expansion into areas of new resources allowed their "extensive" rather than "intensive" development. Had no such frontier existed, demands of the Eastern market would have required digging deeper and deeper into known resources; this would tend to force production into enterprises in which these raw materials could be used. Instead, production in the United States could respond more exactly to demands of the market and of the population's needs. Producers could select from a variety of resources as demand dictated, creating a more diversified economy and one better able to profit from changing demands in world markets. The result benefited both the economy and the spatial frontier, the former by allowing producers to shift their output to meet demands of the market more readily than in less-favored nations, the latter by stimulating the technological innovation needed to hurry economic development.[3]

The interplay of these forces accelerated the rate of national economic growth and helped shape America's affluent society of the twentieth century. They played this role by creating new opportunities for investment that in turn encouraged capital formation.[4] Through the history of the frontier, the growth and spread of population provided opportunities for investors, both in the West and throughout the nation where belief in the opportunity of pioneering encouraged a high birth rate and a steady flow of immigration from abroad. Growth of population, expansion westward, and the influx from Europe in turn accounted for a steady expansion of the economy that was irresistible to investors. As capital flowed westward, it continually opened new areas for investment that lured still more capital. Thus each new transportation route linking East and West encouraged investment in adjacent areas where shipping facilities spelled opportunity for the shrewd producer.[5] This investment stimulated the economy, attracted workers, and created conditions inducing more investment.

These investments, in turn, developed even more capital by stimulating savings. These were possible on frontiers because per capita income was nearly always above the subsistence level, allowing even slight surpluses to be saved, a condition lacking in the underdeveloped countries of the twentieth century. They were encouraged by the predominance of individually owned farms where income was more variable than in most enterprises. The constant threat of crop failures or falling prices encouraged pioneer farmers to put surpluses aside against a rainy day. These funds contributed to the massive accumulation of capital taking place nationally. They were supplemented by a flow of money from abroad to take advantage of the high interest rates paid in new and unstable areas. A no less important source of capital was the savings effected by the sequential exploitation of frontier resources; without these to draw upon more capital would have been sunk in the intensive use of resources already known.[6] All of these conditions released funds for investment and reinvestment, which spurred the economy to a rate of growth unknown elsewhere. From this stemmed a per capita income higher than that of any other nation in the nineteenth century.[7]

This affluence spread slowly, for the "natural wealth" of the frontier had no effect on society until it was translated into "social wealth." Riches buried in the ground were useless until extracted by man; man could make them usable only if he had the technological know-how, suitable transportation outlets, and a political system geared to the equitable distribution of resources among the people. Had frontier America been settled by men unversed in the use of machines or lacking the incentive values of capitalism, the "natural wealth" would have remained untapped. Instead, the West was occupied by pioneers capable of developing technical processes and carrying with them the seeds of democracy.[8] Inherited traits equipped the Americans to become a "people of plenty," but they could not have become a "people of plenty" if nature had not spread a frontier of undeveloped natural resources before them.

They developed these resources at a steadily accelerating rate, determined largely by their emerging technological abilities and incentives. As skills and capital multiplied, generation after generation peeled off successive layers of resources to be fed into the national economy. The first generation removed a very thin slice using primitive techniques; the next a deeper layer employing mechanical processes that were still in their infancy; the third dug still deeper with improved technological means; and so exploitation went on. The process was illustrated in simple form on the mining frontiers; there placer miners with their cradles and sluice boxes skimmed off a bit of surface wealth, quartz miners and river miners dug into the earth or dammed streams to extract a little more, and finally well-financed mining companies with drilling and rock-crushing machinery reached the hard core of precious metal deep in the earth. Sequential stages were needed to utilize nature's resources, but those sequential stages would have been impossible had not a frontier made those resources available. . . .

This abundance, coupled with the urge for self-improvement that was engrained in the Anglo-American character, planted traits and characteristics that have marked the American people for two centuries and that persist today. Pioneering accentuated materialistic attitudes, strengthened a go-ahead philosophy that quickened the pace of life, encouraged reckless wastefulness, and contributed to a proclivity to innovate, especially technological processes. No one of these traits is traceable solely to the frontier experience; all are rooted as much in hereditary as in environmental forces. Yet they have been identified with Americans to an unusual degree, and they have been noted particularly in frontier areas. . . .

That materialism should be a basic tenet in the philosophy of the frontiersman was logical, for his principal energies were directed toward supplying the elementary requirements of life.[9] . . . As a practical individual, the pioneer realized that first tasks must come first; until his land was cleared, his buildings constructed, his drainage system laid, his family's security provided, there was neither time nor energy for expression of other facets of character. In buckling to these practical pursuits he knew that he was creating wealth—wealth that would eventually buy the comforts and culture that were his dream. Riches assumed an importance not only for themselves, but for what they would acquire. Any pioneer who despised money under these circumstances would be, as a traveler put it, a candidate for the lunatic asylum.[10]

In such an atmosphere, the frontiersman was inclined to measure accomplishment by material standards, thinking of his neighbor as worth so many dollars, or judging a building by its size and cost rather than its beauty. No American pioneer could remark, as did an Englishman when told that New York's Woolworth Building was fireproof: "What a pity." To the Westerner, material possessions were the foundation for the good life, the talisman that would flood his future with culture and comforts, and the key to an elevated social status. This did not mean that he scorned the higher aspects of civilization; we have seen that a sizable proportion of the educated elite, at least, were dedicated to transplanting Eastern culture along the frontiers. It did mean that the pioneer's immediate concern was so focused on the accumulation of wealth that material values bulked larger in his life than in the lives of persons who lived in matured societies.

Thus motivated, he was willing to make almost any sacrifices in his pursuit of gain. Leisure was a luxury that could not be afforded; in the United States in general and in the West especially the pace of life accelerated during the nineteenth century. "There is," wrote a pioneer from the Michigan frontier, "so much work to be done, and so few people to do it, that the idea of labor is apt to absorb the entire area of the mind."[11] Everywhere along the frontier travelers noted the restless energy of the people, the feverish speed with which they worked, the reluctance to people, the feverish speed with which they worked, the reluctance to rest. . . . Men were willing to live amidst discomforts and inconveniences; the travel literature is sprinkled with descriptions of miserable hovels, overcrowding, primitive furniture, and littered fields, all endured because every effort was directed into producing goods that could be translated into wealth. The frontiersman, it was observed, would sell his crop and live on unpalatable food so that he could invest surpluses in more land, or forsake a comfortable home to live in a hovel while carving a clearing on a new frontier.[12]

Even the most sacred symbols of culture were corrupted on the frontier, if they stood in the way of material gain. "There is no Sabbath west of the Genesee"—or Missouri—or Pecos—became a byword of the West, because time was too precious to waste a whole Sunday, and work went on as usual. Ministers flattered by an invitation to visit a new community might be disappointed when they found their audience small and the invitation itself prompted by promoters who believed that a church would help sell lots.[13] Even the sanctity of the home suffered, as farmers and merchants neglected their families to spend more time at their tasks. "The exclusive pursuit of gain," sadly noted a traveler, "with the indifference to all which does not aid in its acquisition, are eating up family love and life throughout the West."[14]

Nature's beauty spots were victims of frontier acquisitiveness no less than church and home. Ugliness seemed to be sanctified by the pioneers as they littered their farms with debris, left ugly stumps standing, and neglected village improvements to use every inch of land for profits. A mill was built to utilize the water power at Niagara Falls' Goat Island, marring that stupendous spectacle for years. Mrs. Trollope, admiring a particularly lovely spot along the Erie Canal, was told by a young man that she should return five years hence for "I'll engage there will be by that time, half a score elegant factories—'tis a shame to let such a privilege of water lie idle."[15] . . . As an Easterner wrote from California: "So the seat of empire, in its travel westward, changes its base from soul to stomach, from brains to bowels."[16] No matter where he turned, the Westerner blighted the land's beauty in his drive for wealth.

This pursuit of gain sharpened his materialistic judgments, but it also helped breed in him—and in subsequent generations of Americans—a belief that hard work was the normal lot of man. The compulsion to endless labor is diminishing in twentieth-century America, but it still distinguishes the nation. In the United States no noontime siesta eases pressures as in Latin lands, no leisurely lunch period closes shops as in Britain, no lingering conversation in a sidewalk café provides an interval of relaxation as in France. Instead the American gulps a meal at his desk or in a quick-service restaurant, flirts with speeding tickets as he rushes to business appointments, and glories in the fact that he works harder than his neighbor. . . . The American spends his spare time whacking golf balls to better his score, or slamming tennis balls to best an opponent, or climbing mountains, skiing, sailing, camping, or hunting to prove his prowess. All of this reckless expenditure of energy strikes the European as slightly mad. He treasures moments of rest that the people of the United States cannot comprehend.

Glorification of hard work was noted as an American trait early in the nation's history. "The habits of life," recorded a sensitive observer at the beginning of the nineteenth century, "are those of an exclusively working people. From the moment he gets up, the American is at work, and he is engaged in it till the hour of sleep."[17] Travelers also noted that devotion to hard labor and distrust of leisure increased in a measurable ratio as they moved toward the frontier. "In traveling westward in this country," one wrote, "you may take your longitude by observing the decrements of the time occupied at meals."[18] In the West the pace of life accelerated; all was rush and bustle as men dashed from task to task lest one precious moment be wasted. One visitor believed that Americans lived twice as long as other people because they accomplished twice as much in a lifetime; another felt that they all wanted to perform within a year "what others do within a much longer period. Ten years in America is like a century in Spain."[19] This go-ahead spirit of the West made leisurely pursuits incomprehensible to the pioneers; travelers were frequently questioned as to their business interests because no one could understand that they journeyed for pleasure alone. . . .

This urge to work cannot be explained solely by the frontiering experience, of course; the Anglo-American tradition, the middle-class philosophy of the early settlers, and the Puritan ethic all helped glorify the concept of labor in the United States. Nor was the frontier a catalyst that transformed the indolent into the ambitious; squatters who lived on the outer fringes succumbed to indolence amidst the plenty that existed there, many of them victims of malnutrition or hookworm. Yet the mass of the small-propertied farmers who advanced civilization westward did develop a compulsion to labor that became part of the social environment of the successive Wests. . . . All about were riches galore in the form of untapped resources; only his labor was needed to transform them into wealth. So labor he did as he moved westward, knowing that any relaxation, any squandering of time, would only delay the coming of affluence. Expended energy paid higher dividends in an expanding society than in a static one, and this was the realization that unleashed the locomotive tendency in frontiersmen. . . .

The quest for wealth on America's frontiers contributed to the emergence of another national trait that has persisted into the twentieth century: flagrant wastefulness. No other western nation of the twentieth century so recklessly squanders its resources, or so heedlessly destroys its own creations. The United States, to visiting foreigners, is the land of the throwaway; paper handkerchiefs and paper plates, metal cans and plastic containers, no-deposit-no-return bottles are all made to be used once, then discarded. To a thrifty European the American factory is an assembly line to produce gadgets that will marvelously disintegrate after short use, the

American home a reverse assembly line to reduce those gadgets to basic rubble as rapidly as possible. In Britain a man prides himself on the vintage of his car, in America on its recency. Europeans will never cease to be shocked by the extravagant waste of paper bags in an American supermarket, or by the reckless manner in which nearly new machinery is thrown into the dump heap to make room for something better. They are equally astounded by the reluctance of the United States to preserve its dwindling resources, for not until the twentieth century did a conservation movement attract popular support, and even today nature's bounties are squandered with an abandon unknown in other lands.

Wastefulness came naturally to the frontiersman; who would think of preservation amidst overwhelming abundance? In his eyes nature's riches were so plentiful that their exhaustion was beyond comprehension. Why protect trees in a land where they grew by the billions? Why preserve soil when a move to virgin fields was cheaper than fertilizer? To these questions the pioneer had obvious answers. "Nothing on the face of the broad Earth is sacred to him," wrote an Englishman from the Far West. "Nature presents herself as his slave."[20] So the frontiersman felled forests, mined the soil with his wasteful farming methods, slaughtered game, honeycombed mountains with his mining shafts, overcropped pasturage with his herds, drained lakes, and altered the landscape as he moved in quest of wealth.

On the forested frontiers, trees were particular enemies, symbolizing the wilderness that must be destroyed. . . . All fell before his ax. . . . Travelers along the Old National Road that after 1818 linked the seaboard and the Ohio River complained of the bleakness of the countryside after the pioneers had passed on, leaving a desolate plain behind them. Everywhere the story was the same, because no pioneer was happy until the land was completely naked. "Then he tells you, it looks handsome," wrote a traveler with amazement.[21]

The soils of America suffered the same fate. With land cheap and both labor and fertilizers expensive, pioneers discovered that they could economize by plundering the soil through successive plantings, then move on. "The American," observed one of many British travelers who described this cycle, "seldom or never looks forward to the future and progressive improvement of his land, he uses it as asses are used in this country, worked while they have a spark of life in them, without one care about their support or preservation."[22] Soils were depleted so rapidly that their exhaustion was a primary factor in the westward movement, leaving behind starved fields as their owners pushed on to new frontiers. . . . Oldtimers in Nebraska, so the story goes, used to brag to younger men: "Why, son, by the time I was your age I had wore out three farms."[23]

The habit of wastefulness ingrained in the frontiersmen has been transmitted to later generations in somewhat different form. Today reforestation has restored damaged hillsides, and chemical fertilizers have revitalized butchered soils, but exploitive tendencies were too firmly embedded to be abandoned with the passing of the frontier. The pioneer was reckless with nature's riches because their abundance encouraged waste; the twentieth-century American thinks in terms of planned obsolescence because the plentitude of artifacts and the ease with which he acquires them disinclines him to preserve the old. . . .

Any portrait of the American must depict him not only as a wasteful squanderer but as a consistent innovator, given to experimentation, and inclined to try out new processes or gadgets even when the old are perfectly useful. This inclination was the marvel of the Western world during the nineteenth century. "Would any one but an American," asked an Englishman in the 1860s, "have ever invented a milking machine? or a machine to beat eggs? or machines to black boots, scour knives, pare apples, and do a hundred other things that all other peoples have done with their ten fingers from time immemorial?"[24] Who but an American, he might have added, would have substituted mechanical for human power on the farm by developing gang plows, reapers, threshing machines, seed drills, combines, and a host more? Who but an American would have conceived of the assembly line and the mass-production industries made possible by that labor-saving device? Who but an American would have dreamed of putting the computer to work for mankind so effectively that automation threatened to put half the population out of work? Americans, to Europeans at least, are inventive geniuses whose especial bent is the displacement of men by machines.

Was this the result of the frontiering experience? Visitors from Europe during the eighteenth and nineteenth centuries thought that it was, and Westerners agreed with them. They saw invention as necessary on frontiers, where unique conditions demanded unique artifacts and methods. "The want of those arts and inventions, by which the inhabitants of older countries accomplish their ends," wrote one of the Ohio Valley's most perceptive observers, "renders it necessary for the people of a new state, to invent and substitute others, as emergencies may arise."[25] To Europeans the frontier was "a land of experiment," and the frontiersmen persons with "an extraordinary talent for invention."[26] They acquired those skills through necessity, "having been accustomed to do for themselves in small societies." . . .

In judging the validity of this testimony, we must determine whether conditions in new communities were of the sort to stimulate or retard the inventive process. Innovation, psychologists know, is the achievement of an obstructed wish; an inventor conceives the end that he wishes to achieve, then finds means of overriding the obstacles that stand in his way. These are usually the habits and attitudes acquired by long practice. . . . In a society where the past is venerated or dominates the present completely, traditionalism becomes an insurmountable obstacle. In a new society, where the opposite is true, a break with precedent is far easier. Frontier communities, where people were recruited from a variety of backgrounds and where a strange environment shattered precedents, provided exceptional breeding grounds for innovation.[27]

The testimony of hundreds of visitors and Westerners agrees that lack of fixed practices along the frontiers stimulated invention. They saw the pioneers as newcomers to a way of life as well as to a new geographic location, so unique as to be "almost the termination of existence." "In flying to the wilderness," wrote a traveler, "they fly a thousand constraints which society must always impose." In doing so they turned their faces from the past to the future, and having little to look back upon, were inclined to devise techniques and artifacts best suited to their new way of life. "Nothing," noted a Missourian, "has been venerated or revered merely because it exists or has endured."[28]

No less a stimulant to frontier inventiveness was the sparseness of population, which ruled out division of labor, forcing each pioneer to satisfy his family's needs. "With the first emigration," announced a guidebook, "there are few mechanics; hence every settler becomes expert in supplying his own necessities."[29] Did he need a home, he could not call in a contractor but must build it himself with the aid of neighbors. Did he require a plow, he must fashion it from local materials, buying only the iron parts from a blacksmith. Did his family need clothing, the cloth must be made and the garments sewed by the housewife. Did illness strike, no doctors could be called and reliance must be placed on the advice of the almanac and common sense. As the frontiersman built, so did he experiment, adapting past artifacts to present needs. The evolution of the "Kentucky" rifle or the American ax from their crude European counterparts testified to his skills. This constant practice endowed the pioneer with the mechanical techniques needed for invention, and encouraged him to think in terms of improvement rather than tradition. . . .

The physical climate along the frontiers was as conducive to innovation as the social. Changing geographic environments as population shifted westward meant the outmoding of implements and customs. Scythes suitable to the hilly farms of New England were inefficient on the level prairies of Illinois. Plows used for centuries were unworkable on the heavy sod of eastern Nebraska. Techniques originated in Europe and followed in the humid eastern half of the United States proved outmoded in the semiarid western half. Experimentation became a stark necessity if men were to survive, and with each experiment the bonds of custom were loosened. Practices only a decade old were easier to break than those centuries old.[30] Labor shortages in new communities also stimulated the inventive urge; with manpower lacking as cheap lands absorbed potential farm or factory laborers, mechanical power was the only solution. . . .

Although both logic and contemporary testimony suggest that the frontier was an area of innovation unmatched in Europe or the East, some visitors of that day and some scholars of today have argued that the pioneer was less inclined to experimentation than his fellow Americans in the seaboard states. They point out that improved farming techniques were but coldly received along the frontiers; in the pre-Civil War era reformers who urged practices to preserve and improve soils found readier listeners east of the Appalachians than in the Mississippi Valley. "I find a large portion of our farmers prejudiced against every variety of improvement," wrote a salesman for a farm periodical from Illinois, "particularly where the knowledge of that improvement is to be acquired from books."[31] Even during the Civil War, when manpower shortages encouraged farm mechanization, the frontier adopted labor-saving machinery only slowly.[32] Contemporaries and historians who point this out have also emphasized the pioneers' reluctance to venture into untried regions; frontiersmen, they say, resisted the transition from forest to prairie agriculture for a generation even though English immigrants had demonstrated that the grasslands of Indiana and Illinois made ideal farms. Frontiersmen also, it is argued, lagged in the inventive process; not only most industrial but most agricultural improvements were patented by Easterners rather than Westerners.

Those who hold this position fail to grasp one essential point: changes in human behavior must be measured in relative rather than absolute terms. We can label the pioneer an innovator only if we find him *comparatively* more willing to accept and sponsor change than his Eastern or European cousin. Man is by nature a traditionalist, comfortably following established paths until jolted by some unpleasant necessity. No such urgency turned Mississippi Valley farmers of the pre-Civil War period toward improved farming techniques, for the virgin soils produced all that the market could absorb; only the butchered soils of the seaboard states sparked a demand for reform there. Similarly, the slowness of Americans to adjust to prairie agriculture may shock modern scholars, but to Europeans of that day they adapted with startling rapidity; the transition was made in a single generation while on the Continent farm techniques resisted change for centuries. When goaded by necessity, the pioneer proved a willingness to change that contrasted with the relative lethargy of Easterners.

Our concern, moreover, is with the effect of the frontier on the American habit of innovation, not solely with the frontiersman's contribution in that process. The proper question to be asked is not whether the pioneer devised significant inventions, but whether the *existence* of a frontier in the United States made the American people *relatively* more inclined to experimentation than the Europeans and whether that spirit of experimentation was more noticeable in the West than in the East.

No profound knowledge of mechanical invention is needed to realize that frontiers were ill-suited to produce major contributions. Educational training, wealth, leisure, and the opportunity for intellectual communication among persons of like interests—all essential ingredients in the inventive process—were lacking in pioneer areas. Nor was the frontier's intellectual atmosphere conducive to invention, for the materialistic climate discouraged the abstract theorizing essential to creative thought. Yet the presence of a frontier did stimulate innovation, partly by helping to engender a spirit conducive to experimentation, partly by creating a demand for new products, and partly by fostering an attitude receptive to change as opposed to stability. . . .

A no less important function of the frontier in stimulating innovation was to create a demand for new products that could only be met by invention. Constantly changing conditions as population surged westward challenged inventors throughout the eighteenth and nineteenth centuries; a man who could devise a new product or a new technique suitable to a particular need, or who could substitute a mechanical for a hand-powered implement to offset the perennial labor shortage, stood to make a handsome profit for himself. This was the incentive that sent would-be inventors who lived behind the frontier to their drafting boards, and that inspired thousands of inventions. Travelers in the pre-Civil War era often expressed amazement at the labor-saving machinery used in the West or displayed at county fairs: sulky plows that allowed the farmer to ride, seed planters, threshing machines, mechanical clothes washers, and a hundred more.[33] In the post-war years the advance into the Great Plains offered a new incentive to inventors; they responded by producing wire fencing, improved windmills to suck subsurface moisture to the surface, farm machinery needed for the extensive agriculture practiced there, and dry farming techniques. Inventors in Illinois, Indiana, and other states behind the frontier perfected these wonders, but they did so only because they recognized a market on the frontier.[34] The constantly altering demands of a westward-moving population proved a stimulant to innovation lacking in nonfrontier nations.

Such an incentive would not have existed if farmers on successive frontiers had showed a reluctance to accept new machines and untried gadgets. The reception awaiting any invention is as indicative as the invention itself of the flexibility of the society in which it is developed.

Invention is like a seed falling on different types of soil; the soil may be too wet, too dry, too sandy, too rocky, for the seed to sprout. In the same fashion, an invention will be accepted in one cultural soil, but not in another. The rate of acceptance is determined by the degree of readiness of any society to absorb a modification or addition to its culture.[35] . . .

Studies of the acceptance of innovation in rural areas show that the speed with which farmers modify existing practices is influenced by many factors. The increase in profits to be expected from change is all-important, but scarcely less influential is the nature of the leadership structure of the community. Where an elite class exists and accepts innovation, the remainder of the population usually follows. In terms of the speed with which changes are adopted, farmers can be divided into "innovators" who experiment constantly, "adoption leaders" who accept any proven new device, "later adopters" who follow in large numbers, and "nonadopters." In other words, any community equipped with influential leaders and unrestrained by tradition is particularly receptive to innovations, for the leaders are alert to the greater profits promised and the others are willing to follow their example at varying speeds.[36]

Communities fitting this description were normal near the frontiers. The stratification that occurred early in the history of pioneer settlements elevated an informed group of leaders who were especially alert to profits, sufficiently vocal to make their needs known, and able to influence their neighbors. Perhaps even more important was the fact that these leaders combined knowledge and intelligence to a degree that their error judgments were comparatively few, since every innovation was carefully weighed against local conditions before adoption. This meant that the frontier was not an area of change for change's sake, but a region where change was quickly adopted as soon as greater profits were proved probable. Thus frontiersmen before the Civil War ignored Eastern pressures for improved farming techniques simply because poor transportation facilities precluded the export of extensive surpluses. Why bother with special seeds, manuring, careful soil cultivation, and selective livestock breeding when the pioneer's whole purpose was to maintain a subsistence level until he could sell his lands at a speculative profit? The frontiersman who resisted the advice of farm journals and reformers was not opposed to change; he simply knew that his profits would be high enough without change.[37] With the coming of railroads and the opening of world markets the pioneers of the Great Plains country became more interested in improvements; the vogue of mechanized agriculture and bonanza farming in the 1870s and 1880s testified to that. The frontier farmer was eager to accept innovation just as soon as his community leaders convinced themselves that change would be to their advantage.

A case study of one Iowa county between 1855 and 1885 illustrates this fact. There in the early years of settlement, newspapers, farm journals, and agricultural societies all preached the advantages of new crops, new livestock breeds, and new fencing materials; there "drummers" from the highly competitive farm implement industry peddled their wares so effectively that few farmers were unaware of the latest improvements. Some resisted at first, for the investment demanded was large and the risk of proportionately greater profits high. Opposition soon crumbled when the 110 farmers who occupied the upper rungs of society swung into line. These were the natural leaders, holders of offices in the farm organizations, and dictators of social affairs. More important, most of this group could afford to take risks, for some were absentee owners of considerable wealth, others were large resident operators, and still others were merchant-farmers or stock-dealing farmers who supplemented their income in other ways. All could experiment without fear of complete failure if the new breed of cattle or the new power reaper turned out badly. This group was the first to purchase new products or try new techniques. As soon as the success of the experiment was proved, the rest of the farmers fell into line, motivated by the urge to keep pace with their superiors. If the history of this county is typical, the frontier was an area of cautious experimentation in which innovation was somewhat more common than in older areas.[38]

That the frontiersman was no compulsive experimenter, but that he would change if shown that change was to his advantage, is revealed no less in the history of legal institutions than in that of mechanical inventions. Evidence on this point is ample. Along the frontiers, lawyers and judges alike were usually scantily educated in the common law and distrustful of the pettifogging that seemed designed only to bilk the innocent of their rights. They were inclined to judge issues on the basis of common sense rather than legal precedents. As they applied this philosophy to the unique problems faced in the West, they altered imported practices and in certain areas pioneered a distinctly American law.[39]

One change stemmed from the conflict over land titles that was usual in regions successively occupied by France, Spain, England, and the United States. Untangling this legal skein overtaxed the facilities of the common law; "In many Cases Our practice and policy here, differs widely from their's," observed one justice as he justified the upsetting of an English precedent.[40] Another basic change in procedure stemmed from the need for some legally constituted body to suggest laws that would solve unusual Western problems. The pioneers fastened upon the grand jury to perform this function and expanded its activities in a variety of ways that would have shocked British courts: to relay protests to Washington against actions of the federal government, to voice complaints against territorial officials, to recommend suitable candidates in local elections, as a prod to force legislatures into needed action.[41] Even ordinary juries were endowed with extra power so they could be counted upon to side with debtors against creditors.[42] Beyond the Mississippi the semiarid land required even greater variations of traditional practices, as systems of irrigation law were developed that seriously invaded property rights in the accepted English or Eastern sense. Necessity similarly forced a revolution in legal practices in the mining camps where miners were given the right to use water and extract precious metals without owning a single inch of the land on which they operated—doctrines that Blackstone would have found incomprehensible.[43] All these innovations were eventually given statutory respectability by Congress, and have become an accepted part of American law.

This array of evidence leads inevitably to the conclusion that the existence of a frontier in America during its pioneering period did help promote a climate where innovation was more acceptable than in older societies. The frontiersman, like his fellows everywhere, was more comfortable on a beaten path than on an unblazed trail. But the realities of his life forced him to improvise. The absence of economic specialization in sparsely settled regions and the uniqueness of the situations that he encountered on successive frontiers required new techniques, new instruments, new practices. Less encumbered by tradition, he was free to experiment, and to welcome products or ideas that would make life easier for him. His own jack-of-all-trade inclinations and the challenge that he threw before inventors in the settled areas behind the frontier alike helped create in the United States a social environment less restrained by tradition than in England or Europe, and one in which innovation was more acceptable.

Endnotes

1. The distinction between these two frontiers is discussed in Benjamin H. Higgins, *Economic Development: Principles, Problems, and Policies* (New York, 1959), p. 189.

2. George G. S. Murphy and Arnold Zellner, "Sequential Growth, the Labor-Safety-Value Doctrine and the Development of American Unionism," *Journal of Economic History,* XIX (September 1959), pp. 402-421, is the best discussion of the subjects treated in this paragraph.

3. George G. S. Murphy and Arnold Zellner, "The Turnerian Frontier Process: Generator of Social and Economic Opportunity," paper read at meeting of American Historical Association, December 1959, pp. 1-3, 10-12.

4. Alvin H. Hansen, *Fiscal Policy and Business Cycles* (New York, 1941), p. 360. Hansen estimates that about one half of the nation's net capital formation during the nineteenth century was traceable to population growth and territorial expansion.

5. An excellent case study of the effect of Ohio's canal system on adjacent regions is in Carter Goodrich *et al.*, *Canals and American Economic Development* (New York, 1961). The subject is more broadly discussed in Walter Isard, "Transportation Development and Business Cycles," *Quarterly Journal of Economics,* LVII (November 1942).

6. Murphy and Zellner, "Turnerian Frontier Process," *loc. cit.*, pp. 13-18.

7. Convincing statistical evidence on this point is in Karl W. Deutsch, *Nationalism and Social Communication* (Boston, 1953), pp. 36-45.

8. The best discussion of these subjects is in David M. Potter, *People of Plenty: Economic Abundance and the American Character* (Chicago, 1954), pp. 78-90.

9. This theory is advanced in A. H. Maslow, *Motivation and Personality* (New York, 1954).

10. Combe, *Notes on the United States of North America,* II, 197-198.

11. Caroline M. Kirkland, *Western Clearings* (New York, 1845), p. 88. Another traveler wrote: "Every moment, of every day, the mind, the ingenuity, the exertion, of the settler, are on the stretch, merely to procure just enough to support existence." Howitt, *Selections from Letters,* pp. 44-45.

12. Isaac Weld, *Travels Through the States of North America, and the Provinces of Upper and Lower Canada, during the years 1795, 1796, and 1797* (London, 1807), I, 292.

13. George W. Barnes, "Pioneer Preacher—An Autobiography," *Nebraska History* XXVII (April-June 1946), pp. 79-80; Mrs. Houston, *Hesperos: or Travels in the West* (London, 1850), I, 107-108.

14. Quoted in Robert G. Athearn, *Westward the Briton* (New York, 1953), pp. 93-94.

15. Marryat, *A Diary in America,* I, 209; Trollope, *Domestic Manners of the Americans,* pp. 372-373.

16. Samuel Bowles, *Across the Continent* (Springfield, Mass., 1866), pp. 201-202.

17. Michael Chevalier, *Society, Manners and Politics in the United States* (Boston, 1839), pp. 283-284. For a similar comment see Harriet Martineau, *Society in America* (New York, 1837), II, 136-137.

18. Hodgson, *Letters from North America,* I, 153. Observations on the pace of life in the West are also in Basil Hall, *Travels in North America, in the Years 1827 and 1828* (Edinburgh, 1829), I, 138, and Dwight L. Dumond ed., *Letters of James Gilespie Birney, 1831-1837* (New York, 1938), I, 69.

19. Marryat, *A Diary in America,* I, 18; Francis Lieber, ed., *Letters to a Gentleman in Germany* (Philadelphia, 1834), p. 287.

20. William A. Baillie-Grohman, *Camps in the Rockies* (New York, 1882), p. 21.

21. Francis Wright, *Views of Society and Manners in America* (London, 1821), p. 197. Comparable observations are in Thomas Ashe, *Travels in America, Performed in 1806* (London, 1808), II, 238-239; William N. Blane, *An Excursion through the United States and Canada, during the Years 1822-23* (London, 1824), p. 125; Francis Hall, *Travels in Canada and the United States in 1816 and 1817* (London, 1818), p. 46; Charles J. Latrobe, *The Rambler in North America* (London, 1835), I, 135; Charles Lyell, *Travels in North America* (London, 1845), I, 20-21; and E. Stanley, *Journal of a Tour in America, 1824-1825* (n.p., 1930), pp. 71, 182.

22. Howitt, *Selections from Letters,* p. 200. Similar comments are in Combe, *Notes on the United States of North America,* II, 334; D. Griffiths, Jr., *Two Years' Residence in the New Settlements of Ohio* (London, 1835), p. 65; Frederick L. Olmstead, *A Journey in the Back Country* (New York, 1860), p. 20; and Weld, *Travels through the States of North America,* II, 328.

23. William W. Johnson, *Kelly Blue* (New York, 1960), p. 122.

24. Thomas Nichols, *Forty Years of American Life,* 1820-1861 (New York, 1937), p. 63.

25. Daniel Drake, *Discourse on the History, Character, and Prospects of the West* (Cincinnati, Ohio, 1834), pp. 8-9.

26. Baillie-Grohman, *Camps in the Rockies,*pp. 20-21; Mackay, *The Western World,* II, p. 296.

27. This paragraph is summarized from an extensive discussion in Abbott P. Usher, *A History of Mechanical Inventions,* 2nd ed. (New York, 1954), pp. 56-83.

28. William T. Harris, *Remarks Made during a Tour Through the United States of America, in the Years 1817, 1818, and 1819* (Liverpool, 1819), p. 48; Wright, *Views of Society and Manners in America,* p. 190; John J. Ingalls, *The Writings of John Ingalls* (Kansas City, Kansas 1902), pp. 465-466. Similar comments are in Houston, *Hesperos,* I, 116-117, and Kirkland, *Western Clearings,* p. vii.

29. John M. Peck, *A New Guide for Emigrants to the West* (Boston, 1836), pp. 122-123.

30. Clarence H. Danhof, "American Evaluations of European Agriculture," *Journal of Economic History. Supplement IX* (1949), pp. 61-71.

31. *Western Farmer,* May 1835, quoted in R. Carlyle Buley, *The Old Northwest: Pioneer Period,* 1815-1840 (Indianapolis, Indiana 1950), I, 197-198.

32. Earle D. Ross, "Retardation in Farm Technology Before the Power Age," *Agriculture History,* XXX (January 1956), pp. 11-14.

33. James Caird, *Prairie Farming in America* (New York, 1859), pp. 56-57.

34. Walter P. Webb, *The Great Plains* (Boston 1931), pp. 510-515. This book describes the impact of the Great Plains on invention. His conclusions are challenged in Fred A. Shannon, "An Appraisal of Walter Prescott Webb's *The Great Plains,*" *Critiques of Research in the Social Sciences*: III (New York, 1940), pp. 79-97, which points out that inventions were made behind, not on the frontier. Shannon does not dispute the stimulus to invention provided by the Great Plains frontier.

35. This theme is developed in two works by William F. Ogburn, *Social Change with Respect to Culture and Original Nature* (New York, 1922), pp. 99-102, and *Technology and International Relations* (Chicago, 1949), pp. 16-27.

36. This material is drawn from the excellent article by Allan G. Bogue, "Pioneer Farmers and Innovation," *Iowa Journal of History,* LVI (January 1958), pp. 1-36.

37. Earle D. Ross, *Iowa Agriculture; An Historical Survey* (Iowa City, Iowa, 1951), p. 49.

38. Hamilton County, Iowa, was the subject of this study, the results of which are summarized in Bogue, "Pioneer Farmers and Innovation," *loc. cit.,* pp. 6-36.

39. The best discussions of the frontier's impact on the common law are in Roscoe Pound, *The Spirit of the Common Law* (Boston 1921), and Francis R. Aumann, *The Changing American Legal System: Some Selected Phases* (Columbus, Ohio, 1940), pp. 9-152 and especially pp. 14-16. Both credit the frontier with major importance as a molding force. The opposite viewpoint is argued in a biography of a frontier judge: William B. Hamilton, *Anglo-American Law on the Frontier: Thomas Rodney and His Territorial Cases* (Durham, N.C., 1953). Further discussion of the transfer of legal institutions to the West is in the introduction to the following collections of documents: Francis S. Philbrick, "The Laws of Indiana Territory, 1801-1809," *Illinois State Historical Library Collections,* XXI (Springfield, Ill., 1930); Francis S. Philbrick, ed., "The Laws of Illinois Territory, 1809-1818," *Illinois State Historical Library Collections,* XXV (Springfield, Ill., 1950); and William W. Blume, ed., *Transactions of the Supreme Court of Michigan,* 1805-1837, 5 volumes (Ann Arbor,

Michigan 1935-1940). Some additional information is in John H. Bickett, Jr., "Origin of Some Distinctive Features of Texan Civilization," Philosophical Society of Texas, *Proceedings of the Annual Meeting, Dallas, December 1, 1945* (Dallas, Texas, 1946), pp. 9-48. A competent review article summarizing works on the subject is Clarence E. Carter, "The Transit of Law to the Frontier: A Review Article," *Journal of Mississippi History*, XVI (July 1954), pp. 183-192.

40. Quoted in Carter, "The Transit of Law to the Frontier," *loc. cit.*, p. 191.

41. Richard D. Younger, "The Grand Jury on the Frontier," *Wisconsin Magazine of History*, XL (Autumn 1956), pp. 3-8.

42. Pound, *Spirit of the Common Law*, pp. 120-127.

43. Brief discussions of changes in irrigation and mining law are in Webb, *Great Plains*, pp. 431-446. On mining law see also Rodman W. Paul, *California Gold: The Beginning of Mining in the Far West* (Cambridge, Mass., 1947), pp. 210-216.

6

Does GNP Measure Growth and Welfare?

OSKAR MORGENSTERN

The question posed by the above title raises a number of deep problems of economic science. The question seems simple, yet in those few words—measurement, growth, and welfare—culminate the problems of large areas with which economists have been concerned for centuries. How nice it would be, then, if one could report that now we have one single concept and, indeed, one single number which could summarize variations of growth and welfare. As we shall see, this unfortunately is not the case.

To begin with measurement: All sciences have to come to grips with that problem. It is an extremely difficult one and each science has its own troubles. When a measurement in any field has become possible this is rightly hailed as a great achievement, as a step toward new discoveries and innumerable applications. Even to have a precise measure of time is difficult: Clocks are a late development in human history, and to this day we try to make them more and more accurate, because so much depends on

Oskar Morgenstern, who with John von Neumann wrote *Theory of Games and Economic Behavior* in 1944, was professor of economics at New York University at the time "Does GNP Measure Growth and Welfare?" was written, initially as remarks at the university's Key Issues Lecture Series. It is reprinted by permission from the *Business and Society Review*, Fall 1975, Number 15, pp. 23-31. © 1975, Warren, Gorham and Lamont Inc., 210 South Street, Boston, Mass. All rights reserved.

them. So it is not surprising that when it was recently reported that the rotation of the earth—our finest measure of time—may have slowed down during the last year by one second, this caused great interest in physics and astronomy. From this reaction we also get an idea of the high standards in those sciences. In other fields we measure blood pressure, barometric pressure, the composition of blood, temperature, the speed of light, etc., etc., sometimes crudely, sometimes with extraordinary precision.

Think First, Count Later

Although in the physical and even in the biological sciences a great and firm tradition has been built up over the centuries, the matter of observation and measurement is never closed. Science is never finished; rather, for all time, science is only an approximation of the underlying reality. It may surprise you that in spite of this great tradition Einstein more than once remarked to me, "Most scientists naively think they know what they should observe and how they should measure it." And he had the natural sciences in mind!

How, then, is the situation in the social sciences, in particular in economics? In some manner we seem to be more fortunate than the natural sciences. Nature shows itself to our senses essentially in a qualitative way, and to get to numbers of high precision requires great effort and is a formidable achievement. But in economics we can count the number of inhabitants of a town or a country, the number of motor cars, of checks cashed, of tons of steel produced, of . . . well of almost anything—or so it seems. Since it looks to be so simple to observe and count, there is in economics—as well as in other social sciences—no tradition which would enforce high standards. Counting seems natural, and what is counted is readily accepted. But that is true only up to the point where broader notions are encountered, notions such as "growth" and "welfare." Or even more basic, the question of what is "value" and "utility" promptly causes great difficulty.

Suddenly we see that we have to have sharp concepts, that we must ask questions to which we normally get only qualitative, not—at least not right away—quantitative answers. There is little doubt what an individual is, or a motor car, or a check. But to observe "growth," or "utility," or "welfare" for a whole nation is an entirely different matter. Surely people are involved, or cars that can be counted, or monies changing hands, and so on; but to state how the economy grows, and whether welfare changes and by how much, are entirely different matters. Such words mean very different things to different people. For many, they are abstractions that mean nothing concrete or tangible. It is a long way from that to truly scientific, objective knowledge. What we need are concepts. There is no escape from that, no matter how primitive our approach may be.

Let us first look at "growth." That is clearly a notion that applies to an organism. The human body grows, stops growing, and eventually dies. The body has many parts and many functions. It grows not only all together, as a whole, but parts of it grow at different rates (and not forever, as Galileo knew); and the whole is of unimaginable complexity, which modern biology reveals to us in a rapid though still partial manner. In the whole process of organic growth there is control, genetic planning, and unified function. Can the economy be compared with this so that we can transfer the notion of organic growth from this area to our field? One thing the economy certainly has in common with the human body: The economy is also of the highest complexity. Consequently one must expect that even an adequate qualitative description is correspondingly difficult.

I find, however, that very few people, even few economists—or should I say, regretfully, especially economists—have a real appreciation and understanding of the immense complexity of an economic system. Now, I have used the word *system*, but it is not even clear whether that word is appropriate, because we do not understand fully the organizing principles that make possible the economic life of a nation. One need only observe what happens in an ordinary person's day and what is considered to be absolutely obvious and normal. We take a bus or train in the morning, we go to stores, we buy, the money is accepted with which we pay, or we pay by a check which will be transmitted—by mails about which we have no control whatsoever—to an anonymous institution, possibly far away; the stores order and have things in stock; they set prices on the basis of the expectation of what competitors might be doing; we buy on the basis of expectation as to what our needs might be in the future and how they will be met; we spend our money today because we expect that our salaries, or incomes from other sources, actually will be paid at certain dates in the near or more distant future, etc., etc.

In all this, there is no central genetic regulation, nobody who plans for all, no one to whom everybody is responsible. We carry a great deal of information in our heads, and that which we do not carry we can find in newspapers, which gather information and are printed, again motivated only by their own self-interest, namely, to be published and sold with profit. At present—at this very moment—raw materials are being produced, and there is no conceivable way of telling how they will be finally molded, into which kind of finished products they will be turned. A steel producer has no idea whether his steel will be used for the making of tanks, or ships, or paper clips.

And yet all this works, and works miraculously well, although of course it is easily subject to great disturbances. The astonishing fact is not that the thing works so well, but that it works at all. It is only when we realize the complexity of the economy that we begin to see, and possibly understand, how dangerous it is to interfere in these matters. The economic system is subject to great changes caused by technology, by political events, by changes in the desires and wishes of consumers.

Any living organism is in many ways a very much simpler matter. However, if one knows anything at all about physiology, one finds that statement horrendous, because one can hardly imagine anything more finely tuned and more complicated than, let us say, the human body, not to mention the brain, which, without any doubt, is the most complicated thing . . . in the whole universe, and whose functioning we clearly do not understand, although we have a tremendous amount of knowledge of it. The fact is that the human body has one specific purpose: to stay functioning, to stay alive. We cannot say that the economic system has any such clear purpose.

Introducing a Little Chaos

In the light of such observations, one should be extremely modest in making proposals for policy. In general, I would say that unless we are reasonably sure that we know what the consequences of new policy measures will be—for example, of new taxes introduced, prices regulated, etc., etc.—we should leave things alone. One ought interfere only if one believes that one understands the consequences of the interference. The same is true of medicine: It took a long time to come from the witch doctor to the modern brain surgeon. While presumably the human physiology—or that of any other biological entity—stays practically the same throughout centuries or millennia (although subject to evolution over hundreds of thousands of years), the economic system—to make things still more difficult—is constantly being changed, especially by technology. Technology is an interference from the outside; it is absorbed in a manner which those who bring it into economic existence think to be profitable for them, but whose global effects they neither understand nor care about. Clearly, this compounds the difficulties of policy, because what might have been a suitable measure to achieve desired results at one time may no longer have any validity under present or future circumstances. It takes a long time to develop a scientifically acceptable new idea of policy; and while it is being born, if that happens at all, new features appear in the economic life. For example, Keynesian policy ideas of the 1930s are being adopted by the U.S.

government now—a time when they have virtually no applicability whatsoever.

Thus, the "growth" of an economy is a very different matter from the growth of an organism. The economy has neither a beginning nor an end. In addition, the economy is constantly in flux. So it is perhaps not surprising that, apart from some highly technical and abstract models of economic expansion—which is not the same thing as growth—there simply does not exist a generally accepted scientific concept which would give us the basis for a reliable numerical measurement of the rate of growth.

What About GNP?

But, you say, there is GNP, gross national product, i.e., the turnover in an economy in a unit period—a hallowed notion in contemporary economics. It is used with abandon. I shall say more about it later. For now I want to point out only one of its quantitative features: It is expressed by a single number, a so-called scalar. We discussed organic growth of a human body. Would anybody . . . imagine that there could be a single scalar number which would adequately describe the development of a human from babyhood to maturity to old age: the growth of the body, of the mind, of capabilities? The idea is so ludicrous that we can dismiss it from the outset. We have just seen that the economy, too, is of high complexity; therefore, to think that its description, or rather its changes, could be given and measured—accurately, without the slightest error of measurement— by one scalar number is equally absurd.

Just to show the absurdity and limitation of this popular alleged "concept," consider this: Anything that leads to a transaction in monetary form, where goods or services change hands against money, is recorded as positive. No matter what is being sold, it is added to GNP. It may have been sales of goods already stocked, it may have been a car just coming out of a factory: it does not matter. Neither does it matter what kind of product it is: atomic bombs, drugs, cars, food, aesthetic pollution by new billboards . . . you name it. Clearly, that goes against common sense. Why should all products and services be treated alike? Why should I accept more nuclear weapons as part of the "growth" of the economy? Of course, one could argue that one is interested only in transactions. But then one would have a great deal of explaining to do about how a larger number of transactions can possibly be related to "welfare." Does the uncontrolled increase of cancer cells in a child mean "growth"?

There are other and equally well-known difficulties. Many services are rendered and many goods are produced that never enter a market. Thus they escape GNP. As has been often noted, if housewives were being paid by their husbands GNP would rise, although there would not be one iota of difference in production or services. . . .

Another trouble with the GNP concept is that it measures, or rather expresses, as positive (i.e., as adding to GNP) the malfunctions of the economic system or society. To wit: if we are stuck in one of the thousands of traffic jams, if airplanes are stacked and cannot land on schedule, if fires break out, or other disasters occur that require repair—up goes the GNP. More gasoline is used, fares go up, overtime has to be paid, and so on. It would be difficult to find in any other science a "measure" which simultaneously tells opposite stories of the functioning of a complex system with one single scalar number! If we merely improve the scheduling of airplanes and stagger the times of automobile traffic, and nothing else is changed—down goes GNP! It goes up, on the other hand, if industry pollutes the air and we create other industries to remove the polluting substances.

So we see that there is real trouble with the basic underlying notion of GNP. It is not an acceptable scientific concept for the purposes for which it is used. The fact that it violates common sense might not be considered critical. There are, after all, many concepts in physics which common sense could never create or might reject, such as "curved space." But these concepts are the product of powerful theories and are needed when a scientific field is already well developed. The GNP action, however, is nothing of this kind. It expresses a trivial idea which is clearly accessible to scrutiny by common sense. Therefore its current, indiscriminate uses are suspect, and it is certainly questionable that it should be used to tell us about growth and welfare.

At this point it is proper to recall Einstein's remark that it seems, to many, obvious what one should observe. Surely transactions occur all the time in the economy, but that does not mean that they offer the proper way to describe the functioning of the economy. Perhaps only some transactions—a selection made on the basis of a powerful theory—can give us the desired information. But what we see is that the corrections—or better, the changes—of GNP figures made by elimination of the effect of seasonal variations, price changes, etc.—thereby obtaining a stable base, free of inflation's distortion—in no way touch the fundamental issues and objections.

Smaller Is Better

GNP is a global notion. It is undifferentiated. It falls into the pattern of modern macroeconomics, which attempts to relate, say, the total quantity of money in circulation to total employment, total output of industry, etc. It is tempting to do so, and it would simplify economic reasoning enormously if one could discover strict interdependencies. Yet there is great danger in these efforts: For example, the same increase in the quantity of money will have very different consequences if it goes to consumers rather than to producers. This difference is obliterated when one restricts oneself to the macro entities. (It is interesting to note that modern science goes in exactly the opposite direction: More and more, finer distinctions are made. First, one has a molecule; then an atom; then the electron; then more and more elementary particles; then subparticles; and only by these steps does one arrive at a better understanding of matter.) But GNP as an alleged global measure runs precisely counter to the spirit of modern science. (I am tempted here to quote St. Augustine: "For so it is, oh my Lord God, I measure it, but what it is that I measure I do not know.")

When we talk about "economic welfare" we are entering upon a field where other great difficulties arise. Economists have struggled with the problem of welfare for centuries. Countless volumes have been written about it, but there still is no consensus. It is therefore likely that using a primitive notion such as GNP to measure that much-disputed thing will come to naught. But first let us examine briefly where the difficulties lie with respect to economic welfare. Most of us will think at first of our own, personal situation: possessions, income, stability of income, needs (as perceived), health, obligations to others, prices of the goods and services to be bought over some more or less specified period of time, etc. In short, our personal welfare is composed of many variables. Over time, some variables may go up while others go down. In some cases these movements cancel out: income may rise in the same proportion as the prices of the goods I want and so all stays the same. But when some prices of relevance to us go up and others go down, then it is not so obvious whether and how our individual welfare has been affected.

What Do We Mean by Value?

The principal attribute of individual welfare is, in the last analysis, what value or utility people attach to their possessions and income. What determines value has puzzled economists for ages. Is there an objective value applicable for everyone, in any circumstance, at any time? How is value produced? What affects value? The answers have ranged from the assertion that there are absolute values to the statement that the economic value of an object is only what you can sell it for—"Res tantum valet quantum vendi potest"—which is certainly true in the stock market, although there is also the assertion of an "intrinsic" value which often differs in both directions from the sales value. Though all this may seem to be a confusing situation, there is today no doubt that—apart from the few remaining adherents of the superseded labor-value theory—utility attributed by individuals to goods and services is all that matters. Utility is based on individual preferences, and these are related to the objective, technical characteristics of the desired goods and services. An individual can compare the utilities he expects to derive from goods even though they are all different.

But here we come to an end: Utility is strictly an individual matter. Exactly the same bundle of goods will have a very different utility for different persons.

Of course, it is likely that persons in a given income class have similar needs and are concerned about the prices of similar bunches of goods. But if I take a good from A, for whom it has some utility, and give it to B, for whom also it has some utility, it does not follow that I have diminished A as much as I have improved B's position. The point is, different individuals' utilities are not comparable. There is no known way to find out objectively whether I transfer the same utility (for example, by taxation) from one to the other.

Economists have thought of one way which seems to give us information about general welfare, which is what we are really interested in (and what GNP is somehow expected to measure). It is the Pareto optimum, which says the following: If we look at a community and add a good to one party without at the same time diminishing any other party of that community, then we can say that the welfare of the whole group has increased. This seems plausible and harmless, and we find the Pareto optimum extolled and used in almost every textbook in economics. Yet how can we find out when a person feels diminished? Only by questioning, for there is no objective way of observing the phenomenon. A person might even feel diminished when something is given to him that he does not want or cannot use. And might not A feel diminished when he gets nothing and someone else gets an addition? This can certainly happen—even when nothing is actually taken from him.

If the only way to find out whether someone benefits or is diminished is to ask them, then we face other problems. Do they tell us the truth? Necessarily? Always? May they not be playing a game in order to extract some greater benefit? So we see that this seemingly innocent and seemingly workable concept is applicable at best under severely restrictive conditions which may never exist in reality. In reality, of course, we determine social preferences and act accordingly. We tax people and we transfer income. We build public works, establish museums, run a military force, and so on. But all this is the product of political decision-making processes, based on voting or on dictates, with only vague ideas of what might be good for the society and increase its "welfare." But there is no strictly scientific basis. There is power—or at best persuasion.

The upshot of all this is that welfare is an elusive concept that has great intuitive appeal—but means different things to different people and groups of people. It is a concept that slips through our net the moment we want to make it objective. I say this with all due respect to the many economists, past and present, who have given so much thought to this matter. Many valuable attempts have been made, but, as so often in science, much has to be discarded that was once acceptable. There is a great challenge here to economic science. To find some day a satisfactory description of "welfare" and then also to tell us how to measure it.

A Possible Approach

A promising development is the study of the "social indicators." This movement recognizes that a positively valued social development depends on the simultaneous weighing of several variables. For example, an increase in production is not good if it is accompanied by more pollution; a rise in income is not beneficial if there is deterioration of its present distribution. Incidentally, note that when I speak of "deterioration of income distribution" I appear to be able to tell in a scientifically objective way when a particular income distribution is "better" than another. This would again involve interpersonal comparisons of utility, which we know have to be ruled out. Yet, to take an extreme case, common sense tells us that if 90 percent of the national income goes to 5 percent of the population, that country is no better off than if even a slightly smaller income is distributed more equally among the inhabitants. This clash of insight with our inability to make scientifically acceptable statements is most disturbing.

There are many interrelated factors on which welfare, whether personal or communal, depends. Even to describe them, to enumerate them and put them into a coherent picture, is a difficult task. Any differentiation which forces us to make more and more distinctions and leads us away from simple global expression is in the right scientific spirit.

A poorly defined, hard-to-capture, yet exceedingly important phenomenon, such as welfare is supposed to be measured with extraordinary precision by another phenomenon, GNP, that records nothing better than the total hodgepodge of transactions in the economy. The idea has no chance of finding any scientifically valid justification whatsoever. It is another instance, as was the case in growth, of demanding that a single, scalar number produce wonders of measurement.

Attempts have been made to improve upon the GNP concept, for example, by considering gross domestic product, or attempting to arrive at some measure of net output so that the "productivity of an economy" can be determined. Such efforts to make finer and finer distinctions clearly go in the right direction; however, conceptual difficulties arise then, too. For example, the notion of "productivity" applies easily to processes where we observe physical tangible inputs and outputs. (These can also be expressed in monetary terms, though this is not a simple matter.) However, perhaps only 40 percent of the U.S. economy today involves physical output; the rest is "services." And no one has come forth with good ideas on how to measure productivity of lawyers, doctors, teachers, policemen, hospitals, scientists, musicians, or actors. Yet they all have some kind of "output"—conceivably even a "net" output. But what is it, and how do we compare these heterogeneous services with each other? What is hoped for is, again, a primitive, single, scalar number!

Measuring: Harder Than It Looks

Now let me turn to the way in which one deals with the numbers purporting to measure GNP. Let us forget for the time being all that was said in criticism of GNP. Let us merely look at the measurement itself.

Measurement is demanding, and accurate measurement exceedingly so. It may interest you that even today we do not know the relatively simple matter of the moon's precise distance from earth—though man has visited the moon! What is more, we cannot prove the stability in the large of the moon's orbit around the earth. (We can only prove it "in the small." For the whole proof we would need to know the moon's behavior from the beginning to the end.) Exactly the same is true regarding the entire planetary system. Should not these two considerations make us economists exceedingly modest and cautious when discussing measurement of complex economic-social situations, or the stability of the economic universe?

But what happens in reality?

Mountains of economic statistics pour forth continuously from government and business—millions of numbers, immense detail, comprehensive aggregates, and sophisticated index numbers. Many numbers have been, so to speak, laundered; for example, seasonal variations are eliminated in order to show the alleged "true" movement of some activities. In other cases, numbers are obtained by carefully studied sampling processes; powerful statistical theory is used, and sampling errors are carefully spelled out.

But one characteristic pervades all: We virtually never encounter the words "perhaps," "approximately," "about," "maybe," and so on, or see a sign saying: "± X percent." That is vastly different from the natural sciences, where it is standard to ask immediately what the error of observation might be. (A notable exception is S. N. Kuznets who, in his valuable work on national income, has shown that some of the figures may err by more than 20 percent.) Some things seem easy to measure, e.g., the number of inhabitants in a country. But in the U.S. Census of 1950, about 5 million people—equivalent to a good-sized city, say, Chicago—were not counted! In some Asiatic countries the population count is said to have errors of ±20 percent. Who knows the population of China, or of some African countries? For very gross comparisons this may not matter too much, but the frequently and freely used international per capita income data are often meaningless.

Errors there must be. The extent of admissible error depends on the use for which the measurement is needed. (Cross-section data for nuclear reactors may have an error of ±50 percent. But the reactors work!) Of course, the smaller the error, the better. Reduction of error is usually expensive, and how much one wants to spend on error reduction depends, again, on the use to be made of the measurement or observation. Also, if a good number has to be combined with a poor one, there is not much point in making the good number even better.

Since errors range from very small to very large, is there a generally accepted standard? The answer is that one should always state honestly what error is involved, in whatever field. This is common in physics and, I regret to say, almost totally lacking in economics and the other social sciences. I am referring to the basic errors in variables—i.e., errors in the basic observations, not to sampling errors and the like. There will have to be a change in attitudes, in demands, in standards. No compromise is possible.

The Uses of GNP Figures

Now we come to the point of looking at the calculations made with the GNP figures. It is well to start by quoting one of the greatest mathematicians of all time, C.F.W. Gauss: "The lack of mathematical insight shows up in nothing as surprisingly as in unbounded precision in numerical computations." There are countless illustrations for such activity, not only in economics, but in all social sciences. This is another sign of their lack of maturity compared to the physical sciences. There seems to be a love for a string of decimal places so long as to be meaningless. Yet Norbert Wiener, also an eminent mathematician, observed to me: "Economics is a one-digit science." (I would be inclined to agree in general, but there are a few areas where our power of interpretation is great enough to handle two, perhaps even three, digits.)

GNP figures are principally used to calculate rates of change—presumably rates of growth, because that is what the world has been made aware of. Governments everywhere look hypnotized at these calculations. Systems are judged by the numbers generated even for the short intervals of a quarter year—so brief a period that one must be astonished that all the hundreds of thousands of underlying figures could even be collected, much less collected without any error whatsoever! Or if there are errors, perhaps they very kindly distribute themselves in such manner that they all cancel out? As to both propositions the facts are, of course, quite the contrary. There must be errors: We live in a "stochastic universe," which means that the world is to a large measure indeterminable. And that errors in economic observations would cancel out precisely—well, I shall give an illustration of a "one percent error" in calculation. Suppose you have two consecutive GNP numbers—whatever their absolute values be—such that the second one is 3 percent larger than the first. Now assume that the first is overstated (i.e., errs) by 1 percent, and that the second is understated by the same amount. Then the rate of growth, instead of being +3 percent, is in fact +5.03 percent—a difference of two-thirds! And if the errors are the other way around, so that the first figure is faulty by –1 percent and the second by +1 percent, then the rate of growth is only 0.97 percent. And that is with merely a one-percent error, tiny by almost any standard. (In physics, observations with only a 3 percent error are frequently very good and useful measurements.)

Simple as these considerations are, they are basic. They illustrate precisely the importance of the statement quoted from Gauss. In gathering the thousands of underlying figures, there are delays and corrections. The respective statistical offices naturally want to do a good job, so they correct the initial figures as faults are discovered. (The yearly GNP often requires up to ten years before a final figure is presented.) In the course of these successive revisions, there are plus and minus changes of the order of 2, 3, or sometimes more percent. (Quarterly figures are subject to more and even bigger corrections.) All this plays havoc with the initially calculated rate of change, which is what government and private economists base forecasts and remedial measures on.

Is it not peculiar that governments submit to being judged by numbers as primitive as those here discussed? Not that one would want to deny that some parts of this phenomenon can be expressed numerically. But to proceed as though all can be put into one single number that is free of all possible faults—that is unacceptable. What is more, these numbers are supposed to be comparable internationally. Whether it be India or Sweden or China or the U.S., the "precise" rates of growth are compared with each other—despite the fact that for some countries even the number of inhabitants is only vaguely known. Why would statesmen expose themselves to this kind of evaluation?

Economists have to share in the blame. They have introduced the notion of "fine tuning" the economy, the idea that one can control the whole so precisely as to judge its performance by, and adjust its functionings to, the second digits of growth rates, when in truth even the first digit is in doubt. (One hears a little less, however, about the fine tuning recently in view of the fact that rather gross events—such as high unemployment, high interest rates, and steep oil price increases—are with us.)

We would of course like to know whether, and how much, and in what direction the economy has grown, and how economic welfare has changed. We would like to have good, trustworthy, numerical expressions for these. Alas, the GNP concept is primitive in the extreme, and "social welfare" is still so difficult and controversial that given its inherent, great conceptual difficulties, we have no measure at present which does not involve political, moral, or other prejudices.

7

Neglected Aspects
of Economic Growth

CAMPBELL R. MCCONNELL

There can be no doubt as to the over-all desirability of achieving an adequate rate of economic growth. Domestically, economic growth is the potential source of a higher standard of living and a palliative for many economic problems. Internationally, growth can provide the wherewithal for meeting the Soviet challenge and the acute needs of the underdeveloped nations. Other things being equal, there is no question but that rapid growth is preferable to slow or modest growth. But it must be recognized that rapid economic growth is not free for the asking; nor is it a panacea for all our problems. It is the purpose of this short paper to survey some of the problems, costs, and aspects of economic growth which have been too readily ignored.

1. *Growth as a creator of problems*

It is of considerable importance in assessing the advantages of economic growth to acknowledge the role of growth not only as a palliative for existing economic problems, but, simultaneously, as a creator of, or contributor to, new problems. For example, while economic growth may

"Neglected Aspects of Economic Growth," by Campbell R. McConnell, is reprinted by permission from *Business* (Georgia State University), formerly *Atlanta Economic Review*, July 1963, pp. 10-12. The article is extracted, with abridgement, from a paper presented on April 15, 1961, at the Midwest Economic Association Meeting, Indianapolis.

well take the edge off the long-standing issue of income inequality, it must also be recognized that rapid growth and the affluency stemming therefrom may contain the seeds of the social balance question,[1] not to mention serious problems for adversely affected groups of workers and employers and the myriad of problems associated with rapid urbanization. Furthermore, continued growth brings a nation face-to-face with the question of its responsibilities to the as yet underdeveloped nations and all of the problems of economic policy therein implied. Though the problems created may be less acute than the problems solved, the former can hardly be ignored.

In a broader perspective, it seems decidedly myopic to view growth as a solution to the economizing problem. As Rostow has so succinctly indicated:

> A society like the United States, structurally committed to a high-consumption way of life; committed also to maintain the decencies that go with adequate social overhead capital; committed by its own interests and the interests of those dependent upon it or allied to it to deal with a treacherous and extremely expensive world environment; committed additionally, out of its own internal dynamics, to a rapidly enlarging population and to a working force which must support more old and more young . . . such a society must use its resources fully, productively, and wisely. The problem of choice and allocation—the problem of scarcity—has not yet been lifted from it.[2]

2. Historical relativity of economic concepts

It seems both appropriate and desirable in connection with economic growth that we be aware of the historical relativity of many economic concepts. Concepts, notions, relationships, and policies which may be quite appropriate for a mature nation may be quite inappropriate for an underdeveloped nation, and vice versa.

Some examples may be suggestive of this point. First, Professor Alvin Hansen has contended that the problem of the saving-investment balance is significantly different as between mature and immature nations. The long-run problem in the rich, capital-abundant society may well be that of finding adequate investment outlets for an abundance of loanable funds. In contrast, he argues that many underdeveloped, capital-scarce countries have potentially ample investment opportunities but face a grievous shortage of funds with which to finance this investment. Policywise, Professor Hansen recommends continuous low interest rates to encourage investment spending in advanced nations and high interest rates to induce saving in the underdeveloped lands.[3]

Still another illustration is provided by Professor Hansen. A mature nation may face the choice between slight unemployment and price stability on the one hand, and full employment and slight inflation on the other. However, for an immature nation in the quest of growth, the relevant choice may be between stagnation and unemployment, on the one hand, and rather significant inflation as a technique for forcing saving with which to finance development, on the other.[4]

Similarly, it is well known that the financing of public expenditures by regressive taxation may be an intolerable burden on the peoples of underdeveloped nations, but at the same time prove an extremely useful technique for raising revenue and reallocating resources in an advanced economy with a minimal adverse impact upon incentives.

Furthermore, while limitations upon future growth in the developed nations may well be explainable largely in economic terms, socio-cultural factors may constitute the most pertinent obstacles to growth in some of the underdeveloped nations. Ignorance, superstition, social or religious taboos on commercial activities, and the absence of social cohesiveness in the private sector can have a deadly impact upon any underdeveloped nation's growth prospects, particularly when accompanied by an indifferent, indecisive, or corrupt public sector. The objective of growth may be taken largely for granted in mature economies; but the absence of "the will to develop" may block growth in an immature economy even though its resources are otherwise conducive to the development process.

A final example: the advanced nation finds itself at the technological frontier and therefore is required to devote significant amounts of resources in pursuing this important avenue of growth. In contrast, the primitive economy has the well-known advantage of being able to utilize a vast pool of technological information at little or no cost.

To repeat: Economic ideas, relationships, and policy decisions quite appropriate for the further expansion of already affluent economies may be decidedly out of place in underdeveloped lands which are endeavoring to achieve the preconditions essential for the take-off into economic growth.

3. *The institutional-ideological uniqueness of underdeveloped nations*

The importance of the entire problem of economic growth derives in part from the ideological-institutional competition of the United States and the Soviet Union—a competition which centers upon, and seeks the allegiance of, the emerging and grossly underdeveloped new nations of Africa and Asia.

An implication of this struggle is that most of the emerging nations will adopt an ideological-institutional structure which closely resembles either that of American Capitalism or that of Soviet Communism. However, this supposition may prove to be grossly erroneous. Indeed, there are good reasons to believe that the political and economic arrangements of the new nations should and will vary significantly from both models, possibly utilizing and modifying what seem to be the most appropriate and most useful features of each. We can well expect new economic systems in these developing nations which are unique in many respects and only faintly reminiscent of either mixed capitalism or controlled socialism. There are clearly numerous unexplored hybrids between the two extremes. And, like it or not, there are very compelling reasons why government might play a significantly greater economic role in the developing nations than is now the case in mixed capitalism or democratic socialism. In short, case studies persistently verify the uniqueness of the potentialities and of the problems of underdeveloped countries; this suggests that each will develop significantly different and unique institutions and ideologies.

4. *The costs and disadvantages of economic growth*

It is not at all unlikely that a vast majority of our population hold the clear and unqualified conclusion that rapid economic growth is an unmitigated good, and slow or modest growth is clearly an undesirable state of affairs. However, the very nature of economic science obviously suggests that the pursuit of any economic goal such as growth entails sacrifices and costs. And I refer here not only to the obvious sacrifice of consumer goods, which is essential in accelerating capital formation in a full employment economy, but also to such less apparent costs as the following:[5]

   a. The economic insecurity which rapid change connotes for significant groups of technologically displaced workers and the geographic-social dislocations which re-employment may necessitate can be an extremely important cost associated with growth. Certainly, no small part of these costs are the tremendous problems imposed upon us by the rapid increase in urbanization—costs which economists have too long assigned to the consideration of the other social scientists.

   b. The increased pace of industrial life and concomitant declines in leisure (or at least sacrifices of increases in leisure) which rapid growth implies are important costs of growth. It is well known that the rapid tempo of Soviet industry has contributed to an extremely high ulcer rate in that country.

   c. Under certain conditions rapid economic growth may contribute to greater economic instability. In particular, a context of rapid and uninterrupted growth might lessen the restraints upon union wage demands and upon business price policies, tending to accelerate inflationary pressures.

   d. History suggests that rapid economic growth may be accompanied and nurtured by the wasteful exploitation of natural resources.

e. It is relevant for some underdeveloped countries that economic growth may be achieved only by the political and economic exploitation of certain now-privileged groups in those societies. While American economic growth has not involved any sudden, spectacular redistribution of income and wealth from rich to poor, class struggles may be more pronounced in the embryonic stages of growth in many of the new underdeveloped countries where society aspires to a less leisurely rate of growth. This, of course, is not to cite revolution or violence as a prerequisite of growth, but only to note that substantial class rearrangements may be required and that these entail obvious and significant costs to adversely affected groups.

f. Some very responsible writers[6] have recently expressed the view that in our country the vigorous pursuit of a particularly rapid rate of growth might come at the expense of freedom. Although I am personally hesitant to embrace this view, a potentially great noneconomic cost is obviously involved.

Summary

In summary, some of the neglected facts of economic growth are: (1) growth not only resolves, but it also creates socioeconomic problems; (2) concepts, relationships, and policies relevant and appropriate to advanced nations may be irrelevant and inappropriate to underdeveloped nations, and vice versa; (3) the presumption that the emerging nations of Africa and Asia will necessarily emulate the Soviet or American systems is unwarranted and misleading; and (4) the less evident costs and disadvantages of economic growth must not be ignored in any complete analysis of the growth process.

Endnotes

1. John Kenneth Galbraith, *The Affluent Society* (Boston: Houghton Mifflin Company, 1958).

2. W. W. Rostow, *The Stages of Economic Growth* (New York: Cambridge University Press, 1960), p. 81.

3. Alvin H. Hansen, *Economic Issues of the 1960's* (New York: McGraw-Hill Book Company, 1960), pp. 167-171.

4. *Ibid.*, pp. 173-175.

5. See Martin Bronfenbrenner, "The High Cost of Economic Development," *Land Economics*, May 1953, pp. 93-104; August 1953, pp. 209-218.

6. In particular, see Henry C. Wallich, *The Cost of Freedom* (New York; Harper and Brothers, 1960).

PART II

THE EMERGENCE
OF A MARKET ECONOMY:
COLONIAL
AND REVOLUTIONARY
WAR PERIODS

8

The Contributions
of the American Indian
to Civilization

ALEXANDER F. CHAMBERLAIN

. . . I would seek to tell, in brief terms, the world's debt to the Red Man, what we owe to the race from whom we have snatched a continent. And the debt is, indeed, great. First our language owes him much. Though our unskilled tongues have all-too-often sorely marred them, the whole land is still dotted over with the names he gave. Republic, state, province, county, township, city, town, hamlet, mountain, valley, island, cape, gulf, bay, lake, river, and streamlet are his eternal remembrancers; Mexico, Alabama, Ontario, Multnomah, Muskoka, Lima, Parahiba, Kiowa, Managua, Kootenay, Yosemite, Chonos, Campeche, Panama, hail from as many distinct linguistic stocks as there are individual names in the list. . . .

. . . Of the states and territories of the Union, Alabama, Alaska, Arkansas, Arizona, Connecticut, the Dakotas, Idaho, Illinois, Iowa, Kansas, Kentucky, Massachusetts, (New) Mexico, Michigan, Minnesota, Mississippi, Missouri, Nebraska, Oklahoma, Tennessee, Texas, Utah,

---

"The Contributions of the American Indian to Civilization," by Alexander F. Chamberlain, is reprinted by permission from *Proceedings of the American Antiquarian Society,* new series, XVI (October, 1903), pp. 91-126.

Wisconsin, Wyoming, derive their appellations from the Indian languages of the country. . . . And so many of our rivers, lakes, mountains, and cities too. . . . Some of the terms the Indian has left us, are, doubtless, "jaw-breakers," but most of them are not, and adorn our maps as well as do those inherited from our Aryan forefathers. And where some of the older Indian names of more general application have passed out of use, they have reappeared, sometimes in abbreviated or more euphonious forms, in the appellations of ships of peace and of war, sea-side hotels and country cottages, public parks and private estates, golf clubs, organizations of a political and social nature, etc. . . .

But it is not place-names alone that have come to use from the Indian's store of speech. The languages of all sections of the peoples of European stock dwelling in the New World preserve scores and hundreds of words derived from one or another of the many tongues spoken by the aborigines. This debt to the Indian is, of course, greatest in Mexico, Central and South America, where the natives still exist in very large numbers, and where they have intermixed considerably with the white population, giving rise to millions of *mestizos* and mixed-bloods of various degrees.

To the English spoken and written in the United States and Canada one stock alone, the Algonkian, has furnished at least one hundred and ninety words meriting record in our dictionaries; and a rough count of the words contributed to American English by all the Indian languages north of the Mexican boundary line makes the number about three hundred. The words adopted from the Indian tongues of Mexico, Central and South America would add some two hundred more. Thus, a fair estimate of the total contributions of the American Indian to English speech in America, spoken and written, literary, provincial and colloquial, would be, say, five hundred words. . . . Some sixty selected from this long list will show the character of this aboriginal element in our modern English:

Alpaca, axolotl, barbecue, bayou, buccaneer, cannibal, canoe, caucus, Chautauqua, chipmunk, chocolate, condor, coyote, curari, guano, hammock, hickory, hominy, hurricane, ipecacuanha, jaguar, jalap, jerked (beef), Klondike, llama, mahogany, maize, manito, moccasin, moose, mugwump, ocelot, opossum, pampas, papoose, peccary, pemmican, persimmon, petunia, potato, powow, puma, quinine, raccoon, Saratoga, sequoia, skunk, squaw, Tammany, tapir, tarpon, terrapin, tobacco, toboggan, tomahawk, tomato, totem, tuxedo, vicuna, wahoo, wampum, wigwam, woodchuck, Wyandotte.

What a wide field of thought and experience is represented by these aboriginal words adopted into English! If the Indian had done no more than to give us the terms by which we denote *caucus, Tammany, mugwump, Chautauqua*—four great ideas developed by the Europeans in America—he would have exceeded some of the civilized languages of the Old World in really influencing the future universal speech. Moreover, words like *barbecue, buccaneer, cannibal, hurricane, Klondike, powow, totem,* and so forth, seem to fill "long-felt wants" in our language. . . .

The American Indian contribution to the language of the white man has not been confined entirely to single words. Our colloquial, and even . . . literary speech have been enriched by phrases and expressions which are but translations and imitations, more or less imperfect often, it is true, since the originals were not always completely understood, of aboriginal turns and tricks of thought. Thus we have: Brave, "sun," "moon," fire-water, squaw man, pale-face, "medicine-man," Great Spirit, happy hunting grounds, to bury the hatchet, to smoke the pipe of peace, etc.

. . . From the list of "things Indian" may be selected for special mention: Indian gift, Indian ladder, Indian corn, Indian meal, Indian file, Indian summer. Nor have the squaw and papoose been forgotten, as any dictionary of Americanisms will show. "Indian summer" has now been accepted not alone by our poets, but by those of Old England as well. . . .

When we turn to fiction and romance we find, again, that the American Indian has well served the white race. Defoe, Cooper, Chateaubriand, Marmontel, Mayne Reid, De Alencar, Kingsley, Gerstacker, Lew Wallace, Bandelier, Rider Haggard, Robertson and many others have found inspiration in his history and achievements. In spite of inaccuracy of detail and too frequent and too extensive Anglification and Gallicization, the aboriginal characters of some of these writers stand firmly rooted in our literary memories. We cannot easily forget "Friday," "the last of the Mohicans," "the white God." . . .

Let us now turn from language and literature to more material things.

How readily many of the natives of the New World consented to become guides and porters for the first European travellers and adventurers has been recorded by several of the chroniclers of early colonial days. Roger Williams was particularly cordial in this regard:

> "The wilderness, being so vast, it is a mercy that for hire a Man shall never want guides, who will carry provisions and such as hire them over Rivers and Brookes, and find out oftentimes hunting houses or other lodgings at night. I have heard of many English lost and have often been lost myselfe, and myselfe and others have been often found and succoured by the Indians."

Exploration of the New World was all the easier because almost everywhere, missionary, soldier, adventurer, trader, trapper and hunter followed Indian guides over the old trails. . . .

. . . Professor [Frederick Jackson] Turner does not exaggerate when he says:

> "The buffalo-trail became the Indian trail, and this became the trader's 'trace'; the trails widened into roads, and the roads into turnpikes, and these, in turn, were transformed into railroads. The same origin can be shown for the railroads of the South, the far West and the Dominion of Canada. The trading-posts reached by these trails were on the sites of Indian villages which had been placed in positions suggested by nature; and these trading-posts, situated so as to command the water-systems of the country, have grown into such cities as Albany, Pittsburgh, Detroit, Chicago, St. Louis, Council Bluffs, and Kansas City."[1]

. . . The fact that for so long in American history there was a "frontier" ever receding westward as the tide of immigration advanced, has, as Professor Turner has pointed out, conditioned . . . the development of culture in North America. Had there been no aborigines here the white race would have swarmed over America and civilization would have been much different from what it is now, and the "typical American" would also have been other than he is. The fact that the Indian was here in sufficient numbers to resist a too-rapid advance on the part of the European settlers made necessary the successive Americas, which began with Massachusetts and Virginia and ended with California, Oregon and Alaska. The American is really a composite of the Puritan and the pioneer, with a little of all the races that were here or have since come.

The fur trade and traffic with the Indians generally had no little effect upon the social and political condition of the European colonists; who in these matters learned their first lessons in diplomacy and statecraft. Alliances made often for commercial reasons led to important national events. The adhesion of the Algonkian tribes . . . to the French, and of the Iroquois . . . to the English practically settled which was utimately to win in the struggle for supremacy in America. . . .

From the Indians the early settlers all over America, very naturally, borrowed many ideas and devices relating to hunting and fishing. Hence the fish-weirs of Virginia in the sixteenth and Brazil in the twentieth century; the use of narcotic poisons for killing fish; the employment of the blow-gun for obtaining animals and birds without injuring the skins; catching fish, especially eels and salmon, by torch-light; the "call" for deceiving the moose; methods of trailing and capturing the larger game and wild animals, etc. Also ways of rendering palatable or innocuous many of the plants and vegetables of the tropics. . . .

From the primitive agricultural processes of the American Indians [were] transferred to the whites, particularly in the way of preparing the ground and cultivating the native plants and vegetables . . . New Englanders . . . learned from the aborigines how to treat corn in all its stages. The use of guano in Peru and of fish-manure (menhaden) in northeastern North America, like the burning over of the fields as a preparation for planting, was adopted by the whites from the Indians. From the same source they came to plant corn in hills and pumpkins or beans and corn together. Governor Bradford, in 1621, tells how Squanto, the Indian, came to the relief of the colonists at Plymouth, "showing them both the manner how to set it and after how to dress and tend it. Also, he told them, except they got fish and set with it (in these old grounds) it would come to nothing." And Morton, in 1632, informs us how extensively the white inhabitants of Virginia were in the habit of "doing their grounds with fish."

In the realms of ornament and aesthetics the Indian has also made his influence felt. The wives and daughters of the early European settlers learned from the squaw many a pretty and durable fashion of staining and dyeing their willow and their wooden-ware with juices and extracts of plants, herbs and fruits. . . .

Besides llama wool and alpaca (from Peru) several varieties of cotton (the chief is "Barbados cotton" of which the famous "Sea Island cotton" is the best known type) were known to the aborigines of the warmer parts of America and cultivated by them in pre-Columbian times. Also several kinds of hemps and fibres. . . .

Of Indian inventions and devices for increasing the comfort of man the whites have adopted many—some temporarily, others permanently. The infant of the Hudson's Bay factor in the far north, sleeps safe in the warm moss-bag of the Athapascans, and at the seashore the offspring of the New Englander toddles about in moccasins borrowed from the Iroquois or the Algonkin. The whaler and the Arctic adventurer adapted for their own uses the snow goggles and the dog-sled of the Eskimo. The French ladies in early Louisiana took up the turkey-feather fans of the aborigines and the prospector on the Yukon trail uses the *parfleche* of the plains Indians to transport his few small belongings. In the southwest the white man has not despised the various "soap plants," which the Indians knew before him, while in the northeast he learned from them the uses of the fragrant bayberry wax. In North America basketry, and in South America pottery, made by Indian hands, have served the new-comers long and well, and the "craze" at the present moment for imitating aboriginal art is a just tribute to the race, whose women in California have perfected the art of basketry beyond anything the Old World ever knew. Panama-hats, Navajo blankets, Micmac grass and root-work, and Ojibwa birch-bark all have their vogue among us. . . .

The third day after landing in the New World Columbus saw on the

Bahamas the hamacas, or net-swings, which as hammocks are now in use all over the civilized world. This may be counted the first gift of the aborigines to the strange race that came to them from over-sea. . . .

Recreations, also, the Indian has furnished the white man. The canoe and the toboggan enter largely into American pleasures and sports,—and to the aboriginal ideas have been added the "water-toboggan" and light canoes for women. In Canada and parts of northeastern North America, the healthful game of lacrosse, known of old to the Indians, ranks among our best sports, and among the Creoles of Louisiana still survives raquette, the southern variety of the same invention. The invigorating exercise of snowshoeing comes also from the Indian.

But it is on the food supply of the world that the American Indian has exerted the greatest influence. . . .

Coming not all of them directly through the Indian, but in most cases, largely through his mediation, "Cacao, vanilla, logwood, mahogany, and other useful or decorative timbers, as well as the many ornamental plants of our houses and gardens, have introduced considerable changes in our manners of life."

> Tobacco,—noxious weed, or soothing panacea,—"Sublime to-
> bacco! which, from East to West, Cheers the tar's labor, or the
> Turkman's rest,"

as Byron called it; tobacco, for whose sake Charles Lamb said he "would do anything but die"; solace of Old England's fox-hunting clerics; tobacco, safe refuge of American tariff-tinkers; tobacco, with all it brings of good and of evil, we owe to the Arawaks of the Caribbean. In tobacco the Red Man has long ago circumnavigated and encompassed the globe. The pipe has conquered the high and the low of almost every nation under the sun. With the cigar and the cigarette it has called forth the smoking-car, the smoking-concert, the smoke-talk, while cigar-boxes have contributed to the formation of window gardens, and cigarette-pictures to debase the moral and aesthetic ideals of the youth of the land. Tobacco has been alternately attacked and defended by monarchs, clergymen, laymen, physicians of the soul and of the body individual and politic, poets and men of science, etc. The literature of tobacco, from King James's renowned "Counterblaste" down to the enactments of western legislatures and Congressional reports on protected industries, would certainly form an imposing library. When we consider all these things, and take into account, also, the labor employed, the money invested, the invention stimulated, the trade and commerce encouraged by the growth and development of the tobacco-industry, in its many ramifications, it is clear that the naked redskin who first handed his *cohoba* to the wondering Spaniard and taught him the use of the "weed," though his name be now utterly forgotten, was destined to make a great change in the world's ways and usages, its industries, its pleasures, and, perhaps, also its health. . . .

Concerning another gift we have received from the Red Man there has not been such divergence of opinion. The potato has been little sung by inspired bards or glorified by bishops of a great church,—its humbler task has been to furnish food to the world's hungry millions, and its duty in that respect has been well done. Disastrous, indeed, would be the result were the potato for but a single year to disappear from the food supply of man. . . .

That very useful vegetable, the tomato, was cultivated in Mexico (its name is Aztec) and Peru prior to the European discovery. Since then it has extended even to the Malay Archipelago and the gardens of China and Japan. The opinion that it is poisonous has now died out, and the tomato bids fair to become as popular in the kitchens of the Old World as it is in those of the New. And with it go catchup and "sweet pickles."

The New England dinner of today is incomplete, for a large part of the year, without squash in some form or other; and time was when pumpkin-pie was almost a sacred dish,—there were also pumpkin sauce, pumpkin bread, etc. . . .

Some of our "Boston baked beans," too, had their start from the Red Man, for the common haricot kidney bean, according to De Candolle, was cultivated in America in pre-Columbian times. The Lima bean, as its name indicates, is also American,—and antedates the coming of whites. . . .

De Candolle, also assigns to the New World the origin of the peanut, now more commonly associated with the negro than with the American Indian. . . .

. . . The luscious pineapple, the pawpaw, the persimmon, the agave, the chirimoya, the guava, the sapodilla, the soursop, the starapple, the mammee, the marmalade plum, the custard-apple, the chayote, the cashew, the alligator-pear, etc., are all natives of the New World, and have had their virtues ascertained by the Indians before the discovery, or pointed out by them to the European since.

The artichoke, oca, quinoa, the cacao-bean, arracacha, arrow-root, and red peppers (whence paprika, tabasco sauce, and the like) etc., are other gifts of the American aborigines to those who conquered them. . . .

. . . North America . . . has its succotash, pone, hominy, sagamity, suppawn, etc., name and thing alike adopted from the Indians. Nor must we forget the pemmican of the Canadian Northwest ("pemmican" is now made to order for Arctic expeditions in Europe and America) and the "*jerked* beef," representing the *charqui* of the Peruvian neighbors of the great plains of the Chaco. Indian ways of cooking clams ("Indian bed," e.g.), of preparing fish for eating ("planked shad" etc.), and, in the more southern regions, of boiling, roasting and otherwise cooking and making palatable fruits, roots and herbs, small animals, etc., deserve mention. . . .

The American Indian origin of maple-sugar and maple-syrup has been demonstrated by Professor H. W. Henshaw and the writer of this paper. In the Eastern States and the Canadian provinces of Ontario and Quebec, especially, the production of these articles of food is one of the important industries of the country. Vermont, indeed, has come to be known as "the maple-sugar State." . . .

Famous all over the world is the American habit of chewing gum, which, by reason of the medicinal and hygienic properties attributed to this substance, became soon the fashion among adults as well as among children and youth. Like all fads, the chewing of gum has moderated of recent years, but is still a very prevalent custom and its production a very profitable industry. The basis of the best gum is chicle, obtained from the chiclezapote tree (of the India-rubber family), a native of Mexico. Though Yankee ingenuity is chiefly responsible for the vogue of chewing-gum, it is interesting to learn that chicle was used by the ancient Mexicans in a somewhat similar manner, and that, in the last analysis, the American Indian employment of chicle is the source of our chewing-gum. . . .

. . . There is no doubt of the American Indian origin of "Indian corn," or maize, a plant as useful to civilized man as the cocoa is to savage man. The wild rice of the Great Lakes is another food-plant, which Indian knew before the advent of the whites. . . .

The primitive home of maize was probably in some portion of the Mexico-Isthmian region, whence it has spread wherever man will use or the climate tolerate. Says Mrs. Earle of Old New England:

> "Next to fish, the early colonists found in Indian corn, or Guinny wheat—Turkie wheat one traveller called it—their most unfailing food supply. Our first poet wrote in 1675, of what he called early days:
>
> 'The dainty Indian maize/
> Was eat in clamp-shells out of wooden trays.'

"Its abundance and adaptability did much to change the nature of their diet, as well as to save them from starvation. The colonists learned from the Indians how to plant, nourish, harvest, grind and cook it in many forms and in each way it formed a palatable food."[2]

Take from the New England table during the time that has elapsed since the Indians welcomed the first settlers not merely by word of mouth, but also with agreeable food, its memories of "rye and Indian" with "Boston brown bread," yocake, johnny-cake, pone, suppawn, "Indian pudding," succotash, hulled corn, hominy, mush, and all the other concoctions of "Indian meal," rude and refined, and what a void there would be! And it startles us to think that the American child owes his popcorn to the Indian, to whom must be traced back ultimately such diversified application of the virtues of maize, as is represented by the innumerable uses which the white man has found for the cornstarch extracted from this American plant. Almost every part of the corn plant has been made use of by man for one purpose or another; the boy has his corn-stalk fiddle and his beard of corn-silk; the stalks are employed to make various things, from fuel to baskets; and from them in the green and soft state have been extracted syrup, sugar, brandy, etc.; the husks are used for packing, to stuff mattresses and chairs, to wrap cigarettes, to make paper; out of the fibre of the culm and leaves a sort of yarn has been obtained. . . .

Drinks, too, the Indian has given the white man. . . .

Chocolate (the name, like that of the "bean," cacao, from which it is produced) comes to use from the Red Man, for the cultivation of cacao and the preparation of this useful beverage were known to the natives of Mexico and Central America in pre-Columbian times. From the beans of the cacao-tree are also prepared the long list of nutritious foods and drinks misnamed cocoa, the use of which has spread all over the civilized world. . . .

Medicine owes much to the American Indian. In the early history of the European colonies the "Indian doctor" played a not unimportant role in stanching the wounds and alleviating the pains and aches of the pioneers. . . .

Dr. Bard, in 1894, credited the Indians of California with furnishing "three of the most valuable additions which have been made to the pharmacopaeia during the last twenty years." Two of these are the "yerba santa" (holy plant), Eriodyction glutinosum, used for affections of the respiratory tract; and the cascara sagrada (sacred bark), Rhamnus purshiana, a good laxative. In northeastern North America the lobelia was once the watchword of a local medical school and had an extended vogue as an emetic and cure for asthma. Mexico has furnished jalap, the well-known purgative. The Indians of South America have given the world jaborandi leaves (for dropsy, uraemia, snake-bite), the balsams copaiba, tolu, etc., ipecacuanha, quinine and copalchi, guaiacum (once a famous remedy for syphilis), coca, curari, etc. In this list quinine, coca, and curari deserve more particular mention.

Endnotes

1. See Proc. Wisc. State Hist. Soc., 1889 and 1894. Also, Annual Rept. Amer. Hist. Assoc., 1893.

2. "Customs and Fashions in Old New England," p. 148.

9

From Organization to Society: Virginia in the Seventeenth Century

SIGMUND DIAMOND

ABSTRACT

Virginia in the early seventeenth century may be taken as an example of a social system established in accordance with the model of a commercial organization, in which the behavior of the members was expected to be entirely determined by their positions within the organization. The concessions that were offered to induce them to accept positions within the organization so multiplied the number of statuses they held as to alter decisively their behavior and to transform Virginia from a formal organization into a society. The analysis of the early history of Virginia is an illustration of the way in which historical knowledge may be used to suggest problems of interest to sociological theory.

"From Organization to Society: Virginia in the Seventeenth Century," by Sigmund Diamond is reprinted from *American Journal of Sociology*, Vol. LXIII (March 1958), pp. 457-475. This shortened version is reprinted with the kind permission of Professor Sigmund Diamond.

I

. . . In 1607, when the Virginia Company established a settlement at Jamestown, its population numbered 105; and in 1624, when the crown revoked [the] charter of the Company, the population of Virginia amounted to just over 1,200, despite the fact that the Company had sent more than 5,000 emigrants during that seventeen-year period.[1] But, just as a limited duration of time is no necessary detriment to a study of this kind, because there are periods of history when the rate of change is accelerated, so, too, the limited size of the group affords no accurate measure of the importance of the enterprise. Judged in terms of its outcome, its importance is self-evident. . . .

At its inception—and for a number of years thereafter—it had been a formal organization. . . . Its earlier character . . . is revealed by the instructions given by the Virginia Company to Sir Thomas Gates on the eve of his departure of Jamestown in May, 1609:

> You must devide yor people into tennes twenties & so upwards, to every necessary worke a competent nomber, over every one of w^{c}h you must appointe some man of Care & still in that worke to oversee them and to take dayly accounte of their laboures, and you must ordayne y^t every overseer of such a nomber of workemen Deliver once a weeke an accounte of the wholle comitted to his Charge . . . you shall doe best to lett them eate together at reasonable howers in some publique place beinge messed by six or five to a messe, in w^{c}h you must see there bee equality and sufficient that so they may come and retourne to their worke without any delay and have no cause to complain of measure or to excuse their idleness uppon ye dressinge or want of diet. You may well allowe them three howers in a somers day and two in the winter, and shall call them together by Ringinge of a Bell and by the same warne them againe to worke.[2]

Testifying in 1625 about conditions under the administration of Sir Thomas Dale in 1614-16, Mrs. Perry, one of the fortunates who survived more than a few years in the first quarter-century of Virginia's history, revealed that

> in the time of Sr: Thomas Dales Government An leyden and June Wright and other women were appoynted to make shirts for the Colony servants and had six nelds full of silke threed allowed for making of a shirte, w^{c}h yf they did not p'forme, They had noe allowance of Dyott, and because theire threed naught and would not sewe, they took owt a ravell of ye lower p^{te} of ye shirte to make an end of ye worke, and others y^t had threed of thiere owne made it up wth that, Soe the shirts of those w^{c}h had raveled owt proved shorter then the

next, for wch fact the said An leyden and June Wright were whipt, And An leyden beinge then wth childe (the same night thereof miscarried).[3]

Our first inquiry . . . must be into the characteristics of the original settlement at Jamestown—characteristics which changed so markedly during the course of the next quarter-century.

Virginia was not established as a colony to take its place among the territories governed by the British crown; it was not a state, and, properly speaking, it was not a political unit at all. It was property, the property of the Virginia Company of London, and it was established to return a profit to the stockholders of that company. Under the political and economic conditions of seventeenth-century England, speculators in overseas expansion could count on no support from the government except verbal encouragement and some legal protection—and sometimes precious little of these. Under the circumstances, therefore, colonization had to be undertaken as a private business venture, and the first charge imposed on the property was the return on the shareholder's investment. Traditionally, this episode has been dealt with primarily in terms of the motivation of participants—did they come to establish religious freedom, to seek a haven for the politically persecuted, or to found a "First Republic?"—and it is true that those who joined the Virginia enterprise did so for many reasons. Some, like Richard Norwood, were foot-loose and fancy-free after having completed their apprenticeships. Robert Evelin wrote his mother that he was "going to the sea, a long and dangerous voyage with other men, to make me to be able to pay my debts, and to restore my decayed estate again . . . and I beseech you, if I do die, that you would be good unto my poor wife and children, which God knows, I shall leave very poor and very mean, if my friends be not good unto them." In its promotional literature the Virginia Company took advantage of this broad spectrum of motives and cast its net wide to snare the purses and bodies of all sorts and conditions of persons in support of a venture in which

> . . . profite doth with pleasure joyne,
> and bids each chearefull heart,
> To this high praysed enterprise,
> performe a Christian part.[4]

But, from the point of view of the managers of the enterprise, recruitment was perceived less as a problem of motivation than of achieving an organizational form through which the resources and energies of the participants could be mobilized. The basic objectives of the

promoters in establishing a plantation in Virginia are quite clear: to exploit
the mineral resources which they were certain were there; to search for that
elusive will-o'-the-wisp . . . a water route to the Pacific through North
America . . . and to monopolize whatever local trade existed and whatever
oriental trade would be developed with the opening-up of the northwest
passage.

The organizational form adopted for the venture was not created by the
promoters; the roots of the joint-stock company, though it was still subject
to considerable experimentation, lay deeply imbedded in English history.
Nor were the proprietors themselves totally without experience in the
establishment of plantations or unaware of the experience of others. Sir
Thomas Smythe, a leader of the Virginia enterprise, was one of the
merchant princes of London, a governor of the East India Company, the
Muscovy Company, and many others. And they had before them the
experience—which was . . . not entirely an unmixed blessing—of the
colonizing efforts of Sir Walter Raleigh and Sir Humphrey Gilbert, of the
trading posts established by the great commercial companies, of Spain and
Portugal, and of the founding of plantations in Ireland.[5]

What they established was a business organization; and, though the
form of that organization was changed at various times during the
Company's history, those changes were at all times dictated by the need to
make the business pay, which, in the words of Sir Edwin Sandys, one of the
two great leaders of the Company, was "that wheron all men's eyes were
fixed."[6] Its problems were those of any business organization. It sold
shares, begged contributions, and organized lotteries to raise the necessary
funds; it was concerned to recruit a proper labor force; it had to cope with
the problem of adequate supervision and administration so as to maintain
its authority; and it engaged in a full-scale advertising campaign to sell to
potential adventurers and planters the glories of a land where the "horses
are also more beautiful, and fuller of courage. And such is the extraordinarie fertility of that Soyle, that the Does of their Deere yeelde Two
Fawnes at a birth, and sometimes three." And it was confronted with the
petty harassments of cajoling those whose good will was needed for the
success of the organization. "Talking with the King," wrote the Earl of
Southampton to Sir Robert Cecil, "by chance I told him of the Virginia
Squirrills which they say will fly, whereof there are now divers brought into
England, and hee presently and very earnestly asked me if none of them
was provided for him. . . . I would not have troubled you with this but that
you know so well how he is affected by these toyes."[7]

But though the Company's plans were eminently rational, its grand
design suffered from a fatal flaw; reality was far different from what the
Company expected. Its model had been the East India Company, and its

dream had been to reproduce the Spanish looting of a continent; but conditions in Virginia were not those of India or Mexico and Peru. "It was the Spaniards good hap," wrote Captain John Smith later in the history of the Virginia Company,

> to happen in those parts where were infinite numbers of people, whoe had manured the ground with that providence that it afforded victuall at all times; and time had brought them to that perfection they had the use of gold and silver, and the most of such commodities as their countries affoorded; so that what the Spaniard got was only the spoile and pillage of those countries people, and not labours of their owne hands. But had those fruitfull Countries been as Salvage, as barbarous, as ill-peopled, as little planted laboured and manured, as Virginia; their proper labours, it is likely would have produced as small profit as ours. . . .[8]

But though the error in conception made by the leaders of the Virginia Company was, from their viewpoint, a grievous one, it is also thoroughly understandable. It is true that the late sixteenth and early seventeenth century was a period of rapid expansion in the organization of trading companies; no less than thirty-four were chartered during that time. But the significant point is that the Virginia Company was the eighteenth to be founded, and, of the previous seventeen, whose experience could be taken as models, all dealt with countries within the European seas, with settled communities along the African coast, or with the advanced societies of Asia. For them, the problem was to exploit the already existing labor force of a settled society.[9] For the Virginia Company, the problem—and it is in this that the crucial difference lies—was to recruit a labor force.

It must be understood, therefore, that, in conformity with its objectives and organizational form, the establishment planted by the Virginia Company at Jamestown was a private estate, which, in the absence of an amenable local labor force, was worked on the basis of imported labor. Basic policies were laid down in London by the General Court of the Company, the body of those who had purchased the £12 10 s. shares or who had been admitted for favors in the Company's behalf; the management and direction of affairs were intrusted to agents of the shareholders; and the supervision of those whose labor in Virginia was necessary for the attainment of the Company's objectives was placed in the hands of officials appointed in London.

Under the circumstances there were many potent inducements to English investors to purchase the Company's £12 10 s. shares, a price, incidentally, which was the Company's estimate of the cost of transporting a settler to Virginia. Under the charter of 1606 they were guaranteed that after a five-year period, during which the settlers in Virginia would be supported by a stream of supplies sent at Company expense, the profits gained through trade and the discovery of minerals would be divided among the investors in proportion to the number of shares they held, and grants of land would be made to them on the same basis. But what were to be the inducements to become the labor force of a company trading post?

It should be noted at once that [the] English imitated the Spaniards in attempting to mobilize native labor. For the Company the key to the integration of the Indians into the labor force was in the ease with which, it was anticipated, they could be converted to Christianity and thereby won over as well to the secular values of Europeans. To them would accrue spiritual benefits; the Company, already blessed with those, would receive something more substantial. . . . But though the Company succeeded for a time in exacting some tribute from the local tribal chiefs in the form of goods and weekly labor services, the Indians proved unwilling to accept the Company's spiritual and secular offerings. Long before the Indian uprising of 1622 gave an excuse to the settlers to engage in a campaign of extermination, it was clear that the Virginia Company would be forced to import its own labor force.[10]

Between 1607 and 1609, when its charter was changed, the Virginia Company sent over 300 persons to Jamestown. They were a disparate crew of adventurers and rough-necks, imbued with the hope that after a short period in Virginia they would return home with their fortunes in their purses. The social composition of the original labor force, the tasks they were expected to perform, and the nature of the settlement they were expected to establish can all be inferred from the passenger lists of the first expedition and the three subsequent supplies that were sent out by the Company before its charter was modified in 1609. The original expedition numbered 105 persons, of whom we have the names of 67. Of these 67, 29 were listed as gentlemen and 6 were named to the local council; the rest were listed by occupation—1 preacher, 4 carpenters, 12 laborers, 1 surgeon, 1 blacksmith, 1 sailor, 1 barber, 2 bricklayers, 1 mason, 1 tailor, 1 drummer, and 4 boys—and 2 were unidentified. In the three succeeding supplies, the rather high proportion of gentlemen was not substantially reduced, nor did the range of occupations alter significantly. Seventy-three of the 120 persons in the first supply of 1608 can be identified. In this group, gentlemen exceeded laborers 28 to 21. The remainder was made up of an odd assortment of craftsmen, including jewelers, refiners, and goldsmiths—bespeaking the expectations of the Company—apothecaries, tailors, blacksmiths, and—mute testimony to the fact that gentlemen must be gentlemen whether in the wilds of Virginia or a London drawing room—a perfumer. In brief, the two most striking characteristics of this original labor force are the presence of so high a proportion of gentlemen and the absence of any occupations indicative of an intention to establish a settled agricultural community.[11]

From the point of view of the promoters of the Virginia enterprise, these men were not citizens of a colony; they were the occupants of a status in—to use an anachronistic term—the Company's table of organization, and the status was that of workman. Such other qualities or attributes that they possessed might have been of importance when they were in London, Norwich, or Bristol, but what counted in Virginia was that they should accept the directions of their superiors and that they should be willing to work.

Even under the best of circumstances, the problem of maintaining discipline and authority would have been crucial to the success of the Company. But these were hardly the best of circumstances, for the very social composition of the original labor force intensified what in any case would have been a grievously difficult problem. In the long intervals between the arrival of supplies under the direction of the Company's admiral, Christopher Newport, conditions in Jamestown bordered on anarchy; men were beaten by their officers, plots were hatched to escape the country, and insubordination was rampant. The Company's administrative methods, characterized by the utmost laxness, could not cope with the situation. . . . Nor did the high percentage of aristocrats help matters. Unused to the heavy work of axing timber, they cursed so much at their blisters that the president of the council ordered that at the end of the day's work a can of cold water be poured down the sleeve of each offender for every curse he had uttered. To Captain John Smith, the problem was the presence of too many gentlemen: "For some small number of adventrous Gentlemen . . . nothing were more requisite; but to have more to wait and play than worke, or more commanders and officers than industrious labourers was not so necessarie. For in Virginia, a plaine Souldier that can use a Pickaxe and spade, is better than five Knights."[12]

Clearly, even if the mortality figures had been less gruesome than they were—in July, 1609, between 80 and 100 were alive of the 320 who had been sent since 1607[13]—qualitative considerations alone would have dictated a change in the composition of the labor force. For the Company the situation was brought to a head with the realization that there were to be no quick returns from metals and trade and that profits would have to be made through the exploitation of agricultural resources.

Never did the Company rely fundamentally on the recruitment of involuntary labor, but so desperate were its labor requirements and so necessary was it to keep the good will of those authorities who favored the transportation of undesirables that it felt compelled to resort to forced labor.

As early as 1609, a letter from Lisbon revealed that the Portuguese were transporting fifteen hundred children over the age of ten to the East Indies and suggested that the same be done in the case of Virginia. Shortly thereafter the Privy Council notified the mayor of London that the plagues of the city were due mainly to the presence of so many poor persons and recommended that a fund be raised, with the help of the commercial companies, to send as many of these as possible to Virginia. The Virginia Company promptly gave an estimate of the expenses involved and of the terms that would be offered to the emigrants; but, though a large sum of money was raised, no persons were actually transported at that time. In 1617, however, the City of London raised £500 to pay the cost of shipping one hundred children to Virginia, where they were to be apprenticed until the age of twenty-one, thereafter to be the fee-simple owners of fifty acres of land each. So delighted were the Company and the Virginia planters that they continued the practice, but it is evident that not all the children were equally pleased by the future arranged for them. In January, 1620, Sandys wrote to Sir Robert Naunton, the king's principal secretary, that "it falleth out that among those children, sundry being ill-disposed, and fitter for any remote place than for this Citie, declare their unwillingness to goe to Virginia: of whom the Citie is especially desirous to be disburdened; and in Virginia under severe Masters they may be brought to goodness." Since the City could not deliver and the Company could not transport "theis persons against their wills," Sandys appealed to the Privy Council for the necessary authority. It was quickly given. Exact figures cannot be determined, but, before the demise of the Company in 1624, additional shipments of children had been delivered to Virginia, and it is evident that several hundred must have been involved.[14]

Concerning the shipment of convicts and rogues and vagabonds the information is scanty. Some convicts were certainly in Virginia before 1624, though we do not know how many; but the Virginia Company was antagonistic to the importation of such persons, and, in any case, convict-dumping on a large scale did not become a characteristic of the colonial scene until the second half of the seventeenth century.[15] So, too, was the Company antagonistic to the importation of rogues, possibly because, unlike the case of the London children, it was forced to assume the cost of transportation. It engaged in the practice under pressure from King James I. For one group of fifty boys sent out in 1619, the Company expected to receive £500 in tobacco from the planters to whom they were indentured; but as late as October, 1622, it had received only £275.15.6. . . .[16]

But throughout its history the Company was dependent upon the recruitment of voluntary labor, and especially was this true when it realized that profits would have to be made from agricultural staples and not minerals. The change in objective not only emphasized the necessity of recruiting a larger labor supply but required that it be qualitatively different from the earlier one, for now that the glitter of gold was vanishing the Company needed not soldiers of fortune but sober workmen who would be able to extract from the land the food supplies necessary for their own support and the staples whose export would produce profit for the shareholders.[17] But what could the Company offer as sufficient inducement to motivate large numbers of persons to come to Virginia, especially when—as the evidence indicates—enthusiasm for emigration from England was confined to the wealthy, who themselves were hardly likely to exchange the comforts of life in England for the dangers of life in Virginia?[18]

Clearly, if prospective settlers in Virginia faced "severe discipline, sharp lawes, a hard life, and much labour," substantial concessions would have to be offered to induce them to emigrate. The status the Company was asking them to accept was that of servant, employee of the Company, but it was one thing to create a position and quite another to get men to fill it. Since perpetual servitude was obviously no inducement, the Company was required to limit the period of service and to make other concessions. Every settler over the age of ten, whether he paid his own way or was shipped at Company expense, was promised one share of stock in the Company, with potential dividends from the profits of trade and land grant to be made at the time of the first division after seven years. Every "extraordinarie" man—such as "Divines, Governors, Ministers of State and Justice, Knights, Gentlemen, Physitions" or such as were "of worth for special services"—was given additional shares according to the value of his person. The Company expected, in return for assuming all the costs of maintaining the plantation and providing supplies to the emigrants, that each settler would work at tasks assigned him under the direction of Company-appointed officers. For a period of seven years, all supplies were to be distributed through the Company store, all exports were to be shipped through the Company magazine, and all land was to be held by the Company.[19] In effect, the Company created the status of landowner in order to induce persons to accept the status of non-landowner; it was asking emigrants to accept the present burdens of membership in a lower status in anticipation of the future benefits they would receive upon promotion to a higher status. From the point of view of the structure of an organization, this was simply automatic progression—promotion to a higher position in the table of organization after a limited tenure in a lower position. From the point of view of a society, however, this was a guaranty of social mobility. . . .

But land for the settlers and profits for the stockholders were affairs of the future, and both were dependent upon the skill and speed with which the planters could be molded into an efficient labor force. It was of the utmost importance, therefore, that the Company establish its authority in Virginia and maintain discipline, and for the achievement of these purposes the Company was not content to rely simply on the self-discipline it hoped would be the by-product of the effort to obtain profits. The first step was taken with the issuance of the new charter of 1609. During the first three years in Virginia, the Company felt, "experience of error in the equality of Governors, and some out-rages, and follies committed by them, had a little shaken so tender a body." To avoid the evils of divided authority, "we did resolve and obtain, to renew our Letters Pattents, and to procure to ourselves, such ample and large priviledges and powers by which we were at liberty to reforme and correct those already discovered, and to prevent such as in the future might threaten us . . . under the conduct of one able and absolute Governor."[20] But changes in the formal structure of authority were not sufficient.

Religion, too, was counted upon to do its part in maintaining order. Doctrinal conflict was minimized from the start by the ban on Catholics, but what really distinguishes the role of religion under the Virginia Company was its conscious utilization for disciplinary purposes. No less an authority on colonization than Richard Hakluyt had pointed to the advisability of taking along "one or two preachers that God may be honoured, the people instructed, mutinies better avoided, and obedience the better used."[21] The company was quick to take the hint. Religion was used to screen prospective planters before their arrival in Virginia, and it was used to discipline them after their arrival. "We have thought it convenient to pronounce," stated the Company in a broadside of 1609, "that . . . we will receive no man that cannot bring or render some good testimony of his religion to God."[22] And during the time that Sir Thomas Dale's code of laws was sovereign in Virginia—from May, 1610, to April, 1619—the settlers were marched to church twice each day to pray for relief from dissension and for the showering of blessings upon the shareholders. . . .

In a society of ranks and orders, deference is owed to certain persons by virtue of their social position, and the Company attempted to maximize the potentiality for discipline in such an arrangement by appointing to leading posts in Virginia those persons to whom obedience was due because of their high status. Insofar as it was possible, the Company selected only persons of high birth to be governor; when it was not possible, as in the case of Governor Yeardley, it quickly, and it seems surreptitiously, secured for him a knighthood.[23] And at all times the governors were urged to surround themselves with the pomp and circumstance of high office, the better to impress the governed. . . .

Utimately, however, the Company relied upon a military regimen and upon the imposition of force to obtain labor discipline. Governor de al Warr had been instructed that his men were to be divided into groups and placed under the charge of officers "to be exercised and trayned up in Martiall manner and warlike Discipline."[24] Settlers were forbidden to return to England without permission, and their letters were sealed and sent first to the Company in London before being forwarded.[25] But the full code of military discipline was not worked out until the arrival in Jamestown of Captain Thomas Dale, marshal of the colony, who had been granted a leave of absence from his post in the Netherlands army at the behest of the Company. Dale supplemented the usual list of religious offenses and crimes against the state and the person with a series of enactments designed to protect the Company's interests. Slander against the Company, its officers, or any of its publications; unauthorized trading with the Indians; escaping to the Indians; theft; the killing of any domestic animal without consent; false accounting by any keeper of supplies—all were punishable by service in the galleys or death. Failure to keep regular hours of work subjected the offender to the pain of being forced to lie neck and heels together all night for the first offense, whipping for the second, and one year's service in the galleys for the third.[26]

Moreover, Dale created a military rank for every person in Virginia and specified the duties of each in such a way as to provide us with important clues into the nature of labor discipline and what was expected to provide the motivation to work. . . .

What is so striking about Dale's Code is the way in which it stripped from people all attributes save the one that really counted in the relationship which the Company sought to impose on them—their status in the organization. Behavior was expected to conform to a set of prescriptions the major characteristic of which was that the rights and obligations of persons depended on their position within the organization. In this respect, the contrast between Dale's Code and the first set of laws the settlers were able to enact for themselves at the General Assembly of 1619 is startling. For then, considerations other than status within an organization were fundamental:

> All persons whatsoever upon the Sabaoth days shall frequente divine service and sermons both forenoon and afternoone. . . . And everyone that shall transgresse this lawe shall forfeicte three shillinges a time to the use of the churche. . . . But if a servant in this case shall wilfully neglecte his Mr's commande he shall suffer bodily punishment.[27] . . .

For the planters in Virginia, considerations of length of residence and of varying degrees of freedom now affected the rights and obligations of persons. No longer could relations be determined exclusively by the positions persons held within a single system—the organization of the Company. By 1619 Virginia was becoming a society, in which behavior was in some way determined by the totality of positions each person held in a network of sometimes complementary, sometimes contradictory, relationships. The key to this transformation from organization to society lies in the concessions the Company was forced to offer to induce persons to accept positions in the organizational relationship; for those concessions so multiplied the number of statuses and so altered the status of persons that a system of relationships was created where only one had existed before.

The fact is that the reforms of the Company instituted in 1609 were not sufficient either to swell the supply of labor migrating to Virginia or to motivate the planters who were there to work with the will the Company expected. The Company had hoped that by its reforms it would be able to obtain not "idle and wicked persons; such as shame, or fear compels into this action [but] fit and industrious [persons], honest sufficient Artificers."[28] Yet so unproductive were they that as late as 1616 John Rolfe could indicate to Sir Robert Rich that what had been was still the Company's most serious problem. Our greatest want, he wrote, is "good and sufficient men as well of birth and quality to command, soldiers to marche, discover and defend the country from invasion, artificers, labourers, and husbandmen."[29] And so dissatisfied had the settlers become with their situation that, in a letter smuggled to the Spanish ambassador in London with the connivance of English sailors, Don Diego de Molina, the prisoner in Jamestown, reported that "a good many have gone to the Indians . . . and others have gone out to sea . . . and those who remain do so by force and are anxious to see a fleet come from Spain to release them from this misery."[30] . . .

Nor did the concessions granted to superior colonists in 1614, including a kind of modified right to private property and some relief from the obligation to work on the Company lands, suffice to solve the labor problem.[31] For the simple fact was, as Captain John Smith wrote, that "no man will go from hence to have less liberty there then here."[32] The Company, determined in 1619 to make a final effort to create of Virginia the profitable investment it had always hoped it would be, took his advice to heart. Though it was faced with declining financial resources, with internal bickering, and with increasing evidence that the king was losing patience with its meager achievement, the Company decided to pin its hopes on a quick return. The key to profits, it felt, lay in raising the value of the Company lands through increasing population and in diversifying products through the importation of labor skilled in many trades. The success of the effort, obviously, rested upon the strength of the additional inducements that could be offered to both investors and potential emigrants.[33]

As always, one of the principal devices used by the Company to attract labor and to increase productivity was that of easing the terms on which land could be acquired. The effect of the reform was to create within the Company a new group of statuses differentiated from one another in terms of the amount of property attached to each or the length of time required to obtain land on the part of those who were not yet entitled to it:

1. "Ancient planters" who had come to Virginia at their own cost before 1616 received 100 acres per share in perpetuity rent-free.
2. "Ancient planters" who had come to Virginia at Company expense received 100 acres at an annual rent of 2 s. after the completion of their seven-year period of servitude on the Company's land.
3. All persons who came to Virginia after 1616 at their own expense received 50 acres at an annual rent of 1 s.
4. All persons who came to Virginia after 1616 at Company expense were to receive 50 acres after having worked on the Company's land for seven years, during which time half their produce belonged to the Company and half to themselves.
5. All tradesmen received a house and 4 acres of land so long as they plied their trades.
6. All persons who paid for the transportation of emigrants received 50 acres per person.
7. Company officers not only were entitled to their regular land grants but were supported by the labor of tenants-at-halves on large tracts of land reserved by the Company for that purpose.[34]
8. Indentured servants, whose transportation was paid by the Company or by private associations of investors and who were then sold to planters on their arrival in Virginia, were entitled to "freedom dues"— including a land grant—on the expiration of their servitude.[35]

Nor was this all. Determined to improve the morale of the colonists and, eventually, to relieve the Company of the burdensome cost of transporting labor from England, Sandys also began in 1620 to ship women to Virginia to become wives of the planters. There had been marriages in Virginia before, of course, but the supply of single women, restricted to the few female servants of married couples, was far smaller than the demand. Now, however, the Company organized the shipment of women on a business basis, forming a separate joint-stock company for the purpose. Though the women were, in any case, to be paid for by the planters at the rate of 120 pounds of the best leaf tobacco per person and though the Company conceded that it was dubious as to its authority to control marriages—"for the libertie of Mariadge we dare not infrindg"—it nevertheless discriminated between classes of planters in the bestowal of the women. "And though we are desireous that mariadge be free according to the law of nature," the Company wrote to the Governor and Council of Virginia, "yett would we not have these maids deceived and married to servants, but only to such freemen or tenants as have meanes to maintaine them."[36]

Finally, in a radical departure from previous policy, the Company limited the scope of martial law and ordered Governor Yeardley to convene an assembly of elected representatives from each district in Virginia. The Company did not intend to diminish its own authority, for the Governor was given the right to veto all enactments of the Assembly, and the General Court of the Company in London retained the right to disallow its decisions. Rather was it the Company's hope that the degree of acceptance of its program would be increased if it had the added sanction of approval by representatives of the planters themselves.[37]

In a sense, the Company's reforms succeeded too well. Lured by the new prospects in Virginia, about 4,800 emigrants departed from England between November, 1619 and February, 1625, nearly twice as many as had gone during the entire period from 1607 to 1619.[38] But, while the Company's propaganda could refer blandly to "each man having the shares of Land due to him" and to "the laudable forme of Justice and government,"[39] actual conditions in Virginia were quite different. . . .

Though Company policy was not responsible for all the suffering endured by the settlers, it was responsible for intensifying their sense of deprivation by having promised too much. . . .

No doubt the chasm between expectation and reality contributed to the planters' alienation from the organizational relationship into which they had been lured by the Company's promises. But that relationship was affected even more by the development of a network of relations that followed inevitably from the inducements to get men into the Company.

At one time in Virginia, the single relationship that existed between persons rested upon the positions they occupied in the Company's table of organization. As a result of the efforts made by the Company to get persons to accept that relationship, however, each person in Virginia had become the occupant of several statuses, for now there were rich and poor in Virginia, landowners and renters, masters and servants, old residents and newcomers, married and single, men and women; and simultaneous possession of these statuses involved the holder in a network of relationships, some congruent and some incompatible, with his organizational relationship.

Once the men in Virginia had been bachelors who lived in Company-provided barracks. Now they lived in private houses with their families, and, though the Company attempted to make use of the new relationship by penalizing each "Master of a family" for certain crimes committed by those under his authority[40]—hoping thereby that the master would use his authority to suppress crime—it can hardly be doubted that its action involved the head of the family in a conflict of loyalties.

Once all persons had been equal before Company law, and penalties had been inflicted solely in accordance with the nature of the offense. Now, the General Assembly found that "persones of qualitie" were "not fitt to undergoe corporall punishment."[41]

Once length of residence was irrelevant in determining the obligations of persons to the Company. Now, however, it was enacted that all "ye olde planters, yt were heere before, or cam in at ye laste cominge of Sr. Tho: Gates they and theire posteritie shal be exempted from theire psonall service to ye warres, and any publique charge (Churche dewties excepted)."[42]

Once Virginians had been governed administratively through a chain of command originating in the Company's General Court. Now an authentic political system existed, and the members of the Assembly demanded the same right to disallow orders of the General Court that the Court had with respect to the Assembly.

Once all land had been owned by the Company. Now much of it was owned by private persons, and even more had been promised to them, and the opportunities for the creation of private fortunes involved the planters in a new relationship with the Company. No longer was the planter willing to have his tobacco exported through the Company at a fixed price, when, as a free landowner, he might strike his own bargain with the purchaser. No longer was the planter willing, at a time when labor meant profit, for the Company to commandeer his servants. Even officers of the Company, expected to administer its program in Virginia, saw the chance to subvert it to their own purposes. . . .

The increase in private wealth tended to subordinate status in the Company to status in a different relationship among the planters. The muster roll of early 1625 shows 48 families bearing various titles of distinction, most of which had been earned in Virginia. They alone held 266 of the approximately 487 white servants in Virginia, 20 of the 23 Negro servants, and 1 of the 2 Indian servants.[43] These were the families at the apex of Virginia society, determined to uphold their rights as over against other persons and sometimes going beyond their rights. Acting through the General Assembly, they insisted upon scrupulous enforcement of contracts of servitude, forbade servants to trade with the Indians, and; so as not to lose their labor, regulated the right of their servants to marry. Nor, as the chronic complaints bear witness, were they loath to keep their servants beyond the required time.[44] . . .

But that was only one aspect of the relationship. Conditions in Virginia were now more fluid than they had been, and persons of low estate might also rise. Secretary of State John Pory wrote Sir Dudley Carleton that "our cowekeeper here of James citty on Sundays goes accowtered all in freshe flaminge silke; and a wife of one that in England had professed the black arte, not of a scholler, but of a collier of Croydon, wears her rought bever hatt with a faire perle hat band." The Company was opposed to such unseemly displays of wealth on the part of persons of low estate,[45] but it could not prevent them.

The ultimate stage in the transition of Virginia from organization to society was reached when the settlers came to feel that the new relationships in which they were now involved were of greater importance than the Company relationship, when their statuses outside the organization came largely to dictate their behavior. For at that point they were no longer willing to accept the legitimacy of their organizational superiors.... From general discontent it was but a short step to ridicule of Company officials and outright refusal to accept a Company assignment. . . .

That the Company could no longer expect to command obedience was clear, for even its officers in Virginia perceived themselves as having a set of interests distinct from those of their London superiors and turned their backs to their authority. . . .

In 1607 there had been no "Contrey," only the Virginia Company. It was the Company's fate to have created a country and to have destroyed itself in the process. . . .

II

The generalizations that emerge from our study are of two kinds: those directly tied to the events of the time and place that we have analyzed and those of a more abstract kind that derive from the analysis of these historical particulars but can be stated in such a way as to be of more general applicability.

There seems little room for doubt about some of the conclusions we have drawn: that the character of seventeenth-century North American society was shaped decisively by the fact that, in contrast to the situation in Latin America, the creation of the society was accomplished through the recruitment of a voluntary labor force; that higher statuses in that society were created as a result of the need to induce persons to accept positions in lower statuses; and that the behavior of persons in that society was determined not only by opportunities for advancement, as Whiggish interpreters of our history would have us believe, but, as well, by the fact that these opportunities were less than people had been led to expect.

With respect to more general hypotheses, it may be suggested that the mechanism by which the change from organization to society was accomplished lay in the very effort to apply the blueprint that was intended to govern the relations between persons, for this so multiplied the number of statuses persons held, and therefore the relationships in which they were involved, as to alter their behavior in a decisive fashion.

The testing of these hypotheses, of course, would involve the examination of still other consciously selected historical situations for the purpose of comparison—the experience of the British in establishing other colonies in North America and in coping with a totally different problem in India, of the French in Canada and the Spanish in South America, of the reasons for the difference between the blueprint in accordance with which utopian communities were planned and the outcome of their establishment, and the like. Herein lies the design for a research in historical sociology.

Endnotes

1. Philip Alexander Bruce, *Social Life of Virginia in the Seventeenth Century* (Richmond, 1907), pp. 15, 17-18; "The Virginia Census, 1624-25," *Virginia Magazine of History and Biography*, VII (1899-1900), 364-67; Edward Channing, *A History of the United States* (New York and London, 1905-25), I, 204-5.

2. *Records of the Virginia Company* (Washington, 1906-35), ed. Susan Myra Kingsbury III, 21.

3. "Minutes of the Council and General Court," *Virginia Magazine of History and Biography*, XXIII (1915), 138.

4. Wesley Frank Craven and Walter B. Hayward, *The Journal of Richard Norwood, Surveyor of Bermuda* (New York, 1945); Alexander Brown, *The Genesis of the United States* (Boston and New York, 1897), I, 442; "London's Lotterie," *William and Mary Quarterly*, V (3rd ser., 1948), 259-64.

5. Herbert Levi Osgood, *The American Colonies in the Seventeenth Century* (New York and London, 1904, 1907), I, 32-34; II, 30-32; Philip Alexander Bruce, *Economic History of Virginia in the Seventeenth Century* (New York and London, 1806), I, 3-4.

6. Wesley Frank Craven, *Dissolution of the Virginia Company* (New York, 1932), p. 24. For an account of the structure of the Company see William Robert Scott, *The Constitution and Finance of English, Scottish and Irish Joint-Stock Companies to 1720* (Cambridge, 1910), II, 247-59, 266-88.

7. *A Declaration of the State of the Colonie and Affairs in Virginia* (London, 1620) in Peter Force (ed.) *Tracts and Other Papers, Relating . . . to the . . . Colonies in North America* (Washington, 1836-46), III, 5; Brown, *Genesis*, I, 357.

8. John Smith, *Description of Virginia and Proceedings of the Colonie* (Oxford, 1612), in Lyon Gardiner Tyler (ed.), *Narratives of Early Virginia* (New York, 1907), 178.

9. Susan Myra Kingsbury, "A Comparison of the Virginia Company with the Other English Trading Companies of the Sixteenth and Seventeenth Centuries," *Annual Report of the American Historial Association for the Year 1906* (Washington, 1907), pp. 162-63.

10. Wesley Frank Craven, "Indian Policy in Early Virginia," *William and Mary Quarterly*, I (3rd ser., 1944), pp. 65-82.

11. John Smith, *Description of Virginia*, in Tyler (ed.), *op. cit.*, pp. 125-26, 140-41, 159-60; Thomas Jefferson Wertenbaker, *Patrician and Plebeian in Virginia* (Charlottesville, 1910), pp. 5-9; Bruce, *Social Life*, pp. 39-43.

12. The quotations are in Osgood, *op. cit.*, I, 46-47; Smith, *Generall Historie*, in Tyler (ed.), *op. cit.*, pp. 331-32; John Smith, *The Proceedings of the English Colonie in Virginia* (Oxford, 1612), in the A.G. Bradley edition of Edward Arber (ed.), *Travels and Works of Captain John Smith* (Edinburgh, 1919), I, 149. See also Osgood, *op. cit.*, I, 50, 54-55; Bruce, *Economic History*, I, 197.

13. Channing, *op. cit.*, I, 204.

14. *Calendar of State Papers, East Indies, 1571-1616*, No. 432; Brown, *Genesis*, I, 252-54; E. Ribton-Turner, *A History of Vagrants and Vagrancy* (London, 1887), 141; Kingsbury (ed.), *Records*, I, 304-6, 270, 359; III, 259; *Acts of the Privy Council of England, Colonial Series*, Vol. I, No. 42; Abbot Emerson Smith, *Colonists in Bondage* (Chapel Hill, 1947), pp. 147-49; Richard B. Morris, *Government and Labor in Early America* (New York, 1946), p. 358.

15. A. E. Smith, *op. cit.*, pp. 94-95; Morris, *op. cit.*, p. 323.

16. Kingsbury (ed.), *Records*, I, 520, II, 108; A. E. Smith, *op. cit.*, pp. 139-40.

17. Craven, *Virginia Company*, pp. 29-33; Scott, *op. cit.*, II, pp. 250-52; Philip Alexander Bruce, *Institutional History of Virginia in the Seventeenth Century* (New York and London, 1910), II, 237-41.

18. A. E. Smith, *op. cit.*, pp. 44-46.

19. James Curtis Ballagh, *White Servitude in the Colony of Virginia* ("John Hopkins University Studies in Historical and Political Science, 13th Series," Vols. VII-VIII [Baltimore, 1895]), pp. 15-17; Craven, *Virginia Company*, pp. 29-33; Craven, *Southern Colonies*, pp. 85-90; A. E. Smith, *op. cit.*, pp. 8-10; Kingsbury, "Comparison," *op. cit.*, pp. 163-69.

20. *A True and Sincere Declaration* (London, 1609), in Brown, *Genesis*, I, 352.

21. Quoted in Craven, *Southern Colonies*, p. 64.

22. Appendix to *A True and Sincere Declaration*, in Brown, *Genesis*, I, 352.

23. Kingsbury (ed.), *Records*, III, 216-19.

24. *Ibid.*, p. 27.

25. *Ibid.*, p. 22.

26. For the full text of the code see *For the Colony in Virginea Britannia, Lawes Divine, Morall and Martiall, Etc.* (London, 1612), in *Force* (ed.), *op. cit.*, Vol. III.

27. Kingsbury (ed.), *Records*, III, 173, 160.

28. Appendix to *A True and Sincere Declaration* (1609), in Brown, *Genesis*, I, 352; Virginia Company broadside of 1610, in Brown, *Genesis*, I, 439.

29. Quoted in Charles M. Andrews, *The Colonial Period of American History* (New Haven, 1934-38), I, 113-14.

30. Brown, *Genesis*, II, 648-49.

31. Ballagh, *op. cit.*, pp. 22-23; Osgood, *op. cit.*, I, 75-77; Bruce, *Economic History*, I, 212-15; Craven, *Southern Colonies*, 116-17; A. E. Smith, *op. cit.*, pp. 10-11.

32. Quoted in Miller, "Religion and Society," *op. cit.*, p. 37.

33. Craven, *Virginia Company, passim,* but esp. pp. 168-71; Craven, *Southern Colonies,* pp. 145-47; Scott, *op. cit.,* II, 266-88; Susan Myra Kingsbury, *An Introduction to the Records of the Virginia Company of London* (Washington, 1905), pp. 34-35, 40-41, 94-95.

34. "Instructions to Governor Yeardley, 1618," *Virginia Magazine of History and Biography,* II (1894-95), 161-62; Bruce, *Economic History,* I, 226-33, 511-14; Ballagh, *op. cit.,* pp. 25-28, 31; Craven, *Virginia Company,* pp. 50-57; Craven, *Southern Colonies,* pp. 127-29.

35. A. E. Smith, *op. cit.,* pp. 11-17; Ballagh, *op. cit.,* pp. 28-30; Bruce *Economic History,* II, pp. 41-48; Morris, *op. cit.,* p. 395.

36. Kingsbury (ed.), *Records,* III, 115, 493-94, 505.

37. Thomas Jefferson Wertenbaker, *Virginia Under the Stuarts* (Princeton, 1914), pp. 38-39; Craven, *Virginia Company,* pp. 70-80; Craven, *Southern Colonies,* pp. 127-29; "Proceedings of the First Assembly in Virginia, Held July 30, 1619," in *Colonial Records of Virginia* (Richmond, 1874).

38. Samuel H. Yonge, "The Site of Old 'James Towne,' 1607-1698," *Virginia Magazine of History and Biography,* XI (1903-4), 399-400.

39. *A Declaration of the State of the Colony* (1620), in Force (ed.), *op. cit.,* III, 5-6.

40. Proclamation of Governor Wyatt, June, 1622, in Kingsbury (ed.), *Records,* III, 659.

41. Act of March, 1623/24 (*ibid.,* IV, 584).

42. Act of March, 1623/24 (*ibid.,* IV, 582).

43. The figures are derived from the muster rolls in John Camden Hotten, *The Original Lists of Persons of Quality; Emigrants, Religious Exiles . . . Who Went from Great Britain to the American Plantations, 1600-1700* (London, 1874).

44. A. E. Smith, *op. cit.,* pp. 226-29; Kingsbury (ed.), *Records,* IV, 128-30.

45. Pory to Carleton, September 30, 1619, in Tyler (ed.), *op. cit.,* p. 285; Kingsbury (ed.), *Records,* III, 469.

10

A Counterblaste to Tobacco

KING JAMES I, of ENGLAND

. . . Many in this kingdom have had such a continual use of taking this unsavory smoke, as now they are not able to forbear the same, no more than an old drunkard can abide to be long sober, without falling into an uncurable weakness. . . .

It is, as you use, or rather abuse it, a branch of the sin of drunkenness, which is the root of all sins: for as the only delight that drunkards take in wine is in the strength of the taste, and the force of the fume thereof that mounts up to the brain; for no drunkards love any weak or sweet drink; so are not those (I mean the strong heat and the fume) the only qualities that make tobacco so delectable to all the lovers of it? . . .

And for the vanities committed in this filthy custom, is it not both great vanity and uncleanliness, that at the table, a place of respect, of cleanliness, of modesty, men should not be ashamed to sit tossing of tobacco pipes, and puffing of the smoke of tobacco one to another, making the filthy smoke and stink thereof, to exhale athwart the dishes and infect the air, when very often men that abhor it are at their repast?

Surely smoke becomes a kitchen far better than a dining chamber, and yet it makes a kitchen also oftentimes in the inward parts of men, soiling and infecting them with an unctuous and oily kind of soot, as hath been found in some great tobacco takers that after their death were opened. . . .

"A Counterblaste to Tobacco," James I, of England, 1604, in *English Reprints*, ed. by Edward Arber, London, 1869, pp. 99-112.

The public use whereof at all times and in all places hath now so far prevailed, as divers men, very sound both in judgment and complexion, have been at last forced to take it also without desire, partly because they were ashamed to seem singular . . . and partly to be as one that was content to eat garlic (which he did not love) that he might not be troubled with the smell of it in the breath of his fellows.

And is it not a great vanity, that a man cannot heartily welcome his friend now, but straight they must be in hand with tobacco? Now it is become in place of a cure, a point of good fellowship, and he that will refuse to take a pipe of tobacco among his fellows (though for his own election he would rather feel the savor of a sink) is accounted peevish and no good company. . . . Yea the mistress cannot in a more mannerly kind entertain her servant than by giving him out of her fair hand a pipe of tobacco. . . . A custom loathsome to the eye, hateful to the nose, harmful to the brain, dangerous to the lungs, and in the black stinking fume thereof, nearest resembling the horrible Stygian smoke of the pit that is bottomless.

11

New England Merchants in the Seventeenth Century

BERNARD BAILYN

In social origins the transplanted London tradesmen were unique among the settlers. Most of the colonists had known only life on the land, either as gentlemen, independent farmers, tenants, or laborers; consequently, both the magistrates and the majority of the population brought with them the attitudes and desires of rural Englishmen. To them land meant not so much wealth as security and stability, tradition and status. Shaken out of their familiar ways by economic and political disturbances, caught up in varying degrees by the cause of religious reform, most of the 20,000 Englishmen who migrated to America in the 1630s sought to recreate the village and farm life they had known. They accepted and probably welcomed the medieval social teaching of orthodox Puritanism if only for its inspiring support of the idea of the close-knit community that existed for the good of all its members and in which each man was his brother's keeper.[1]

Reprinted by permission of the publishers from *The New England Merchants in the Seventeenth Century* by Bernard Bailyn, (Cambridge, Mass.: Harvard University Press), copyright 1955 by the President and Fellows of Harvard College, pp. 39-44.

For the merchants, bred in London and the bustling outports, these needs and ideas were less urgent. The great metropolis was a hothouse of new values and attitudes. In contrast to that of the average agriculturist, the life pattern of merchants who, like Thomas Savage and Robert Keayne, could boast of having received "no portion from my parents or friends to begin the world withal," and, after a career of constant striving, having emerged triumphant from financial losses "sufficient to have broken the backe of any one man in the Country"—such life patterns were characterized by geographical and social mobility.[2] To such men the authoritarianism of Winthrop's government, which suggested security and status to most of the settlers, tended to imply constriction and denial. Freed from the complexities and competition of the Old World cities and trained in some aspect of the production and distribution of goods, the merchants experienced a release of energies in America which frequently struck the Puritan leaders as brashness and insubordination. Conflict between men who had risen through the struggles of city life and the leaders of the Puritan Commonwealth was implicit from the start.

Yet the right of the merchants to participate fully in the community life was not challenged. All of them were received into a church and made freemen of the corporation. The difficulty took the form of a series of clashes between the merchants and the public authorities. Some of these were trivial and easily handled by the usual processes of law.[3] Others led through subtle ways to serious trouble. In a society where theology and political theory were interwoven, thin lines of doctrine were often the threads upon which rested the justification for the use of power. Dissatisfaction with the magistracy stemming from different assumptions as to the right of self-expression, political and economic as well as religious, could be voiced in hair-splitting theological disputes. . . .

The divergence between the merchants and most of the rest of the Puritan population manifested itself . . . particularly in public condemnations for malpractices in trade, particularly overcharging, usury, taking advantage of a neighbor's need. The public clamor that accompanied one such incident grew to such proportions as to indicate that an important source of discontent had been touched.

Robert Keayne was a typical self-made tradesman of London.[4] Starting as a butcher's son in Windsor he had risen through apprenticeship in London to prominence as a merchant tailor. Transplanted to New England in 1635, he was received into the church, made a freeman of the corporation, and immediately assumed a leading position in local affairs. He moved into a house and shop on the southwest corner of Cornhill and King streets in the heart of Boston, one lot distant from the First Church and facing the central market square. Drawing on the "two or 3000 lb in good estate" he had brought with him, he reestablished contact with his

London friends and commenced his career as a retailer of imported manufactures. For four years he rode the wave of the inflation, selling badly needed goods to the immigrants for whatever prices he could get. But in November 1639 he was struck down by both church and state. Keayne was charged in General Court with "taking above six-pence in the shilling profit; in some above eight-pence; and in some small things, above two for one."[5]

It had all started with a bag of nails he had sold at what he claimed was a perfectly reasonable price. Once this single charge had exposed the merchant to public censure, a variety of other accusations, such as overcharging for "great gold buttons," a bridle, and a skein of thread, were fired at him. Haled before the highest court he was made to face a barrage of denunciation. So agonizing were the resulting wounds that in drawing up his Last Will and Testament fourteen years later he referred again and again to the incident as if to ease the pain of that "deepe and sharpe censure that was layd upon me in the Country and carryed on with so much bitterness and indignation . . . contrary or beyond the quality and desert of the complaynts that came against me." The public ire was expressed not so much in the court's conviction of the merchant as in the fact that the fine was fixed at no less than £200. But even that was cheap considering the state of public feeling. Keayne later wrote that "if some could have had their wills they would have had the fyne mounted up to 1000 lb yea 500 lb was too little except some co[r]poral punishment was added to it, such as my mans [sic] standing openly on a market day with a Bridle in his mouth or at least about his necke, as I was credibly informed. Here was well guided zeale."[6]

So far only the civil sword had struck. The church then took up the matter. The elders studied "how farr I was guilty of all those claymors and rumors that then I lay under," and exposed his defense to a most "exquisite search." Though he escaped excommunication, a fact he later boasted of, he was given a severe admonition ". . . in the Name of the Church for selling his wares at excessive Rates, to the Dishonor of Gods name, the Offence of the Generall Cort, and the Publique scandall of the Cuntry." It took a "penetentiall acknowledgment" of his sin to regain full membership in the church.[7]

To Keayne the most painful part of this episode (and also of his more famous involvement three years later with Goody Sherman and her sow)[8] was not the fine or the admonition but the public insistence that he was a sinner.

> . . . the newnes and straingnes of the thing, to be brought forth into an open Court as a publique malefactor, was both a shame and an amazement to me. It was the greife of my soule (and I desire it may ever so be in a greater measure) that any act of mine (though not justly

> but by misconstruction) should be an occasion of scandall to the Gospell and profession of the Lord Jesus, or that my selfe should be looked at as one that had brought any just dishonor to God (which I have endeavored long and according to my weake abilities desired to prevent) though God hath beene pleased for causes best knowne to himselfe to deny me such a blessing, and if it had beene in my owne power I should rather have chosen to have perished in my cradle than to have lived to such a time.[9]

The merchant was as devout a Christian by his lights as his brother-in-law, the Reverend John Wilson. He had dedicated himself to the life of the spirit in the most befitting way. Not only had he been regular in his church attendance but he had kept notes on the sermons he had heard that he might refer to them later. He had studied the sacred books far into the night and left as the fruit of his labor "3 great writing bookes which are intended as an Exposition or Interpretation of the whole Bible . . . as also a 4th great writing booke which is an exposition on the Prophecy of Daniel, of the Revelations and Prophecy of Hosea . . . all which Bookes are written with my owne hand . . . and worth all the paines and labour I have bestowed upon them, so that if I had 100 lb layd me downe for them, to deprive me of them, till my sight or life should be taken of me I should not part from them." He had followed the Calvinist precepts of personal conduct. Never had he indulged in "an idle, lazie, or dronish life" or allowed himself "many spare houres to spend unprofitably away or to refresh myself with recreations." Naturally, he had prospered despite all the malice of his adversaries.[10]

Finding evidence in the social teachings of Calvinism for the rectitude of his life, he could impute only sinfulness to those who attempted to blacken his name. But his enemies also drew upon religious ideas for the justification of their attack. To them it seemed clear that by all the relevant Calvinist standards of justice in business, Keayne had sinned. In his scramble for profit he had trampled underfoot the notion of a just price. He had dealt with his debtors usuriously. He had put the increase of his own wealth above the common good. No amount of public benefaction could make up for such evil practices.

The original charge against the distraught merchant fell like a spark into an incendiary situation. The settlers, predisposed to believe middlemen parasites, found themselves utterly dependent on them for the most essential goods and equipment. Incapable of understanding or controlling the workings of the economy, they sought to attribute the cause of the soaring prices and the shortage of goods to human malevolence. Instances of merchants taking advantage of the situation[11] confirmed them in their belief that only the most rigorous discipline of the businessmen could save them from misery. In the same Calvinist social teachings that had justified his life to Keayne they had a grammar for the translation of economics into morality, and in the machinery of the Puritan church and state a means of effecting these ideas. From the same texts the Puritan magistrates and the merchants read different lessons. The former learned the overwhelming importance of the organic society which subordinated the individual to the general good. Keayne learned the righteousness of those individual qualities whose secondary but attractive virtue it was to aid in the fight for success in business. Keayne's advice to the "Reverend Eldrs of this Country" that they "be as easily perswaded to yeeld in civill and earthly respects and things as they expect to prevayl with any of us when they have a request to make of us" would have implied to Winthrop the severance of the moral sinews in the body of Puritan society.[12]

Keayne's Last Will and Testament expresses the dilemma of the first Puritan import merchants. Its 50,000 words were written under the compulsive need to gain final approval from a generation that seemed to confuse diligence with avarice. To be both a pious Puritan and a successful merchant meant to live under what would seem to have been insupportable pressures. It meant to extend to the life of business a religious enthusiasm which must be continuously dampened lest it singe the corners of another's life. It meant to accumulate as much wealth as one righteously could, only to dispose of it, like a steward, according to the principle *uti non frui*. It demanded against the natural desire to live spontaneously and heedlessly the total rationalization of life. Above all, it required an amount of self-discipline that only great faith could sustain.

Endnotes

1. For a moving example of this ideal in practice, see the Pilgrims' pledge of 1617 to remain as they were, "knite togeather as a body in a most stricte and sacred bond and covenante of the Lord . . . straitly tied to all care of each others good, and of the whole by every one and so mutually." Bradford, *History*, I, 76.

2. "The Last Will and Testament of me, Robert Keayne . . . 1653 . . .," A [Tenth] *Report of the Record Commissioners of the City of Boston, containing Miscellaneous Papers* (Boston, 1886), pp. 47, 16.

3. For example, Edward Bendall, who crossed in the Winthrop Fleet, was fined and imprisoned for failure to "acknowledge the justice of the Court." *Mass. Records*, I, 176.

4. For a full account of Keayne and his troubles, see Bailyn, "Keayne."

5. "Last Will," p.47; *Winthrop's Journal*, I, 215.

6. "Last Will," pp. 27, 34. *Mass. Records*, I, 281. The fine was later reduced to £80. *Mass. Records*, I, 290. Winthrop had little sympathy for Keayne: the "corrupt practice of this man . . . was the more observable because he was wealthy and sold dearer than most other trades-

men, and for that he was of ill repute for the like covetous practice in England. . . ." *Winthrop's Journal*, I, 316.

7. "Last Will," p. 34; Records of the First Church of Boston (handwritten copy in the Massachusetts Historical Society), pp. 12, 14.

8. Most of the documents bearing on this case, which resulted in the separation of the General Court into two houses, will be found in A. P. Rugg, "A Famous Colonial Litigation," *A.A.S. Procs.*, new series, XXX (1920), 217-250.

9. "Last Will," p. 34.

10. "Last Will," pp. 5, 42.

11. For other cases, see *Winthrop's Journal*, I, 77; *Mass. Records*, I, 163, 208, 279, 317; *Plymouth Records*, I, 137.

12. "Last Will," p. 15.

12

British Policy and Colonial Growth: Some Implications of the Burden from the Navigation Acts

Roger L. Ransom

Very few issues in American economic history have stirred as many contrasting views as the debate regarding the effects of the British Navigation Acts on the Thirteen American Colonies. The most recent entry in the long argument is Robert Thomas' analysis of the problem.[1] Thomas constructs quantitative estimates of the impact of the Acts which are designed ". . . to measure, relative to some hypothetical alternative, the extent of the burdens and benefits stemming from imperial regulation of the foreign commerce of the 13 colonies."[2] He presents these estimates to test the hypothesis that: ". . . membership in the British Empire, after 1763, did not impose a significant hardship upon the American Colonies."[3] Thomas has employed new data in constructing his estimates, and he has carefully brought economic theory explicitly into the discussion. His framework requires the construction of a "counterfactual" hypothesis against which to evaluate the impact of policy. As he views it: "The only

"British Policy and Colonial Growth: Some Implications of the Burden from the Navigation Acts," by Roger L. Ransom is reprinted by permission from *Journal of Economic History*, XXVIII (Sept., 1968), pp. 427-435.

reasonable alternative in this case is to calculate the burdens or benefits of British regulation relative to how the colonists would have fared outside the British Empire, but still within a mercantilist world."[4] Given such a model, the value of the burden and benefit is estimated in terms of market prices and the pattern of trade which would have emerged had the colonies been free in 1763.

His results, summarized in Table 1, show that the absolute magnitude of the burden was quite small. Expressed as a sum per capita, the "net burden" averaged only 26 cents during the decade 1763-72; for the single year 1770 it was 42 cents. How much difference could such a small sum make in the level of colonial welfare? If, as Thomas supposed likely, the level of income at that time was about $100 per head, then the answer is that the burden would make very little difference, indeed. . . .

Table 1: **Thomas' estimates of burden**

Estimate	1763-72	1770
Gross		
Burden	£451,000 ($2,255,000)	£532,000 ($2,660,000)
Benefit	£351,000 ($1,775,000)	£351,000 ($1,775,000)
Per capita		
Burden	$1.20	$1.24
Net burden	$0.26	$0.42

Notes: Net burden is the per capita difference between the burden and the benefits.

Source: Robert Thomas, "A Quantitative Approach to the Study of the Effects of British Imperial Policy upon Colonial Welfare," *Journal of Economic History* XXV (Dec. 1965), Table 2, p. 637.

The largest estimated loss on this basis is .42 of one percent of per capita income, or 42 cents on a hundred dollars. Suppose for a moment that my estimates are off by 100 percent; then, in that case, the burden would be slightly more than one percent of national income. It is difficult to make a convincing case for exploitation out of these results.[5]

Thomas has very ingeniously combined theory and data to enlarge considerably our appreciation of the quantitative effects of the Acts. And, as he points out, a quarter of one percent is such a small figure that even a substantial error would leave the level of colonial welfare virtually unchanged. Yet one is left with a nagging suspicion that the impact of a 2½ million dollar distortion of the colonial economy should not be dismissed so lightly. Using Thomas' estimates of the burden, this article presents some points which, while they do not represent a convincing case for exploitation, nevertheless indicate that a sizable portion of the colonial economy did suffer from the enforcement of the Navigation Acts. One object in doing this is to point out that *changes in those Acts* might have affected income in the Colonies. My discussion centers on three points connected with Thomas' work: (1) some difficulties with the very broad nature of his hypothesis, (2) the different regional affects of the Acts, and (3) the relative size of the burden in the light of new evidence about the level of income in the Colonies at the end of the Colonial Period.

I

Any number of possible hypotheses can be constructed with regard to the impact of the Navigation Acts. Thomas chose to deal with the broad issue of whether the Colonies were significantly worse off as a result of being in the British Empire. In this case, the "burden" from regulations imposed by Britain must be weighed against the "benefits" of being British; the counterfactual alternative is that of a free economy. In the context of the atmosphere of the late 1770's, a break with England does appear to be the most plausible alternative. Yet it may not be the most useful for analytical purposes. Such a broad formulation of the problem brings in many other factors which tend to obscure the role of any single set of forces (such as the Navigation Acts) in generating friction between the Colonies and England. Table 2 shows the sources of the burden and benefits as computed by Thomas. Whereas all of the items connected with the burden stem from provisions of the Navigation Acts, the benefits all involve the overall obligation of Britain to defend her Empire. These services were of a very different nature than the regulations on trade. Protection of British subjects and the rights of these subjects to enjoy the opportunities afforded by participation in the Empire were not adjusted in response to particular groups; all members of the system shared them. They did not, in other words, represent a "policy variable" in the hands of the British government. The Navigation Acts, on the other hand, were a set of specific regulations enacted by the Parliament. They could be—and were—adjusted from time to time to meet particular situations.[6] Thus, while the source of the burden changed with shifts in policy, the source of the benefits remained the same. A "Net Burden"—the concept employed by Thomas to test his hypothesis—cancels these two opposing effects against each other without taking into account the differing nature of each.

Lawrence Harper, in his study of the burden of the Acts, concentrated on a narrower question. As he put it, his task was "merely to determine what price the colonists paid for what they received."[7] For each hypothesis that one puts forward there are a myriad of counterfactual alternatives. In

Table 2: **Sources of the burden and benefit from British policy (thousand pounds sterling)**

I. Burden[a]		
A. *Net loss* from export restrictions		−411
1. *Loss* from enumeration of goods	−449	
2. *Gain* from preferential duties	+55	
3. *Gain* from bounties on colonial exports	+33	
B. *Loss* from restrictions on imports		−121
C. *Net loss* from restrictions on shipping		0
1. *Loss* from forgone shipping earnings	−( )[b]	
2. *Gain* from monopoly shipping rights in Empire	+( )[b]	
Total burden		−532
II. Benefits[a]		
A. *Gain* from military protection of British Army		+145
B. *Gain* from naval protection on high seas		+206
Total benefits		+351
III. Net burden		−60

[a] "−" implies a cost imposed by that policy; "+" implies a benefit to the Colonies from that policy.

[b] Thomas estimated the gains from monopoly to be about £77,000 in 1770. He felt that this would be more than offset by the losses implied by the lower volume of traffic carried under the Navigation Acts. Hence the net effect of I.C.1 and I.C.2, above, is zero. (Thomas, p. 633).

Source: Burden—Robert Thomas, "A Quantitative Approach to the Study of the Effects of British Imperial Policy upon Colonial Welfare," *Journal of Economic History* XXV (Dec. 1965), p. 626; Benefits—Thomas, *ibid.*, pp. 633-36.

this case both Harper and Thomas use the same hypothetical model—a free market for colonial exports and imports—with which to weigh the impact of the Acts.[8] However, Harper's question focuses attention on the *gross burden* rather than the *net burden*. Such a separation of costs and gains is, it seems to me, desirable. It allows us to judge whether or not changes in regulations would make any difference to the Colonies. This article will *examine the extent to which changes in the Navigation Acts could have significantly affected economic activity in the Colonies*. To do so, it will concentrate on showing the *maximum effect* which could result; that is, suppose that the restrictive clauses of the Acts were removed altogether. The estimated *gross burden* will then represent this maximum influence which adjustments in commercial policy could exert on the colonial economy.

While the counterfactual hypotheses with regard to trade restrictions are essentially the same in this formulation and Thomas', the fact that the Colonies would not be outside the Empire if only the provisions of the Acts were altered means that they would not necessarily lose the positive effects from policies. The gains from preferential duties (I.A.2 of Table 2), from bounties on colonial exports (I.A.3 of Table 2), and from monopoly shipping rights within the empire (I.C.2 of Table 2), are all balanced off against the losses from restrictions on exports and imports in Table 2. The total burden of £532,000 therefore understates the actual gross burden from the Acts. Preferential duties were for the most part associated with the costs of enumeration, and it seems fruitless to try and break out that portion of the gain which might not have been directly involved with enumeration. I assume that these preferences would be adjusted along with any relaxation of enumeration; hence it remains as a positive element in the gross burden. The bounties, on the other hand, are clearly a separate aspect of mercantilist policy. Since there is no reason to expect that Britain would not still subsidize these items, the £33,000 in bounties (I.A.3 of Table 2) should not be omitted from the gross burden. The effect is to increase my estimate of the gross burden from £532,000 to £565,000 as shown in Table 3.

Table 3: **The southern burden in 1770 (thousand pounds sterling)**

	Total burden	Adjustment factor[a]	Southern burden
Exports			
Tobacco	326	1.00	326
Rice	120	1.00	120
Other	53	0.75	40
Less preferences	−55	0.75	−40
Imports	121	0.48	59
Total burden	565		505

[a] Share of total allocated to the South.

Source: Robert Thomas, "A Quantitative Approach to the Study of the Effects of British Imperial Policy upon Colonial Welfare," *Journal of Economic History* XXV (Dec. 1965), p. 626.

The question of the monopoly gains from protection of shipping within the Empire is more difficult to deal with. Thomas calculated these gains to be in the neighborhood of £75,000 in 1770. Clearly they would still remain, and thus would not offset the losses of shipping revenue from the restriction on trade (I.C.1 of Table 2). I shall not attempt to include an adjustment for the effects which a loosening of trade regulations would have on shipping earnings. Suffice it to point out that these earnings would expand if the volume of trade expanded, and therefore my estimate of the gross burden is an understatement of the total effect.[9]

II

Perhaps the greatest advantage of separating the benefits and costs of British policy is that one can better note the regional impact of the Acts. A glance at the estimates of Table 2 shows that the enumeration of colonial exports accounts for most of the burden. The purpose of enumeration was to monopolize the trade in colonial staples for the Mother Country. Thus, despite the presence of potentially lucrative markets elsewhere, southern staples such as rice and tobacco had to be shipped directly to Britain. It is clear that the South bears a greater share of this cost than the other Colonies. Table 3 presents an estimate of the burden placed upon the southern colonies. All of Thomas' estimated burden for tobacco and rice was allocated to the South; the remainder was allocated on the basis of southern trade with Britain.[10] The figures show that in 1770 about £505,000 ($2.5 million)—almost 90 percent of the total burden—fell on the South.

If we consider that the provisions of the Acts were concentrated on a single sector of the economy—foreign trade—then the relative size of the burden in southern trade appears quite large. Southern exports to Britain amounted to £770,000 in 1770.[11] This means that exports to the Mother Country might have *expanded by nearly two-thirds* in that year. Since exports to Britain remained relatively steady over the entire decade, the importance of such a burden on British-Colonial trade would be of a comparable magnitude in any year.[12] Even if it is acknowledged that the export sector of the southern colonies represented only a portion of total activity, this was the area which was most oriented to the market. Decisions with regard to incremental changes in production would be geared to this market; the overall effects of a 67 percent increase in exports might be quite substantial indeed.

III

The absolute magnitude of the burden does not tell us the impact on the economy. In assessing the relative importance of the burden, Thomas considered it as a proportion of income. He assumed that the per capita income during the period was $100. This estimate was based on the conclusions of George Rogers Taylor regarding the failure of income to rise substantially between 1775 and 1840, and on Albert Fishlow's comment that income in 1790 could not have been much less than $100 per head.[13] More recently, Paul David has constructed some very rough estimates of the level of income around 1800.[14] He insists that per capita income in 1800 was between $60 and $65 in 1840 dollars, and his conjecture for 1790 places it around $55 in 1840 dollars.[15] The evidence of Fishlow and Bjork on the post-Revolutionary Period suggests that the standard of living in 1790 was not appreciably higher than in 1770; it may have been slightly lower.[16] If we adjust for price changes, this evidence suggests a per capita income in 1770 of between $75 to $85 (in current dollars.)[17] This is, to be sure, only a rough approximation to the actual level. However, it is substantially below the $100 employed by Thomas in his remarks, since he did not adjust for changes in prices between 1840 (the basis of the Fishlow-Taylor estimate) and 1770. An income of $100 in 1840 dollars would be equivalent to about $135 in 1770 prices.

When David's revised income estimate is used, the gross burden of $2.8 million could have represented as much as 1.8 percent of income in 1770. In the southern colonies, the loss would amount to just over 2.5 percent of the regional income.[18] This is not an inconsequential amount; to the southern planter it might have seemed large relative to the less tangible benefits from British rule. Certainly it was large enough to warrant complaints against the policy on the part of southern planters.

Thomas' estimates of the absolute size of the burden are only approximates, and David's figures for per capita income are highly conjectural. Can manipulation of such estimates tell us much about the impact of the Navigation Acts? Our difficulties of estimation should not obscure the fact that the issue is clearly a quantitative one. The extent to which the Acts seriously constrained all or part of the colonial economy depends on the magnitude of the distortions they introduced. We know very little about the nature of aggregate economic activity in Colonial America, and with this limited knowledge we can hardly construct an economic (or econometric) model which would indicate the full dynamic effects of a burden imposed over a considerable period of time.

Yet, if Thomas' estimates of the gross burden indicate even a correct *order of magnitude*—and they are certainly the best figures which we have at the moment—then it is by no means obvious that the effects of the Navigation Acts are negligible. To consider the simplest case, the imposition of a burden of "x" percent would result in the loss of this fraction of income each year. The gap between realized income and income that would exist without the restrictions would grow over time as the "burden" for each year failed to be compounded into future growth of the economy and as the absolute size of the burden rose with income.

IV

The intent of this article has been to indicate whether changes in the Navigation Acts could have had much effect on the Colonial economy. Three main conclusions seem to emerge from the study: (1) For the economy as a whole, changes in the Acts (particularly the relaxation of enumeration of colonial staples) would have a perceptible, though not overwhelming, effect on income. My interpretation of the burden implies that removal of the restrictions in 1770 would have caused income to rise by something on the order of 1.5 to 1.8 percent. (2) It is clear that the impact of any change in policy would fall largely on the southern colonies, since they bore the brunt of the burden. The loss to the South amounted to some 2.5 percent of income in 1770. (The *net burden* implied by Table 3 would be close to 1.5 percent of income, well above the level for the economy as a whole[19]). (3) Finally, the trade of the southern colonies was considerably affected by the provisions of the Navigation Acts. In 1770 exports might have been 67 percent higher without the restrictions. Additional effects would have appeared through an incease in shipping earnings as trade expanded.

The fact that the Navigation Acts represented a noticeable burden on the colonial economy hardly provides a basis for arguing that the Colonies should leave the Empire to escape that burden. Oliver Dickerson insists that the Navigation Acts were not an important force in the arguments for independence.[20] Lewis Gray points out that the tobacco interests did not complain about the Acts; he argues that:

> After the industry had become thoroughly adjusted to these restrictions it is doubtful if they bore severely on colonial producers, and . . . there is little official opposition by the tobacco colonies to the Navigation Acts.
>
> In short, while British policy was formulated with a view to appropriating the golden egg made available by . . . the tobacco trade . . . it was careful to nourish and sustain the colonial goose.[21]

These views are not inconsistent with the findings of this article; the Acts *did* distort the economy, but this distortion may not have been so great as to warrant the drastic action of leaving the Empire.

Until we can conjecture more meaningful predictions regarding the long-run effects of a burden of "x" percent per year, it will be difficult to say very much more on the question of a break with England. Moreover, estimating the "benefits" of British colonial rule may be a much more formidable task than the one set forth here. As Thomas correctly asserts to leave the Empire is to move into a *mercantilistic world*, not a world of free trade. The confusion following the American Revolution shows how substantial an impact such a move could have. Britain in the eighteenth century controlled a very large and wealthy area within which trade could move with reasonable freedom. It is quite obvious that the American Colonies were major participants in that trade by the 1770's.[22] Breaking away from this trading community involved a host of uncertainties, and the "costs" were substantial. The pessimism regarding the economic outlook of the Colonies as late as 1790 shows the magnitude of the adjustments required.[23]

The implications of quantitative analysis must not be pushed too far, for the broadest measurement of "burdens" or "benefits" from British rule still focuses on a narrow aspect of the issues prompting the colonists to revolt in 1775. Even the more limited attempt to assess the role of the Navigation Acts as a contributing factor to the American Revolution involves much more than a measurement of "economic" costs. Charles Andrews summed up the situation well when he argued that the *political* as well as the *economic* development of the colonies had proceeded to the point where the colonies were:

> . . . qualified to co-operate with the mother country on terms similar to those of a brotherhood of free nations such as the British world is becoming today (1926). But England was unable to see this fact, or to recognize it, and consequently America became the scene of a political unrest which might have been controlled by a compromise, but was turned to revolt by coercion. The situation is a very interesting one, for England is famous for her ability to compromise at critical times in her history. For once at least she failed.[24]

If my analysis is correct, the regulations on trade, commerce, and industry comprising the Navigation Acts represented an area in which, had she chosen to, Britain could have offered a meaningful compromise. It seems most unlikely that changes in these regulations alone would have stemmed the tide of revolution in 1775. But—in conjunction perhaps with other evidence of compromise—it certainly might have helped at an earlier date.

Endnotes

1. R. Thomas, "A Quantitative Approach to the Study of the Effects of British Imperial Policy Upon Colonial Welfare," *Journal of Economic History* XXV (Dec. 1965). The first

quantitative estimates were constructed by Lawrence Harper in "The Effects of the Navigation Acts on the Thirteen Colonies," reprinted in H. N. Scheiber, ed., *United States Economic History* (New York: Knopf, 1964), pp. 42-78.

2. *Ibid.*, p. 615.

3. *Ibid.*, p. 616.

4. *Ibid.*, p. 616.

5. *Ibid.*, p. 638. The original text incorrectly read ".54 of one percent" and has been corrected in accordance with a letter from the author.

6. The arbitrariness of such adjustments to favor particular groups was a source of irritation to the Colonies, but they did not always lose by these changes. Thus, the relaxing of restrictions to allow rice to be shipped directly to points south of Cape Finisterre increased the returns to that staple after 1731. Major adjustments of this sort were rare; the point is that they could be made.

7. Harper, "The Effects," p. 70.

8. Douglass C. North, in *Growth and Welfare in the American Past* (Englewood Cliffs, N.J.: Prentice-Hall, 1966), p. 47 argues that Harper "did not use a single consistent hypothetical alternative" against which to measure the impact of the Acts. I think it is clear, however, that with regard to I.A. and I.B. of Table 2 Harper considers a free access to the world market as his hypothetical alternative. This is the same result as Thomas' assumption that the colonists are free.

9. Thomas estimates these gains to be about £90,000 on an increased volume of 53,000 tons in 1770, assuming the colonists left the Empire. Remaining in the Empire would increase this to about £100,000 since the colonial share of the trade would increase the tonnage by some 10 percent.

10. In 1770 the southern colonies accounted for 75.4 percent of the total colonial exports to Britain, and 47.8 percent of the imports. *Historical Statistics of the United States* (Washington, D.C.: U.S. Government Printing Office, 1960, series Z 21-34), p. 757.

11. *Ibid.*, p. 757.

12. Over the decade 1763-72 the value of southern exports to Britain averaged £924,000 per year (*Historical Statistics*, p. 757). Thomas estimates a smaller burden for the decade average (see Table 1); thus the increase would be closer to 45 percent of the exports. However, Jacob Price argues that the entire period of the late 1760's and early 1770's is an interval characterized by low tobacco exports. He feels that Thomas' decade estimate understates the magnitude of the burden in later years. See J. Price, "Comment," *Journal of Economic History* XXV (Dec. 1965).

13. G. R. Taylor, "American Economic Growth Before 1840: An Exploratory Essay" and A. Fishlow, "Comment" (on Bjork), *Journal of Economic History* XXIV (Dec. 1964).

14. P. David, "The Growth of Real Product in the United States Before 1840," *Journal of Economic History* XXVII (June 1967).

15. *Ibid.* For 1800 the figure is from Table 8; for 1790 in footnote 69, p. 187. It should be emphasized that both figures are highly "conjectural," and that the 1790 figure is less reliable than the 1800 figure.

16. G. Bjork, "The Weaning of the American Economy: Independence, Market Changes, and Economic Development" and A. Fishlow, "Comment" (on Bjork), *Journal of Economic History* XXIV (Dec. 1964).

17. The level of income in 1770 was taken to be $55-60 in 1840 prices. The Warren-Pearson index of wholesale prices was used to convert the estimate to current dollars (*Historical Statistics*, p. 116).

18. Using the per capita income figures above, southern income would be between $101 million and $108 million. Population was 1,345,000, including slaves.

19. The net benefit for the South was derived by allocating the $1,775,000 of total benefit to the southern colonies on the basis of population in 1770. The total implied benefits would then be $1.07 million for the South.

20. Oliver Dickerson, *The Navigation Acts and the American Revolution* (Philadelphia: University of Pennsylvania Press, 1951), pp. 118-22.

21. L. C. Gray, *A History of Agriculture in the Southern United States to 1860* (Baltimore: Waverly Press, Inc., 1933), p. 258.

22. See Thomas, pp. 618-19, for comments relating to the importance of trade with Britain to the Colonies in 1769. In 1772-73, "North America" received 25 percent of all British exports and accounted for 13 percent of all British imports (*Abstract of British Historical Statistics* [Cambridge, (Eng.): The University Press, 1962], p. 312. This does not account for the very large trade with the West Indies. Price makes the same point in his comment on Thomas' paper, pp. 656-57).

23. See D. C. North, *Economic Growth of the United States, 1790-1860* (Englewood Cliffs, N.J.: Prentice-Hall, 1960), pp. 17-23, especially the quote by Thomas Jefferson.

24. Charles Andrews, "The American Revolution: An Interpretation," *American Historical Review* XXXI (Jan. 1926), p. 232.

13

The American Revolution Considered as an Economic Movement

CLARENCE L. VER STEEG

Historians for a generation or more have been so sensitive to economic influences during the Revolutionary period that a modern scholar places his reputation in jeopardy if he fails to take account of such forces, regardless of what phase of political, social, or cultural life he is investigating. Although this sensitivity did not have its birth with the notable works of Charles A. Beard, they assuredly stand as an unmistakable landmark. The results, in the main, have been good. Our perspective of the Revolutionary generation has broadened, our understanding deepened; and the main stream of events has often been magnificently illuminated.

In contrast, historians have tended to neglect the other side of the coin, giving relatively little, if any, attention to the influences that political, social, and cultural forces might have had upon economic development. Even studies embracing what are normally considered "economic" subjects—such as the role of merchants, the course of trade, the change in the land systems—have almost invariably been oriented toward a distinct

"The American Revolution Considered as an Economic Movement," by Clarence L. Ver Steeg, is reprinted by permission from *Huntington Library Quarterly*, XX (August 1957), pp. 361-371.

vantage point: What effect did a change in land policy have upon social structure? How did the course of trade affect diplomatic policy? How significant was the position of the merchant in the formulation of political decisions? As illuminating as such studies have been, the results have given us only a partial view, for we have yet to answer the questions which arise when economic developments are approached from the reverse, and what many economists would call the proper, perspective. Did the modification of political institutions affect the economy? Did political action influence economic change? Were social theories produced that modified the actions of merchant and planter capitalists? Did American society by its very structure circumscribe or direct the course of economic change? How significant was the American Revolution generally upon the rise of capitalism in America? If historians are to assess the impact of the American Revolution upon the whole of American life, these questions and others of equal importance need more precise answers than we now possess.

To illustrate the lack of balance in current historical writing, one need only compare the emphasis given by scholars to the social rather than the economic consequences of the Revolution. Numerous monographic and more general works covering the period could be cited to support this point, but textbooks in United States history give as reliable a testimony as one would wish. Whereas none would be considered complete without its section neatly entitled "Social Impact of the Revolution," or something similar, followed by appropriate paragraphs of description and analysis, no textbook examined by the writer has a similar section devoted to the economic impact. Indeed, it is rare when the possibility of economic results is so much as mentioned. The textbooks in American economic history offer little more. A chapter on the Revolution is seldom included. When it is, too often its focus is "economic causation"; in fact, most economic histories are organized in such a way that one would scarcely realize that a revolution had taken place. Let it be quickly said that this comparison casts no reflection whatsoever on the textbook writers; the texts, quite properly, merely show the trend of scholarship. Although individual scholars, treating isolated subjects, have sometimes attempted to evaluate the economic effect of the Revolution, no major attempt has been made to bring together the existing material, much less to strike out into unexplored areas where fresh insights and new material would provide the ingredients for a solid synthesis. The only possible exception in the literature of the Revolution is Evarts B. Greene's helpful chapter on "The War's Economic Effects" in his *The Revolutionary Generation, 1763-1790* (New York, 1943). Greene gives a useful summary of some of the scholarship, but his approach is rather limited. Furthermore, Greene's chapter has never caught the attention of scholars; it has not been a departure point for new investigation.[1]

What becomes increasingly obvious, therefore, is that this significant theme, the impact of the Revolution upon the course of economic development, rates a thorough book-length study. This article can be little more than an introduction to an exciting historical problem. Its primary purpose is to focus attention upon the importance of the theme in terms of an area for research and in terms of a more complete understanding of the Revolutionary epoch. It will also attempt to indicate possible approaches to the problem, to make a preliminary assessment of some of the existing material, and, on occasion, to suggest additional theses that might help to define the problem. Part of the following discussion, therefore, will view familiar material from a somewhat different perspective, while other parts will suggest areas that seem to deserve more elaborate consideration if historians are eventually to make a realistic evaluation, and to see the Revolution in its fullest context.[2]

One of the most obvious, but largely overlooked, changes brought by the Revolution, carrying with it the broadest economic implications, was the new relationship between the rights of private property and mineral rights or, to use a broader term, natural resources. A careful study of this transition has never been made, but it is clear that whereas mineral rights in colonial times resided with the sovereign, to be granted or reserved as circumstances dictated, the Revolution saw such rights brought eventually within the purview of private property. The control of natural resources, therefore, was secured more firmly by private enterprisers.

It will be recalled that the charters of most colonies, though granting the rights to minerals and mines, contained a clause reserving the fifth part for the crown. This figure was more than a token; it represented an acknowledgment that the crown, when it disposed of land, possessed the power to grant or retain natural resources under the soil. That such grants were made at all merely indicates that the crown did not believe such resources existed in quantity, and, in consequence, it could be generous with an added "inducement" to colonization. As a result, there was some mining activity in the majority of colonies before the Revolution. It is interesting, however, to speculate how magnanimous the crown would have been in granting any mineral rights if precious metals, the priority minerals of the seventeenth and eighteenth centuries, had suddenly been discovered in the colonies; given the basic mercantile position of the mother country it is safe to say that its terms would have been somewhat less liberal.

From the point of view of this article, it is significant that the sovereign right of the central government over mineral resources, though retained as a matter of form, apparently was not preserved in substance. So far as my investigation goes, there seems to be no discussion of this point in the exhaustive debates that took place on the land question during the Revolution. The Land Ordinance of 1785, it is true, reserved "one-third part of all gold, silver, lead, and copper mines" for the national government, but if a scholar relies on the standard monographs on the national land system, nothing seems to have come of it. Although the problem requires more exhaustive study, it would seem that one of the legacies of the Revolution, established almost by default, made an incalculable impact on American society where the command of critical natural resources—coal, iron ore, oil and gas, precious metals, and many others—has been a key factor.

Two of the basic elements in eighteenth-century economic life, farming and land policy, were also greatly influenced by the Revolution. Quite naturally, the celebrated Land Ordinance of 1785 comes immediately to mind, for it was largely responsible for "institutionalizing" the basic productive unit in Midwestern agriculture, the family farm. What this meant for the course of economic development is significant; interestingly enough, arguments are still raging as to the merits of the established family farm as compared with a much larger unit, seemingly more suitable to the complex economy of modern times. The Land Ordinance is only the most obvious of more subtle changes from the land practices of the colonial period, some of them procedural and others substantive, depending upon the region studied. Moreover, the stimulus given to land speculation by some of the interstate and international business groups—an area in which additional research would clarify many issues—is of great importance in itself.[3]

Farming, at least in two regions, the South and New England, underwent a profound change. That historian of agriculture, Lewis C. Gray, whose discriminating analysis and careful judgment commands respect if not always agreement, goes so far as to assert: "For the South it [the American Revolution] was also a great economic Revolution."[4] He particularly emphasizes that general farming, as distinguished from the production of staples in certain areas, was stimulated; and he stresses the importance of the new internal lines of communication and trade. Gray has received additional ammunition from Professor Lawrence Harper who has traced the relative production of specific staples. Indigo, for example, ceased to be produced soon after the Revolution, not so much because indigo failed to enjoy the British subsidy of colonial times, but rather because the British subsidy after the Revolution, applying as it did only to producers within the empire, resulted in a price advantage that the South could not meet.[5] It is also well to remember that the damage caused by the fighting—the crops and livestock destroyed, and the wasted fields—

meant that the South needed time to rebuild its plantation economy, especially in South Carolina and Georgia. Indeed, the desperate search for new staples to replace the loss of indigo, together with the limited geographical area where rice could be produced, helps to explain the renewed interest in cotton, which had been experimented with for a century previous to independence but never produced in quantity.

Although the New England farmer generally was not asked to face the ravages caused by military engagements, the Revolution had a profound effect upon New England agriculture. The decisive change that occurred when its customary marketing outlets were eliminated, especially those to the West Indies, was not immediately apparent, for until 1780 war-born markets took up the slack. With the sharp cutback in wartime markets starting late in 1781, and with no comparable peacetime markets to replace them, the New England farmer suffered a blow from which he never fully recovered. It is highly probable that the despair and discontent of agrarian New England in the 1780's is largely explicable in terms of the economic consequences of the Revolution.[6]

Trade, as well as agriculture and land policy, was never the same as a result of the Revolution. In some areas it was greatly broadened; in others it was sharply restricted. Furthermore, the lines of trade were modified and mercantile connections were altered to meet the new circumstances. Although this effect of the Revolution has received some attention, more exacting studies are needed before it can be adequately measured.

The opening of the China trade, for example, was a direct consequence of the Revolution. In colonial times, the British imperial system made any notion of such a trade an unattainable dream. With the elimination of the British restrictions, this new vista was opened; and the business enterprisers of the new republic, anticipating its promise of rich rewards, rushed to exploit it. It matters not that their hopes were, in part, built upon illusions, for these illusions were quickly dispelled. What is significant is that the Asiatic trade introduced new products, created new demands, and, in some respects, educated this country's merchants in new trading techniques. William B. Weeden's apt statement deserves to be quoted; he asserts that the Revolution marked a break where one passes "from the Peter Faneuils, the negro and rum dealers of the middle century, to the Derbys, Perkinses, Thorndikes. . . . These men brought the far Eastern world home to its new counterpart in the West."[7] The influence of this trade, of course, was not confined to New England. It was a Pennsylvanian, Robert Morris, who was mainly responsible for outfitting the first American ship to Asiatic waters, and it was a New Yorker, John Jacob Astor, whose career was built upon the rewards of this trade.

Whereas the Pacific trade was opened, the Caribbean trade was sharply reduced. Many factors were responsible, not the least of course being the

British and French imperial systems, which automatically established a barrier against commodities from the new nation. Where the West Indies had served as an important market for fisheries, livestock, lumber, rum, and other goods during the colonial period and had acted as the crucial entrepôt during the War of Independence itself, it was suddenly closed to American products. How significant this result was for the economy of the new country has often been suggested, but it is a theme that still requires more elaborate and precise investigation.[8]

When trade is basically modified, it is axiomatic that mercantile connections are modified as well. As the most casual reading of the recently published volumes on eighteenth-century merchants will testify, the impact of the Revolution was profound. Some trading connections were completely changed; in others the nature of the trade itself was altered; in still other cases, a particular merchant or merchant group either won or lost its relative position in the trading community. The Pepperrells of Piscataqua, remaining loyal to Britain, abandoned American shores; the Browns of Providence, though they maintained their important position in the trading community, modified their business connections and adjusted their manufacturing interest to suit the new era; in New York City, James Beekman, whose business was seriously crippled during the Revolution when he was forced to flee from New York City to escape the British, found after the war that the pattern of trade relationships he used with success before 1776 was no longer applicable; Robert Morris, whose relative position within the mercantile community had improved so significantly that he could properly be called the Prince of Merchants, found it not only necessary after 1783 to establish a new network of business partnerships to adjust to the times, but also advantageous to expand his business operations and diversify his investments.[9]

General business organization, as well as the careers of individual merchants, were influenced by the Revolution. Robert East's indispensable book has demonstrated the intricate connections between business groups during the Revolution; but he was primarily interested in their political and to some extent social impact.[10] Using some of the identical material, it is possible to reverse the coin and see the results upon economic life: the rise of multiple partnerships and the beginnings of the corporate structure; the expansion of business groups to include every major marketing center; and the modification of these connections to meet new trade and business opportunities. When the Revolution so profoundly affected so many of its most representative mercantile leaders and the structure of business generally, how can it ever be said that it had little impact upon the economic development of the United States or the rise of commercial capitalism in the young republic!

A discussion of trade during the Revolution inevitably leads to the subject of interstate commerce, especially of course to the fact that its control was placed within the framework of the national government. This subject has become so commonplace that there is a tendency to dismiss it without relating its significance to the rise of commercial capitalism. During the first six decades of the eighteenth century one of the key signs of economic maturation and of developing commercial capitalism was the increased specialization that occurred within the colonies. Each region— New England, the Middle Colonies, and the South—was producing commodities for market that were best suited to its resources. This specialization, among other things, stimulated intercolonial trade. When the Revolution placed its blessing upon this development by giving control of interstate commerce to the national government (the Articles of Confederation in allocating this power to the individual states were actually running counter to the colonial experience and, it should be added, to reality) the consequences were so significant as to be almost incalculable. An unlimited, unfettered, internal market not only stimulated the fruition of commercial capitalism, but also laid down the basic pattern that was to provide an expanding market for the industrial America that would eventually emerge.

The problem of money and money supply and its relation to economic development is a theme that runs through American history, but we still need an evaluation of the effect of the financial experience and policies of the Revolution upon the economic development of the nation. For a nation based upon a money economy, the mere act of transfer, shifting the financial problems from Britain to the United States, is obviously important for the direction of economic development, but scholars have yet to study the finances in this context.

There are, however, other promising approaches, one of which could focus around the concept of an expanding economy. It is possible, for example, that the extensive use of paper money—far outreaching any colonial experience—stimulated general economic activity, although this thesis requires a more precise examination before it can be accepted. Moreover, a number of alert minds during these formative years explored the relationship between national credit and an expanded national economy—Peletiah Webster, Robert Morris, Gouverneur Morris, and Alexander Hamilton, to cite the most obvious. Still another part of the story is the creation of commercial banks, made possible only by the act of Independence. Although the Bank of North America, chartered in 1781, was first, it was quickly imitated by banks in Massachusetts and New York and plans were laid to create others. The critical role played by these institutions is a matter of record, particularly in their credit experience and their role in the expansion of the economy. Without question, such ideas, practices, policies, and institutions in financial affairs—the result of the Revolution—played a significant role in the economic development of the period; indeed, it is possible that careful study and analysis will find that not nearly enough stress has been placed on their far reaching effects.

Another area requiring further research is manufactures.[11] At first glance this plea may appear unnecessary, for numerous historians assert that manufacturing was greatly extended, often supporting such claims with some specific illustrations. What is overlooked, however, is how often historians are merely quoting each other. The few basic economic studies that have included a section on manufacturing—so far as the writer knows, no single monograph on manufacturing in the Revolution exists—are sadly in need of revision. In addition, scholars have failed to distinguish between an increase in production and an increase in total "plant" capacity, a crucial feature of the industrial expansion in the First and Second World Wars. It is logical to assume that the demand for guns, wagons, tents, clothing, and other articles brought an expansion in total productive capacity, but the evidence is not conclusive; nor is there so much as a well-informed estimate as to the degree of expansion.

Another factor that remains virtually unnoticed is the expansion of foreign investments in the United States during and after the Revolution. Before independence, quite naturally, neither French nor Dutch capital was invested in American enterprise; almost immediately upon the outbreak of war, however, key figures in both countries appeared to exploit the opportunities opening up in the new nation. In France such great names as that of Chaumont were prominent; in Holland, the Willinks and the Van Stapenhorsts. Some of the investment was purely speculative—the "investments" in currency, for example. In other cases, it was geared to more lasting enterprises, such as the French financial backing given to several new commercial houses. It can also be assumed that foreign investment in American securities must have played some part in capital formation during this period, but there has not been so much as a scholarly guess as to how significant a part. More important, the question of British investment has been neglected. Leland Jenks's fine study of the migration of British capital to the United States begins too late to throw much light on the Revolutionary epoch, with the result that our information is less than sketchy for the prewar as well as the immediate postwar period. Although historians have not given the entire subject of foreign investment its due, and in consequence we cannot speak of the results with confidence, it most certainly is an area of almost limitless possibilities.

Another promising approach, but one that has attracted little attention, is to use material normally discussed in terms of social history. The abolition of primogeniture and entail is a case in point. In most discussions the social consequences of these acts are emphasized; making the stratification produced by a set land system more flexible and thereby encouraging democratization. Seldom, if ever, is the abolition of primogeniture and entail considered in terms of its economic impact, a perspective of equal, if not greater, importance. To encourage a flexible land system where more efficient producers using up-to-date techniques can thrive, in contrast to a static system that settles for the status quo, is surely a matter of importance. Indeed, it is instructive that historians have recently discovered that the abolition of primogeniture and entail in Virginia had minor social significance and that support for this act was more universal than had been assumed.[12] It might well be another way of saying that these acts were more important for economic than for social results. More study is needed before a final conclusion can be drawn, but it is evident that a number of topics customarily considered in a social context will be rewarding avenues of exploration for the historian evaluating the economic consequences of the Revolution.

In fact, the number of essential questions requiring answers that only a thorough investigation can provide is a bit overwhelming. Historians have acknowledged that recent depressions, that of the 1930's in particular, have brought about some profound changes, but they have yet to appraise the lasting effect of the immediate postwar depression upon the course of economic development. Historians have written about the rise of the port of Baltimore, when the British blockade of Philadelphia brought new opportunities to its Maryland neighbor, but they have yet to assess the total effect of the Revolution upon the marketing centers of the new nation, including New York City. Historians have noted the decline of fisheries in New England, the change that took place in whaling, and the move from the outports of Massachusetts to Boston, yet they have been slow to determine whether or not the economy of one region of the nation received a more durable impress from the Revolution than did the others. Historians talk about American society with confidence, but they have never asked whether it contained within itself certain special characteristics that would decisively determine the course of economic life in the New Nation.

These considerations re-emphasize not only the importance of the theme but also the vast number of questions that will need to be asked—and, if possible, answered—if we are to assess the full impact of the Revolution. Although this article is merely an introduction rather than a *summa* and any conclusions are, at best, tentative, the evidence concerning the economic consequences of the Revolution is impressive. It is entirely possible that when scholars have completed their investigations, they will conclude that the American Revolution is of greater importance for its economic consequences, where the surface has scarcely been scratched, than for its social consequences, where the research in the Revolution has been concentrated in recent decades. To use the celebrated phrase of that pioneer in the field, J. Franklin Jameson, as a model, a phrase that has made scholars acutely conscious of the social aspects of the Revolution— the time seems overdue for historians to recognize and develop the idea of "The American Revolution Considered as an Economic Movement."

Endnotes

1. It will be interesting to see whether or not the volume in Rinehart's series on the *Economic History of the United States*, covering the period 1776-1815, will grapple with this problem or whether it will be a straight narrative. There are three places where a summary of the general economic development for these years can be found: Edward Channing, *History of the United States* (New York, 1912), III, ch. iii; Clarence L. Ver Steeg, *Robert Morris, Revolutionary Financier* (Philadelphia, 1954), ch. iii, stressing the period up to 1781; and Merrill Jensen, *The New Nation* (New York, 1950), pp. 179-244, stressing the Confederation period.

2. Because of the exploratory nature of this article, only a few citations have been made.

3. Payson J. Treat's standard monograph, *The National Land System, 1785-1820* (New York, 1910), ch. ii, makes some comparison between colonial land systems and those that evolved after the Revolution. It is entirely possible, however, that the "New England influence" on the national land system has been overstated. It was a thesis that was given wide currency before new research revised some previously accepted assumptions on eighteenth-century New England land policy.

4. Lewis C. Gray, *History of Agriculture in the Southern United States to 1860* (New York, 1941), II, 613.

5. Lawrence A. Harper, "The Effect of the Navigation Acts on the Thirteen Colonies," in *The Era of the American Revolution*, ed. R.B. Morris (New York, 1939), pp. 24-25, and n. 61.

6. There is some difference of opinion among scholars who have recently surveyed this problem. Oscar and Mary Handlin's *Commonwealth: A Study of the Role of Government in the American Economy: Massachusetts, 1774-1861* (New York and London, 1947), pp. 1-52, is a good evaluation for the whole New England economy. Percy Bidwell and John Falconer's *History of Agriculture in the Northern United States to 1860* (Washington, 1925), is of no help.

7. William B. Weeden, *Economic and Social History of New England, 1620-1789* (Boston and New York, 1890), II, 821-822.

8. Merrill Jensen believes that there was less disruption to the West India trade than most scholars have asserted (*op. cit.*, pp. 198-199).

9. Byron Fairchild, *Messrs. William Pepperrell: Merchants at Piscataqua* (Ithaca, N.Y., 1954); James B. Hedges, *The Browns of Providence Plantations; Colonial Years* (Cambridge, Mass., 1952), pp. 285-286, 306. Philip L. White, *The Beekmans of New York* (New York, 1956), pp. 441-530; Clarence L. Ver Steeg, *Robert Morris, Revolutionary Financier* (Philadelphia, 1954), ch. x.

10. *Business Enterprise in the American Revolutionary Era* (New York, 1938), passim.

11. It is of interest to note that J. Franklin Jameson, *The American Revolution Considered as a Social Movement* (Princeton, 1926), spends an entire chapter on "Industry and Commerce," although it is difficult to see how he relates it directly to social change, except to state that the "Revolution brought ultimate benefit to the agriculture, the manufactures, and the commerce of the United States of America" (p. 114). The focus of this article, in contrast, is upon those areas where the Revolution may have altered the direction or emphasis of economic development.

12. A choice example is to trace the increasing firmness with which this new thesis is accepted in the works of Irving Brant on Madison and Dumas Malone and Nathan Schachner on Jefferson.

PART III

THE CHANGING ECONOMY
FROM THE FRAMING
OF THE CONSTITUTION
TO CIVIL CONFLICT

14

The Constitution:
Was It an Economic Document?

HENRY STEELE COMMAGER

. . . Some 45 years ago Charles A. Beard propounded an economic interpretation of the Constitution—an interpretation which submitted that the Constitution was *essentially* (that is a crucial word) an economic document—and that it was carried through the Convention and the state ratifying conventions by interested economic groups for economic reasons. "The Constitution," Mr. Beard concluded, "was essentially an economic document based upon the concept that the fundamental private rights of property are anterior to government and morally beyond the reach of popular majorities."

At the time it was pronounced, that interpretation caused something of a sensation, and Mr. Beard was himself eventually to comment with justifiable indignation on the meanness and the vehemence of the attacks upon it—and him. Yet the remarkable thing about the economic interpretation is not the criticism it inspired but the support it commanded. For within a few years it had established itself as the new orthodoxy, and

"The Constitution: Was It an Economic Document?" by Henry Steele Commager is excerpted from *American Heritage*, Vol. X (December, 1958), pp. 58-61, 100-103 and is reprinted by permission of Dr. Commager.

those who took exception to it were stamped either as professional patriots—perhaps secret Sons or Daughters of the Revolution—or naive academicians who had never learned the facts of economic life.

The attraction that the economic interpretation had for the generation of the twenties and thirties—and that it still exerts even into the fifties—is one of the curiosities of our cultural history, but it is by no means an inexplicable one. To a generation of materialists Beard's thesis made clear that the stuff of history was material. To a generation disillusioned by the exploitations of big business it discovered that the past, too, had been ravaged by economic exploiters. To a generation that looked with skeptical eyes upon the claims of Wilsonian idealism and all but rejoiced in their frustration, it suggested that all earlier idealisms and patriotisms— even the idealism and patriotism of the framers—had been similarly flawed by selfishness and hypocrisy.

Yet may it not be said of *An Economic Interpretation of the Constitution* that it is not a conclusion but a point of departure? It explains a great deal about the forces that went into the making of the Constitution, and a great deal, too, about the men who assembled in Philadelphia in 1787, but it tells us extraordinarily little about the document itself. And it tells us even less about the historical meaning of that document.

What were the objects of the Federal Convention? The immediate objects were to restore order; to strengthen the public credit; to enable the United States to make satisfactory commercial treaties and agreements; to provide conditions in which trade and commerce could flourish; to facilitate management of the western lands and of Indian affairs. All familiar enough. But what, in the light of history, were the grand objects of the Convention? What was it that gave Madison and Morris and Wilson and King and Washington himself a sense of destiny?

There were two grand objects—objects inextricably interrelated. The first was to solve the problem of federalism, that is, the problem of the distribution of powers among governments. Upon the wisdom with which members of the Convention distinguished between powers of a general and powers of a local nature, and assigned these to their appropriate governments, would depend the success or failure of the new experiment.

But it was impossible for the children of the eighteenth century to talk or think of powers without thinking of power, and this was a healthy realism. No less troublesome—and more fundamental—than the problem of the distribution of powers, was the problem of sanctions. How were they to enforce the terms of the distribution and impose limits upon all the governments involved? It was one thing to work out the most ideal distribution of general and local powers. It was another thing to see to it that the states abided by their obligations under the Articles of Union and that the national government respected the autonomy of the states and the liberty of individuals.

Those familiar with the Revolutionary era know that the second of these problems was more difficult than the first. Americans had, indeed, learned how to limit government: the written constitutions, the bills of rights, the checks and balances, and so forth. They had not yet learned (nor had anyone) how to "substitute the mild magistracy of the law for the cruel and violent magistracy of force." The phrase is Madison's.

Let us return to the *Economic Interpretation*. The correctness of Beard's analysis of the origins and backgrounds of the membership of the Convention, of the arguments in the Convention, and of the methods of assuring ratification, need not be debated. But these considerations are, in a sense, irrelevant and immaterial. For though they are designed to illuminate the document itself, in fact they illuminate only the processes of its manufacture.

The idea that property considerations were paramount in the minds of those assembled in Philadelphia is misleading and unsound and is borne out neither by the evidence of the debates in the Convention nor by the Constitution itself. The Constitution was not *essentially* an economic document. It was, and is, *essentially* a political document. It addresses itself to the great and fundamental question of the distribution of powers between governments. The Constitution was—and is—a document that attempts to provide sanctions behind that distribution; a document that sets up, through law, a standing rule to live by and provides legal machinery for the enforcement of that rule. These are political, not economic functions.

Not only were the principles that animated the framers political rather than economic; the solutions that they formulated to the great questions that confronted them were dictated by political, not by economic considerations.

Here are two fundamental challenges to the Beard interpretation: first, the Constitution is primarily a document in federalism; and second, the Constitution does not in fact confess or display the controlling influence of those who held that "the fundamental private rights of property are anterior to government and morally beyond the reach of popular majorities."

Let us look more closely at these two contentions. The first requires little elaboration or vindiction, for it is clear to all students of the Revolutionary era that the one pervasive and overbranching problem of that generation was the problem of imperial organization. How to get the various parts of any empire to work together for common purposes? How to get central control—over war, for example, or commerce or money—without impairing local autonomy? How, on the other hand, to preserve personal liberty and local self-government without impairing the effectiveness of the central government? This was one of the oldest problems in political science, and it is one of the freshest. . . .

The British failed to solve the problem of imperial order; when pushed to the wall they had recourse to the hopelessly doctrinaire Declaratory Act, which was, in fact, a declaration of political bankruptcy; as Edmund Burke observed, no people is going to be argued into slavery. The Americans then took up the vexatious problem. The Articles of Confederation were satisfactory enough as far as the distribution of powers was concerned, but wholly wanting in sanctions. The absence of sanctions spelled the failure of the Articles—and this failure led to the Philadelphia Convention.

Now it will be readily conceded that many, if not most, of the questions connected with federalism were economic in character. Involved were such practical matters as taxation, the regulation of commerce, coinage, western lands, slavery, and so forth. Yet the problem that presented itself to the framers was not whether government should exercise authority over such matters as these; it was *which* government should exercise such authority—and how should it be exercised?

There were, after all, no anarchists at the Federal Convention. Everyone agreed that *some* government had to have authority to tax, raise armies, regulate commerce, coin money, control contracts, enact bankruptcy legislation, regulate western territories, make treaties, and do all the things that government must do. But where should these authorities be lodged— with the state governments or with the national government they were about to erect, or with both?

This question was a political, not an economic, one. And the solution at which the framers arrived was based upon a sound understanding of politics, and need not be explained by reference to class attachments or security interests.

Certainly if the framers were concerned primarily or even largely with protecting property against popular majorities, they failed signally to carry out their purposes. It is at this point in our consideration of the *Economic Interpretation of the Constitution* that we need to employ what our literary friends call *explication du texte*. For the weakest link in the Beard interpretation is precisely the crucial one—the document itself. Mr. Beard makes amply clear that those who wrote the Constitution were members of the propertied classes,[1] and that many of them were personally involved in the outcome of what they were about to do. He makes out a persuasive case that the division over the Constitution was along economic lines. What he does not make clear is how or where the Constitution itself reflects all these economic influences.

Much is made of the contract clause and the paper money clause of the Constitution. No state may impair the obligations of a contract—whatever those words mean, and they apparently did not mean to the framers quite what Chief Justice Marshall later said they meant in *Fletcher v. Peck* or *Dartmouth College v. Woodward*. No state may emit bills of credit or make anything but gold and silver coin legal tender in payment of debts.

These are formidable prohibitions, and clearly reflect the impatience of men of property with the malpractices of the states during the Confederation. Yet quite aside from what the states may or may not have done, who can doubt that these limitations upon the states followed a sound principle—the principle that control of coinage and money belonged to the central, not the local, governments, and the principle that local jurisdictions should not be able to modify or overthrow contracts recognized throughout the Union?

What is most interesting in this connection is what is so often overlooked: that the framers did not write any comparable prohibitions upon the United States government. The United States was not forbidden to impair the obligation on its contracts, not at least in the Constitution as it came from the hands of its property-conscious framers. Possibly the Fifth Amendment may have squinted toward such a prohibition; we need not determine that now, for the Fifth Amendment was added by the *states* after the Constitution had been ratified. So, too, the emission of bills of credit and the making other than gold and silver legal tender were limitations on the states, but not on the national government. There was, in fact, a lively debate over the question of limiting the authority of the national government in the matter of bills of credit. When the question came up on August 16, Gouverneur Morris threatened that "The Monied interest will oppose the plan of Government, if paper emissions be not prohibited." In the end the Convention dropped out a specific authorization to emit bills of credit, but pointedly did not prohibit such action. Just where this left the situation troubled Chief Justice Chase's Court briefly three-quarters of a century later; the Court recovered its balance, and the sovereign power of the government over money was not again *successfully* challenged.

Nor were there other specific limitations of an economic character upon the powers of the new government that was being erected on the ruins of the old. The framers properly gave the Congress power to regulate commerce with foreign nations and among the states. The term commerce—as Hamilton and Adair (and Crosskey, too!) have made clear—was broadly meant, and the grant of authority, too, was broad. The framers gave Congress the power to levy taxes and, again, wrote no limitations into the Constitution except as to the apportionment of direct taxes; it remained for the most conservative of Courts to reverse itself, and common sense, and discover that the framers had intended to forbid an income tax! Today, organizations that invoke the very term "constitutional" are agitating for an amendment placing a quantitative limit upon income taxes that may be levied; fortunately, Madison's generation understood better the true nature of governmental power.

The framers gave Congress—in ambiguous terms, to be sure—authority to make "all needful Rules and Regulations respecting the Territory or other Property" of the United States, and provided that "new states may be admitted." These evasive phrases gave little hint of the heated debates in the Convention over western lands. Those who delight to find narrow and undemocratic sentiments in the breasts of the framers never cease to quote a Gouverneur Morris or an Elbridge Gerry on the dangers of the West, and it is possible to compile a horrid catalogue of such statements. But what is significant is not what framers said, but what they did. They did not place any limits upon the disposition of western territory, or establish any barriers against the admission of western states.

The fact is that we look in vain *in the Constitution itself* for any really effective guarantee for property or any effective barriers against what Beard calls "the reach of popular majorities."

It will be argued, however, that what the framers feared was the *states*, and that the specific prohibitions against state action, together with the broad transfer of economic powers from state to nation, were deemed sufficient guarantee against state attacks upon property. As for the national government, care was taken to make that sufficiently aristocratic, sufficiently the representative of the propertied classes, and sufficiently checked and limited so that it would not threaten basic property interests.

It is at this juncture that the familiar principle of limitation on governmental authority commands our attention. Granted the wisest distribution of powers among governments, what guarantee was there that power would be properly exercised? What guarantees were there against the abuse of power? What assurance was there that the large states would not ride roughshod over the small, that majorities would not crush minorities or minorities abuse majorities? What protection was there against mobs, demagogues, dangerous combinations of interests or of states? What protection was there for the commercial interest, the planter interest, the slave interest, the securities interests, the land speculator interests?

It was Madison who most clearly saw the real character of this problem and who formulated its solution. It was not that the people as such were dangerous: "The truth was," he said on July 11, "that all men having power ought to be distrusted to a certain degree." Long before Lord Acton coined the aphorism, the Revolutionary leaders had discovered that power corrupts. They understood, too, the drive for power on the part of individuals and groups. All this is familiar to students of *The Federalist*, No. 10. It should be familiar to students of the debates in Philadelphia, for there, too, Madison set forth his theory and supported it with a wealth of argument. Listen to him on one of the early days of the Convention, June 6, when he is discussing the way to avoid abuses of republican liberty—abuses which "prevailed in the largest as well as the smallest [states]." . . .

> . . .And were we not thence admonished [he continued] to enlarge the sphere as far as the nature of the Government would admit. This was the only defence against the inconveniences of democracy *consistent with the democratic form of Government* [our italics]. All civilized Societies would be divided into different Sects, Factions & interests, as they happened to consist of rich & poor, debtors and creditors, the landed, the manufacturing, the commercial interests, the inhabitants of this district or that district, the followers of this political leader or that political leader, the disciples of this religious Sect or that religious Sect. In all cases where a majority are united by a common interest or passion, the rights of the minority are in danger. . . . In a Republican Govt. the Majority if united have always an opportunity [to oppress the minority. What is the remedy?] The only remedy is to enlarge the sphere, & thereby divide the community into so great a number of interests & parties, that in the first place a majority will not be likely at the same moment to have a common interest separate from that of the whole or of the minority; and in the second place, that in case they should have such an interest, they may not be apt to unite in the pursuit of it. It was incumbent on us then to try this remedy, and . . . to frame a republican system on such a scale & in such a form as will controul all the evils which have been experienced.

This long quotation is wonderfully eloquent of the attitude of the most sagacious of the framers. Madison, Wilson, Mason, Franklin, as well as Gerry, Morris, Pinckney, and Hamilton feared power. They feared power whether exercised by a monarch, an aristocracy, an army, or a majority, and they were one in their determination to write into fundamental law limitations on the arbitrary exercise of that power. To assume, as Beard so commonly does, that the fear of the misuse of power by majorities was either peculiar to the Federalists or more ardent with them than with their opponents, is mistaken. Indeed it was rather the anti-Federalists who were most deeply disturbed by the prospect of majority rule; they, rather than the Federalists, were the "men of little faith." Thus it was John Lansing, Jr., of New York (he who left the Convention rather than have any part in its dangerous work) who said that "all free constitutions are formed with two views—to deter the governed from crime, and the governors from tyranny." And the ardent Patrick Henry, who led the attack on the

Constitution in the Virginia Convention—and almost defeated it—complained not of too little democracy in that document, but too much.

The framers, to be sure, feared the powers of the majority, as they feared all power unless controlled. But they were insistent that, in the last analysis, there must be government by majority; even conservatives like Morris and Hamilton made this clear. Listen to Hamilton, for example, at the very close of the Convention. Elbridge Gerry, an opponent of the Constitution, had asked for a reconsideration of the provision for calling a constitutional convention, alleging that this opened the gate to a majority that could "bind the union to innovations that may subvert the State-Constitutions altogether." To this Hamilton replied that

> There was no greater evil in subjecting the people of the U.S. to the major voice than the people of a particular State. . . . It was equally desirable now that an easy mode should be established for supplying defects which will probably appear in the New System. . . . There could be no danger in giving this power, as the people would finally decide in the case.

And on July 13, James Wilson, another staunch Federalist, observed that "The majority of people wherever found ought in all questions to govern the minority."

But we need not rely upon what men said; there is too much of making history by quotation anyway. Let us look rather at what men did. We can turn again to the Constitution itself. Granted the elaborate system of checks and balances: the separation of powers, the bicameral legislature, the executive veto, and so forth—checks found in the state constitutions as well, and in our own democratic era as in the earlier one—what provisions did the framers make against majority tyranny? What provisions did they write into the Constitution against what Randolph called "democratic licentiousness?"

They granted equality of representation in the Senate. If this meant that conservative Delaware would have the same representation in the upper chamber as democratic Pennsylvania, it also meant that democratic Rhode Island would have the same representation as conservative South Carolina. But the decision for equality of representation was not dictated by considerations either economic or democratic, but rather by the recalcitrance of the small states. Indeed, though it is difficult to generalize here, on the whole it is true that it was the more ardent Federalists who favored proportional representation in both houses.

They elaborated a most complicated method of electing a Chief Executive, a method designed to prevent the easy expression of any majority will. Again the explanation is not simple. The fact was that the framers did not envision the possibility of direct votes for presidential candidates which would not conform to state lines and interests and thus lead to dissension and confusion. Some method, they thought, must be designated to overcome the force of state prejudices (or merely of parochialism) and get an election; the method they anticipated was a preliminary elimination contest by the electoral college and then eventual election by the House. This, said George Mason, was what would occur nineteen times out of twenty.[2] There is no evidence in the debates that the complicated method finally hit upon for electing a President was designed either to frustrate popular majorities or to protect special economic interests; its purpose was to overcome state pride and particularism.

Senators and Presidents, then, would not be the creatures of democracy. But what guarantee was there that senators would be representatives of property interests, or that the President himself would recognize the "priority of property"? Most states had property qualifications for office holding, but there are none in the Federal Constitution. As far as the Constitution is concerned, the President, congressmen, and Supreme Court justices can all be paupers.

Both General Charles Cotesworth Pinckney and his young cousin Charles, of South Carolina, were worried about this. The latter proposed a property qualification of $100,000 (a tidy sum in those days) for the Presidency, half that for the judges, and substantial sums for members of Congress. Franklin rebuked him. He was distressed, he said, to hear anything "that tended to debase the spirit of the common people." More surprising was the rebuke from that stout conservative, John Dickinson. "He doubted," Madison reports, "the policy of interweaving into a Republican constitution a veneration for wealth. He had always understood that a veneration for poverty & virtue were the objects of republican encouragement." Pinckney's proposal was overwhelmingly rejected.

What of the members of the lower house? When Randolph opened "the main business" on May 29 he said the remedy for the crisis that men faced must be "the republican principle," and two days later members were discussing the fourth resolution, which provided for election to the lower house by the people. Roger Sherman of Connecticut thought that "the people should have as little to do as may be about the Government," and Gerry hastened to agree in words now well-worn from enthusiastic quotation that "The evils we experience flow from the excess of democracy." These voices were soon drowned out, however. Mason "argued strongly for an election . . . by the people. It was to be the grand depository of the democratic principle of the Govt." And the learned James Wilson, striking the note to which he was to recur again and again, made clear that he was for "raising the federal pyramid to a considerable

altitude, and for that reason wished to give it as broad a basis as possible."
He thought that both branches of the legislature—and the President as
well, for that matter—should be elected by the people. "The Legislature,"
he later observed, "ought to be the most exact transcript of the whole
Society."

A further observation is unhappily relevant today. It was a maxim with
John Adams that "where annual elections end, there tyranny begins," and
the whole Revolutionary generation was committed to a frequent return to
the source of authority. But the framers put into the Constitution no limits
on the number of terms which Presidents or congressmen could serve. It
was not that the question was ignored; it received elaborate attention. It
was rather that the generation that wrote the Constitution was better
grounded in political principles than is our own; that it did not confuse, as
we so often do, quantitative and qualitative limitations; and that—in a
curious way—it had more confidence in the intelligence and the good will
of the people than we seem to have today. It is, in any event, our own
generation that has the dubious distinction of writing into the Constitution
the first quantitative limitation on the right of the majority to choose their
President. It is not the generation of the framers that was undemocratic; it
is our generation that is undemocratic.

It is relevant to note, too, that the Constitution contains no property
qualification for voting. Most states, to be sure, had such qualifications—
in general a freehold or its equivalent—and the Constitution assimilated
such qualifications as states might establish. Yet the framers, whether for
reasons practical or philosophical we need not determine, made no serious
efforts to write any property qualifications for voting into the Constitution
itself.

The question of popular control came up clearly in one other connection
as well: the matter of ratification. Should the Constitution be ratified by
state legislatures, or by conventions? The practical arguments for the two
methods were nicely balanced. The decisive argument was not, however,
one of expediency but of principle. "To the people with whom all power
remains that has not been given up in the Constitutions derived from
them" we must resort, said Mason. Madison put the matter on principle
too. "He considered the difference between a system founded on the
Legislatures only, and one founded on the people, to be the true difference
between a *league* or *treaty* and a *Constitution*." Ellsworth's motion to refer
the Constitution to legislatures was defeated by a vote of eight to two, and
the resolution to refer it to conventions passed with only Delaware in the
negative.

Was the Constitution designed to place private property beyond the
reach of majorities? If so, the framers did a very bad job. They failed to

write into it the most elementary safeguards for property. They failed to write into it limitations on the taxpower, or prohibitions against the abuse of the money power. They failed to provide for rule by those whom Adams was later to call the wise and the rich and the wellborn. What they did succeed in doing was to create a system of checks and balances and adjustments and accommodations that would effectively prevent the suppression of most minorities by majorities. They took advantage of the complexity, the diversity, the pluralism, of American society and economy to encourage a balance of interests. They worked out sound and lasting political solutions to the problems of class, interest, section, race, religion, party.

Perhaps the most perspicacious comment on this whole question of the threat from turbulent popular majorities against property and order came, *mirabile dictu*, from the dashing young Charles Pinckney of South Carolina—he of the "lost" Pinckney Plan. On June 25 Pinckney made a major speech and thought it important enough to write [it] out and give to Madison. The point of departure was the hackneyed one of the character of the second branch of the legislature, but the comments were an anticipation of De Tocqueville and Lord Bryce. We need not, Pinckney asserted, fear the rise of class conflicts in America, nor take precautions against them.

> The genius of the people, their mediocrity of situation & the prospects which are afforded their industry in a Country which must be a new one for centuries are unfavorable to the rapid distinction of ranks. . . . If equality is . . . the leading feature of the U. States [he asked], where then are the riches & wealth whose representation & protection is the peculiar province of this permanent body [the Senate]. Are they in the hands of the few who may be called rich; in the possession of less than a hundred citizens? Certainly not. They are in the great body of the people. . . . [There was no likelihood that a privileged body would ever develop in the United States, he added, either from the landed interest, the moneyed interest, or the mercantile.] Besides, Sir, I apprehend that on this point the policy of the U. States has been much mistaken. We have unwisely considered ourselves as the inhabitants of an old instead of a new country. We have adopted the maxims of a State full of people . . . The people of this country are not only very different from the inhabitants of any State we are acquainted with in the modern world; but I assert that their situation is distinct from either the people of Greece or of Rome . . . Our true situation appears to me to be this—a new extensive Country containing within itself the materials for forming a Government capable of extending to its citizens all the blessings of civil & religious liberty—capable of making them happy at home. This is the great end of Republican Establishments. . . .

Not a government cunningly contrived to protect the interests of property, but one capable of extending to its citizens the blessings of liberty and happiness—was that not, after all, what the framers created?

Endnotes

1. "A majority of the members were lawyers by profession.

"Most of the members came from towns on or near the coast, that is, from the regions in which personalty was largely concentrated.

"Not one member represented in his immediate personal economic interests the small farming or mechanic classes.

"The overwhelming majority of members, at least five-sixths, were immediately, directly, and personally interested in the outcome of their labors at Philadelphia, and were to a greater or less extent economic beneficiaries from the adoption of the Constitution." Beard, *An Economic Interpretation of the Constitution.*

2. It has happened twice: Jefferson v. Burr (1801) and J. Adams v. Clay, Jackson, and Crawford (1825).

15

Success and Failure Factors; American Merchants in Foreign Trade in the Eighteenth and Early Nineteenth Centuries

STUART BRUCHEY

Why one man succeeds in business and another man fails is a difficult problem at any time. The difficulty lies not so much in our ignorance of the general factors involved as in tracing their complex interaction. Intelligence and good luck, for example, are certainly fundamental: but can we say with confidence where the one ends and the other begins? What of other elements of success, such as prudence, persistency in will, good housekeeping habits, and the aids of the business community? Can we be sure of the part played by each of these factors in particular business

"Success and Failure Factors; American Merchants in Foreign Trade in the Eighteenth and Early Nineteenth Centuries," by Stuart Bruchey, is reprinted by permission from *Business History Review*, Vol. XXXII (Autumn, 1958), pp. 272-292. Copyright 1958.

decisions? If so, are sufficient case histories of businessmen available to warrant general conclusions?

I believe the answers to these questions are very largely negative. For one thing, far more records of success than of failure have survived the attrition of history. Even the success stories have their limitations. The bookkeeping records of foreign traders, for example, do not as a rule permit correlation between a specific investment decision and a specific gain or loss, for merchants did not usually compute the results of particular shipments.[1] We know well, however, that some men made only a living, while others made fortunes. Still others, such as the New York merchant Victor duPont, went bankrupt.[2] Most of the Jacksons and Lees of Massachusetts "at some time or other [in the eighteenth century] either failed in business or came to the very brink of such a disaster."[3] In March, 1803, Robert Oliver, merchant of Baltimore, noted that "upwards of 100 failures have . . . taken place in this City in the last three years. . . ."[4] An increasing number of studies of American merchants illuminate some of the areas of difference between them which have led to these varying results. Many of the studies also show that the merchants themselves had definite ideas concerning the qualities making for success.

Let us first consider the factor of prudence. It is undeniable that the same man sometimes plunges and sometimes reins in. On the other hand, some men appear temperamentally disposed to caution, others to an easier trust that things will come right. James B. Hedges clearly sets forth the difference between the merchant John Brown of Providence and his brothers, Moses and Nicholas. John was eager to reinvest each year's profits in an expanding business. But Nicholas, "cautious, [and] conservative by nature," probably approved the terms in which Moses rejected the plan: " 'who Ever plays any Game the Rubbers, or plays the last for the Value of the whole gain of the Preceding many, will Sooner or Later Loose the Whole at one Throw.' "[5] Miss Virginia D. Harrington has written that the proportion between speculative and revenue-producing holdings of real estate in the hands of the colonial merchants of New York depended partly "on the temper of the individual."[6] Miss Elva Tooker concludes of the Philadelphia merchant Nathan Trotter: "Nothing is clearer throughout Trotter's business career than his prudence, caution, and moderation."[7] Prudence lay near the center of the business values of Robert Oliver & Brothers. They "desired to have an accurate knowledge of the length and breadth of their obligations," a contemporary merchant later wrote about the most extensive operation in which the Olivers ever participated, "before the scheme could be set in motion."[8] Oliver repeatedly showed his concern for security as well as profit potentiality. By curtailing his investments in trade and by choosing not to send "a large amount in any one Vessel" he twice enabled his house to survive deflationary shock waves that toppled many of his Baltimore confreres.

To Oliver, the opposite of prudence was a "sanguine speculative disposition." ". . . before you can expect much business in the Commission line," he once advised an apparent beginner in trade, "you must establish a reputation for real industry & prudence & quit visionary Schemes." He thought Richard Caton of Baltimore "too sanguine," "too speculative."[9] Caton surely resembled John Brown of Providence, who had an "inclination toward undue risk-taking."[10] According to Oliver, Aquila Brown, Jr., of Baltimore, lost "upwards of 140,000 Dollars in two years by bad debts on the Sale of Linens."[11] But no doubt an ability to draw learning from loss has proved an important factor in the final success of some men. John Jacob Astor, according to his biographer, partly owed his fortune to that ability.[12]

Probably most men who have entered business have desired to succeed. But some men have hitched their wills to the traces of a single-minded drive. The records of Robert Oliver supply evidence of an extraordinary attentiveness to the life of trade. "You can hardly fail to succeed," he once advised a younger man, "if you will abandon Politicks, *think only of your business*, follow it with unremitting industry and depend on yourself instead of others." . . . Oliver once used the occasion of a visit to Philadelphia, presumably made for the purpose of attending the funeral of the man to whom he owed most, to purchase ninety boxes of Havana sugars. On a later trip to New York, again for unstated purposes, he bought over $160,000 worth of nankeens.[13] The man from whom he bought them, John Jacob Astor, undoubtedly exemplifies even more clearly than Oliver a single-minded devotion to the goal of success. "Astor's life," to use the words of Miss Henrietta Larson, "was business, and he had a passion for profits and an abhorrence of waste or loss."[14] A contemporary merchant, Vincent Nolte, once remarked of Astor: "His mind was incessantly busied with the increase of his resources, and had no other direction."[15]

We know from Kenneth W. Porter's careful study that Nolte's characterization exaggerates, and that Astor found time for family, friends, and a variety of cultural interests.[16] Yet it is clear that Astor's business schemes sometimes incubated during nonbusiness hours, while riding around Manhattan on his horse, for example. Perhaps this explains why he reputedly " 'did not bestow at his countinghouse more than half the time most merchants feel compelled to give their concerns.' " But no doubt for the majority the countinghouse represented "a chance to think, to plan, to work out policies, to arrange for others to do the detailed work."[17]

Yet it must be admitted that we have little satisfactory evidence of the length of time spent by merchants in their countinghouses. The natural assumption, that it depended upon the volume of trade, would appear from Astor's instance not always to hold. Samuel Eliot Morison has supplied additional reason for questioning the dependence: despite a considerably increased volume of trade the merchant patriciate of Federalist Boston can hardly have spent more than three hours a day in their places of business.[18] We know that the "busiest years" of Colonel William Pepperrell of Piscataqua and of his son lay in the decade following the Peace of Utrecht, which was "one of expanding trade," but the evidence does not permit a situating of the Colonel in his countinghouse any specified number of daily hours.[19] Neither does it in the case of Robert Oliver for such a year as 1807, during which the Baltimore merchant dispatched vessels twenty-six times to Vera Cruz, Lisbon, Barcelona, Amsterdam, Trieste, and New Providence.[20] In other instances, oblique evidence provides support for the possibility of sizable stretches of time in the countinghouse. Business, for Thomas Hancock, was "his one engrossing interest." During 1771-1772, at least, his nephew John was "spending less and less time in the countinghouse, and more and more in bed or the general assembly." The biographer of Gerard G. Beekman, a New York merchant whose trade at least touched "four continents," reports that Beekman "abstained from such pleasures [as hunting] in his early years, preferring to devote his energies to trade."[21] . . . By the mid-nineteenth century, at any rate, the merchants of New York, according to Scoville, spent considerable, if leisurely stretches of time in the "throne-room" of their enterprises.[22]

In that throne-room lay the bookkeeping records which made it possible for all the strings of diverse enterprise to be controlled by the hand of the resident merchant. "Considerable judgment was needed," as Miss Harrington has said, "to juggle remittances, returns and investments successfully."[23] Accounts informed that judgment, at least for men with good housekeeping habits. How carefully did eighteenth-century merchants keep their accounts? W. T. Baxter believes that colonial bookkeeping was in general "dilatory" and that a leading reason for this was the "tiny scale of business."[24] The association between care in record-keeping and scale of business seems to me persuasive. But I believe Baxter's generalization has two weaknesses: (a) it appears to rest largely upon an examination of the records of small-scale firms whose proprietors were primarily storekeepers rather than merchants and (b) does not take into account changes in the scale of business which occurred as the eighteenth century advanced.[25] . . .

There is reason to believe that as the volume of trade increased, earlier eighteenth-century laxness in record-keeping often gave way to a careful practice of double entry. In this respect as in others, furthermore, the evidence is clear that one merchant differed from another. The beginnings of change appear to have accompanied an early increase in trade volume between 1720 and 1740, and they have been described as follows by Carl Bridenbaugh:[26]

> In every colonial port this period brought a marked advance in the methods and extent of trade. The increased sums of money and larger number of items handled made it necessary for merchants to maintain staffs of clerks in their counting houses. Bookkeeping by "Double Entry, Dr. and Cr., the best Method," came into wide use everywhere except at Newport by 1733, and schools gave instruction in shorthand and the Italian method of keeping books. Accountants offered their services in all the larger towns. . . .

. . . Accounts might inform the judgment of an uncle but not of his nephew: "Thomas [Hancock] knew as much about his own affairs from an accounting standpoint as was possible in mercantile capitalism, while John was generally hopelessly swamped."[27] Or one cousin and not the other: "James [Beekman] was as meticulous in keeping records as Gerard was careless."[28] . . .

Miss Harrington finds that "most" New York wholesale houses on the eve of the Revolution appear to have used double-entry bookkeeping, and that a "fairly high level of proficiency must have been maintained." The ledger and wastebook of the Livingstons, for example, are "models of the double-entry books."[29] . . .

Just as merchants differed in respect to prudence, will, and housekeeping habits they differed also in intelligence. It is, of course, impossible to exhibit this difference except in terms of varying reactions to similar situations. And it hardly need be said that variety in reaction itself depends not only on intelligence, but also upon knowledge, and upon such other factors as capital or credit status, liquidity and knowledge of the extent of it provided by orderly accounts, prudence, force of will, and so forth. Furthermore, the situations themselves are very numerous, far too numerous for consideration here. In changing contexts provided by government action or inaction and by rising and falling markets in peacetime and war, merchants had to decide such questions as what commodities to invest in and where to buy them, where and when to ship them and in what assortments, whether to consign their goods to ship captain, supercargo, or resident merchant, whether to invest in vessels or freight space, what goods to have purchased as returns, whether to invest part of the proceeds of the outward cargo in bills of exchange, where to dispose of return cargoes: by reshipment or by sale in the local market, and, if the latter, what credit terms to give and what men to trust; and finally, how to employ the proceeds of business: i.e., how to balance investments between ships or ship-shares, commodities, warehouses, bonds or notes, real estate, and, later, stocks.

Numerous as were the decisions to be made, almost all of them called for the exercise of judgments with respect to foreign markets. Residing in one port as they did, and not accompanying their wares to market, all merchants depended considerably upon other members of a wide mercantile community, upon ship captains and supercargoes (especially in the East Indian trade), and upon other merchants resident in foreign (and often domestic) ports. The interdependence of resident merchants throughout the commercial world rested upon a mutual need for services almost indispensable to the conduct of trade. Resident merchants not only supplied each other with the information upon which investment decisions often rested, but performed other services, such as advancing part of the value of goods prior to their sale and holding them for better times. . . .

Hedges found in the Brown Papers "many illustrations of the care with which [the Browns] gathered all possible information before embarking upon a new venture."[30] As the case of Gerard G. Beekman illustrates, a merchant might seek information from another American city: "In the season of 1753-54 Gerard began to exchange information with a resident correspondent of Philadelphia, Townsend White."[31] Or he might seek it abroad. Robert Oliver in 1807 went so far as to propose (successfully) to an English house giving him keen competition in trade to Vera Cruz that the two firms exchange information in regard to the nature and value of their shipments, the number of vessels and voyages made, the nature of exports from the United States, and the condition of the Vera Cruz market![32] Far more typical was the routine exchange of price and market information between two merchants residing in different ports. Acting on the basis of such information every merchant was at one moment principal, at another commission agent.

Agency relationships typified eighteenth-century commerce between Europe and America, as well as between many of the ports of Europe itself. According to Sombart and Max Weber the growth of consignment trading "was the outstanding feature of eighteenth century trading." The commission agent, says Charles Wilson, was the "real representative" of the trade between Amsterdam and the ports of England, Spain, and other countries. W. T. Baxter finds the agent to have been "the keystone of New England's foreign trade." "The London commission merchants with whom the Trotters [of Philadelphia] did business," Miss Tooker observes, "were in effect their representatives abroad."[33]

The ship captain-agent, however, dominated colonial trade with the

West Indies. According to Kenneth W. Porter, "Participation by local merchants in the sale and purchase of cargoes in the West India trade is not conspicuous." Hedges reaches a similar conclusion, for "only occasionally were factors employed to assume part of the burden of buying and selling." In the West Indies, Miss Harrington has noted, "the market, though steady, varied from island to island." John Hancock's "instructions to captains show that it was often undesirable to draw up rigid plans regarding the route to be followed. . . ." Instead, as Christopher C. Crittenden has observed, the master might be instructed to proceed to a particular island, such as Martinique, and upon arrival "to inquire concerning the condition of the markets both there and in other islands to the leeward, and . . . to sell where, everything considered, the greatest profit could be reaped." Or he might, Hedges emphasizes, enjoy even greater leeway by embarking on "a huckstering voyage with cargo to be sold wherever he could find a market." Richard Pares believes that the majority of colonial West Indian shipments were consigned to captains.[34] . . .

This widespread reliance upon ship captains in the West Indian trade is attributable to a variety of circumstances. Miss Martin has pointed out that many merchants "had received their early mercantile training as captains of vessels engaged in that trade and were well-acquainted with market conditions both in the West Indies and in adjacent Central and South American ports." Only a limited number of commodities were imported—principally sugar, rum, molasses, and coffee—and these were "much simpler to select and appraise" than European manufactured goods would have been. Furthermore, goods were often bartered against goods, "which eliminated the necessity of a commission merchant to provide short-term credit." In addition, as Pares reminds us, except for lumber nearly every article of North American produce was perishable in the tropics, and hence could not be stored for long to await an upturn in the market. Advances by agents, although sometimes made pending the sale of an outward cargo, were therefore not as important as they would otherwise have been. An even more basic reason for consignments to captains was the necessity for giving them leave to take their cargoes in search of markets that were not glutted. "Only three ports—Bridgetown in Barbados, Kingston in Jamaica, and above all the Dutch island of St. Eustatius, were markets of conspicuous size or wide commercial connections. The capitals of the lesser islands were glutted by a very few cargoes— still more so the smaller towns like Spikestown, Barbados." Certainly in the earlier colonial years probably few merchants did sufficient business with any one port to permit active relations with an agent there. . . .[35]

In the 1790's an increase in variety was added to the increased volume of goods exported to the West Indies. During most of the colonial period articles of domestic produce or manufacture had made up the list of exports, e.g., the timber and fish of Piscataqua, the bread and flour of New York, the candles turned out by the " 'Spermacetic Works' " of Obadiah Brown of Providence, or various goods picked up in coasting voyages by Rhode Islanders lacking in a tributary back country. After the outbreak of the Continental Wars in 1793 had seen a superior British fleet wipe enemy shipping from the high seas, American merchants began to import such goods as nankeens (from China) and German linens (especially from Hamburg and Bremen) not only to supply domestic American markets but also to provide, via neutral shipping, for the total needs, and not merely part of the provisioning needs, of the Caribbean islands. . . .[36]

Rising demand must have made more and more possible the services of resident commission agents in the West Indies. Let us consider why this should be so. News of need for an article in the islands often took three or three-and-a-half weeks to arrive in Baltimore, and even if a merchant there had a supply of the article on hand and a vessel outfitted and ready for sea it required another three or three-and-a-half weeks for it to reach market. In earlier colonial times these six or seven weeks would have permitted some huckstering, island-hopping ship captain or two, dispatched to the West Indies with cargoes of familiar commodities suited to an habitual commerce, to stumble luckily upon the demand and fill it. But would not this situation have occurred more readily in 1750 than in 1800, and in 1700 than 1750? In the later years was it not increasingly possible for a resident merchant to say to his agent, as Samuel Smith of Baltimore said to one of his in 1788: "We hope your next [letter] may encourage the return of our Brig[an]t[ine] to you"?[37] In the later years, in short, even if an agent informed correspondents in several North American ports of high prices in his market, it seems quite possible that those prices were supported by a demand of sufficient depth to accommodate without loss more cargoes than in the earlier years. Could not merchants increasingly, therefore, avoid the wasteful and time-consuming ventures of their huckstering ship captains and base their investment decisions on price information from a number of alternative markets? If so, it became increasingly important for men like the Olivers to place their business "in the hands of Men of Stability, *good information* & undoubted integrity."[38] For there can be no question that the larger profits "depended on having first knowledge of a market and arriving before the crowd."[39]

The preceding discussion seems to me to suggest the possibility that the eighteenth-century merchant became more and more able by forethought to narrow down the area of impotency ruled by luck. This interpretation must, however, meet a widely held view that slow and unsure means of communication placed a heavy discount upon the value of planning.

"Despite the merits of the agency system," says Baxter, "it involved very weak control by a merchant over his foreign trade. He had perforce to trust his agents blindly." Not only was "skill at bookkeeping and auditing so rare that he had little check on their transactions" (a point which we have seen is open to question), but his messages to them traveled "at a snail's pace." Hedges also emphasizes "the leisurely pace of commerce in the eighteenth century," and the "guesswork and uncertainty involved in transacting business at such a distance" as that between Providence and Surinam. When a vessel arrived, Byron Fairchild concludes, was "chiefly a matter of wind and weather."[40]

It is my opinion that far too much emphasis has been placed upon the irregularity and uncertainty of communications. It is true that copies of letters and bills of exchange were sometimes sent in triplicate, or even in quadruplicate. But these acts of insurance attest only to the possibility that important documents might miscarry: in themselves they shed little light on the question of how great was that possibility. Similarly, one might cite many examples of long passages and delayed arrivals. But their typicality must await adequate statistical evidence of sailing times, and it may be that definite answers are impossible to attain. . . .

The fact that these Baltimore merchants could say that voyages were "often performed" in a specified time, or that a voyage "should not have" exceeded a given number of days, seems to me to point to the distinct possibility that regularity in communications was the rule and not the exception. It would therefore seem to me justifiable to place less stress upon wind and weather and more on the intent of the merchant shipper, less on fortuity and more on forethought. If there was relatively little forethought in early colonial times and more dependence upon lucky strikes by wandering ship captains was it not possibly because the volume and nature of the West Indian demand rather than the elements blunted the point of planning?

Since forethought depended so much on fresh information from many market centers I suspect that it became increasingly important in the advancing eighteenth century to acquire and retain good agents—and not by any means for West Indian trade alone. . . .

Because of the key role they played in eighteenth-century commerce, ability to manage one's agents with skill often affected the outcome of investments. As is to be expected, merchants displayed varying abilities in this regard. The Pepperrells' biographer concludes that "an important element" in the success of the Piscataqua merchants "was their ability to maintain satisfactory relations with their correspondents." But that luck cannot be ruled out as a factor in that success is evident from the fact that when William Pepperrell's agent at Antigua complained that the sale of lumber cargoes was tedious, Pepperrell "agreed with what the latter had to say . . . thanked him for not giving up his business, and then went on sending more lumber." Thomas Hancock "did not scruple" to send his London supplier "a rival correspondent's prices, demanding a rebate." . . .

In sum . . . an eighteenth-century merchant might do much to influence the outcome of his investments in foreign trade. To do so, he necessarily relied on the aid of his agents, chosen and managed with varying degrees of skill. Indeed, if it be true, as seems quite possible, that an increased West Indian trade was accompanied by an increased use of agents, the area of business amenable to control widened during the course of the eighteenth century. To be sure, communications were slow, they were sometimes irregular, and decisions once taken might later appear mistaken in the light of changed conditions, or of factors previously unknown. Yet when such a situation developed we often find an Oliver, a Beekman, an Astor, or a Brown dispatching follow-up letters in the wake of a departed ship captain.[41] . . .

Some merchants, as I trust the preceding pages have made clear, had more wit and perseverance, more prudence and better housekeeping habits than others. In general and in the long run possession of these qualities must have played significant if imponderable roles in the achievement of business success. But having said this I would reaffirm my sense of the impossibility of demarcating between these factors themselves, or between all of them, on the one hand, and, on the other, luck. The luck (it is not always this, of course) of having the right relatives is a case in point. Gerard Beekman "profited in many ways from the assistance of his relatives in getting started," and for his cousin James "the family tie was [also] beneficial." Porter has extensively discussed "Kinship and Business" as a "conspicuous feature of business in early Massachusetts [that appeared] in all its aspects." I agree with Robert K. Lamb's thesis that the "extended kinship family" must be emphasized as a factor in the success of entrepreneurs. Certainly no one familiar with the story of Robert Oliver would be inclined to minimize the role of luck. Two nearly incredible sets of brother-in-law relationships gave him an opportunity to make from trade to Vera Cruz in 1806-1807 a nearly incredible net profit of $775,000 in 18 months. But no reader of the record of those months can fail to be impressed with the intelligence and vigor (and also occasional unscrupulousness) with which Oliver proceeded to make the most of his opportunity, or with the extent of his dependence upon a faithful agent.[42] Here, as elsewhere, it is a case of the man and the moment, and while, with an ear to what a poet once said about the outcome of the best-laid plans, I would give luck its due, I would also give man his, especially, in this narrow case, the business community of man.

Endnotes

1. Richard Pares, *Yankees and Creoles* (Cambridge, 1956), p. 139. Pares finds this "strange." But except for the necessity of dividing profits with joint investors no such calculations were required; merchants based their investment decisions not upon records of past gain or loss but upon fresh market information; S. Bruchey, *Robert Oliver, Merchant of Baltimore*, 1783-1819 (Baltimore, 1956), pp. 135-141.

2. In 1805. From this and other information about the duPonts I wish to express my gratitude to Dr. Norman B. Wilkinson, Research Associate of the Eleutherian Mills-Hagley Foundation in Wilmington, Delaware.

3. Kenneth W. Porter, *The Jacksons and the Lees* (Cambridge, 1937), Vol. I, p. 4.

4. Oliver Record Book (hereafter ORB) 5, pp. 42-44, to P. Godeffroy Sons & Co., et al., March 22, 1803 (Maryland Historical Society—hereafter Md. Hist. Soc.).

5. James B. Hedges, *The Browns of Providence Plantations* (Cambridge, 1952), p. 13.

6. Virginia D. Harrington, *The New York Merchant on the Eve of the Revolution* (New York, 1935), p. 133.

7. Elva Tooker, *Nathan Trotter, Philadelphia Merchant*, 1787-1853 (Cambridge, 1955), p. 57.

8. Vincent Nolte, *Fifty Years in Both Hemispheres or, Reminiscences of the Life of a Former Merchant* (New York, 1854), p. 97.

9. Bruchey, *op. cit.*, pp. 364-365.

10. Hedges, *op. cit.*, p. 11.

11. ORB 5, pp. 42-44, to P. Godeffroy Sons & Co., et al., March 22, 1803 (Md. Hist. Soc.).

12. Kenneth W. Porter, *John Jacob Astor, Business Man* (Cambridge, 1931), Vol. II, p. 610.

13. Bruchey, *op. cit.*, pp. 363-364.

14. N. S. B. Gras and Henrietta M. Larson, *Casebook in American Business History* (New York, 1939), p. 78.

15. Nolte, *op. cit.*, p. 143.

16. Porter, *Astor*, Vol. II, Chap. 23.

17. Gras and Larson, *op. cit.*, pp. 78, 6.

18. Samuel Eliot Morison, *The Maritime History of Massachusetts* (Boston, 1921), pp. 130-131.

19. Byron Fairchild, *Messrs. William Pepperrell: Merchants at Piscataqua* (Ithaca, 1954), pp. 47, 49.

20. See list of sailings in front of ORB 6 (Md. Hist. Soc.).

21. W. T. Baxter, *The House of Hancock, Business in Boston*, 1724-1775 (Cambridge, 1945), pp. 146, 281-282; Philip L. White, *The Beekmans of New York in Politics and Commerce*, 1647-1877 (New York, 1956), p. 218.

22. Cited by Robert G. Albion, *The Rise of New York Port* (New York, 1939), p. 264. The word "throne-room" is Miss Larson's (*op. cit.*, p. 6).

23. Harrington, *op. cit.*, p. 116.

24. W. T. Baxter, "Accounting in Colonial America," in A. C. Littleton and B. S. Yamey, *Studies in the History of Accounting* (Homewood, Ill., 1956), p. 280. Baxter believes that

"colonial accounting" lasted well into the 19th century. "By say 1820, the modern look is beginning to creep in: cash appears more often, debtors can sometimes be distinguished from creditors, and the double-entry structure is less incomplete." (pp. 286-287).

25. Baxter cites not only the records of a "general store," but also those of an innkeeper and blacksmith (pp. 275, 278, 280). It is true that a merchant was also a storekeeper, but I disagree with Baxter's conception of the storekeeping function as the focal point of the merchant's business activity, an activity in which ventures in foreign trade are regarded as "sidelines to his principal business" (p. 280). Baxter first elaborated this conception in his interpretation of Thomas Hancock as driven to engage in a variety of trading enterprises by the necessity for obtaining sterling exchange with which to pay for the goods he imported from London for sale in his store. In my opinion, it is infelicitous to envisage Hancock's "little bookshop" as the "nerve-center of a complex and far-flung business," which included shipowning, mining and paper mill projects. (Baxter, *House of Hancock*, pp. 45-48, 62.) I believe Hancock to have been a typical 18th-century merchant in the sense that he sought profits from investments in diverse enterprises.

26. Carl Bridenbaugh, *Cities in the Wilderness* (New York, 1938), p. 359.

27. Editor's preface (N. S. B. Gras), in Baxter, *House of Hancock*, p. xxii.

28. White, *op. cit.,* p. 656. But James was certainly not a meticulous bookkeeper all his business life (cf. p. 352 with pp. 469, 490, and 492).

29. Harrington, *op. cit.*, p. 96.

30. Martin, *op. cit.*, p. 124; Hedges, *op. cit.*, p. 330; to Francis Johonnot, Feb. 15, 1784 (Letter Book, Johnson, Johonnot & Co., 1783-1785, Md. Hist. Soc.).

31. White, *op. cit.*, p. 243.

32. Bruchey, *op. cit.*, p. 317.

33. For Sombart and Weber, see Harrington, *op. cit.*, p. 68; Charles Wilson, *Anglo-Dutch Commerce & Finance in the Eighteenth Century* (Cambridge, 1941), p. 11; Baxter, *House of Hancock*, p. 197ff., 300ff.; Tooker, *op. cit.*, p. 75.

34. Porter, *Jacksons and Lees*, Vol. I, p. 48; Hedges, *op. cit.*, p. 27; Harrington, *op. cit.*, p. 91; Baxter, *House of Hancock*, p. 56; Christopher C. Crittenden, *The Commerce of North Carolina*, 1763-1789 (New Haven, 1936), p. 109; Hedges, *op. cit.*, p. 9; Pares, *op. cit.*, p. 77.

35. Martin, *op. cit.*, p. 133; Pares, *op. cit.*, pp. 84, 78. It is my conclusion, rather than Pares', that advances were therefore not as important as they would otherwise have been.

36. Bruchey, *op. cit.*, pp. 80, 190, 194-195.

37. Ltr. to Messrs. P. Burling & Co., Nov. 6, 1788 (Smith Ltr. Bk., II, in Md. Hist. Soc.).

38. ORB 4, pp. 29-31, to J. & F. Baring & Co., July 22, 1800. (My italics.) (Md. Hist. Soc.).

39. Harrington, *op. cit.*, p. 87.

40. Baxter, *House of Hancock*, p. 302; Hedges, *op. cit.*, p. 28; Fairchild, *op. cit.*, p. 51.

41. ORB 3, pp. 81-82, to Hall & McIntosh, Aug. 16, 1797 (Oliver); White, *op. cit.*, Vol. I, p. 272, to John Bennit, Jan. 28, 1756; Porter, *Astor*, Vol. I, p. 431; Hedges, *op. cit.*, pp. 78-80.

42. White, *op. cit.*, pp. 534 (Gerard Beekman), 347 (James Beekman); Porter, *Jacksons and Lees*, Vol. I, p. 88; Robert K. Lamb, "The Entrepreneur and the Community," in *Men in Business*, W. Miller, ed. (Cambridge, 1952), p. 93; Bruchey, *op. cit.*, Chap. 6 (Oliver).

I wish to express my thanks to Professor Arthur H. Cole of Harvard University whose searching questions about merchants led me, at his suggestion, to undertake this article. I also wish to thank Professor Frederic C. Lane of Johns Hopkins for his helpful comments upon a first draft of it. I, of course, assume sole responsibility for the conclusions reached.

16

Slavery:
The Progressive Institution?

PAUL A. DAVID
and PETER TEMIN

Time on the Cross[1] brings to a close an historiographic cycle that began
with the publication of Ulrich Bonnell Phillips' *American Negro Slavery*
(1918). According to Robert William Fogel and Stanley L. Engerman, the
material conditions under which plantation slaves lived and worked
compared favorably to those of free workers in the agriculture and
industry of the time. Slavery, then, was not a physically harsh, labor-
degrading regime. But neither was it an unprofitable system irrationally
supported by paternalistic planters. It was good business practice in a
highly competitive industry to care for and seek to make the most
productive use of the competent and industrious workforce—particularly
when abusive treatment of so valuable an asset would be at the economic
expense of the slaveowners themselves. The system that had grown up
around the holding of human chattels was not riddled with "internal
economic contradictions" or verging upon "collapsing under its own

Paul A. David and Peter Temin, "Slavery: The Progressive Institution?" *Journal of
Economic History*, Vol. XXXIV (September, 1974), pp. 739-783. Excerpted, and reprinted
by permission of The Economic History Association and the authors.

weight." On the eve of the Civil War, slavery was a commercially vigorous and highly efficient mode of agricultural production, and the slave plantations formed the leading sector in the rapidly developing regional economy of the antebellum South.

Obviously, this is an ambitious and imposing book. Unlike most works of the new economic history, it has been featured in *Time, Newsweek* and many other popular journals and newspapers. The broad argument has been well projected to reach the general public, but the specific details of the authors' historical research are presented in a way that precludes comprehension by that readership. Indeed, much of the underlying technical economic and statistical methodology has been made so unnecessarily difficult to follow that without further elucidation it will remain inaccessible to all but a tiny number of the book's readers.

It is obligatory upon our profession, therefore, to furnish general historians and other scholars with an appraisal of *Time on the Cross* as a technical work of economic history. This extended review essay is part of that process of evaluation. It contains four parts. The first undertakes to restate Fogel and Engerman's theses in the context of the recent literature on Negro slavery in America. Their arrestingly novel assertions about the material treatment of the slaves, and the relative efficiency of agriculture based on slave labor are shown to occupy a central place in the logical design, as well as in the rhetorical fabric of the book. The second and third parts of the review accordingly examine the evidence adduced in support of each of these assertions, taking them in turn. Although the authors' text forcefully argues that by comparison with free workers the plantation slaves were materially well-off and highly productive, both claims appear to lack an adequate scientific foundation. This is not just a matter of undue literary license having been taken in restating esoteric technical findings for popular consumption. The seemingly "neutral" numbers generated by Fogel and Engerman's quantitative methods carry a persistent bias, portraying slaveowners, and the conditions and work performance of the blacks they held in bondage, in a more favorable light than would be cast by a more complete analysis.

The fourth and concluding part of our review turns from technical criticism of the evidence actually adduced, and questions the basic conceptual approach Fogel and Engerman have applied in re-evaluating the economic performance of the peculiar institution. Paradoxically, the authors of *Time on the Cross* appear to have adopted a framework of analysis that leads them systematically to overlook the economic essence of slavery, namely that the slaves lost the freedom to exercise choices as producers and consumers.

The Argument in Context

Fogel and Engerman do not help the reader to place their work on the economics of American Negro slavery within its larger historiographic context. They do not suggest that many of the "corrections" they would make in the neoabolitionist portrayal of the peculiar institution form part of the broader reinterpretive trend in recent contributions to black history. The authors are promoting a particular methodological approach which they fervently oppose to the conventional, "un-social-scientific" study of history. This mission disposes them to gloss over the ebb and flow of debate in the historical literature of the last three decades, and to construct a fictitious protagonist against whom the arsenal of quantitative methods can be shown off as totally devastating, and hence "revolutionary" in its impact upon the interpretation of slavery. . . .

The considerable scholarship of Phillips and his followers was devoted to rehabilitating the progressive image of white supremacist society in the antebellum South; it provided a generally sympathetic and sometimes blatantly apologetic portrayal of slaveholders as a paternalistic breed of men. These planters, it turned out, had borne the economic (and ultimately the military) burden of trying to maintain a commercially moribund but socially benign institution; they had contributed to the making of America the control and instruction that was required for the gradual cultural and industrial acclimatization of inherently incompetent African savages. Through the perfection of plantation slavery the masters had managed a difficult problem of racial adjustment which had been thrust upon them by historical circumstances.

The reaction of the late 1930's and 1940's against the sort of racial bigotry which drew support from Phillips' work effected a complete reversal of the moral light in which the question of slavery was viewed. The vantage point correspondingly shifted from that of the master to that of his slave. The reversal culminated in Kenneth M. Stampp's *The Peculiar Institution* (1956), which rejected both the characterization of blacks as a biologically and culturally inferior, childlike people, and the depiction of the white planters as paternal Cavaliers coping with a vexing social problem that was not of their own making. The slaveholders, said Stampp, had built the system consciously bit by bit, decision by decision. They had done so for profit, and they had been duly rewarded. Despite the unspeakable oppression to which the resulting regime had subjected the slaves held within it, American blacks somehow had remained uncrushed in spirit. Their resistance was not that of mass rebellion, of vain insurrection, but a day-to-day affair; the meek, smiling ones who many thought were "contented though irresponsible" had protested their bondage "by shirking their duties, injuring the crops, feigning illness, and disrupting the routine." In the end the slave had remained unbroken as a person, "a troublesome property."

In 1958 Alfred Conrad and John R. Meyer's now-renowned paper on the economics of slavery provided rigorous support for Stampp's (and before him Lewis C. Gray's) insistence that the ownership of slaves represented a profitable private investment in the antebellum South. But it was Stanley Elkins' *Slavery: A Problem in American Institutional and Intellectual Life* (1959) that carried the rejection of Phillips still further. The personal and societal consequences flowing from the trauma of enslavement and the deprivations of slavery could not be comprehended within the terms of a mere point-by-point response to Phillips' account of a fundamentally genial regime rather like a boarding school. Think instead, suggested Elkins, of the phenomenon of mass personality distortion produced by a total institution like the Nazi concentration camp. Unfettered capitalism had created on the mainland of North America a peculiarly harsh and hopeless system of slavery, which left the typical bondsman broken in spirit—a psychologically "infantilized" inmate described by the stereotype of "Sambo."

From this high-water mark reached in the late 1950's, the tide of the anti-Phillips reaction began to recede. Comparative studies of slavery in the New World contradicted Elkins' presupposition that the Sambo stereotype was a peculiarity of the North American historical experience.[2] Doubts were raised about his assertion that the system of slavery developed there was—in its actual operation, as distinct from its legal provisions and restraints—significantly more "closed," and correspondingly more harsh than that which had evolved in Latin America. The a priori plausibility of this last comparative proposition appeared to be still further reduced by the results of Philip Curtin's (1969) meticulous examination of the available quantitative evidence relating to the Atlantic slave trade.[3] Of the Africans carried to the New World, all but a small fraction were absorbed in the comparatively high mortality environments of the Caribbean sugar islands and Brazil; those brought to the northern mainland not only reproduced themselves, but grew in number at a rate not very different from the free, white population.

The emphasis given by Stampp and Elkins to the masters' systematic recourse to physical cruelty and unrelieved material deprivation—in pursuit of the related objectives of profit and psychological domination of the blacks—also came in for criticism from Eugene D. Genovese. In *The Political Economy of Slavery* (1965) he suggested that the former interpretive emphasis improperly deflected attention from the precapitalistic, aristocratic, patriarchal aspects of the southern slaveowning class, and obscured the many paternalistic features of plantation life. Subsequently, in a bold reversal of Elkins, Genovese argued that paternalism constituted the more serious, more insidious mode of assault upon the autonomy of black culture and the slave's personality.

This broadening line of counter-argument indicated that Elkins, and perhaps also Stampp, had under-represented the extent of the psychological and cultural breathing-space which had been allowed American Negro slaves. J. W. Blassingame's *The Slave Community* (1972), based largely on a cautious re-examination of published slave narratives, portrays plantation life as holding out positive incentives as well as providing negative inducements to cooperate in the ostensible commercial undertakings of the organization. Within the structure of controls, moreover, the slaves found it possible to maintain greater stability of family life than has often been supposed, as well as to create and preserve their own religion, folklore, and music.

However much the vantage point and the moral tone diverged from that of Phillips, the paternalistic aspects which were so prominent in his description of plantation life had thus begun to make their way back into the historical literature during the 1960's. Recognition of these outwardly more genial qualities of the peculiar institution now was enlisted in the effort to retrieve for American *blacks* some "usable past," some reconstruction of history that would leave them more than victims of a social tragedy, brutally infantilized, cut off from their cultural roots, dependent upon white society.[4]

For this purpose, however, a full rehabilitation of the system of slavery did not seem required. Indeed, Genovese's attention to planter paternalism was initially coupled with his dismissal of Stampp's and Conrad and Meyer's point about the private profitability of slaveownership as unilluminating; in *The Political Economy of Slavery* he sought to recast in Marxian terms the traditional Phillipsian representation of slavery as an economically dysfunctional system of production. In the resulting account of southern "backwardness," the derived precapitalist ideology of the ruling planter class, the unsuitability of the mode of plantation organization for the conduct of diversified farming, and slavery's distorting effects upon the distribution of income and the structure of demand within the region, all served to obstruct the economic modernization of the South. The slaveholders made, and ultimately fought vainly to preserve, a quasi-feudal political and social order based upon a distorted, non-progressive economy; the era of the planters' hegemony and tutelage could hardly have been expected to provide Afro-Americans any useful preparation for assuming a place in modern urban-industrial society, even if it had allowed them some considerable decency and dignity in the terms of their bondage.

Time on the Cross has finished the work of up-ending Elkins and

Stampp. It asserts that through the unseen operation of competitive market forces a private vice, the planter's greed for profit, became a (comparative) social virtue. Unfettered capitalism in America led to a form of slavery which was peculiarly benign insofar as concerns the social and material circumstances of its human chattel. Equipped with this explanation for the manifestations of paternalism so central to Phillips' view of plantation life, the authors turn on Genovese and proceed to marshall [sic] the research of many other economic historians in order to contradict his representation of the antebellum southern economy as necessarily backward and stagnant.

Much of this second aspect of their thesis therefore should be familiar enough to professional readers. Richard Easterlin's (1961) compilation of regional income estimates for the United States had shown us that the South was not falling behind the rest of the nation in the period 1840-1860, and had attained high levels of GNP per capita on the eve of the Civil War. Charles Wesley's (1927) work on the urban Negro labor force, Robert Evans' (1962) study of the slave hire market, and, more recently, Robert Starobin's *Industrial Slavery in the Old South* (1970) provided ample evidence that slaves could be, and were, utilized in non-agrarian pursuits. Studies of the distribution of income and wealth in the antebellum period by Robert Gallman (1969) and Lee Soltow (1971) suggested that the degree of inequality among the free population was not notably greater in the South than in the North. The effect of the presence of the planter class in the rural South was counterbalanced by the comparative smallness of the southern urban population, urban wealth-holding being typically more concentrated than rural irrespective of region.[5]

To this sweeping revision of Genovese's picture of the slaveholders' economic milieu, *Time on the Cross* adds two arrestingly bold and essentially novel propositions. Both have a close connection with the authors' contention that the material conditions of life and labor were not especially harsh or degrading to the typical plantation slave. First, it is their view that the consumption standards at which slaves were maintained compared favorably with those of contemporaneous free agricultural labor in the South, and even approached the economic condition of urban industrial workers in the North during the latter half of the nineteenth century. . . .

The second novel proposition is that as an agricultural system plantation slavery was more efficient in its use of the factors of production than the free family farm typical of the North. Fogel and Engerman assign economies of scale only partial responsibility for the greater measured productivity of southern plantation agriculture. Instead they argue that the comparative industriousness and personal efficiency of the Afro-American laborers vis-à-vis the free work force must have been the principal cause underlying their findings on this score. The conclusion complements the propositon that the typical slave was a well-cared-for productive asset.

Having stood both Elkins and Stampp on their heads as far as concerns the harshness of slavery under pure capitalism, and having concluded that black bondsmen must have been more efficient workers than free whites, Fogel and Engerman are thus in a position to dismiss the Sambo stereotype as utterly without objective basis in either the circumstances or behavior of the typical slave. They brand it as merely another pernicious myth, created as much by the latent prejudices of abolitionist propagandists as by the open bigotry of southern white supremacists. . . .

The paradox of *Time on the Cross* is that its laudable announced aim of rectifying a historiographic injustice and restoring to American Negroes today a source of justifiable pride in their cultural heritage has led the authors to the excesses of an utterly sanguine reappraisal of the peculiar institution. The commercial success of capitalistic slavery somehow emerges as the most fitting subject for modern black pride. Few readers will miss the irony that this book, whose passionate title is meant to convey the depth of the authors' moral condemnation of slavery, in substance actually transcends even U. B. Phillips' rehabilitative intentions. Cool, detached social science, we are told,[6] requires one to face up to the fact that Negro slavery in its time was a "vigorous, deeply entrenched, and rapidly growing economic system"—indeed, putting "purely moral" considerations aside, a comparatively benign institutional arrangement worthy of a progressive America. . . .

The keystones of this reinterpretive edifice, and the proximate sources of the theoretical confusions that impart to the book a puzzling and paradoxical quality, are not hard to locate. They are found in the assertions Fogel and Engerman advance concerning the material conditions of the slaves' lives, and the latters' willing, industrious efficiency as workers. These two propositions, as we already have seen, underlie the truly novel arguments that *Time on the Cross* contributes to revising the macro-economic portrait of the antebellum South as a backward, agrarian region. Further, taken in combination with Stampp's and Conrad and Meyer's point about the private profitability of slaveownership, these same propositions form the empirical basis upon which Fogel and Engerman construct new characterizations for the *dramatis personae*. The patriarchal Cavalier has been turned into the shrewd master, an enlightened capitalistic manager of personnel. And Sambo's place is now occupied by the keen, "achieving" slave who strives for some measure of self-improvement within the considerable breathing space allowed him by competitive capitalism.[7]

What evidence and arguments support these two tenets of Fogel and

Engerman's bold reinterpretation? Are these, perhaps, the "most telling revisions" which "turn on technical mathematical points, points which despite their obscurity are vital to the correct description and interpretation of the slave economy"? Just how have they been derived from "the new techniques and hitherto neglected sources" which the authors rather dauntingly allude to in their opening chapter on "Slavery and the Cliometric Revolution"?

Alas, the full text of *Time on the Cross* may be studied endlessly without learning the answers to these questions. To understand how this could be, one first must grasp the format of the book. It is presented in two volumes, the first (Volume I) being the text and an index thereto, the other (Volume II) comprising a bibliography and various appendices—including, as Appendix B, an extended set of technical notes pertinent to assertions made in the text.

Although the reader of the text is initially cautioned to "keep in mind [the] distinction between the principal findings of the cliometricians and our attempt to interpret them" (Vol. I, p. 10), this is not so easily done when only "interpretations" are being presented. We do not allude here to the deep epistemological problems raised by Fogel and Engerman's desire to distinguish cleanly between findings of "fact" and their "interpretation." A more immediate difficulty is that the published findings of other historians, as well as their new empirical results described in Appendix B, are not invariably reported in the same terms by the narrative discussion of the text. The "primary volume" of *Time on the Cross* offers a popularized account, which has only slightly more of a claim to faithfully represent the nature of the authors' own research contributions than were it to have been prepared by someone else altogether.

Fogel and Engerman's text itself is utterly unencumbered by documentation. Curiously, conventional historians who initially have reviewed the first volume seem to have been so unnerved by "the rattle of electronic equipment" and the tramping legions of research assistants "heard off stage" that they failed to complain of this omission. The absence of footnotes, bibliographic citations, discussion of sources, explicit mention of methodological problems, in short, of the standard critical apparatus of works of professional history, is intended on this occasion "to encourage the widest possible discussion of the findings of the cliometricians" (Vol. I, pp. 11-12). But a heavy burden thereby has been placed upon any scholar who undertakes to inform "popular" discussions by critically examining these findings and relating them to the authors' conclusions.

The problem is that the second volume, subtitled *Evidence and Methods*, simply does not set out the bushels of footnotes which, one might imagine, had studded an original, unpruned version of the text. The author's introductory essay (Appendix A) on the roles of ideology, humanism and science in the historical study of slavery discloses that only as much as they have been able to learn about slavery using the method of the social sciences, and no more, has been set down in Appendix B. Yet, to produce the reinterpretation offered by their first volume, something more was needed: "We were obliged to invoke assumptions which, though plausible, cannot be verified at present, and to rely on additional evidence which is too fragmentary to be subjected to systematic statistical tests" (Vol. II, 4). One has to turn to Appendix B remembering that it does not pretend to fully document the text, but only the portions (extensive as these are) for which Fogel and Engerman have felt able to present a suitably social-scientific basis.

And on these, Appendix B proves to be tough going indeed. Throughout the appendices the authors deploy an elaborate, sometimes bewildering system of internal cross-references and numerical bibliographic citations whose general effect is accurately conveyed by the following item:

> 4.11.1 The various points on the curve in figure 41 are the values of the right-hand terms of equation 4.7 for each value of t from 0 to 75. The values of the variables entering equation 4.7 were estimated in the manner described in 3.4.9 and 4.10.1 except that an allowance of 26 percent was added to basic income to cover the average amount of "extra" income received by slaves (see 6.7.1.2). The resulting figure ($42.99) was the average value of M. Atwater's weights [366, pp. 52-53] were used to convert the average value of M into age and sex specific values. (Vol. II, p. 120)

Quite obviously, Appendix B has not been written for anyone to sit down and read. It is neither a full set of conventional footnotes nor a self-contained technical monograph that can justly be evaluated on its own merits. It does not make available to other historians any of the original data from the probate records or the manuscript censuses upon which Fogel and Engerman have drawn. Far from undertaking to explain to conventional historians the cliometric methods that the authors espouse, the logic of their economic arguments (and their demographic analyses, about which we will say little) is made unnecessarily hard to follow, and the descriptions of the actual quantitative methods employed oscillate between the extremes of frustrating imprecision and ostentatious overformalism.

But, the details of Fogel and Engerman's difficult second volume, and the mysteries of Appendix B in particular, must be our main preoccupation. . . . Clearly it is important to know how seriously to take the authors' prefatory admonitions to keep in mind the difference between the cliometric "findings" discussed by the supporting technical volume, and their attempt in the text at a broader interpretation of the historical experience of American Negro slavery. But it is no less vital to determine whether the claim implied in this warning can be safely accepted. Has cliometrics really provided startling "findings of fact" about which there is little room for argument? Do the key empirical propositions advanced by Fogel and Engerman—those regarding the comparatively favorable material conditions of life, and the greater efficiency of slave labor—possess an objective "scientific" status that derives from the methods employed in securing them?

The remainder of this review is geared to respond to these questions. From the detailed examination of the authors' evidence and methods on the material treatment and the productive efficiency of slaves, presented in the two following sections, we think it will become apparent just how unwarranted it is to accept their empirical "findings" as scientifically incontrovertible. But the closing section of the review takes up the still more fundamental point that many of the defects revealed by a close reading of the supporting, technical volume turn out to be conceptual rather than narrowly methodological. No greater degree of analytical rigor or meticulousness of scholarship on the authors' part could really have redeemed the claim to have arrived at an ethically neutral economic appraisal of the "performance" of a social institution, let alone the institution of chattel slavery. The entire conception of producing a "scientifically objective" or "value free" reappraisal of the economic welfare consequences of slavery seems to us to be peculiarly ill-founded. For the ethical and behavioral premises upon which modern economic welfare analysis rests are immediately inconsonant with the degree of personal involition which remains the defining attribute of the institution in question. In this respect, we shall argue, the strain of paradox and confusion which runs through *Time on the Cross* involves more than a mere problem of rhetoric.* . . .

On Welfare-Efficiency and the Morality of Slavery

Some broader patterns begin to emerge from the welter of details sampled for discussion in the foregoing, admittedly incomplete methodological appraisal of *Time on the Cross*.

Although the authors present their empirical "findings" as objective

---

*Because of severe space limitations the next two sections: "Methods and Evidence on Material Treatment" and "Evidence and Methods on the Relative Efficiency of Slave Agriculture" are omitted. In the original article, these sections were dealt with between pages 749 and 778.

economic statements uncontaminated by any judgments about the "morality" of slavery, their cliometric investigations have been conducted within a conceptual framework whose ethical perspective seems peculiarly one-sided. The authors consider the diet of slaves as given and assess its caloric worth without asking whether blacks under freedom would have chosen to work hard enough to require so much food energy, or whether the intake allowed them was adequate for *their* actual energy needs. The authors do not inquire how poor a free man—say, a freed black in the Reconstruction period—might have to have been before he chose to obtain such a level of food energy in the carbohydrate-intensive way the slaves were compelled to obtain theirs. Nor do the authors ask how impoverished a free family would have to have been in the nineteenth century before the husband, wife, and children "chose" to toil the number of hours expected of slave families. In reckoning what was being "expropriated" by the masters the authors start by accepting the fact that blacks as slaves were not financially responsible for their own offspring; thus they tacitly suppose that each generation would in any event have had to finance its own upbringing, paying interest charges for loans obtained against future earnings. And, finally, in measuring the comparative "efficiency" of the agricultural system based on slavery, the authors have in effect accepted the contemporary market valuations as measuring the social-welfare benefits derived from the specific goods produced by slave labor—while failing to count the longer average hours worked, that is, the additional leisure lost by slaves, as among the social resource costs incurred for that worthwhile "output."

Thus, in quantifying the economic dimensions of the experience of slavery, Fogel and Engerman recurringly slip into a tacit acceptance of the status quo of black bondage as the appropriate point of departure for making their evaluations. The resulting work looks at the "economic performance" of the system of slavery mainly from the perspectives of the owners of the human capital and the consumers of the commodities that it produced; the condition of freedom is not correspondingly adopted as an alternative which might be systematically employed in quantifying the economic welfare burdens imposed upon the slave population.

In a brief, concluding exercise (cf. Vol. I, p. 244) Fogel and Engerman do present a measure of welfare costs to the blacks of the "non-pecuniary disadvantages" of laboring under the slave plantation's gang system: $75 per head, annually. But this estimate is conceptually inadequate and empirically unfounded. To derive it they argue that the difference between the post-Emancipation earnings of freedmen employed on labor gangs and the earnings of black sharecroppers provides a pecuniary measure of the blacks' distaste for the system in which they were compelled to work under slavery.[8] But beyond Fogel and Engerman's factual misconstruction of

C. E. Seagrave's evidence on this point, it hardly seems adequate to represent the "non-pecuniary" disadvantages of being "driven" by *slave*-drivers as measurable in terms of the difference between the earnings obtained under two alternative systems of *free* labor. And to cap it off, the authors have reckoned the net economic burden imposed on the slaves by deducting—from this inappropriate measure of the gross burden—an allowance for the fictitious pecuniary advantage which slaves allegedly enjoyed in comparison with free agricultural workers. (Cf. Vol. I, pp. 244-245, particularly Table 3.)

For reasons such as these it is unfortunately not possible to accept the sanguine belief that the quantitative methods applied in writing *Time on the Cross* truly have fulfilled the authors' expectations by providing "a more *accurate and complete* portrayal of slavery than was previously available."[9]

That the tacit ethical orientation of Fogel and Engerman's "cliometric" contributions should have defeated this aspiration to completeness as well as to accuracy really is not so surprising. In an important respect the slant of their quantitative work reflects the economist's professional habits of mind, and the methodological pull of the tradition established by Conrad and Meyer's studiously *de-personalized* approach to the issue of slavery's profitability. Those two pioneers of the "new economic history" stressed that the analytical problems of determining the profitability of holding slaves were not different from those met in determining the returns from investments in machines or cattle. Trouble comes, however, from adhering to this bent when venturing beyond the quantification of profitability—a dimension of the institution's performance which certainly was of more immediate interest from the vantage point of some members of antebellum society (the masters) than from that of others (the slaves). In defining what is meant by the *social* "optimality" of resource allocation, or in devising criteria for comparing the allocative "efficiency" of different economic systems, the natural predisposition of economists is to consider how affairs appear to the human agents who are capable of acting so as to better satisfy their wants. Modern economic welfare theory simply does not encourage one to view life also from the standpoint of the lathes and the livestock.

Certainly *Time on the Cross* makes it perfectly clear that it is *not* any insensitivity on the authors' part to the moral evil of slavery which has led them to re-evaluate the economic performance of the institution by reference to standards that tend to embrace the viewpoint of the owners of productive assets, rather than that of the assets in question. The immorality of slavery for Fogel and Engerman is unquestionable; it is a fundamental ethical precept which can be, and is, asserted categorically—regardless of their supposed exoneration of slavery from the "economic indictments" falsely brought against it by abolitionist propaganda. "Even if slavery did produce, on the average, better material conditions than obtained for free Negro laborers, or white laborers for that matter, the *moral* indictment of slavery still prevails" (Vol. II, p. 222). Indeed, we are warned that the historian of slavery who persists in the neoabolitionist penchant for "continually linking the issue of morality with physical cruelty, with sexual abuses, or with mistreatment in respect to food, clothing and shelter," runs the grave risk of having "obfuscated rather than clarified the profound immorality of the *system*."[10]

What is one to make of this effort to separate "economics" from "morality?"[11] A dichotomy works two ways: the author's insistence that economic matters should not be permitted to becloud issues of "pure morality" also suggests that no prior ethical judgments have contaminated the "purely economic" findings upon which *Time on the Cross* is based. But do the methods of welfare economics enable one to carry through an ethically neutral re-examination of the comparative social efficiency of the system of slavery? Is it possible to conduct the sort of "value-free" inquiry which Fogel and Engerman appear to envisage as establishing the economic facts concerning the consequences of this particular institutional arrangement, the objective historical truths about which moral judgments subsequently may be made?

The brief answer is that modern welfare theory is quite incapable of supporting such an undertaking. Not only does the central analytical concept of the "welfare efficiency" of a specific pattern of resource allocation have a distinct ethical content, but the ethical premises upon which it rests make this a peculiarly inappropriate framework within which to comprehend systems based on varying degrees of personal involition.

The notion that questions concerning the allocative efficiency of alternative economic arrangements can be usefully separated from concerns with other aspects of those arrangements, such as the distribution of wealth, income, and ultimately of the human happiness that may be derived from them, is fundamental in modern economic welfare theory. But this notion rests on the idea that maximization is good; that states of the world in which more of an inherently desired thing is available to be (potentially) shared by all are "better"—in some widely shared sense of the word—than states in which there is less. By moving to such a state at least some individual could be given more of what he desired (made "better off") without necessarily rendering anyone worse off. To such a change reasonable men freely would assent. Economists describe states where any individual's further gain must come at someone else's expense to be welfare-efficient, or Pareto-efficient, and a move toward such a position is said to be "Pareto-safe."

Pareto efficiency, then, is not an ethically neutral concept. It rests on the premise that each individual's desires (preferences among goods, and between goods and leisure, and goods today vs. goods tomorrow) should be allowed to count. Thus Pareto-safe moves are only ethically safe for the "scientific" economist to recommend because maintaining the new position presumably would require no coercion. Indeed it is because one presumes that all commodities "consumed" are voluntarily chosen, and all efforts and sacrifices made for the production of commodities are freely rendered, that the commodities ethically can be called "goods." But, once the presupposition of autonomous individual preferences is seriously questioned, it becomes unclear how truly voluntary "choice" is. The serious possibility that what individuals seem to want may be systematically shaped by what they have been allowed to have therefore undermines the ethical foundations of normative welfare analysis. If people who had been long enslaved eventually "chose" to continue in the security of their chains, should we unhesitatingly say that this test revealed bondage to be a "better" condition than freedom?

Welfare analysis based on the search for Pareto optimality not only subscribes to the complex ethical character of that criterion, but "counts" individual preferences only as these can be expressed through market behavior. Recommendations of Pareto-safe changes in the pattern of resource allocation therefore must implicitly accept the past and the existing distribution of income and wealth, the institutional working rules, and the larger social and political power structure. The criterion applies to consensual, "no injury" changes from whatever status quo has come to prevail as a result of the past economic and non-economic processes.

But because the prior specification of property rights can, and usually does exercise a powerful role in determining whether a particular change is deemed Pareto-safe, the rule of unanimity itself carries a strong bias in favor of the status quo. A slave set free might not be able, given his prior lack of training, to earn sufficient income to both compensate his master for the loss of his services and improve his own economic welfare. The two parties could not agree on manumission. Yet if a prospective master were obliged to fully compensate a free man for the welfare loss entailed in entering perpetual bondage, it is unlikely that the two could agree to that change either. So in determining which, between slavery and freedom, is the more welfare-efficient economic system, the thing that may well matter most is whether the new economic historian will start from an ethical presumption of the human right to freedom, or accept a factual status quo which finds a people already "stolen" and held in bondage.

Modern welfare economics is grounded on the supposition that all market and nonmarket transactions of interest between individual actors are voluntary. Involuntary transactions, in which goods are wrested from unwilling "sellers" or forced upon unwilling "buyers," amount to theft and extortion, respectively. Such a theory is not helpful for deriving any precise statements about the welfare consequences of changes which entail the introduction or further extension of involuntary transactions of the sort essential to slavery. As the ethical premise that each individual's preferences must count underlies the notion that the only "Pareto-safe" (welfare-efficiency justified) changes are those to which there would be unanimous assent, it is difficult to use this apparatus to assess the *comparative* economic welfare efficiency of slave and free societies. For in imagining the change from one to the other one must acknowledge that the entailed redistribution of property rights violates the ethical premises for making formally justifiable statements about the resulting change in social welfare. When people are enslaved, *welfare necessarily is transferred* to their masters, and there is no ethically neutral way to compare the welfare efficiency of the resulting institution with the set of outcomes characterizing an alternative institution under which that particular interpersonal welfare transfer need not take place. Any such comparison would require weighing the slaves' losses against the masters' gains.

There would be no difficulty conducting an analysis of economic welfare efficiency that treated slaves as objects, mere instruments of production whose condition was excluded from the purview of welfare considerations except insofar as it impinged on the well-being of the actors whose preferences *did* count. Economic theory is thus well set up to guide us in making coherent statements about the welfare efficiency of slavery from the standpoint of everyone but the slaves. If this were what *Time on the Cross* had set out to do, it would be both a less-arresting and a less misleading book.

Endnotes

1. *Time on the Cross*, Vol. I: *The Economics of American Negro Slavery*, by Robert William Fogel and Stanley L. Engerman, 286 pp. (Boston: Little, Brown and Company), $8.95. Vol. II: *Evidence and Methods—A Supplement*, by Robert William Fogel and Stanley L. Engerman, 267 pp. Boston: Little, Brown and Company, $12.50.

2. Cf., e.g., the essays by Sidney W. Mintz, Marvin Harris, David Brion Davis, Arnold S. Sio, and others in Laura Foner and Eugene D. Genovese, eds., *Slavery in the New World* (Englewood Cliffs, N. J.: Prentice-Hall, 1969).

3. Phillip D. Curtin, *The Atlantic Slave Trade: A Census* (Madison: University of Wisconsin Press, 1969).

4. Cf. David B. Davis, "Slavery and the Post-World War II Historians," *Daedalus* (Spring 1974), 9-10, for this imputation of purpose.

5. Cf. R. A. Easterlin, "Regional Income Trends, 1840-1950," in Seymour Harris, ed., *American Economic History* (New York: McGraw-Hill, 1961); C. H. Wesley, *Negro Labor in the United States, 1850-1925* (New York: Vanguard Press, 1927); R. Evans, Jr., "The Economics of American Negro Slavery," in *Aspects of Labor Economics* (Princeton: National Bureau of Economic Research, 1962); R. S. Starobin, *Industrial Slavery in the Old South* (New York: Oxford University Press, 1970); R. E. Gallman, "Trends in the Size Distribution of Wealth in the Nineteenth Century: Some Speculations," in *Six Papers on the Size Distribution of Wealth and Income*, ed. Lee Soltow (New York: Columbia University Press, 1969); L. Soltow, "Economic Inequality in the United States in the Period from 1790 to 1860," *Journal of Economic History*, XXXI (December 1971), 822-839.

6. *Time on the Cross*, Vol. II, p. 16.

7. The role of these new characterizations in the overall structure of *Time on the Cross*, as well as the evidence adduced for them, are discussed in P. A. David and P. Temin, "Capitalist Masters, Bourgeois Slaves," *Journal of Interdisciplinary History* (forthcoming, Winter 1975).

8. Despite gang wages 2.11 to 2.42 times as large as the earnings of sharecroppers (on 4 Louisiana plantations during 1865-1866), say Fogel and Engerman, "planters found it impossible to maintain the gang system once they were deprived of the right to apply force," and sharecropping became the predominant mode through which southern Negro labor was mobilized. (Cf. Vol. I, pp. 238-239; Vol. II, p. 160.) Yet, as the source they cite for these Louisiana earnings differentials makes clear, during the two years in question the weather was miserable and the sharecroppers took a particularly bad financial beating. Moreover, it is noted there that the high wages set in these Louisiana parishes by the Freedman's Bureau *did succeed in recruiting black gang labor:* in May, 1866 only 21 percent of the Negroes under the supervision of the Bureau in Louisiana were sharecroppers instead of working under various types of wage contracts. This "anomalous" preponderance of the system of paying wages for gang labor seems to have persisted in the Louisiana sugar-growing regions. Cf. C. E. Seagrave, "The Southern Negro Agricultural Worker: 1850-1870" (unpublished Ph.D. dissertation, Stanford University, April, 1971), pp. 41-42, 53-54.

9. Vol. II, p. 19, emphasis added. Undoubtedly Fogel and Engerman are right in identifying the validity of this methodological claim as "the real question."

10. Vol. II, p. 222. Kenneth Stampp is charged with having thus "inadvertently obfuscated" the true immorality of slavery, and with having failed "to stress that proof of good treatment was insufficient to remove the moral brand" from the institution.

11. It is the thesis of Fogel and Engerman's Ch. 5 ("The Origins of the Economic Indictment of Slavery," Vol. I, esp., pp. 158-161) that the "moral purity" of the eighteenth-century radical Quaker position against slavery subsequently was diluted by the addition of an "economic indictment" constructed to meet the propaganda needs of nineteenth-century abolitionists. But as an essay in intellectual history this seems quite incorrect. Cf. D. B. Davis, *The Problem of Slavery*, pp. 291-309, 316-317, on the elements of rational analysis in Quaker theology, reflected in a willingness to examine Biblical texts in the light of reason and human standards of justice, as well as for the inclusion in early Quaker tracts of arguments concerning slavery's social and economic consequences. Davis (p. 317) explicitly cites an American Quaker pamphlet of 1713 as anticipating Hinton Rowan Helper's (1857) warning that Negro bondage would promote economic divergences and political conflicts between rich slaveholders and poor whites.

17

The Legend of Eli Whitney and Interchangeable Parts

ROBERT S. WOODBURY

In some legends the story is such that from its very nature we can never establish its truth or falsity; in others patient historical work—usually external to the legend—can ascertain whether the events actually happened or not. The legend of Eli Whitney's part in interchangeable manufacture is, however, unique in that the clues and even much of the evidence for its refutation are part of the legend as customarily recited. It is also unique in that the legend is not merely a popular one nor even a story given "authority" by inclusion in conventional textbooks. This legend has been retold at least twice with all the paraphernalia of historical scholarship—footnotes, elaborate bibliography, discussion of the sources, and even use of archival material.[1] But in both cases we find the same failure to evaluate the evidence critically, to follow leads to other sources, and to question basic presuppositions. These same faults extend back to the origins of the legend. . . .

"The Legend of Eli Whitney and Interchangeable Parts," by Robert S. Woodbury, *Technology and Culture* I (Summer, 1960), pp. 235-253. Copyright 1960, Wayne State University Press; reprinted by permission of the University of Chicago Press.

I

The Contract

Whitney's contract of June 14, 1798 to manufacture arms for the Federal Government is the focus of a number of elements of our legend. His motives in this undertaking have been interpreted as those of a prudent businessman doing his patriotic duty and as those of a genius anxious to put into execution a new scheme of manufacture for the good of this country in a time of crisis. His actual motives were quite different.

In 1798 Miller and Whitney had lost all their suits to obtain their cotton gin patent rights in the courts of the South. What little legal merits these decisions had stemmed from a defect in the Patent Law of 1793; clearly nothing further could be done until Congress corrected this defect. The efforts of Whitney and others did not finally result in a new patent law until 1800. The intervening years could be seen as a lull in the affairs of Miller and Whitney. But Whitney could hardly look forward to any relaxation, for their financial affairs were in desperate straits. Every source of credit had been exhausted by both partners.[2] Certainly Whitney himself was on the verge of a nervous breakdown. Although some have tried to find in this situation a frustrated love for Catherine Greene, a more careful reading of his letter of October 7, 1797 to Miller indicates rather that Whitney's high hopes of financial security, respected position, and prestige have not only come crashing to the ground, but the disgrace of bankruptcy is staring him in the face. . . .

Whitney needed a new opportunity—any opportunity. But, more important, he needed credit—credit to save Miller and Whitney from bankruptcy, credit to enable him to fight for his rightful profit and for his good name lost in the cotton gin suits. When he heard that the Congress was "about making some appropriations for procuring Arms etc. for the U.S.," here was a heaven-sent opportunity.[3] This would at least keep his manufactory going until he could get his cotton gin rights. The opportunity was so great and Whitney's situation so desperate that he was willing to promise "ten or Fifteen Thousand stand of Arms," a fantastic proposal! Whitney even promised to begin delivering "in a short time" and he "will come forward to Philadelphia immediately. . . ." New hope for a desperate man!

Why was such a rash proposal not rejected at once by such prudent men as President Adams and Timothy Pickering, the Secretary of War? The failure of the Pinckney mission had caused public concern, and French privateers were rumored to be off the coast. Even Washington was called out of retirement to head the armed forces. On the 4th of May 1798 Congress voted $800,000 for the purchase of cannon and small arms.

When on the 24th of May Whitney arrived at the seat of government the plum was not only ripe and juicy but begging to be picked. Public sentiment was aroused, and the highest officials must do something—and that right promptly. Both sides could not close the contract quickly enough. Only the Purveyor of Public Supplies, Tench Coxe, seems to have kept his head—"I have my doubts about this matter and suspect that Mr. Whitney cannot perform as to time."[4] . . .

Certain features of the contract deserve closer examination. . . . There *was* something special about Whitney's contract—it contained a paragraph six not included in any of the others. It was this paragraph that was crucial for Whitney. Having quickly sized up the situation in which the high officials found themselves, the shrewd Whitney saw his chance, consulted Baldwin as to the form the contract should take,[5] and at one stroke solved all his immediate problems. This paragraph reads:

> 6th. "Five thousand dollars shall be advanced to the party of the second part on closing this contract, and on producing satisfactory evidence to the party of the first, that the said advance has been expended in making preparatory arrangements for the manufacture of arms, Five Thousand dollars more shall be advanced. No further advances shall be demanded until One thousand stands of Arms are ready for delivery, at which time the further sum of Five thousand dollars, shall be advanced. After the delivery of One thousand stands of arms, and the payment of the third advance as aforesaid, further advances shall be made at the discretion of the Secretary of the Treasury in proportion to the progress made in executing this contract. It is however understood and agreed by and between the parties to this instrument, that from time to time, whenever the party of the second part shall have the second thousand ready for delivery he shall be intitled to full payment for the same, so with respect to each and every Thousand until he shall have delivered the said Ten thousand stands."

Here was credit at last! Here was financial standing which assured further credit! Five thousand dollars at once, and five thousand more on terms which could be easily fulfilled by using his cotton gin laborers and machines. And assured payment for each thousand stands of arms upon delivery—to a total of $134,000. Little wonder that Whitney wrote to his friend Stebbins: "Bankruptcy and ruin were constantly staring me in the face and disappointment trip'd me up every step I attempted to take, I was miserable . . . Loaded with a Debt of 3 or 4000 Dollars, without resources, and without any business that would ever furnish me a support, I knew not which way to turn. . . . By this contract I obtained some thousands of Dollars in advance which saved me from ruin."[6]

No wonder that in his eagerness to read paragraph six of the contract, Whitney evidently skimmed rapidly over the incredible terms of paragraph one.[7] Whitney had contracted to deliver 4000 stands of arms by September

30, 1799, and 6000 more by September 30, 1800. Four thousand stands of arms in 15 months, from a factory yet to be built, and made by laborers as yet untrained, and by methods as yet unknown! And 6000 more in the following year! In his desperation Whitney had thrown all caution to the winds. He was no experienced manufacturer, as his deliveries of the relatively simple cotton gin indicate. He was aware that he knew nothing of arms making. And a prudent man would have expected at least some of the setbacks with which he fills his later letters to Wolcott, together with requests for further credit, contrary to the provisions of the contract. In short, despite his vague claims of new methods and what could by done by "Machinery moved by water," Whitney had only the vaguest idea of how he would actually fulfill the contract. He was not able to deliver even the first 500 muskets until September 26, 1801, and the contract was not actually completed until January 23, 1809. Further, the records of the Springfield Armory, now in the National Archives, show that even during the period 1815 to 1825, when his plant was fully established, Whitney never delivered muskets at the rate promised in his contract of 1798. . . .[8]

III

Manufacture by Machinery

We have thus far taken the term "manufacture by interchangeable parts" to have a clear meaning, based upon Blanc's, Whitney's, and Hall's dramatic demonstrations in assembling arms out of parts taken at random. This is a concept based upon characteristics of the product. It of course raises the question of how closely the parts must fit to be interchangeable. The usual answer is that the tolerances allowed must be sufficiently small for the product to work as designed and no more, since closer tolerances will merely increase cost. But this is rather vague. A more significant concept of interchangeable parts results from an examination of the actual methods by which such parts are produced. In this sense modern interchangeable parts require these elements: (1) precision machine tools, (2) precision gauges or other instruments of measurement, (3) uniformly accepted measurement standards, and (4) certain techniques of mechanical drawing. We do not, of course, expect Whitney to have all these elements, but we can estimate the contribution he may have made by comparing his work to them.[9]

In what sense were the Whitney firearms interchangeable? A test of a number of known Whitney arms in at least one collection proved that they were *not* interchangeable in all their parts! In fact, in some respects they are not even approximately interchangeable![10] The answer to this paradox is to be found partly in the actual means of establishment of standards for their manufacture. Each of the contractors of 1798 (and the later contractors as well) was given two or three samples of the Charleville model of 1763, and his contract specified that these were to be followed exactly. This method meant that at best the output of one plant would be interchangeable, but the muskets of a given contractor would not necessarily be interchangeable with those of the other contractors. In short, our third and fourth elements of interchangeable parts—uniform standards of measurement, and working from adequately dimensioned drawings—were absent. In fact, they were not to appear for two more generations. . . .

The list of machine tools in the inventory of Whitney's estate is detailed and tells us much about the tools he had in use at the time of his death in 1825, but lists nothing not already in use at Springfield and Harper's Ferry. In fact, the large number of files listed as on hand would suggest that for much of his work Whitney used only a filing jig or fixture to guide a hand operated file as his principal means of producing uniform parts for the locks of his muskets. But Polhem had done this two generations earlier.

The Whitney papers at Yale also include a number of drawings, none of them dated, signed, or even identifiable as definitely made by Whitney; these drawings are quite possibly those of Whitney's nephews, for Benjamin Silliman, writing in 1832, says: "The manufactory has advanced, in these respects [machinery], since it has been superintended by Mr. Whitney's nephews, the Messrs. Blake, and to them it is indebted for some valuable improvements."[11] They had been in charge for about five years before Whitney's death.

The legend includes one specific machine—the milling machine discovered in 1912 by Professor Joseph W. Roe of Yale, and now in the collection of the New Haven Colony Historical Society. It was identified by Eli Whitney's grandson of the same name as having been made by his grandfather and as the first one ever made. His authority for this identification was that he remembered having seen it as a boy and having been told this story by workmen in the old Whitneyville plant. Roe dated this machine as of 1818 merely because of a statement in the *Encyclopaedia Britannica* that "the first milling machine was made in a gun manufactory in 1818." All this hardly seems adequate evidence. The first reference we have to the use of milling by Whitney is in his letter to Calhoun of March 20, 1823. But by 1818 we have clear evidence that milling was in common use in both national armories, and by at least Robert Johnson and Lemuel Pomeroy of the private contractors.[12]

In short, we really know practically nothing of what Whitney actually had in his manufactory at Mill Rock; what little we do know of was clearly not an innovation; and we have good evidence to show that all that

Whitney claimed as his own contribution was at least independently innovated by others, particularly in the national armories. Whitney's claims of originality seem to have been the exact opposite of the truth. Certainly no one is justified in stating that Whitneyville was the site of "the birth of the machine tool industry," much less the birthplace, even in America, of manufacture by means of interchangeable parts.

IV

The Birth of American Technology

There can be no doubt that what became by the 1850's widely known abroad as the "American system of manufacturing" had its origin in this first quarter of the nineteenth century and that its principal features were developed in the northeastern section of the United States. The American system included mass manufacture, by power-driven machinery, by machinery especially designed to serve its particular purpose, and by the use of the principle of interchangeable parts.

The legend says that all this stems from Eli Whitney. We have seen enough to indicate that we actually know very little of what he really did; hence there is no clear beginning from which we can tell what later developed from Whitney's work. It is also clear that other men were working along these very lines in the manufacture of arms at the same time.

The legend also claims that from Whitney stemmed the application of the American system of manufacture to many light metalworking industries—Colt and his revolver, Jerome's clocks, Waltham watches, Yale's locks, Singer's sewing machines, and so on. Even if we knew exactly what Whitney did, there is little evidence to support this application of the-great-man-in-history hypothesis. About all that can be said is that further applications of interchangeable parts would *logically* seem to follow from Whitney's broad *claims*. But this is not the same as proof that Whitney actually had methods similar to those of later innovators, much less that they really did derive their ideas and methods from his. Certainly many other men contributed as much or more than Whitney, and evidence for their work can be found, far more convincing than Whitney's boasting claims. The legend says, for example, that the influence of Whitney was the basis of the Colt Armory methods of manufacture. In fact, it was E. K. Root who was the technical genius behind the manufacture of the Colt revolver, and his work stems directly from that of John Hall at Harper's Ferry. Whitney's influence on the manufacture of clocks, watches, and sewing machines is equally open to question.

We know so little of Whitney's actual methods of manufacture that his contribution to interchangeable parts is difficult to assess. What little we do know indicates, if anything, that Whitney was on the wrong track anyhow. John Hall's methods can be fairly clearly established, at least sufficiently for us to be sure that modern interchangeable manufacture derives far more from his inventive genius at Harper's Ferry than from Eli Whitney's manufactory at Mill Rock.[13] Actually one is led to find the origins of the "American system of manufacturing" in the culmination of a number of economic, social, and technical forces[14] brought to bear on manufacture by several men of genius, of whom Whitney can only be said to have been *perhaps* one.

V

Conclusion

This analysis of the Legend of Eli Whitney and Interchangeable Parts raises more questions than it answers. We have by no means arrived at the truth about the legend, much less about the advent of manufacture by interchangeable parts. However, I hope it is clear that the whole question needs re-examination—a more critical analysis of presuppositions and of the evidence which is known, and a more careful search for other sources.

But why not let this nice convenient legend go on? Were it Whitney alone that concerns us, that might be well enough. But the issue is larger than that. The history of our industrial growth is of first importance to the understanding of our American heritage. That industrial development cannot be properly understood without careful consideration of its technological basis. Therefore the true story of the "Birth of American Technology" is of prime concern to us. We should make certain that the baby is perfect and legitimate.

Endnotes

1. J. Mirsky and A. Nevins, *The World of Eli Whitney* (N.Y., 1952); C.M. Green, *Eli Whitney and the Birth of American Technology* (Boston, 1956).

2. Miller to Whitney, Dec. 2, 1796 and May 11, 1797.

3. Whitney to Wolcott, May 1, 1798.

4. *The Report and Estimate of Tench Coxe, Purveyor of Public Supplies*, June 7, 1798.

5. Whitney to Baldwin, May 27, 1798.

6. Whitney to Stebbins, Nov. 27, 1798.

7. Whitney admitted as much in his letter to Wolcott of Oct. 17, 1798, and again June 29, 1799. He had already admitted in a letter to Stebbins: "I have now taken a serious task upon myself and I fear a greater one than is in the power of any man to perform in the given time—but it is too late to go back."

8. Note that when Whitney had his plant fully established and his contract of 1798 was about to run out, he wrote to Major Rogers (Oct. 28, 1809) looking for a new contract: "I would contract to deliver 2000 or 2500 per year for seven or ten years." Experience had sobered his promises.

9. For a more complete analysis of the concept of interchangeable parts and for a detailed history of its development see the author's forthcoming monograph *History of Shop Precision of Measurement and Interchangeable Parts.*

10. C.E. Fuller, *The Whitney Firearms* (1946), p. 156.

11. Silliman, *loc. cit.*

12. For further details see R. S. Woodbury, *History of the Milling Machine* (Cambridge, Mass., 1960).

13. For this story see the author's forthcoming monograph *History of Shop Precision of Measurement and Interchangeable Parts.*

14. See J. E. Sawyer, "The Social Basis of the American System of Manufacturing," *Journal of Economic History* (1954), especially pp. 369-79.

18

Society in America

HARRIET MARTINEAU

. . . The young men of New England migrate in large numbers to the west, leaving an over-proportion of female population, the amount of which I could never learn. Statements were made to me; but so incredible that I withhold them. Suffice it that there are many more women than men in from six to nine States of the Union. There is reason to believe that there was much silent suffering from poverty before the institution of factories; that they afford a most welcome resource to some thousands of young women, unwilling to give themselves to domestic service, and precluded, by the customs of the country, from rural labour. . . .

The first cotton-mill that I saw was at Paterson, New Jersey. It was set up at first with nine hundred spindles, which were afterwards increased to fifteen hundred; then to six thousand. Building was still going on when I was there. The girls were all well-dressed. Their hair was arranged according to the latest fashions which had arrived, via New York, and they wore calashes in going to and fro between their dwellings and the mill. I saw some of the children barefooted, but carrying umbrellas, under a slight sprinkling of rain. I asked whether those who could afford umbrellas went barefoot for coolness, or other convenience. The proprietor told me that there had probably been an economical calculation in the case. Stockings

Harriet Martineau, *Society in America*, London, Saunders and Otley, 1837, vol. II, pp. 242-255.

and shoes would defend only the feet; while the umbrella would preserve the gloss of the whole of the rest of the costume. . . .

I visited the corporate factory-establishment at Waltham, within a few miles of Boston. The Waltham Mills were at work before those of Lowell were set up. The establishment is for the spinning and weaving of cotton alone, and the construction of the requisite machinery. Five hundred persons were employed at the time of my visit. The girls earn two, and some three, dollars a-week, besides their board. The little children earn one dollar a-week. Most of the girls live in the houses provided by the corporation, which accommodate from six to eight each. When sisters come to the mill, it is common practice for them to bring their mother to keep house for them and some of their companions, in a dwelling built by their own earnings. In this case, they save enough out of their board to clothe themselves, and have their two or three dollars a-week to spare. Some have thus cleared off mortgages from their fathers' farms; others have educated the hope of the family at college; and many are rapidly accumulating an independence. I saw a whole street of houses built with the earnings of the girls; some with piazzas, and green venetian blinds; and all neat and sufficiently spacious.

The factory people built the church, which stands conspicuous on the green in the midst of the place. The minister's salary (eight hundred dollars last year) is raised by a tax on the pews. The corporation gave them a building for a lyceum, which they have furnished with a good library, and where they have lectures every winter—the best that money can procure. The girls have, in many instances, private libraries of some merit and value.

The managers of the various factory establishments keep the wages as nearly equal as possible, and then let the girls freely shift about from one to another. When a girl comes to the overseer to inform him of her intention of working at the mill, he welcomes her, and asks how long she means to stay. It may be six months, or a year, or five years, or for life. She declares what she considers herself fit for, and sets to work accordingly. If she finds that she cannot work so as to keep up with the companion appointed to her, or to please her employer or herself, she comes to the overseer, and volunteers to pick cotton, or sweep the rooms, or undertake some other service that she can perform.

The people work about seventy hours per week, on the average. The time of work varies with the length of the days, the wages continuing the same. All look like well-dressed young ladies. The health is good; or rather (as this is too much to be said about health anywhere in the United States) it is no worse than it is elsewhere. . . .

The shoe-making at Lynn is carried on almost entirely in private dwellings, from the circumstance that the people who do it are almost all farmers or fishermen likewise. A stranger who has not been enlightened upon the ways of the place would be astonished at the number of small square erections, like miniature school-houses, standing each as an appendage to a dwelling-house. These are the "shoe shops," where the father of the family and his boys work, while the women within are employed in binding and trimming. Thirty or more of these shoe-shops may be counted in a walk of half-a-mile. When a Lynn shoe manufacturer receives an order, he issues the tidings. The leather is cut out by men on his premises; and then the work is given to those who apply for it; if possible, in small quantities, for the sake of dispatch. The shoes are brought home on Friday night, packed off on Saturday, and in a fortnight or three weeks are on the feet of dwellers in all parts of the Union. The whole family works upon shoes during the winter; and in the summer, the father and sons turn out into the fields, or go fishing. I knew of an instance where a little boy and girl maintained the whole family, while the earnings of the rest went to build a house. . . .

There seems to be no doubt among those who know both England and America, that the mechanics of the New World work harder than those of the Old. They have much to do besides their daily handicraft business. They are up and at work early about this; and when it is done, they read till late, or attend lectures; or perhaps have their houses to build or repair, or other care to take of their property. They live in a state and period of society where every man is answerable for his own fortunes; and where there is therefore stimulus to the exercise of every power. . . .

There are troubles between employers and their workmen in the United States, as elswhere; but the case of the men is so much more in their own hands there than where labour superabounds, that strikes are of a very short duration. The only remedy the employers have, the only safeguard against encroachments from their men, is their power of obtaining the services of foreigners, for a short time. The difficulty of stopping business there is very great; the injury of delay very heavy: but the wages of labour are so good that there is less cause for discontent on the part of the workmen than elsewhere. All the strikes I heard of were on the question of hours, not of wages. . . .

19

Railroads as an Analogy
to the Space Effort:
Some Economic Aspects

ROBERT W. FOGEL

Introduction[1]

Viewed as an investment, the central issue posed by the space effort is: Will the increase in national income made possible by the space program exceed the increase in income that would be obtained if the same resources were invested in other activities? To answer this question one has to know the increment to national revenue that will follow from space activities in all future years. Given this information, the present value of the stream of returns can be computed and compared with the cost of the program. If the present value of the returns exceeds the cost then it should, from the purely

Robert W. Fogel, "Railroads as an Analogy to the Space Effort: Some Economic Aspects," is abridged from the chapter in *The Railroad and the Space Program; An Exploration in Historical Analogy*, ed. by Bruce Mazlish, M.I.T. Press, 1976, pp. 74-106. Reprinted by permission of the American Academy of Arts and Sciences, © 1976.

economic view, be undertaken. If not, it should, on the same view, be abandoned. Of course, it is possible that political or military factors might dictate a course of action different from that implied by purely economic considerations. Political and military issues, however, are beyond the scope of this chapter.

If a study of the influence of railroads on American economic growth is to contribute to an evaluation of the investment decisions posed by the space effort, two conditions must be met. First, the analysis of railroads must focus on the incremental contribution of this innovation. Discussions merely of things the railroad did are of no use unless we know whether these services represent more or less than would have been contributed by alternative investments. Second, one must be able to show how the effects of the space program may conform to, or deviate from, the types of effects attributable to railroads both in magnitude and in quality. While this chapter focuses primarily on the first of the aforementioned conditions, a concluding section will deal with some aspects of the second one.

From an economic point of view the central or primary feature of the railroad was its impact on the cost of inland transportation. Obviously, if the cost of rail service had exceeded the cost of equivalent service by alternative forms of transportation over all routes, and for all items, railroads would not have been built and all of their derived consequences would have been absent. The derived consequences of railroads can be divided into two categories. The "disembodied" consequences are those that followed from the saving in transportation costs per se and which would have been induced by any innovation that lowered transportation costs by approximately the amount attributable to railroads. The "embodied" consequences are those that are attributable to the specific form in which the railroads provided cheap transportation services.

The Effect of Railroads on the Availability of Resources

The change in the availability of resources is perhaps the most important of the disembodied effects of the railroad. Of course, all parts of the nation would have been physically penetrable even in the absence of railroads. However, without this innovation the cost of transportation to and from some areas might have been so great that, from an economic point of view, large sections of the land mass would have been nearly as isolated as the moon is from the earth. By reducing the cost of transportation, railroads increased *the economic accessibility* of various parts of the natural endowment of the United States. The question is: Which endowments were so affected and by how much?

Agricultural Land

Agricultural land was the most valuable of the natural resources of the United States in 1890. It was also more widely dispersed than coal, iron ore, oil, and other mineral deposits. Land in farms occupied one-third of the national territory in 1890. . . . One would expect to find that railroads were more essential in obtaining access to farmland than to other resources.

Even in the case of farmland . . . certain factors suggest that the incremental contribution of railroads was limited. One of these is the experience of the half century following the ratification of the Constitution. The occupation not only of the territory east of the Appalachians but also of that lying between the Appalachians and the Mississippi River was well under way before the coming of the railroad. As Kent T. Healy has pointed out, it was "water transportation, available first on natural waterways and later on canals" which made possible the "astonishing redistribution of population and economic activity" during the first four decades of the nineteenth century. By 1840, "before a single railroad had penetrated that area from the coast, some 40 per cent of the nation's people lived west of New York, Pennsylvania and the coastal states of the South."[2] . . .

The fact that the initial occupation of the trans-Appalachian lands was based almost exclusively on waterways is suggestive; but it by no means proves that waterways could have sustained later developments. The acreage of agricultural land in the North and South Central states underwent a fourfold expansion between 1850 and 1890.[3] It is therefore necessary to devise a method of determining how much of the land settled after the advent of railroads would have been settled in their absence.

Without railroads the high cost of wagon transportation would have limited commercial agricultural production to areas of land lying within some unknown distance of navigable waterways. It is possible to use the theory of rent to establish these boundaries of feasible commercial agriculture in a nonrail society. Rent is a measure of the amount by which the return to labor and capital on a given portion of land exceeds the return the same factors could earn if they were employed at the intensive or extensive margins. Therefore, any plot of land capable of commanding a rent will be kept in productive activity. It follows that, even in the face of increased transportation costs, a given area of farmland will remain in use as long as the increased costs incurred during a given time period do not exceed the original rental value of that land.

Given information on the quantity of goods shipped between farms and their markets, the distances from farms to rail and water shipping points, the distances from such shipping points to markets, and the wagon, rail and water rates, it is possible to compute the additional transportation cost that would have been incurred if farmers attempted to duplicate their actual shipping pattern without railroads. In such a situation shipping costs would have risen not because boat rates exceeded rail rates but because it usually required more wagon transportation to reach a boat, than a rail shipping point. In other words, farms immediately adjacent to navigable waterways would have been least affected by the absence of rail service. The further a farm was from a navigable waterway the greater the amount of wagon transportation it would have required. At some distance from waterways the additional wagon haul would have increased the cost of shipping by an amount exactly equal to the original rental value of the land. Such a farm would represent a point on the boundary of feasible commercial agriculture. Consequently, the full boundary can be established by finding all those points from which the increased cost of shipping by alternative means the quantities that were actually carried by railroads is equal to the original rental value of the land.

This approach, it should be noted, leads to an overstatement of the amount of land falling beyond the "true feasible" boundary. A computation based on the actual mix of products shipped does not allow for adjustments to a nonrail technology. In the absence of railroads the mix of agricultural products would have changed in response to the altered structure of transportation rates. Such a response would have lowered shipping costs and hence extended the boundary. The computation also ignores the consequence on the level of prices of a cessation in agricultural production in areas beyond the feasible region. Given the relative inelasticity of the demand for agriculture products the prices of such commodities would have risen in the absence of railroads. The rise in prices would have led to a more intensive exploitation of agriculture within the feasible region, thus raising land values. The rise in land values would have increased the burden of additional transportation costs that could have been borne and shifted the boundary of feasible commercial agriculture further away from water shipping points.[4]

The method outlined above has been used to establish the boundary of feasible commercial agriculture for 1890. In this year the relative advantage of railroads over alternative forms of transportation was probably greatest. During the half century that preceded it, increases in productivity reduced the cost of railroad transportation more rapidly than that of boats and wagons. The selected year also precedes the emergence of motor vehicles as an effective alternative. It thus appears likely that the incremental contribution of railroads to the accessibility of agricultural lands was at or near its apex in 1890.

Analysis of the relevant data indicates that in the absence of railroads the boundary of feasible commercial agricultural would have been located at an average of about forty "airline" miles from navigable waterways. Forty-mile boundaries drawn around all natural waterways used for navigation in 1890, as well as all canals built prior to that date, brought less than half of the land mass of the United States into the feasible region.[5] However, as Table 1 indicates, the feasible region includes 76 per cent of all agricultural land by value. The discrepancy is explained by the fact that over one-third of the United States was located between the hundredth meridian and the Sierra Nevada Mountains. While this vast area fell almost entirely beyond the feasible range, it was of extremely limited usefulness for agricultural purposes. By value the area represented only 2 per cent of all agricultural land in use in 1890.

Table 1 also shows that barely one-quarter of 1 per cent of the lost agricultural land was located in the North Atlantic region, while only 6 per cent was in the Mountain states. About 75 per cent of the loss was concentrated in the North Central region. Indeed more than half of all the land lost by value was located in just four states: Illinois, Iowa, Nebraska, and Kansas. This finding does not support the frequently met contention that railroads were essential to the commercial exploitation of the prairies. The prairies were occupied at a time when the railroad had achieved clear technological superiority over canals. Consequently, the movement for canals that played so important a part in the development of the Eastern states was aborted in the prairies. The fact that major loss of land was concentrated in a compact area suggests an entirely different conclusion: a relatively small extension of the canal system would have brought into the feasible region most of the productive land that Table 1 puts outside of it.

Indeed, it would have been possible to build in the North and South Central states a system of thirty-seven canals and feeders totaling five thousand miles. These canals would have reduced the loss of agricultural land occasioned by the absence of railroads to just 7 per cent of the national total. The system would have been technologically feasible and economically profitable. Built across the flatlands of the middle west, the average rise and fall per mile of the proposed waterways would have been less than that which prevailed on all canals successful enough to survive railroad competition through 1890. The water supply would have been more than ample. And in the absence of railroads, the social rate of return on the cost of constructing the system would have exceeded 45 per cent per annum.[6]

The loss in agricultural land could have been further reduced by improvements in common roads. According to estimates published by the Office of Public Roads in 1895, regrading and resurfacing of public roads

Table 1: **Farmland lying beyond the feasible region of agriculture, 1890* (thousands of dollars)**

Region*	1 Value of farmland 1890	2 Value of farmland beyond feasible region 1890	3 Column 2 as per- centage of column 1	4 Value of land beyond feasible region as percentage of value of all agricultural land
North Atlantic	1,092,281	5,637	0.5	0.07
South Atlantic	557,399	117,866	21.1	1.45
North Central	4,931,607	1,441,952	29.2	17.75
South Central	738,333	158,866	21.5	1.96
Mountain	129,655	123,016	94.9	1.51
Pacific	671,297	95,200	14.2	1.17
United States	8,120,572	1,942,537	23.9	23.91

* For sources and method of computation see Fogel, *op. cit.*, Chapter 3, especially Table 3.7.

† The states included in each of the regions are *North Atlantic:* Maine, New Hampshire, Vermont, Massachusetts, Rhode Island, Connecticut, New York, New Jersey, Pennsylvania; *South Atlantic:* Delaware, Maryland, District of Columbia, Virginia, West Virginia, North Carolina, South Carolina, Georgia, Florida; *North Central:* Ohio, Indiana, Illinois, Michigan, Wisconsin, Minnesota, Iowa, Missouri, North Dakota, South Dakota, Nebraska, Kansas; *South Central:* Kentucky, Tennessee, Alabama, Mississippi, Louisiana, Texas, Arkansas; *Mountain:* Montana, Wyoming, Colorado, New Mexico, Arizona, Utah, Nevada, Idaho; *Pacific:* Washington, Oregon, California.

could have reduced the cost of wagon transportation by 50 per cent. This implies that the boundary of feasible commercial agricultural would have fallen eighty miles from navigable waterways. Together with the proposed canals, road improvements would thus have reduced the loss of agricultural land to a mere 4 per cent of the amount actually used in 1890.[7]

It thus appears that while railroads did increase the availability of agricultural land, their incremental contribution was—even at the apex of railroad influence—quite small.

Iron Ore and Coal

Unlike agricultural land, which in 1890 occupied nearly one million square miles of territory in over two thousand countries in every state of the nation, the mining of iron ore was highly localized. . . .

As for the Lake Superior ores, their exploitation, beginning in 1854, preceded the construction of railroads in the northern parts of Michigan and Wisconsin. Five years later, although the region was still without railroad service, its mines accounted for over 4 per cent of the national production of iron ore.[8] . . .

Many of the smaller deposits of iron ore were also well located with respect to water transportation. . . .

The production of coal, like that of iron ore, was highly localized. Nine states accounted for about 90 per cent of all coal shipped from mines in 1890. And within these states production was further localized in a relative handful of counties. Forty-six counties shipped 76,000,000 tons—75 per cent of all of the coal sent from mines in the nine states. Moreover, all these counties were traversed by navigable rivers, canals actually constructed, or the proposed canals discussed above. In this case, too, many of the smaller deposits were well located with respect to water transportation.[9] Hence, it seems likely that a nonrail society could have had low-cost access to all of the coal it required.

The Position of Railroads in the Market for Manufactured Products

While the railroad was the chief vehicle by which late nineteenth-century society actually achieved access to natural resources, other mediums could have fulfilled essentially the same function. However, the low-cost services of these alternative forms of transportation were embodied in forms of equipment and structures different from those characteristic of railroads. Hence, it is still possible that railroads profoundly affected the course of economic growth because of the specific inputs, particularly of manufactured goods, required to produce railroad services.

Railroad input requirements could have affected the productivity of manufacturing in two ways. First, the railroad's incremental consumption of the output of various industries could have been so large that it moved these industries to a level of production permitting significant economies of scale. Second, the railroads could, uniquely, have induced changes in the technology of manufacturing processes that affected the production not only of railroad goods but also of goods consumed by other sectors of the economy. This section examines the first line of possible influence. The next section deals with the nexus between railroads and technological innovation.

The Ante Bellum Period

Iron is frequently cited as the classic ante bellum case of an industry raised to modern status by railroad purchases. Hofstadter, Miller, and Aaron, for example, report that the railroad was "by far the biggest user of iron in the 1850's," and that by 1860 "more than half the iron produced annually in the United States went into rails" and associated items.[10] Such statements, however, are not based on systematic measurements but on questionable inferences derived from isolated scraps of data. Casual procedures have led to the use of an index that grossly exaggerates the rail share, to the neglect of the rerolling process, and to a failure to consider the significance of the scrapping process. . . .

The neglect of the replacement process has also served to exaggerate the importance of railroads in the market for iron. Replacements became a major factor in rail consumption very early in the history of railroads. In fifteen of the thirty years following 1839, replacements represented more than 40 per cent of total rail requirements; in five of these years replacements accounted for two-thirds of requirements. However, most replaced rails were scrapped. The availability of such scrap metal spurred the development of the rerolling of old rails. As early as 1849, one-fourth of all domestically produced rails were rerolled from discarded ones. By 1860, rerolling accounted for nearly 60 per cent of domestic rail production.[11] Thus, although replacements rapidly became a substantial part of total rail consumption, replacement demand had little effect on the growth of blast furnaces. Replacements generated their own supply of crude iron. And scrapped rails that were not rerolled supplanted pig iron as an input in the production of other products.

When corrections are made for the bias of traditional indices, and when account is taken of the replacement process, it turns out that the net addition to pig-iron production attributable to rails during 1840-1860 amounted to less than 5 per cent of the output of blast furnaces. The significance of the railroads appears somewhat greater if account is taken of all forms of railroad consumption of iron from all sectors of the iron industry. On this basis railroads accounted for an average of 17 per cent of total iron production during the two decades in question. While it is true that the railroad share rose to 25 per cent in the final six years of the period, more germane is the fact that during the quinquennium ending in 1849 railroad consumption of domestic crude iron was just 10 per cent of the total. Even if there had been no production of rails or railroad equipment whatsoever, the domestic crude iron consumed by the iron industry would have reached an average of 700,000 tons in the second quinquennium. The rise over the previous quinquennium would still have been 338,000 tons— an increase of 94 per cent, as opposed to the 99 per cent rise that took place with the railroads. Clearly the new high level of production attained by the iron industry during 1845-1849 did not depend on the railroad market.[12]

Furthermore, the demand for iron by industries other than railroads was more than adequate to permit a firm size capable of realizing the economies of scale in the production of nonrailroad iron that were actually achieved prior to 1860. The average capacity of blast furnaces prior to the Civil War was 4,800 tons; and the capacity of the largest furnace was under 10,000 tons. Similarly, except for rolling mills engaged exclusively in the rolling of rails, no firm appears to have produced more than 13,000 tons; but even if one assumes that the optimum firm capacity was 20,000 tons (the product of the largest rail firm in 1856 was 18,600 tons), the nonrail production of rolled iron at the time would have permitted seventeen firms of such size.[13]

Railroads occupied an even more modest position in the markets of other ante bellum manufacturing industries. In the case of lumber, railroads purchased a minuscule share of total output—this despite the large quantities of wood consumed as fuel and in the construction of track. . . .

The share of the output of the transportation equipment industry purchased by railroads is also surprising. From 1850 through 1860 some 26,300 miles of new track were laid. During the same time, about 3,800 locomotives, 6,400 passenger and baggage cars, and 88,600 freight cars were constructed. Yet, value added in the construction of railroad equipment in 1859 was only $12,000,000, or 25.4 per cent of value added by all transportation equipment. The output of vehicles drawn by animals was still almost twice as great as the output of equipment for the celebrated iron horse.[14]

As for other types of machinary, railroads directly consumed less than 1 per cent. Again, the situation does not change appreciably if indirect purchases at more remote levels of production are considered. . . .

The transportation-equipment, rolling-mill, blast-furnace, lumber, and machinery industries were the main suppliers of the manufactured goods purchased by railroads. Using value added as a measure, railroads purchased slightly less than 11 per cent of the combined output of the group in 1859. Since these industries accounted for 26 per cent of all manufacturing in that year, railroad purchases from them amounted to a mere 2.8 per cent of the total output of the manufacturing sector. Railroad purchases from all the other manufacturing industries raised the last figure to just 3.9 per cent.[15] This amount hardly seems large enough to attribute the rapid growth of manufacturing during the last two ante bellum decades to the requirements for building and maintaining railway systems.

The Post-Civil War Era

Since the real capital stock of railroads increased at approximately the same rate as the real output of manufacturing, a detailed survey of changes in the position of the railroad in the market of most industries between 1859 and 1899 need not be undertaken in this paper.[16] The iron and steel industry, however, requires further consideration. It is frequently said that the introduction of the Bessemer process radically reduced the cost of producing steel and ushered that industry into a new era. As measured by value added, the production of basic steel products rose from 4 per cent of the output of the iron industry in 1859 to 23 per cent in 1880.[17] Moreover, the consumption of steel was dominated by rails. . . . In 1871 some 52 per cent of all steel ingots were consumed in the production of rails. The rail share rose steadily from that date until 1881, when it stood at 87 per cent, after which it declined to 50 per cent in 1890.

The fact that the rail share of steel production fluctuated between 50 and 87 per cent for a period of twenty years suggests that the market for rails was indispensable to the emergence of a modern steel industry in the United States. This opinion also seems to have been nourished by the inverse relationship between the average output of Bessemer mills and the prices of the products of these mills (see Table 2), a relationship that suggests economies of scale.

There is, however, another way of looking at the data contained in Table 2. Stress on the share of total output consumed by rails in any given year beclouds the extremely rapid rate at which nonrail steel consumption grew and the rapidity with which that type of consumption exceeded the total steel production of a given year. . . . The time required for the nonrail consumption of steel to exceed the total production of a given year varied from two to nine years, the average being about six years. Consequently, if the nonrail demand for steel was inelastic over the range of price involved,

Table 2: **The average product of Bessemer steel mills and the average price of steel rails**

Year	1 *Average product of Bessemer mills (in thousands of net tons)*	2 *Average price of Bessemer steel rails in dollars of 1890 (dollars per net ton)*
1870	21	73
1880	90	62
1890	99	36

Column 1: The 1870 entry refers to a calendar year while the entries for 1880 and 1890 represent production in census years. In computing average product, furnaces using the Clapp-Griffith and Robert-Bessemer processes were excluded. Thomas Dunlap, ed., *Wiley's Iron Trade Manual* (New York, 1874), p. 187; A.I.S.A., *Annual Report*, 1896, p. 69; *Eleventh Census, Manufacturing*, Part III, pp. 411-412.

Column 2: Calendar year prices were deflated by the Warren-Pearson wholesale index. The current dollar prices for the three years were $120, $76, and $36 per net ton. A.I.S.A., *Annual Report*, 1896, p. 84; U.S. Bureau of the Census, *Historical Statistics of the United States, Colonial Time to 1957* (Washington, D.C.; 1960), p. 115.

the observed scale of operations could have been achieved with an average lag of six years even in the absence of rails.

It is possible to estimate the maximum gain to the nation made possible by rail-induced economies of scale. The computation turns on the availability of the open-hearth furnace. The optimum plant size of the open-hearth mill was about one-tenth that of a Bessemer mill.[18] In 1880, open-hearth mills had an average production of only 3,500 net tons; in 1890, the average product was 9,000 net tons.[19]

If the absence of rails reduced the scale of operation to such a level that the cost of Bessemer steel exceeded the cost of open-hearth steel, consumers of Bessemer steel would have made their purchases from open-hearth mills. Hence the maximum gain to society from the economies of scale in Bessemer plants induced by rails was the price differential between Bessemer and open-hearth steel. In 1880, the average differential in the delivered price of Bessemer and open-hearth steel was $10.19 per ton. Nonrail consumption of Bessemer steel was 112,200 net tons. Hence the maximum gain due to economies of scale induced by the railroad in the production of nonrail steel was only $1,144,000, or 0.01 per cent of gross national product. By 1890, the average price differential fell to $4.02 per ton, while the production of nonrail Bessemer steel rose to 1,740,000 net tons. The indicated maximum gain attributable to railroad-induced economies of scale in 1890 is thus $6,995,000, or 0.06 per cent of gross national product.[20]

It appears that a modern steel industry would have emerged even in the absence of a demand for rails. While the increase in the scale of operations may have lagged behind that actually observed, it does not appear likely that the average lag would have exceeded six years. In any case, the maximum social loss of a slower growth in the scale of operations would have been barely one-twentieth of 1 per cent of gross national product. . . .

The Effect of Railroads on Technological Innovations

In discussing the effect of railroads on the introduction and diffusion of inventions, a distinction has to be drawn between innovations limited exclusively, or largely, to the operation of railroads and innovations that had a major impact outside of the railroad industry. The former category of devices will be denoted by the term "restricted," the latter by the term "transcending."

Most inventions which arose out of the operation or construction of railroads fall into the category of restricted devices. Such items as air brakes, block signals, car trucks, automatic-coupling devices, track switches, pullman cars, and equalizing bars were mere appurtenances. While they may have been important to the efficient operation of railroads, they had no significant application outside of this industry during the nineteenth century. Nor did the railroads' demand for these items induce the rise of industries or production processes of transcending economic significance. They made no independent contribution to economic growth. Rather they defined the conditions under which railroads operated— conditions that in varying degrees explain how it was that railroads were able to produce low-cost transportation service.

There are, however, certain innovations associated with railroads to which transcending significance has been attached, and which therefore require further consideration. The two that will be considered here are cheap methods of producing steel, and the telegraph.

The belief that the railroads' demand for improved rails was responsible for the inventions that led to low-cost steel production rests on shaky foundations. It was not the problem of how to produce better rails that led Henry Bessemer into the series of experiments that eventuated in the Bessemer converter. As J. S. Jeans has pointed out, Bessemer's experiments stemmed from a desire to improve the effectiveness of artillery. A major obstacle to such improvement was the inadequacy of cast iron for cannon firing heavy projectiles. Bessemer pursued his research on metallurgy with the aim of "producing a quality of metal more suitable than any other for the construction of heavy ordnance."[21] William Kelly, who independently discovered the Bessemer process in the United States, was engaged not in the production of heavy rolled forms but in the production of cast-iron kettles.[22] And the immediate factor that stimulated the Siemens brothers to develop the open-hearth furnace was their desire to find industrial applications for their earler discovery, the regenerative condenser.[23]

The point is that metallurgical research in the mid-nineteenth century was induced by the rapidly growing demand for iron in a wide variety of production processes. Cheap steel had potential marketability not only for the fabrication of rails but also for ships, boilers, bridges, buildings, ordnance, armor, springs, wire, forgings, castings, chains, cutlery, etc. Metallurgical innovators could have been, and were, lured to search for improved products and processes by the profit that was to be earned from sales in all markets for iron, and not just in the railroad market.

It is, of course, true that during the initial decades following the discovery of the Bessemer process, most of the steel that poured from converters was destined for the fabrication of rails. From 1867 to 1883, about 80 per cent of all Bessemer steel ingots were so consumed.[24] This fact seems to suggest that railroads played an essential role in making cheap steel available on a large scale. . . .

But in fact some Bessemer steel was used for nonrail products. In 1880, 8.9 per cent of all such metal was turned into bars; 5.7 per cent into rods; 0.2 per cent into structural shapes, sheets, and boiler or other plate. In total, 169,645 net tons of Bessemer steel were rolled into products other than rails.[25] While some of these shapes were also consumed by railroads, it may be assumed that the bulk are not. . . .

At the time when Bessemer steel was most rapidly displacing wrought iron as the basic raw material for rails, it was unable to dislodge wrought iron from its dominance as an input in the production of other products of rolling mills. According to Peter Temin, Bessemer steel "was subject to mysterious breakages and fractures that made people prefer iron" for most nonrail purposes.[26]

In later years the fall in the relative price of steel led to a situation in which most rolling-mill products were made from this material. By 1909, over 89 per cent of rolling-mill output other than rails was made from steel. However, most of this steel came not from converters but from open hearths. In the production of those forms for which demand was increasing most rapidly—plates, sheets, structural shapes, wire, etc.—open-hearth steel was preferred because of its superior qualities and its competitive price.[27]

Thus superior alternatives to Bessemer steel for nonrail uses were available at comparable prices through the end of the nineteenth century. Bessemer steel does not appear to have provided the basis for the remarkable growth of productivity in other industries that it did in the railroad sector.[28] Although the rapid expansion of Bessemer production between 1867 and 1890 is attributable to the market for rails, the Bessemer process appears to have been a restricted rather than a transcending innovation.

Unlike the case of Bessemer steel there was little connection between the railroads and the early growth of the telegraph industry in the United States. The first telegraph line was established in 1844. Just eight years later the nation was laced with lines totaling 17,000 miles.[29] By 1852, the telegraph network connected all of the major eastern and southern cities. St. Louis, Milwaukee, Chicago, Detroit, and Toledo had telegraphic connection with the Atlantic coast well before the completion of the railroad link. . . .

The demand that induced the remarkably rapid rate of construction emanated not from railroads but from other businesses. Bankers, stock brokers, commodity brokers, and newspapers were the largest purchasers of telegraphic service.[30] The railroads did not try to employ the new device systematically until the basic wire network had been completed. The Erie Railroad, which began to use the telegraph for the dispatching of trains in 1851, was the first to do so. Despite its successful experience, most other railroads did not immediately become convinced of the advantages of the system. . . .

What then is the basis for the view that railroads played a fundamental role in the growth and diffusion of the telegraph? It appears to rest primarily on the operating efficiencies achieved as a result of the alliance between the two systems. Once the alliance was formed, telegraph companies could utilize railroad men "to watch the line, straighten poles, re-set them when down, mend wires and report to the telegraph company."[31] Consequently, by making use of railroad trackwalkers and other railroad maintenance men, telegraph companies were able to reduce maintenance costs below what they would have been. Such savings were, no doubt, reflected in lower rates that probably stimulated the growth of telegraphic service. Given the existence of railroads, the telegraph was no doubt aided by the alliance. However, it by no means follows that the observed rate of growth of the telegraph industry was higher than it would have been in the absence of railroads. It must be remembered that by speeding up the distribution of mail, railroads provided consumers with a better substitute for the telegraph than would otherwise have been available. . . .

The Social Saving of Railroads[32]

It is possible to set an upper limit on the increase in national income attributable to the reduction in transportation costs made possible by railroads. The main conceptual device used in this computation is the "social saving." The social saving in any given year is defined as the difference between the actual cost of shipping goods in that year and the alternative cost of shipping exactly the same goods between exactly the same points without railroads. This cost differential is in fact larger than the "true" social saving. Forcing the pattern of shipments in a nonrail situation to conform to the pattern that actually existed is equivalent to the imposition of a restraint on society's freedom to adjust in an alternative technological situation. If society had had to ship by water and wagon without the railroad, it could have altered the geographical locus of production in a manner that would have economized on transport services. Further, the sets of primary and secondary markets through which commodities were distributed were surely influenced by conditions peculiar to rail transportation; in the absence of railroads some different cities would have entered these sets, and the relative importance of those remaining would have changed. Adjustments of this sort would have reduced the loss of national income occasioned by the absence of the railroad. . . .

Using . . . estimates of tonnages shipped, rates and distances it appears that the actual cost of the interregional agricultural transportation in 1890 was \$87,500,000, while the cost of transporting the same goods by water would have been only \$49,200,000. In other words, the first approximation of the interregional social saving is negative by about \$38,000,000. This odd result is the consequence of the fact that direct payments to railroads included virtually all of the cost of interregional transportation, while direct payments to water carriers did not. In calculating the cost of shipping without the railroad one must account for six additional items of cost not included in payments to water carriers. These items are cargo losses in transit, transshipment costs, wagon-haulage costs from water points to secondary markets not on waterways, capital costs not reflected in water rates, the cost resulting from the time lost when using a slow medium of transportation, and the cost of being unable to use water routes for five months of the year. . . .

When account is taken of the neglected costs, the negative first approximation is transformed into a positive social saving of \$73,00,000 (see Table 3). Since the actual 1890 cost of shipping the specified commodities was approximately \$88,000,000, the absence of the railroad would have almost doubled the cost of shipping agricultural commodities

Table 3: **The social saving in the interregional distribution of agricultural commodities**

First approximation	$ –38,000,000
Neglected cargo losses	6,000,000
Transshipping	16,000,000
Supplementary wagon haulage	23,000,000
Neglected capital costs	18,000,000
Additional inventory costs	48,000,000
Total	$ 73,000,000

interregionally. It is therefore quite easy to see why the great bulk of agricultural commodities was actually sent to the East by rail, with water transportation used only over a few favorable routes.

While the interregional social saving is large compared to the actual transportation cost, it is quite small compared to annual output of the economy—just six-tenths of 1 per cent of gross national product. Hence, the computed social saving indicates that the availability of railroads for the interregional distribution of agricultural products represented only a relatively small addition to the production potential of the economy. . . .

. . . The entire first approximation of the alpha estimate of the social saving—which amounts to $300,000,000—is attributable not to the fact that railroad charges were less than boat charges but to the fact that railroads reduced the amount of expensive wagon haulage that had to be combined with one of the low-cost forms of transportation. . . .

Three indirect costs do have to be added to the first approximation. These are cargo losses, the cost of using a slow medium of transportation, and the cost of the limited season of navigation. . . . These neglected items amount to only $37,000,000, which, when added to the first approximation, yields a preliminary alpha estimate of $337,000,000, or 2.8 per cent of gross national product.

The preliminary estimate of the agricultural social saving is based on the severe assumption that in the absence of railroads all other aspects of technology would have been unaltered. It seems quite likely, however, that in the absence of railroads much of the capital and ingenuity that went into their perfection and spread would have been turned toward the development of other cheap forms of land transportation. Under these circumstances it is possible that the internal-combustion engine would have been developed years sooner than it actually was, thus permitting a reduction in transportation costs through the use of motor trucks.

While most such possibilities of a speed-up in the introduction and spread of alternative forms of transportation have not been sufficiently explored to permit meaningful quantification at the present time, there are two changes about which one can make fairly definitive statements. These are the extension of the existing system of internal waterways, and the improvement of common roads. Neither of these developments required new knowledge. They merely involved an extension of existing technology.

As has already been pointed out, in the absence of railroads it would have been technologically and commercially feasible to build canals in the North and South Central states. A five-thousand-mile system of such canals would have brought all but 7 per cent of agricultural land within forty "airline" miles of a navigable waterway. In so doing, these waterways would have reduced the combined inter- and intraregional social saving from $410,000,000 to $287,000,000. Similarly, improvement of roads could have cut the cost of wagon transportation by 39 per cent, thus still further reducing the total agriculture social saving to $214,000,000. . . .

It is probable that 35 per cent of the $214,000,000 should be assigned to the social saving induced by railroads in transporting products of mines, forest, and factories. In other words, the "pure" agricultural social saving is about $140,000,000. Given that 20,000,000,000 ton-miles of railroad service were required for the shipment of agricultural commodities in 1890, the agricultural social saving per ton-mile of railroad service was $0.0070.

Second, available evidence suggests that the social saving per ton-mile was less on nonagricultural products than on agricultural ones. Products of mines dominated the nonagricultural commodities carried by railroads. Coal alone represented 35 per cent of the nonagricultural tonnage in 1890. Iron and other ores brought the mineral share to over 50 per cent. As has previously been shown, a relatively small extension of the canal system could have brought most mines into direct contact with waterways. Thus, very little supplementary wagon transportation would have been required on these items. Moreover, the cost of increasing inventories to compensate for the slowness of, and interruptions in, water transportation would have been quite low. The total value of products of mines was well below the value of the agricultural commodities shipped from farms. As a consequence, the opportunity cost of the increased inventories of minerals would have been well below that found for agriculture. Additional storage charges, if any, would have been trivial. Minerals required neither very expensive storage facilities nor shelters. They were stored on open docks or fields.

These general considerations are supported by estimates compiled by Albert Fishlow, which reveal that in 1860 the social saving per ton-mile on nonagricultural commodities was only 46 per cent of that for agricultural goods.[33] This ratio applied to the figure of $0.0070 indicates that in the case of nonagricultural freight the social saving per ton-mile in 1890 was $0.0032. On this basis the social saving made possible by the

59,000,000,000 ton-miles of nonagricultural freight service provided by railroads in 1890 was $189,000,000. The last figure added to the "pure" agricultural saving yields a total of $329,000,000 on all commodities. Thus, the availability of railroads for the transportation of commodities appears to have increased the production potential of the economy by about 3 per cent of gross national product.

Implications for the Space Effort[34]

If space activities should make a major contribution to economic growth it seems highly unlikely that this will take the same form as the contribution made by railroads. The central feature of the developmental impact of the railroads was not so much that they induced or made possible new economic activities but that by reducing transportation costs they facilitated processes and activities which were well under way prior to their advent. The cheap form of inland transportation service purveyed by railroads speeded the commercialization of agriculture, widened the market for manufactured goods, and promoted regional specialization. While the scope of these effects and the net benefit accruing to the economy from them was much less than is usually presumed, they were nonetheless large enough to warrant the investment made in railroads. . . .

With respect to the development of technology, the experience of the railroads offers little basis for assuming that the devices required for space transportation will lead to innovations that markedly affect productive techniques in other spheres of activity. Most of the devices invented to improve railroads had no significant applications outside of this industry. And in the case of Bessemer steel, a product with many applications that was clearly promoted by railroad requirements, the economy independently produced an extremely effective substitute, namely, open-hearth steel.

It is also important to keep in mind that the huge investment devoted to railroad construction may, by diverting resources, have retarded technological development in other fields. A case in point is the relatively late realization of commercially useful motor vehicles. The decisions that led society to invest billions of dollars in railroads between 1830 and 1890 while allocating paltry sums to the perfection of motor vehicles may have delayed the advent of motor transportation by several decades. . . .

. . . One cannot at this point foreclose the possibility that in the absence of railroads more capital and talent would have been devoted to the perfection of the horseless carriage, and that as a result the engineering knowledge and technical skills required to produce effective motor vehicles would have emerged decades sooner than they actually did. In weighing the benefits of technological innovations such as telemetry, compact power sources, reinforced plastics, and new metal alloys that have been induced or accelerated by the space effort, one must take into account alternative devices that could have been developed if the resources devoted to the space effort had been applied to other activities.

The preceding discussion does not necessarily imply that the space effort will fail to contribute to the expansion of the nation's production potential. There is a very important asymmetry between the railroads and rockets. While railroads increased the area of economically accessible territory, it did not affect physical accessibility. All parts of the earth's surface were penetrable before the invention of railroads. Indeed the various territories of the world were explored by man before they were traversed by rails. It is impossible, however, to explore the solar system without rocket ships. The development of spacecraft, unlike the railroad, thus offers man access to knowledge that cannot be obtained in any other way. The knowledge gained from space exploration may have enormous consequences for the biological and physical sciences. The advances in these sciences made possible by space exploration may in turn lead to a technological and commercial revolution far more portentous than that which followed from the scientific breakthroughs of the seventeenth, eighteenth, and nineteenth centuries. In this respect the space effort has a chance of affecting economic life far more radically than did the railroads. Examination of the railroad experience cannot aid in predicting the value of the scientific knowledge that may be gained from space exploration.

Endnotes

1. This chapter draws on concepts and empirical findings developed in my book, *Railroads and American Economic Growth: Essays in Econometric History* (Baltimore: The Johns Hopkins Press, 1964). I am grateful to The Johns Hopkins Press for permitting me to make use of these findings, I have also benefited from comments by Raymond Bauer, Albert Fishlow, Edward Furash, Bruce Mazlish, and Peter Temin.

2. Kent T. Healy, "American Transportation before the War between the States," *The Growth of the American Economy*, ed. Harold F. Williamson (New York: Prentice-Hall, 1944), p. 187.

3. *Eleventh Census, Agricultural*, pp. 92, 100.

4. For a more detailed discussion of the theoretical issues involved in, and of the computational methods employed for, the establishment of the feasible boundary see Fogel, *op. cit.*, Chapter 3.

5. A map of the area falling within the feasible region is given in *ibid.*, Figure 3.4.

6. *Ibid.*, pp. 92-100, 218.

7. *Ibid.*, p. 110.

8. Dunlap, *op. cit.*, p. 462; U.S. Bureau of the Census, *Eighth Census of the United States, 1860: Manufactures of the United States in 1860*, p. clxxvii; Frederic L. Paxson, "The Railroads of the 'Old Northwest' before the Civil War," *Transactions of the Wisconsin Academy of Science, Arts and Letters*, XVII (1914), 266.

9. *Eleventh Census, Mineral Industries*, pp. 347, 348, 355-417; Fogel, *op. cit.*, Figure A-1.

10. Richard Hofstadter, William Miller, and Daniel Aaron, *The American Republic* (2 vols.; Englewood Cliffs, N.J.: Prentice-Hall, 1959), Vol. I, p. 557.

11. Fogel, *op. cit.*, p. 194.

12. *Ibid.*, pp. 130-135, 199.

13. American Iron and Steel Association, *Bulletin of the American Iron Association* (Philadelphia, 1856-1858), pp. 58-63, 79, 103, 107, 155, 171, 173.

14. *Ibid.*, p. 139.

15. *Ibid.*, p. 145, 146.

16. Albert Fishlow, "Productivity and Technological Change in the Railroad Sector, 1840-1910," unpublished paper presented to the Conference on Research in Income and Wealth, Chapel Hill (September 1963), Table 6; Robert E. Gallman, "Commodity Output, 1839-1899," Conference on Research in Income and Wealth, published in *Trends in the American Economy in the Nineteenth Century*, Vol. 24 of *Studies in Income and Wealth* (Princeton: Princeton University Press, 1960), p. 43.

17. *Eighth Census, Manufacturing*, pp. clxxviii, clxxx, clxxxiii, clxxxv, clxciv; U.S. Bureau of the Census, *Tenth Census of the United States, 1880: Report on the Manufactures of the United States*, II (1883), 748, 749, 753, 755, 757, 758, 759, 760. The term "iron industry" as used here includes forges, bloomeries, blast furnaces, rolling mills, and steel mills.

18. Peter Temin, *Iron and Steel in Nineteenth-Century America* (Cambridge: M.I.T. Press, 1964), p. 141.

19. *Tenth Census, Manufacturing*, pp. 743, 756; Temin, *op. cit.*, p. 174; *Eleventh Census, Manufacturing*, Part III, p. 412.

20. A.I.S.A., *Annual Report*, 1896, p. 69; *Eleventh Census, Manufacturing*, Part III, p. 417; *Historical Statistics*, p. 139. Even the small figures indicated in this computation overstate the

gain attributable to railroad-induced economies of scale. The computations assume that the superior quality of open-hearth steel was of no value to consumers of the Bessemer product. One would expect that for at least some purchasers of Bessemer steel there was a positive value to the superior features of open-hearth steel, although they obviously believed that the incremental benefit was less than the price differential between the two products. The computations also assume the existence of a completely inelastic demand curve for nonrail Bessemer steel. However, if the demand curve had some degree of elasticity, then to some consumers the incremental value of steel over other alternatives was less than the observed differential in the price of Bessemer and open-hearth steel.

21. J. S. Jeans, *Steel: Its History, Manufacture, Properties and Uses* (London, 1880), pp. 44-45.

22. *The National Cyclopaedia of American Biography* (46 vols., New York, 1898-1963), Vol. XIII, p. 196.

23. Leslie Stephen and Sidney Lee (eds.), *The Dictionary of National Biography* (22 vols.; Oxford, 1921-1922), Vol. XVIII, pp. 241-242.

24. A.I.S.A. *Annual Report*, 1889, pp. 63, 65; Note to Table 3.2, Column 2.

25. *Ibid.*; also *Tenth Census, Manufacturing*, pp. 743, 758.

26. Temin, *op. cit.*, p. 217.

27. *Ibid.*, pp. 141-145, 217, 224-230, 279-280. It should be stressed that only a negligible proportion of open-hearth steel was used for the production of rails. In 1880 the figure was 10 per cent, by 1890 it had fallen to less than 1 per cent.

28. According to Albert Fishlow ("Productivity and Technological Change," *op. cit.*) the substitution of steel rails for iron rails, the increased power of locomotives, and the increased capacity of freight cars account for 50 per cent of the increase in total factor productivity between 1870 and 1910. He further indicates that steel rails were a necessary condition for the utilization of heavy engines. They may also have been a necessary condition for the larger capacity of freight cars.

29. U.S. Bureau of the Census, *Report of the Superintendent of the Census for December* 1, 1852 (1853), pp. 111-113.

30. Robert Luther Thompson, *Wiring a Continent* (Princeton: Princeton University Press, 1947), pp. 47, 242.

31. *Ibid.*, p. 213.

32. Unless otherwise stated, Fogel, *op. cit.*, Chapters 2 and 3, is the source for all of the computations presented in this section.

33. Albert Fishlow, *Railroads and the Transformation of the Ante Bellum Economy* (forthcoming, Harvard University Press, Fall, 1965), Chapter 2; Fishlow, "The Economic Contribution of American Railroads Before the Civil War," unpublished doctoral dissertation, Harvard University, 1963, Table A-5. Fishlow estimates that the social saving on passenger traffic in 1890 was $300,000,000 (see Fishlow, *Railroads*, Chapter 2).

34. It is worth repeating the caveat stated at the beginning of this chapter. No evaluation of the impact of railroads on American development can be complete without a consideration of the cultural, political, military, and social consequences of such an innovation. I have focused on economic aspects of railroads, and my consideration of the implications of the railroad experience for the space effort is limited to the economic effects outlined in the preceding pages.

20

The Role of the State
in American Economic
Development, 1820-1890

HENRY W. BROUDE

Economic change in the United States during the nineteenth century
followed a pattern which, although set at an early stage by Great Britain,
soon became distinctly American in characteristics and timing. The rate of
growth increased with an impetus stemming from the simultaneous
emergence of new technology and expansion of the domain under the aegis
of the United States. The period has been described as typifying extensive
and independent growth. Hoselitz has characterized the American setting
as expansionist (almost unlimited natural resources), dominant (relatedly
self-sufficient, self-reliant approach to economic development), and
autonomous (minimal intervention by the state in economic activity).[1] The
appropriateness of the characterization as expansionist is evident not only

Henry W. Broude, "The Role of the State in American Economic Development, 1820-1890,"
in *The State and Economic Growth*. Papers of a Conference held on October 11-13, 1956,
under the auspices of the Committee on Economic Growth, edited by Hugh G. J. Aitken. New
York: Social Science Research Council, 1959, pp. 4-25. Excerpted, and reprinted by
permission of the Social Science Research Council.

as reflected in the advance of the frontier,[2] but also in the burgeoning "American system of manufacturing," unique in itself.[3] . . .

The first part of the discussion below is concerned with the character and degree of governmental intervention in the economy. Next we present evidence on what might be termed positive aspects of the state's role. Finally, observations are made regarding the validity of the characterization and the potential usefulness of the American example in a framework of typical growth patterns.

Character and Degree of Intervention

An appraisal of the degree of private enterprise in the development of a given economy might begin with specification of its industry sectors and estimates of each sector's share of output originating under the control of private establishments. For America in the nineteenth century, this would give a picture of overwhelming proportionate dominance of the private sphere. . . .

Definition of the limits within which governmental intervention is considered to be passive and minimal plays an important part in evaluating the American situation, for the really significant role may be found to lie outside the defined function of "consciously allocating productive factors in a specified direction." One finds in aggregated data on governmental shares of national wealth (Table 1) or income realized from the government sector (Table 2) that the proportionate shares of government were

Table 1: **Percentage shares of government in total reproducible wealth, United States***

Year	Structures		Equipment	
	Current prices	1929 prices	Current prices	1929 prices
1805	3.4	3.9	—	—
1850	2.9	3.1	—	—
1880	2.4	2.7	0.8	0.6
1890	2.8	2.8	0.9	1.0
1900	3.5	3.5	1.2	1.2

Source: Raymond W. Goldsmith, "The Growth of Reproducible Wealth of the United States of America from 1805 to 1950," Table I, pp. 306-307, in International Association for Research in Income and Wealth, *Income and Wealth of the United States: Trends and Structure*, Income and Wealth Series II (Cambridge, England: Bowes & Bowes, 1952).

* Including nonprofit institutions, but excluding military inventory data not available.

Table 2: **Realized income from government, by kind, United States, 1799-1900**

Year	Realized income from government (million $)	Percentage of total realized national income	Production income from government (million $)	Other income from government (million $)
1799	6	0.9	6	—
1809	11	1.2	11	—
1819	17	1.9	15	2
1829	21	2.2	20	1
1839	39	2.4	37	2
1849	58	2.4	57	1
1859	101	2.3	100	1
1869	290	4.2	271	19
1879	322	4.5	284	38
1889	558	5.2	486	72
1899	1,005	6.5	910	95
1900	1,052	6.5	957	95

Source: Robert F. Martin, National Income in the United States, 1799-1938 (New York: National Industrial Conference Board, 1939), p. 87.

relatively low, although on the rise during the nineteenth century.[4] An examination of federal finances shows federal expenditures to be a small portion of gross national product, and years in which budgetary surpluses existed were frequent in the earlier part of the century.[5] . . .

From the early differences regarding governmental intervention there emerges a picture of men with ideological appetites for a laissez-faire menu, but one highly seasoned with selective exceptions. The record shows that up to the end of the nineteenth century the wage and price system, usage of resources, credit creation, and provision of capital,[6] as well as other elements of the entrepreneurial function were kept within and held to be within the province of the private sector of the economy. Government effected a land tenure policy for the country, controlled immigration policy (conditioning the supply of labor), maintained intervention in the banking system (varied over the period),[7] established protection of trade through tariff and patent legislation, performed the roster of services "rightfully" governmental, and represented and strengthened the particular legal framework within which private business was organized.[8] Despite the acknowledged dominance of the autonomous sector of the economy, however, the record does indicate that at the end of the century calls for governmental aid had resulted in the holding by government of approximately 7 percent of the nation's capital assets and the employment by government of approximately 4 percent of the national labor force.[9] . . .

. . .There was tacit acceptance of an ideology; yet within it there were notable internal paradoxes and there were extensive departures from it in practice on a "selective" basis. This perhaps stresses the obvious but indicates the linked relationship, typically traced in discussions of economic growth, between investment (as the focal point in a dynamic industrial economy) and entrepreneurial action (responsive to expectations and the accessibility of usable funds).[10] Interwoven in such analysis is a link between ideology and growth and, hence, between the attitude of the entrepreneur toward the political climate and the state's role as it relates to the economic sphere. The pertinent question is whether the internal paradoxes and departures from the ideal that existed in the nineteenth century were at variance with the American entrepreneur's economic objectives or supplemental to them. Departure from a laissez-faire ideology means, of course, intervention of government. What must be established is whether intervention left the "representative" entrepreneur hostile, neutral, or perhaps with positive sentiments. If it appears that most "interventions" were compatible with the goals of the entrepreneur, it may be suggested that in evaluating the role of the state in economic growth we cannot consider only (or merely) the amount of income generated in the government sector of the economy, or the cases where impediments to activity in the private sector had been removed by government. Rather we must consider what the entrepreneur saw as the accommodation potential of the political structure in aiding him in his pursuit of his "special" needs along an uncertain and hazardous course.[11]

The next section presents examples of three aspects of government's positive role: giving specific and direct support to industry in the private sector; taking initial risks, leading the way, and removing bottlenecks; and creating a favorable climate which had salutary effects on expectations in the private sector.

Positive Aspects of the State's Role

The range of possible government actions affecting the economy is so wide that any discussion could become a mere exercise in cataloging. It seems preferable, therefore, to consider particular episodes that illustrate "positive" action. Positive is here contrasted with passive or minimal, and a complete roster of such positive action in the nineteenth century would include attempts to modify the physical environment and the level and skill of the labor force, the introduction of new techniques, and the direct undertaking of business ventures, as well as support of industry in the private sector.[12]

A survey of the many dimensions of economic participation open to political units in the nineteenth century impresses one with the extensive functional range of these activities at all levels of government. Yet discussions of governmental intervention often implicitly emphasize government at the federal level. It is advisable, therefore, to differentiate explicitly between state and federal action as their effects were felt during the century.

Before the Civil War, government intervention in economic life was widespread but it was concentrated at the state level. The recent studies by the Handlins, Hartz, Heath, Pierce, and Primm[13] all present evidence not only of the extent of government intervention but of the fact that respective states held the center of the stage.[14] In his study of expenditures on railroads in the South, Heath concludes that public investment should be credited with more than 55 percent of total investment in that area (based on the total value of its railroads in the Census of 1860). He indicates that 4.7 percent of total public expenditures were federal, 56.7 percent were state, 26.0 percent municipal, and 12.6 percent county. In addition to direct expenditures, there was aid in the form of services of public officials and property, grants of rights of way, public lands and building sites, materials, tax exemptions, banking facilities, and other privileges.[15] There was activity at the local level also. Martin, in his study of living standards in 1860, points out that before 1860 local government expenditures were called forth, in part at least, by increased needs for goods and services.[16]

The nature and scope of the role of the respective states in the earlier part of the century is reflected in conclusions by Hartz:

> ... the mixed enterprise program ... embracing both profit and control objectives ... had more than simply a promotional significance. Originating in the banking field in the late eighteenth century, it flourished with increasing strength for half a century, eventually being extended to transportation and embracing various types of enterprise there. In 1844 over one hundred and fifty mixed corporations were currently listed in the official records of Pennsylvania, with public investments ranging from a few shares of stock to several thousand. It is hard to view such a policy as an incidental phase of state action worthy of only marginal notice.
>
> Nor is it easy to regard as incidental the role of the state as entrepreneur exclusively in its own right.... It was with the inception of the public works in the 1820's, where a process of steady expansion and increasing investment was premised at the outset, that the entrepreneurial function of the state assumed major proportions.[17]

Writing of government action at the various levels in unlocking the reservoirs of national wealth, Potter calls attention to the rejection of "public capitalization of a great economic asset" in favor of "widespread access to wealth." Yet, as he notes, the potential for economic development depended not only on the now available land, but also on access to markets. Government participation in providing such access was extensive, taking the form of furthering internal improvements to facilitate communication with markets. Sometimes the federal government directly undertook projects, such as construction of the Cumberland Pike; sometimes the state government took responsibility as New York did with the Erie Canal; and there were many cases of indirect participation through offers of public credit or the power of eminent domain, as well as direct financial support of entrepreneurs.[18] Hibbard has pointed out that land grants as part of a program of internal improvements were "a major part of the whole episode of conscious development of the nation through public action. It was believed that private action was likely to be too uncertain and too slow."[19] Indeed there was an approach to conscious economic planning, which is reflected in President Fillmore's assertion, on signing the Land Grant Act in 1850, that it could be "expected to help undeveloped regions of West and South."

Controversy has long existed over how to evaluate a policy that transferred the disposal of resources to one industrial sector at the expense of alternative uses. Welfare criteria brought to bear on this discussion would have to weigh against the rapid expansion of a transportation system and the unifying effects on the nation such considerations as the episodes of waste, mismanagement, and erratic growth patterns.[20]

Characterization of specific activities and policies in an appraisal of the state's role must take account of continuing governmental action to make resources and areas more readily accessible as the economy developed. Initially, reference was made to internal improvements with emphasis on communication. However, as changing technology brought new resources (coal, iron, waterpower, oil) and new methods of production into use, government's role in "facilitating growth" covered the range of activities typically discussed in a survey of American developmental history: a legal structure conducive to corporate ownership of production units with guarantees of equal advantage in internal competition and, through tariff barriers, protection against competition from abroad.[21] Aitken has suggested that the temptation to minimize the role of tariffs in this respect should be resisted for two significant reasons: they have the effect of redistributing income among sectors of the economy and serve as means of reducing the uninsurable risks for private investment. Inclusion of these considerations in the American picture would depend on whether tariff protection effectively blocked sources of competition for American producers, whether entrepreneurial willingness to undertake certain amounts of production would have been affected at the margin by a risk element removed by the existence of the tariff barrier, and whether protection did not insulate enterprise from stimuli to greater growth than took place. The last possibility appears to be the one on which the firmest assertion can be made: it seems reasonable to say that stimulus to growth was not wanting and that, unlike France, for example, the existence of protection did not result in stifling the dynamic potential of the period. Also, assurance of domination of domestic markets and the ensuing reduction of risk and promise of increased returns affected the rate of capital formation and the areas of the economy to which it was directed. . . .

Government records give abundant evidence of the part played in removal of such obstacles as those in the Red River. Examples of providing links and easing the way are easy to find. . . . There is evidence also in the sponsorship by Congress of scientific expeditions and surveys throughout the period. This pathfinding was certainly motivated in part by military needs,[22] but also by the desire to open areas for settlement and to increase communication and commerce. In these efforts should be included river surveying, well digging, resource surveying, wagon-road building, as well as cartography and other aspects of scientific exploration.[23] Congress approved a survey, largely under army leadership, of a possible railroad route between the Mississippi and the West Coast; and during 1853-55 five surveys were made between the 32nd and the 49th parallels. The resulting empirical material was not only useful for railroad building but also added much to scientific knowledge of the area.[24] . . .

Finally, there is the somewhat elusive factor—the psychological impact of government's presence. Fleeting references in historical material acknowledge that this influence was of critical importance in conditioning the rate of growth. Part of the effect was due to the "credit standing" of the government. For example, commenting on the inability of private corporations to command a supply of capital in the years before 1840, Callender pointed out that "There was no body of private individuals in the country well enough known and with sufficient influence in the business world to establish the credit of a corporation so that it could command the confidence of both these classes of investors. The only securities that could do this were public securities, or the securities of corporations which were guaranteed or assisted by the government. American public credit had been raised to the highest pitch by the debt-paying policy of the federal government; and it was inevitable that the American people should turn to the only means in their power to provide for their needs."[25]

The psychological factor affected entrepreneurial expectations. The individual investor was reluctant to venture into the West alone; but his attitude was different with the government at his side, or more likely ahead of him. The effect was to encourage more and larger entrepreneurial undertakings. Many of the ventures that preceded the government into "uncharted" territory were unsuccessful, and this lesson was heeded by the entrepreneur. Certainly at early stages in American economic expansion, the presence of the government, usually in the form of the army, meant a tie with less primitive aspects of society. This tie was evidenced through the exchange of physical goods with governmental outposts, but it had a psychological impact as well in sustaining those who had moved to remote areas. . . .

Leverage Effects of Governmental Intervention

Several observations on the general nature of American economic development seem important within the context of the present discussion; and in discussion of comparative development one must say something about *uniqueness*—particularity, rather than generality, emerges from a survey of the nineteenth-century American scene.[26] The word "pattern" should perhaps be avoided. As must be clear from preceding sections, the West, the revolution in transportation, and the continuing flow of new techniques in production dominate the picture. In the literature various hypotheses provide general developmental frameworks and direct special attention to a particular aspect or factor, for example, the frontier and abundance.[27] Taken separately or looked on as parts of a "total explanation," they provide a basis for illustrating the uniqueness of the American situation. They delineate development of a country with an expanding geographical area, in a position to use the know-how gained through the path-breaking of another country, and to do so in an environment with a growing labor force and a growing market—all in what appears to be nearly optimal concomitance. The highly special set of circumstances that existed over the period should make one hesitant to generalize from the American experience. The constraint becomes all the more forbidding when, to these contextual factors, a series of specific *events* unique in character and having immediate impact on the course of economic change in America are added. These events include, of course, the conflicts arising from regional tensions (East vs. West, as well as Civil War and reconstruction), the pattern of settlement of the West, the role of foreign capital, the emergence of combinations in business, and the events conditioning the social and political milieu. These episodes and factors affected the attitudes of the entrepreneur and resulted in a conception of his social role quite different from that in other cultures. These ramifications reinforce the aspect of uniqueness.[28]

After reference to the role of the state in the development of the American West, there remains the task of pulling together the characterization of the West's impact on the East and hence on national economic growth. This can be done without re-evaluating the issues in the Turner controversy.[29] Nevertheless, in the literature on the Turner thesis there is implicit acknowledgment of the accelerator impact of the West on the East, with little recognition of what might be called the leverage effects of Eastern expenditures on the Western border and in areas newly opened to settlement.[30] Ready availability of land and the emergence of markets did act as stimuli to expansion of plant in the East, but more than this was involved: as Duesenberry has pointed out, it is likely that the *extension* of national economic activity over a wide and geographically remote area resulted in the need to duplicate as well as enlarge capacity.[31] Thus there were induced increments to national wealth. Along with the activity that generated income in areas that had been dormant (the West), there was stimulus for the already active areas with associated multiplier effects throughout—all as a result of the regionally focused expansion.[32]

Martin states that "to introduce the question of whether additional expenditures for military purposes would have 'raised' the level of living is futile."[33] This seems somewhat harsh; if the raw data were available and if the multiplier effects seemed conceptually useful enough to warrant a quantitative indication of the force of new expenditures in the area,[34] available analytical tools could aid in this research.

In more descriptive terms, evidence can be found in the multiplier effects of various governmental undertakings (in addition to railroad buildings and land policy): for example, in exploration and survey; in the use of local facilities to sustain governmental operations, as in the purchase of forage and subsistence items for the Army from farmers in the vicinity of a post; and in sutlers' activities.[35] All these were responsible to some degree for the introduction of new money into the remoter areas, giving rise to higher expectations and to subsequent investment activity.

In the light of the foregoing discussion and in conclusion, it may be well to return to the appropriateness of the designation "autonomous." The question does arise whether the factor so central to our discussion, i.e., the presence of the West, the advancing frontier, and its impact on the American experience, may not be the very condition that contributed most to the aptness of the general and ultimate characterization of the American pattern as one of autonomous growth. It is the view of some, for example, that because of the particular circumstances of expansionism in America (the open frontier combined with the ideological biases that were part of nineteenth-century America), the role of the central government was smaller than it might otherwise have been. They would argue that the very factors that placed America in the expansionist category were functionally linked in the case of the United States with placing it in the autonomous category. This suggests that the expansionist attribute in itself might contribute to minimization of the government's positive role in the economic life of the country. There is need for further study of this question.

There is, of course, need for detailed analysis of the functional role of government at different periods, not only of the various aspects of a positive role, but also in terms of changing functions and possible negative effects on development. Further study may show that the effects on allocation were more significant than the leverage effects.

Nevertheless, and even in the light of the argument referred to above, there appears to be good reason to hesitate before allowing the United States experience for the period 1820-90 to be placed, without qualification, in the autonomous category. For reasons suggested in this paper, it seems advisable to use caution in applying the American experience in analogies of growth; to emphasize the need for qualitative interpretation of governmental activity at both the state and federal levels, particularly because of the possible leverage effects of government action; and finally, to assert that the role of the state in American economic development in the nineteenth century was surely more than minimal. The effects of the action and presence of government on growth were significant and were manifested throughout the period.

Endnotes

1. Bert F. Hoselitz, "Patterns of Economic Growth," *Canadian Journal of Economics and Political Science*, 21:416-432 (November 1955).

2. From Turner's vantage point (in 1893), "The fall line marked the frontier of the seventeenth century; the Alleghanies that of the eighteenth; the Mississippi that of the first quarter of the nineteenth; the Missouri that of the middle of this century (omitting the California movement); and the belt of the Rocky Mountains and the arid tract, the present frontier."—Frederick J. Turner, *The Frontier in American History* (New York: Henry Holt and Company, 1921), p. 9.

3. John E. Sawyer, "The Social Basis of the American System of Manufacturing," *Journal of Economic History*, 14(4): 361-379 (1954), especially 368ff.

4. Limitations of the data available for periods before 1880 are well known; nevertheless, reference to early series for an indication of relative magnitudes is useful for our purposes.

5. Cf. Albert S. Bolles, *The Financial History of the United States from 1789 to 1860* (New York: D. Appleton and Company, 1883), especially pp. 203-216, 538-566, 576-609.

6. As to facilitating the availability of capital, Spengler has noted: "The state can contribute to the augmentation of equipment per worker by preventing waste of resources, by creating a milieu favorable to saving and capital formation, by facilitating the provision of an efficient

banking system, by emphasizing investment rather than consumption expenditures in its anticyclical policies, and in general by fostering the increase of per capita output and of the fraction of this output devoted to capital formation. It should be noted that, for technical and economic reasons, a state's power to increase equipment through the importation of capital is quite limited."—Joseph J. Spengler, "The Role of the State in Shaping Things Economic," *Journal of Economic History*, Vol. 7, Suppl. (1947), p. 135.

7. Early discussion of government intervention in this sphere is cited by Victor S. Clark: "After the War of 1812, when other means to promote manufacturing than the tariff were under discussion, attention was drawn mainly to the difficulty of procuring capital for their support. 'Some thought it would be best for the Government to establish manufacturers and carry them on at public expense by managers and superintendents to be appointed by the Executive.' [Quoted from the *Aurora* updated, in Carey Clippings, VI, 281.] The Secretary of the Treasury suggested the expedient of a Government circulating capital, to be loaned without interest to manufacturers and to be repaid by them as conditions admitted [*American State Papers, Finance*, II, 430, 431]."—*History of Manufactures in the United States*, Vol. I, 1607-1860 (Washington: Carnegie Institution, 1916), p. 369.

8. Fabricant classifies government services "in terms of their ultimate objectives: (1) maintenance of order; (2) promotion of economic activity; (3) production to meet current needs; (4) development of the nation's capacity to defend itself and satisfy its needs; and (5) distribution of the nation's income."—*Op. cit.*, p. 48.

9. *Ibid.*, p. 7. Assets cited are "exclusive of roads and streets and most military and naval equipment."

10. "Further analysis seems to be called for, at least so far as American capitalism is concerned, analysis that will come to closer grips with the special features of American social structure and the various influences which made for a strong entrepreneurial bias in the 'social character' of the nineteenth-century American."—Leland H. Jenks, "Railroads as an Economic Force in American Development," in Frederic C. Lane and Jelle C. Riemersma, eds., *Enterprise and Secular Change* (Homewood, Ill.: Richard D. Irwin, 1953), p. 179.

11. Spengler has provided a basis for examining governmental effect on national income aggregates, dividing the range of state action into three subcategories. He states that distribution of income "is governed (a) by the functional division of net output among the co-operating productive agents, which depends, under simple competition, upon the comparative rates of growth of the several classes of human and nonhuman productive agents, and upon the elasticity of substitution of each type of productive agent for other agents; (b) by the distribution of the ownership of economically significant talents, output-creating factors, and income-generating institutional relations not otherwise covered; and (c) by the changes produced, by gifts and taxation, in income distribution as determined by (a) and (b) alone."—*Op. cit.*, p. 132.

12. A condensed survey of government activity in business (1789-1932) was made by Warren Persons, who was concerned with evaluating the relative "success" of undertakings (he found them unsuccessful); in the course of this evaluation he surveyed the range of activity. See his *Government Experimentation in Business* (New York: John Wiley & Sons, 1934).

13. Oscar and Mary F. Handlin, *Commonwealth: A Study of the Role of Government in the American Economy: Massachusetts, 1774-1861* (New York: New York University Press, 1947); Louis Hartz, *Economic Policy and Democratic Thought: Pennsylvania, 1776-1860* (Cambridge: Harvard University Press, 1948); Bray Hammond, "Banking in the Early West: Monopoly, Prohibition, and Laissez Faire," *Journal of Economic History*, 8: 1-25 (May 1948); Milton S. Heath, "Public Railroad Construction and the Development of Private Enterprise in the South before 1861," *Journal of Economic History*, Vol. 10, Suppl. (1950), pp. 40-53, and *Constructive Liberalism: The Role of the State in Economic Development in Georgia to 1860* (Cambridge: Harvard University Press, 1954); Harry H. Pierce, *Railroads of New York: A Study of Government Aid, 1826-1875* (Cambridge: Harvard University Press, 1953); James N. Primm, *Economic Policy in the Development of a Western State: Missouri*

1820-1860 (Cambridge: Harvard University Press, 1954). Material presented in Pierce's study shows intervention well after the Civil War. Cf. Howard R. Lamar, *Dakota Territory, 1861-1889: A Study of Frontier Politics* (New Haven: Yale University Press, 1956).

14. For a nineteenth-century perspective on the relative success of state aid to early railroad development (and of attempts at internal improvements by the states), see John L. Ringwalt, *Development of Transportation Systems in the United States* (Philadelphia: published by the author, 1888), pp. 79-82.

15. Heath, "Public Railroad Construction and the Development of Private Enterprise in the South Before 1861," *op. cit.*, pp. 40-43.

16. "The old voluntary fire and police departments were totally inadequate. A municipal water supply was essential to a crowded population, and sewers had to be provided. Greater distances and heavier traffic called for better streets and sidewalks, bridges, and (in other local divisions) roads."—Edgar W. Martin, *The Standard of Living in 1860: American Consumption Levels on the Eve of the Civil War* (Chicago: University of Chicago Press, 1942), pp. 280-281.

17. Hartz, *op. cit.*, p. 290.

18. Cf. David M. Potter, *People of Plenty: Economic Abundance and the American Character* (Chicago: University of Chicago Press, 1954), p. 124; also Carter Goodrich, "American Development Policy," *Journal of Economic History*, 16: 449-460 (1956).

19. He continues: "Beginning with wagon road and canal grants in the twenties, followed closely by river improvement grants, the plan of granting the land to the states was devised. These specific grants extended over a period of about forty-five years, from 1823 to 1869. A more general plan was embodied in the half-million acre grants, mainly for the same, or at least similar, purposes in the act of 1841.

". . . The grants for railroads, the most liberal donations ever made for the encouragement of private enterprise, reached the figure of 129,000,000 acres, and even this is somewhat short since other lands granted to states, not specifically for railroads, were turned over to them nevertheless. Minor grants, and grants to states for miscellaneous purposes, run well into the millions."—Benjamin H. Hibbard, *A History of the Public Land Policies* (New York: P. Smith, 1939), p. 267. Cf. James A. Maxwell, *Federal Grants and the Business Cycle* (New York: National Bureau of Economic Research, 1952).

20. Gates makes the point: "At the very moment when Congress was promising free land to settlers, it was enacting measures which gave to railroads, in order to aid in their construction, an area three times the size of New York State. Congress was also giving lands to states as subsidies for education in universities, vocational, and grade schools. These lands were not to be given to settlers but instead were to be sold at the highest possible price. Furthermore, despite the advent of free homesteads in 1862 Congress neglected to repeal measures providing for unrestricted sale of public lands. Consequently, many million acres continued to be sold to speculators, lumber barons, cattle kings, and land companies, who secured the profits in rising land values that the Homestead Act had intended to assure the small man. In keeping old policies and superimposing upon them the new and more generous policies, Congress was moving away from the well-organized, consistent, and coherent policies of the past into a complex maze of inconsistent and inharmonious measures that minimized greatly the benevolent character of the new program."—Paul W. Gates, *Fifty Million Acres: Conflicts over Kansas Land Policy, 1854-1890* (Ithaca: Cornell University Press, 1954), pp. 13-14. Cf. also his "The Homestead Act in an Incongruous Land System," *American Historical Review*, 41: 652-681 (July 1939); Thomas C. Cochran, "Land Grants and Railroad Entrepreneurship," *Journal of Economic History*, Vol. 10, Suppl. (1950), especially pp. 55, 64, 67; and Jenks, *op. cit.*

21. Cf. Potter, *op. cit.*, pp. 124-125.

22. Cf. William A. Ganoe, *The History of the United States Army* (rev. ed.; New York: D. Appleton-Century Company, 1942).

23. Cf. William H. Goetzmann, "The Corps of Topographical Engineers in the Exploration and Development of the Trans-Mississippi West," unpublished Ph.D. dissertation, Yale University, 1957.

24. "Payments from the Treasury, expenditures on account of public lands, surveys, administration, salaries, etc. from January 1, 1785, to June 30, 1880, were (estimated) $46,563,302.07. . . . The expenses of the Indian Department, on account of holding treaties, etc. and including yearly payments for annuities and other charges, which are, in fact, in consideration for surrender of occupancy-title of lands to the Government, from July 4, 1876, to June 30, 1880, was $187,328,903.91"—Thomas C. Donaldson, *The Public Domain: Its History, with Statistics* (Public Land Commission, 1881), pp. 18, 20. Cf. Forest G. Hill, "Government Engineering Aid to Railroads before the Civil War," *Journal of Economic History*, 11: 235-246 (Summer 1951).

25. Guy S. Callender, "The Early Transportation and Banking Enterprises of the States in Relation to the Growth of Corporations," *Quarterly Journal of Economics*, 17:45 (November 1902).

26. Cf. Simon Kuznets, "Measurement of Economic Growth," *Journal of Economic History*, Vol. 7, Suppl. (1947), pp. 29-30; and Warren C. Scoville, "Discussion—Factors in Modern Industrial Development," *American Economic Review*, 41: 275 (May 1951).

27. Turner, *op. cit.*; Potter, *op. cit.*

28. Sawyer, *op. cit.*

29. See bibliography in Oscar Handlin and others, *Harvard Guide to American History* (Cambridge: Harvard University Press, 1954), p. 21.

30. For an exception to this see Clarence H. Danhof, "Economic Validity of the Safety-Valve-Doctrine," *Journal of Economic History*, Vol. 1, Suppl. (1941), p. 106.

31. "It is to be emphasized that the services in question [specialized medical, legal, and personal] cannot be imported. The facilities for producing them have to exist in the region in which the demand exists. The existence of such facilities in the East was of no use to the farmers of the Midwest. In consequence of this situation trading communities sprang up in strategic locations throughout the developing area. The people of these communities provided services to their agricultural hinterland."—James S. Duesenberry, "Some Aspects of the Theory of Economic Development," *Explorations in Entrepreneurial History*, 3:98-99 (December 1950).

32. Aitken suggests that perhaps the very act of acquisition of new territory constituted "the most important single contribution of the government to economic growth."

33. Martin, *The Standard of Living in 1860*, pp. 280-281.

34. ". . . the multiplier for any sector is the ratio of the final change in its receipts to the initial disturbance. If each sector's marginal propensity to spend to every sector is known, it is possible, mathematically, to calculate the value of the multiplier."—John S. Chipman, *The Theory of Inter-Sectoral Money Flows and Income Formation* (Baltimore: Johns Hopkins Press, 1951), p. 22.

35. For a description of the extent of sutlers' operations, see William N. Davis, Jr., "Post trading in the West," *Explorations in Entrepreneurial History*, 6: 30-40 (1953-54), especially p. 31.

PART IV

THE SHAPING
OF THE NATIONAL ECONOMY:
1860 TO THE TURN
OF THE CENTURY

21

Economic Change
in the Civil War Era

CHAIRMAN HAROLD F. WILLIAMSON
and PARTICIPANTS

General Discussion of the Conference

WOOD GRAY: . . . We have seen the impact of the period and the Civil War on the American economic system. I have the feeling that the impact of the War itself has been undersold.

Certainly one of the chief changes in nineteenth-century America was the rise of the big businessman. But we have not talked about the tax structure in terms of the tax on manufacturers, which is said to have encouraged consolidation of production into the single factory. Nor have we emphasized the recession of the politician as an admired father figure, and the rise of the businessman to take his place and make the politician increasingly his errand boy. I think the War itself had even more impact than perhaps we have recognized here.

"General Discussion of the Conference" and "Summary" by Harold F. Williamson, in *Economic Change in the Civil War Era; Proceedings of a Conference on American Economic Institutional Change*, 1850-1873, and the *Impact of the Civil War*, held March 12-14, 1964 edited by David T. Gilchrist and W. David Lewis, Greenville, Delaware: Eleutherian Mills-Hagley Foundation, 1965, pp. 166-174. Excerpted and reprinted by permission of Eleutherian Mills-Hagley Foundation Incorporated.

. . . I note that two speakers are listed here as working on the new series of volumes and bibliographies about the impact of the War sponsored by the Civil War Centennial Commission. Are we selling short or are we insufficiently informed about the impact of the War on economic factors which are inseparable from political and social factors? I wonder if those people, Professors Bruce and Elazar, and perhaps others who are working on this series, would tell us what the series and the bibliographies are going to do about filling in some of these still neglected aspects of the Civil War. . . .

DANIEL J. ELAZAR: So far as the project as a whole is concerned, I am becoming more and more impressed that the series may come out with a majority of the authors saying what this Conference has said: that the War itself had relatively little impact, and that such impact as it had was supplementary rather than primary; but that the period 1850-1870 was of great importance, with many primary changes, not War-related, taking place.

I can't say much yet about the tax structure, but I can say something about politicians. Again, the change is not due to the War. The politician had already ceased to be a kind of father figure, as you put it, by the beginning of the War period. Although we produced the greatest political father figure of our history during the War—Lincoln—he was not such a figure while President, at least not until the very end of his service. Indeed, he was anything but that if the records of the time are to be accepted. I would prefer to call the type you are describing the virtuoso individual politician. The first Jacksonians were the last generation in which this kind of person figured as a common type. This older type was frequently not from an aristocratic background—often one who had become an "aristocrat" in the society of one of the newly settled regions and had entered national politics with aristocratic pretensions. This type of virtuoso political performer was much like the business tycoon who became the central figure a generation later. The virtuoso individual politician falls before the new-style party organization in the 1830's and 1840's. He is displaced by the professional politician who rises through the party organization by serving it faithfully and who very rarely triumphs over the organization. You have at least half a generation of politicians, none of whom are commanding figures, representing this new type before the Civil War. The series of Presidents after Polk symbolizes this new "organization man," who is chosen from the professional party organization or from the outside by the professionals simply because he is clearly unable to become strong enough to interfere with or replace the organization. . . . The War did not initiate this trend. It dates back to the emergence of the Whigs and Democrats as organized parties in the several states back in the 1830's. If anything, the "organization man" was found in politics a generation before he emerged in the business world.

ROBERT V. BRUCE: I might add, since I have been brought into this, too, that I agree with Professor Elazar. What was going on was a process of crystallization, to borrow a term from technology. In the terms of this metaphor, the Civil War may serve us best as the fracture which enables us to examine the crystalline structure of the American system. The violent and dramatic dislocations brought by the War probably led contemporary observers to describe and measure and weigh prewar tendencies and relationships which might otherwise have been taken for granted, and so only half seen.

HAROLD F. WILLIAMSON, Chairman: May I ask Professor Gallman if he has any comments to make regarding this period, which he has been studying?[1] In other words, does the Civil War seem to make a break or was it part of a trend?

ROBERT E. GALLMAN: In addition to what I have already said, I think that the impression given by Professor Chandler about the pace of industrial growth is quite correct. The rate of growth is high before the War. The level of industrialization in 1859 is impressive. I don't know when the period of rapid growth began. Barry Poulson has just developed an index from the data of the 1809 census and from the 1839-1879 census materials that I've worked up.[2] The impression the index gives is that the rate of growth from 1809 to 1839 is lower than the rate thereafter. But whether the period of rapid industrial growth began with the forties or a decade or two earlier, I don't know. One piece of evidence that impresses me about the mid-thirties to mid-forties as a period for the beginnings of rapid growth is the large number of new industries and new products which developed during that period.

One final point with respect to the Civil War: I do think the rate of growth for the Civil War decade was low. There was a higher rate of growth from 1839 to 1859, a lower rate from 1859 to 1869, and then a higher rate from 1869 for several decades.

One way in which the Civil War may have promoted growth is through changes in the distribution of income. Professor Bruce and I were talking about this on the way over. What were the changes in the distribution of income regionally; industrially, of course; and more importantly, among income groups, classified by size of income? I am wondering if the Civil War had the effect of channeling income into the hands of those who would be prepared to invest, and whether it had its main result not during the War period, but in the subsequent decades.

WILLIAMSON: It seems to me that Professor Cochran's article in the *Mississippi Valley Historical Review* was in many ways the inspiration for this Conference. He ought to have a chance to defend himself or to comment. Have you, Professor Cochran, changed your mind as a result of these meetings?

THOMAS C. COCHRAN: Those of you who have read this article may remember it was entitled "Did the Civil War Retard Industrialization?" What was advanced in it was simply quantitative evidence, reaffirmed by Dr. Gallman today, which indicates recession in general, recession of rates of advance, during the decade of the sixties. I put the question mark in my title because I wasn't prepared to say there weren't institutional factors that might have entered into this situation.

During the course of the Conference I was afraid we might find that there was an institutional factor which would lead me to decide that there was probably a great stimulus to economic development in this particular change. As I listened and you listened to the various speakers, no such factor appeared. This morning Alfred Chandler, the last of the speakers, failed to produce such a factor. Possibly the Civil War was a prima donna who hasn't held her audience during this discussion. The War seems to have sunk into the background very much.

Ironically enough, through further statistical study it is possible that some institutional factor will be found that will slightly alter this view. But I can't help but feel that this Conference has indicated that growth and change are of longer range, and the processes of institutional interactions aren't usually violently disturbed by the events of four or five years.

Another thing has struck me in listening to the discussion. We are in the grip of the decadal census. We can't get around thinking in terms of the 1850's, 1860's, and 1870's. While what we really have done from the very beginning of this discussion . . . is to point out the tremendous significance of the period 1846-1855. With the great upsurge of immigration, the rapid westward migration, and the peak of the transportation revolution, this period was, as I am sure Professor Gallman would agree, one of the three sharpest upswings in gross national product in our history.

This is a rather negative conclusion about the Civil War, but a very satisfactory one to me because I wasn't hoping for anything positive.

GRAY: Growth isn't the whole thing. We may be concentrating too much on gross national product and that sort of thing, and not enough on the distribution of income or the centralization of business control—in short, the political economy.

Summary

by Harold F. Williamson

There are few subjects of greater interest to students of American economic history than the one selected for consideration at this Conference. One hundred years later, the extent to which the Civil War affected our economic institutions is still a subject of spirited debate. To give historical perspective to this question, planners of the Conference wisely asked the participants to consider the economic impact of the Civil War within the framework of the evolution of the economy from the 1840's to the 1870's, a relatively unexplored period of American economic development.

In his public address, Professor Taylor provided an excellent introduction and setting for the Conference discussion. His original and provocative paper contributes to a better understanding of the development of the nation's economy between 1840 and 1880. Of particular interest was his conclusion that, whatever immediate impact the Civil War may have had on our economic institutions, there is little evidence to suggest that such changes affected the long-run growth trend of the economy during the period covered by his analysis.

By its very nature, however, Professor Taylor's broad coverage of the period left unanswered a number of critical questions. As Professor Gray observed, the use of economic growth as a measuring rod of performance may fail to reveal important qualitative changes in economic institutions. It is possible that changes which occurred during a span of forty years had significant effects on the cyclical behavior of the economy. It is also possible that important changes took place which on balance either canceled each other out insofar as their effect on economic growth was concerned or, alternatively, may have significantly stimulated or retarded the growth trend. There is the further question of the impact of the Civil War. Were there any important changes in economic institutions during the War? If so, to what extent were they a function of the War and to what extent were they the result of trends that originated earlier? Finally, what effect did changes associated with the War have on the operation of the economy during the conflict and afterward?

It is evident from the published account of the Conference proceedings, that there was general agreement among the participants that the area of commercial banking was most obviously affected by the War. As outlined by Professor Sharkey, the two most important changes were the shift in the type of assets held by banks and the formation of the National Banking System. His account was supplemented by Dr. Redlich's succinct analysis of the relationship between the problem of marketing Union securities and the legislation establishing the National Banking System. In evaluating the significance of these changes, Professor Sharkey emphasized their influence on a shift in the balance of financial power between classes and sections, while Dr. Redlich called special attention to the tendency under the National Banking System for central-bank assets to become liquid during periods of financial stringency.

In his discussion of the relationships between business and government, Professor Hartz noted that there were persuasive elements of truth in the traditional interpretation that the Civil War was a primary factor in the nationalization of the economy, i.e., the growth of federal political power relative to the position of state and local governments. As a more significant interpretation, he suggested the provocative thesis that the Civil War era provided the setting for the Republicans to take over the egalitarian appeal of the Democrats and to establish the Horatio Alger "myth." But, according to Professor Elazar, an increase in governmental activities at the federal level during the War was primarily the extension of a prewar trend that was matched by a similar increase in governmental activity affecting the economy at the state and local levels.

The remaining principal speakers and critics generally agreed that the Civil War had relatively little or no effect on the particular economic institutions they were asked to discuss. Professors Pierce and Carosso, for example, were in agreement that, aside from the fact that the flow of foreign capital into the United States declined substantially during the War, the conflict itself had no significant impact on the structure and operation of the international market for American securities as it had evolved over the preceding decades.

Professor Rothstein likewise argued that marketing innovations commonly associated with the War were, at most, modifications of an already highly commercialized and efficient international marketing structure. Without disagreeing with this general interpretation, Professor Parker did suggest that Professor Rothstein had failed to evaluate the possible significance of changes in ideas and practices which may have affected the operation of the international market for commodities. Professor Parker did not indicate, however, whether he felt such changes could be associated with war.

In their discussion, Professors Dupree and Bruce advanced somewhat different interpretations of the relationships between science and technology during the nineteenth century. Both agreed, however, that no important scientific advances were made during the War, nor were there any significant technological breakthroughs associated with the war effort.

To Professor Chandler, the factory, mass production of durable goods, and the use of the corporation as an administrative device to control and manage large-scale enterprises were the most significant characteristics of transportation and manufacturing to evolve during the 1850-1873 period. Essentially they were the result of new modes of transportation introduced a decade or so before the Civil War and were little influenced by the conflict. Professor Johnson did not challenge this general interpretation. On the contrary, he suggested that Boston merchants had already solved many of the complex problems of controlling and managing relatively large amounts of capital, material, and labor well before the advent of the railroad dramatized the use of the corporation for this purpose.

On the whole, it may be said that the most significant and positive contributions to the Conference resulted from the analysis and discussion by well-qualified scholars of the origin and long-run evolution of particular economic institutions or sectors of the economy in the years prior to and following the Civil War. Even so, not all participants were prepared to accept the preponderant interpretation of the principal speakers that, aside from commercial banking, the Civil War appears not to have started or created any significant new patterns of economic institutional change.

Professor Gray, for example, was not alone in feeling that the full impact of the War on economic institutions had been undersold. In addition to reservations about the adequacy of long-run growth data to measure such changes, he explicitly noted the absence of any consideration of the possible relationship between the wartime tax structure and the subsequent rise of large business units. Professor Gallman raised a closely allied question regarding the effect of the way the War was financed on the distribution of income and the possibility that inflation may have channeled large funds into the hands of individuals prepared to invest in postwar expansion. Interestingly enough, none of the business historians present volunteered information that would tend to confirm or negate this hypothesis.

These unresolved differences in interpretation and analysis testify to the success of the Conference in providing an opportunity for scholars to exchange ideas and to discuss topics of common interest. Even more important, the Conference undoubtedly achieved the major objective of its planners, which was to stimulate further research and analysis concerning this important period in American economic and social history.

Endnotes

1. Professor Gallman had pushed back the Kuznets type of national income statistics to earlier decades. His article, "Gross National Product in the United States, 1834-1909," will be published in Volume 29 of the National Bureau of Economic Research series, *Studies in Income and Wealth*. The reader is also referred to Simon S. Kuznets, *National Product since 1869* (New York, 1946).

2. Barry W. Poulson, "Industrialization in the American Economy, 1809 to 1839" (unpublished M.A. thesis, Ohio State University, 1964).

Pioneering in Investment Banking:
Financing the Civil War and Western Development

22

Jay Cooke: Private Banker

HENRIETTA M. LARSON

Jay Cooke's Place in the History of American Business

In the history of American business, Jay Cooke ranks as an outstanding leader. Not that he always built well; like the typical pioneer he was likely to advance ahead of his time—even as a banker he was still in his heart a frontiersman always eager to push on westward. But he towered high in his generation and left his mark on American business, both in the work he did and in the practices and institutions which he handed down to the generation which followed him. Jay Cooke's part in the financing of the Civil War still stands as a remarkable financial achievement and a great patriotic service, and his work in railroad finance contributed to the development of the Northwest. His importance in the history of American business lies especially, however, in his leadership in a very significant transition that came in investment banking in the 1860's and 1870's. He was the first in America to stand out dramatically and effectively as an active investment banker operating on a large scale. Though his firm was destroyed in his effort to finance the Northern Pacific, he demonstrated the

Reprinted by permission of the publishers from *Jay Cooke: Private Banker*, by Henrietta M. Larson, Cambridge, Massachusetts: Harvard University Press, © 1936 by the President and Fellows of Harvard College, pp. 427-433.

possibilities of aggressive investment banking, revealed some of its problems, and pointed to their solution. Though he himself failed, those who later followed his general strategy succeeded.

It was the Civil War which turned Jay Cooke in the new direction. When the leading bankers of the country, men of experience and considerable resources who lived by the old tradition, had showed that they could no longer furnish the government with sufficient means for conducting the war, Jay Cooke, almost single-handed and without much prestige or capital or even much encouragement from the leading bankers, conducted loan campaigns which supplied the Treasury with adequate funds.

The investment banker operating on a large scale must have a considerable market and a good distribution system. Jay Cooke succeeded in getting both in war finance. Contrary to both American and English practice, he turned to the people, rather than the big bankers, in the sale of the war loans. By his results he demonstrated to American bankers the importance of the small investor. He brought the great democracy into the bond market; in the language of today, he popularized the baby bond. To reach the small investor it was necessary to develop a new method of security distribution. Bankers and capitalists could be reached directly, but it took entirely different methods to reach the small buyer. Jay Cooke, accordingly, introduced aggressive advertising and publicity into security selling; he brought thousands of small bankers, insurance men, and leading citizens into his selling organization, and he even used traveling agents, forerunners of our door-to-door salesmen. Thus arose large-scale, high-pressure selling of bonds in the United States. The development of this new method of retail distribution was an important contribution to American investment banking technique.

Driven by necessity and by his success in the war, Jay Cooke was caught in the post-war railroad boom. Like two earlier leaders in national finance, Robert Morris, the financier of the Revolution, and Nicholas Biddle of the second Bank of the United States, both of whom had made a great reputation and had acquired great self-confidence, Jay Cooke turned to speculative promotion. In financing the Northern Pacific, he used the methods which had proved so successful during the war. Though Jay Cooke as railroad financier was less successful than as war financier, it was in the railroad field that he did his most significant experimenting in the new role of the active investment banker.

Jay Cooke was right in believing that only aggressive methods would succeed in selling Northern Pacifics. But he evidently did not have a clear comprehension of the necessity of protecting his own organization from the heavy risks which such a method would involve. He made the mistake of committing his own firms to the project before he had built proper defenses against failure. In his feeling out for new devices he was a leader;

his weakness lay in not perfecting the mechanism required by the new type of leadership.

In his handling of the big bankers he was especially unfortunate. He tried to win the support of the Rothschilds before he finally committed himself to the project, but they were of the old, passive type of investment banker and would have nothing to do with a promotion scheme like the Northern Pacific. Jay Cooke, therefore, fell back upon the old practice of relying on bankers as distributors only. That he did not have a clear comprehension of his problem is seen from the fact that he was willing to go ahead without any guarantee of support from bankers. He even failed to enlist the aid of strong bankers as distributors. He had clearly overestimated his own strength with bankers, both at home and abroad. In forming our final judgment of Jay Cooke as a financier, we should remember that, while he stood high among the smaller people in finance, he never gained leadership among leaders. In the Northern Pacific, as in the war, his work was grounded on faith rather than on economic reality, which not only made no appeal to his realistic compeers but must even have made them suspicious of the Philadelphian. Moreover, the outstanding bankers, both in America and Europe, were of the passive type which was suspicious of the banker who took so aggressive a position in the promotion of a large enterprise.

Failing to secure the aid of the bankers, Jay Cooke fell back on the market on which he had depended during the war. But with the small investor, also, he overestimated his influence. The war securities had appealed to patriotism in a national crisis, while the railroad bonds were judged on the strength of their investment value. In the earlier instance, moreover, increasing incomes from an inflated war business made people ready to purchase securities, while in the later case Jay Cooke had to work against the decreasing investment power of the small investor who was suffering from post-war deflation in many lines of business and decreased income. Jay Cooke not only failed to realize where business was in reference to the cycle, but he also failed to see that we were in a long-time downward trend. In fairness to him it must be noted that this observation is based on information which he did not have.

After he had failed to win the support that he had anticipated, Jay Cooke should have withdrawn from active promotion of the Northern Pacific, but by that time he and his firms had virtually become underwriters of the road. Their contract with the Northern Pacific actually placed only a moderate amount of responsibility on Jay Cooke & Co., but Jay Cooke's handling of his firm's banking relations with the road led them into a position which had not clearly been defined from the beginning and from which it would have been dangerous, if not impossible, to withdraw.

Jay Cooke made a grave mistake in assuming responsibility for such a venture as the Northern Pacific. The project was a rank promotion scheme; the road had an extensive land grant but it had no capital and no immediate prospect of traffic or income from the sale of land. In judging Jay Cooke it must be remembered that, with the great resources of the United States, its heavy immigration, and the rapid technological advance then in progress, he saw good times ahead for business. He made the common error of confusing the well-being of business with social and economic growth.

Though only the most able management could under the circumstances have carried the project to success, the Northern Pacific had neither responsible nor efficient heads. Jay Cooke had not foreseen that, in assuming such an active position in the sale of the road's bonds, he might have to give consideration to its management. He had no intention, at the beginning, of participating in the management of the concern, and in this he was rightly recognizing the limitations of his own experience and energies. Under those circumstances he should have followed the Rothschilds' rule not to undertake to sell securities for any project which might involve risk or trouble in management. What long experience had taught the Old-World bankers, Jay Cooke had not yet learned.

The situation was made especially difficult because Jay Cooke had allowed himself and his firm to become enmeshed in several conflicting responsibilities. As investor through the direct investments of Jay Cooke & Co. in the Northern Pacific and other railroads and through loans to them, as leader of a group of partners, as a banker and as a holder of extensive deposits, as sponsor and virtual underwriter of the enterprise, and finally as trustee for the bondholders, Jay Cooke found himself in a serious dilemma when trouble came. He has been severely criticized for sacrificing the depositors of his banking firm to the bondholders of the Northern Pacific; it is very important to remember that as a trustee he had not only a moral but also a legal responsibility for the interests of the bondholders. His mistake was not so much in choosing between conflicting responsibilities when trouble arose as in assuming them in the first instance.

By the time Jay Cooke realized the full implications of his position, it became almost impossible for him to save himself. A long-continued and increasing stringency in the money and bond markets drove him to support the road by loans from Jay Cooke & Co. At this point the Cookes felt the full force of a fundamental weakness in their set-up: they did not have an adequate firm capital for the business they were doing. This arose, Jay Cooke explained in his Memoirs, from an injudicious mode of distributing annual profits. Instead of being retained by the firm in the form of cash securities, their profits had been distributed among the partners, who had made them unavailable for emergencies. So strongly did Jay Cooke feel later about this weakness of his firm that he said that, if he were to pass through the same experience again, he would capitalize all profits except moderate living expenses and thus acquire large and independent means for his business. It is a significant commentary on American business that this weakness has prevailed so extensively in American banking. . . .

The lack of an adequate capital forced the Cookes to depend largely on their deposits for working capital. Since they followed the common practice of paying interest on demand deposits, the New York house, especially, had come to hold deposits which were virtually the reserves of inland banks. The employment of those deposits in advances to the Northern Pacific could lead only to trouble under the condition of business in 1873. Here was a striking instance of that use of bank reserves in investment banking which caused so much trouble in American business. . . .

The way in which Jay Cooke became involved in the affairs of the Northern Pacific demonstrated forcibly the vulnerability of the banker as promoter. It showed that one house could not alone stand the risk of sponsoring so great an enterprise. Bankers could, of course, in the future desist from active participation in promotion, but that was not to be in keeping with the opportunities nor the spirit of the time. The bankers had seen what could be done, and they would not turn back if it were possible to go forward.

Jay Cooke had pointed the way along which they could go forward with some degree of safety. Through his experience he had not only demonstrated that the active investment banker would have to look to his own defences by strengthening the base on which he stood and by establishing some control over the project which he was financing; in his successful use of the underwriting syndicate in the government loan of 1871 he had also showed how bankers could, by co-operating in risk-bearing and aggressive marketing, go far toward minimizing the dangers in the promotion of large enterprises.

The full significance of the work of Jay Cooke and other contemporary bankers of his type can be seen only through developments after 1873. Then came a most rapid exploitation of American resources, an unprecedented increase in wealth, and a remarkable growth in business activity and organization. Whether or not this rich economic development was healthy, it is not the function of this study to consider. It is important to observe, however, that in this remarkable period the active bankers played a significant, even a dominant, role. The leaders among these bankers were the Morgans, Drexels, Mortons, Seligmans, and Kuhn, Loebs, all of whom had strong support abroad. They particularly developed the technique for protecting themselves, spreading their risks by the use of the underwriting syndicate and employing aggressive marketing methods.

They also reached out for a measure of control of management and thus brought a degree of order into a chaotic competitive system. By such means, men like J. Pierpont Morgan and Jacob H. Schiff raised the active banker to his highest power and effectiveness in the United States. They built on the foundation which Jay Cooke had helped to lay.

23

Immigration and the Labor Force

A. ROSS ECKLER
and JACK ZLOTNICK

In an appraisal of the relationship of immigration to the manpower needs of the country, the total number of immigrants is perhaps the most striking of the statistics to be considered. Since 1820, the earliest year official immigration figures were tabulated, about 39 million immigrants have been admitted to the United States. In the decade of the 1840's, the number of immigrants topped the million mark, and in every decade thereafter until 1930, the number admitted was counted in the millions. In the 1880's, it was 5 million, and in the first decade of the twentieth century it reached the all-time high of nearly 9 million. Many of the immigrants, it is true, returned to their native lands; but about 70 percent, it has been estimated,[1] remained in this country.

Immigration and Population Growth

The successful absorption of this large number of immigrants into the American economy is testimony to the manpower needs of the country. It

"Immigration and the Labor Force," by A. Ross Eckler and Jack Zlotnick is reprinted by permission from the authors and The American Academy of Political and Social Science. The article appeared in *The Annals* of The Academy, Vol. 262 (March, 1949), pp. 92-101. At the time of its publication, Dr. Eckler was assistant director of the Bureau of the Census; Mr. Zlotnick was a member of the staff of the Population Division of the Bureau of the Census.

is pertinent to observe, however, that the manpower needs which immigrants to America met were in part needs which they themselves created. As workers they added to the supply of labor. At the same time (to give the argument advanced by Professor Alvin Hansen and other proponents of the "mature economy" thesis), the population increase for which immigration was partly responsible created an increased demand for housing, transportation facilities, and industrial expansion which called for more labor and encouraged more immigration.

In view of this interpretation of the effect of immigration on population growth, it is perhaps in order to mention that not all analysts agree that immigration really contributes to population increase. Malthus and Pearl, although they formulated quite dissimilar population theories, both subscribed to the position that, over the years, immigration does not add to a country's population growth. Toward the end of the nineteenth century, when the question of immigration was becoming a lively topic of political discussion, Francis A. Walker of the Bureau of the Census presented statistical evidence to support the contention that the population of the United States would have been just about what it was even if there had been no large-scale immigration into the country—that the effect of immigration was to curtail the rate of natural increase and to substitute the foreign for the native stock.

The statistical interpretations of General Walker appear doubtful in the light of recent evidence, and many population analysts have challenged the view that immigration merely involves the substitution of one kind of population growth for another. The downward fertility trend in some countries which experienced net outmigration, for example, has been cited along with other evidence to oppose the thesis that immigration was the factor which was most responsible for America's declining birth rate. If those who contest General Walker's view are correct, immigration did contribute to population growth and tended thereby to increase the supply of labor in the United States.

Preponderance of Males

The particular importance of immigration to the Nation's manpower did not arise entirely, however, from the addition immigration provided to the size of the population. The increase to the labor force due to immigration was relatively greater than the addition to the population. One reason was the preponderance of males among the immigrants. Table 1 shows the proportion of males among immigrants in every decade from 1820 to 1940. Only in the last decade, when the flow of immigration had

Table 1: **Immigration into the United States and percentage of male immigrants: 1820 to 1940 by decades**

Period	Total number of persons	Percent males
1820	8,000	69.8
1821 to 1830	143,000	70.9
1831 to 1840	599,000	64.6
1841 to 1850	1,713,000	59.5
1851 to 1860	2,598,000	57.5
1861 to 1870	2,315,000	60.8
1871 to 1880	2,812,000	61.4
1881 to 1890	5,247,000	61.1
1891 to 1900	3,688,000	62.3
1901 to 1910	8,795,000	69.9
1911 to 1920	5,736,000	63.5
1921 to 1930	4,107,000	55.6
1930 to 1940	528,000	43.4
Total, 1820 to 1940	38,291,000	62.5

Note: Individual figures are rounded to the nearest thousand without being adjusted to total, which is independently rounded.

Source: U.S. Bureau of the Census, *Historical Statistics of the United States, 1789-1945.*

considerably lessened, the remaining immigrants being in large measure relatives of persons already in this country, did the number of female immigrants exceed the number of males.

Age Groupings

Another reason for the special importance of immigration to the country's manpower needs is that most of the immigrants have been young adults. The very old and the very young have been relatively few. Unfortunately, the available statistics on age of immigrants classify them by very broad age groups, and the limits of the age groups are unhappily not consistently maintained over the years. The statistics, nevertheless, as presented in Table 2 for the years 1899 to 1914 are sufficiently indicative of the very high proportion of immigrants of working age. Although only half of the Nation's population consisted of persons 14 to 44 years old, the proportion in this age range among immigrants was about four-fifths. Only about an eighth of the immigrants were children under 14 years of age, as compared with a third of the Nation's population.

Table 2: **Percent distribution by age of immigrants into the United States 1899 to 1914 and of the population of the United States for 1900 to 1910**

Year	Under 14 years old	14 to 44 years old	45 years old and over
Immigrants into the United States:			
1899	14.1	79.6	6.3
1900	12.2	82.5	5.3
1901	12.8	81.3	5.9
1902	11.4	83.1	5.5
1903	12.0	83.3	4.7
1904	13.4	80.9	5.7
1905	11.2	83.3	5.5
1906	12.4	83.0	4.6
1907	10.8	85.6	3.6
1908	14.3	80.6	5.1
1909	11.8	83.1	5.1
1910	11.6	83.4	5.0
1911	13.4	81.4	5.2
1912	13.6	80.9	5.5
1913	12.3	82.3	5.4
1914	13.0	80.6	6.4
Population of United States:			
1900 Census	34.5	47.7	17.8
1910 Census	32.2	49.0	18.8

Source: U.S. Bureau of the Census, *Historical Statistics of the United States, 1789-1945.*

Effect of Immigration on General Labor Supply

The percentage of the labor force consisting of foreign-born persons offers a measure of the importance of past immigration in adding to the Nation's manpower. . . .

The available data indicate that immigration was responsible for a substantial addition to the Nation's supply of labor after the Civil War. Table 3 presents the statistics on the proportion of foreign born among the gainfully occupied in each of the decennial years from 1870 to 1930. The statistics probably understate the true proportion of foreign born; for many personal reasons, respondents did not always disclose the fact of foreign birth to census enumerators. The figures in the table refer generally to white foreign-born persons rather than to all foreign-born persons, since

Table 3: **Gainful workers and per cent foreign born: 1870-1930**

Year	All gainful workers	Per cent foreign born[a]
1870	12,506,000	21.6
1880	17,392,000	20.1
1890	23,318,000	22.0
1900	29,073,000	19.7
1910	38,167,000	20.5
1920	41,614,000	18.6
1930	48,830,000	15.2

[a]The statistics of foreign-born gainful workers from 1890 to 1930 exclusive of nonwhite persons. The 1930 figures for foreign-born gainful workers are also exclusive of whites born in Mexico. The omission of nonwhite persons and those born in Mexico from the statistics of foreign-born gainful workers does not significantly affect the percentages in this table.

Source: U.S. Bureau of the Census Decennial Reports.

many of the census tabulations do not classify the nonwhite workers by nativity. Nonwhite persons, however, have been relatively few among immigrants, so that the omission of the nonwhite-foreign born does not affect the general conclusions presented below.

The evidence of the figures in Table 3 is that, in the absence of immigration, the Nation's labor force in the period between the Civil War and World War I would have been at least one-fifth less than it actually was. This figure of one-fifth would seem to be a conservative estimate of the contribution of immigration to the Nation's labor supply during this period. It is an estimate based on the hypothesis that, in their own generation, immigrant workers constituted an addition to the labor supply. A modification of the hypothesis to allow for descendants of immigrants would raise the estimate above one-fifth. The estimate would be further raised by an allowance for the under-enumeration of foreign-born persons in the decennial censuses. The evidence seems clear that immigration provided a very substantial addition to the Nation's manpower in the half-century of rapid industrial development before the First World War.

Immigration and the Business Cycle

Although the long-time economic growth of the United States has required a generally expanding labor force, the demand for labor has been subject to considerable cyclical variation. Periods of prosperity when labor was in high demand have contrasted with periods of depression when the demand for labor was not enough to provide jobs for everyone who wanted to work. These fluctuations in the country's manpower needs have very often been associated with corresponding variations in the volume of immigration.

The late Professor Harry Jerome, in his study on *Migration and Business Cycles*, prepared for the National Bureau of Economic Research, observed a clear correlation between immigration and fluctuations of business activity. Generally, immigration has tended to increase in periods of prosperity and to decline during depressions. The correlation, as might be expected, was most apparent during the years after the Civil War. Before the Civil War, when the country was predominantly agricultural and land was cheap, immigrants found it relatively easy to take their place as farmers; leading more self-sufficient lives than wage-earners, they were less affected by and less concerned with business fluctuations. After the Civil War, with the gradual disappearance of free land, new immigrants had to rely more heavily on opportunities in industry, and partly for this reason were more responsive to the fluctuating labor demands of the business economy. After the outbreak of World War I, the association of immigration with business fluctuations was impaired first by the interruptions in international movement caused by the war and second by the enactment of restrictive immigration legislation.

. . . The evidence is clear that, as a rule, immigration increased during periods of business expansion and declined during periods of contraction.[2] Exceptions to the rule obtained in some years when immigration increased despite a downturn in business activity (in the fiscal years 1888, 1891, and 1900 for example), but the extent of the recession in these years was moderate.

The conjuncture of high immigration with periods of prosperity suggests that the inflow of persons into this country has in considerable part been related to the Nation's manpower needs, the stream swelling as the demand for labor increased and contracting as the demand for labor diminished. One reason for this close association of phenomena may have been the intensification of the desire to come to America as reports of opportunities multiplied during good times. A second reason helps account for the immigration of persons with relatives who had previously arrived in this country. Particularly in the case of women and children, immigration was often made possible by financial assistance from family members already in the new land. Such assistance was most likely to be forth-coming during periods of good wages and steady employment. Labor agents also actively recruited immigrants during much of this period, the level of their activity more or less coinciding with the business cycle.

Occupations of Immigrants

In the preceding sections, the analysis attempted to relate immigration to the demand and supply of labor generally. Labor, however, is not a homogeneous commodity. There are wide differences among occupations, and immigration has not by any means affected all occupations uniformly. Immigration statistics have classified immigrants by broad occupation categories (professional, commercial, skilled, farmers, servants, laborers, and miscellaneous) according to the occupation followed before coming to this country. In every decade from 1841 to 1930, laborers have constituted the largest group among immigrants reporting an occupation. In this country, such immigrant laborers could expect little better initially than low-paying jobs requiring little skill. Indeed, even the skilled and semiskilled among the foreign born, beset by language barriers, anti-foreign prejudice, and personal difficulties of adjustment in the new land, often failed to utilize previous training and accepted jobs as unskilled workers.[3]

Perhaps the most comprehensive analysis of data on the occupations of foreign-born persons is that prepared by Dr. Joseph E. Hill of the Bureau of the Census in a study of tabulations from the 1900 Census which he prepared for the Sixty-first Congress.[4] Dr. Hill's report tends to confirm the impression that immigration answered the Nation's needs for unskilled rather than skilled manpower. Table 4 summarizes some of the data in Dr. Hill's study.

Laborers

The figures for laborers (not specified) refer to persons returned in the 1900 Census as laborers, day laborers, or general laborers, without specification as to the kind of work on which they were employed. Generally, the work of persons in this classification was unskilled manual labor, requiring little in the way of education or previous experience and paying comparatively low wages. Table 4 clearly shows that the proportion of laborers among the foreign-born workers was much higher than the percentage among native white workers. The approximately similar percentages shown for the native white workers whose parents were born abroad and those whose parents were born in this country suggest the importance of continued immigration in adding to and maintaining the Nation's supply of common unskilled labor. It would seem that the economic effects of immigration restrictions may have been particularly favorable to the competitive position of common laborers, tending to enhance their wages relatively to those of the more skilled workers. No

Table 4: **Number of male gainful workers and per cent in specified occupations, by nativity and color: 1900**

Occupation	All classes	Native white, native parents	Native white foreign or mixed parents	Foreign-born white	Nonwhite
Total gainful workers—number	23,958,000	12,014,000	4,143,000	4,887,000	2,914,000
per cent	100.0	100.0	100.0	100.0	100.0
Laborers (not specified)—number	2,516,000	961,000	357,000	706,000	491,000
per cent of total	10.5	8.0	8.6	14.4	16.9
Miners and quarrymen—number	570,000	184,000	96,000	249,000	40,000
per cent of total	2.4	1.5	2.3	5.1	1.4
Iron and steel workers—number	287,000	94,000	78,000	103,000	12,000
per cent of total	1.2	0.8	1.9	2.1	0.4
Building trades—number	1,213,000	597,000	258,000	310,000	49,000
per cent of total	5.1	5.0	6.2	6.3	1.7
Clerical workers—number	754,000	413,000	236,000	98,000	8,000
per cent of total	3.1	3.4	5.7	2.0	0.3
Professional service—number	833,000	534,000	147,000	119,000	33,000
per cent of total	3.5	4.4	3.6	2.4	1.1
All other occupations—number	17,785,000	9,231,000	2,971,000	3,303,000	2,281,000
per cent of total	74.2	76.8	71.7	67.6	78.3

Note: Individual figures are rounded to the nearest thousand without being adjusted to total, which is independently rounded.

Source: U.S. Senate, Reports of the Immigration Commission, Vol. 28 (Washington: Government Printing Office, 1911).

more than the statement of a tendency, however, is justified; there are too many other factors, such as the advance of mechanization and the increased strength of labor organizations, which have affected wage scales.

Miners

The miners and quarrymen constitute another occupation group in which immigrants have been important. In the 1900 Census, more than two-fifths of the miners and quarrymen were of foreign birth; the proportion of foreign parentage was three-fifths. Approximately 5 per cent of the foreign-born workers in this country in 1900 were miners or quarrymen; the proportion among native white workers of native parentage was only 1.5 per cent. In the mining states, these proportions were of course higher. In Pennsylvania, for example, 21 per cent of the foreign-born workers were miners or quarrymen as compared with 3 per cent of the native white workers of native parents. The figures in Table 4 indicate clearly that the immigrant was an important source of labor supply to the mining industry; probably the restriction of immigration has strengthened the bargaining position of the mine workers in their negotiations for higher wages.

Iron and Steel Workers

Among iron and steel workers, the foreign born were not quite so important as among miners and quarrymen, but Table 4 shows that during the period of large-scale immigration, they did constitute over one-third of the total. The number of foreign workers among iron and steel workers was larger than the number belonging to any other nativity group. Of all the foreign-born workers in the country, about 2 per cent were iron and steel workers, more than twice the corresponding percentage for native white workers of native parents.

Second-generation Americans

Differences in the percentages shown by the different nativity groups should be interpreted with some caution since they may reflect in part differences in the age distribution of persons in each group. However, if it may be accepted that by and large the percentage of second-generation workers engaged in a particular occupation as compared with the percentage of foreign-born workers indicates movement to or away from the occupation, then it would seem that the children of immigrants were attracted less by the skilled manual occupations than by white-collar jobs.

Table 4 shows that 6 per cent of the second-generation workers were engaged in the building trades (carpenters, masons, painters, plasterers, plumbers, roofers, etc.) or about the same as the percentage of foreign-born workers. Clerical occupations, on the other hand, were followed by 5.7 per cent of the second-generation workers, as contrasted with 1.9 per cent of the foreign-born workers. The clerical occupations were those of clerk, copyist, stenographer, typewriter, bookkeeper, and accountant, pursuits which call for an educational background which the children of immigrants were much more likely to possess than their parents. Similarly, in the case of gainful workers engaged in professional service, the difference in the percentages shown in Table 4 for the second-generation Americans and for the foreign-born is probably explained by the superior educational background of the children of immigrants.

It is noteworthy that the proportion of second-generation Americans in the clerical occupations (5.7 per cent) was higher than the proportion of native Americans of native parents (3.4 per cent). The higher percentage for second-generation Americans is partly explained by the fact that they were relatively most important in the urban areas of the north where opportunities for clerical jobs were most numerous. Some 60 per cent of the second-generation white Americans were living in urban areas in 1900, as compared with only 30 per cent of the native white Americans of native parentage. The proportion of second-generation white Americans living in cities of half a million or more population (20 per cent) was approximately four times that (5 per cent) of native white Americans of native parents. It is not unlikely that as a result of the much decried tendency of immigrants to congregate in large cities, their children may have had access to greater educational advantages than did the average American child. Indeed, the United States Census figures for 1900 reveal that only 1.6 per cent of the native whites of foreign parentage were returned as illiterate, as compared with 5.7 percent of the native whites of native parentage. These advantages of education encouraged the shift by second-generation Americans away from the occupations of their parents and into the white-collar jobs.

Implications of the Occupation Data

A consideration of the economic implications of immigration must take account of the fact that immigrants added more to the supply of unskilled and semiskilled than of skilled labor. Did this influx of cheap labor from abroad tend to hinder or encourage American industrial development?

The reasoning that explains the profitability of employing capital in terms of the alternative costs of utilizing labor or capital might tend to the conclusion that the increase in the supply of cheap labor discouraged mechanization. A thoughtful analysis, however, would consider the many forms that mechanization has taken. Sometimes unskilled manual labor was eliminated as by the introduction of hoisting, conveying, and loading equipment. Sometimes, on the other hand, specialized machinery was introduced to accomplish as far as possible each operation of the skilled workman's craft; the consequent job simplification in many industries economized the use of skilled labor and called for the hiring of semiskilled operatives. In such industries, the capital expansion attendant upon the introduction of machinery was encouraged by the profit possibilities seen in the employment of untrained immigrants.

Industries Particularly Affected by Immigration

The nature of the immigrant's response to his adopted country's manpower requirements was generally quite narrowly circumscribed by the limits of his own skills, by the character of his ambitions, and by the experience of previous immigrants from his native land. The effect was to encourage the movement of some nationality groups into certain industries, and in time the foreign-born workers in these industries, together with their children, came to constitute the greater part of the working force. Table 5 lists the larger industries in which immigrants constituted a high percentage of the male workers at the time of the 1910 Census.

These percentages are for the entire country. For many individual areas, the percentages were much higher. In New York City, immigrants predominated in the clothing industry to an even greater extent than the figure in Table 5 indicates. Similarly in many coal mining counties, the working force was overwhelmingly foreign born.

Sometimes the contribution of a national group was so distinctive as to influence the work pattern of a particular industry and thus to affect its subsequent manpower requirements. The clothing industry provides an example of such a development.

In the 1890's Jewish immigrants from Poland and Russia began to enter the clothing industry in large numbers. Their entry was facilitated by the fact that many of them had prior experience as tailors and by the fact that they were able to obtain employment from Jewish clothiers of German origin, who had already attained to some prominence in the industry.

The typical Jewish immigrant aspired to the proprietorship of his own enterprise, and in the clothing industry, the Jewish people furthered the development of the system of contracting and subcontracting, a system which multiplied the number of entrepreneurs. The manufacturer or

Table 5: **Percentage of foreign-born whites among male workers in selected industries: 1910**

Industry	Per cent foreign-born white
All industries	20.5
Coal mines	48.3
Copper mines	65.4
Iron mines	66.8
Quarries	45.2
Lime, cement, and gypsum factories	40.0
Marble and stone yards	44.2
Clothing factories (suits, coats, cloaks, and overalls)	75.9
Clothing factories (except suits, coats cloaks, and overalls)	72.2
Hat factories (wool and felt)	42.4
Bakeries	50.5
Slaughter and packing houses	45.8
Car and railroad shops	45.6
Tanneries	52.9
Breweries	49.2
Piano and organ factories	43.2
Brass mills	45.8
Blast furnaces and steel rolling mills	51.0
Carpet mills	48.3
Silk mills	46.5
Textile, dyeing, finishing and printing mills	48.7
Woolen and worsted mills	50.2
Rubber factories	40.3
Construction and maintenance of streets, roads, sewers, and bridges	46.0

Source: U.S. Bureau of the Census, *Thirteenth Census of the United States, Population*, Vol. IV.

wholesale merchant provided the contractor with cloth, and the latter undertook to employ his own labor to produce the finished garments. Since the business of contracting required but very little investment (not much more than a few sewing machines), the field was overcrowded with the new Americans, who competed feverishly among themselves to provide the garments to the manufacturers at the lowest possible cost.

The pressure to cut costs had temporarily unfortunate effects on working standards until the labor organizations of the industry successfully exerted their own counterpressures. More enduring were the effects on production methods; the contractors recruited their working forces from each new throng of immigrants and utilized their limited skills by furthering the development of division of labor. Cutters, machine operators, basters, finishers, and pressers combined their operations to produce garments more cheaply and more quickly than the custom tailors. The consequent expansion of the market for ready-to-wear clothing provided more jobs for more immigrants. The history of the clothing industry illustrates part of the role the immigrant played in expanding the manpower needs of his adopted land. The immigrant himself was an active participant in the American industrial expansion which provided employment for the ever increasing labor force.

Summary

Although the effectiveness of immigration in contributing to the Nation's population growth has been called in question, the importance of immigration in increasing the Nation's labor force is unmistakable. The reason is twofold: first, immigrants into the United states up to 1930 were predominantly males, and second, they were in the most productive working ages. In the period of industrial expansion between the Civil War and World War I, the Nation's supply of labor in the absence of immigration would have been at least one-fifth less than it actually was.

The relation of immigration to the country's fluctuating manpower needs is evidenced by the variations in annual immigration which, after the Civil War, corresponded to the cyclical ups and downs of business activity. The causal relationship between volume of immigration and rate of business activity is debatable, but the close association of phenomena is striking.

Generally, immigrants entered the unskilled and semiskilled occupations. A large number took jobs as common laborers; a considerable proportion became miners. The children of immigrants, on the other hand, enjoying the superior educational advantages open to residents of urban communities, tended more to enter the white-collar occupations.

Following in many cases the example of their fellow countrymen who had preceded them to America, the immigrants tended to enter certain selected industries. The mining and textile industries, for example, drew a large part of their labor supply from the foreign-born population. In specific industries, such as clothing, the foreign born constituted a predominant element of the working force and were responsible for much of the industrial advance which provided employment for themselves and the immigrants who came after them.

Endnotes

1. Walter F. Willcox, *Studies in American Demography* (Ithaca, New York: Cornell University Press, 1940), p. 390.

2. See the business cycle chronology prepared by Arthur F. Burns and the late Wesley C. Mitchell and published in their volume on *Measuring Business Cycles*.

3. For an analysis of relationships between occupations prior to immigration and subsequently, see Louis Bloch, "Occupation of Immigrants Before and After Coming to the United States," *Quarterly Journal of the American Statistical Association*, Vol. 17 (June 1921), pp. 750-64.

4. U.S. Senate, *Occupations of the First and Second Generations of Immigrants in the United States*, Report of the Immigration Commission, Vol. 28, S. Doc. 282, Washington: Government Printing Office, 1911.

24

Nationalizing
the American Economy, 1870-1910:
The Play of Technology
on Resources

HARVEY S. PERLOFF and OTHERS

For practical purposes, the joining of the Union and Central Pacific railroads in Utah on May 10, 1869, may be said to symbolize the beginnings of a truly nation-wide economy.[1] Subsequent preoccupation with the vast resource potential made accessible by the completion of the railroad network did not mean, of course, that the country severed its close ties with the Atlantic economy. On the contrary, the movements of population, capital and goods across the Atlantic reached unprecedented levels during the late nineteenth century. The pace and character of American growth, however, were no longer determined so largely by the size and kinds of overseas demand. Exports rose in volume throughout the rest of the century, but they were an increasingly smaller portion of total American output. More significant, though the United States remained

"Nationalizing the American Economy, 1870-1910: The Play of Technology on Resources," in *Regions, Resources and Economic Growth* by Harvey S. Perloff and others, was published for Resources for the Future, Inc. by The Johns Hopkins University Press, Baltimore, 1960, pp. 191-221, and is reprinted by permission of The Johns Hopkins University Press.

the world's largest debtor, its economic development was now less dependent upon continuing imports of European capital. Billions of dollars flowed into the economy concurrently with millions of immigrants, but indigenous capital formation seldom comprised less than 95% of investment increase in any one year. Industrial Europe, meanwhile, became more and more dependent on supplies of American farm staples. Technical developments over these years enabled the United States to meet its mounting foreign obligations with a declining proportion of its greatly enlarged output.

The forces of population growth and of technical and economic progress that had been operative in the crucial political-economic decision of the sixties were now free to shape the continental framework of the nation's economic growth.[2] On average, net national product per capita increased over 10% per decade over the years 1870-1910. After 1890, when the so-called "frontier of settlement" finally disappeared, the advertising of numerous products was undertaken on a nation-wide scale, and by the early years of the 20th century the domestic market embraced all the population.

Some historians have suggested that in the years after 1860 the urban-industrial Northeast imposed its way of life upon a defenseless rural America. But this essentially "political" point of view exaggerates the consensus among Northeastern manufacturers in regard to such issues as tariff and monetary policy; the interests of New England textiles and Pennsylvania iron in these issues, for example, were by no means identical. Moreover, a national banking system, land grants to transcontinentals, and the easing of state incorporation laws were not so much examples of "sectional imperialism" as of belated and, on the whole, successful efforts to create institutions by means of which productive activities could be organized on a continental scale. If sectional conflicts persisted, and for a while at least they were aggravated by agrarian politics, they were nevertheless a waning influence, complicating administration and policy, but always giving way before the surge of industrial growth. By the early years of this century modern urban-industrial America had been achieved: a powerful continental economy made up of a complex of differentiated regions that could offer families in every part of the country a more abundant material life.

This enormous transformation was not, of course, effected merely by the impersonal forces of industrial revolution. It was also the lifework of millions of men and women whose motivations and mores were moulded in turn by the social process they helped forward. No period of American history has produced a more dramatic human spectacle than the decades following the Civil War; at no other time perhaps did "economic" man so completely dominate the American scene. But the heroes of this "age of enterprise" were no longer provincial merchants gathering in a material surplus for trade beyond the seas; they were the promoters of continental empires in transportation, finance, natural resources, and manufactures. The Astors were no longer an exceptional breed; they were followed by a generation of energetic and ruthless "national businessmen" who made an indelible impression on the course of American development. The Havemeyers in sugar, the Dukes in tobacco, the Weyerhaeusers in lumber, the Armours and Swifts in meat-packing, the Carnegies and Fricks in steel, the Harrimans and Hills in transportation, the Cookes and Morgans in finance, the Rockefellers in oil, became the effective arbiters of national growth. For a period, at least, they acquired for themselves and their corporate dynasties huge portions of the land, resources, and wealth of the nation. They managed its democratic politics in the interest of bounties, franchises, tariffs, and immunities from taxes or public regulation. If their formal residences were usually on the Northeastern seaboard, their creative energies were oriented away from the harbors and shipping lanes towards the railroads and freightyards of the interior. Such men thought and acted in continental terms, for the entire country had become a stage on which to play out the continuing drama of their quest for wealth.

To focus only on the achievements of the star performers would be as serious a distortion as to neglect the human factor altogether. On every hand were a host of lesser lights, smaller figures whose profit horizons were limited to the region or locality in which they lived, yet whose strength lay in association or competition with others of their kind. They were no mere local chorus echoing the grand themes of acquisition stated by the principals; they spoke their own lines and originated private roles within the continuity of the general plot. They also served in opening up the new territories and reaped rich harvests on their personal account; their modest capital or credit went into small companies and partnerships, into the plant and machinery which heightened the play of technology on resources. Then, too, there were the vast majority who made up the crowd scenes, both participants and spectators, producers and consumers, who took their cues from the main actors or from the contagion around them. As they moved west with the surge of population and industry, their expectations rose and their efforts were redoubled. Like Tocqueville a half century before, Lord Bryce found them in the greater West of the eighties "reaching forward to and grasping at the future."[3]

What had occurred since the relatively calm midcentury to release this flood of energies in continental development? Did productive possibilities in the West of the late nineteenth century differ in any important respect from productive possibilities in the West of earlier years? Judged by the type and volume of activities, the answer must be that, with few exceptions, it offered little that was essentially new; grazing lands, copper ores, petroleum deposits, and great stands of timber were by this time hardly novelties. The absolute volume of resource inputs, of course, was greatly expanded as a consequence of Western development. But the greatest gains in output were obtained not from increased quantitites of materials but from the reorganization of production functions along capital-intensive lines—that is, by industrialization. Industrialization was a process that involved and affected all regions. Multiplication and differentiation of areas and activities within the continental system widened and deepened technological influences in every aspect of American life; all areas were made accessible to each other through increasingly refined networks of transportation and communications; agriculture was reorganized into specialized "type of farming" areas; remote sources of minerals and lumber were made available in order to sustain the growth of industrial manufactures. Thus it was the extension of industrial technique and organization, not only to manufacture and distribution, but to agriculture, mining, and forestry as well, that made Western resources economically significant at this point in the nation's history. These resources eased the course of industrialization in all parts of the country. But they did not determine its pace or its direction; this was a function of demand.

In early phases of industrialism, the character of demand is usually shaped by the requirements of industrialization itself, by the need to accumulate stocks of capital goods—plant, machinery, materials, and various forms of "social overhead" such as transport services, urban housing, and utilities. In the American case, however, many authorities have pointed to the unprecedented demands of war after 1860 as imparting a momentum to economic growth that sufficed to industrialize the Northeast and carry industrial influences across the continent. No doubt, the task of supplying the Union armies with food, clothing, and munitions did create opportunities in agriculture, mining, and heavy manufactures; mechanization of some branches of agriculture and some sections of the men's garment industry was accelerated. The outcome of the war removed certain political obstacles to completion of the transcontinentals and liberalized the conditions of public support for important economic interests. Nevertheless, even before the war, industrialization had already taken hold in both the New England and the Middle Atlantic states and the process of regional differentiation had gone far. It was probably railroad construction and operation, both East and West, that after 1850 gave greatest impetus to economic development and set in motion new patterns of resource utilization.

Technology and Resources: The Role of the Railroads

The first construction of railroads into the older West had begun as early as 1853 and, if anything, the prosperity of the later war years attracted capital away from what had already proved to be a risky venture. Little new construction was attempted during the war years beyond the double-tracking of routes into the coal and ore producing districts of the Middle Atlantic states. But the manufacture of iron rails alone absorbed almost two-thirds of the increased pig iron output during the years 1860-64; and by the end of the war, the total railway use of iron exceeded 42% of the nation's output. Half the incremental coal product of the war years likewise went into fuel supply for rail manufacture or was consumed by the locomotives themselves. *It was railroad building on this scale which quickly revealed critical limits to the industrial raw material potential of the Middle Atlantic and New England states.* By the end of the war some 13% of all iron was being derived from ores extracted in the Great Lakes region; small inroads were also being made upon the forests and bituminous coal fields of this region in order to meet the demands of industry in the rapidly developing Northeast.[4]

The most spectacular surge of railroad construction was reserved for the post-war period, when cheaper rails made from Bessemer steel were introduced. In 1866, rails absorbed less than 1% of the nation's minute steel output and steel rails were twice as expensive as iron rails; but in little more than a decade, nearly 70% of the greatly enlarged steel output went into rails and steel rails cost only one-third more than their iron counterpart. Meanwhile their superior strength and quality had permitted the development of larger and heavier locomotives and had raised the freight potential of the emergent railroad network. By the late seventies, also, railroad construction and operation were absorbing from 12 to 15% of all coal output and around 10% of the annual lumber cut. At the end of the century, when for all practical purposes the great continental rail net had been completed, more than 20% of the pig-iron total was being rolled into railroad bars.[5]

Railroad construction generated unprecedented demands for capital, land, and labor; larger lines such as the Central Pacific, Union Pacific, and Illinois Central employed upwards of 10,000 men each in their peak years of construction. One authority estimates that the national figure for railroad construction workers probably reached a maximum of 200,000 during the eighties. By that time the census reported employment in railroad transportation service in excess of a quarter of a million. Similarly, the mobilization of funds for railroad investments had become the major concern of financiers on two continents and enforced a wholesale adaptation of financial institutions and techniques. Experience with railway finance trained a key generation of specialists in the business of manipulating huge aggregations of mobile capital. Up to World War I, in fact, railroads remained the second largest consumer of capital, second only to the construction of buildings for residence and business.[6] Thus, in Leland Jenks' words, "the initial impetus of investment in railway construction led in widening arcs to increments of economic activity over the entire American domain, far exceeding in their total volume the original inputs of investment capital."[7]

These increments of activity across the nation are the essential contribution of the railroad to the dynamics of regional growth. The railroad carried the industrial revolution into every part of the continental interior. Historians have stressed the role of the railroad in reducing the cost of freight and speeding the flow of goods, but from the present standpoint at least three other features are of equal significance. First, the railroad liberated the course of economic growth from the relatively fixed and narrow channels of the coastal and inland waterways systems. The import of this "emancipation" had been evident in some areas during the era of sectional rivalry before the war, but in the years after 1870 its influence was paramount everywhere. Second, the penetration of the railroad into the trans-Mississippi West brought a heavy-duty, high-capacity transport service into regions of untold resource potential which otherwise could have acquired little economic significance. Finally, the physical task of building railroads across boundless plains and high mountain passes from the Great Lakes to the Gulf and Pacific coasts fostered a growth of heavy manufactures and a consequent demand for raw materials beyond the capacity of older resource regions to supply. Railroad building in the Plains and Western Great Lakes states, for example, necessitated some tapping of the ore, fuel, and forest resources of these areas concurrently with their agricultural settlement.

Railroad mileage in operation during the calendar years 1870, 1880, 1890, 1900, and 1910 in each of the eight regions is shown in Table 1, together with percentage increases in track over each intervening decade. After 1880 the bulk of the nation's increased facilities appears to have been constructed in the South and trans-Mississippi West, although increases in the Great Lakes states remain sizable down through 1890. After 1890, however, railroad building falls off relatively in the Great Lakes region and also in the Plains. In all Western regions the penetration of the railroad seems closely associated with agricultural settlement; but in the Mountain and Southwest regions, changes in the rate of mileage increase also follow the general increase or decrease in mining employment; changes in the general level of business activity seem to have had a greater influence on

Table 1: **Railroad mileage in operation during calendar years and percentage increases by decades, by region, 1870–1910**

Region	1870 Mileage	1880 Mileage & % increase	1890 Mileage & % increase	1900 Mileage & % increase	1910 Mileage & % increase
United States	52,922	93,267 (76)	163,596 (75)	193,348 (18)	240,438 (24)
New England	4,494	5,982 (33)	6,718 (12)	7,521 (12)	7,921 (5)
Middle Atlantic	10,577	15,147 (43)	19,745 (30)	22,464 (14)	23,777 (6)
Great Lakes	14,701	25,109 (71)	36,924 (47)	41,007 (11)	44,928 (10)
Southeast	11,843	16,328 (38)	31,785 (95)	41,134 (29)	55,932 (36)
Plains	8,046	19,094 (137)	38,354 (101)	42,988 (12)	49,730 (16)
Southwest	711	4,640 (553)	12,248 (164)	15,302 (25)	25,391 (66)
Mountain	873	3,236 (271)	9,330 (188)	11,634 (25)	15,550 (34)
Far West	1,677	3,731 (122)	8,492 (128)	11,298 (33)	17,209 (52)

Source: Poor's Railroad Manual; Interstate Commerce Commission, *Statistics of Railways in the U.S.*

Western railroad building in the nineties than in the seventies. By 1900, except in the Mountain region, probably few farms were more than ten miles or so from a railroad. Meanwhile, the nation was already entering the automobile age.

Differentiation in Agriculture

The new accessibility of the trans-Mississippi West, together with the growth of foreign and domestic markets for farm produce, effected a radical transformation in the location of agricultural activities over the decades following the Civil War. Already by 1860 the Plains region was contributing about 9% of all wheat threshed in the United States, but the heart of the wheatlands still lay in Wisconsin and Illinois. A decade later the Plains region's share of wheat threshed had risen to 23% and by 1890 reached 37% (see Table 2). Its share of the corn harvested for grain in the United States rose from 21% of the total in 1870 to more than 48% two decades later. In 1870 very little milk was sold from farms in the Plains, but by 1890 that region (mostly Minnesota and Iowa) contributed one-fifth of the greatly expanded national milk supply. Cattle had likewise become a major concern in some Plains states by 1870, but by 1890 the region had more than doubled its share of all cattle population and had over 27% of the national total. The cattle industry of the Southwest had meanwhile received a comparable stimulus as the railroad penetrated further into Texas. Over the first half of the decade 1870-80 Texas had also risen to second place after Mississippi among the nation's cotton producers, with Arkansas ranked third. The spread of the cotton culture into Texas was almost wholly a consequence of railroad development, since most of the fertile cotton lands were far removed from the Gulf coast.[8] . . .

The introduction of fast-freight service and refrigerated cars . . . facilitated the movement of dairy products over longer distances: a series of triumphs at national dairy shows soon secured the state (Wisconsin) a reputation for prime produce. Not all branches of the emerging dairy industry, of course, were equally specialized at this time. Farmers who did not yet have cheese factories in their vicinity were advised to make butter and since this was a relatively simple process there was less need for skilled operatives or factory organization. As a consequence, Wisconsin butter-making remained a domestic chore until well into the eighties when technical advances in cream separation combined with price changes in regional dairy markets to foster a rapid growth of creameries. Since Wisconsin had largely pre-empted leadership in cheesemaking, dairymen in the adjacent states of Minnesota and Iowa concentrated their first

Table 2: **Regional distribution of selected farm products, 1870-1950**

Wheat (Threshed)

(000's bushels)

Region	1870	1890	1910	1930	1950
United States	287,746	468,374	683,379	800,649	1,006,559
	100%	100%	100%	100%	100%
New England	0.35	0.07	0.01	—	—
Middle Atlantic	14.19	8.87	5.98	4.18	3.84
Great Lakes	44.35	31.33	17.74	12.64	16.50
Southeast	10.30	8.06	4.61	2.44	2.42
Plains	23.40	37.28	56.18	46.83	38.30
Southwest	0.27	1.01	2.54	12.49	15.86
Mountain	0.37	1.30	4.16	12.00	14.02
Far West	6.77	12.08	8.78	9.42	9.06

Corn (Harvested for Gain)

(000's bushels)

Region	1870	1890	1910	1930	1950
United States	760,945	2,122,328	2,552,190	2,130,752*	2,778,190*
	100%	100%	100%	100%	100%
New England	0.97	0.29	0.32	0.07	0.03
Middle Atlantic	9.81	3.96	3.62	2.94	2.98
Great Lakes	36.49	27.10	33.12	25.09	35.75
Southeast	28.49	16.91	16.87	18.01	14.63
Plains	21.24	48.23	39.04	47.39	43.73
Southwest	2.79	3.30	6.71	5.40	2.34
Mountain	0.04	0.08	0.23	0.98	0.46
Far West	0.17	0.13	0.09	0.12	0.08

*excluding silage corn.

(Continued on next page)

Table 2: **Regional distribution of selected farm products, 1870-1950 (continued)**

All Cattle

Region	1870	1890	1910	1930	1950
United States	23,820,608	57,648,792	61,803,866	63,895,826	76,762,461
	100%	100%	100%	100%	100%
New England	5.71	2.45	2.18	1.98	1.42
Middle Atlantic	16.17	7.58	7.41	6.69	5.69
Great Lakes	22.75	15.67	15.89	16.63	15.87
Southeast	23.93	15.56	16.61	13.95	17.51
Plains	12.32	27.00	28.54	31.12	28.88
Southwest	14.94	20.24	17.46	16.35	15.99
Mountain	0.70	7.00	5.99	7.26	7.92
Far West	3.48	4.50	5.92	6.02	6.72
	37.51	28.64	27.71	32.08	27.66

efforts on buttermaking. Meanwhile in Illinois the expansion of the Chicago milk shed caused many farmers to direct their output into the more profitable market for fluid milk.

. . . The revolution in dairy organization, technique, and markets gradually disrupted the older modes of production and enlarged the element of skill in the new. Under a double compulsion to preserve the fertility of the soil and raise the return on its use, dairy farmers of Wisconsin and adjacent areas concentrated on the improvement of feeds and breeds in order to achieve an increased flow of milk at lower costs per unit. This was accomplished between 1870 and 1890 by a more balanced crop program and by extending lactation through the winter months. Ensilage (silos) provided the long-sought solution to winter dairying problems while research, at the State University and in other parts of the country, related the cow's yield of milk to her intake of digestible nutrients. Further experiment, based on German examples, resulted in the development of a "balanced dairy ration" which combined the several feed components in the correct proportions required by the flow of milk. Finally in 1890 the celebrated Babcock fat-test provided at once the first cheap, accurate measure of milk quality and a more equitable basis for making payments for milk at the factory; it compelled even closer attention to scientific breeding and better feeding practices.[9]

The continuing revolution in dairy farm management led, in turn, to more numerous and larger manufacturing establishments. A series of technical and scientific developments permitted even greater control over manufacturing processes. By the nineties, improvements in milk sanitation and pasteurization helped reduce the hazards of fluid milk consumption, condenseries had obtained a foothold in northern Illinois and southeastern Wisconsin, and hence a growing share of the regional milk supply was being diverted to lucrative market milk outlets in midwestern cities. Milk sold as whole milk or cream to city milk dealers (or condenseries) generally displaced milk manufacturing (cheese and butter) in areas close to large urban populations, where land values and most other cost factors (except transportation) were usually high. Cheese and butter manufactures slowly relocated in belts beyond the market milk zones. In Wisconsin, climatic conditions and resultant crop programs usually gave milk sold for cheese an edge over milk sold for butter, but in southwestern parts of the state and adjacent sections of Iowa and Minnesota, butter-making in conjunction with hog raising and corn-growing proved more viable.[10] Thus competition for milk among the different branches of dairying gradually enforced a pattern of local specialization within the dairy belt of the Great Lakes and Plains regions as it had done somewhat earlier in the more populous Middle Atlantic and New England regions.[11]

. . . The wheat belt gradually moved further west, eventually settling in the western Plains, Southwest, and Mountain states and becoming increasingly dissociated from the corn belt. Meanwhile livestock activities concentrated more intensively in the rich corn belts and grasslands of the Great Lakes and eastern Plains states. The corn-hog-cattle complex, for example, located in southern parts of these regions where growing seasons are notably longer, while the grass-cattle-dairy complex tended to concentrate north of the corn-belt. Local adjustments within this over-all pattern have occurred from time to time during the present century but they do not appear related to the expanding transportation system or, for that matter, to the taking-up of new land. They have more to do with changes in demand, wartime needs for food and fibers, and government policies for agriculture. Nevertheless, some adjustments have stemmed from improvements in technique—the introduction of new breeds of cattle (important in the South), the development of hybrid corn (important in areas with short growing seasons), and the extension of irrigation (important in semi-arid areas of the Southwest and Far West).[12]

Differentiation in Mining Activities

Regional developments in mining activities in the late nineteenth century were, perhaps, even more spectacular than those in agriculture. At the close of the Civil War, for example, the Great Lakes region was providing about 13% of the nation's iron and a somewhat larger proportion of its iron ore. By 1870 some 30% of the iron ore total originated in this region, and by 1890 the proportion had risen to 48%.

Over the same period the mining of Alabama-Tennessee ores raised the Southeast's share of national ore production from 2% to almost 20%. It was no coincidence that this great expansion in Southern mining, like that in the Great Lakes states, accompanied two decades of rapid railroad building both regionally and nationally. In the Southeast, moreover, it was a genuine regional expansion in the sense that, although much of the enterprise and capital came from outside, much of the demand for iron products originated in the region itself. For a period, at least, the Southern iron manufacture benefited from its low-cost production, which ranged as much as 26% below Pittsburgh. The ores were not suited to the Bessemer process of steelmaking, yet their proximity to cheap coal and improved access to growing markets for foundry iron sufficed to insure their lively development.

In contrast to the Great Lakes and Southern iron fields, the great ore reserves of the northern Plains were largely unaffected by the national demand for iron and steel products. As late as 1890 the entire Plains region supplied less than 8% of the nation's ore requirements. There were, to be sure, certain processing problems connected with the soft and crumbly hematite of Minnesota which probably retarded Plains development; on the other hand, the ore was admirably suited to the newer stripping and steam shovel techniques used in selective mining. It required only the linking of the local Mesabi mine railways to the Great Northern system in the late nineties to release this ferric treasure for American industry.[13] Unlike the earlier exploitations of iron ore in the Middle Atlantic, Great Lakes, and Southeast regions, however, the rapid development of the Minnesota ores did not result in any great upsurge of local pig-iron production. The proximity of the mines to cheap water routes on the Great Lakes made these new fields a tributary to the iron and steel manufacture of the Great Lakes and Middle Atlantic states.[14]

Lead mining was perhaps even more profoundly affected by railroad development than iron. In 1870 about 60% of the lead produced in the United States came from the Great Lakes region and about 34% from newer developments in the Plains. At this time no significant amounts of lead were reported from the Mountain region. But a decade or so later, after branch lines from the mines had linked up with major systems, Colorado, Utah, and Nevada supplied more than 66% of the enlarged national lead requirements.[15] Meanwhile production of recoverable lead in the Great Lakes region had declined to a trickle. In the Plains region, on the other hand, Missouri has continued as a major producer of lead down to the present; and since 1910 Far Western production has assumed a modest importance as older regions have declined. . . .

Differentiation in Iron and Steel Production: the Dominance of Fuels

The dynamic influences of science and technology were not, of course, confined to the processes of mining and smelting ore; they pervaded almost every branch of productive activity. The record of iron and steel, thought by many observers of the late nineteenth century to be the epitome of economic progress, reveals the influence of technology on processing and fabricating to be at least as significant as on the extraction and treatment of ores. If the development of the Minnesota iron ranges marked a profound shift in the regional pattern of ore supplies, changes in the location of iron and steel production were affected by other forces, more especially by developments in metallurgical science and fuel supply. Compared with either lead or copper, iron production was not critically dependent on the provision of new railroads.[16] Thus, as Table 3 shows, the regional pattern of iron manufacture, apart from expansion in the South, was not drastically changed down to World War I (or, for that matter, thereafter). Regardless of shifts in ore production, the Middle Atlantic and Great Lakes regions dominated pig-iron production throughout the period 1870-1910 and have declined only moderately since, notwithstanding the recovery of the South and more recent developments in the Mountain and Far Western regions. The impact of Mesabi ores after 1890 was felt not in the Plains or even the western Great Lakes states, but in Ohio and other manufacturing centers linked to the ports along the southern shores of Lake Erie.

In steelmaking the growing ascendancy of the Great Lakes region within the larger Northeastern industrial belt was already apparent before 1910, though its rise to dominance was delayed until the interwar years. The attraction of the cheap water route from Minnesota was no doubt a factor in the decisons of steel men to move the Lackawanna plant from Scranton to Buffalo (1901) and to locate the new Gary works in Indiana, as it was in the still earlier proliferation of Bessemer plants around Chicago. However, more potent factors can be found in the superior access of Lake sites to the westward-moving steel market (Buffalo also provided cheaper access to some Eastern markets) and in the growing complications of the fuel supply. The persistence of an iron and steel complex in southern Illinois and eastern Missouri after the virtual impoverishment of local ores is further testimony to the importance of fuel and market considerations in the steel geography of the period before 1910.

Over the decades 1870-1890 larger and more efficient blast furnaces raised average furnace output sixfold, while the Bessemer convertors multiplied in areas with access to non-phosphoric ores. But already in the seventies the industry was confronted with the critical inadequacy of its principal charcoal and anthracite fuels. Uncoked bituminous coals had been used in Pennsylvania during the 1840's and many new furnaces in the eastern Great Lakes states had also adopted this fuel, but conversion to coke (often in conjunction with anthracite) was not common until the Civil War decade. By 1871 about 30% of the total iron output was produced with so-called "beehive" coke, and within the next few years the proportion produced with coke fuel surpassed the combined proportion produced with anthracite and charcoal.[17] . . .

Mass Production for National Markets

By the opening decade of the twentieth century the economy of the United States was effectively nationalized. Both resource and processing

Table 3: Pig iron production, by region, 1870-1950

Region	1870	1890	1910	1930	1950
United States	1,832,878[a]	9,202,703[a]	27,303,567[a]	31,752,169[a]	57,666,937
	100%	100%	100%	100%	100%
New England	1.68	.28	.06	—	—
Middle Atlantic[b]	66.53	54.89	50.55	39.42	34.90
Great Lakes[c]	25.44	27.13	36.57	44.36	43.94
Southeast[d]	6.35	17.35	11.25	13.69	17.05
Mountain[e]	—	.23	—	2.53	—
Far West[f]	—	.12	1.57	—	4.11

[a]Includes ferro-alloys.

[b]Includes Massachusetts after 1910.

[c]Includes Missouri in 1890, Minnesota in 1910 and 1950.

[d]Includes Texas after 1870 and Maryland in 1950.

[e]Includes Wisconsin, Minnesota and Iowa in 1930.

[f]Includes small amounts in Missouri and Colorado in 1910, and Colorado and Utah in 1950.

Source: U.S. Census 1870, Vol. III, p. 603; American Iron and Steel Association, *Annual Statistical Reports, 1890*, p. 62 and 1910, p. 95; American Iron and Steel Institute *Annual Statistical Reports, 1930*, p. 4 and 1950, p. 18.

activities were slowly and selectively adjusting to the conditions of a nationwide market. The railroad network extended to every part of the continental territory and in some regions was supplemented by a somewhat dilapidated system of inland waterways. Coastal shipping had recently witnessed a notable revival, and the early efforts of Standard Oil to prevent the growth of a system of oil pipelines in competition with their captive railroads had failed.[18] Already the promise of the automobile was stimulating interest in the long-neglected public highways and would shortly result in a burst of construction in and between the major metropolitan centers. Of course, spatial frictions had not been eliminated; but all parts of the country were now accessible—at a price.

Endnotes

1. A transcontinental telegraph was opened in October 1861. Before that time it required at least three weeks for mails to reach San Francisco from the Mississippi Valley by the Overland Mail or from the Atlantic seaboard via the Pacific Mail and Panama route. The "Pony Express," inaugurated in 1860, could carry urgent communications in about eight days, but heavy duty freight movements from coast to coast were impossible except by long ocean passage.

2. At the turn of the century the *Final Report* of the U.S. Industrial Commission (Washington: Government Printing Office, 1902), Vol. 19, p. 1, concluded that the country had been occupied and that remaining "areas of unsettled country" were chiefly (1) mountainous regions unsuited to agriculture or inaccessible to markets; (2) swamp and lake regions; (3) timber lands; and (4) arid lands. In fact, more land was taken up under terms of the Homestead Act and its successors after 1890 than ever before. As late as 1913 the Secretary of Agriculture reported that less than 60% of arable land was under cultivation and that, of this, not more than 12% was yielding "reasonable full returns." See D. F. Houston, *Eight Years with Wilson's Cabinet* (New York: Doubleday Page and Co., 1926), p. 200; L. P. Jorgenson, "Agricultural Expansion into the Semiarid Lands of the West North Central States During the First World War," *Agricultural History*, Vol. 23 (January 1949), pp. 30-40.

3. All the passionate eagerness of people in the West was directed towards the development of their country: "to open the greatest number of mines . . . to scatter cattle over a thousand hills, to turn the flower-spangled prairies of the Northwest into wheat fields, to cover the sunny slopes of the Southwest with vines and olives: this is the end and aim of their lives, this is their daily and nightly thought. . . ." J. Bryce, *The American Commonwealth*, Vol. II (London: Macmillan and Co., 2nd edition revised, 1891), p. 700.

4. P. H. Cootner, *Transport Innovation and Economic Development: The Case of the U.S. Steam Railroad*, unpublished Ph.D. thesis, M.I.T. (June 1953), Chap. V, pp. 13-14.

5. *Ibid.*, Chap. VI, pp. 10a and 12.

6. T. C. Cochran, *The American Business System: A Historical Perspective, 1900-1955* (Cambridge, Mass.: Harvard University Press, 1957), pp. 29, 32-35.

7. L. H. Jenks, "Railroads as an Economic Force in American Development," *Journal of Economic History*, Vol. 4 (May 1944), p. 7.

8. On the relation of transport developments to increased farm production and regional marketing problems, see U.S. Industrial Commission, *Report on Agriculture and Agricultural Labor*, Vol. 10 (Washington: Government Printing Office, 1901), pp. X-XV, and relevant testimony.

9. Henceforth cows were tested for their individual yields and herds were slowly up-graded. By 1900, Holstein and Channel Islands' breeds were preferred above all others; public and private efforts were joined to eliminate the scourge of bovine tuberculosis from Wisconsin herds; the interrelation of technical and economic forces in the growth of dairying is discussed at length in the forthcoming volume, E. E. Lampard, *The Rise of the Dairy Industry: A Study of Agricultural Change in the Midwest, 1820-1920* (Wisconsin State Historical Society, Madison, Wis.).

10. Skim milk from creameries, or separated on the farm, provided an important supplement to hog feed. Corn quickly became the staple animal feed, hence beef cattle were also well-suited to states in which corn was the principal grain. Corn-hog-beef production at this time was usually more profitable than dairy farming, but its geographical spread was limited by the exacting climatic requirements of corn culture.

11. E. Brunger, "Dairying and Urban Development in New York State, 1850-1900," *Agricultural History*, Vol. 29 (October 1955), pp. 169-74.

12. L. Haystead and G. C. Fite, *The Agricultural Regions of the United States* (Norman: University of Oklahoma Press, 1955); E. S. Dunn, Jr., *The Location of Agricultural Production* (Gainesville: University of Florida Press, 1954).

13. J. W. Thompson, "The Genesis of the Great Northern's Mesabi Ore Traffic" *Journal of Economic History*, Vol. 16 (December 1956), pp. 551-57. In 1906 James J. Hill claimed that "never in the whole world has the same amount of track moved the same tonnage, or approached it." Between 1896 and 1900 shipments of iron ore from Lake Superior ports doubled, from 9,600,000 tons to 18,600,000 tons: 80 per cent of this ore was received by ten ports on the lower shores of Lake Erie; Industrial Commission, Vol. 19, *op. cit.*, pp. 472-74.

14. The opening of the Lake Superior ore district appears to have coincided with the abandonment of the high-cost production of the Appalachian range. Experts of the U.S. Geological Survey estimated that, at the prevailing rate of output of the early 1900's, production would reach a maximum in the next thirty years and begin to decline; National Conservation Commission, *Report* (3 vols., Washington: Government Printing Office, 1909), Vol. I, pp. 95-110; Vol. III, pp. 483-520. If anything, their concern for the coal supply at the time was even greater, since, unlike the iron, fuel could only be used once; *ibid.*, Vol. III, pp. 426-446.

15. U.S. Industrial Commission, Vol. 19, *op. cit.*, pp. 229, 242-46; W. R. Ingalls, *Lead and Zinc in the United States* (New York: Hill Publishing Co., 1908).

16. Iron ore moved over some 200 miles of railroad, in addition to its voyage on the Lakes, to reach the furnaces of the manufacturing belt. Coal, limestone, ore, and pig loomed large in the bulk of railroad freight in the Great Lakes region. Until 1860 Pennsylvania was the largest iron ore producer, but by 1902 it had fallen to sixth place among the states. Iron manufactures in the Atlantic coastal states benefited from their seaboard location, and ore imports rose rapidly in the late nineteenth century. By 1913 they exceeded 2,500,000 tons, most of which came from Cuba and Chile. Isaac Lippincott, *Economic Development of the United States* (New York: D. Appleton and Co., 1921), pp. 176, 330-32.

17. Charcoal had remained the principal American smelting fuel until about 1855 and the persistence of "obsolescent" technique is underlined by the fact that as late as 1917 some 376,525 tons of pig were made in 18 blast furnaces using charcoal fuel. American Iron and Steel Institute, *Annual Statistical Report*, 1917, p. 21.

18. G. R. Taylor and I.D. Neu, *The American Railroad Network*, 1861-1890 (Cambridge:

Harvard University Press, 1956); A. M. Johnson, *The Development of American Petroleum Pipelines: A Study in Private Enterprise and Public Policy*, 1862-1906 (Ithaca, N.Y.: Cornell University Press for The American Historical Association, 1956); Inland Waterways Commission, *Preliminary Report*, (*Senate Document* No. 325, 60th Congress, 1st Session [Washington: Government Printing Office, 1908]), pp. 177-312; U.S. Commissioner of Corporations, *Transportation by Water in the United States: Report* (Washington: Government Printing Office, 1909), Vol. I, pp. 149-380 and Vol. II, pp. 249-80. The extension of coastwise shipping regulations to Alaska, Hawaii, and the Philippines helped raise the Pacific registered tonnage 120%, 1897-1909. Total coastwise tonnage, including Lakes and Western river vessels, in 1909 was 6,500,000 or eight times the tonnage registered for ocean trade. Also, H. U. Faulkner, "The Decline of Laissez-Faire, 1897-1917" in *The Economic History of the United States* (New York: Rinehart and Co., 1951), Vol. 7, pp. 220-48.

25

Jay Gould

The Railroad Gazette (New York), Dec. 9, 1892

By the death of Jay Gould the socialists and anarchists have lost their mightiest ally. His work has done more for their cause than all the arguments of Marx or the diatribes of Most. It was precisely such work as his that gave those arguments and diatribes whatever force they may have possessed. The essential feature, common to socialism and anarchism, is a protest against modern business methods. Whoever develops those methods in the right direction weakens the socialistic party; whoever develops them in the wrong direction strengthens it. Jay Gould developed business methods in the wrong direction; he brought out their possibilities of evil rather than their possibilities of good. He thereby gave point to the charges of the socialists against our commercial system; and the community, so far as it tolerated his methods and acquiesced in this development, in some measure pleads guilty to the charges.

There are two radically distinct conceptions of business. Under the older one it was regarded as a contest between buyer and seller, in which each party sought to gain at the expense of the other. The buyer was anxious to pay less than the article was worth, the seller to charge more than it was worth; the latter by his superior knowledge being on the whole likely to come out ahead. This conception of trade is still held by the socialists. But

"Jay Gould," an editorial, *The Railroad Gazette*, Vol. XXIV (Dec. 9, 1892), pp. 924-925.

in the world as a whole it has been replaced by a broader view. We no longer regard business as a fight between buyer and seller, but as a means of mutual service. If the merchant can sell at a good price, it is because his wares meet an actual want. If he can make a profit in so doing, it is because he knows how to organize production to advantage. If prices at any moment seem too high, the community can end the trouble soonest by letting businessmen find the most efficient means of supplying the want. To a man who looks at matters in this way, the capitalist appears not as an extortioner, but as a public servant. It is not too much to say that the whole structure of modern society is based upon this view of business. We give the capitalist control of industry because we believe that in intelligently serving himself he serves others also. It is because of the essential soundness of this idea that the pursuit of wealth is an honorable ambition, instead of a base matter of avarice. The man who makes money legitimately has presumably made it by serving his fellow men; and the power which its possession confers is, in its best and truest aspect, the power of rendering additional service to society on a yet larger scale than before.

Of the truth of this view we need seek no better examples than Vanderbilt or Scott, or Edgar Thomson, or a number of no less honorable names among those who have succeeded them. Vanderbilt served himself in serving his stockholders and the public. He made money by doing an enormous business at low rates, with methods of far sighted economy. He made his money not by raising charges but by lowering them. His fortune, however large, was small in comparison with the pecuniary benefits which he conferred upon producers and consumers. He made, perhaps, a hundred millions; but he gave new life to the trade of the United States, and cheap food to the world.

But side by side with Vanderbilt were other men who exemplified the older and worse conception of business; who regarded it as a fight, or, at best, as a game, in which the gains of one man were to be sought in the losses of another. Such men sought success quite as often by mismanaging the property intrusted to their charge as by managing it well. Breach of faith, so long as the law could not punish it; appropriation of trust funds, so long as it did not land the perpetrators in states prison; legislative and judicial corruption, so long as the influence to be purchased was worth the price charged—all were regarded by these men as legitimate, if only they were crowned with success in money getting. What should have been a means of serving society was made an end, and every other end was subordinate to it. The story of the operations of men like this, in our worst period of commercial abuse, has been told with unrivaled force by Charles Francis Adams in his "Chapters of Erie."

It is fair to say that even in the worst days society was not quite satisfied with transactions of this sort. The men who engaged in them felt this.

Some, like Daniel Drew, tried to propitiate public opinion by attendance on prayer meetings and gifts to religious objects. Others, like Fisk, went to the opposite extreme, and set public opinion at defiance, by a career of reckless libertinism. Gould made neither of these mistakes. He neither sought to defy society nor to propitiate it. It may be that he was so interested in the game of money-making that he was actually indifferent to everything else. It may be that he believed that, if he was successful in money-making, society would ultimately condone the means used. If so, he was partly wrong and partly right. Public opinion was never quite ready to pardon some of his worst offenses. Laws were made to prevent their repetition, and the enforcement of these laws was watched with a care that would have made the repetition of some of the chapters of Erie impossible. But in Gould's central conception of corporate finance as a game instead of a trust, society has on the whole acquiesced. Society has improved the rules of the game from year to year, and has held the umpires up to a strict performance of their duty; but it looks with leniency on violations of fair play that do not infringe the rules in such a way as to attract the umpire's notice. This conception has degraded not only our finance, but our politics and our law. Lawyers who would repel the very suspicion of personal corruption do not hesitate to take large fees for advising the representatives of corporations as to the manner in which they may evade their moral duty as trustees of the business interests of the country without coming into direct conflict with the law. So far as a man accepts this conception of business he becomes a partner in the public wrongs of men like Gould, even though he refuses to profit by their private ones. He becomes a sharer in their responsibility, if not in their guilt. His responsibility may be less than theirs, but in the face of the freshly-closed grave it is more seemly for society to pass judgment upon the survivors than to preach against the dead.

Three hundred years ago, there lived at Florence a man named Benvenuto Cellini, who was regarded by the Italians of his day as having made a signal success of his career. An accomplished politician, a brilliant artist, a fast and furious liver, he attained what his contemporaries most coveted, and literally "drank life to the lees." A propensity to commit murders sometimes threatened to interfere with his career, and even to bring him to the scaffold, but he had influence with the authorities, and it took so long to catch him that the was usually able to plead the statute of limitations. He wrote a curious and apparently truthful autobiography, in which he recounts his crimes with great candor. There is no evidence that he or his contemporaries regarded murder as anything but an ordinary incident in the career of an active businessman—not a pleasant incident, perhaps, and a dangerous one at best, but withal something that was to be judged with great leniency, especially if you escaped being hanged or beheaded for it. It is obvious that if we should judge Cellini by the standards which we should apply to a murderer of the present day, we should make a great mistake. When society acquiesced in murder and tolerated it, it transferred from the individual murderer to itself no small part of the responsibility.

In the three centuries that have since elapsed public opinion on the subject of murder has become stricter. No man could run a course like that of Cellini without making himself an outlaw. The weak point of the decalogue is now to be sought in the eighth commandment rather than the sixth. People have learned not to tolerate deeds of violence nor to expect such toleration for themselves. They have not learned the necessity of an equally intolerant attitude toward fraud. The nineteenth century extends to deeds like those of Gould the same easy judgment which the sixteenth century extended to Cellini. Yet it is from precisely these deeds that our century has most to fear. An unscrupulous financier may readily do more harm than any burglar, or perhaps than any murderer, though neither he nor his associates see it.

Take the case of the Kansas Pacific transactions, for which Jay Gould has been recently commended by resolution of the directors of the Western Union. What were the leading facts in this case, omitting certain darker side transactions connected with it? Gould bought the stock of a number of small lines at a low figure, made use of his position in the Union Pacific to sell them at an unduly high figure, and thus loaded the Union Pacific with burdens and himself with dollars. Now, if we can get ourselves sufficiently away from our nineteenth century standpoint, let us see what this means. He not only took money from the investors to enrich himself, but he made use of a position of trust to despoil those who had trusted him; and, worse than all this, he was false to the duties of the still wider position of trust which society had given him as a leader in the business of the country. The excuse that he and his associates did not look at things in this way may relieve him of some of the personal blame, but renders the transaction itself all the more dangerous. It is not from avowed law-breakers like Fisk, whose careers throw odium upon their commercial transactions, that society has most to fear, but from men who maintain a respectability of private character which wins toleration for their breaches of public trust.

With the extension of business in recent years, and the development of new industrial and commercial methods, our rich men have attained a power of directing the world's affairs such as they never had before. The only thing in history which can be compared with it is the power which Napoleon attained in directing the political and military forces of the civilized world. He acquired that power by using his talents in the service of France. He yielded to the temptation of making power an end and not a means. In the pursuit of war and politics as a game he ceased to regard his power as a trust. We know what happened to him and to France. Jay Gould has been called the Napoleon of Finance. Let us beware that the parallel does not hold true to the bitter end. Our financiers, as a class, past and present, have won their power as a public trust, in the public service. They have been allowed to direct the industries of the country, because such direction enriched others as well as themselves. A career like that of Jay Gould's where one man has enriched himself phenomenally at the expense of others, and not in the service of others, is at once a breach of public trust, and a menace to existing institutions.

26

Presidential Veto of House Bill No. 10203, February 16, 1887

PRESIDENT GROVER CLEVELAND

EXECUTIVE MANSION, February 16, 1887.

To the House of Representatives:

I return without my approval House bill No. 10203, entitled "An act to enable the Commissioner of Agriculture to make a special distribution of seeds in the drought-stricken counties of Texas, and making an appropriation therefore."

It is represented that a long-continued and extensive drought has existed in certain portions of the State of Texas, resulting in a failure of crops and consequent distress and destitution.

Though there has been some difference in statements concerning the extent of the people's needs in the localities thus affected, there seems to be no doubt that there has existed a condition calling for relief; and I am willing to believe that, notwithstanding the aid already furnished, a donation of seed grain to the farmers located in this region, to enable them

Grover Cleveland to the House of Representatives, February 16, 1887, in *A Compilation of the Messages and Papers of the Presidents, 1789-1897*, compiled by James D. Richardson, Washington, Government Printing Office, 1898, Vol. VIII, pp. 557-558.

to put in new crops, would serve to avert a continuance or return of an unfortunate blight.

And yet I feel obliged to withhold my approval of the plan, as proposed by this bill, to indulge a benevolent and charitable sentiment through the appropriation of public funds for that purpose.

I can find no warrant for such an appropriation in the Constitution, and I do not believe that the power and duty of the General Government ought to be extended to the relief of individual suffering which is in no manner properly related to the public service or benefit. A prevalent tendency to disregard the limited mission of this power and duty should, I think, be steadfastly resisted, to the end that the lesson should be constantly enforced that though the people support the Government the Government should not support the people.

The friendliness and charity of our countrymen can always be relied upon to relieve their fellow-citizens in misfortune. This has been repeatedly and quite lately demonstrated. Federal aid in such cases encourages the expectation of paternal care on the part of the Government and weakens the sturdiness of our national character, while it prevents the indulgence among our people of that kindly sentiment and conduct which strengthens the bonds of a common brotherhood.

It is within my personal knowledge that individual aid has to some extent already been extended to the sufferers mentioned in this bill. The failure of the proposed appropriation of $10,000 additional to meet their remaining wants will not necessarily result in continued distress if the emergency is fully made known to the people of the country.

It is here suggested that the Commissioner of Agriculture is annually directed to expend a large sum of money for the purchase, propagation, and distribution of seeds and other things of this description, two-thirds of which are, upon the request of Senators, Representatives, and Delegates in Congress, supplied to them for distribution among their constituents.

The appropriation of the current year for this purpose is $100,000, and it will probably be no less in the appropriation for the ensuing year. I understand that a large quantity of grain is furnished for such distribution, and it is supposed that this free apportionment among their neighbors is a privilege which may be waived by our Senators and Representatives.

If sufficient of them should request the Commissioner of Agriculture to send their shares of the gain thus allowed them to the suffering farmers of Texas, they might be enabled to sow their crops, the constituents for whom in theory this grain is intended could well bear the temporary deprivation, and the donors would experience the satisfaction attending deeds of charity.

GROVER CLEVELAND

*Farmer Discontent
and the Free Silver Campaign of 1896*

27

Bryan, Bryan, Bryan, Bryan

VACHEL LINDSAY

I

I brag and chant of Bryan, Bryan, Bryan
Candidate for president who sketched a silver Zion
The one American Poet who could sing outdoors.

. . . .

It was eighteen ninety-six, and I was just sixteen
And Altgeld ruled in Springfield, Illinois,
When there came from the sunset Nebraska's shout of joy:
In a coat like a deacon, in a black Stetson hat
He scourged the elephant plutocrats
With barbed wire from the Platte.
The scales dropped from their mighty eyes.
They saw that summer's noon
A tribe of wonders coming
To a marching tune.

. . . .

These creatures were defending things Mark Hanna never dreamed:
The moods of airy childhood that in desert dews gleamed,
The gossamers and whimsies,
The monkeyshines and didoes
Rank and strange
Of the canyons and the range,
The ultimate fantastics
Of the far western slope,
And of prairie schooner children
Born beneath the stars,
Beneath falling snows,
Of the babies born at midnight
In the sod huts of lost hope,
With no physician there,
Except a Kansas prayer,
With the Indian raid a-howling through the air.

. . . .

And all these in their helpless days
By the dour East oppressed,
Mean paternalism
Making their mistakes for them,
Crucifying half the West.
Till the whole Atlantic coast
Seemed a giant spiders' nest.
And these children and their sons
At last rode through the cactus,
A cliff of mighty cowboys
On the lope,
With gun and rope.
And all the way to frightened Maine the old East heard them call,
And saw our Bryan by a mile lead the wall
Of men and whirling flowers and beasts,
The bard and the prophet of them all.
Prairie avenger, mountain lion.
Bryan, Bryan, Bryan, Bryan,
Gigantic troubadour, speaking like a siege gun,
Smashing Plymouth Rock with his boulders from the West.

. . . .

II

When Bryan came to Springfield, and Altgeld gave him greeting,
Rochester was deserted, Divernon was deserted,

Mechanicsburg, Riverton, Chickenbristle, Cotton Hill,
Empty: for all Sangamon drove to the meeting—
In silver-decked racing cart,
Buggy, buckboard, carryall,
Carriage, phaeton, whatever would haul,
And silver-decked farm-wagons gritted, banged and rolled,
With the new tale of Bryan by the iron tires told.

. . . .

III

Then we stood where we could see
Every band,
And the speaker's stand.
And Bryan took the platform.
And he was introduced.
And he lifted his hand
And cast a new spell.
Progressive silence fell
In Springfield,
In Illinois,
Around the world.
Then we heard these glacial boulders across the prairie rolled:
"The people have a right to make their own mistakes. . . .
You shall not crucify mankind
Upon a cross of gold."

. . . .

IV

July, August, suspense.
Wall Street lost to sense.
August, September, October,
More suspense,
And the whole East down like a wind-smashed fence.
Then Hanna to the rescue,
Hanna of Ohio,
Rallying the roller-tops,
Rallying the bucket-shops.
Threatening drouth and death,
Promising manna,
Rallying the trusts against the bawling flannelmouth;
Invading misers' cellars,
Tin-cans, socks,

Melting down the rocks,
Pouring out the long green to a million workers,
Spondulix by the mountain-load, to stop each new tornado,
And beat the cheapskate, blatherskite,
Populistic, anarchistic,
Deacon-desperado.

. . . .

V

Election night at midnight:
Boy Bryan's defeat.
Defeat of western silver.
Defeat of the wheat.
Victory of letterfiles
And plutocrats in miles
With dollar signs upon their coats,
Diamond watchchains on their vests
And spats on their feet.
Victory of custodians,
Plymouth Rock,
And all that inbred landlord stock.
Victory of the neat.
Defeat of the aspen groves of Colorado valleys,
The blue bells of the Rockies,
And blue bonnets of old Texas,
By the Pittsburg alleys.
Defeat of alfalfa and the Mariposa lily.
Defeat of the Pacific and the long Mississippi.
Defeat of the young by the old and silly.
Defeat of tornadoes by the poison vats supreme.
Defeat of my boyhood, defeat of my dream.

. . . .

28

The Electric Light and the Gas Light: Innovation and Continuity in Economic History

HAROLD C. PASSER

I

When Thomas Alva Edison gave the signal to start the dynamo in the Pearl Street Station, New York City, on September 4, 1882, a new system of light supply had its commercial beginnings in the United States. The development of the American economy during the nineteenth century with attendant industrialization, urbanization, and new methods of transport, had greatly enlarged the demand for light. To meet this increasing demand, methods of lighting had slowly changed. Candles had been replaced by oil lamps, oil lamps in turn by kerosene lamps, and finally, in the larger cities, gas had become the accepted means of illumination. But gas, too, was to be supplanted as an illuminant. The central station incandescent lighting

Harold C. Passer, "The Electric Light and the Gas Light: Innovation and Continuity in Economic History," *Explorations in Entreprenerial History*, Vol. I (March, 1949), 1-9. Reprinted by permission of Dr. Passer.

system which replaced it is one of the major innovations of the nineteenth century.

The obvious fact that the electric light differs from the gas light in important respects will not be of prime concern in this paper. Rather, I shall stress the continuity in the development of the business of selling light and how the electric system evolved out of the gas system. The striking similarities between the two systems serve as the main focus here. Edison's clear and complete understanding of the gas industry gave rise to his desire to design a method of electric light supply as much like it as possible. This choice of goal is the principal reason for the very substantial and early success achieved by his electric lighting ventures.

The first electric light to be of commercial importance was not Edison's incandescent light but the arc light. This light is produced by an arc formed between two carbon rods inserted in an electric circuit. The arc light was fairly satisfactory and in many ways a great improvement over gas. It flickered considerably, however, and the carbon rods, which gave off ill-smelling fumes as they burned, had to be replaced frequently. But its chief disadvantage was its intensity. Nobody had been able to make an arc lamp of less than 1000 candlepower, which meant the light could be used only in outdoor areas or in very large rooms. Beginning about 1878, arc lights were used as street lights and in factories, hotels, and auditoriums. In nearly all these cases, the dynamo and the lights were owned and operated by the light consumer himself. In the case of street lights, a separate company was usually formed to operate them under contract from the municipality. Arc lights were series-connected and hence had to be all turned on or off at once. But this was no great handicap because they were only used in places where it was the usual desire that all the lights be burning at once. No meter was needed in the arc light system because in those few cases where the owner of the equipment was not the consumer of the light, a contract for specified hours of lighting was easy to arrange. The system was thus very simple and elementary—no meters, no fuses, and almost no accessories were needed.

Edison first began experimenting with the electric light in 1877 but he soon laid it aside to perfect the phonograph which occupied him until the middle of 1878. At that time he turned again to the electric light. The arc light did not interest him, however, because of its unsuitability for domestic and office illumination. Edison knew that ninety percent of the gas industry revenues came from interior lighting and that the really profitable electric light would be one of small candlepower, suitable for the home. His problem, therefore, was to "sub-divide the electric light"—a problem considered by many respectable scientists to be as incapable of solution as the invention of a perpetual motion machine.

Edison first made a very careful study of the gas industry. He is quoted as having said in 1878, "I started my usual course of collecting every kind of data about gas; bought all the transactions of the gas engineering societies, etc., all the back volumes of the gas journals. Having obtained all the data and investigated gas-jet distribution in New York by actual observations, I made up my mind that the problem of the subdivision of electric current could be solved and made commercial."[1] Edison's conception of the problem before him is shown by entries he made in one of his notebooks (no. 184) about this same time. "Object, Edison to effect exact imitation of all done by gas so as to replace lighting by gas by lighting by electricity. . . . Edison's great effort—not to make a large light or a blinding light but a small light having the mildness of gas."[2]

Edison's basic plan, which is suggested in the above quotations, was to imitate the gas system as closely as possible. He believed that the methods, devices, and practices which had gained wide consumer acceptance in the sale of gas should be used in an electric lighting system wherever possible. His goal was to develop a system of light supply which would differ from gas only in that it provided a superior and hence more desirable light.

II

The similarities between the Edison system and the gas system can be analyzed from both the technical and commercial points of view. The technical features common to the two systems stem directly from the fact that Edison was looking for an electrical analogue to the gas system. It is hard to appreciate how revolutionary an idea this was. To refuse to consider as relevant the technical aspects of the arc light system, which was the only electric lighting system known, and to see instead an analogy with gas was truly remarkable. At that time electrical phenomena were very imperfectly understood. Edison stands out as a scientist who had grasped the fundamental laws of electricity and thus was able to make sound comparisons between electrical pressure and gas pressure and between resistance to the flow of electricity and resistance to the flow of a gas.

Edison decided on a system of central supply with mains (copper conductors) carrying the electric energy to the lights in the houses. This is exactly how gas was distributed and entirely different from the isolated plant method which had so far been used in arc lighting. The novelty of Edison's approach is emphasized by the opinion of Sir William Preece, the most prominent English electrician of that period, who wrote in 1882 that each house would have its own dynamo driven by a gas motor and that "it is in this direction that the practical illumination of houses will be carried out."[3] That Preece was wrong and Edison right can be attributed to Edison's perception of the gas system analogy.

Edison decided to put his conductors underground like the gas mains instead of on poles like the telegraph, telephone, arc light, and fire alarm circuits of that day. He realized that the similarity between his conductors and the gas mains was far greater than any similarity between his conductors and the common electrical conductors. When questioned about putting his mains underground, Edison replied, "Why, you don't lift water pipes and gas pipes up on stilts."[4] The decision to put the mains underground necessitated that the Edison Electric Illuminating Company be incorporated under the gas statutes of the State of New York for only then could it have the power to break up the streets. Designing and installing the underground mains was a difficult, expensive process but the essential wisdom of this method is indicated by the fact that within ten years no overhead wires were permitted in New York City.

Gas was distributed under constant pressure with each jet controlled independently of the others. Likewise, in Edison's system, the electric current is delivered at constant pressure (parallel system) and each light can be controlled independently. This is in sharp contrast to the arc light systems which were series systems and which had a different voltage at each light. And, as mentioned above, the arc lights were all turned on and off together with no independent control.

The gas consumption of each user was measured by a meter located on his premises. Edison decided that his system also should have a meter. Here is another instance where the extent of the novelty of Edison's idea is hard to imagine. At that time, electricity was a mysterious force which could be measured only crudely and imperfectly in the laboratory. To suggest that this force could be measured in some simple, reliable, and inexpensive way seemed fantastic in the extreme. Yet such measurement was necessary if electric lights were to become a commodity.

The gas meters had a dial mechanism where pointers indicated the cubic feet of gas consumed. Edison realized the advantages of such a direct-reading type of meter from the consumer's point of view. He tried to perfect an electric meter which was direct-reading and measured electricity used in cubic feet (like gas) but failed.[5] The meter he finally worked out fulfilled all the requirements except that it was not direct-reading. It was a chemical device and contained plates which were removed each month and taken to the central station where they were weighed. The customer could learn nothing about his consumption of electricity from the meter and had to trust the company to be accurate and honest. For this reason, these chemical meters were never completely successful and eventually were replaced by direct-reading, mechanical-type meters.

As to the candlepower of the electric light in the Edison system, it is sufficient to say that it was designed to produce 16 candlepower, which was equivalent to the standard gas jet of the 1880's.

The thinking of Edison in developing the technical features of his system is brought out very clearly when his reasons for rejecting the storage battery are examined. It was thought by some electricians that the most practical system of light distribution would involve storage batteries in each house to be charged during the daytime by the central station dynamo which could then supply current to other lights—say street lights—at night. This method has the following advantages: 1. While the battery would be discharged at a low voltage suitable for inside a home, it would be charged at a high voltage—thus reducing the energy lost in transmission from the central station; 2. the central station could have a much steadier load and therefore lower cost per unit of electrical energy.

Edison was interviewed on January 28th, 1883 by a *Boston Herald* reporter and made the following remarks on the storage battery: "In 1879 I took up that question and devised a system of placing storage batteries in houses connected to mains and charging them in the daytime, to be discharged in the evening and night to run incandescent lamps."[6] Edison went on to say that he found this system unworkable.

The reporter next asked, "Then you consider storage batteries wholly impracticable? Is there no hope for their doing good, legitimate work?"

Edison replied, "None whatever. Except in a very limited number of cases, storage of gas could be made analogous to storage of electricity. One of the principal outlays of a gas company is for pipes. The average diameter of their mains is five or six inches. But under pressure greater than they now force the gas through their mains, an inch pipe would answer under the storage principle of having a small gasometer in every house. The difference saved to the company by this arrangement would be about $15 for pipes from house to house, 25 to 30 feet apart. But the gasometer would cost a great deal more in each house than the 25 feet of pipe buried in the street. Besides, gasometers might not be just the thing in the hands of the public; there might be explosions; some of them might not have room. The gasometer would require some little mechanism to reduce the pressure down to a limit where it could be burnt. Now, these little mechanisms are uncertain."[7]

Edison's reasons for rejecting the battery method, apart from technical difficulties which might have arisen from batteries as such, were based, therefore, on his analysis of why the gas companies had never adopted the corresponding method in gas distribution. Considerations of safety, reliability, and convenience applied equally to both. The reservoir of gas in each home would be a potential source of fire or explosion just as the battery, especially its high voltage side, would be a potential cause of fire or personal injury. The gasometers and the batteries were both costly and unreliable to the extent that any savings in cost of gas pipes or electric conductors would be more than offset. If there would be inconvenience to a household in having space occupied by the gas reservoir, there would also be inconvenience in having space occupied by the coffin-sized battery.

With the conception of the electrical analogue to the gas system in his mind, Edison and his associates worked for nearly four years designing the components of his system and perfecting the details. In essence this meant inventing a suitable dynamo; a system of underground mains; switches, sockets, and junction boxes; a fusing device; and, of course, the incandescent lamp itself. What Edison finally achieved was a system of light supply vastly superior to the gas system from a purely technical point of view. The light was of much better quality. It did not flicker or vitiate the atmosphere or give off a noticeable amount of heat. The system was much safer, too, in that there was no open flame, no danger of explosion or suffocation, and almost no chance of personal injury or fire. The Edison meter was extremely accurate and marked a great improvement over the gas meters which were, at times, notoriously inaccurate.[8]

III

Commercially, the Edison system showed the same similarity to the gas system as it did technically. The estimates of the demand for light in the area of New York City chosen for the first central station were based on the number of gas jets in use. Edison had men thoroughly canvas the district to obtain information on the number of gas jets burning at each hour up to three in the morning. A house-to-house survey was made later which provided complete data on exactly how many jets were in each building, the average hours of burning, and the cost of this light to consumers. These estimates served as the basis for determining the size and quantity of electrical equipment needed.

The Edison electric light was priced to equal the price of gas light. In one of his surveys, Edison asked the gas consumers whether or not they would take the electric light if its price were the same as gas. All but 850 of the 16,000 gas users answered in the affirmative.[9] There remained the question of exactly how much these consumers had paid for gas light with the price of gas at $2.25 per 1000 cubic feet. To determine this, Edison collected some 24 books containing gas light bills of consumers in the district.[10]

On the assumption that a 16 candlepower jet consumes 5 cubic feet per hour, the price of 16 candlepower-hours of light, when gas is $2.25 per 1000 cubic feet, is 1.125 cents. The price of light supplied by the Edison central station was set at 1.2 cents per 16 candlepower-hours (with the central station supplying the light bulbs as well as the electric energy). Thus the price of the electric light was almost exactly the same as the price of gas light, the commodity it was designed to replace.[11]

Edison was aware that if his system were really effective, the gas companies might conceivably reduce the price of gas. In an 1882 interview,[12] he explained that he had calculated that the cost of the gas which sold for $2.25 per 1000 cubic feet was 90 cents—of which 45 cents was variable production cost and 45 cents overhead. Even if the price of gas was reduced to $1, Edison was confident that he could get one-half of the lighting business in the district by setting the price of electric light equivalent to gas at $1.50. With their volume cut in half, the gas companies would find their cost to be $1.28 and Edison did not consider them strong enough to sell below cost for very long. By the time several years had elapsed, the Edison people became more confident and expressed the belief that the electric light customers could be held at the existing price no matter what happened to the price of gas. They made the comparison with the success of the gas companies in retaining their customers in the face of lowered kerosene prices some years before.[13]

In the business methods adopted by the Edison Electric Illuminating Company, every effort was made to simulate the practices and terminology of the gas companies. Monthly bills were rendered and the Edison lights were often referred to as burners. The consumer was billed for light-hours instead of for electric energy to avoid confusing him with mysterious terminology and to stress the fact that he was buying light.

Edison did not expect to find much of a market for light distributed from a central station in communities too small or too poor to support a gas company. The areas of the nation which were considered as possible locations for Edison central stations once their commercial feasibility had been demonstrated in the New York district were those chosen with reference to the gas industry. Here again can be seen Edison's hesitation to depart very markedly from the business practices of the gas companies.

IV

The similarities between the Edison central station light supply system and the gas light supply system indicate how closely Edison was able to achieve his goal—the electrical analogue of the gas system. But the impact of the gas industry does not end with the conception and design of the electric light system. Once this system had been placed in operation in the

New York City district, the Edison company had to take account of the gas companies in its policies and decisions. In this section I shall discuss the actions and tactics of an innovating firm in view of the competition from the product that the innovation is designed to replace.

The location of the first central station was so chosen (by accident or by design) that gas was placed at the greatest quality disadvantage possible. At a time when water-gas (as against coal-gas) was forbidden by law in New Jersey and Massachusetts, lower Manhattan was furnished with this poisonous, inferior gas. The *London Journal of Gas Lighting*, December 12, 1883, contained the following comment: "One thing that will operate in Edison's favour, when he gets to work in earnest to light the downtown district, is that this section of the city is supplied with water-gas. This gas gives a great deal of trouble by causing the burner tips to become stopped up with carbon; the result, of course, being a miserable forked flame. Further, people are beginning to realize that carbonic oxide is not so harmless a substance as they have been led to believe. The truth is, the number of deaths caused by water-gas in New York alone, during the past few months, is simply appalling. The *Sanitary Engineer* stated that 14 deaths have occurred in the city in the consequence of the use of this gas, since the 1st of July. If there is to be a fight between gas and electricity, this is a heavy load for the gas industry to carry to the conflict."[14]

The proposition that Edison chose lower Manhattan because of the water-gas use there cannot be proved on the basis of available evidence. He could hardly have chosen it on the grounds of a large lighting demand, however, because even in 1882 lower Manhattan was a business district where most buildings were dark after 6 P.M. There are some indications that Edison may have chosen the Wall Street area in order to impress the prominent capitalists at first hand. Whatever the reason for the choice, the electric light was able to demonstrate its superiority over water-gas much more easily than if it had been competing with coal-gas.

The advertising and sales efforts of the Edison company in trying to expand the use of incandescent lights were directed almost entirely toward showing its superiority over gas. In the Bulletins of the Edison Electric Light Company and the Edison Company for Isolated Lighting which were published every month or so during the years 1882-1886, explosions, fires, and deaths due to gas in New York and elsewhere were reported with monotonous regularity. Incidents of gas supply failure were cited to give the impression that gas was unreliable. The reader of these Bulletins learned that the heat given off by a gas light was uncomfortable and impaired the acoustical qualities of theaters; that the gas light was sooty and grimy; and that the clean, cool, steady Edison light had none of these disadvantages. The gas light was pictured as inconvenient and limited in use because it required a match to be lighted, could not be turned on from a distance, could not burn inverted, and could not burn in a wind.

In one Bulletin, a comment was headed "The Electric Light Cures Shortsightedness" and an English journal was quoted as follows: "Remarking the number of students who are afflicted with shortsightedness, Professor Pickering has lately examined some physical causes that may bring about this abnormal condition of the eye. He finds that it is not the light so much as the heat that is mainly concerned in the developing of prejudicial effects. . . . Ordinary gas burners give out a considerable amount of heat by the energetic combustion of hydro-carbons and hence their injurious effect. In this respect, the electric light is not open to the same objection, for although the light may be rendered as intense as desirable, still there is very little heat produced."[15]

V

The relationship between a new product (the incandescent electric light) and the product it displaces (the gas light) is seen to have two important aspects. How is the new product like the old and how is it different from the old? The similarities between the two express the continuity in economic development; the differences are the discontinuities, the abrupt changes, in economic development. From the standpoint of the innovator, the time to be especially conscious of the continuity elements is in the period when the new product, its production, and its marketing are conceived and worked out. The time to be especially conscious of the differences is when the new product is marketed and is facing the competition of the old product.

One of the key factors in Edison's success in the New York City electric lighting venture was his ability to select from the gas system those elements which could serve in his system. His original conception of an electric analogue for gas carried him to exceedingly sound judgments in the design of his electrical light system. How sound they were is proven by the test of time. The size of the area he chose for one central station is still used for distribution purposes although now the immediate source of electric energy in each such district is a sub-station which contains transformers and converters. His choice of voltage (110 volts) and the constant pressure parallel system are standard throughout the United States. The bamboo filament of the Edison light has been replaced by a metallic filament and the glass is commonly frosted now, but the physical size of the incandescent light, its electrical characteristics, its life, and other features are not radically different from the originals of 1882. Edison's decision to put the conductors underground and his original work in the accessories of the system—the fuses, the switches, the underground mains, the sockets— were also correct anticipations of the future course of the industry.

The meter, it will be recalled, was satisfactory except that unlike a gas meter it was not direct-reading. Inventions in the late 1880's and the early 1890's made possible a mechanical-type direct-reading meter which replaced nearly all the chemical meters by 1900. The one important respect in which Edison failed to imitate the gas industry turned out to be a source of consumer complaint which was not remedied until a gas-type of direct-reading meter was finally perfected.

Endnotes

1. Martin, T. C., *Forty Years of Edison Service*, New York, 1922, p. 9.

2. *Ibid.,* p. 11.

3. "Progress of the Electric Light in England," a report submitted to the House of Commons, Ottawa, Canada, March 10, 1882. Quoted in the Edison Electric Light Company *Bulletin* no. 9, May 15, 1882, p. 16.

4. Martin, *Forty Years of Edison*, p. 38.

5. This meter can be seen in the restored Menlo Park Laboratory, Edison Institute, Dearborn, Michigan.

6. The Edison Electric Light Company *Bulletin* no. 16, February 2, 1883, p. 31.

7. The Edison Electric Light Company *Bulletin* no. 16, February 2, 1883, pp. 33, 34.

8. The Cincinnati Water Works installed an electric light plant in 1884 and for a period of several months used almost no gas. But its gas bill each month was the same as before. *Cincinnati Enquirer*, February 16, 1885. Quoted in the Edison Company for Isolated Lighting *Bulletin for Agents* no. 6, September 15, 1885, p. 3.

9. *American Gas Light Journal*, July 3, 1882, p. 5.

10. *Ibid.*

11. It might be argued that by coincidence the cost of electric light may have been equal to the price of gas light and that no inference can be drawn from the fact of identical prices of gas and electric light. My cost data and calculations are not yet complete but they indicate that the cost of electric light was substantially below the price set.

12. *American Gas Light Journal*, July 3, 1882, p. 5.

13. *Edison Electric Light Company booklet*, 1884. In the historical file of the General Electric Company, Schenectady, New York.

14. Quoted in Edison Electric Light Company *Bulletin* no. 17, April 6, 1883, pp. 21-22.

15. The Edison Electric Light Company *Bulletin* no. 9, May 15, 1882, pp. 6-7.

29

Power and Morality; American Business Ethics, 1840-1914

SAUL ENGELBOURG

Two questions are crucial. First, did business morality change at all, in either theory or practice, between 1840 and 1914? Second, if business morality changed and, more than that, for the better, what brought about change? The toughest problem is deciding whether business became more ethical or society became more sophisticated. . . .

Dishonesty lessens when the rules are clarified and enforced.[1] This is one of the reasons why it is likely that business morality moved to a new plane during the three-quarters of a century with which this study is concerned. Precedent was piled upon precedent, law was piled upon law, and administrative ruling was piled upon administrative ruling. At the same time businessmen were increasingly exposed to the glare of publicity. Again and again they were called upon to make an accounting of their actions to themselves and to the public at large. As a result, in at least

Saul Engelbourg, "Power and Morality; American Business Ethics, 1840-1914," in *Contributions in Economics and Economic History*, Number 28, Westport, Connecticut: Greenwood Press, 1980, pp. 134-143, 164-165. Excerpted and reprinted by permission of the Greenwood Press.

certain areas and circumstances, businessmen were less prone to act in 1914 as they did earlier on the five issues I have examined.

. . . This study has not attempted to treat the evolution of business morality in general but instead has dealt with five specific business practices, and I have accorded only peripheral attention to other aspects of business morality. Second, the most marked transformation in the behavior of businessmen in all probability occurred in those areas in which businessmen interact with each other as insiders in conflict-of-interest situations. In such areas, the standard of honesty has risen as a concomitant of economic growth, because complex enterprises demanded it. Also, there was an extension of the time horizon, which meant that a good reputation was more valuable in the long run than a quick killing in the short run.

Certainly those who doubt the growth of morality can be safely challenged, at least on those topics I have examined here, although the historian, like the jurist, deals only with those who are caught. At the end of the period there was less conflict of interest than there had been earlier. Restraint of trade was delimited, although the structure of the American economy was not affected. Competitive tactics were modified, and certain practices virtually disappeared. Stock watering diminished in the railroads, although it continued to flourish elsewhere. Financial reporting improved, although much remained to be done. Although government left the internal affairs of large-scale enterprises quite alone until 1933, it regulated their external affairs much earlier.

To explain why there was change is another matter. Despite the mass of evidence of a descriptive nature, it is difficult to speculate confidently on the causes of historical change because so little can be known for sure about the motives of men. . . . In any culture there are enormous pressures, both visible and invisible, making for stability; and yet cultures do change, in part because of the opportunities for moral creativeness. The one under examination, American business society, changed profoundly. . . .

Self-interest was (and still is) a guide to action. Never was it the sole guide, but it was certainly a fundamental point of departure for Americans generally during the period from about 1840 to 1914. . . . All societies, traditional and modern, agricultural and industrial, have laws or rules that set limits on the pursuit of self-interest, and business as a subsociety is no exception. To account for moral change is indeed difficult. Some men act largely in response to something in their own nature independent of their culture.[2] It is this category that is always the most difficult to account for, and yet it is at the heart of change.

No wholly satisfactory explanation of internally derived change exists, but there are some possibilities. One reason is the range of behavior within the business culture. Each industry, indeed each firm, is a subculture with its own code, and this makes it easier for an individual to be morally creative, to be a determinant of business morality as well as a product of it, but it says nothing about why a particular individual was creative. Different social groups of businessmen have different codes, which may compete, conflict, or overlap. Codes applicable to insiders may not be applicable to outsiders.[3] If stockholders as outsiders emerge victorious in a struggle for control with insiders, they might impose new ethical standards.

The possibility of internal change arising from individual creativity was limited by competition. It was difficult to eliminate bad actors and to unite an entire industry for self-regulation because tactics commonly condemned as immoral did win competitive advantages.[4] Much of self-regulation either by a businessman or in conjunction with his fellows is not based on a self-sacrificing internalization of the views of the community but rather on a more selfish desire to remain one step ahead of the law. . . .

Internal changes in business morality did occur regarding conflict of interest. One decisive turn of events, the Burlington's revolution of 1875, was in no way related to the passage of new laws. Much more to the point was anxiety on the part of insiders lest revelations about conflict of interest investment by the public.[5] . . . In general, legislation was of little consequence in the later diminution of conflict of interest, although legislation affecting the life insurance industry, passed in the aftermath of the Armstrong investigation, represents a notable exception. The main reason for change as to conflict of interest was the increase in the size and financial strength of enterprises that adopted their own rules. The Louisville & Nashville, for example, imposed such a rule in 1876 although the railroad had been in operation for more than two decades.[6] This reason was coupled with the pragmatic fact that honest management, in the long run, had perceptible advantages in the capital market. Perkins uttered a cry from the heart: "We railroad men had bad [enough] reputations to stagger under before, but the Boston management [of the Burlington] had been beyond suspicion. Now the public thinks we are all thieves!"[7] Such evidence suggests that Forbes and those who sided with him during the revolution of 1875 were not exclusively concerned with abstract notions of right and wrong. They were concerned with a kind of fiduciary relationship established with their investors; to act as both buyer and seller was to jeopardize that relationship. . . .

There was a shift in the so-called permanent or quasi-public enterprises toward the long-term view on the maximization of profits and on the belief that good business pays in the long run. The pursuit of short-term self-interest often means not only the moral but also the economic long-term disadvantage.[8]

For the most part the pressures for change in business morality came from outside. Most men do not have such finely tuned consciences that they will act against what they perceive as their own self-interest. Defenders of business argued for reliance on good men rather than good laws, while critics of business insisted that business immorality required action by government.[9]

The opportunities for business transgression were lessened during the period under study. The separation of the stock register from the stock transfer agent prevented management from converting the proceeds of the sale of securities to its own purpose. As the financial strength of railroads increased, they used outside rather than inside construction companies. Change in business morality occurred quite frequently because society, instigated largely by aggrieved customers, colleagues, and competitors, adopted the contention of the critics.

Internalization can frequently be delayed and change retarded in business morality by obstacles that arise from self-interest. There has been less change in business morality concerning restraint of trade than in the other business practices under discussion. An examination of restraint of trade necessitates the conclusion that, to the extent that there has been any change at all, it has been derived from the Sherman Antitrust Act as amended and as interpreted by the courts; however, there are numerous examples of breaches of the antitrust law, which itself constitutes a minimum standard of morality. . . .

The forces for the reform of competitive tactics were augmented by businessmen. Virtually no businessman could, for example, compete without accepting rebates if his competitors avidly sought them, but he could and did mobilize in order to secure the sanction of law. "From every standpoint," wrote Mark Sullivan, "it was to the advantage of the better class among these to have the dangerous and dishonest practices of their unscrupulous competitors curbed." The reform movement was intricately criss-crossed with motives entertained by various groups of businessmen.[10] As a result of the attack on big business, many businessmen gradually substituted the code of the outsiders for that of the insiders in evaluating themselves and their peers. Some chose not to sell patent medicine; others declined to avail themselves of the benefits of freight rate discrimination, and still others campaigned actively against it. Management continued to decide what a shareholder might know about his company, but some managements provided more information in their financial reports than either the law or custom required. As an illustration that change was by no means linear, the Louisville & Nashville furnished better financial reports prior to 1875 under Albert Fink than it did in the early 1880s under less able and less moral management.[11] . . .

The motives of men are obscure indeed, and Thomas C. Cochran, one of the ablest students of American business society, expressed his view as a reasoned act of faith: "There is no theoretical reason why important innovations in role behavior could not arise from inner-conditioning independently of all immediate exogenous factors. It is merely the bias of my historical observation that I think such instances rare."[12] The evidence presented here tends to support this conclusion that change in business morality was preponderantly derived from external rather than internal sources.

The process of external change was by no means simple. The key element in the drive for external change in business morality, at least in terms of initiating the process, was the victim. The historical mechanism thereafter was the expansion of the victim's moral outrage by publicity and the activities of crusaders to make it the public conscience. Government investigations hastened the crystallization of public and business opinion concerning alleged good or evil methods or results in business.[13] . . . Once the public conscience was successfully aroused, then the perpetrator of the deed to which the public voiced objection was placed on the defensive. Eventually the aid of government as the agent of society was invoked and appropriate legislation was enacted. The provisions of legislation and decisions interpreting the law define the new morality, identifying the permitted and prohibited actions. . . .

Changing business morality requires something more than a legislative enactment. There must also be internalization of the rule by the individual, which is a gradual and intermittent process. If this does not materialize, then the violations may become endemic, and the rule will fail to accomplish its purpose.

What determines whether the new rules on paper become new rules in behavior? The answer to this crucial question is sanctions. All moral codes are violated to some extent, and the strength of the sanctions determines the link between the code and social action. What punishments are inflicted by the individual upon himself (guilt) or by society (ostracism, fines, or prison) if an individual transgresses? Is the way of the transgressor hard? Certain business behavior, such as railroad rebates, ceased to be a matter of social concern, because the sanctions became strong and well established. On the other hand, restraint of trade violations by giant enterprises are still so frequent (although in varied forms) that the moral objective of the rules is not fully translated into behavior in this area. Nevertheless, while in the short run the sanctions of the insiders may prevail, in the long run those of the outsiders are more likely to prevail.[14]

Power and morality are inseparable. Considerations of the evolution of business morality without reference to the restructuring of economic power are invalid. The inequality of power in the market place that came to the fore with the rise of the giant enterprise created implications of business morality because of the failure of morality to be commensurate with power. . . .

Standard Oil failed to realize that power confers responsibility and that practices that might be acceptable in a small firm were regarded as unfair if applied by a dominant firm.[15] This was indeed the course of events; the largest enterprises attracted the greatest notoriety. A century ago prices were set by the interaction of substantially equal buyers and sellers, and each transaction was a bargain struck by buyer and seller. But large buyers and large sellers possessed an enormous advantage as compared with other and less fortunate competitors. It was the inequality of power, and not the presumed immorality of price discrimination, that caused the demand for a one-price policy. For that matter, bargaining was replaced by a one-price policy in retailing for purely practical reasons that had nothing to do with morality.

The business leadership of each generation is something other than an exact replica of the one that preceded it and has somewhat varying notions of right and wrong. . . . The laws violated by businessmen are recent and lack a firm foundation in public ethics, and sometimes the law is in conflict with business ethics. Therefore the public (and the businessmen) do not regard them in the same light as burglary.[16] A violation of the legal code is not necessarily a violation of the business code. Businessmen do not conceive of themselves as criminals when they violate the law. The most persistent and relevant illustration of this idea is the antitrust laws. Businessmen do not regard those involved in such actions as having lost prestige.[17] . . .

The normative business morality of the historically noteworthy titans I have cited was in a state of flux in the span of the seventy-five years during which America became the world's leading producer, although more decisively for some business practices than for others. Men in general, and goal-oriented businessmen in particular, are incapable of a rapid rate of self-improvement. The tendency to test the limits of moral and legal authority is all but universal. Therefore, the prime impetus for raising the standard of business morality came from the disaffected. Self-interest was as much as ever a guide to action for the businessman, who continued to define it in terms of achievement, but the choice of weapons was narrowed. All was never fair in business, although society, as it acquired greater understanding, in some instances came to accept what it had opposed earlier. Still, more became unfair with each passing generation. The ends remained constant but the means dramatically changed.

Endnotes

1. Richard C. Cabot, *Honesty* (New York: Macmillan, 1938), p. 89.

2. Kenneth Wiggins Porter, *The Jacksons and the Lees* (Cambridge, Mass.: Harvard University Press, 1937), 1:100-01, 110.

3. Fritz Redlich, "Sanctions and Freedom of Enterprise," *Journal of Economic History* 11 (Summer 1951): 266-70.

4. J. Owen Stalson, *Marketing Life Insurance* (Cambridge, Mass.: Harvard University Press, 1942), p. 406.

5. David P. Gagan, "The Railroads and the Public, 1870-1881: Charles Elliott Perkins' Business Ethics," *Business History Review* 39 (Spring 1965): 51.

6. Maury Klein, *History of the Louisville & Nashville Railroad* (New York: Macmillan, 1972), p. 203.

7. Gagan, "The Railroads and the Public," p. 43.

8. Stalson, *Marketing Life Insurance*, p. 295.

9. Irwin G. Wyllie, *The Self-Made Man in America* (New Brunswick, N. J.: Rutgers University Press, 1954), p. 76.

10. Mark Sullivan, *Our Times* (New York: Scribner's, 1929), 2:521, n. 1.

11. Klein, *Louisville & Nashville Railroad*, pp. 199-200.

12. Thomas C. Cochran, "The Entrepreneur in Economic Change," *Explorations in Entrepreneurial History/Second Series 3* (Fall 1965): 36-37.

13. Stalson, *Marketing Life Insurance*, pp. 294-95.

14. Redlich, "Sanctions and Freedom of Enterprise," pp. 266-70.

15. Ralph W. Hidy and Muriel E. Hidy, *Pioneering in Big Business* (New York: Harpers, 1955), p. 716.

16. Edwin H. Sutherland, "Is 'White Collar Crime' Crime?" *American Sociological Review* 10 (April 1955): 138; Marshall B. Clinard, *The Black Market* (New York: Rinehart, 1952), p. 230.

17. Edwin H. Sutherland, *White Collar Crime* (New York: Dryden, 1949), pp. 219, 222; Clinard, *The Black Market*, p. 306.

PART V

LARGE-SCALE ENTERPRISE, FINANCE CAPITALISM AND THE ROLLER-COASTER ECONOMY, 1900-1945

30

Recent Developments in American Business Administration and Their Conceptualization

ALFRED D. CHANDLER, JR. and FRITZ REDLICH

I

The evolution of large-scale, twentieth-century-style business organization raises certain problems for the economic theorist who deals with the personal element in business and economic development. This is because in the all-important process of decision-making for business enterprise change was reflected in two different ways. Or to put it in other words, two trends have appeared simultaneously in this connection, trends which will but contradict each other.

On the one hand, the decision-making process in large-scale corporations has become increasingly complicated as more and more persons

Alfred D. Chandler, Jr. and Fritz Redlich, "Recent Developments in American Business Administration and Their Conceptualization," *Business History Review*, Vol. XXXV (Spring, 1961), pp. 1-27. Excerpted and reprinted by permission of the *Business History Review*.

participate in it, while at the same time the *preparation* of decisions has turned into a more pressing and critical function to be carried out by the officers and employees plus outside advisers. When their work is completed these men report facts and figures, analyzing and submitting them in such a form that conclusions can easily be drawn by the "top management" actually making the decisions. Those preparing them select what they consider important information and drop what they consider of no immediate interest and concern. By molding the result into a digestible form, they gain, often unbeknown to themselves as well as to the top personnel, an extraordinary influence on decision making.

If the theorist then starts from the inherited concept of the entrepreneur as the decision-making man or team of men, he runs into difficulties. More and more unidentifiable employees below the top level participate in the process just described, or at least prejudice it by actions of their own. If we consider them part of the entrepreneurial team, the latter term loses its significance, for one can speak of a team only where there is personal contact among the members. If, on the other hand, we use the word "team" so loosely as to exclude that criterion, the concept of the "entrepreneur" becomes a mere symbol for human interplay within the large-scale corporation. . . .

If this were the only answer possible, the consequences would be serious. Those interested in pertinent empirical studies and historians who use the theoretical terms of entrepreneur and entrepreneurship are usually interested in the personal element in business and economic development. By that concept, they hope to identify the men who are or were the leaders within enterprises, the men molding them and fitting them into the market and the national economy; at the same time, if creative individuals, they are or were also the leaders in economic development. . . .

The second avenue to the solution of our problem lies in resolutely taking a step further in an ideological process by which the "entrepreneur" was developed out of Adam Smith's "capitalist." . . .

With the coming of the business corporation, the providing of capital split off from that of running the enterprise, and Jean Baptiste Say was the first to recognize what he called the "entrepreneur" as separate from the capitalist. In Say's days, the "entrepreneur" was the counterpart of a man doing a fairly extensive business by using other people's capital. As we would say today, he was a manager-entrepreneur who, like the eighteenth-century merchant, had occasionally to make a strategic decision and for the rest managed his plant, industrial, commercial, or what have you. . . . Some mid-nineteenth-century economists sensed intuitively that the type needed further analysis. The latter became urgent with the development of a new kind of large-scale enterprise in the late-nineteenth and early twentieth centuries. In such enterprises, men were needed to spend time preparing and making an increasing number of strategic decisions for the solution of major problems arising in their concerns, while they left their daily round of work to another set of men. For the latter, the term "managers" came to be used to distinguish them from the former, the "entrepreneurs." To the "entrepreneurs" an enterprise appeared as an organism to be kept alive, to the "managers" as a mechanism to be kept in working order. Here, of course, we deal with an analysis of two functions which in reality overlap.

By 1960, however, new steps in economic development had come to be reflected in new forms of business organization. . . . The early twentieth-century concept of "entrepreneur" needs further splitting up, so that new tools may emerge with which to handle mid-twentieth-century reality. However, before we can start our theoretical reasoning, we must present in the next two sections of the paper a description of the development of mid-twentieth-century large-scale business organization and business administration in the United States out of earlier nineteenth-century forms.

II

A historical survey of American business points to the development in this country of three types of enterprise.[1] The oldest one prevailing a hundred years ago was what one might call the single-function firm, i.e., a firm fulfilling one function only. The mercantile house only bought and sold goods. The shipping company as well as the canal and turnpike companies were interested in the single activity of transportation; while the mining concerns specialized in extracting raw material from the ground. Finally, the manufacturing firm only produced goods and, at the same time, produced only a single line of goods. Like the plantation owner, the mid-nineteenth-century manufacturer purchased the necessary materials from and sold his output to commission agents or a few wholesalers. Thus we can characterize a manufacturing firm of that period as a single-product, single-function concern. To be sure, the phrase used above, "fulfilling one function only," should not be taken literally. It means only that one function dominated or dominates a certain kind of enterprise; all others were or are subordinated to the main one and, as far as possible, left to other independent enterprises. . . .

The years between the Civil War and the turn of the century witnessed the evolution and rapid growth in manufacturing of what can be characterized as multi-function enterprises. Under the stimulus of the development of a national market, created with the help of the railroads and becoming quickly and increasingly a predominantly urban market, manufacturing firms not only came to have plants in different parts of the country but also took upon themselves the simultaneous handling of different activities. Many industrial enterprises developed an elaborate marketing organization dealing directly with consumers. They thereby freed themselves from the dependence on the wholesaler. Simultaneously they started producing one, several, or all of the raw materials needed in the process of manufacturing. In taking over what can be called the procurement function, they again freed themselves from the dependence on wholesalers and at the same time from that on the producers of raw material. Some manufacturing firms even took over the control of the transportation of their raw materials and finished goods. To a lesser extent, mining and marketing firms moved into manufacturing. Yet, as should be stressed, nearly all such multi-functional manufacturing concerns operated within the confines of one industry: they produced one major line of products and a few by-products. Thus they must be characterized as single-product, yet multi-function industrial concerns.

During the first half of the twentieth century, a new stage in the development was being reached. Many single-product, multi-function industrial enterprises in meeting the needs and opportunities created by a highly dynamic technology developed different lines of products, each with its own set of by-products. From single-product, multi-function manufacturing enterprises, they now grew into multi-product and multi-function industrial concerns, the maintenance and expansion of which required the tackling of more complicated tasks and the solving of more difficult problems than those involved in operating the older types.[2] The different ranges of decisions in these three types of enterprises—single product and single-function, single product yet multi-function, and multi-product and multi-function—led to three different types of industrial administration. (*Mutatis mutandis* this was the case also in other lines of business besides manufacturing.)

Modern structure and administration of industrial enterprise began in the United States with the geographical dispersion of such firms. That is, it began when manufacturing enterprises came to possess a number of factories by building or buying new units or by combining with other firms. Geographical dispersion was the initial step in making modern industrial enterprise, because it made necessary the distinction between headquarters and field. This distinction implies that the executives responsible for a firm's affairs had, for the first time, to supervise the work of other executives, those charged with managing the factories or branch offices in the field. The leading men at headquarters also had to coordinate the activities of the several field-units, that is to say, they had to standardize the procedures for these various units. The development of such procedures as well as the planning for expansion, maintenance, or contraction of the activities in the field became part and parcel of setting the goals and objectives of the firm in question.

The new trend gained momentum after the Civil War as the expanding market permitted an increased volume of manufacturing and marketing. In this period, evolving modern industrial enterprise was fortunate in that it could draw on the administrative experience gained in another type of dispersed and single-function enterprise, railroading. In this area the development had started as early as the 1850's, when the rapidly growing railroads demanded far more capital, equipment, and professionally trained personnel than did enterprises typical of the time. They were more complex than other contemporary, geographically dispersed single-function firms because of their need for careful, minute to minute, coordination and supervision of the operating sub-divisions. Such control was necessary to assure not only effective use of existing operating equipment, but also the efficient movement of goods and the safety of the passengers.

In the early railroads, the key decisions were usually made by the so-called general manager, a full time specialist, acting in close consultation with the representatives of the large investors. Like the manager of a contemporary textile mill, he made the major operational decisions, but was also responsible for the basic strategic ones, such as those on expansion, rates, and so forth. Moreover, he was one of the very first American businessmen to work out an explicit operating structure, that is, to establish clearly the channels of authority and communication within the organization. Naturally the executives of a railroad, sprawled out over a large geographical area and employing, as early as the 1850's, as many as five or six thousand men, could hardly supervise personally all of their company's activities.[3]

To deal with their new problems, the basic structure of American railroad corporations was worked out during the 1850's. In running a railroad its executive had to supervise three sets of activities—the moving of the trains, getting freight and passengers, and handling the financial transactions involved. Therefore, the organization of most railroads consisted of three major departments, transportation, traffic, and finance.[4] The most important department, transportation, in turn, was divided into three functional sections—transportation, maintenance of way, and maintenance of motor power. Because the moving of trains was the critical task, the officials in charge of transportation had to assume the authority and responsibility for all operating decisions. They became communication centers both on the local and central levels. On the former, namely, the level of the so-called division, which covered usually two to four hundred miles and was the smallest operating unit, headed by a "division manager," those who handled motor power and maintenance of way as well as the conductors and freight agents, were made responsible to the division's transportation manager. On the central level, the manager in charge of transportation was senior to the heads of the other two departments. He and the division managers, reporting to and receiving orders from the general manager, came to be called line officers and the others to be considered as staff men.

After the Civil War and the great expansion of the railroad networks, the railroad system rather than the individual road became the dominating operating organization. The more complex became operations, the more an explicit overall structure was needed. On such great systems as the Pennsylvania, the Vanderbilt roads, the Illinois Central, the Chicago and Northwestern, the Louisville and Nashville, the Rock Island, the problems of coordination, appraisal, and over-all policy planning became too complex to be handled by two to three men who had operational and other duties as well. Thus it became necessary to devise new organizational structures. These, formed at the time when the great systems emerged in the 1870's and 1880's, had characteristic features in common and consisted of a central office and several operating units, each of which was comparable to a single large railroad company.[5] The Pennsylvania had three such units—the lines east of Pittsburgh, west of Pittsburgh, and those to St. Louis.

. . . The general managers of these operating units now became primarily concerned with the mechanics of day-to-day activities, while the central office team took over the responsibility for those over-all decisions which we have come to call entrepreneurial. The central office became responsible for assuring effective coordination or traffic flow between the different major operating units. It appraised operating performance and took executive action on such appraisals. The most vital task of the general officers, however, was to consider the major strategies of new construction and of purchases and sales of lines.

Nevertheless as time passed, these senior officers did not stay clear from, but became again increasingly involved in operational duties. There were several reasons for this relapse. First and foremost, as the systems were rounded out and completed, the need to buy and build lessened and strategic problems became fewer. They decreased further as the Interstate Commerce Commission took over rate setting. In addition, systems of appraisal and coordination worked out in minute detail became more and more routinized. Thus by the early twentieth century, the duties of the railroad central offices assumed more of a routine character and the men occupying these positions handled anew operating functions.

We shall return to this subject in the fourth section of this paper after we have developed theoretical concepts by which we can better explain administrative progress in one period of railroading and administrative relapse in a later one. Suffice it here to sum up in empirical language what is essential from the point of view of this paper. While modern business administration evolved in the field of railroading, the character of that business forbade carrying the achievement to its logical conclusions. For a time, separation of operational functions from strategy determination was attempted. It did not become permanent. Major decisions in either area remained unseparated in the hands of the same top personnel.

We are now ready to turn to the single-product yet multi-function *industrial* enterprise that developed out of the single-product and single-function organization which dominated the American industrial scene until about 1860. A typical industrial enterprise such as a textile works, rolling mill, or shipyard of the ante-bellum days manufactured only one product or a single line of products and sold, usually in bulk, to one sales agent or a very few wholesalers. Even after such an enterprise expanded its operations in the 1870's and 1880's to include a number of geographically dispersed plants, it remained a single-function activity. Twenty years later, however, major sectors of American industry were dominated by great single-product yet multi-function firms. As these consolidated enterprises, the result of vertical integration, came to do their own marketing, their own purchasing from the primary sources and often their own producing of raw materials, *the different functional activities soon became organized into different departments.*

In a typical single-product yet multi-function firm, each functional department was as important as the others. The line and staff set-up of the railroads had little relevance for the over-all structure here. The major departments might have their own auxiliaries like engineering in manufacturing and advertising in sales. But each department head was a specialist and supreme in his own sphere. Usually a vice-president, he had his managing director for dealing with the routine activities of his department. The vice-presidents, as individuals, planned the broader developments within their functionally determined departments. Collectively, together with the president and chairman of the board, they guided the destinies of their vast business empires. For this purpose, the men concerned usually cooperated in so-called executive committees. In making the distinction between vice-president and manager or managing director, the corporations in question were defining the difference between policy-making and operations.

The executive committees of the single-product yet multi-function enterprises had the same underlying duties as the "general managers" of the railroad systems. But as the nature of their business was different, so was the nature of the appraising, coordinating, and policy-making duties. Appraisal was the least different from that of the railroads. It meant constant concern for the development of increasingly meaningful profit and loss figures. But because more basic and quite different functions were involved, the over-all determination of profit and loss proved more difficult. So, too, the senior officers in those enterprises had to assess performance, not just in one, but in nearly all major parts of the over-all industrial process.

Coordination of the enterprise's various activities was more complex than in a geographically dispersed single-function firm, including even the large railroads. A steady flow of product through the different departments—from the raw materials to the ultimate consumer—had to be assured. The rate of flow depended on market demand. Thus coordination of interdepartmental activity with market demand was necessary if for no other purpose than for making effective use of the company's total facilities and resources. Therefore, coordination became a critical central office function. Yet where the markets and sources of supply remained fairly unchanged, as was true after 1900 in many of the agricultural processing and metal industries, it became increasingly a routine task.

Even more critical was planning for the maintenance and expansion of the enterprise as a whole. This meant that the senior officers had to make basic decisions with respect to the several very different functional activities. The executive committee had to allocate funds among departments and thus decided whether to expand or contract in sales, manufacturing, the control of raw materials, engineering, etc. In so doing, it had to face a new specific difficulty. Since this top committee was made up of department heads, i.e., of functional specialists, the final policy tended to be the result of negotiations and compromise between the different departments. In addition, the top level team, so composed, had neither enough time, nor enough impartial information to handle over-all problems satisfactorily. Its members spent most of their working day on departmental matters, and the information on which the executive committee acted was biased just because it was framed by these executives in their capacities as functional operating officers. Factual and analytical reports were usually presented so as to favor one of the alternatives under discussion, although this was not always done consciously.

In some single-product yet multi-function industries, just as in railroading, the administrative pattern froze once it had been elaborated. As long as the enterprise in question sold one major line of goods manufactured from one group of raw materials by means of one relatively simple marketing technique and in a comparatively unchanging and steady market, the questions and problems decided by the top team became relatively simple as time went on. This held true of the steel, copper, nickel, and some other metal industries, of meat packing, tobacco processing, distilling, flour milling, and other agricultural processing industries. But resting on one's oars was not possible where the decision-making remained difficult, because markets, production techniques, or sources of supply were changing continuously or rapidly.

Let us sum up what is essential from the point of view of this article: the administration of single-product yet multi-function industrial enterprises pivoted and pivots around functional departments whose heads—specialists—together with the corporation president and chairman of the board formed and form an executive committee. That is to say, the committee, set up to make strategic decisions, consisted and consists of men who were and are themselves rooted in the fulfillment of certain functions. Once more, major decisions in two fields, operations and strategy, rested or rest in identical hands.

By 1910, the *threshold* of a new administrative development was being raised in those industries which came into the orbit of the two new generators of power, the internal combustion engine and the electrical motor. The development gained momentum with the rapid growth of the science-based industries. By 1940, however, it was still concentrated in five major industries: electrical and electronics, power machinery including the automobile, rubber, petroleum, and chemicals. It resulted primarily from product diversification, based on new and expanding technologies. After 1900, Allis Chalmers, for example, moved from building steam machinery to making electrical apparatus and equipment, to developing trucks and other commercial vehicles, and finally into the producing and selling of tractors and farm machinery. International Harvester, after applying the internal combustion engine to farm implements, moved to making tractors and then trucks and commercial vehicles. As new lines were developed in individual enterprises, it became increasingly hard to handle the purchasing, manufacturing, and marketing of each within the same centralized, functionally departmentalized operating organization. Marketing was particularly difficult since the new products went to quite different types of customers.

In the electrical and chemical industries, the continuous development of new products raised even more intense difficulties, for their markets were still more varied. By the mid-1920's, companies like General Electric, du Pont, and Union Carbide had not only moved into the making of quite different producers' goods, ranging from metal products to plastics, but also had begun to sell consumers' goods. The chemical enterprises sold paints, batteries, and antifreeze directly to consumers, and the great electrical firms began to move into the same broad market by making appliances such as refrigerators, washing machines, vacuum cleaners, and stoves. In the rubber and oil industries, there was less strain on the existing functionally departmentalized organizations. Although revolutionized by the coming of the automobile, some leading companies tended to stay within the bounds of a single industry. On the other hand, firms like Goodrich and United States Rubber, when taking up the production of a broad variety of rubber products, including rubber chemicals, and the oil companies developing petro-chemicals, faced structural problems initially comparable to those met by the electrical and chemical firms.

The strategy of diversification and concomitantly the development of the multi-product and multi-function industrial enterprise quickly demanded a new form of organization. The old functional departments were wholly unable to handle the problems arising from the engineering, producing, and marketing of entirely different goods, to say nothing of those of supplying materials for the manufacture of each. *Consequently, as the enterprises moved into the new lines, the administration of each major line was organized on a multi-function basis.*[6] In other words, the major operating unit within the enterprise came to be based on a product line, not a function. Each head of a product division had under his control a full set of functional departments—manufacturing, sales, finance, purchasing, engineering, and research and development. Within the bounds and limits, i.e., the policy established by the central office, the chief officers of those product units made major decisions. These, however, must be distinguished from those emanating from headquarters.

Within the framework of central policy, the duties of a division head were quite comparable to those of a senior executive of a single-product yet multi-function enterprise. Divisional performance was appraised by the financial success (return on investment) and to a lesser extent by the share in the market which the division chiefs could conquer or maintain. From these units, data flowed continuously to the headquarters in the form of statistics, charts, reports, etc., supplemented by oral communications during visits, both of unit heads to headquarters and of the central office executives to the operating units.

A relatively small team of four to a dozen men, located in adjoining offices in the central headquarters, now became responsible for the enterprise as a whole. The team's functions were appraisal, coordination, and the determination of policy both for the enterprise as a whole and for its multi-function, product-based operating units. In carrying out these duties, the general officers at central headquarters had the assistance of a staff of specialists. Normally, the new advisory staff had offices pertaining to one or several of the major functions to be performed, such as advertising, marketing, production, purchasing, engineering, labor relations, public relations, research and development, and so forth.

In such a structure, then, the top team is an easily identifiable group, and it is recognizable by what it does—by its functions and activities—rather than by the personality traits of its members. It cannot be stressed strongly enough, as did Sombart and other researchers, that such business executives are not necessarily possessed of *charisma*. Personally unknown to the possibly tens of thousands of workers and employees, they need no *charisma* and usually have none. If one of them has this quality, it may show up in his relations to the other members of the team, in his political influence, and in his role in trade associations and the like.

This team communicates directly and interacts only with the men responsible for operations, but is in no way the latters' captive. In making *critical* decisions as to the maintenance and expansion of the enterprise, its alternatives are *sui generis* and not forced on it by the operators. Its decisions are concerned with balancing conflicting interests between the operators whose demands are determined by the products and/or functions for which they are responsible. In making those decisions, the top team has data and opinions presented by the functional staff specialists at headquarters who have little or no divisional connections or biases.

This new type of organization started immediately after World War I at General Motors and du Pont. A few others followed in the 1920's and 1930's. But it was only with the great economic expansion during and after World War II, with the rapid increase of systematic research and development, and with the demands of the present-day economy and technology, that this modernized, decentralized type of structure became widespread. Increasingly used by multi-product and multi-function firms in the five industries already listed, it was taken over also by some of the older agricultural processing companies, such as Armour [and] Procter and Gamble, to the extent that they too moved into chemicals and built highly diversified product lines.

We can consider as the characteristic feature of the newest kind of business administration that not only are operations (management) and policy-making separated but that also a middle level which has essentially administrative functions has been inserted. We will return to this matter in the fourth and analytical section of this paper. Suffice it to stress here . . . that the delegation of functions by the top team has not left it without tasks. New ones had to be and were added to the traditional functions. While, for example, in a single-product enterprise, the question of what to produce is solved once and for all with the establishment of the works and reappears only in cases of critical reorganization, the current determination of what to produce becomes a major type of strategic decision in the modern multi-product and multi-function industries.

Goal determination takes the time and energy of the top team. And since its members are no longer responsible for operations and administration, they are psychologically more committed to seeing the concern as a whole. They have the time for planning and, last but not least, they have excellent information. The steady flow of relevant data assembled by the central staff, supplemented by those on the performance of the divisions and by regular visits with the administrators, provides such information as is necessary for policy-making.

A General Motors report of 1937 is of the greatest interest in this context. It stated that the administration was being left to the divisions and the formulation of policy to the central headquarters, and it defined the distinction in this way.[7] "By 'administration' is meant the daily conduct of the Corporation's affairs. By 'formation of policies' is meant both the establishment of the broad principles by which administration is to be guided and the determination of the fundamental concepts of the business. The prime objectives of the business; the scope of its operations, both as to products and markets; the desirability of expansion, horizontally or vertically or both; the provision of the essential capital for its operations, and the question of distribution of its profits as between the amount paid in dividends and the amount retained in the business—all are problems involving 'formation of policies' and illustrate the principle involved."

III

We have painted with broad strokes of the brush the development of American business organization between about 1850 and 1950. From our point of view, the significant finding can be characterized as the evolution of a three-level out of a two-level organization. We have now to look for the tools which were developed parallel with the organizational evolution, for the tools which made the latter possible. Critical and crucial was progress in the field of communication, the more so the closer we come to our own time. As the top team of our day became increasingly concerned with over-all policy and strategy and less involved in the day-to-day conduct of the business and as both the operating and administrative structures of the firms concerned became larger and more intricate, the need grew for free flowing and efficient channels of communication between the top team and the various levels of the organization. At the same time and on all levels, more and more precise data were also needed concerning the all but bewildering external situation, particularly in the markets. And, naturally, as the business units grew in size and the activities in complexity parallel with the spreading industrialization and urbanization of the nation, and as the industrial technique and its scientific basis became more and more involved, effective communication became harder and harder.

Two methods could be used for improving communication lines between the top team and the lower levels or for guaranteeing at least a steady flow of communication. One was to define more clearly the *channels* of communication and authority; the other was to develop more useful *kinds* of information to move through the channels. Thus began systematic, periodic reports, operating statistics, forecasts, and so forth. In this country, the creation of the first precise internal channels of communication and of detailed operating statistics was again the work of the railroads. Contemporary mercantile houses or textile or iron mills had as little need for a detailed reporting system as for formal operating structures, as has been described. Nor would they have been able to get much information on the external situation other than prices current or shipping news.

In the early years of railroad expansion, particularly in the decade of the 1850's, much thought was given not only to formal organization, but also to the development of operating statistics. While many companies defined their lines of communication and authority, in an *ad hoc* way, i.e., as particular problems had to be worked out, some attacked them more systematically. The Erie had a detailed organization chart by 1854; the Pennsylvania a printed organization manual by 1858.[8] In 1889 when the Illinois Central, planning a reorganization, made a survey of twenty-two major railroads, it found that one third of these had printed codes or rules "defining the power and duties of (their) officers."[9] Some others had carefully regulated their organizations, although the result had not been published and was not available for distribution. The rest still operated under informal codes of "usages and procedures," built up over time.

Statistics as first developed by the railroads reflected, like their organizational structure, the basic need of assuring the safe and efficient running of the trains. Hence the roads assembled a wealth of satisfactory *operating* data. Reporting and statistical procedures worked out as early as the 1850's came into common use after the Civil War.[10] Railroad officers were soon to learn the value of these data for determining cost and with it profits, an extremely difficult problem. By the early 1870's, Albert Fink and other railroad men had worked out quite sophisticated techniques for establishing cost per ton mile operated.[11] By the end of the century, the term "control through statistics" was regularly used in railroading.[12]

But this control remained operational rather than anything else. The railroads developed satisfactory data for appraising past performance, but they did almost nothing to work out forecasts, budgets, or statistical procedures as might be used to plan ahead. This lack can undoubtedly be explained by the fact that after 1900 strategy and planning became less important in railroading. . . . The existing data and procedures were sufficient to carry out the major central office functions of appraising the performance of the different operating units and of coordinating traffic flow between the units.

Little of what the railroads had achieved in this field was carried over into the single-product yet multi-function manufacturing enterprise because of the different character of its business. However, by the turn of the century, in working out a specific structure of its own, it also had to develop lines of communication and authority that suited its own needs. In so doing, some of the big enterprises proceeded quite systematically.[13] Questions relating to structure and the means of sustaining it came to be discussed by the end of World War I in the business and industrial literature of the day, such as trade journals and other periodicals and even in textbooks.[14] At the same time, the data flowing through the more clearly defined channels were being greatly improved. In industrial enterprises, unlike the railroads, internal statistics grew out of the need for cost analysis rather than for detailed day-to-day operating information. Effective means for allocating overhead and for determining variable costs led, in turn, to the recognition that variable costs are closely related to volume and that realistic cost analysis called for the determination of expected future as well as past performance.

The needs of interdepartmental coordination also brought pressure on the large-scale enterprise to predict its future in addition to gauging its past performance. Ultimately the total of product flow through various departments depended on demand. The more accurately demand could be forecast, the more evenly the flow could be channelled, and thus the overall organization could be operated closer to maximum capacity. The importance of forecasting demand for the purpose of determining quantities to be produced, of coordinating product flow, and of finding variable costs was greater for firms operating in the mass-consumer market than it was for those making producers' goods, and greater also in the production of consumer durables than in that of consumer perishables. The great meat packers like Armour and Swift could maintain flow by keeping a constant telegraphic communication between the sales managers of the branch houses in the great eastern metropolises and the buyers of cattle and other livestock in the stockyards of western cities.[15] On the other hand, General Motors discovered, right after World War I, that the maintenance of any kind of steady flow and with it the steady use of plant and personnel called first of all for careful forecasts of annual demand and the development of detailed production schedules based on these estimates.[16] Then came the need to work out procedures to make possible the *adjustment* of the forecasts and production schedule to the *actual conditions* of the changing market. This was done at General Motors by obtaining reports every ten days from the dealers as to the actual number of cars sold and also frequent reports on new car registrations. After 1925, the year in which General Motors started basing nearly all its activities on expected market demand, the use of forecasts and of statistics for anticipating market behavior was becoming a fairly widespread practice in American industry.

The needs of planning, like those of coordination and appraisal, equally turned American industrialists to acting on the basis of anticipated rather than past performance. The development and expansion of the different functional activities and the resulting problems of allocating funds among departments and within departments led in many enterprises to the systematizing of appropriation procedures. Senior officers asked that each request for capital expenditure include carefully worked out cost information, indicate an estimated return on investment on the proposed project and the project's relation to the over-all program of the operating unit involved and of the company itself. Soon comparable reports were requested for estimated operating as well as capital expenditures.

Both came to be combined into regular—semiannual or annual—budgets. The budget became both a means of supervision and an expression of policy. As to the former, operating performance could be checked against the estimates and proposals in the budget. As to the latter, the budget by its allocation of available funds set the limits on the departmental or divisional activities, and at the same time it indicated the areas where the senior officers believed the company should expand or contract its activities. The budget was and is considered more as a guide than as an unadjustable schedule to be followed without questioning. Budget-making forced firms, as early as World War I, into forecasting the financial and economic conditions outside of the companies concerned, so that financial planning and the allocation of funds might be put on a rational basis. In those same years—those immediately following World War I—periodicals and books on business came to take an increasing interest in the discussion of forecasting, budgeting, techniques of inventory, production, and marketing control.[17]

The coming of the multi-product and multi-function enterprise brought, besides increasing stress on formal structure, a further refinement of existing statistical and other communication techniques. The problem of structure in this new type of enterprise was essentially one of redefining channels of authority and communication to meet the new complexities. In addition, statistical procedures were refined in two new ways. There was the need of getting *precise* information in as *compact* a form as possible. Otherwise the general officers at headquarters would not have found the time to make effective use of it in appraising performance, coordinating the units, and making over-all policy. Secondly, statistical techniques had to be *perfected* so that the *rapidly increasing* amount of all kinds of information on production, purchasing and marketing could be used more effectively on all levels, particularly in the administrative divisions. Also the reports and personal visits between the policy-makers at the center and the administrators on a lowel level became more and more important in assuring communication between central headquarters and the administrative divisions. In the development of those new statistical techniques and procedures, the central staff played a more significant role than did the operating units.

These practices then provided the executives with data essential to supervising and maintaining control over their increasingly intricate enterprises in an external situation growing always more complex. Statistical and financial controls made possible the delegation of major decisions to the men in charge of the multi-functional product divisions. Through constant objective checks on divisional performance, errors and mistakes of these subordinates could usually be caught before major harm was done to the over-all enterprise. The senior men could take action because they controlled the selection of executive personnel and because, through budgeting, they allocated the funds to the operating divisions. In the way they allocated their resources—capital and personnel—and in the promotion, transferral and retirement of operating executives, they determined the framework in which the operating units worked and thus put into effect their concept of the long-term goals and objectives of the enterprise. . . .

IV

When we examine our material from another point of view, it becomes evident that the two kinds of business administration which were developed to fit the needs of the older forms of enterprise are two-level affairs, while that corresponding to the most modern type of enterprise takes place on three levels. The first two levels are operations (management) on the one hand, and coordination of operations, goal determination, and planning, on the other. In the multi-product and multi-function enterprise, however, the top level was split up by the delegation of one of its activities—the coordination of operations of the various functional departments within the major lines of products. The coordination of these functional units, working possibly in the most disparate fields, demanded such special care that it became necessary to give full time attention to administering the operators (managers) of these units. This then became the task of a new, middle level of business administration. For want of a better word, we will characterize it as the *locum-tenential* level, because certain officers other than the top team, but *in lieu* of it, undertake to administer on their own responsibility particular lines of product, a situation which implies supervision and coordination of the functional operators concerned. Thereafter, the top team could specialize on goal determination and planning. . . .

One cannot emphasize too strongly that operator (manager), "locum tenens," and entrepreneur are ideal types with which the generic figures of reality must be compared, if analysis of reality is desired. Of course, while a theoretical model must be clear-cut to serve as a useful tool for the analysis of reality, reality itself never is precise. The performers of any one of those critical functions fulfill other, i.e., noncritical ones also. Moreover, those working on the higher levels may also have a hand temporarily or permanently in the performance of the typical functions of the one just below. Vice versa, an able man serving on a lower level may, because of his ability or insight, be called to advise the next higher level. Yet the larger the enterprise tends to be and the nearer to the present time, the clearer becomes the separation of functions. . . .

Once the conceptual frame here proposed is adopted, new light can be thrown on several phenomena, two of which are of interest here.[18] First, we can see that the initial steps towards a three-stage business administration were taken in railroading, and in stressing this fact we take up an earlier thread. As early as the 1870's we find the planning entrepreneur at headquarters in railroad enterprises. The heads of the regional units stood for the "locum tenens" of theory, while the heads of the various departments corresponded to the operators (managers) of theory. The relapse into a simpler and, from the point of view of the historian, older type of administration, described earlier, can then be explained by the need for fewer decisions once the railroad net was practically completed with the concomitant and continuous systematization of day-to-day operations. Railroads could return to the simpler two-stage administration with only headquarters and field organized in functional departments.

Secondly, the phenomenon of decentralization comes up for a new interpretation. The term of "decentralization" has been used to denote geographical as well as administrative decentralization. Of these, only the latter type is of interest to us. Within our conceptual frame, administrative decentralization predicated on the delegation of functions, i.e., the power to make decisions in the delegated field, appears on two levels—the operational (managerial) and the "locum-tenential." The former is historically the older one. In large-scale, nineteenth-century enterprise, certain decisions were made at headquarters, others in the "field." A historically later and different kind of decentralization appeared first in the 1920's when the middle level of business administration, the "locum-tenential," became semi-independent. Consequently, today we find in some enterprises two levels of decentralization, a fact which has only begun to be recognized by researchers. Operators and "locum tenentes" have in common a concern with day-to-day activities, while the top team, being rather remote from these, acts, one might say, from year-to-year and intermittently. But in this connection, one needs to guard against a misunderstanding. Day-to-day actions are by no means synonymous with routine. . . .

To repeat, in the study of business enterprise the difference between entrepreneur, "locum tenens," and operator (manager) is one between tasks to be performed by these various cooperating and complementary figures. This holds true even though it would appear at first glance that they have one task in common, namely, coordination. But a mere word should not deceive us. On every level of the hierarchy, different kinds of coordination take place. On the operational (managerial) level, executives—plant managers, heads of branch offices, or groups of product salesmen, purchasing agents, or scientists—are coordinated to carry out a single basic function—manufacturing, sales, purchasing, or research. On the "locum-tenential" level, functions relating to the processing of a major line of products, all the way from the raw material to the consumer, are coordinated. Finally, the top team (the entrepreneur) coordinates the various lines of products in the best interest of the enterprise.

The performance of the various tasks is reflected in the different horizons of the officers in question. The operator (manager) thinks in terms of a single function, the "locum tenens" in terms of a line of products or an industry, while the entrepreneur has the national economy and even the whole world in his mind in making his decisions.

Administrative problems of course are solved by decisions. Consequently, to our three kinds of business administration there correspond three levels of business decisions: operational (managerial), "locum-tenential," and entrepreneurial, the last term to be used if we stick to the tradition and call the top team "the entrepreneur" whenever we speak in theoretical terms. Correspondingly, as there are three levels of business administration, three horizons, three levels of tasks, and three levels of decision-making, so there are three levels of policy. There is the operational (managerial), "locum-tenential," and entrepreneurial policy. . . .

Taking a cue from military language, we can designate operational (managerial) and "locum-tenential" decisions as tactical in contrast to entrepreneurial as strategic decisions. In military science, specifically in Clausewitz's language, tactics implies the leading of forces for the purpose of a battle, while strategy connotes the conducting of battles for the purpose of war. Or, as was taught in German military schools, tactics implies leading forces *in* battle, strategy leading forces *into* battle. If we adapt this terminology to the study of business administration, we could say: strategic decisions are those that allocate the means of production, including available liquid funds and available manpower, particularly skilled personnel, according to the purpose of the enterprise; while tactical decisions apply allocated means and manpower for the purpose of administering those units which are under the care of the "locum tenentes" and managers. Or to put it more pointedly, the difference is one between the allocation as against the application of means of production.

This then is the place to show how reality, i.e., what the businessman calls "top management," deviates from the ideal type, the model of "the entrepreneur." When a businessman reaches a certain place in the administrative hierarchy of enterprise, he becomes a member of "top management" and remains so until he retires. In theory, however, entrepreneurship, i.e., the participation in the goal-determining and planning team, is actualized only in making a *particular* decision. Outside of the intermittent process of making strategic decisions, any given person is a member of the entrepreneurial team only potentially while the specific entrepreneurial decisions in large-scale business enterprise are made by an ever slightly varying team.

The discussion of decisions has brought us to that of business policy. Here again the development of large-scale industry and of appropriate forms of business administration has been accompanied by historical change. Leland Jenks has shown in another context that in the nineteenth century, problems of business administration were solved *ad hoc*.[19] In such a situation, business policy could develop only slowly; and by business policy we mean a consistent sequence of decisions, even if not recognized as such by the men concerned. The fact of *conscious* policy determination is established in railroading for the 1850's and in industry for the 1880's.[20] Actually, business policy seems to be the natural concomitant of geographically dispersed enterprise. In no other way can widely scattered operating decisions be coordinated and supervised. Ultimately, in the course of a hundred years of administrative development, the more or less conscious consistency of decisions has emerged until, at least on the entrepreneurial level, business policy has become equivalent to a master plan. To this master plan, i.e., entrepreneurial policy, "locum tenentes" as well as operators (managers) must adhere and adherence is enforced by budgetary procedures.

At this point, then, we meet a crucial problem. We have designated the functions of the top team as goal determination and planning. These functions can be performed only by men who are in control of the concern's capital, allotted and unallotted alike. Thus the function of goal determination and planning is underpinned by that of fund allocation or budgeting (synonymous terms in modern enterprise). As a matter of fact, the first appearance of a budget in business enterprise cannot be overestimated in its historical importance. It is an indicator of emerging bureaucratization of business, the correlative to modern large-scale enterprise. The budget sets a goal, while traditionally business enterprise was satisfied with gauging the result once a year by a profit and loss statement. The function of fund allocation (budgeting) which goes with that of goal determination and planning is the factor which determines the locus of ultimate authority in enterprise. . . .

Ultimate authority in business enterprise, as we see it, rests with those who hold the purse strings, and in modern large-scale enterprise, those persons hold the purse strings who perform the function of goal setting and planning. . . .

Our findings can be summed up thus: if in theoretical contexts we wish to conceptualize the top team which keeps modern large-scale business alive, we cannot start from the difference between innovation and routine. Nor can we see as essential characteristics of the top team the making of decisions or the determining of policy. Like some earlier theorists, we can see as the criterion the making of *strategic* decisions, provided it is well understood what we mean by "strategic." We can and should start from the specific functions which the top team performs—goal determination, planning, and budgeting. We can and should stress that the team holds the ultimate authority in the enterprise concerned. If then, in line with tradition, we wish to use the term "entrepreneur" to designate that top team, here are the elements to define it.

Endnotes

1. The following section is based on a historical analysis of the changing corporate structure and strategy in the United States. It includes case studies of organizational innovations made by du Pont, General Motors, Jersey Standard, and Sears, Roebuck; and also a broader investigation of the experience of more than seventy of the largest industrial and transportation companies in the United States. Preliminary results of this investigation can be found in Alfred D. Chandler, Jr., "Management Decentralization: An Historical Analysis," *Business History Review*, vol. XXX (Boston, Mass., 1956), pp. 111 ff. Chandler, "The Beginnings of 'Big Business' in American Industry," *ibid.*, vol. XXXIII (1959), pp. 1 ff. Chandler, "Development, Diversification and Decentralization," in *Postwar Economic Trends in the United States*, ed. Ralph E. Freeman, American Project Series, Center of International Studies, Massachusetts Institute of Technology (New York, 1960), pp. 235 ff.

2. The term "multi-product firm" will be used in this paper to refer to one making quite different product lines, each with its own set of by-products, for quite different markets. An

example of such a multi-product firm would be a large chemical company which has such different lines as plastics, film, textile fibers, polychemicals, explosives, paints, pigments, rubber products, electro-chemicals, and photographic products.

3. Thomas C. Cochran, *The Railroad Leaders, 1845-1890: the Business Mind in Action* (Cambridge, Mass., 1953), chaps. 5-9. Alfred D. Chandler, Jr., *Henry Varnum Poor—Business Editor, Analyst, and Reformer* (Cambridge, Mass., 1956), chap. 7.

4. Ray Morris, *Railroad Administration*, Appleton's Railway Series (New York and London, 1910), chaps. 2-3.

5. *Ibid.*, chap. 4. The following is based on a survey of the annual and other reports of the Pennsylvania Railroad and the New York Central system.

6. This same type of organization was developed by the single-line firm, particularly large oil companies, whose activities had become world-wide—or multi-regional—in scope. The head of each regional unit usually managed the several functions of the business and operated quite autonomously within the framework set by the central office.

7. *Twenty-ninth Annual Report of General Motors Corporation, Year Ended December 31, 1937*, Prepared for Presentation to the Stockholders at the Annual Meeting to Be Held in Wilmington, Delaware, Tuesday, April 26, 1938, p. 37.

8. Chandler, *Henry Varnum Poor*, pp. 147 ff. *Pennsylvania Railroad Company, Organization for Conducting the Business of the Road, Adopted December 26, 1857* (Philadelphia, 1858).

9. "Minutes of the Meeting of the 'Board,' Appointed by the Resolution of the Illinois Central Board of Directors, May 15, 1889, Held at the General Offices in Chicago, Friday, June 21, 1889, 11 A.M.," from the Illinois Central Railroad Company's files.

10. Chandler, *Henry Varnum Poor*, pp. 137 ff., 145 ff.

11. Particularly valuable in this connection is the *Annual Report of the Louisville and Nashville Railroad for the Year Ending June 30, 1874*, written by Albert Fink.

12. Ray Morris, *Railroad Administration*, has a chapter entitled "Control Through Statistics."

13. Some of the large companies which had systematically worked out their structures before World War I included United States Rubber Company, International Harvester, American Smelting and Refining, Westinghouse, Allis Chalmers, General Electric, and Bethlehem Steel.

14. A brief examination of the first volumes of the journal, *Management and Administration* (New York), which began publication in 1921 is useful in this connection. So also is Leon Carroll Marshall, *Business Administration* (Chicago, Ill., 1921), one of the best anthologies of business literature. Two of the best early books on structure are Russell Robb, *Lectures on Organization* (privately printed [Boston?], 1911), and Dexter S. Kimball, *Principles of Industrial Organization* (New York, 1913), p. 22.

15. *Report of the Commissioner of Corporations on the Beef Industry* (Washington, D.C., 1905), p. 21.

16. Donaldson Brown, "Pricing Policy in Relation to Financial Control," a series of articles appearing in *Management and Administration* in the spring of 1924. Also C. S. Mott, "Organizing a Great Industrial," *ibid.*, pp. 527 ff.; Albert Bradley, "Setting Up a Forecasting Program," American Management Association, *Annual Convention Series No. 41 (March, 1926); and Donaldson Brown, "Decentralized Responsibilities With Centralized Coordination," ibid.*, No. 57 (Feb., 1927).

17. Again the articles in the early numbers of *Management and Administration* are particularly revealing.

18. The following is a schematic somewhat oversimplified sketch.

19. Leland Jenks, "Some Early Phases of the Management Movement," *Administrative Management Quarterly*, vol. V (Ithaca, New York, 1960/61), p. 424.

20. Ralph W. and Muriel E. Hidy, *History of Standard Oil Company* (New Jersey), vol. I, *Pioneering in Big Business* 1882-1911 (New York, 1955), p. 62.

31

The Decline of Laissez Faire, 1897-1917

HAROLD U. FAULKNER

In following the yearly variations in the business cycle one may easily miss the fundamental economic revolution which took place during these years. This was no less than a shift in the control of American economic life from industrial to financial capitalists. Unregulated and virtually unhindered, finance capitalists achieved a power hitherto unknown in American history and probably never reached again even in the lush years of the 1920's. This power had not appeared overnight, but had been the result of long development. From the settlement of Jamestown to the end of the nineteenth century, wealth had accumulated in America, but it was largely in fixed form. When America during these three centuries needed large amounts of liquid capital it had sought them in Europe. Such great European firms as Baring of London, Hottinguer of Paris, and Hope of Amsterdam had floated American securities and kept in close touch with the American money market through their agents in this country.[1]

In the meantime surplus liquid capital increased in America, coming mainly from the profits of the wealthy and the savings of the prosperous

Harold U. Faulkner, *The Decline of Laissez Faire*, 1897-1917. Volume VII, The Economic History of the United States, New York: Rinehart & Company, Inc., 1951, pp. 35-45. Reprinted by permission of Pamela Faulkner (Mrs. Frank T.) Mansure.

middle class. National wealth increased from $88,500,000,000 in 1900 to $351,700,000,000 in 1917, and national income from $18,000,000,000 to $51,300,000,000. Assets of financial institutions including national banks, savings banks, private banks, loan and trust companies, and life insurance companies rose from $9,156,000,000 in 1897 to $27,795,000,000 in 1911. There can be no doubt that the volume of individual savings grew rapidly in the early years of the present century. When to individual savings were added foreign investments, undistributed business earnings, and the expansion of bank credits, it is clear that the sources of income both from capital expansion and from the purchase of securities were expanding. Foreign investments, which had remained at a low level during the early nineties, increased rapidly in the intense industrial expansion after 1897. Moreover, the percentage of banking funds invested in securities rose from 18.0 in 1890 to 27.7 in 1910. During the nineteenth century most of the surplus capital had gone into the westward movement and into transportation facilities. After 1897 large amounts continued to go into railroads, but the investment market now widened to include public utilities, industrial enterprises, foreign properties, and the bonds of local and state governments and those of the federal government.[2]

By the 1890's there were sufficient investment funds to promote business for large American investment houses, and American as well as European money was drawn upon heavily for industrial and transportation projects. Such concerns, primarily interested in the early years in the sale of securities, included J. P. Morgan & Co., Kuhn, Loeb & Co., J. and W. Seligman & Co., Speyer, and Brown Brothers of New York; Kidder, Peabody & Co., and Lee, Higginson & Co. of Boston; and Drexel & Co. (a Morgan affiliate) of Philadelphia. Although American capital increased, European money continued to flow to America, and these investment houses were concerned with both sources. As this capital found its way into an increasing number of stocks and bonds, facilities for the ready purchase and sale of such securities expanded. The number of stocks listed on the New York Stock Exchange increased from 143 in 1870 to 426 in 1910, and the number of bonds from 200 to 1,013.[3] A million-share day was reached in December, 1886, and on April 30, 1913, the volume rose to 3,281,226 shares, a record to that date.

The shift of power from the industrial to the finance capitalist came when the expansion of industry reached a size beyond the resources of individual entrepreneurs or banks, and when the movement for consolidation reached a stage where the services of a central investment house became necessary to handle the finances involved. The technique was worked out by J.P. Morgan, who entered railroads in the 1880's to salvage various lines that had been wrecked by high financing and the speculative wars of Drew, Fiske, Gould, and other "robber barons." Morgan's first great success was in 1879, when he saved control of the New York Central for William Vanderbilt by selling 250,000 shares of New York Central stock in Great Britain without breaking the market. Morgan's reward was $3,000,000 and a representation on the board of directors. Thereafter he was the banker for that railroad.[4]

Refinancing and reorganization accompanied by rich rewards and a share in the future management were the usual steps to power taken by finance capitalists. Along with this were the profits, prestige, and power which came from organizing "trusts" during the great period of consolidation. Note will be taken later of the large returns which went to the Morgan firm for underwriting the United States Steel Corporation and other consolidations. From the time that it organized United States Steel, J.P. Morgan & Company dominated the corporation. When it is remembered that in these three years—1899, 1901, and 1902—79 great trusts were formed with a total capitalization of more than $4,000,000,000, the almost unlimited possibilities opened to finance capitalists are apparent. It should be noted that in the development of finance capitalism, bankers and investment houses worked closely together.

These investment bankers, as Louis Brandeis points out, were not content merely to deal in securities:

> They desired to manufacture them also. They became promoters, or allied themselves with promoters. Thus it was that J.P. Morgan & Company formed the Steel Trust, the Harvester Trust and the Shipping Trust. And, adding the duties of undertaker to those of midwife, the investment bankers became, in times of corporate disaster, members of security holders' "Protective Committees"; then they participated as "Reorganization Managers" in the reincarnation of the unsuccessful corporations and ultimately became directors. It was in this way that the Morgan associates acquired their hold upon the Southern Railway, the Northern Pacific, the Reading, the Erie, the Père Marquette, the Chicago and Great Western, the Cincinnati, Hamilton and Dayton. Often they insured the continuance of such control by the device of the voting trust; but even where no voting trust was created, a secure hold was acquired upon reorganization. It was in this way also that Kuhn, Loeb & Co. became potent in the Union Pacific and in the Baltimore and Ohio.[5]

And when a banker once entered a board of directors, "his grip proves tenacious and his influence usually supreme; for he controls the supply of new money."[6] The imperious Morgan represented this power at its greatest extent. "Wherever Morgan sits on a board is the head of the table even if he has but one share," said a railroad president in 1905.[7] Charles S. Mellen, president of the New York, New Haven and Hartford Railroad, testifying before the Interstate Commerce Commission, admitted that the board "used to vote as a rule pretty near where Mr. Morgan voted.... There were strong men on the New Haven Board other than Mr. Morgan, but I do not recall anything where Mr. Morgan was determined, emphatic, insistent—I recall no case in which he did not have his way."[8] Morgan's way, incidentally, brought financial ruin to the [New Haven] railroad.

The extension of investment banker control into industry by the technique just described was not wholly new. What was significant was the speed with which it was accomplished and the extent to which it was practiced. What made the latter possible was a simultaneous penetration into the nation's sources of credit. Although J. P. Morgan & Co. operated its own private bank with sizable resources, the extent of its operations was so great that it quickly stretched out to gain control of many of the leading banks of New York City and thus control of larger resources. Morgan first acquired direct control of the National Bank of Commerce, then purchased part ownership in the First National Bank. These two banks, in cooperation with the House of Morgan and by means of stock ownership and interlocking directorates, then secured control of the Liberty, Chase, Hanover, and Astor National Banks. Since the trust companies could operate under the state law more freely than the national banks under federal law, Morgan interests organized the Bankers Trust Company and by 1903 were in control of five others. Morgan himself was a large stockholder in the First National Bank of Chicago and his associates were directors in other important out-of-town banks.[9] It looked for a time as if the new era of finance capitalism would be largely centered in the hands of J. P. Morgan and his close associates, the most powerful of whom were George F. Baker, president of the First National Bank, James J. Hill, president of the Great Northern, and John A. McCall, president of the New York Life Insurance Company.

The House of Morgan, however, did not go unchallenged. By the 1890's the huge surpluses of the Standard Oil had piled so high that there was no need for much of them in the oil business itself. In the skillful hands of William Rockefeller, Henry H. Rogers, Oliver H. Payne, William C. Whitney, and others, this wealth began to penetrate into railroads, mining, public utilities, and investment banking. Closely allied with the investment banking house of Kuhn, Loeb & Co. and with James Stillman's National City Bank, the Rockefeller interests controlled the Second National Bank, the Farmers' Loan and Trust Company, and others. The resources of Standard Oil were already so vast that it was virtually independent of the banks, but it nevertheless found them a convenience. "While the House of Morgan," said Lewis Corey, "represented finance penetrating industry,

Standard Oil represented the transformation of industrial capitalists into financial capitalists."[10] And this transformation was far-reaching. A banker returning from a tour of the country remarked that "wherever he went he found by scratching beneath the surface a Standard Oil connection with some leading bank in the locality."[11] Said one New York banker in despair: "With them [the Standard Oil group] manipulation has ceased to be speculation. Their resources are so vast that they need only to concentrate on any given property in order to do with it what they please. . . . There is an utter absence of chance that is terrible to contemplate."[12]

John Moody, who was thoroughly conversant with Wall Street, was convinced in 1904 that the economic power of the nation rested in the financial hands of Morgan and Rockefeller. Even these two powers, he believed, would eventually combine. Around the Morgan-Rockefeller interests, wrote Moody

> . . . or what must ultimately become one greater group, all other smaller groups of capitalists congregate. They are all allied and intertwined by their various mutual interests. . . . Viewed as a whole, we find the dominating influence in the Trust to be made up of an intricate network of large and small capitalists, many allied to one another by ties of more or less importance, but all being appendages to or parts of the greater groups, which are themselves dependent on and allied with the two mammoth, or Rockefeller and Morgan groups. These two mammoth groups jointly . . . constitute the heart of the business and commercial life of the nation.[13]

One more important step was still to be taken in the development of finance capital and its domination of the nation's economic life—the integration of the great insurance companies with the investment bankers. Through the payments of millions of small policy holders, the life insurance companies provided a never-failing reservoir of capital; the three largest, the New York Life, the Mutual of New York, and the Equitable, had aggregate bond investments of over $1,019,153,000 on January 1, 1913, and at least $70,000,000 in new money to invest every year. Although other investment bankers had maintained close relations with the insurance companies, and had drawn heavily upon them, it was J. P. Morgan & Co. which eventually got control of the big three. For Mutual and the New York Life, interlocking directorates or an exchange of officers and partners provided the means. A notable case was that of George W. Perkins, vice-president of New York Life, who became a partner of Morgan. While Perkins held both positions, New York Life bought from J. P. Morgan in four years $38,805,000 in securities. Testifying before an Armstrong Legislative Committee investigating the life insurance scandals, Perkins insisted that in one of these transactions he had secured a bargain. "Did you bargain with any person other than yourself?" inquired Charles E. Hughes, the lawyer of the committee. Answered Perkins, "I think I did it with myself, probably."[14]

Controlling stock in the Equitable was owned for some years by Thomas F. Ryan, an active promoter and speculator. Some of it he had sold to Harriman, and this had been purchased by Morgan after Harriman's death (1909). Morgan now forced Ryan to sell the rest to him, paying $3,000,000 for stock which had a par value of $51,000. Since dividends were limited, the stock had a yield of one-eighth of 1 per cent on the purchase price. Although Morgan later refused to admit anything to the Pujo Committee, it was clear enough that he, like Ryan, was interested in control, not immediate financial return. Three years later Equitable owned $48,000,000 of securities issued by J. P. Morgan & Co.

A further link between the insurance companies and the investment bankers was disclosed by the Armstrong investigation. Although the purchase of stock by life insurance companies was closely restricted, they were allowed to invest in bank stock. Large purchases of stock in national banks and trust companies brought insurance directors and investment bankers together in the ownership and management of banks, and allowed insurance companies to profit indirectly from financial operations and speculations which they might not carry on directly. The insurance companies in this manner entered the business of banking and speculation as well as insurance. After the Armstrong investigation the New York legislature enacted a law ordering the insurance companies to sell their holdings in bank and trust companies within five years, but later extended the time. A few years later the Pujo Committee discovered that the stocks had been sold to the investment bankers who controlled or were closely associated with the insurance companies.[15]

As finance capitalists became more powerful and gradually took over control of the banks, the center of banking interest shifted increasingly from commercial to investment banking. The banks themselves became more interested in buying bonds for their own portfolios and they naturally bought them from the investment brokers who owned the banks. Likewise, loans to brokers and to individual investors and speculators became an increasingly important part of the banking business. Only one step remained to enter completely into investment banking—the selling of securities themselves. This began in 1908, when the First National Bank, the "keystone of the Morgan system of commercial banks," initiated the First Securities Corporation by declaring a dividend in the form of stock in the new company. Technically separated, they were bound together by an organization agreement between George F. Baker on behalf of the trustees and J. P. Morgan acting for the stockholders.[16] Two years later the National City Bank formed the National City Company by declaring a 40 per cent dividend to provide $10,000,000 of stock for the new company.

These security affiliates, of course, were organized to allow commercial banks to conduct a business denied to them by the banking laws. This technique of conducting business illegal in spirit if not in fact by the organization of a security affiliate, one writer has described as "a masterpiece of legal humor."[17] It may have been humorous to lawyers and bankers, but it led to abuses so intolerable, particularly in the 1920's, that Congress in the Banking Act of 1933 ordered all banks in the Federal Reserve System and all insuring with the Federal Deposit Insurance Corporation to relinquish their security affiliates and limit themselves to a strictly banking business.

During the great period of industrial consolidation it was not difficult to see what was happening and to sense the danger to the small businessman and the consumer. The consolidation and integration of finance, which proceeded simultaneously with that of industry, was not so obvious. In retrospect it is clear that two important financial developments were taking place during the early years of the twentieth century. The first was a rapid and tremendous concentration of capital; the second was a shift of power from industrialists to financiers and banking houses. The former was soon sensed and resulted in the famous investigation of the "money trust" by the Pujo Committee of the House in 1913. The second, which meant a shift in the control of economic life from farmers, merchants, and manufacturers to bankers, was a logical outcome of the concentration of capital and marked a new era in American economic history.

The investigation by the Pujo Committee was skillfully done and its work carefully evaluated. The result was a clear picture of the concentration of control of money and credit and how it had developed.[18] It had been effected, said the committee, chiefly through the consolidation of competitive or partially competitive banks and trust companies; through interlocking directorates and stockholdings; through the influence of the powerful investment houses, banks, and trust companies brought to bear upon insurance companies, railroads, and industries; and, finally, through partnership arrangements between a few of the banking houses in the purchase of security issues, which had the effect of virtually destroying competition. The committee named J. P. Morgan & Co., the First National Bank of New York, and the National City Bank as the most powerful banking units, placing their combined assets in New York City, including seven subsidiary banks controlled by them, at over $2,000,000,000. In addition to the interests named, the committee believed that Lee, Higginson & Co., Kidder, Peabody & Co., and Kuhn, Loeb &

Co. were the principal banking agencies through which the corporate enterprise of the United States obtained capital for their operations. Four allied financial institutions in New York City, it affirmed, held 341 directorships in 112 banks, transportation, public-utility, and insurance companies, whose aggregate resources were $22,245,000,000.[19]

Summarizing the committee's findings, the *Report* asserted:

> If by a "money trust" is meant an established and well defined identity and community of interest between a few leaders of finance which has been created and is held together through stock holdings, interlocking directorates, and other forms of domination over banks, trust companies, railroads, public service, and industrial corporations, and which has resulted in a vast and growing concentration of control of money and credit in the hands of a comparatively few men—your committee has no hesitation in asserting as a result of its investigation that this condition, largely developed within the past five years, exists in this country today.[20]

The Pujo Committee may not have proved without cavil the existence of an absolute money trust, but it did prove a tremendous concentration and control of capital, so great and far-reaching as virtually to dictate the obtaining of large amounts of money and the terms upon which such funds would be granted. Moreover, this concentration was much greater in 1913 than it had been a few years earlier. The Rockefeller capitalists, more interested in industrial expansion than in financial domination, engaged in no open battle with Morgan after the Northern Pacific struggle, and they gradually disintegrated as a united group. After 1906 Standard Oil devoted its resources chiefly to developing the mid-continent oil fields. Harriman's death in 1909 removed the most active challenger to Morgan's control. Stillman's National City Bank, the instrument of the Harriman and Rockefeller groups, gradually drifted into the Morgan orbit. Lesser rivals in New York had been weakened or destroyed in the panic of 1907. There existed strong financial groups in the economic provinces, notably the Mellon interests of Pittsburgh, but they avoided conflict with the Morgan power. Bankers in Boston and Chicago generally cooperated with Morgan & Co. At the time of his death in 1913 Morgan was the acknowledged financial dictator of the century.[21]

Concentration of control over credit and with it the penetration of banker control over industry marked the dominance of finance capitalism. Whether this domination conferred any economic benefit on the nation is hard to say. Morgan undoubtedly believed that he was contributing to the "rationalization" and "stabilization" of business. In a sense monopolization is a stabilizing factor. On the other hand, as Brandeis points out, the control of credit made it possible for the "banker-barons" to levy "through their excessive exactions, a heavy toll upon the whole community; upon owners of money for leave to invest it; upon railroads, public service and industrial companies, for leave to use this money of other people; and, through these corporations, upon consumers."[22] More serious was the fact that the money trust was able to suppress competition. Efforts to break or prevent private monopolies had little chance of succeeding with the control of credit as concentrated as it had become in the United States. In effect it was a supermonopoly of money dominating other monopolies in industry, transportation, utilities, and almost every economic activity of the nation.

Outside and beyond the problem and effects of financial monopoly was the significance of banker control of the nation's economic life. American economic history shows but little aid or encouragement given by bankers to the initiation or early development of great economic projects. Inventors and individual capitalists have generally started them. Only after success was proved have the bankers entered to participate and often to gain control. The process of taking over control was often accompanied by overcapitalization of assets, deterioration in the quality of the securities based on these assets, impoverishment of the property for the benefit of bankers, and a disregard of the welfare of stockholders and the community.

Having gained control, banker management has frequently tended to be inefficient, unimaginative, and often ruinous.[23] At its best, banker control meant domination by men usually unacquainted with the business they were directing. At its worst, it resulted in the ruination of a property. The classic example of the latter was Morgan's use of the assets of the New Haven to build a transportation monopoly in New England which resulted finally in the financial collapse of the railroad.[24] Except for its function of sometimes saving a concern from bankruptcy and providing funds for rehabilitation, finance capitalism had little to contribute.

Endnotes

1. Margaret G. Myers and Others, *The New York Money Market* (New York: Columbia University Press, 4 vols., 1931-1932), Vol. I, Chaps. II, IV.

2. Harold G. Moulton, George W. Edwards, James D. Magee, and Cleona Lewis, *Capital Expansion, Employment, and Economic Stability* (Washington: The Brookings Institution, 1940), pp. 4-30; George W. Edwards, *The Evolution of Finance Capitalism* (New York: Longmans, Green and Co., 1938), pp. 183-184, 416, 422.

3. Edwards, *The Evolution of Finance Capitalism*, p. 167.

4. Lewis Corey, *The House of Morgan* (New York: G. Howard Watt, 1930), pp. 141-146.

5. Louis D. Brandeis, *Other People's Money and How the Bankers Use It* (New York: Frederick A. Stokes Company, 1913, new ed., 1932), pp. 9-10.

6. *Ibid.,* p. 11.

7. Quoted by Frederick Allen, *The Lords of Creation* (New York: Harper & Brothers, 1935), p. 81.

8. *New York Times*, May 20, 1914, p. 4.

9. Corey, *The House of Morgan*, pp. 255-258.

10. *Ibid.,* p. 259.

11. Sereno S. Pratt, "Who Owns the United States?" *World's Work*, VII, No. 2 (December, 1903), 4264-4265.

12. Clews, *Fifty Years in Wall Street*, p. 746.

13. Moody, *The Truth about the Trusts*, p. 493; Corey, *The House of Morgan*, pp. 258-161.

14. State of New York, *Report of the Joint Committee of the Senate and Assembly of the State of New York Appointed to Investigate the Affairs of Life Insurance Companies* (Albany: 1907), *Testimony*, p. 1218. See also Burton J. Hendrick, "The Story of Life Insurance," *McClure's Magazine*, XXVII, No. 1 (May, 1906), 36-49, and following numbers; and Edwards, *The Evolution of Finance Capitalism*, pp. 171-195.

15. Brandeis, *Other People's Money*, pp. 16-17; *Report of the Committee Pursuant to House Resolutions 429 and 504 to Investigate the Concentration of Control of Money and Credit, House Report* No. 1,593,62 Cong., 3 Sess., p. 135, generally referred to as the report of the "Money Trust Investigation" or the "Report of the Pujo Committee."

16. Edwards, *The Evolution of Finance Capitalism*, p. 171; House Banking and Currency Committee, *Investigation of the Financial and Monetary Conditions in the United States*, 62 Cong., 3 Sess. (Washington: Government Printing Office, 29 pts., 1913), Pt. 20, p. 1423.

17. Allen, *The Lords of Creation,* p. 174.

18. Louis Brandeis, *Other People's Money*, is based on the Pujo Report.

19. "Money Trust Investigation," pp. 55-56, 87-88, 89-90; reprinted in H. U. Faulkner and Felix Flügel, *Readings in the Economic and Social History of the United States* (New York: Harper & Brothers, 1929), pp. 597-700.

20. "Money Trust Investigation," p. 130.

21. Corey, *The House of Morgan*, pp. 349-354.

22. Brandeis, *Other People's Money*, pp. 46-50.

23. *Ibid.,* Chaps. IX-X.

24. *Ibid.,* pp. 189-208.

32

Behind the Throne: A Non-Morgan View of the Panic of 1907

SAUL ENGELBOURG

According to the orthodox version of the panic of 1907, J. P. Morgan, almost singlehandedly, staved off total disaster. It is in this fashion that countless authors of scholarly and popular treatments, of general works and biographies, have related the events of the dramatic fortnight that began late in October 1907 and ended early in November. Morgan and those closely associated with him and his firm have been the subjects of other studies. No attempt is made here to denigrate the very real and significant achievements of Morgan; he could not do it alone and Stillman, among others, took part. James Stillman has been the subject of only one biography, sponsored by the family more than forty years ago. An adequate biography is unlikely ever to be written because of the loss or unavailability of the necessary documentation. However, a more balanced view of the panic of 1907, using for the first time the relevant Stillman papers which are newly available, is now possible.

"Behind the Throne: A Non-Morgan View of the Panic of 1907," by Saul Engelbourg is excerpted and reprinted by permission from *Revue Internationale d'Histoire de la Banque* (Geneva, Switzerland), 1971, pp. 141-157.

Morgan was the natural leader around whom others rallied but no rescue effort could be successful without the resources, and the resources were in the great commercial banks, among which Stillman's National City Bank was pre-eminent. In an era when there was no central bank with its power to expand the money supply, resources were as essential as leadership, a fact recognized by Stillman's contemporaries but until now seemingly disregarded by historians. . . .

The panic was precipitated by an unsuccessful attempt by several speculators, who were also officials of New York banks and trust companies, to corner the stock of a copper company. When it failed, depositors in the institutions controlled by the men involved became fearful that the banks would fail and withdrew their money with such frequency and in such amounts as to constitute a run.[1] This both set the stage for the next act in this drama and set the pattern for all those that followed. In a fire in a crowded public place people are more likely to be trampled in the panic than burned to death and so it is in a bank run; it is the panic that is usually responsible for such losses as occur both for the depositors and for the stockholders of banks. . . .

The manner in which the onset of the panic of 1907 manifested itself should not obscure another aspect of its fundamental character, i.e., the banking system and in particular the banking system in New York. There was a concentration of funds in the major New York City banks because the country banks held much of their reserves in their correspondent banks. The ultimate reserve of the banking system was held by the six bankers' banks (led by the National City Bank headed by Stillman). Two more or less distinct and competing segments comprised the New York banking community: the national banks and those few trust companies which had an associate membership in the New York Clearing House and, secondly, the non-member trust companies which expanded their banking business in the decade prior to the panic of 1907. These trust companies maintained cash reserves which were so notoriously inadequate that not much more than faith protected the depositor, a risky policy which was attractive because of the potentially higher rate of return. These trust companies did not have a clearing house of their own nor did they have membership in the clearing house for the national banks; instead they usually cleared through a national bank which served as their agent. Lacking a central bank, the monetary system was unable to expand and contract the supply of money in accordance with the needs of the economy.

The fact that trouble was brewing was obvious to observers with foresight as well as to those with the more common hindsight. Those who were apprehensive of an economic downturn had their forebodings seemingly confirmed with the break in the stock market in March 1907 and again in August. . . .

James Stillman, president of the National City Bank, New York and the nation's largest, was one of those who had foreseen trouble. Observing the characteristics of a boom, late in 1906 Stillman called the attention of Arthur Balfour to the tight money situation and the consequent rise in interest rates: ". . . it may cause liquidation in the stock market and consequently lower prices." He prophesied that this would be temporary and ". . . will not be of serious consequences to a serious investor."[2] . . .

In reaction to the downturn Stillman returned to the United States from one of his customary sojourns in Paris to resume his post as helmsman for the National City.[3] . . . By late in August 1907 the cloud had become for Stillman larger than a man's hand. . . . Stillman was perplexed early in September: "I wish I were a prophet . . . but unfortunately I am not."[4] The news from day to day continued to be mixed but caution was the watchword.[5]

The decline in the price of copper (among other commodities) resulted in the failure of a speculative venture in the stock of a copper mining company and provided the spark that ignited the conflagration. The first banking institution to be affected was the Mercantile National Bank whose president was the leader of this coterie of speculators; he owned a majority of its stock and had become president at the beginning of 1907. The Mercantile National hardly had the best reputation, and ". . . distrust of his [the president's] methods led many depositors to withdraw their accounts after the change in management."[6] Six months before the panic Vanderlip had reported to Stillman on this "outlaw" bank which he judged "presumably" to be "perfectly solvent."[7]

The Mercantile National applied to the New York Clearing House Association for aid on Wednesday, October 16. The Clearing House, while nominally only performing the clearing function for its members, also served as a quasi-public regulatory agency and mutual aid society. Stillman had been chairman of the Clearing House Committee for 1907 (his term ended before the panic) and he remained a member of the Committee during the panic. Despite its unsavory past, the Mercantile National was able to receive assistance from the Clearing House the following day, thus proving that a chain can sometimes be stronger than its weakest link.[8]

Stillman's analysis at that moment in a cipher cablegram was: "In my judgment New York banks perfectly sound and excellent with the exception of one which has capital surplus and shareholders' liability equal to its deposits. U.S. Controller thinks it is all right."[9] It was probably on the basis of both Stillman's information and his judgment that the Clearing House acted. . . .

From the Mercantile National Bank the pressure was transmitted to the Knickerbocker Trust Company (its president was linked with the copper speculators), which was the third largest trust company in New York. On Monday, October 21, the National Bank of Commerce, which had served as the clearing agent in the New York Clearing House Association for the Knickerbocker, declined to perform this function. That night, in a classic example of ineptitude which allowed the news of the Knickerbocker's difficulty to spread like wild-fire, a more or less open meeting was held at Sherry's restaurant by its directors. . . .

There was a run on the Knickerbocker the next day, and the company appealed to Morgan for money. The chain of command extended from Morgan to Henry Davison, vice-president of the First National Bank, who in turn appointed Benjamin Strong of the Bankers Trust Company as the head of a committee to determine the solvency of New York's banking institutions. It is worth noting that it later developed that the Knicker-bocker was financially sound but not immediately liquid.[10] "The cash was all gone and Mr. Baker, Mr. Morgan, Mr. Woodward [president of the Hanover National Bank] and Mr. Stillman were awaiting some word from us [Davison and Strong] as to what we found."[11] The plea for help by the Knickerbocker was denied by Morgan because the hurriedly prepared report of these two men as his examiners was unfavorable;[12] the Knickerbocker failed on that day.

It has been alleged, but no direct evidence exists to support the allegation, that the dominant money powers could have chosen to save the Knickerbocker but instead deliberately allowed it to fail. (Note that the Knickerbocker Trust Company resumed business in March 1908 and its depositors were repaid in full.) Until the last moment the Knickerbocker refused to submit to an examination by an unofficial committee and this all but precluded action. In short, although the post-mortem would indicate an obvious delay in handling the crisis, this can be plausibly, if not conclusively, explained. First, Morgan did not return to New York until the morning of Sunday, October 20. Second, there was no way of predicting the severity of the crisis; even Stillman, with the matchless economic intelligence at his command, could privately underestimate the gravity of the crisis and be far more optimistic than was warranted in the light of later events. Third, under the rules of the day there was no provision for the automatic rescue of a bank. This was something that had to be earned; a banking institution had the right to fail especially if that was the reasonable consequence of its own actions.

That three men constituted a rescue committee, unofficial though it was, there can be no denying. J. P. Morgan was the head of J. P. Morgan & Co., the leading investment banking firm, George F. Baker had long been a close associate of Morgan and was the president of one of the great commercial banks and James Stillman was the president of the National

City Bank, the largest commercial bank. George W. Perkins, a Morgan partner, later observed: "It would be impossible to chronicle or recall the tremendous rapidity of events during this week [October 20-26]; what people said, what they did, and how they felt; but Mr. Morgan and Mr. Stillman and Mr. Baker stand out clearly as the three strong men in the situation."[13] Of these, Morgan led all the rest. Even Vanderlip, Stillman's fair-haired boy, acknowledged that Morgan was captain.[14]

"But for the powerful influence of Mr. J. P. Morgan it is probable that no united action would have been taken."[15] Morgan's prime contribution was personal—his charismatic leadership; to this Stillman and Baker were able to add the unparalleled resources of their banks. These three men had had a long and continuous association and trouble brought them even closer together. Directly and indirectly, they controlled vast sums of money. This, plus their adroit financial management, enabled them to limit the 1907 financial crisis.

The National City Bank, the nation's largest bank, numbered among its directors some of the most prominent industrialists, and its gold reserve was second only to that of the United States Treasury. It held deposits from some two hundred correspondent banks. The influence of this bank and of its president, James Stillman, who was its largest stockholder and owned almost one-fifth of its capital, approached that of a European central bank. The aura of stability that radiated from this bank perhaps helps to account for the fact that it even managed to grow during the panic year of 1907.[16] This enhanced Stillman's ability to play from strength.

It is by now a commonplace that the panic of 1907 primarily affected trust companies rather than commercial banks. Still, a word of explanation is in order. National banks had rigid reserve requirements established by law, whereas trust companies, which also did a banking business, did not, and this fact invited disaster. James Stillman, among others diagnosed this before the panic: "The Trust Company as a bank is wrong and as long as people will use them as banks I admit it's a problem and in the crash we will lose money, but if by able and judicious management we have money to help our dealers when trust companies have suspended, we will have all the business we want for many years."[17]

In addition to not having a reserve requirement, the trust companies had another potential weakness; that is, overwhelmingly they were not members of the Clearing House nor did they have an equivalent organization of their own for mutual aid. They therefore had no institutionalized means of obtaining assistance when confronted with widespread bank runs. . . .

"The suspension of the Knickerbocker Trust Company on October 22 marks the beginning of the panic of 1907."[18] . . . On the following day all trust companies had runs.[19] The chief victim of this loss of confidence on the part of depositors was the Trust Company of America, which was even larger than the Knickerbocker, and another was the Lincoln Trust Company.[20] Morgan called an *ad hoc* meeting of Baker, Stillman and himself on Wednesday, October 23, while the run on the Trust Company of of America was at its height. The three top financial leaders decided that some form of cooperation was necessary in order to protect and save solvent institutions. They constituted the general staff with Davison and Strong as their subordinates. After a somewhat hasty examination, they judged the Trust Company of America to be solvent and decided that this was the place to start. The three then agreed that they would that day supply the cash necessary to stop the run on the Trust Company of America.[21] Now was the time for all good bankers to come to the aid of their community, and a positive decision by Stillman was essential.

Strong later recounted: "Mr. Stillman sat at the telephone in the adjoining room [of J. P. Morgan & Company] communicating with his bank, and Mr. Morgan and I sat at a big table while Mr. Oakleigh Thorne [president of the Trust Company of America] and his clerks spread out the securities and their values were determined for the purpose of securing the first loan to the Trust Company of America. Mr. Morgan had a pad in front of him making figures as we went along, and when he was satisfied that collateral had been delivered for an advance, he would ask Mr. Stillman to telephone over to the National City Bank to send over currency for the amount determined upon. This went on until three o'clock when about $3,000,000, as I recall, had been sent over to the Trust Company of America. This cash, under the arrangement, was to be furnished by the three banks [National City, First National and Hanover National] and J. P. Morgan & Company."[22]

After a late afternoon meeting of trust company presidents failed to provide a satisfactory solution for the rescue of the Trust Company of America it was scheduled to reconvene that night. "Then [after dinner] I [Perkins] went to Mr. Stillman's house to talk over the coming meeting of the Trust Company Presidents and to urge him to be present. He finally consented and he, together with Mr. Vanderlip, Vice-President of the City Bank, started downtown in my cab. Mr. Stillman was in some doubt about his going into the meeting of the Trust Company Presidents, so I suggested that he stop off at the Union League Club and I would send for him at the critical moment, which moment I felt sure we were going to reach. Mr. Vanderlip and I went down to the meeting. One after another the Presidents gathered and began to discuss the situation. After this discussion had lasted for one-half or three-quarters of an hour a motion was made to adjourn until the next morning. At this point, I asked Mr. King [Edward King of the Union Trust Company], the Chairman, if he would step into another room that I might say a word to him and, in passing out I asked Mr. Vanderlip to hurry up and get Mr. Stillman. I kept Mr. King engaged in conversation until Mr. Stillman came in, almost immediately followed by Mr. Morgan."[23] The result of this meeting was that the trust companies united to support the Trust Company of America by putting up the necessary cash.[24] "The saving of the Trust Company of America at the critical moment on Wednesday [October 23] was the crisis of that day."[25] Further cash was needed by the Trust Company of America throughout the panic, however, and it was not finally able to pay depositors without assistance until days later.[26] . . .

Although assistance for the Trust Company of America had been pledged by the trust companies the previous evening, time ran out on the morning of October 24, before all the procedures were completed in order to provide the cash that would enable that concern to open for business. In this crisis Davison and Strong obtained cash from the National City Bank in a matter of minutes, on what constituted an emergency loan without collateral, and once again saved the day.[27]

Far more significant than the continued run on the Trust Company of America was the decline in the stock market and the unavailability of call money to stop bankruptcies among brokers.[28] Evidently alarmed by the run on three trust companies, the other trust companies were strengthening their cash position and refusing to issue loans.[29] At the juncture Ransom H. Thomas, president of the New York Stock Exchange, went to see Stillman, hoping to eliminate both the call money shortage and the jump in the interest rate. Stillman referred him to Morgan,[30] who called a meeting of the presidents of the leading banks and tried to organize a money pool to relieve the stringency and prevent further failures. "Mr. Stillman, of the City Bank, promptly spoke up and offered Five million dollars and other banks fell into line with from One and one-half millions to One half million dollars."[31] Stillman was the first willing to back his judgment with money. But Morgan apparently took responsibility for calling the meeting. In Perkins' judgment, "The saving of the Stock Exchange was the crisis of Thursday [October 24]."[32] . . .

The general pressure on all fronts continued; no more than that, but that was enough. A silent movement seemingly as irresistible as the outward movement of the tide was in process. Just as no single banking institution can withstand a loss of confidence on the part of its depositors and pay all of them at once, neither can the banking system. Cash was being withdrawn by depositors from banking institutions of all types and not redeposited, but hoarded. The very awareness of this led to a ". . . more desperate scramble for money." Not only did ordinary depositors demand cash but in addition banking institutions outside New York retrieved whatever cash they could from New York and held it.[33] Hundreds of millions in cash were hoarded.

Prior experience indicated the desirability of issuing clearing house loan certificates to members on acceptable collateral as a means of relieving the shortage of cash by expanding the means of payment at least for the purpose of settling inter-bank balances. Stillman had opposed a central bank in 1903 but clamored for one in the throes of the panic.[34] A central bank could serve as the leader of last resort. Vanderlip commented years later in his autobiography: ". . . if the Federal Reserve System had been in existence in 1907, the thing that brought about the financial paralysis, the mad scramble for individual reserves would not have occurred; there would have been no panic in 1907."[35] The knowledge that banks could obtain cash would diminish their desire for it. From the panic of 1907 which so sharply etched the defects of the banking system, the sequence of reform of the banking system progressed from the Aldrich-Vreeland Act of 1908 to the National Monetary Commission (Aldrich) of 1910-1911 to the Federal Reserve Act in 1913.

Four days were allowed to elapse between the failure of the Knicker-bocker Trust Company on October 22 and the authorization of the issuance of clearing house loan certificates.[36] The repeated money pools had not been enough. A noted monetary economist concluded just a few years after the panic was over: "The strenuous efforts that were made to relieve the situation were but partially successful, because they lacked the authority and backing of the Clearing House Association . . . the relief afforded was of a piecemeal character without any certainty of its continuance."[37] . . .

From the vantage point of history the delay in the issuance of Clearing House certificates was excessive and unwise. Admittedly the evidence is shaky and inferential in character, but the New York bankers apparently equated the issuance of Clearing House certificates with a suspension of specie payments (which in fact occurred simultaneously), and delayed, hoping that the crisis would subside. It should be realized that although Clearing House certificates had been issued during previous crises they possessed an aura of extralegality. Morgan publicly expressed the fervent hope (perhaps naive, but not unreasonable), the depositors would leave their money on deposit and not hoard cash; however, the public sucked up money like a sponge. It is always a problem, even assuming that one knows the appropriate economic medicine, to know at precisely what moment it should be administered.

A day later more money was needed on the Stock Exchange and another money pool was created, but this time the amount forthcoming fell far short of the amount requested. . . . Finally, after the repeated use of money pools, facilitated to such an extent by the government that about half of the money was the result of federal deposits in national banks,[38] Clearing House certificates were authorized on Saturday, October 26.[39]

Another few days passed without incident worthy of mention and then a new weak spot appeared. As before there was a fundamental weakness exposed under pressure. On at least four separate occasions, only days before the panic broke in full fury, Perkins wrote letters to J. P. Morgan, Jr., calling attention to the fact that the finances of New York City were in trouble.[40] On Monday, October 28, the trio at the helm and Perkins met with New York City officials to arrange a means of extricating the city from its fiscal plight. Morgan proposed a solution and Baker and Stillman accepted and agreed to execute it. Morgan wrote the agreement the next day. According to this plan J. P. Morgan & Company, the First National Bank, and the National City Bank agreed to lend New York City the money which it so desperately needed. "Mr. Stillman and Mr. Baker scrutinized the paper very carefully as a business proposition."[41] . . . But they also believed that the preservation of the credit of New York City was essential to the financial community at large, since by this time any bad news, however slight, might be more than could be withstood.

Having fought the good fight up to this point Stillman summarized the turmoil: "The past week has been one of great excitement, which none of us had anticipated. . . . While the local situation is steadily improving, the worst being undoubtedly over here, the trouble is extending all over the country and we will doubtless see numerous failures and a greater falling off in the volume of business than was expected. . . .

"I was much gratified at being able to report to the Directors of The National City Bank, at their weekly meeting yesterday, that the bank had loaned during the past ten days $35,000,000 at 6% interest, with the exception of a small amount loaned at a higher rate through its contribution to a money pool for the relief of brokers, over which it had no control, and that the bank had not called one dollar for payment and in addition, had imported $8,000,000 of gold.[42]

The most publicized scene of this drama occurred in what was to be the last act of the panic of 1907. A prominent brokerage firm, Moore & Schley (Grant B. Schley was the brother-in-law of George F. Baker), was in trouble. Schley was a member of a syndicate which had bought the controlling shares of the Tennessee Coal & Iron Company. Some of the stock had been deposited with banks as collateral for loans. It was difficult for Moore and Schley to repay their loans as they matured because of the general decline in the stock market. Also, the sale of any appreciable amount of Tennessee Coal & Iron stock would have further depressed its price. If Moore & Schley had failed the strain on similar houses and on the New York Stock Exchange would have increased and the banking structure would also have been placed in great peril. Morgan and others were concerned about the possible effects of the failure of Moore & Schley;

impending disaster was prevented by the acquisition of Tennessee Coal & Iron Company stock by the United States Steel Corporation.

Simultaneously, another money pool was created to accomplish the final rescue of the Trust Company of America. This scene in the Morgan Library began on the night of Saturday, November 2, and its participants included everyone involved in stemming the panic of 1907 from the stars to the spear carriers.[43] . . .

It had been a continuing day by day struggle to keep alive the trust companies that had been weakened. On Thursday, October 21, before the curtain rose on the climax, Perkins assessed the drama in this way: "It was not because we [the leaders of the banking world] were particularly in love with these two Trust Companies [Trust Company of America and the Lincoln Trust Company] that we wanted to keep them open; indeed, we hadn't any use for their management and knew that they ought to be closed, but we fought to keep them open in order not to have runs on other concerns and have another outburst of panic and alarm."[44] The fate of the two trust companies was finally settled at the Morgan Library, where so many other fateful decisions had been made, on the night of Tuesday, November 5.[45] Perkins reported: "Mr. Morgan, Mr. Stillman and I had mapped out a plan during the day by which we were to try to raise Fifteen millions for the Trust Company of America and Five millions for the Lincoln Trust Company."[46] After a good deal of travail the plan was put into effect, and by Wednesday, November 6, the panic was over.[47]

With a note of exultation Perkins then wrote *finis*: "The market opened buoyantly. A tremendous change for the better had taken place and at last we had one day when everyone was hopeful, and all talk of failure and collapse ceased."[48] One could perhaps declare that the panic was officially over and calm restored when, in January 1908, Stillman cabled to Lord Revelstoke in England: "Sailing today Lusitania,"[49] as he returned to Paris, the second home of his semi-retirement.

Endnotes

1. F. L. Allen, *The Lords of Creation*, New York, 1935, pp. 112-113, 118-119, 121; F. L. Allen, *The Great Pierpont Morgan*, New York, 1949, p. 241; W. C. Mitchell, *Business Cycles and Their Causes*, Berkeley, 1941, pp. 75-76; O. M. W. Sprague, *History of Crises under the National Banking System*, National Monetary Commission, 61st Congress, 2nd Session, Senate Doc. 538, Washington, 1910, pp. 247-249; A. R. Burr, *The Portrait of a Banker: James Stillman* 1850-1918, New York, 1927, p. 220.

2. Stillman to A. Balfour, December 14, 1906, James Stillman MSS, Columbia University.

3. F. A. Vanderlip, *From Farm Boy to Financier*, New York, 1935, p. 173.

4. Stillman to Madame Alice von Andre, September 3, 1907.

5. Stillman to Gaspard Farrer, September 5, 1907; Stillman to Sir Ernest Cassel, September 6, 1907; Stillman to Poniatowski, September 9, 1907, October 7, 1907; Stillman to Dr. Crosby C. Whitman, September 13, 1907; Stillman to John J. Hoff, September 23, 1907; Stillman to Frederick H. Allen, October 11, 1907; Stillman to Nicholas Murray Butler, October 11, 1907.

6. O. M. W. Sprague, *History of Crises*, cit., p. 247.

7. Vanderlip to Stillman, April 19, 1907, Vanderlip MSS.

8. F. L. Allen, *The Lords of Creation*, cit., pp. 112-113, 118-119, 121; F. L. Allen, *The Great Pierpont Morgan*, cit., p. 241; W. C. Mitchell, *Business Cycles*, cit., pp. 75-76; O. M. W. Sprague, *History of Crises*, cit., pp. 247-249; A. R. Burr, *The Portrait of a Banker*, cit., p. 220; A. D. Noyes, *Forty Years of American Finance*, New York, 1909, pp. 365-366.

9. Stillman to Poniatowski, October 17, 1907, Cablegram, cipher, translated.

10. F. L. Allen, *The Lords of Creation*, cit., pp. 122-126; F. L. Allen, *The Great Pierpont Morgan*, cit., pp. 245-246; L. V. Chandler, *Benjamin Strong, Central Banker*, Washington, 1958, p. 27; M. Friedman and A. J. Schwartz, *A Monetary History of the United States* 1867-1960, Princeton, 1963, pp. 159, n. 37, 166; J. A. Garraty, *Right-Hand Man*, cit., p. 199; W. C. Mitchell, *Business Cycles*, cit., p. 76; H. L. Satterlee, *J. Pierpont Morgan*, New York, 1939, pp. 465-466; O. M. W. Sprague, *History of Crises*, cit., pp. 251-253.

11. Benjamin Strong to Thomas W. Lamont, December 22, 1924, Baker Library MSS, Harvard University, p. 6. This Lamont manuscript consists of a cover letter and eighteen typewritten pages. It was used by Lamont in his biography of Henry P. Davison and written for that purpose.

12. *Ibidem*.

13. Columbia University, Perkins MSS, p. 22.

14. F. A. Vanderlip, *From Farm Boy to Financier*, cit., p. 168.

15. O. M. W. Sprague, *History of Crises*, cit., p. 255.

16. A. R. Burr, *The Portrait of a Banker*, cit., pp. 206, 252; T. C. Cochran, *The American Business System*, Cambridge, 1960, pp. 81, 86-87; F. Redlich, *The Molding of American Banking, Men and Ideas*, Part II, 1840-1910, New York, 1951, p. 391; P. B. Trescott, *Financing American Enterprise, The Story of Commercial Banking*, New York, 1963, pp. 74, 194; F. A. Vanderlip, *From Farm Boy to Financier*, cit., pp. 141, 154-155, 162; J. K. Winkler, *The First Billion: The Stillmans and the National City Bank*, New York, 1934, p. 171.

17. Stillman to Vanderlip, February 12, 1907.

18. W. C. Mitchell, *Business Cycles*, cit., p. 123.

19. A. D. Noyes, *Forty Years of American Finance*, cit., p. 366.

20. W. C. Mitchell, *Business Cycles*, cit. p. 76.

21. F. L. Allen, *The Lords of Creation*, cit., pp. 126-129; L. V. Chandler, *Benjamin Strong, Central Banker*, cit., p. 27; M. Friedman and A. J. Schwartz, *A Monetary History of the United States*, cit., p. 159; J. A. Garraty, *Right-Hand Man*, cit., pp. 200-202; T. W. Lamont *Henry P. Davison*, New York, 1933, pp. 74-75; A. D. Noyes, *Forty Years of American Finance*, cit., p. 672; Columbia University, Perkins MSS, pp. 7-10; H. L. Satterlee, *J. Pierpont Morgan*, cit., pp. 468-472, 478; O. M. W. Sprague, *History of Crises*, cit., pp. 253-254; Baker Library, Lamont MSS, pp. 8, 11-12, 20.

22. Baker Library, Lamont MSS, p. 9

23. Columbia University, Perkins MSS, p. 10.

24. *New York Times*, October 24, 1907, p. 1.

25. Columbia University, Perkins MSS, p. 13.

26. F. L. Allen, *The Lords of Creation*, cit., p. 131; J. A. Garraty, *Right-Hand Man*, cit., pp. 213-214; Columbia University, Perkins MSS, p. 11.

27. Baker Library, Lamont MSS, pp. 14-15.

28. J. A. Garraty, *Right-Hand Man*, cit., pp. 204-205; A. D. Noyes, *Forty Years of American Finance*, cit., p. 372; H. L. Satterlee, *J. Pierpont Morgan*, cit., pp. 474-475.

29. Columbia University, Perkins MSS, p. 12.

30. F. L. Allen, *The Lords of Creation*, cit., pp. 131-132; E. Lefevre, *Reminiscences of a Stock Operator*, New York, 1923, p. 124; United States Congress, House Committee on Banking and Currency, *Money Trust Investigation* (Pujo), House Res. 429 and 504, Washington, 1913, I, p. 355.

31. Columbia University, Perkins MSS, p. 12.

32. *Ibidem*, p. 13.

33. W. C. Mitchell, *Business Cycles*, cit., pp. 77, 83; A. D. Noyes, *Forty Years of American Finance*, cit., p. 374; F. A. Vanderlip, *From Farm Boy to Financier*, cit., p. 170.

34. P. M. Warburg, *The Federal Reserve System*, New York, 1930, I, pp. 18-19.

35. F. A. Vanderlip, *From Farm Boy to Financier*, cit., p. 181.

36. F. L. Allen, *The Lords of Creation*, cit., p. 133; H. L. Satterlee, *J. Pierpont Morgan*, cit., pp. 476-477; O. M. W. Sprague, *History of Crises*, cit., pp. 257-258, 271, 314.

37. O. M. W. Sprague, *History of Crises*, cit., p. 256.

38. O. M. W. Sprague, *History of Crises*, cit., pp. 263-264.

39. Columbia University, Perkins MSS, p. 20.

40. J. A. Garraty, *Right-Hand Man*, cit., pp. 207-209; Perkins to J. P. Morgan, Jr., October 3, 1907, October 12, 1907, October 15, 1907, October 16, 1907; Columbia University, Perkins MSS, pp. 27-29, 31, 34-35; H. L. Satterlee, *J. Pierpont Morgan*, cit., p. 482.

41. Columbia University, Perkins MSS, p. 31.

42. Stillman to Poniatowski, October 30, 1907.

43. F. L. Allen, *The Lords of Creation*, cit., pp. 135-138; J. A. Garraty, "A Lion in the Street" in *American Heritage*, VIII, June 1957, p. 100; *New York Times*, November 6, 1907; H. L. Satterlee, *J. Pierpont Morgan*, cit., p. 487; Baker Library, Lamont MSS, pp.17-19; A. B. Paine, *George Fisher Baker*, New York, 1920, pp. 227-228, privately printed.

44. Columbia University, Perkins MSS, p. 38.

45. F. L. Allen, *The Lords of Creation*, cit., p. 137; J. A. Garraty, *Right-Hand Man*, cit., pp. 213-214.

46. Columbia University, Perkins MSS, p. 54.

47. J. A. Garraty, *Right-Hand Man*, cit., pp. 213-214.

48. Columbia University, Perkins MSS, p. 56.

49. Stillman to Lord Revelstoke, January 10, 1908, cablegram.

33

The Evolution of Managerial Ideas in Industrial Relations

EDWIN E. WITTE

Industrial Conditions in the Early Twentieth Century

In the years when management emerged as a distinct factor in the American economy—at the turn of the century—industrial relations did not occupy much of its attention. By that time, there had been labor unions in the United States for nearly a century. Unions were of undoubted legality and "economic" strikes also were clearly legal. Even the closed shop was not unknown and was held legal in New York and some other jurisdictions. Labor-management agreements were new, but not unknown. Unions, however, were of real importance only in a few industries—on the railroads, in building construction, coal mining, printing, cigar-making, and a few smaller industries. Strikes were fairly numerous and often were accompanied by much violence. But most managements gave little thought to labor unions and labor troubles, and even less to the labor supply.

Edwin E. Witte, *The Evolution of Managerial Ideas in Industrial Relations*, ILR Bulletin No. 27, Ithaca, N. Y.: New York State School of Industrial and Labor Relations, Cornell University, 1954, pp. 3-15. Excerpted and reprinted by permission of ILR press.

The explanation was that labor was in abundant supply. Earlier, both labor and capital were very scarce. Adam Smith in his pioneer treatise, *The Wealth of Nations*, written in the year of the Declaration of Independence, 1776, commented upon the scarcity of labor in colonial New York and attributed to this factor the relatively high wages in the Colonies compared with those in England and Scotland. But in each decade following the Civil War, we had more and more immigrants, with the peak being reached in the first decade of the twentieth century. This heavy immigration, plus a strong movement of younger people from the country to the cities, changed the labor supply situation in industry from one of scarcity to surplus. Moreover, the bulk of the immigrants after 1890 were from a different part of the world and from other races and religions than the earlier immigrants from whom the bulk of Americans were then descended. Those of this period were mainly peasants from southern and eastern Europe but, unlike the earlier immigrants, they did not settle on farms but found employment in industry. Not knowing English, generally illiterate, and always timid, they counted for but little in public affairs and were pushed around in the factory. If there was any management policy toward labor it was "to treat them rough." The selection, training, direction, and dismissal of the worker were left to the tough Irish foreman. The foreman himself was regarded as an employee, not as part of management, but had almost unlimited authority in dealing with the production workers. Management had many more difficult problems to deal with, in financing and marketing, and seldom had to concern itself with what we now call industrial relations.

This situation changed fundamentally in the years following World War I. The outbreak of that war in 1914 shut off immigration from Europe and after its close we adopted the restrictive policy which has kept immigration to a trickle. The second generation of the southern and eastern Europeans in this country were no longer foreigners, but Americans, gradually winning recognition in industry and in public affairs. In the years following World War I, there occurred also a marked rise in the educational equipment of the new entrants into industry. Before World War I, most native-born Americans entered industry at 14, if not younger. Few states then had higher educational qualifications for child labor permits than completion of the fifth grade, or six years of school attendance. In contrast, the 16-year age limit for employment in factories and completion of the eighth grade, or at least nine years of attendance in school, have become the generally prevailing standard. And in all sizable cities we now have vocational schools for young people who do not like the regular elementary and secondary schools or who drop out for any reason, and for the part-time education of employed children. . . .

Many people ascribe the great growth of unions to legislation and governmental favoritism, but probably a more important factor has been the profound change in our labor force. Changes in the supply and character of the labor force also account, in large part, for the increased importance accorded industrial relations and the improved techniques of supervision developed by management in dealing with the workers. Plus this, industry has become both more specialized and interrelated, depending for its successful operation upon the whole-hearted cooperation of all who are concerned in any manner with production. This factor, too, has contributed to the development of the newer management attitudes, techniques, and philosophies in dealing with the production workers.

Scientific Management

The earliest of these was scientific management. This was advocated by Frederick W. Taylor, one of the greatest names in the development of managerial ideas. Taylor promulgated the gospel of scientific management in the first decade of the twentieth century, but it was not widely practiced in industry until the next decade and it did not become general until World War I.

Scientific management was essentially an engineering approach to industrial relations. It was motivated by the desire to reduce costs of production. It sought to apply scientific methods to industrial relations problems—to simplify and clearly define jobs, to improve the physical conditions of work, to set up operations in such a way as to minimize waste time and lost motions, and to provide an incentive to increased production through methods of pay based on worker productivity.

Scientific management made many important contributions to the betterment of industrial relations. It stimulated industrial accident prevention, and improved lighting and sanitation in industry. It stressed rational arrangement of processes in production and the rationalization of jobs, and promoted the adoption of methods of pay based upon the amount and value of the worker's production. Beyond question, it contributed to increased production and to the reduction of costs.

Scientific management still is practiced widely in industry—in fact, more so now than at the time when it was talked about much more. At that time, it was bitterly denounced by union people as being only a "speed-up"—more work, with no lasting increase in pay. Legislation was introduced in Congress to prevent methods of payment based on production from being applied in government arsenals and navy yards. But, long since, labor has become reconciled to scientific management, although incentive rates still are a frequent cause of labor troubles and at times result in lessened, rather than increased, production. Like all other developments in management ideas relating to industrial relations which I shall note, scientific management has had profound influences upon the management practices of the present day. Scientific management is today accepted practice, but management no longer regards it as all-sufficient to assure the lowest possible production costs.

Developments of the Twenties

The 1920's were a period of quite diverse developments in industrial relations. During this decade, production increased rapidly, although the number of people employed in manufacturing remained constant, as did prices. This was the time when assembly-line methods of mass production came into their own and with them a great increase in semiskilled, specialized jobs in industry. Very important for industrial relations was the cessation of immigration and the improvement in the educational equipment of the new entrants into industry, which I believe to have been among the most important factors necessitating the increased attention now given industrial relations by management.

Two basically different methods of dealing with the development problems of industrial relations were manifest at this time—both often adopted by the same firms. One of these was to fight unionism with every weapon that management could command. Even before World War I this was the attitude of the National Manufacturers' Association, the National Metal Trades Association, some other employers' associations, and of quite a few individual firms. But it was after that war, which witnessed a meteoric rise in union membership from only a little more than a million in 1914 to six million in 1919, that management most extensively and bitterly fought the unions and with great success. The twenties were the only extended period of prosperity in the last century in which unionism lost ground. By 1929, there were scarcely four million union members and at the depth of the depression in 1932 and 1933 less than three million. Even such a previously well-organized industry as coal mining became largely nonunion, as did the nonoperating crafts in railroading, with quite extensive losses in union membership occurring also in the building trades. This was the period of widespread resort to discrimination against workers for union membership and activities, blacklisting, and the yellow-dog contract. It was also the era of the most extensive employment by management of strikebreakers, armed guards, and industrial spies—all supplied by dozens of private detective agencies, doing a nationwide business. The aid of government also was enlisted by many managements in fighting unions. The twenties witnessed the most extreme decisions by the courts against labor, severely restricting the right to strike, to picket, and the freedom of organization. This was the time of the most widespread resort to injunctions against unions and of the most extreme injunctions. It is now generally recognized that the excesses of many managements in the 1920's in fighting unions were a major factor in creating a more favorable public opinion toward the unions, which found expression in the legislation of the 1930's to protect and encourage unionism. This change in public opinion had already been manifested in the Railroad Labor Act of 1926 and in the decision of the United States Supreme Court in the Railway Clerks Case in 1930, which held company-controlled unions to be an invasion of the right of self-organization of the workers, a right guaranteed by this legislation and the Constitution. It was President Hoover, in 1932, who signed the Norris-LaGuardia Act, which put an end to yellow-dog contracts and the abuse of injunctions against labor, as far as the federal courts are concerned.

Employee Welfare Programs

Unrestricted warfare on unions was only one aspect of the industrial relations policy of many managements in the 1920's. Another was employee welfare. This was motivated, in part, as a countermove against the unions. In part, also, it resulted from a developing realization that productivity depended, to a great extent, upon the workers' attitudes and loyalty. These employee welfare programs included recreational activities; credit unions; loan funds; employee stock ownership; company housing developments; company nurses; industrial medical programs; some employee health, welfare, pension, and profit-sharing programs; and many industrial representation plans independent of the unions and generally restricted to a single plant or company. As it was evident that the employees' productivity depended quite as much upon their environment and lives in the fourteen hours away from work as in the ten hours while at work, many of these programs reached beyond the factory into the homes of the employees and included also their wives and children.

It was this aspect of employee welfare which to a considerable extent defeated its purpose. Employees, then as now, resented employer attempts to control what they should do during what they regarded as their own time. Some other welfare programs backfired later. Stock purchased in the boom years at a discount and at that time a source of goodwill became almost worthless in the depression and produced bitter feelings toward the company. Employee representation plans, conceived as a method of keeping out the unions, in numerous instances were taken over by the unions when unionism became popular in the thirties. Many of the welfare plans of the twenties did not survive the thirties.

But, viewed in broad perspective, employee welfare has become a part of the recognized industrial relations policies of many large and medium-sized establishments. Not all of the several programs first developed extensively in the 1920's are at all common today, but most of them survived as the "fringe benefits" of today and are much more widespread than ever before. Management now, however, commonly counts them only as costs, forgetting that at least many of them have morale-building value and often serve to attract employees in a tight labor market. Scarcely anyone now thinks of employee welfare programs as all that is necessary for a sound industrial relations policy.

Personnel Management

It was during the 1920's also that personnel management became popular in management, although it is somewhat older in a few firms. It differed from scientific management in its emphasis upon the human factor in production, as distinguished from engineering and physical factors. It developed because it came to be appreciated that however good the working conditions might be, and the arrangements of work and methods of pay perfectly scientific, the hoped-for lowest possible costs of production often were not realized. The main reason why this was so was seen in the failure of the individual workers to put forth their best efforts. By this time, being tough with the workers seemed no longer to produce the desired results. This belief accounted, to some degree, for the establishment of employee welfare programs, but even more directly for the establishment of personnel departments in charge of personnel managers—today often known as labor relations departments and directed by labor relations managers or vice presidents in charge of labor relations.

Personnel management was concerned with the selection and training of employees. Where developed most fully, it emphasized the need for treating workers with the fairness and dignity to which all men and women are entitled. It led to the replacement of the foreman by the personnel department in hiring and still more in firing and disciplining of workers or, at least, in the review by higher authority of the foreman's action in such matters. The personnel department usually had responsibility for the employee welfare programs, for workmen's compensation and industrial safety, and for the hiring, at least, of juveniles to reduce the hazards of conflicts with the child labor laws. While generally not accorded very high rank in the hierarchy of executive authority, the personnel manager was charged with responsibility for keeping the workers contented and getting them to cooperate wholeheartedly with management in attaining maximum production at minimum costs.

In the 1920's, personnel management almost always was treated as an overhead cost. When, with the onset of the depression, the cutting of costs became a vital necessity, many companies reduced and even discontinued their personnel departments. But personnel management never died out and came back strong when business conditions improved. The personnel practices developed in the 1920's have become pretty standard in American industry. To the work performed by the personnel departments of the twenties, there has been added, in many companies, participation in dealings with labor unions in the negotiation of labor-management agreements, and, more commonly, primary responsibility for representing management in the many issues which are almost certain to arise during the life of such contracts concerning the meaning and application of their provisions. Often included in present-day personnel management is the matter of developing and maintaining orderly wage structures and equitable incentive methods of pay.

Related to personnel management and also first attracting attention in the 1920's were industrial psychology and psychiatry. The concern of these specialties was principally with the abnormal employees, the troublemakers, and the people with psychoses and emotional troubles which affected their attitude toward the company and their productivity. Even in large firms, this aspect of industrial relations seldom led to the establishment of special departments. Instead, this work was done by consultants from the universities and by private practitioners operating on a professional fee basis.

Industrial psychology and psychiatry have survived to this day and have gained in popularity. The former has come to be concerned above all else with the study and experimentation related to worker attitudes and with the analysis of particular jobs and training therefor. Industrial psychiatry is still largely concerned with the special problem employees, but some attention is being given to the emotional problems and reactions of the mass of the employees. Industrial psychology and psychiatry are even today largely performed on a consulting basis.

The Depression in Its Impacts upon Industrial Relations

The Great Depression, which began in 1929 and did not end until we became directly involved in World War II, had pronounced effects upon industrial relations and on management's ideas and practices. One

consequence was a great lowering in the prestige of American industrialists. Business, particularly big business, was in low repute. It was
unable to provide employment to millions of workers normally dependent
upon industry. Like agriculture and labor, business turned to government
for assistance and financial aid. A political party, holding the hopes of the
masses but distrusted by business, came into power and remained in the
White House for a total period of twenty years. While able to get Congress
to adopt its legislative program on domestic issues only for a few years
after it first came into office, its New Deal legislation crowded within these
few years changes in the economy which had taken over a generation in
western European lands. Even more far-reaching was the new construction
of the Constitution which the Supreme Court adopted after the administration failed in its attempt to change the Court itself. Viewed from the
perspective of fifteen years and after the previously long-entrenched
opposition party has been returned to power, without making any serious
attempt to turn back the clock, the changes of the depression years seem
much less revolutionary than they did to many while they were occurring.

As regards industrial relations, the most important development was the
pronounced growth of unionism, which began in 1933 in the depth of the
depression. The membership of American unions increased from less than
3,000,000 in 1933, to 8,500,000 in 1940, to above 14,000,000 at the end of
World War II, and by more than another 1,000,000 before the enactment
of the Taft-Hartley Act in 1947. Of even greater significance than this
growth in membership was the ability of the unions to win recognition and
contracts in several of our major mass-production industries—steel,
automobiles, rubber, electrical manufacturing, and meat packing—which
occurred shortly before World War II.

It is customary in management circles to attribute the great gains of the
unions in the New Deal period to the Wagner Act and governmental
favoritism. That the political climate was favorable to unionism after
Roosevelt became President cannot be gainsaid. But long before the
Wagner Act and the preceding Section 7(a) of the NIRA, unions,
economic strikes, and peaceful picketing were all legal. The changes in
substantive law made in this New Deal legislation were restricted to the
prohibition of acts of discrimination against union members, company
control of unions and the requirement that employers must bargain
collectively with representatives of their employees if a majority of them so
desire. Neither at that time nor since has the government ever directly
assisted unions in organizing, as it long has assisted farmer cooperatives. It
is not without significance that the left-wing unions took the position that
both the NIRA and the Wagner Act were worthless frauds upon labor. It
was the conservative business unionists who made the most of this

legislation—a good example being John L. Lewis (who, except in 1936, has always supported Republican candidates for President) who, entirely on his own, the minute the NIRA became law sent organizers into all the unorganized coal fields with the cry, "Roosevelt wants you to organize," and within a short period got pretty nearly the entire industry organized. As my colleague at the University of Wisconsin, the labor historian, Selig Perlman, has expressed it, "The New Deal got labor off dead center," and labor took full advantage of the more favorable political climate to recoup its losses of the 1920's and to attain a strength it never had had previously.

But probably even more important in explaining the growth of unionism in the 1930's were the changes in the composition of the labor force and the statesmanship of some leaders of industry in the ranks of management, who concluded that the times called for giving unionism a trial. The major mass-production industries were no pushover for the unions in the late thirties. They fought unionism stubbornly, but not to the bitter end. When World War II came most of them were dealing with unions, but collective bargaining was still very new when the war interrupted its normal development.

It was at the time of its triumph that unionism lost favor in public opinion. Americans are ever inclined to support the underdog. When labor was weakest, in the 1920's and in the deepest depression, public opinion swung in its favor. When labor had the Wagner Act and when this was sustained by the Supreme Court and given the widest possible application and when it increased its membership by leaps and bounds and won contracts from the great mass-production industries, in the late thirties, it got into the doghouse with public opinion and to date has never recovered its favor. For this labor itself, at least in part, was responsible. Sit-down strikes and considerable violence in labor disputes antagonized the public. The bitter hostility of the two groups into which labor was split at this time and the reckless disregard of public convenience and interests exhibited in this contest prejudiced the neutral public against the unions. If management brought on the Wagner Act and forfeited the support of public opinion by its excesses in fighting unions in the 1920's, labor lost tremendously by its excesses of the late 1930's, when it was registering its greatest advances.

Elton Mayo and His Human Relations Approach to Industrial Relations

It was in this environment that Elton Mayo publicized his Hawthorne experiments and developed the approach to industrial relations which has had the greatest influence upon management thought of any studies ever conducted. The Hawthorne experiments—so named from the Hawthorne Works of the Western Electric Company in a suburb of Chicago—were undertaken because that company could not get satisfactory production, in spite of great efforts to improve conditions of employment and scientific methods of remuneration. Elton Mayo was an Australian-born industrial sociologist, teaching in the Harvard Graduate School of Business Administration. He began his Hawthorne studies in the late 1920's but did not complete them until well into the thirties.

What Mayo discovered is not easy to set forth simply. He proved by experiments that production is not solely a matter of individual effort, equipment, and conditions of work. He found that the workers' attitudes and, specifically, their productivity were largely determined by norms established by the group. While each worker is an individual, he is also a member of a group and to most everybody what matters most is the favorable opinion of the group. Many times this expressed itself in rigid adherence to limits on production set by the group, although the Hawthorne Works were at that time entirely free of unionism. To Mayo, the factory was a social organism and within it were many smaller groups, which largely determined the production of the individual employees and their attitudes toward the company. More than anything else production depends upon human relations, and human relations are largely a matter of group reactions. Management's task is to mold group opinion in directions favorable to increased production.

It is understandable why Mayo assigned no role to the unions in his Hawthorne studies. There was then no union in this plant. Nor did Mayo in any of his later studies ever attribute any functions to unions in relation to production. Some of his followers "discovered" unions, but saw in them only obstacles to maximum production. Others concluded that it is not the unions but the much smaller groups into which the workers naturally divide themselves that matter. Others, not directly connected with Elton Mayo, recognized the union as, perhaps, the most important of all groups influencing the attitudes of the individual workers toward the company and production. They pointed out that, in organized plants, getting the cooperation of the union is a major task facing management desirous of increasing output and reducing costs. But such views were developed only after the Hawthorne experiments had been widely publicized.

The appeal of the Hawthorne experiments and what came to be known to many managements as the "human relations" approach of Elton Mayo lay in the hope they seemed to offer of being able to avoid the dreaded unionism, then "in the air," by appealing to and working with the smaller groups to be found in all establishments. That was by no means Mayo's central idea, but in the troublesome times of the thirties it was the application of his emphasis upon the importance of the group in securing results desired by management which accounted for much of its early popularity.

In the long run, what proved most significant was probably Mayo's insistence upon research and experimentation to discover all the facts applicable to each industrial relations situation. Satisfactory industrial relations is not a matter of following some formula or doing what someone else has done. It presents a problem for which there is never a perfect or final answer, but one calling for the exercise of the best intelligence management can muster and, above all, for recognition that this is basically a human problem with group, no less than individual, aspects.

Human relations as preached by Elton Mayo and his followers continues to this day as the central core of the approach of many progressive managements to sound industrial relations. There have been numerous refinements and additions since Mayo conducted his experiments, but his influence continues to be very great upon American management in many aspects of industrial relations. . . .

34

Industrial Life Insurance in the United States

JACK BLICKSILVER

Industrial life insurance was introduced into the United States during the 1870s by a few young, farsighted insurance executives. Predominant among this group of pioneers were John F. Dryden of Prudential, Joseph W. Knapp of Metropolitan Life and Stephen H. Rhodes of John Hancock. In pioneering in the new field of Industrial insurance, their motivations were both humanitarian and economic.

A reference regarding Stephen Rhodes could be applied readily to the senior executives of Prudential and Metropolitan Life: "It was part of his vision of service that the benefits of life insurance should be made available to all people."[1] In practice this meant devising a system of sale and service that would make private life insurance protection—then confined to the wealthy few—practicable for the growing mass of low income Americans, including women and juveniles.

There was little doubt of either the deepening need or the expanding market potential for this kind of basic life insurance protection during the decades following the Civil War. In the 1870s population was pushing

Jack Blicksilver, *Industrial Life Insurance in the United States*, Life Insurers Conference, Richmond, Virginia, 1968, pp. 12-28.

toward the fifty million mark. A quarter of a million or more immigrants entered annually to join miners, cattlemen, and farmers in filling out the last frontier between the Mississippi River and the Rocky Mountains; they also settled in increasing numbers in the larger towns and cities where they competed for jobs with farmers' sons and daughters who were swelling the exodus from rural America in search for greater economic opportunity and a higher standard of living. (In 1870, eight million Americans resided in communities with 8,000 or more inhabitants; the number grew to 11.3 million in 1880, 18.2 million in 1890 and 25.0 million in 1900.)[2]

Life for the low income masses in American cities during the late nineteenth century while undergoing improvement was still short and brutish. The average death rate (20.38 per thousand during the 1880s) was one-third higher in cities than in the countryside; it was considerably higher for citizens of foreign parentage than for those of native white parents; it was much higher for Negroes than for whites in all parts of the nation. (The average expectation of life in the United States at birth in 1900 was 48.2 years for white males and 51.1 years for white females; it was 32.5 years for nonwhite males and 35.1 years for nonwhite females.)[3]

The life span of adult males and females was shortened by the high incidence of consumption, pneumonia, typhoid and paratyphoid fevers. Millions of infants were doomed to an early death by a spate of unchecked childhood diseases: diphtheria, measles, whooping cough, scarlet fever.

Confronted with the cold reality of their situation, low income Americans developed a deep-rooted yearning for sufficient financial security to defray the costs of a final illness and to assure a decent Christian burial. The need for private financial security was accentuated by the impersonality of urban life and the minimal role of government. Close-knit ties promoted by long residence and kinship relations so characteristic of farm and small town living were broken in the big, indifferent city. Little in the way of welfare payments could be expected of government in an era in which social Darwinism (survival of the fittest) reigned supreme. . . .

Within this socio-political environment the low income masses turned to the private sector, and to Ordinary insurance. They soon found that tradition-bound Ordinary insurance could not meet their needs. True, in the post-Civil War years a few Ordinary companies began to solicit business among the working class, offering contracts with a face value as low as $100. But their annual or semi-annual terms of premium payment seemed an insuperable barrier to men whose weekly incomes barely covered the cost of basic necessities for their families. Furthermore, only a few policies were issued on women—who as widows with dependent children or as white collar clerical and retail sales employees constituted a growing segment of the potential life insurance market—and none on juveniles. As a result, fewer than four per cent of Americans purchased

Ordinary life insurance during the late nineteenth century. The average size Ordinary policy in force in 1900 was $2,233, virtually the same as in 1950. And not a single one of the 25 leading Ordinary companies as of 1870 ever developed Industrial life insurance business.[4]

The low-income Americans, continuing their search for basic life insurance protection, turned to fraternal and assessment associations, which enjoyed a great wave of popularity in the years after Appomattox. But the great fraternal orders restricted their membership to specific social, religious and racial groups. Cooperative assessment societies tended to be plagued by poor management and suffered a high failure rate. It became increasingly clear that fraternal and assessment associations both failed to fulfill their promise to provide a stable source of life insurance protection to the masses. The insurance commissioner of Massachusetts in 1873 urged the replacement of cooperative societies with proprietary Industrial insurance companies. By the mid-1870s leading insurance journals throughout the nation joined in advocating the introduction of Industrial insurance.[5]

Industrial insurance was first issued in the United States in Newark, New Jersey, on November 10, 1875. Newark, with a population of 120,000, ranked among the nation's fifteen largest cities; heavily industrialized, a high proportion of its labor force depended upon weekly wages. The year 1875 saw many business failures and a high rate of unemployment as the economy continued to struggle through a prolonged depression. (The depression adversely affected the life insurance industry, as it did many others; between 1873 and 1877, the number of insurance companies operating in New York State was reduced from 71 to 34.) In the midst of this period of economic distress, Industrial insurance was introduced by an obscure proprietary company, The Prudential Friendly Society, founded by John Dryden, the 36-year-old son of a Maine farmer.[6]

Dryden clearly conceived both the need for low cost of life insurance protection and the practices necessary to make it economically justifiable. The Prudential's prospectus stated that the policies it was making available were "designed for persons of limited needs." The indigent, the improvident, the unemployable were not to be solicited. The Industrial contract's principal purpose was to provide a burial fund for adults and children and a modest pension in old age. (An additional purpose, to provide protection against sickness and accidents, was soon abandoned by the Prudential in favor of a straight life policy. Combination health and life insurance contracts were made available, however, by a number of companies formed after 1875.)

The major contribution of Dryden, continued by companies following the lead of Prudential, was to establish sound and sensible business practices in the realm of limited cost life insurance. These practices included providing minimum protection policies for low income classes, sold at rates that would cover long-term costs; selling policies upon a premium basis which best suited the income arrangements of its patrons; and collecting premiums in a manner that would offset as much as possible the natural temptation of persons with marginal incomes to be lured by the siren-call of semi-luxuries, and therefore to neglect or forget their insurance needs. An additional deviation from orthodoxy lay in the mass coverage approach of Industrial insurance. Issued without medical examinations, Industrial insurance protection was made available to all members of the family. (Of the first 1,000 applications received by Prudential, one-third were on women and one-third were on children below the age of ten.) . . . Therefore, at a time when the United States was making rapid strides in the direction of the mass production of industrial commodities and the mass marketing of consumer goods, the large-scale sale of low-unit life insurance policies was entirely appropriate.[7]

(In successfully introducing Industrial insurance into the United States, Dryden side-stepped the pitfalls that plunged many assessment and cooperative societies into bankruptcy. In doing so, he drew heavily upon the proven practices of British Industrial insurance.

(The Prudential Assurance Company of London began selling Industrial insurance in 1854. Organized six years earlier—1848—the company was transacting Ordinary life insurance business, with modest success, when in 1853 a committee of the House of Commons disclosed the many defects of British friendly societies and burial clubs. The committee's report stressed the need for extending dependable life insurance to the lower income groups.

(The directors of the London Prudential accepted the challenge and opened an Industrial branch in 1854. Policies were issued initially on persons between the ages of 10 years and 60 years, with premiums varying by age at issue and computed on the level premium basis. Medical examinations were dispensed with. Premiums were payable weekly and were collected by representatives who called at the home of policyholders.

(Progress was slow at first; not until 1861 did the Company show a profit. But once accepted by the British public, Industrial insurance grew rapidly, spurred by a liberalization in the table of rates and by the introduction of a policy for infants. When John Dryden arrived in 1874 to study its operations, the London Prudential could boast of having almost two million policies in force. Deeply impressed, Dryden resolved to transfer the Prudential's policy contract and basic business techniques to the United States, then experiencing an economic development comparable to that of Britain two decades earlier.)[8]

During the first three decades following its introduction into the United States in 1875, Industrial life insurance became firmly established, expanded at a substantial pace and spread throughout the nation. By 1890, nine life insurance companies marketing Industrial contracts had 3.8 million policies in force, with a total value in force of $428 million. By 1905, the number of Industrial life insurance companies had grown to 20; the policies in force to 16.8 million, and the insurance in force to $2,278 million.[9]

In this period three companies gained a dominant position within the Industrial segment of the life insurance industry. In addition to The Prudential Insurance Company, the "big three" included Metropolitan Life Insurance Company and The John Hancock Mutual Life Insurance Company. The latter two companies began to issue Industrial insurance policies on the weekly premium plan in 1879. All three became combination companies, selling both Industrial and Ordinary insurance. But the Industrial portion of their business loomed larger, especially for Prudential and Metropolitan Life. In 1905, the Met alone controlled 49 per cent of the nation's Industrial insurance business. Together, the "big three" held 88 per cent of the business, while the other 17 companies shared the remaining 12 per cent. The bulk of the business controlled by the larger companies was concentrated in the highly industrialized northeast and midwest.[10]

In the south, still characterized by the scattered countryside and the crossroads town, small, regional companies were organized in the 1880s and 1890s. Offering, primarily, combination health and burial fund policies, they became increasingly popular with persons of "moderate means" unable to pay the high rates of Ordinary policies sold by old line companies. In some instances, southern based companies catered exclusively to the large Negro market.[11]

During its formative years Industrial insurance was subjected to sporadic and, at times, intense criticism. In England the attack centered on charges of heavy administrative costs and high lapse rates. (The criticism culminated in legislation in 1865 which empowered the Postmaster General to conduct a life insurance business. The scheme failed to win wide popularity; by 1918 fewer than 30,000 contracts had been written; subsequently, the plan was abandoned as an acknowledged failure.)[12]

In the United States, criticism concentrated at first on the charge of infanticide. During the 1880s a number of state insurance commissioners came to the stout defense of Industrial insurance, and criticism on this score soon waned.[13]

Sporadic attacks on Industrial insurance, involving a wide spectrum of charges, continued during the final decades of the nineteenth century and finally culminated in investigation by the Armstrong Committee of the New York State legislature, beginning September 6, 1905. Although the investigation concentrated on the practices of the large Ordinary companies, committee attorney Charles Evans Hughes in his questioning of witnesses aired all the by-then familiar complaints against Industrial insurance: the cost of Industrial contracts compared to Ordinary; the smaller benefits; the high lapse rate; and low earnings of agents.

Against these charges, leading industry representatives mounted a strong defense. The higher cost of protection, it was pointed out, was determined both by the higher mortality rates of the class of persons insured and also by the considerably higher cost involved in selling and servicing this type of business. John R. Hegeman, president of Metropolitan Life, testified as to the "immense amount of detail work required. . . . It is selling insurance at retail rather than at wholesale. It is on a par with the selling of coal by the pail instead of by the ton." Industry spokesmen conceded the higher-than-Ordinary lapse rate (although the trend was definitely downward and the spread was narrowing). Lapses of Industrial policies were to a large extent due to policyholder income instability, which also made it difficult for low income families to sustain mortgage payments and installment payments on consumer purchases over an extended period of time. Lapses which occurred in the first year after purchase constituted a net loss to the company, while the policyholder enjoyed life insurance protection during the limited time the policy was in force. As for the agency force, it was generally conceded that the average Industrial insurance agent was poorly paid. President Hegeman stated that Metropolitan agents earned "on the average less than the mechanics and people among whom they go." No feasible remedy for this situation was suggested.[14]

The Armstrong committee report, made public on February 22, 1906, summarized the recognized weaknesses of Industrial insurance, but declined to suggest changes. The report stated:[15]

> The most serious evils . . . to wit, the excessive premiums, the enormous lapse rate and the hardships of the agents, seem to be inherent in the system. . . . The alternative seems to be presented either of prohibiting altogether industrial insurance by private corporations or of permitting its continuance substantially upon the present basis, subject to those regulations designed to secure economical administration applicable to all companies alike.

Compared to its bitter attack upon the practices of the large Ordinary insurance companies, the Armstrong committees's conclusions concerning Industrial insurance came close to being a complete vindication. Certainly its mild censure of some industry features failed to shake confidence in Industrial insurance among the low income masses. Several months following the Armstrong committee's final report, a publication of the United States Department of Labor expressed wonderment "that people who are barely holding body and soul together, and who are so sorely

pressed by the demands of the present, will surrender a part of the income
. . . to the purchase of a benefit that can accrue only in the future."[16]

Sales of Industrial life insurance surged during the years following the
Armstrong investigation. In the decade 1906-1915 Industrial policies in
force in the United States increased from 17 million to 32 million, and
Industrial life insurance in force also almost doubled, increasing from $2.3
billion to $4.3 billion. Rapid growth was sustained during the years of
World War I and post-war adjustment. In 1920, there were 48 million
Industrial policies in force in the United States with an aggregate value of
$6.9 billion.[17]

Although satisfied by the substance and tone of the Armstrong report,
leaders within the Industrial life insurance industry recognized that self-
improvement was essential if more severe criticism was to be avoided in the
future.

Consequently, in the years after 1906, the industry began to take stock of
itself and to introduce some significant changes, beneficial to its clients.
Industrial insurance rates were repeatedly and sharply reduced during the
decade after 1906; the aggregate reduction totaled about 20 per cent.
(Developments making the reduction possible included better business
methods and improved mortality. Lowered mortality rates, especially
striking at infantile ages, followed the wide-spread acceptance of the 1906
Standard Industrial Mortality Table.) Soliciting methods were considerably improved, leading to lower lapse rates. (The ratio of policies lapsed
and surrendered during the year to mean policies in force fell from 23.4 per
cent in 1900, to 18.7 per cent in 1905, to 14.4 per cent in 1915, and to 9.3 per
cent in 1920.) Furthermore, policy provisions were liberalized by introducing a number of innovations in Industrial policies: paid-up insurance, cash
surrender values, extended insurance, incontestability and full death
payments to policyholders who died during the first policy year.[18]

In a further attempt to enhance the value of Industrial insurance, while
improving persistency and cutting down claims, a number of insurers
moved into the sphere of social welfare work. During the decades of the
1910s and 1920s, millions of pieces of literature on health, safety and infant care were distributed; some of the larger companies organized a nursing service, making home care freely available to their Industrial
policyholders. The movement was spearheaded by Metropolitan Life
which launched its separate welfare division in 1909; many other Industrial insurers, on a somewhat smaller scale, through publications and the
weekly contacts of their agents, performed an invaluable service in supplying sound advice and financial guidance to their clients. During the
1930s, the rising cost of private social welfare work and the increasing role
of public efforts led to the phasing out of nursing and other formal
services. . . .

While the large northern-based companies took the lead in establishing ambitious social welfare programs, smaller southern companies, less well-equipped financially to follow suit, pursued the path of cooperative action in the years after 1906. They were spurred on by the Armstrong hearings, which by spot-lighting the abuses of the giants in the industry gave an impetus to the growth of regional companies. . . . Responsible insurance executives became alarmed by the criticism directed against Industrial life insurance by Louis D. Brandeis and other reformers. They were alert to the manifold benefits to be gained through periodic meetings and the mutual sharing of information and experiences.

These fears and feelings found fruition in December, 1910 when officers representing 18 Industrial insurance companies met in Atlanta, Georgia, and organized the Southern Casualty and Surety Conference. Its stated purpose was "the cultivation of friendship, the promotion of harmony, and the betterment of conditions affecting their particular classes of business." Beginning as a loosely-organized regional association of companies concerned with Industrial debits, the Conference evolved over the years into a highly effective association of combination life insurance and multi-line companies with interests affecting the entire industry and with ramifications extending beyond the nation's borders. Renamed the Industrial Insurers' Conference and later, at its 39th annual meeting in 1948, the Life Insurers Conference, the association's 98 members home based in 22 states, Washington, D.C., Puerto Rico, and Bahamas by 1967 had more than 58.7 million policies in force with an aggregate insurance in force approaching $125 billion.[19]

Beginning in the 1920s Ordinary and Industrial life insurance began to draw closer together and some overlapping of policy categories began to take place. Prior to the mid-1920s Industrial insurance was written only on a weekly premium basis and Ordinary insurance only on a quarterly or less frequent basis. A number of companies then commenced to market Ordinary insurance on a monthly premium basis. At the same time, combination companies began to issue Ordinary policies with monthly premiums of less than $10 by servicing them on a debit basis. These companies also extended the issue of monthly premium insurance to amounts less than $1,000.[20]

Simultaneously, a movement developed on the part of smaller southern companies which had previously restricted themselves to offering a combination policy—providing protection against injury and sickness, with a small death benefit—to issue straight life Industrial insurance policies. (Indeed, a "straight life craze" swept the south during the 1920s, forcing some hesitant insurance executives to join the movement or be left behind.)

During the 1920s, a decade of widespread prosperity, particularly for the urban, industrial segment of the economy, Industrial life insurance maintained its popularity among the lower income classes. Industrial life policies in force increased from 48 to 86 million during the decade while Industrial insurance in force more than doubled, growing from $6.9 billion to $17.9 billion. In line with rising incomes, and influenced by a modest increase in the cost of living following the extensive inflation of the World War I years, the average size Industrial policy increased from $150 in 1920 to $210 in 1930.

The depression decade of the 1930s was a time of trial for the life insurance industry in the United States, and no less so for the the Industrial segment than for the Ordinary. The number of Industrial policies in force dropped from 86 million in 1930 to 78 million in 1933; it rose again to 85 million by 1937, and leveled off at that figure for several years until a wartime impetus sent it surging again. The insurance in force figure followed the same trend. From a peak of $17.9 billion in 1930, Industrial life insurance in force in the United States declined year by year to a nadir of $16.6 billion in 1933; it then began to climb slowly but steadily, reaching a level of $20.8 billion in 1940.[21]

It is significant that although Industrial insurers suffered losses during the worst years of the depression, Industrial insurance in force fell less and recovered more rapidly than did Ordinary insurance. As of December 31, 1937, Industrial insurance accounted for 19 per cent of life insurance in force in the United States, 23.4 per cent of the amount paid in premiums to life insurance companies and 72 per cent of the number of policies in force. As many as fifty million Americans held industrial insurance policies. The billions of dollars paid out in cash surrender values to Industrial policyholders during the course of the long depression helped pull many lower income families through difficult times.[22]

As the depression finally waned during the latter part of the 1930s, Industrial insurance, along with most other sectors of economic life, was subjected to a searching scrutiny by the Temporary National Economic Committee, authorized by the 75th Congress of the United States. A subcommittee of TNEC was appointed to hold hearings on Industrial insurance, with the Securities and Exchange Commission in charge of the presentation of evidence. Hearings were held in February and November, 1939, and a final report was made public in March, 1941.

A spate of information on the character and procedures of the industry was gathered. It revealed, among other things, that Industrial insurance in the late 1930s was still heavily concentrated in the hands of the "big three" companies. Metropolitan Life and Prudential together held 73 per cent of Industrial insurance in force; John Hancock held 8 per cent; and the remaining 19 per cent of the business was divided among about 135 small companies.

The testimony itself traversed well-trodden ground and revealed little about Industrial insurance that was not well known. But the tone of the hearings was harsh and the summary recommendation was severe: "A fundamental change in the conduct of Industrial insurance should occur. Otherwise its eventual elimination may be necessary." The impact of the recommendation was softened, however, by leaving to the states and the individual companies responsibility for effecting the change.[23] . . .

The extensive liberalization of Industrial life insurance policies during the decades of the 1920s and 1930s made possible an era of unparalleled growth beginning in 1940. The number of Industrial policies in force rose steadily during the World War II years, from 85 million in 1940 to 101 million in 1945; during these years, Industrial insurance in force increased from $20.8 billion to $27.6 billion.[24]

A survey conducted at the end of the war confirmed the importance of Industrial life insurance to its policyholders. It provided the only funds for the cost of the final illness and burial in three-fourths of all cases where death benefits became payable. In addition, such death benefit payments provided about six months income in the majority of instances in which the head of the family had died. Secondly, as much as $3 million was paid annually to Industrial policyholders who had lost one or more limbs or the sight of one or more eyes. Finally, the survey disclosed that the owners of Industrial policies, whether they were endowment contracts or not, had a systematic means of saving which in most cases was their only means of saving, and in other cases was the backbone of the modest family savings.[25] . . .

Endnotes

1. John Hancock Mutual Life Insurance Company, *The First Seventy-Five Years* (n.p., n.d.), p. 10.

2. U.S. Department of Commerce, *Historical Statistics of the United States* (Washington, 1960), *passim*.

3. *Ibid.*; *Census of the United States*: Population, 1890, 1900.

4. J. Owen Stalson, *Marketing Life Insurance: Its History in America* (Cambridge, Mass., 1942), pp. 462-463; Davis, *Industrial Life Insurance in the United States*, chapter 1; *Life Insurance Fact Book*, 1948, p. 12.

5. Stalson, *Marketing Life Insurance*, tables pp. 805-807; R. C. Buley, *The American Life Convention*, 1906-1952; *A Study in the History of Life Insurance* (New York, 1953), volume I, pp. 107-108.

6. Frederick L. Hoffman, *History of The Prudential Insurance Company of America*, 1875-1900 (Prudential Press, 1900), chapters 1-4; Earl C. May and Will Oursler, *A Story of Human Security, The Prudential* (Garden City, N. Y., 1950), chapters 1-3.

7. *Ibid.; Fifty Years of the Prudential; The History of a Business Charged with Public Interests*, 1875-1925 (Newark, N. J., 1927), pp. 12-14.

8. Arnold Wilson and Hermann Levy, *Industrial Assurance, An Historical and Critical Study* (London, 1937), pp. 34-39; Dermot Morrah, *A History of Industrial Life Assurance* (London, 1955), chapter II.

9. Stalson, *Marketing Life Insurance*, table, p. 809; *Life Insurance Fact Book*, 1967, p. 19.

10. May and Oursler, *The Prudential*, pp. 76-130; Marquis James, *The Metropolitan Life, A Study in Business Growth* (New York, 1947), pp. 73-139.

11. See, for example, *Annual Report of Insurance Department of State of Georgia*, Comptroller-General Office, *Report of 1896-1897* (Atlanta, 1897), pp. 217-218; Buley, *American Life Convention*, p. 110.

12. Morrah, *A History of Industrial Life Assurance*, pp. 31-35.

13. Buley, *American Life Convention*, pp. 111-112; James, *Metropolitan Life*, pp. 86-87.

14. James, *Metropolitan Life*, pp. 140-160; May and Oursler, *The Prudential*, pp. 129-141.

15. Quoted in James, *Metropolitan Life*, p. 162.

16. Quoted in *Fifty Years of the Prudential*, p. 14.

17. *Life Insurance Fact Book*, 1967, p. 19.

18. Brandeis, *Business—A Profession*, pp. 185-187; *Life Insurance Fact Book*, 1946, p. 29.

19. Atlanta *Constitution*, December 10, 11, 1910; A. B. Langley, "The Three Decades of the Conference," *Proceedings of the 31st Convention of the Industrial Insurers' Conference*, May 15-17, 1940, pp. 33-36; H. C. E. Johnson, "President's Address," *Proceedings of the 40th Annual Convention of the Life Insurers Conference*, April 27-29, 1949, pp. 9-13; *The Insurance Field*, June 4, 1960, pp. 26-27; *Proceedings of the 57th Annual Meeting of the Life Insurers Conference*, April 10-12, 1967, pp. 130-136.

20. M. E. Davis, "Industrial Life Insurance—History and Operation," *Examination of Insurance Companies, A Series of Lectures Delivered Before the Examiners of The New York State Insurance Department* (New York, 1955), Volume VI, chapter 4.

21. *Life Insurance Fact Book*, 1967, p. 19.

22. T. N. E. C., *Study of Legal Reserve Life Insurance Companies* (Monograph No. 28), p. 248.

23. See Investigation of Concentration of Economic Power, *Hearings Before the Temporary National Economic Committee*, 76th Congress, 1st Session, Part 12, Industrial Insurance (Washington, 1940); James, *Metropolitan Life*, pp. 346-361.

24. *Life Insurance Fact Book*, 1967, p. 19.

25. Survey cited in talk by Bruce Batho at Savannah Life Underwriters Association, January 25, 1947 and printed in *The LOG* (Atlanta, Georgia), May, 1947.

35

Recent Economic Changes in the United States, A Review

WESLEY C. MITCHELL

The Prime Factor Making for Prosperity

Past experience has taught us that a period of depression will presently be followed by a business revival. But when this revival will come, and whether it will develop into full-blown prosperity, are matters which the past does not tell. Each cycle has its special features which require special explanations. How the United States managed to attain a higher per capita income in 1922-1927 than ever before, though conditions in most other countries were not favorable, and though its basic industry, agriculture, was depressed, is the outstanding problem of the cycles of 1921-1924, 1924-1927 and 1927 to date.

. . . Since 1921, Americans have applied intelligence to the day's work more effectively than ever before. Thus the prime factor in producing the

Wesley C. Mitchell, "A Review," *Recent Economic Changes in the United States*, by the President's Conference on Unemployment, Herbert Hoover, Chairman. New York: McGraw-Hill Book Company, Inc., 1929, pp. 841-910. Excerpted and reprinted by permission of McGraw-Hill Book Co.

extraordinary changes in the economic fortunes of the European peoples during the nineteenth century is the prime factor in producing the prosperity of the United States in recent years. The old process of putting science into industry has been followed more intensively than before; it has been supplemented by tentative efforts to put science into business management, trade-union policy, and Government administration.

Concrete instances of technical improvements [are evident] in many mining, metallurgical, and fabricating processes. The remarkable results achieved are demonstrated statistically from census data showing output per worker. Similar, though less striking, instances appear in the chapter on construction. Without help from any extraordinary invention, the railroads also have attained a higher level of operating efficiency.[1] In farming there is an intriguing report of new machines and new methods coming into use. Here too, the record of average output per worker shows considerable gains.

All this means that since 1921 Americans have found ways of producing more physical goods per hour of labor than before. They have received larger average incomes because they have produced more commodities and services.[2] That is true in the aggregate, although not all who have contributed to the increase in physical production have shared in the increase of real income. . . .

The reality of the gains made by improving the technique of farming, railroading, manufacturing, and building seems to be established beyond question. There is room for doubt only concerning the pace of recent progress in comparison with earlier spurts of technical improvement. Comparisons between output per worker in later years and in 1919 often show sensational gains. But that is largely because 1919 made a wretched record of physical inefficiency. . . . But doubts whether the rate of improvement in the past six years is unprecedented are not of great moment. It remains clear that the Industrial Revolution is not a closed episode; we are living in the midst of it, and the economic problems of today are largely problems of its making.

While the details of the latest technical advances always possess thrilling interest, perhaps there is more of promise . . . [in] recent changes in economic policy. The efforts to apply scientific methods to such matters are in an early stage of development. The sciences which underlie these efforts—psychology, sociology, economics—are far less advanced than physics and chemistry. The experts who are making the applications—personnel managers, advertising specialists, sales directors, business economists, and statisticians—are less rigorously trained than engineers. It is even harder to measure the results they achieve than to determine what difference a new machine makes in unit costs. Nor are business executives so generally convinced of the practical value of the rather intangible services which the new professions can render as they are of the indispensability of engineering advice. Yet it is conceivable that applications of the social sciences, now in their tentative stage, will grow into contributions of great moment to economic welfare. . . . [E]nterprising business concerns and some enterprising trade unions are trying new policies, and often getting results which they deem good.

Perhaps none of the changes reported here will prove more important in the long run than the change in the economic theories on which the American Federation of Labor and certain outside unions are acting. That organizations of wage earners should grasp the relations between productivity and wages, and that they should take the initiative in pressing constructive plans for increasing efficiency upon employers, is not wholly without precedent; but the spread of such ideas and the vigor with which they are acted on by large organizations must startle those who have believed that trade unions are brakes upon economic progress.

Scarcely less significant is the report from the employing side. Our investigators believe that the art of business management turned a corner in 1921, cultivating since then more skillful understanding of the whole situation and nicer adjustment of means to the immediate environment. Numerous corporations and some trade associations are maintaining research bureaus of their own. Among the managerial devices experimented with are co-ordinated staffs in place of one "big boss," bonus payments to executives and "incentive wages" for the rank and file, operating budgets, forecasts of business conditions, close inventory control, personnel management, and employee representation. Most of these devices are attempts to understand and to utilize the psychological forces which control human behavior, or the economic forces which control business activity. . . .

Marketing—traditionally the part of business in which native shrewdness, experience, and "personal magnetism" have been held all-important—even marketing is being permeated by applied psychology. Costly investigations of "consumer appeal," of advertising "pull," of "sales resistance"—the very terms would have been unintelligible to our fathers—show that sales managers are trying to base their planning upon factual studies of human behavior. And the rapid spread of chain stores and of installment selling shows that marketing methods are no more standing still than is industrial technique.

By the side of these rather definite changes in trade-union and in business policy, we may set the influence of certain general ideas which have gained wide currency in the last years. . . .

More publicity concerning business operations and closer co-operation among business enterprises should also be noted as characteristic of the day. These are features of American practice which impress all our foreign visitors; the older rules of secretiveness and rivalry seem to have maintained themselves more rigidly in other countries. Perhaps the growth of trade associations and the expansion of their programs is the clearest evidence of the new attitude. No doubt every industry has its recalcitrants who, for one reason or another, refuse to play on the team; but certainly there is a marked increase of readiness to join co-operative programs of research and publicity, to interchange trade information, to standardize products where standardization is good business, to consult about methods and practices—in short, to treat the industry for many purposes as a unit in whose prosperity all members have a common interest, and to inspire good will in the public by open dealings.

. . . Belief in the economy of high wages has become prevalent among the abler business executives, much as belief in increasing productivity has become prevalent among the abler trade-union leaders. To find a market for the wares turned out by mass production and urged on consumers by national advertising, it is patently necessary to have corresponding purchasing power in the hands of consumers. Since studies of the national income have demonstrated that wages constitute by far the largest stream of personal income, it follows that wages per man—or rather, wages per family—must be increased as production is expanded. Perhaps most people would have accepted this argument in the abstract at any time in the last hundred years. But many employers in the past would have retorted with the assertion that high wages undermine the moral stamina of the masses. To-day such talk is far less common in the United States. Not only do many business executives admit the general principle that paying high wages is good policy; they are ready to assume what they consider their share of the responsibility for putting the principle into practice. . . .

To repeat: all of the changes making for prosperity . . . can be summed up under a single head—applying fresh intelligence to the day's work. From the use of abstruse researches in pure science to the use of broad economic conceptions and the use of common sense, the method of American progress in 1922-1928 has been the old method of taking thought. Peace let us turn our thoughts to common matters, the hard times of 1921 spurred our efforts, and the complicated consequences our efforts produced have kept us thinking.

Hardships Caused by Increasing Efficiency

Among the consequences which improvements in industrial technique or in business methods produce in an individualistic state, are hardships of various kinds. The victims are partly business competitors who are a bit slow in adopting new methods; partly industries or geographic regions affected indirectly; partly individuals who find their services no longer needed. To follow all the complicated difficulties produced by recent economic advances in the United States is out of the question; but a few chains of cause and effect may be traced link by link. For the queer mixture of prosperity and depression noted at the outset of this chapter is due largely to the pressure which some group's growing efficiency puts upon other groups. . . .

. . . The reduction in unit costs, and the increase in the supply of wares turned out by improved methods, combined with international forces to keep the American price level from rising buoyantly in the active years of our period, as it has done in most periods of prosperity. Presumably, the international factors have been more potent than the domestic factors in producing the results. Yet we may count the reductions in cost by industrial leaders and the increases in output among the manifestations of efficiency which have contributed to the difficulties of making money in this period.

Sagging prices make it harder to conduct business with profit because many of the expenses of an enterprise are fixed by long contracts or by understandings hard to alter, and cannot be cut to offset a reduction in selling rates. Above, we noticed how the rapidly rising prices of the war and of 1919 swelled paper profits and reduced bankruptcies. Also we noted how the sudden fall of prices in 1920-1921 turned profits into losses and swelled bankruptcies. In 1922-1927, we find an intermediate result. Concerns in the van of technical progress have done handsomely. But the prices at which they could market their large outputs with profit to themselves have meant loss and even failure to less aggressive rivals. . . . The average number of failures in 1922-1927 has actually exceeded the number in 1921, but the total and the average liabilities have grown smaller.

. . . One expects a period of unusually rapid increase in efficiency to be a period of more than usual inequality of profits. This expectation has been borne out by the experience of 1922-1927. As a whole, corporate incomes reported to the Internal Revenue Bureau . . . have been large in the latest years for which we have data; but they have not equaled the records of 1916-1919.

Whether the enterprises which have lagged behind in cost reductions and in earnings are mainly smaller enterprises, as has been contended, is less sure. Of course this contention tends to become true with the lapse of time, for the simple reason that the exceptionally profitable enterprises grow exceptionally fast. The profitable enterprises of to-day tend to become the large enterprises of tomorrow. But Dr. Thorp's [discussion] . . .

shows that there is no close relationship between large size and low unit-cost, or between large size and high rates of profit. It seems to be middle-sized enterprises, rather than small ones, which have felt the severest pressure. But the facts, as the census shows them, are complicated and cannot be adequately presented in a brief statement.

The Competition of New Products and New Tastes

Scarcely less characteristic of our period than unit-cost reductions is the rapid expansion in the production and sale of products little used or wholly unknown a generation or even a decade ago. Among consumers' goods, the conspicuous instances are automobiles, radios, and rayon. But the list includes also oil-burning furnaces, gas stoves, household electrical appliances in great variety, automobile accessories, antifreezing mixtures, cigarette lighters, propeller pencils, wrist watches, airplanes, and what not. Among producers' goods we have the truck and the tractor competing with the horse and the mule, reinforced concrete competing with brick and lumber, the high-tension line competing with the steam engine, fuel oil competing with coal, not to mention excavating machines, belt conveyors, paint sprayers, and "automatics" of many sorts competing with manual labor.

Changes in taste are in large part merely the consumers' response to the solicitation of novel products, effectively presented by advertising. But that is not all of the story; the consumer is free to choose what he likes among the vociferous offerings, and sometimes reveals traces of initiative. . . . Americans are consuming fewer calories per capita; they are eating less wheat and corn but more dairy products, vegetable oils, sugar, fresh vegetables, and fruit. More families than ever before are sending their sons and daughters to college—surely that is not a triumph of "high-powered" salesmanship. Young children, girls and women, are wearing lighter and fewer clothes. The short skirt, the low shoe, the silk or rayon stockings, "athletic" underwear, the soft collar, sporting suits and sporting goods, have an appeal which makers of rival articles have not been able to overcome. And, in a sense, every consumers' good, from college to candy, is a rival of every other consumers' good, besides being a rival of the savings bank. . . .

Geographical Shifts in Industry and Trade

Just as definite a gain may be made in productivity by shifting factories to better locations, or by reorganizing channels of supply, as by installing automatic machines. Besides the drift of cotton manufacturing to the South, of which everyone thinks, and the more recent drift of shoe manufacturing to the West, [there has been] a prevailing tendency toward geographical decentralizing of production. The proportion of the output of many goods coming from the old headquarters is on the decline. . . . [A]griculture indicates a parallel development in farming. The cotton belt is stretching west, the wheat belt west and northwest; the dairying and the market-garden areas are moving in various directions. Finally, . . . marketing shows a concentration of trade in cities and towns at the expense of villages.

Doubtless these changes are to the advantage of those who make them. If they proved unprofitable, they would be abandoned. But it is equally clear that we have here another feature of increasing efficiency which brings losses as well as gains. New England may not lose as much as North Carolina and St. Louis gain from the shifts in the cotton and shoe trades—that is a question of the totals. And New England may devise new ways of using her labor, her capital, her manufacturing sites, and her ingenuity, more profitable than the old—necessity is often the mother of invention. If these efforts succeed, they may create fresh difficulties felt elsewhere. Similar truisms might be recited concerning the other cases in point. But whatever happens in the future, we must not let the dazzle of the high lights blind us to the sectional shadows.

"Technological Unemployment"

Among all the hardships imposed by increasing efficiency, most publicity has been given to the decline in the number of wage earners employed by factories. That is a matter of the gravest concern in view of their slender resources. To it special attention has been paid in this investigation.

The new phrase coined to describe what is happening, "technological unemployment," designates nothing new in the facts, though the numbers affected may be large beyond precedent. . . .

The number of the unemployed has varied from year to year with cyclical changes in business activity. It surpassed all previous records in the depression of 1921; it declined rather slowly in the revival of 1922; even in the busy year 1923 it remained higher than in 1920; it rose in the mild recession of 1924, declined on the return of activity in 1925-26, and then mounted again in 1927. The final estimates . . . may be summarized as [shown in Exhibit 1].

It must be emphasized that these figures are merely the best estimates which it is possible to make from the scattered and imperfect materials

Exhibit 1: **Estimated average minimum volume of unemployment in the United States, 1920-1927**

Year	Nonagricultural wage and salary earners	Average minimum number unemployed	Percentage unemployed
1920	27,558,000	1,401,000	5.1
1921	27,989,000	4,270,000	15.3
1922	28,505,000	3,441,000	12.1
1923	29,293,000	1,532,000	5.2
1924	30,234,000	2,315,000	7.7
1925	30,941,000	1,775,000	5.7
1926	31,808,000	1,669,000	5.2
1927	32,695,000	2,055,000	6.3

available. They are subject to considerable margins of error. They minimize the seriousness of unemployment. Finally, even as minimum figures, these estimates do not profess to show the high points reached by unemployment in bad seasons—they give only yearly averages.

One may wonder at the versatility, initiative and mobility of Americans, as evidenced afresh by their prompt shifting of occupations on so great a scale in recent years. One may wonder also at the rapid expansion of the trades which have absorbed some five million employees in seven years without reducing wage rates. But one must not forget that these shiftings have been compulsory in large measure; men have been forced out of farming and forced out of factories as well as pulled into automobile services, shops and restaurants. And the employment balance is on the unfavorable side. While our economic progress has meant larger per capita earnings for all workers taken together, it has imposed severe suffering upon hundreds of thousands of individuals.

The Domestic Difficulties of Agriculture

It was noted above that American farming owes part of its difficulties in 1922-1927 to reductions in foreign demand and increases in foreign supply. It must now be added that fresh difficulties have been created for farmers by changes in domestic demand, and by the successful efforts of farmers to increase their own efficiency as producers. . . .

The Interrelations Among Economic Changes

. . . So far, the contrasts noted at the outset of this chapter between the economic fortunes of different income groups, different industries, and different sections of the United States in 1922-1927, have been traced to three factors—or rather to three great complexes of factors. (1) Foreign conditions on the whole have been none too favorable to American business, and they have been eminently unfavorable to American agriculture. Important branches of industry have enjoyed a large increase in foreign sales; but had Europe been prosperous, American prosperity would have been less "spotty" and more intense. (2) Such prosperity as we have enjoyed has been earned by many-sided and strenuous efforts, in which millions of people have shared, to improve our technical methods, our business management, our trade-union policy, and our Government administration. (3) While increasing efficiency has added to real income, it has put pressure, often rising to severe hardship, upon competitors, direct and indirect. The factory hand competing with the "automatic" machine, the horse farmer competing with the tractor farmer, the lumber industry competing with the cement industry, the New England cotton mill competing with the North Carolina cotton mill, the independent retailer competing with the chain store, the clothing trade competing with the makers of automobiles and radios for slices of the consumers' dollars, have had a hard time. . . .

Retardation in the Growth of Population and Its Effects

The additional factor to be taken into account concerns population growth. . . .

This reduction of birth rates has been going on during our period in most of the states of the Union. The decline seems to be more rapid than the decline in death rates. Moreover, first the war and then legislation restricted immigration. [Exhibit 2 sums up] the results. Combined, the

Exhibit 2: **Decline in net immigration totals**

	Net immigration into the United States	Average per year
Prewar period		
July 1, 1907-June 30, 1914	4,645,590	663,656
War and early postwar period		
July 1, 1914-June 30, 1921	1,253,652	179,093
Quota-restriction period		
July 1, 1921-June 30, 1927	1,873,311	312,219

birth-rate and death-rate changes and the changes in migration reduced the average annual increase of population from 1,800,000 in 1920-1925 to 1,545,000 in 1925-1928. . . .

. . . Had there been no legal check on immigration in 1922-1927, unemployment would have attained large proportions, and the difficulty of maintaining wage rates would have been greater.

Moreover, it seems sound to ascribe a part of the gains in technical efficiency, which have been so characteristic of recent years, to the high price of labor. An employee to whom one pays high wages may represent low labor cost. But if he is to be so efficient as to be cheap, he must be provided with good equipment and aided by good management. . . .

. . . Had there been no reduction in birth rates and no restriction of immigration, the United States would contain several millions more people than it does. As large or a larger fraction of the greater population would be "engaged in gainful occupations," and, despite more unemployment and a less advanced stage of industrial technique, the workers would probably be producing a greater volume of goods. Thus, the national income would be rising faster than it is; but per capita income would be growing slower than it is. Since birth-rate restriction seems to be voluntary, and since immigration restriction certainly is, we must conclude that Americans are preferring to raise the economic level of average life rather than to maximize national wealth. . . .

How Matters Stand in the Spring of 1929

Forecasting the future is no part of the present task. But we should not close the record without noting that recent developments may appear less satisfactory in retrospect than they appear at present.

Even on the face of affairs, all is not well. Americans have seen more uniformly fortunate times. . . . The condition of agriculture, the volume of unemployment, the textile trades, coal mining, the leather industries, present grave problems not only to the people immediately concerned, but also to their fellow citizens. How rapidly these conditions will mend, we do not know. Some may grow worse.

Nor can we be sure that the industries now prosperous will prolong indefinitely their recent record of stability. That we have not had a serious crisis since 1920 or a severe depression since 1921 is no guarantee that we shall be equally prudent, skillful, and fortunate in the years to come. If we are to maintain business prosperity, we must continue to earn it month after month and year after year by intelligent effort. The incomes disbursed to consumers, and to wage earners in particular, must be increased on a scale sufficient to pay for the swelling volume of consumers' goods sent to market. The credit structure must be kept in due adjustment to the earnings of business enterprises. Security prices must not outrun prospective profits capitalized at the going rate of interest. Commodity stocks must be held in line with current sales. Overcommitments of all sorts must be avoided. The building of new industrial equipment must not be overrapid. These and the similar matters which might be mentioned present delicate problems of management which will find their practical solutions in the daily decisions of business executives. Perhaps errors are being kept within the limits of tolerance. Perhaps no serious setback will occur for years to come. But we are leaving 1921 well behind us, and there are signs that the caution inspired by that disastrous year is wearing thin.

Whether the recent rate of progress in the arts of industry and business can be maintained is another uncertainty. Past experience ... suggests that the pace will slacken presently, and that years may pass before we see such another well-maintained advance. But that is a matter in which experience is not a trustworthy guide. Scientific research, industrial invention, and business pioneering all lead into the unknown. They are fascinating ventures which energetic minds will ever be trying, whether the tangible rewards prove great or small. All that is certain is that whatever progress in efficiency we continue to make must be won by the same type of bold and intelligent work that has earned our recent successes.

Endnotes

1. Dr. Julius H. Parmelee, director of the Bureau of Railway Economics, has kindly furnished a backward extension of the "index of railway operating efficiency," mentioned by Professor Cunningham in a preceding chapter. The yearly averages, on a 1920-1924 base, run as follows: 1920, 99.7; 1921, 95.3; 1922, 96.5; 1923, 103.5; 1924, 104.8; 1925, 109.4; 1926, 113.5; 1927, 115.2; 1928, Jan.-Nov., 118.1.

2. Increased productivity per man at work does not necessarily mean larger real income per head of the population. In some industries the output per worker rises in periods of business depression when total output falls; because the less efficient hands have been laid off; because the men kept on the payroll are afraid of discharge when new jobs are scarce and so work harder than usual; because only the best-equipped or best-managed plants can keep running at all; or for other reasons. As will presently be shown more at length, the number of men at work in two of our greatest branches of industry—farming and manufacturing—has been reduced. But the reductions in numbers at work have not offset the increases in output per remaining worker, even in these branches. There remains a net gain in real income per capita for the whole country.

36

The Permanent New Deal

WALTER LIPPMANN

It would be useful to know whether the many experiments of the past six years are merely a response to a passing emergency or whether they signify lasting changes in the relation between government and the economic order. A satisfactory answer to this question would not stop with a general conclusion that this is a rapidly changing world. The answer ought to carry conviction only if it identifies an important new function of government, defines it, and demonstrates the reason why there is a presumption of permanency. . . .

. . . We have to deal with the impression that the two Administrations are so radically different that they have nothing important in common. The partisans of both have tried to fix this opinion in the public mind. They would like us to believe that a new era began on March 4, 1933. They would have us believe that Mr. Hoover was the faithful defender of the established traditions and that Mr. Roosevelt is the revolutionary pioneer of a New Deal. Though it will outrage the supporters of both men, I must argue that this is not history but partisan mythology: that though the two Presidents have somewhat different sympathies and allegiances, though they profess somewhat different purposes, though they have somewhat

Walter Lippmann, "The Permanent New Deal," *The Yale Review*, Vol. XXIV (June, 1935), pp. 649-667. Excerpted, and reprinted by permission of Harvard University, Office of the General Counsel.

different constituencies to please, though they have resorted to somewhat different devices, yet in their fundamental conceptions of the functions of government they are much nearer to one another than either is, let us say, to Calvin Coolidge or to Grover Cleveland.

I shall have to contend that if there has been anything in the nature of a sharp break with the past, the break occurred not in March, 1933, when Mr. Roosevelt was inaugurated but in the autumn of 1929 when, with the collapse of the postwar prosperity, President Hoover assumed the responsibility for recovery. No doubt, it was inevitable that he should have done this since he had been elected on the promise of four more years of prosperity. But that does not alter the fact that the policy initiated by President Hoover in the autumn of 1929 was something utterly unprecedented in American history. The national government undertook to make the whole economic order operate prosperously. In the language of Burke the state attempted to direct by the public wisdom a recovery in the business cycle which had hitherto been left with as little interference as possible to individual exertion. President Hoover, let us remember, did not merely seek to create an atmosphere of confidence in which private initiative could act; he intervened at every point in the national economy where he felt that something needed to be done.

For that reason, it may be said, I believe, that his historic position as a radical innovator has been greatly underestimated and that Mr. Roosevelt's pioneering has been greatly exaggerated. It was Mr. Hoover who abandoned the principles of *laissez faire* in relation to the business cycle, established the conviction that prosperity and depression can be publicly controlled by political action, and drove out of the public consciousness the old idea that depressions must be overcome by private adjustment.

Whether that was good or bad, necessary or unnecessary, does not concern us here. The point is that a radically new conception of the functions of government was established in the autumn of 1929. The subsequent course of events becomes utterly unintelligible if we accept naively what the partisans of Mr. Hoover and of Mr. Roosevelt say today. Only those who have forgotten the inclusive and persistent experimentation before March 1933 can, I think, fail to see that most of President Roosevelt's recovery programme is an evolution from President Hoover's programme; and that there is a continuity of principle; and that both programmes are derived from the unprecedented doctrine that the government is charged with responsibility for the successful operation of the economic order and the maintenance of a satisfactory standard of life for all classes in the nation. After October, 1929 that doctrine was the major premise of the Hoover Administration. It is the major premise of the Roosevelt Administration. Never, except in time of war, has it been the major premise in the policies of any other President. Did Harding in 1921 or Cleveland in 1893 or Grant in 1873 suppose that it was the President's duty to tell farmers and businessmen and bankers, debtors and creditors, employers and employees, governors and mayors, what to do in order to restore prosperity, or that he had a right to draw upon all the powers of government and all the resources of the nation?

Yet that is precisely what President Hoover, beginning in the autumn of 1929, took to be his duty and his right. Not until his time had any American president assumed this specific responsibility with all the expansion of the functions of government which it necessarily implies. Yet when the change occurred, there was almost no comment. Almost no one raised his voice to challenge Mr. Hoover on the ground of the individualistic tradition or of the accepted limitations of the federal power. So we have a strong presumption that the great change was generated by historic circumstances that are stronger than the ordinary opinions of men.

On August 11, 1932, in accepting his renomination, President Hoover declared that when "the forces of destruction" invaded the American economy and brought about "bank and business failures, demoralization of security and real property values, commodity prices and employment, . . . two courses were open. We might have done nothing. That would have been utter ruin. Instead, we met the situation with proposals to private business and the Congress of the most gigantic programme of economic defense and counter-attack ever evolved in the history of the republic."

Mr. Hoover made it perfectly plain that he had departed from the individualistic doctrine that depression must be liquidated by individual adjustment. "The function of the federal government in these times," he said, "is to *use its reserve powers* and its strength *for the protection of citizens and local governments* by support to our institutions *against forces beyond their control.*" He was insistent that this defensive and compensatory action by the government should not destroy but should on the contrary revive private and local enterprise and responsibility. But he had no doubts, theoretical or practical, indeed he proudly declared that "we have not feared boldly to adopt unprecedented measures to meet the unprecedented violence of the storm."

He then went on to describe his unprecedented measures. He had called the leaders of business and of labor and of agriculture "to meet with me and induced them, by their own initiative, to organize against panic":

(1) "To uphold wages until the cost of living was adjusted."
(2) "To spread existing employment through shortened hours."
(3) "To advance construction work, public and private, against future need."

He then described how he had mobilized the relief agencies and "when it became advisable to strengthen the States who could no longer carry the full burden of relief to distress, I held that the federal government should do so through loans to the States." He said that "in aid to unemployment we are expending some six hundred millions in federal construction and such public works as can be justified as bringing early and definite returns"; that in addition he had made "provision of one billion five hundred millions of loans to self-supporting works so that we may increase employment in productive labor."

He went on to tell how he had used government credit (1) to strengthen the capital of Federal Land Banks, (2) to lend money to farmers co-operatives to protect farm prices and to home-owners in danger of foreclosure, (3) to set up the Reconstruction Finance Corporation "with a capital of two billions to uphold the credit structure of the Nation."

He stated that "we expanded the functions and powers of the Federal Reserve Banks that they might counteract the stupendous shrinkage of credit due to fear, to hoarding and to foreign withdrawals."

He pointed out how, parallel with his expansion of the extraordinary expenditures of the government, he was seeking to retrench on the normal expenditures and to increase taxes to balance them.

Finally, he announced that "I am to-day organizing the private and financial resources of the country to cooperate effectively with the vast governmental instrumentalities which we have set in motion."

When Mr. Hoover declared that "these programmes" were "unparalleled in the history of depressions in our country and in any time," he had perhaps overlooked a few other countries, but his claim was quite correct when confined to the United States. His programme was unparalleled. But what interests us about it is that it lays down the fundamentally new principle that it is "the function of the federal government in these times to use its reserve powers and its strength" to regulate the business cycle, and that in applying this general principle Mr. Hoover formulated a programme which contains all the more specific principles of Mr. Roosevelt's recovery programme.

Let us fix in mind the working principles of Mr. Hoover's recovery programme:

(1) To counteract deflation by a deliberate policy of inflating the base of credit.

(2) To draw upon the government credit in order to supplement the deficiency of private credit.

(3) To reduce the normal expenses of government but to incur extraordinary expenditures covered not by taxation but by deficit financing.

(4) To expand public works in order to create employment.

(5) To have the federal government assume the ultimate responsibility for relief of destitution where local or private resources are inadequate.

(6) To reduce the hours of labor while maintaining wage rates.

(7) To peg farm prices and encourage farmers to organize to curtail production.

(8) To organize industry with a view to adopting common policies in respect to wages, hours, prices, and capital investment.

Apart from the Roosevelt measures of reform, which we shall have to examine later, all the main features of the Roosevelt programme were anticipated by Mr. Hoover.

The only important difference between the monetary policies of the two Administrations is that Mr. Hoover attempted to regulate the internal value of the dollar whereas Mr. Roosevelt is attempting to regulate its external value as well. Mr. Hoover was just as eager as Mr. Roosevelt has been to bring about a rise in the wholesale prices of staple commodities, particularly the politically sensitive farm products and raw materials whose prices are fixed by international competition. He was just as eager to stop the general deflation and to bring about a reflation. Nor did he hesitate to use monetary measures, sometimes called "currency tinkering."

The measures he used consisted in expanding the base of credit by open-market operations in the Federal Reserve system and in lowering the discount rates. This was the policy of the President, of the Treasury, and of his appointees on the Federal Reserve Board. It was carried out in spite of some opposition from some of the Federal Reserve Banks, and though the government's right to regulate the volume of credit was not formally avowed, as it is in Governor Eccles's banking bill, the power was, in fact, exercised.

Mr. Roosevelt has continued this policy. He has supplemented it by measures designed to regulate the international value of the dollar in terms of gold, silver, and the foreign exchanges. But the major premise, which was that the regulation of the purchasing power of money is a function of government and is not automatic, was accepted and acted upon by the Hoover Administration. However great may be the differences of opinion as to how the purchasing power of money should be regulated, however much men may disagree as to who shall exercise the power to regulate, it would therefore seem reasonable to assume that the effort to manage the purchasing power of money will continue to be a function of government.

Legally it has, of course, always been a function of government, and ever since the war we have had a managed monetary system. Neither Mr. Hoover nor Mr. Roosevelt invented a managed currency. Yet they have changed the conception of what the object of management should be. It had previously been assumed though not with entire consistency, that the dominant purpose of management should be to keep the currency stable in terms of gold. Mr. Hoover did that though he wished at the same time to regulate the currency in terms of its purchasing power. When the value of gold changed violently between 1929 and 1933, he was caught on the horns of a dilemma. If he regulated the currency to maintain a stable gold content he had a currency which was catastrophically unstable in its purchasing power. Mr. Roosevelt resolved the difficulty in 1933 by abandoning stability in terms of gold in order to achieve control in terms of purchasing power. But in 1934 he returned to stability in terms of gold, and ever since the American price level has once more been under the disturbing influence of the instability of gold itself. The effort to manage the value of gold by manipulating the value of silver followed. It is too early to judge the experiment when this is written. Whether it fails or succeeds, whether the outcome is a new international gold standard, or bimetallism, or a second abandonment of the gold standard is outside this discussion. The idea that it is a function of public authority to regulate the purchasing power of money is not likely to be abandoned, whatever may be the fate of the particular measures now used to regulate it.

The use of the national credit to support and to supplement local and private credit is not, strictly speaking, a radically new innovation. It was practiced during the World War and in the first post-war depression. President Hoover adopted the policy on a grand scale when he created the Reconstruction Finance Corporation and various farm credit agencies. Mr. Roosevelt has continued the policy and has extended it. A substantial part of the deficits incurred in both Administrations is due not to the expenses of government but to this banking operation. Neither President has believed that the money borrowed by the government for this banking operation should be balanced by taxes. Both have acted on the principle that this banking operation should be supported by deficit financing. It is reasonable to suppose that this principle will become orthodox and that in future emergencies government borrowing will be resorted to when private credit is deficient.

The questionable element of the Roosevelt budgetary programme is in that part of the deficit which is being deliberately incurred in irrecoverable expenditures—for relief and for public works that are not "self-liquidating." Mr. Hoover had deficits of this sort. But he had a bad conscience about them, whereas Mr. Roosevelt has seemed to look upon them as preferable in principle to the deflationary effect of greatly increased taxes or of drastic retrenchment. But while Mr. Hoover was not in favor of deficits to finance public works, he was, of course, an early and conspicuous promoter of the idea that government enterprises should be expanded when private enterprises contract. He formulated the principle during the depression of 1921, acted upon it in 1930, and pointed to it with pride in 1932. Mr. Hoover believed in the principle of "pump-priming." In actual fact, he financed his pump-priming with deficits just as Mr.

Roosevelt has done. In theory, he would presumably have preferred to finance them by taxes in order to keep the budget in balance, and presumably he would today prefer to give up the pump-priming in order to balance the budget.

In their relations to agriculture and to industry there is no sharp break between the two Administrations. Both have recognized that the agricultural staples have unsheltered prices whereas most manufactured goods have sheltered prices, and that this produces a disparity which it is a function of government to correct. The superior position of industry lies in the fact that it can benefit by the tariff, that much of it is under a centralized control in which prices can be maintained by regulating the supply through curtailment of production. The agricultural staples, on the other hand, cannot without special devices take advantage of tariffs, and the farmers are the most highly individualistic and competitive of all producers. President Hoover made many attempts to remedy this disparity. He increased the tariff on farm products. He used government money in an effort to control the supply offered in the markets. He advised the farmers to curtail production, and he contemplated the government rental or purchase of marginal lands in order permanently to reduce production. The Roosevelt agricultural policy has followed those same principles. It has used government money to regulate the supply offered for sale. It has supplemented Mr. Hoover's advice to curtail production by levying a tax to pay farmers who follow the advice, and it is withdrawing marginal lands permanently. Both Presidents recognized that a satisfactory domestic solution of the farm problem is very unlikely; both have wanted to see a revival of foreign markets; neither was able or willing to expand agricultural exports by reducing the tariff on industrial goods.

As regards their relations to industry, if we strip the N.R.A. of its ballyhoo, of the more or less unenforceable and unenforced labor provisions, we find the trade associations (which Mr. Hoover did so much to promote as Secretary of Commerce) freed of the menace of the anti-trust laws (which Mr. Hoover as President did so little to enforce). The N.R.A. extended the principle of organization to industries and trades that had not been organized previously. It tightened up the organization all along the line. It made price-fixing and production control and marketing quotas more general, more effective, more respectable. But in embryo, in all its essential features, the substance of N.R.A. existed before the Blue Eagle was hatched. The National Industry Recovery Act was little more than the substitution of legal for companionate marriages in the realm of private monopoly.

Even the wage policy of N.R.A. was a continuation of a policy inaugurated by Mr. Hoover in the autumn of 1929 and maintained by him throughout his term. It consisted in the preservation of the rate of wages regardless of the income received by the wage-earner. Mr. Hoover threw the whole weight of his influence against reduction in the rate of wages, as Mr. Roosevelt did in 1933 and until very recent times. He believed what the labor leaders believed, what the N.R.A. economists believed, what Mr. Roosevelt in his first year believed, that the purchasing power of labor could be maintained by a high hourly rate. That the high hourly rate in the face of falling prices was a sure way to increase and perpetuate unemployment was denied in both Administrations, though I suspect that neither Mr. Hoover nor Mr. Roosevelt would deny it to-day.

In rough fashion, this covers the ground usually marked out as the recovery programme. I do not see how one can fail to conclude that in all essential matters of policy—monetary management, the budget, the agricultural disparity, and industrial "stabilization"—there has been no break in principle, and that the Roosevelt measures are a continuous evolution of the Hoover measures.

What about the reforms? In one sense the most radical of all the reforms are these very recovery measures themselves: the acceptance by the government of responsibility for recovery, and the corollaries of that—the resort to monetary management, the use of government credit, the expansion of government enterprise, and the organization of agriculture and of industry under government auspices for the control of production and of supply in the markets. These mark great changes in a political system which until 1929 was committed to the general doctrine of *laissez faire*.

The measures that are specifically called the "reforms" are distinguished from the others by the fact that, except as a response to the challenge of popular discontent, they were not dictated by the emergency and might have been imposed later and in more leisurely fashion. But it is clear, I think, that though the reforms might have been delayed, and though they might have been different in detail, their essential principles are derived directly and inevitably from the fundamental assumption of the whole period since 1929, that we have a national economy and not a mere aggregation of individual enterprises.

The reforms extend into new fields: the regulation of private enterprises, on the one hand, and the expansion of government enterprises, on the other. Some of the new regulation is merely the logical development of well-established principles. The clearest example in this category is the legislation as to buses and trucks and other common carriers in order to bring about parity of competitive conditions with the railroads. Another example in the same category is the proposal to bring gas and electricity under more complete regulation. These reforms involve no new principles, and the fundamental questions they raise are not novel and are not radical.

In the present Administration we come soon, however, to regulations which are novel and radical. In the Securities Act and in the Stock Exchange Act and in certain parts of the Banking Act of 1933, the orbit of public authority is enlarged. In substance, these reforms lay down the principle that corporations financed by public subscription are publicly accountable. They require a disclosure, particularly of the whole process of capital investment, which is intended to take from private management much of its former privacy. The underlying theory of the legislation is that when the ownership of corporations is widely diffused, when corporations are financed out of the savings of large masses of people, it is an anomaly that those who control and manage them but do not own them should have the kind of privacy in their corporate conduct which men have in their genuinely personal affairs and in the handling of truly personal property. The legislation in these three Acts is not socialism. It does not substitute government ownership or government management for private ownership and management. It lays down the rule that private management shall operate in the public view in order to make it accountable to the great mass of its owners, its creditors, its customers, and its employees.

The officers of corporations are in effect required to submit to the same standards which they would have to meet if they were public officials. The doctrine that public office is a public trust is supplemented by the doctrine that corporate office is a public trust. From this doctrine there follow inevitably the prohibitions in the new laws against being on both sides of a transaction. Just as a public official may not have a private interest in a contract with the government, so under the new laws bankers may not sell to their depositors securities which they have issued; utility holding companies may not sell services at their own price to operating companies they control; it is made hard for the officers and directors of corporations to use their special knowledge for their private advantage, and they are required to disclose their private interests in the corporations they manage.

That this development of public policy is the logical consequence of the corporate form of industry seems plain. It might have come more slowly had the public not suffered such losses after 1929, and if there had not been so many flagrant examples of the abuse of positions of trust. But once so important a part of the property of the nation became organized in large corporations, it was only a question of when and of how they would be recognized as being public institutions in all their essential relations.

The transition to this new conception of policy might possibly have been delayed a few years had the accidents of politics brought a conservative rather than a progressive Administration into power in 1933. The impulses of reform generated in the upheaval of the Nineties were held back for a few years by the reaction against Bryanism and the distraction of the Spanish War. They became effective about 1902 and were not exhausted until the World War introduced a new diversion of the national energy. The reforms of Theodore Roosevelt and of Woodrow Wilson brought under some regulation large areas of private enterprise: the railroads, the central banking function, the public domain and natural resources, foods and drugs. These present reforms extend to private finance, generally, and to the capital market, the underlying assumptions which were applied to railroads and central banking in the preceding era of reforms.

In addition to this extension of the regulatory functions of government, there has been an extension of government enterprise. A part of it is simply a development of the conservation movement. Reforestation, measures against soil erosion, the protection of water courses are not new in principle: it has long been recognized that there were certain kinds of capital investment which because they could not be profitable to private enterprise, had to be undertaken collectively. Mr. Roosevelt has, however, made a departure in at least two important directions. The first is represented by the Tennessee Valley Authority; here collective enterprise has been deliberately undertaken for the purpose of making a competitive demonstration against the electric utility companies. The second is the social insurance programme: here the federal government enters a field heretofore left to individual or local action.

It would be an exaggeration to say that either of these Roosevelt reforms represents a clean break with the past. No other President, it is true, ever sought to regulate electric utilities by forcing them to face the competition of government-owned utilities. But other Presidents have sought to regulate railroad rates by building canals, and President Hoover himself promoted the St. Lawrence Seaway as a competitor with the railroads. As for social insurance, while it represents a new function of the federal government, it is not a new function in state government, and Republican leaders, including Mr. Hoover, have endorsed it in principle.

We must conclude, I think, that however startling they may have seemed, however inadvisable or inexpedient it may have been to impose them at this time, the Roosevelt reforms are far less novel or radical in their implications than is the recovery programme which Mr. Hoover and Mr. Roosevelt have both followed. To regulate large corporations and high finance, to extend government enterprise into fields unoccupied by private enterprise, to use government enterprise as a threat to compel private monopoly to reduce its rates, to insure the weaker members of the community by collective action—none of these things is new in principle. They are all the continuation of a movement in American politics which goes back at least fifty years, and there is little if anything in the New Deal reforms which was not implicit in the New Nationalism of Theodore Roosevelt or the New Freedom of Woodrow Wilson.

The recovery programme, on the other hand, is new and is radical. For here we have an assumption of responsibility for the operation of the whole national economy and the conviction that all the reserve power of government and all the resources it can command may and must be used to defend the standard of life of the people "against forces beyond their control."

This represents a far more radical change in the conception of government in America than is to be found in any of the reforms. For if it is now the responsibility of the government to protect the people against the consequences of depression, then inevitably the government must regulate the prosperity which precedes depression and produces it. If government is responsible for the downward phase of the business cycle, it has a responsibility in the whole business cycle. If it is fitting and necessary to manage the currency, the national credit, budgetary expenditures, and the like to counteract deflation, then it is fitting and necessary that they may be managed to counteract inflation.

It would seem that the decision which Mr. Hoover took in the autumn of 1929 is irreversible: he committed the government to the new function of using all its powers to regulate the business cycle. With this precedent established it is almost inconceivable that any of his successors should in another depression refuse to act. The knowledge that the government will have to act to offset depression compels it to act to prevent depression. Because Mr. Hoover and Mr. Roosevelt have regulated a slump, their successors will also have to regulate a boom. The business cycle has been placed within the orbit of government, and for *laissez faire* and individual adjustment and liquidation there has been substituted conscious management by the political state.

It is perhaps possible to go further and indicate why it is that this very great new duty has been imposed upon the state. The recovery programme since 1929 has rested on the basic assumption that the "fixed costs" in a modern economy are rigid: that debts, contracts, wage rates, taxes cannot be reduced quickly or easily or sufficiently to liquidate the depression. Part of the recovery programme under both Mr. Hoover and Mr. Roosevelt has in fact been a defense of rigid wage rates and debts. The classic remedy, the only remedy known to *laissez faire*, is therefore impracticable. But if "fixed costs" are rigid, then flexibility must develop somewhere else in the economy if there is not to be complete paralysis followed by a social collapse. The flexibility to compensate for the rigidity of "fixed costs" has been found in the currency, in the national budget, and in public expenditure.

Unless one is to suppose that the proportion of fixed debt in the modern economy will be drastically reduced, that long-term contracts and rentals will become easily amended, that salaries, wages, and pensions will become easily adjustable, we may take it as certain that we shall not return to *laissez faire* in the business cycle. If we do not return to it, then the management of money and the use of the national credit to expand and to contract government expenditures must be regarded as permanently new functions of the American government.

No one will imagine that I am saying that the particular devices employed by Mr. Hoover or Mr. Roosevelt were well conceived or effectively administered. To judge them, they would have to be examined on their merits. But I am saying that when we examine them, we are compelled to judge them on the presumption that, because our economy has become too rigid to readjust itself by individual action, it will henceforth be a normal function of government to attempt to regulate the business cycle. We have come on to a new plateau from which it is not likely that we shall easily descend. On this plateau the issues of the near future will be fought out, and there it will be determined whether a system of private enterprise, which has lost much of its power to adjust itself, can be preserved in working equilibrium by the compensatory action of the state.

37

Why the Depression Lasted So Long

GILBERT BURCK and CHARLES E. SILBERMAN

The Spiral Begins

The depression had begun . . . because of several basic weaknesses in the outwardly strong "New Era" economy of the 1920's. Among them were an increasingly lopsided distribution of the benefits of rising productivity, declining population growth, and relatively ineffective marketing techniques; because of these weaknesses, expenditures on consumer durables began to slide off in the mid-Twenties, and expenditures on home building fell sharply. Farm prices and income also fell. These declines made a correction practically inevitable.

But the correction, which might have been moderate had it occurred in 1928, was temporarily forfended by the stockmarket boom, which erected false props of prosperity under the economy. It artificially stimulated certain forms of consumption as well as capital spending. Stocks kept soaring up even after business had turned down. Thus the boom in stocks, by postponing the correction and creating overcapacity, made a moderate correction impossible. The patient was in a bad way, but the heady philter of speculation deluded him into thinking he had never felt better. His first reaction, after his fortune changed for the worse, was that he would get better soon. But it was not long before his basic weaknesses exacerbated his illness and all but ruined him.

At first, many observers argued that the stock market crash would affect only those who had lost money in it. Even these were a considerable deflationary force. Millions of people, rich and poor, even those who did not have to pay off margin accounts out of income, were forced to economize. The luxury market began to soften rapidly. And the great soft spots in the economy—consumer durables, housebuilding, and farm prices—grew softer still.

What is more important, the whole nation was heavily and precariously in hock to itself, and falling prices and the liquidation of security and real-estate values made the burden intolerable. In 1929 the interest on corporate debt took 40 per cent of all corporate profit before taxes, against about 10 per cent today. Nonfarm mortgage debt—most of it callable in five years—was equal to 50 per cent of disposable income against only 36 per cent now, and interest rates in 1929 were 50 to 100 per cent higher than they are now. Farm mortgage debt came to more than 150 per cent of farm income, compared to 63 per cent now.

The banking system, despite the creation of the Federal Reserve in 1913, was not half so strong as most people thought it was. It was still a frontier system, hospitable to boom and vulnerable to bust. It contained too many small and weak banks, and only a third of all banks were members of the Federal Reserve. There was no deposit insurance. Too many bankers had acquired the habit of manipulating and promoting "securities." Even in the prosperous 1920's about one out of every five commercial banks failed. Now the banking system was up against challenges that would have strained the strongest one.

When the stock and real-estate markets cracked, the banks already had nearly 25 per cent of their assets in security loans and 10 per cent in real-estate loans. The colossal decline in value of securities—$45 *billion*, or more than 50 per cent, by 1931, for those on the New York Stock Exchange alone—weakened the banks immeasurably. So did the real-estate decline. Farm prices and incomes collapsed, and the defaults on farm mortgages brought down many farm banks with them. Inflated urban real-estate values, on which mortgage debt was based, also collapsed. As Secretary of the Treasury Andrew Mellon told Herbert Hoover in the early stages of the depression, "There is a mighty lot of real estate lying around the United States which does not know who owns it."

In the meantime, every intelligent businessman, watching inventory accumulate and sales and profits drop sharply, knew he had to retrench. So business cut back purchases of inventory and capital goods, and industrial production declined 20 per cent within a year after the crash. Although business responded to President Hoover's pleas and for a while maintained wage rates, it laid off workers across the board. Not only did all these cutbacks contract the consumer market, the consumers who still had high incomes worried increasingly about their jobs, and began to cut their own spending. Few seemed willing to mortgage an uncertain future to buy durables like cars and appliances. And so business was forced to retrench still more.

Flight of Gold

Thus, for a full year and a half, the whole economy slid downward. But in the spring of 1931 there seemed to be signs that the worst was over. Industrial production and gross national product, which had declined 30 per cent and 15 per cent respectively, actually turned up slightly. Stock prices rose, and President Hoover was quoted as saying that prosperity was just around the corner.

Even as he spoke, however, ominous tidings were coming from overseas. Europe's economies, which had been buoyed up during much of the 1920's by U.S. loans and large U.S. imports, were confronted with a virtual cessation of both. The big problem of these economies, too, was debt—not only to one another, but to the U.S. Their ability to pay those debts was not helped by the passage of the ill-famed Hawley-Smoot Tariff of 1930, which, signed reluctantly by Hoover, gave the rest of the world notice that it would have a difficult time earning the dollars to pay the U.S. As the situation worsened, gold and foreign exchange—"hot money"—moved frantically from country to country, looking for a refuge and wrecking credit systems in the process. The Kredit Anstalt, the largest bank in Austria, suddenly closed its doors in May, 1931, and every bank in Europe trembled. Business declined sharply, and even the cartel-dictated price structures began to crack.

Although Hoover met this challenge with imagination and resolution—he personally drafted and sold to key members of Congress an international moratorium on debts, described by the London *Economist* as the gesture of a great man—the gesture availed little. By September 1931, Britain was forced off the gold standard. Fears that the U.S. would follow, plus the fact that U.S. production had turned down again, led to panic flights of foreign capital from the U.S. and of U.S. gold into foreign coffers and hoards at home. In slightly more than a month, beginning in mid-September, the U.S. lost $725 million worth of gold.

The Federal Reserve, which had previously adopted an easy-money policy to stimulate business, found its gold reserves threatened, and elected to protect the gold standard in the traditional way. On October 9, 1931, as though fighting inflation, it raised its rediscount rate from 1.5 to 2.5 per cent, and a week later to no less than 3.5 per cent. This served to check gold movements, but at the sacrifice of any chance of domestic recovery. Interest rates rose, stock prices dropped abruptly, production declined, and banks tightened credit—and the credit-tightening process started liquidation all over again. And, of course, the banks' attempts to "get liquid" made it steadily harder for everybody to "get liquid."

Bank failures, which had numbered 158 in August, rose to 522 in October—the largest number in any month before or since. It was at this point that fear, Roosevelt's "nameless, terrifying fear," gripped the country. Hoarding rose $500 million in two months. Unemployment rose still higher while industrial production fell still lower—12 per cent in three months. What had capped the crisis, what had turned it into the most serious financial panic in U.S history, seemed to be Herbert Hoover's determination to remain on the gold standard in the face of the world financial crisis.

In the Depths

This is not to say that Hoover's policy, as so many believe, was one of doing nothing. Contrary, too, to popular myth, Hoover's economics were not incorrigibly *laissez faire.* Many of his associates, particularly Andrew Mellon, urged him to let things alone, arguing that the liquidation would end quickly, as previous liquidations had ended, if only left alone. But Hoover pointed out that the vast majority of Americans no longer lived and worked on the land, and no longer could sit out a depression on the farm; the depression meant heavy unemployment in the cities, and untold and unprecedented suffering. So he had announced late in 1929 that recovery was the government's responsibility. In 1930-32 he actually introduced many of the important measures that later became the bases of Roosevelt's recovery program. Through RFC he supplemented private credit for business with government credit. He created a little employment through public works. He plugged for high wage rates. He tried to cope with farm surpluses by withholding them from the market. And he tried to expand credit.

Having done all this, however, Hoover stuck doggedly not only to the gold standard but also to the balanced budget, which remained for him the categorical imperatives of the free-enterprise system. Their abandonment under any circumstances was something that could be seriously considered only by knaves, collectivists, or crackpots. It was primarily to save the gold standard that he pushed through the Glass-Steagall Act of February, 1932, which allowed the Federal Reserve to use government bonds to back the currency, and so released $1 billion in gold for possible export. Although Hoover ran deficits in 1931 and 1932, these were largely involuntary. And it was to balance the budget that he persuaded the American Legion to forgo demanding a bonus, vetoed a direct relief bill, and took a resolute stand against "squandering the nation into prosperity."

To be sure, practically everybody in 1931 and 1932 thought as Hoover did—including Franklin Roosevelt. Practically nobody understood what today is commonly understood—that a deficit, if it occurs when a nation's resources and labor force are only partly utilized, need not be inflationary. Although John Maynard Keynes was already arguing in the press that deficit financing could cure the depression, it was not till 1936 that he launched the "Keynesian Revolution" with his *General Theory of Employment, Interest, and Money*, which, among other things, popularized the notion that a government's finances should be managed primarily in terms of their effect on the economy's stability.

Another and less academic partisan of deficit spending was a then obscure Utah banker named Marriner Eccles, who had never read Keynes. What the government should do, he told his scandalized banker friends, was not merely to loosen credit, not merely to devalue, but to spend more than it took in, in order to increase the nation's buying power. The government of 1930-32, he argued, was like the stewards on the doomed *Titanic*, who locked all the staterooms so that nothing could be stolen as the ship sank. . . .

Cross of Gold

By the close of 1932 . . . industrial production stood at only 50 per cent of its mid-1929 level, and gross national product had fallen 40 per cent, to $67 billion (1929 dollars). Nearly 13 million men—some estimates ran to 15 million or 16 million—were out of work, not counting several million more on short weeks. Wages and salaries had fallen 40 per cent.

Since people always stop buying postponable things first, the worst decline was suffered by the durable-goods business, which had boomed early in the 1920's. Unlike the volume of non-durables and services, which in real terms declined no more than 15 per cent, that of durable consumer goods dropped 50 per cent. . . . Auto production fell from 4,600,000 in 1929 to 1,100,000 in 1932. Residential construction withered away to less than

25 per cent of its 1929 volume; only 134,000 new nonfarm units were started in 1932, compared to 509,000 in 1929, and 937,000 in 1925, at the peak of the residential boom. Because corporations (taken together) lost $2 billion in 1932 and again in 1933, and because excess capacity was depressing prices in almost every industry, business cut its purchases of capital equipment (producer durables) by 50 per cent, and cut industrial and commercial construction 70 per cent.

Meantime, the financial crisis grew more acute. The Dow-Jones average dropped to 40, mortgage foreclosures rose sharply, and bank failures mounted. In the first two months of 1933 hoarding increased by $900 million, and the merest rumor was enough to start a run on a bank. Farm-mortgage riots spread all over the Midwest as farmers took over foreclosure sales and forced the resale of foreclosed properties to mortgagees for a few dollars. . . .

The Roving Quarterback

When Roosevelt took office his advisers were full of ideas, many conflicting, about what had gone wrong—the nation's capital stock had been overexpanded, prices had been "managed," labor hadn't got a fair share of income, public utilities had been antisocial, and so on. But at first Roosevelt and his Administration had one important broad, fixed objective: to raise production by stimulating purchasing power, and to achieve this objective they were willing to try anything plausible. In a press conference Roosevelt compared himself to a football quarterback who can call only one play at a time, and must decide each play on the basis of how the previous one worked.

This pragmatic, experimental approach was perhaps the only intelligent one in those early days of the New Deal, and for a time it worked very well. Roosevelt's cheerful ignorance of economics, far from being a handicap, was if anything an advantage, for it made him receptive to the new and unorthodox. The trouble came later on, when it became necessary to stop improvising and choose a sound approach to the nation's problems and stick to it.

But the earliest measures of the new Administration, in March, 1933, were consistent enough. In his 1932 campaign Roosevelt had, much to his later embarrassment, argued eloquently against an unbalanced budget. "Stop the deficits," he had implored. "I accuse the Administration of being the biggest spending Administration in peacetime in all our history." And the first thing the New Deal had to do, after reopening the solvent banks, was to "restore confidence" by demonstrating that it could cut expenditures and balance the budget. An economy act was passed, and federal salaries and other costs were cut. What would have happened if this deflationary course had been followed to the bitter end is hard to say, but even most businessmen by this time were afraid to let it happen.

The Multiple Attack

At all events, the Administration reversed itself and moved rapidly toward credit expansion, monetary inflation, price and wage rises, relief payments, and public works. The most important decision was to go off gold, and the decision was in effect forced on Roosevelt by an inflation-minded Congress. On April 20, 1933, Roosevelt placed an embargo on gold, and thus in effect took the country off the gold standard.

There followed, between 1933 and 1937, a continuous avalanche of congressional acts and executive orders dealing with recovery. There were steps primarily designed to raise prices and boost purchasing power—though some of them involved various reforms. There was, of course, pump priming by means of a bewildering succession of public works and relief measures. There was the Federal Emergency Relief Administration, the Civilian Conservation Corps, the Civil Works Administration, and PWA, which under "Honest" Harold Ickes spent so little money that WPA had to be formed under Harry Hopkins. Partly as a result of these measures . . . federal expenditures rose from $3.7 billion in 1932 to $8.2 billion in 1936 (in 1929 dollars).

There was TVA, which got the government into the power business in a colossal way. There were aids to agriculture like "parity" prices and the AAA, which raised prices by paying farmers to restrict production. There were several labor measures, discussed later, which raised union membership from about two million in 1932 to over 11 million in 1941. There were a variety of measures easing home and farm mortgages. And there was the social-security system, founded in 1936.

Among the solidest early achievements of the New Deal were the laws reforming and strengthening the banking system, such as the Banking Act of 1933, which provided for deposit insurance and for the divorce of investment and commercial banking; the Banking Act of 1935, which centralized Federal Reserve power, particularly over open-market operations; and the Securities and Exchange Acts of 1934-35, which reformed the issuing and buying and selling of securities. Sidney Weinberg, who fought hard against the Securities and Exchange Acts, now says he would go on a crusade against any move to repeal them. And professor Milton Friedman of the University of Chicago, one of the leading orthodox economists, argues that the Federal Deposit Insurance Corporation is by all odds the most important of the changes affecting the cyclical characteristics of the American economy, perhaps even more important than the establishment of the Federal Reserve.

The Bright Blue Eagle

The most inconsistent New Deal creation, the one that remains the supreme example of the Administration's let's-give-it-a-try, all-things-to-all-men approach was NRA, or the National Recovery Administration, created in 1933. NRA was a kind of state-run supercartel, with a genially ferocious dictator in the person of General Hugh ("Ironpants") Johnson in charge and a new national flag in the form of the "bright badge" of the Blue Eagle. Had NRA survived and succeeded, it would have accomplished publicly all that any group of European cartelists, meeting behind closed doors and puffing big cigars, has ever been able to accomplish. It would have wiped out the antitrust acts and committed the whole nation to planned restrictionism, with government, capital, management, and labor restricting together. . . .

The labor provisions of the act started a wave of unionization, and they, too, encountered employer resistance. Section 7a of the dead NRA, however, was quickly replaced by the National Labor Relations Act (the Wagner Act), which specifically authorized collective bargaining, defined unfair employer practices, and set up the National Labor Relations Board to help enforce the act.

The Controversial Lag

For all their inconsistencies, the New Deal's early measures did achieve their major aim; they raised farm and industrial prices and wages, and so stimulated consumption and industrial production. Gross national product . . . rose just about as fast as it had declined, and by the third quarter of 1937 stood 5 per cent above its mid-1929 level. Industrial production had also passed the 1929 peak, and volume of consumer non-durables was 10 per cent above 1929. This, however, was not full recovery. Because the national working force had increased 10 per cent and its productivity 15 per cent, true recovery, that is, fairly full employment, would have meant a G.N.P at least 25 per cent higher than in 1929. As it was, there were still more than seven million unemployed early in 1937.

What blocked full recovery, and so perpetuated mass unemployment, was the fact that the durables sector of the economy hardly recovered at all. By 1937 the volume of residential construction was still 40 per cent below its 1929 level, industrial and commercial construction . . . was 50 per cent below 1929, and producer and consumer durables were 5 and 6 per cent below 1929, respectively. Why did they lag?

The story of residential construction may be told simply. There had been considerable overbuilding in the 1920's and the low incomes and low household formation of the Thirties created little additional demand. The birth rate fell 19 per cent and people doubled up. And so long as lenders feared that new houses would have to compete with houses on which they had foreclosed, or held shaky mortgages, they were reluctant to give mortgages for new construction. Then, too, building costs did not fall so much as costs in general.

The stagnation in capital spending—on industrial and commercial construction and producers' goods—is not so simple a story. The volume of commercial construction was so great in 1929 that it was not equaled again until 1954; thus the overbuilding and speculative real-estate inflation of the 1920's were among the main reasons why 1937's volume remained only half of 1929's volume. Then, too, commercial construction is closely related to the rate of home building, which was low.

Even the fact that the 1937 volume of producers' goods was only 5 per cent below its 1929 volume was disappointing. For there was (and is) occurring a long-term shift in capital spending from plant to equipment, and thus the volume of producers' equipment relative to the trend was actually low. And why did not this capital spending on equipment and plant recover?

Too Many Adjustments

One answer popular in the late 1930's was Alvin Hansen's theory of secular stagnation, which blamed oversaving at a time when investment opportunities were declining, thanks to the economy's "maturity." What seems today a more plausible reason is that business probably was not able to adjust to all the changes that confronted it in a few short years:

> The reform of the credit system, as well as SEC regulations, were badly needed, but probably discouraged new-issue flotation.
> Legalized unionization elevated wage rates 41 per cent in 1933-37. Even harder to accept, for many businessmen, was that unions had to be recognized and bargained with.
> Increasingly higher taxes altered the calculations on which investments had been based. In his attempts to balance the budget, Hoover had raised tax *rates* drastically in 1932. The New Deal raised them further, and added new taxes—e.g., excess-profits taxes, social-security taxes, and the undistributed-profits tax. It had also closed many loopholes, such as personal holding companies. As business and income picked up, therefore, tax payments rose even more.

Federal receipts more than tripled between 1932 and 1937, rising (in 1929 dollars) from $2 billion to $6.8 billion, or nearly double the 1929 figure of $3.8 billion.

Banking regulations, unionization, and higher taxes, of course, are commonplace enough today. But the speed with which business had to adjust to them had a lot to do with its reluctance to make capital investment. Its adjustment problems were not eased by the increasingly uncompromising attitude of President Roosevelt. He had provocation, it is true. Some businessmen were venting a virtually psychopathic hatred of "that man." Roosevelt went on to assume that all businessmen, save a few New Deal "captives," were enemies of the people. His 1936 message to Congress was studded with such fighting phrases as "entrenched greed" and "resplendent economic autocracy," and his campaign speeches were even less conciliatory. "They are unanimous in their hate of me," he boasted with a certain accuracy of those who opposed him. But then he added childishly: "I welcome their hate."

Not Enough Spending?

Yet there remains one other important circumstance that probably contributed greatly to the lag in capital goods. What really shapes business decisions to buy capital goods is not a vague sense of confidence or doubt, not necessarily even an inflationary or deflationary government policy, but the outlook for sales and profits. Partly because of rising wages, partly because of rising taxes (and partly because 1929 profits were unusually high), profits in the 1930's did not recover so fast as wages and production. Corporate profits in 1937, after taxes, were 43 per cent below their 1929 level, and the sales outlook for the durable industries was still bad. But could anything have been done about *that*? The government could have kept taxes down by running somewhat bigger deficits. And why didn't this high-spending government run bigger deficits? Simply because Roosevelt was constantly plagued by the ideal of a balanced budget and by congressional advocates of sound money, and never seemed to understand quite how an unbalanced budget need not be inflationary (though he actually needed some inflation). Thus is irony defined.

Here We Go Again, Boys

And it was the lack of a consistent New Deal fiscal policy that was partly if not largely responsible for the disheartening recession of 1937-38, the steepest economic descent on record. In a few months the nation lost half the ground it had gained since 1932; industrial production fell 30 per cent, unemployment passed ten million. Stocks plummeted; e.g., New York Central declined from 41½ to 10 in about six months.

The reasons for the recession seem clear enough today. The 1936-37 boom, fed by the 1936 soldier's bonus, pushed up industrial production, commercial loans, and stock prices. Settlement of the automobile sitdown and other strikes led to a rash of wage increases. Businessmen, fearing that rising wages would mean higher prices, and expecting the government to continue to run a deficit, put their money into goods, speculatively placing orders for both current and future needs, and touching off an inventory boom. Yet raising wages did not increase consumption enough to stabilize the economy, and they did not because the government's irresolute fiscal policy in 1937 reduced its contribution to the nation's buying power by $3.2 billion, or more than the inventory accumulation and more than the aggregate wage increase.

How did this happen? It happened because in 1936 Roosevelt had begun to worry about inflation and the mounting pressures of business and the press, and had tried to balance the budget. He had even vetoed the 1936 soldier's bonus. But Congress had passed a $1.7 billion bonus over his veto, so in 1936 the government ran a deficit of $3.4 billion (1929 dollars).

In 1937, however, the government had no bonus to pay, and so spent $1.2 billion less than it did in 1936. At the same time, moreover, it collected $1.5 billion in new social-security taxes, practically none of which it disbursed. So for all practical purposes Roosevelt and Secretary of the Treasury Morgenthau balanced the budget. And thus it was that they reduced the government's contribution to the nation's buying power by more than $3 billion. Businessmen, seeing their inventories mount while sales (especially of durables) fell, curtailed orders. By the late summer of 1937, the landslide began to gather way.

Franklin Roosevelt, who had been so hospitable to the new economics (up to a point), now found himself in the same frustrating, discouraging position that Herbert Hoover had been in five and six years before. For the first time in his associates' memory, Roosevelt was unable to make up his mind quickly on an important issue. Even while Secretary Morgenthau was promising another balanced budget, Roosevelt was conferring and discussing and mulling over the problem. Finally, on April 14, 1938, a full seven months after the recession began, he countermanded Morgenthau and asked Congress to appropriate $3 billion for relief, public works, housing, and flood control. The economy revived quickly as inventories were rebuilt, and by late 1939 most of the lost ground was recovered. But full employment was not restored until 1942, when World War II was in full swing. . . .

38

The Life and Times of Rosie the Riveter

M. C. DEVILBISS

The Life and Times of Rosie the Riveter
Clarity Education Production, Inc.
Franklin Lakes, New York, 1980.

The Life and Times of Rosie the Riveter is a 1-hour 16mm colour documentary distributed by Clarity Educational Productions, Inc., which deals with the experience of women workers in the U.S. during the World War II era. The film has had featured screenings both in the United States and has received critical acclaim in *Film Comment*, *The New York Times* and *Ms*.

The director of *Rosie the Riveter* describes it as an attempt 'to record on tape and film the work and home life experience of women who worked in heavy manufacturing during World War II and to examine the process of mobilizing and demobilizing women into and out of the trades.' It seeks to do this not with a traditionally narrated historical film with archival

"The Life and Times of Rosie the Riveter" a film review, by M. C. Devilbiss, *Women's Studies International Forum*, Vol. 5, No. 3/4 (1982), pp. 389-390. Excerpted and reprinted by permission of Pergamon Press, Inc.

footage, but with five women narrators who lived through the experience personally. No traditional interviewer sits and asks questions to which the women respond; rather the women are seen in their present surroundings simply talking, as to a friend or interested person who did not have this experience in a reminiscent yet clearly realistic fashion. The women's stories are supplemented by film clips, photos, posters, magazine advertising, and, especially, songs of the period which help to bring the women's works to life in quite dramatic fashion. Indeed, after viewing the film, one feels as though one has lived for an hour in an earlier era (with the benefit of present day retrospective analysis) and has known as friends the five women whose life the film portrays.

Who exactly was 'Rosie the Riveter' and how does this film present her 'Life and Times'? In the 1940s, a newly industrialized United States felt an unprecedented need for skills and personnel to meet the rapidly increased production demands of a wartime economy. Because a substantial percentage of *man*power was being taken away from the civilian sector for service in the armed forces, alternate personnel resources were needed (some 220 of military personnel were women, but their number was restricted by both law and policy as it is today). The war was not to be a relatively brief conflict, fought principally in domestic lands and waters. Thus, methods and material had to be devised to supply and support extremely large armies for prolonged periods of time far removed from the United States. Directors of defense plants and factories as well as the government itself undertook campaigns to mobilize womanpower for the war effort. Thus, Rosie the Riveter was born, and became a national heroine during the 1940s, immortalized forever by Norman Rockwell in his May 29, 1943 cover of *The Saturday Evening Post*.

"Rosie" was the personification of the millions of women working in manufacturing and heavy industry, in such settings as aircraft, shipbuilding, and munitions plants. These kinds of jobs involved hot, hard, heavy, manual labour and were often very dangerous, sometimes leading to injuries and fatalities. Why, then, did women take these jobs? Probably there were many reasons, as the film attempts to show. Clips from the period show the government and business appealing to women to 'do the job he left behind,' emphasizing patriotism and national need and stressing that a *national* effort by *all* citizens was the way in which the war could be shortened, victory gained, and the husbands, fathers, brothers, and lovers of 'Rosies' returned home. Women have always been asked to sacrifice those that they loved to wars, now they were being asked to contribute in yet another way: to give their labour so that the lives of those they loved— and others like them—might potentially be spared. Selected spots contained in the film illustrate this point quite graphically.

But there were other reasons that women took 'war jobs' and this is best depicted by the personal statements of the five 'Rosies' in the film. A driving incentive for each of these women was an economic one. The jobs being offered to women in industrial production were skilled and relatively high paid (as compared to wages women had been getting in other types of work). Formerly classified as 'men's work,' the jobs would previously have been closed but were now legitimated for women because of extremely pressing shortages of men. Each of the five 'Rosies' in the film explains her reason for taking a war job; it was an opportunity, a chance to learn new skills and to do a job which had paid substantially higher wages than other types of work they were able to get. (This was especially the case for black women.) Thus, the film accurately shows us that there were indeed two 'Rosies'—the housewife who entered the work force during this period for the first time and the woman already in the work force who was suddenly able to get a different and better job.

The Life and Times of Rosie the Riveter poignantly shows the difficult and often hazardous conditions under which these women (and men) worked and the viewer is often hard-pressed to imagine what, if such an environment was an improvement, the former jobs and working conditions were like for these people. The film also deftly depicts shifts in attitude: when women were reclassified from a marginal to a basic labour supply; when they were needed to do work formerly considered a 'man's job,' Rosie the Riveter was praised and efforts were made to help her in her new role, e.g. women were granted union membership and benefits, day care centres were established, and women's 'advisors' were appointed to plant management staffs. But the viewer also sees, through the words of the Rosies and through the advertisements of the period the assumption that women worked a 'double day.' After their work at the plant, there were still shopping, housekeeping and child care responsibilities to discharge that were theirs alone. Interestingly, no connection was made between such burdens and the absenteeism managers were continually trying to reduce. Finally, the viewer sees that although many women wished to continue working after the war in jobs using their newly acquired skills, they were forcibly laid off their jobs to make room for the returning male veterans. Much public opinion at the time (created by and reflected in industry and Madison Avenue speeches and slogans) supported this view. The five Rosies in the film in their individual stories show us what happened in this post-war period: women either (a) remained in the labour force, but shifted back to other types of jobs and lower wages, i.e. did not retain their highly paid industrial jobs nor utilize the new skills they had acquired, or (b) dropped out of the labour force to bear and rear children (the post-war 'baby boom'). Some then came back to work when their children were older, but they returned to different types of work, as they were unable to find or were not allowed to be employed in jobs at the skill and pay levels they had achieved during the war. The film illustrates clearly that, however praised they were for doing certain jobs when there was a need, when it seemed that circumstances no longer 'warranted' their participation, women were forced out: they were manipulated in and manipulated out of skilled jobs.

The film *The Life and Times of Rosie the Riveter* has much to recommend it. It is well-designed, produced, and presented; through its approach of a blend of oral history and archival footage, the story of Rosie the Riveter—then and now—comes vividly alive. The film makes several points quite soundly: the photographs and films of women in what we might refer to as non-traditional jobs explodes the myth that women are incapable of performing these jobs or that it is inappropriate for them to do so. We also see, however, that in the era which the film depicts womenpower was viewed as a flexible, non-permanent resource, that is, the prevailing assumption (of both women and men at the time) was that in war, women *temporarily* fill roles otherwise and at other times reserved for men. The film also clearly shows a traditional feminine role in war, i.e. in war, women participate individually, making implements of war and making personal sacrifices to it.

It is perhaps the film's strongest point that it describes the situation of women in defense industries in the 1940s to an audience in the 1980s who have the privilege of retrospective analysis. The viewer can compare, for example, attitudes and assumptions about women's work and roles, largely unquestioned in an earlier era to those same attitudes and assumptions that are being challenged to a greater extent today and thus become more finely attuned to the process of social evaluation. For those who view history as cyclic, the '40s and the '80s provide an apt comparison: in the modern era with its permanent arms industry yet shortage of manpower in skilled labour jobs, will women once again become the alternative source of labour supply as these roles become 'legitimated' for them? And, once again, will they be told, like their mothers and grandmothers before them, that being a patternmaker is similar to cutting out dresses, that operating a lathe is no more difficult than running a sewing machine?

If the film has some drawbacks, it is in its perhaps biased selection of and portrayal of Rosie the Riveter. Obviously, the five women chosen to appear in the film are articulate, pleasing personalities whose experience in defense production work was very important to them personally, both at the time and in its consequences for their lives. Perhaps this was the view of most Rosies, but perhaps it was not: many other former Rosies may have viewed the experience as insignificant or marginal in their lives. Also (this is of particular importance in the classroom) the film had no guide or materials to set it in context, to give more background, or to pose questions for discussion. To its credit, however, a study guide to accompany the film is presently in the works by the film's production staff. Also, a larger oral history project, currently being conducted by Sherna Gluck (of the *Rosie* advisory board) which focuses upon women production workers in the aircraft industry in Los Angeles attempts to take a more comprehensive look at the Rosies of the past and to include women for whom this experience was not necessarily significant/meaningful as well as those for whom it was.

The Life and Times of Rosie the Riveter is a 1-hour adventure into an earlier time. It is a fascinating, educational, and well-made film which tells a story that has been ignored and which explodes many stereotypes. If you wish to spend an hour watching a film that will make you think, and may make you change your mind, be sure to see it. The film is entertaining and yet disquieting—perhaps because it makes us wonder whether women have 'come a long way' or not, after all. . . .

39

The Economy, Liberty and the State

CALVIN B. HOOVER

The War and Postwar American Economy: The Changed Economic System Assumes Permanent Form

The outbreak of the war in Europe was a milestone in the transformation of the American economy. The further extension of the powers of government over the economy ceased to have the purposes which had previously motivated the Roosevelt administration. Thereafter, until the end of the war in 1945, there was to be no New Deal-type legislation designed to prevent or overcome depressions or to redistribute the national income or to provide economic security for lower-income groups. Scarcely any of the New Deal legislation was repealed, however, though some of it was reversed in purpose. Governmental support prices for farm products were employed during the war to stimulate production, rather than to restrict it in order to help sustain prices. Governmental control of the prices of manufactured goods in wartime was designed to keep prices from rising rather than to keep them from falling as in the days of N.I.R.A. Wage controls were similarly reversed in intent.

From Calvin B. Hoover, *The Economy, Liberty and the State*, pp. 211-285, © 1958 by the Twentieth Century Fund, New York.

Yet the effect of United States participation in the war was to increase greatly the area and the intimacy of governmental control. Such a network of controls is of course an inevitable concomitant of waging modern wars, as the experience of World War I had demonstrated. Experience under the New Deal, by accustoming industrialists, farm leaders and labor leaders to operate under a network of governmental controls, greatly facilitated the transition to a highly regulated wartime economy. The experience of industrialists in the war economy, many of whom served as governmental administrators, in turn conditioned them to accept a degree of governmental intervention and control after the war which they had deeply resented prior to it. Thus the removal of wartime controls, even though it meant no more than a reversion to the level of controls and intervention in the prewar New Deal economy, was to seem like a return to old-style, laissez-faire capitalism. Further, the combined experience of operating the Code Authorities of the National Recovery Administration in the early New Deal days, even though these had been unpopular with most industrialists, and of operating sections of the W.P.B. and similar agencies during the war was significant psychologically in habituating industrialists to thinking in industry-wide terms rather than in terms of their own particular corporations. This wartime experience thus became a factor in the further evolution of the American economy away from old-style competition, just as experience with the N.R.A. Code Authorities had left behind a legacy of cooperation among the executives of corporate industry even after the act had been declared unconstitutional.

After the death of President Roosevelt and the end of the war, some effort was made through the "Fair Deal" of President Truman to expand the legislative program of the New Deal concurrently with the gradual dismantling of wartime controls.[1] In essence, however, the "Fair Deal" consisted in adapting the economic and political policies and legislation of the New Deal to the postwar economic situation. . . .

The Employment Act of 1946 embodied in legislation for the first time the "responsibility of the Federal Government to use all practicable means consistent with the needs and obligations and other essential considerations of national policy . . . to coordinate and utilize all its plans, functions, and resources" for the stated purpose of the act—maximum production, employment and purchasing power.[2] The act did not state the particular means by which the government was to carry out the goal of maximizing production and employment. Although the Council of Economic Advisers was set up, this body had no executive or administrative power over the economy, only analytical and advisory powers. All the means by which the purposes of the act were likely to be carried out had been utilized by the government at one time or another to attain these same ends. However, the purposes for which those means had been used in particular instances had not always been admitted, nor had there ever previously been a legislative mandate for combining various specific measures to carry out the declared purposes of the act.

Though the specific powers of the federal government over the economy were not extended by the Employment Act, its powers and influence could now be exerted more freely, in a more coordinated fashion and for purposes which had not previously been explicitly stated. For example, the level of governmental expenditures required to maintain full employment, the taxation or borrowing required to meet these expenditures, and the extent to which a budgetary surplus or deficit could be expected to have inflationary or deflationary effects could now appropriately be considered by the executive and legislative branches of the government in exercising their fiscal functions and responsibilities. The goal of maximizing production and employment may not be the main determinant of whether the federal budget is or is not going to be balanced at a particular time. Yet the recognition of the legitimacy of this purpose was of the greatest importance in the development of the powers of the government over the economy. The level of governmental support for agricultural prices, the attitude of government officials toward raising wage rates either through collective bargaining or through minimum-wage legislation, the question of whether corporate taxes or the personal income tax exemption is to be raised or lowered, may now be considered in relation to maximizing production and employment.

The passage of the Employment Act of 1946 did not specifically increase the powers of the federal government over the Federal Reserve System, and many of the devices for implementing monetary policy depend upon action by that organization rather than by the federal government itself. Yet actions of the Federal Reserve System with respect to the rediscount rate, reserve ratios, open market policy and the like are, to an important degree, determined by the wishes of the administration in power. The legislative mandate which assigned an increased degree of responsibility for the maintenence of optimum levels of production and employment to the federal government unquestionably implied that government officials would furnish more guidance to the Federal Reserve System in exercising monetary powers to the extent that they affect production and employment.

Furthermore, when proposed new legislation in the economic field comes before a congressional committee for consideration, government officials appearing as witnesses are likely to be much freer in arguing, for example, that raising or lowering particular tax rates would expand production and employment.[3] If a member of a congressional committee rebukes such a witness by saying that taxes are levied to meet the expenses of government and not to interfere with or affect the level of production and employment, the witness is now on much safer ground, for he can cite the language of the Employment Act of 1946. . . .

. . . Apart from the effects of World War II, it is possible to attribute the recovery from the depression of the 1930's and the maintenance of substantially full employment after the war in considerable degree to New Deal policies intended to maintain mass purchasing power. The principal factor in these policies was deficit financing. During the Truman administration, resort to a budgetary deficit whenever substantial unemployment occurred had become permanent governmental policy. To the extent that this policy was responsible for the maintenance of full employment and to the extent that the employment of persons who would otherwise have been unemployed reduced inequality in income distribution, the New Deal can be credited in some degree with the reduction in inequality. In so far as New Deal policies were responsible for raising real wages, for increasing incomes to farmers through subsidies of many diverse kinds, and for increasing the shares of low-income receivers through relief payments financed either out of income taxes at much more progressive rates or by budgetary deficits, these policies may be credited with some direct effect upon income distribution. To the extent that these measures were favorable to the maintenance of purchasing power in the economy, they helped to keep up the volume of employment as well and thus indirectly increased the income of many persons who would have had much lower incomes or no incomes at all.[4]

In summary, under the Truman administration the New Deal economic legislation which had been initiated by President Roosevelt and which was partially in abeyance during World War II gave evidence of having become an integral part of the American economic system. The process of price and wage determination in industry had become one involving large corporations and large labor unions. It could no longer be considered substantially an approximation of the purely and perfectly competitive process assumed as characteristic of laissez-faire capitalism. In agriculture, government had come to intervene in the pricing and resource allocation process with the somewhat confused goal of restoring prices and resource allocation to a normality which it was assumed they would have had under old-style competitive pricing. By the Employment Act of 1946 government took over responsibility for the maintenance of full employment in the economy. It had been assumed that full employment would automatically exist in a purely and perfectly competitive laissez-faire economy, but under the changed character of the economy this no longer could be taken for granted. The marked decline in the inequality in distribution of the national income which had manifested itself by the time of the Truman administration could not be attributed directly to the legislative measures enacted with this intent by the Democratic administrations. Nevertheless, the decline in income inequality was attributable in part directly and in considerable degree indirectly to changes in the economic system inaugurated by the New Deal. In any event, this decline in inequality was likely to prove one of the factors which would insure popular support for the continuance of these modifications of the American economic system in the future.

Thus it was during the two terms of President Truman that the new economic system of the United States began to take on an air of permanency. It has been pointed out that the corporate organizational form in industry had transformed old-style, individual-enterprise capitalism long before the New Deal. What the New Deal did was simultaneously to prop up collapsing corporate capitalism, make deficit financing respectable, tremendously strengthen the economic and political power of labor and farm organizations, throw down the shield of inviolability which the courts in the United States had placed over private property, establish the precedent for widespread governmental intervention in the economy, set up a program of social security, and modify the distribution of income in the direction of greater equality.

Yet these great economic changes of the New Deal had not been based upon a previously developed ideology or upon a comprehensive plan. Some of the changes had been represented as only temporary. Consequently, conservatives had hoped that, after the unemployment of the Great Depression was over and after the end of World War II, most of the New Deal measures could be repealed and the old economic systems could be restored. But the consolidation of the economic measures of the New Deal under President Truman and his re-election meant that, even in peace-time and even when there was little or no unemployment, politicians could win popular majorities by supporting this new economic system. Politicians now came to feel little hope that popular majorities could be obtained by a conservative party unless the mass of the voters were offered economic inducements as appealing as those of the New Deal and its Fair Deal successor.[5] But if these inducements were offered, could there be any restoration of the economic system to what it had been before the New Deal? The Eisenhower administration had to face this question. . . .

The Conservative Acquiescence in the Changed American Economic System

Conservative businessmen who initially have viewed the complex of New Deal economic measures as a fundamental impairment of "free enterprise capitalism" doubtless believed that the repeal of these measures would be the first order of business after the Republican victory at the polls, if this happy event should ever take place. Long before the Democratic Party gave way to the Republican Party in the election of 1952, however, conservative businessmen had begun to abandon their position that the New Deal had fatally impaired the capitalistic system. Of course, they had never believed that by the early 1930's competition was already so altered by quasi-monopolistic forms of giantism in industry as to reflect a fundamental change in the economic system. During the war and postwar period American industrialists began to push into the back of their minds the changes wrought by the New Deal and to point again with pride to the tremendous productivity of what they were once more coming to think of as *their* American capitalism. They had, for example, seized the opportunity afforded by the Marshall Plan to package advice with aid and to urge European countries both to eschew the evils of industrial monopoly and to refrain from further socialization of their national economies that they might also enjoy the high productivity of "free enterprise capitalism."[6]

It would be incorrect to say that American businessmen had gradually become convinced of the virtues of the economic changes brought about under the New Deal, although even this was partly true for some. American businessmen had, however, learned that they could live with what was once considered the "New Order" and had largely come to take it for granted. The conditioning effect upon some industrialists of their own experience in administering economic controls as wartime governmental officials, on the one hand, and their relief at the elimination of some of the most severe and cumbersome controls after the war, on the other, have been pointed out in the previous chapter. Those New Deal measures which were nevertheless still distasteful were tolerated in recognition that substantial corporate profits could still be earned even though this legislation remained in force. Unquestionably, however, some conservative businessmen had adjusted themselves to this legislation only because the popular support enjoyed by the Democratic administrations of Roosevelt and Truman left them no choice. After the Republican victory in 1952 these conservatives found that they were still not free to dismantle this structure; hostages had been given to fortune in the course of the political campaign by accepting a substantial part of the New Deal legislation.

Thus the newly inaugurated administration found little of the complex of New Deal economic measures which it seemed politically feasible to have repealed. Social security legislation could certainly not be repealed; instead, it was to be broadened. No one any longer advocated substantial modification of legislation regulating the issuance of securities and the security exchanges. The enactment of legislation providing for "flexible" price supports in agriculture, in claimed contrast with "rigid" price supports at some fixed percentage of parity, represented only a minor divergence from the legislation passed under the Truman administration, which had also provided some degree of flexibility. The Eisenhower administration even proposed to amend the Taft-Hartley Act in an effort to render it more acceptable to labor. Since the proposed amendments did not go far enough to satisfy labor leaders, the act—which had originally been passed over the veto of President Truman—remained in force. It is true that labor leaders could not, as under the Truman administration, count upon the intervention of government in collective bargaining to increase wages. Real wages nevertheless rose, nor did the share of labor in national income decline. Managements of industrial corporations did not stubbornly resist wage increases, since they were eager to attract political support for the Eisenhower administration from among industrial workers by demonstrating that their standard of living would be at least as high under a Republican as under a Democratic administration. This rise in real wages was for a time facilitated by the temporary stabilization of consumer prices, the result of a slight rise in the prices of manufactured goods and a fall in farm prices. While the agricultural price decline was politically most unfortunate, it did serve to mitigate the effect on the cost of living of rising wages and rising profits in industry.

An effort by the more conservative wing of the Republican Party to eliminate the Council of Economic Advisers through failing to appropriate funds for its maintenance, and thus allow the Employment Act of 1946 to fall into disuse, was frustrated by the President. A vigorous effort to reduce expenditures and to balance the budget was indeed made by the new administration. In some degree this represented a change in policy from that of the previous Democratic administrations. But it inevitably became the operative policy of the Eisenhower administration that the budget should be balanced only during a period of high employment. It gradually became apparent that, if economic recession threatened, the federal budget would be left in deficit or again allowed to become unbalanced. With the onset of the short-lived recession in the fall of 1953, the President announced that he would use all of his constitutional powers to prevent a depression. The restrictive credit policy of raising interest rates to discourage business expansion and other associated anti-inflationary measures which had been inaugurated during the early days of the administration were hastily and temporarily reversed as soon as unemployment began to increase and gross national product began to decline. There is little doubt that taxes would have been lowered with the hope of stimulating both investment and consumer expenditures, in accordance with the New Deal-Fair Deal tradition of budgeting for a deficit to prevent unemployment, if this had proved necessary to halt the recession. . . .

The transfer of governmental control from Democratic to Republican hands did not result in a return to an individualistic, free-enterprise economic system. Governmental spending was somewhat curtailed, the expansion of the governmental bureaucracy was slowed down, the extension of governmental activity into new areas was at least temporarily halted, and the powers of government could no longer be counted upon to settle wage disputes in favor of labor unions. There was, however, no significant withdrawal of governmental power in the monetary and fiscal field nor even a basic change in policy in this field. Governmental controls over production and prices in agriculture continued in effect with only slight modifications. . . .

Thus the Eisenhower administration, having inherited the evolutionary transformation of the organization and control of industry which gave rise to the New Deal and Fair Deal and having accepted most of the economic measures of the New Deal and Fair Deal, in its actual economic policies signalized the permanence of the changed economic system. This new system might be variously called the Mixed Economy, Welfare Capitalism, Progressive Capitalism or simply the Organizational Economy, to distinguish it from the individual-enterprise, laissez-faire, private-property economy of old-style capitalism.

The changed system in the United States, characterized by a great relative improvement in the standard of living of the former lower-income classes, a sharp increase in the power of labor organizations, a diminution in the degree of absolute authority of management over workers in industry, a far greater role of the state in the economy, a substantial shrinkage in the rights of private property, the acceptance by the state of responsibility for full employment plus a wide system of social security, was not easily distinguishable from the economic system existing in the United Kingdom under the Conservative government which succeeded the postwar Labor government. . . .

Endnotes

1. For instance, the proposal for a system of health insurance.

2. Edwin G. Nourse, *Economics in the Public Service*, Harcourt, Brace, New York, 1953, p. 125.

3. A government official was once sharply rebuked by a member of Congress for arguing that the reduction of trade barriers would shift resources into more productive uses. He was

advised that there was no legislative authority whatever for his trying to decide what domestic industries should be curtailed or expanded for the purpose of increasing national income.

4. All these factors which add to purchasing power are, of course, simultaneously factors which can produce inflation.

5. This age-old dilemma of the conservatives was well illustrated when Cato in 62 B.C., against all his principles, widened the privilege of obtaining cheap bread-grains at state-subsidized prices in order to win the votes of the masses. Caesar, as the leader of the radical *Populares*, completely outbid the conservative *Optimates* four years later when corn was given out free.

6. In 1947, some members of the President's Committee on Foreign Aid, commonly referred to as the Harriman Committee, urged that Marshall Plan aid should not be advanced to those countries which proposed further nationalization of their industries. This recommendation was opposed by the majority of the Committee, of which the writer was a member, and it was not adopted.

PART VI

THE MIXED ENTERPRISE ECONOMY IN TRANSITION, 1945-PRESENT

40

The American Economy
in Transition: A Review Article

WALTER S. SALANT

The Flexibility of the Economy
in Responding to Dynamic Changes

The foregoing review of postwar changes in the American Economy has
not addressed frontally one major general question: What changes if any,
have occurred in its ability to adapt to change? No single paper in the book
addresses this question, either, although several papers refer to the
responsiveness of specific variables to changes in conditions that directly
affect them. The general question is of great importance for the present and
future operation of the economy.

The major failure in the operation of the economy has been the
emergence of stagflation—the failure of the general level of prices and

Walter S. Salant, "The American Economy in Transition: A Review Article," *Journal of
Economic Literature*, Vol. XX (June, 1982), pp. 564-584. Reprinted by permission of the
American Economic Association and Dr. Salant. *The American Economy in Transition*,
edited by Martin Feldstein, was published by The University of Chicago Press for the
National Bureau of Economic Research in 1980.

money wages to decline and even to stop increasing when the growth of nominal aggregate demand fell below the growth of potential output; an increasing proportion of the response to given changes in nominal aggregate demand appears to have taken the form of decrease in real output. Downward price adjustments have apparently not disappeared entirely; in many markets, especially those for primary commodities and for unorganized labor, prices and wages continue to respond to decreases in demand, but the proportion of the economy that responds in this way apparently has diminished and the responses are slower. This increase in resistance to downward price adjustments shows up not only in a change in the relation between responses of the price level and of total output but in less obvious ways. The failure or sluggishness of the international balance of goods and services in responding to deficits in the balance of payments under fixed exchange rates, increasing the preference for altering the relation between national price-and-cost levels by changes of exchange rates rather than by changes in prices and costs expressed in national currencies, is a manifestation of this development. So is the persistence of high differentials between the unemployment rates of youth and older workers and between those of white and nonwhite workers.

This is not to say that the economy has entirely lost its capacity to adjust to shifting market forces. Not only do some prices and wages still respond to decreases in demand, as has already been noted, but the allocation of resources continues to respond to such shifts, although perhaps only sluggishly. This responsiveness is noted in several papers in this book. For example, increases of wages were greater for the more educated and more skilled workers than for those less educated and less skilled in the first two decades and were less during the 1970s, evidently in response to changes in supply and demand conditions. But insofar as changes in relative prices have to be effectuated almost entirely through increases in the nominal prices of goods and labor for which demand increases relative to supply because prices fail to decrease where demand falls relative to supply, an upward bias has been imparted to the price level. The effort to combat this inflationary tendency reduces actual output in relation to potential output.

What has changed the responsiveness of prices and of the economy, to the extent that it has changed? I have already noted that Okun, in discussing Gordon's paper, points out how the growth of government's role may have contributed to reducing downward adjustment of money prices and wages or to slowing them.[1] Other factors that are believed to have contributed are the size and duration of unemployment compensation; the level of minimum wages; floors under farm prices; the increased prevalence of multi-year labor contracts, which delay the response of wage rates to changes in conditions in the relevant labor markets; the increased tendency to bail out large firms in financial difficulties to protect investors against failures and employees against shutdowns; and the possibility that the setting of prices of goods and wages of labor with a view to maintaining firm long-run relationships between buyers and sellers, analyzed by Okun (1981), has increased. Underlying many of these changes, some within the market sector and others in the relation between it and the non-market sector, is the greater concern for the security of individuals and the increasing vigor and effectiveness of resistance to change.[2]

Theses changes in adaptability must have had adverse effects on the growth of productivity, although there is no basis for assessing the magnitude of those effects. But they have also had their benefits. They are largely a response to felt needs. That the society responds to these needs more than it did in pre-war and especially in pre-Depression years is itself a major change.

Concluding Comments

I have stressed the importance of the flexibility of the economy's response to dynamic changes because the structure and the mode of operation of the U.S. economy, like those of other national economies and of the world as a whole, are in constant flux. The tendency to treat these characteristics of the economy and the more conspicuous changes in it— and, indeed, of the society as a whole—in the most recent years as though they alone were worthy of study appears to be common but is certainly mistaken. Today's economy differs in some important aspects of structure and method of operation from that of, say, a decade ago, and in more aspects, and generally also in greater degree, from those of several decades ago. Undoubtedly changes in important characteristics will continue and the economy of the future will differ in important respects from that of today.

Change requires adjustment of plans and policies, both private and public. But that is a gradual process and, because of lags in adjustment, so is the effect of changes in plans and policies on the outcomes they are intended to influence. It is important, therefore, to recognize change, to try to understand the interrelations and causes of the changes that have occurred, and so far as possible to foresee those that will occur in order to take timely account of them. Awareness of change is also necessary to appreciate how short-lived may be the validity of quantitative estimates of structural relations based on data for short periods.

A first step in understanding change and in foreseeing its effects and policy implications is to recognize it when it has occurred. To do this requires descriptive and historical work of a sort that economists have tended to neglect. This is especially necessary in the case of changes that are persistent but too gradual to be noticed by the casual observer. Next steps are to devote more attention to analyzing the forces influencing long-term economic change, and the effects that such changes, in turn, have on these forces, which requires theoretical analysis and judgment.

As I noted earlier . . . studies of data over long periods cast doubt on whether the relationships between the price level and some demand variables first believed to have changed greatly really did change much or at all, and have suggested that price behavior may have changed for other reasons. The behavior of prices is only one illustration of the value of studying periods of several decades or more. Such historical work may not only reveal changes not apparent from data covering only a decade or so; it may also reveal that the alleged causes of some changes have been incorrectly identified, or may at least cast doubt on an accepted explanation. It may show that a supposed change in one variable previously assumed to be strategic may not have occurred and that a change in some other variable, previously unnoticed because it remained constant over a decade or so, played an important role in the change of behavior. The papers in this book by Easterlin on demography and Blinder on the size distribution of income and the more recently published work on price behavior illustrate the value of using historical data to test existing hypotheses and develop new ones.

It is a virtue of *The American Economy in Transition* that its essays present descriptive historical work of the kind that is needed and so greatly neglected. The essays and some of the comments identify many differences between the economy of the first postwar years and that of the late 1970s: the boom and bust in fertility rates, the distribution of the population by age, geographical region, and between urban and rural areas; the enormous increase in the percentage of women in the labor force and the decline in the percentage of men over 65 years of age (intensifying a long-existing trend); the halving of the share of output bought by the federal government since the Korean War and the less-than-offsetting rise in the share of state and local government; the shift from private to public shoulders of much of the burden of supporting the elderly and the handicapped and the consequent enormous rise in the federal government's transfer expenditures for those and other social purposes; the shift of employment from manufacturing to the service industries and the public sector; the decline in the fear of depression as the cyclical instability of the economy and the fraction of the population with experience of the depressed 1930s both diminished and gave way to accelerating inflation, and the increasing awareness and expectation of inflation as the fraction of the population that had no mature experience of a stable price level increased; the rise of real output; the maintenance of rapid productivity advance and then its rapid fall; the decrease in the pre-eminence of the United States in international trade and in the world economy generally from the early postwar years; the general increase in international economic interdependence, and other changes, too. About some of these changes, and also about some things that turn out on examination to have changed very little, if at all, the book tells us a great deal. It is a gold mine of information and it contains valuable studies of some specific sectors or aspects of the American economy and a great deal that is instructive about the problem of analyzing some of them. Indeed, some authors are so attentive to detail that an equally attentive reader is likely to have difficulty in getting an impression of postwar changes, apart from the growth in the importance of government and demographic change.[3]

About some other aspects of the structure and operation of the economy, especially those that cut across the designated sectors, such as flexibility and adaptability to change discussed above, it tells us less. Some things are not discussed at all, among them the resource character of technological change and the vast increase in our quantitative information about the economy and its effects. There is little explicit recognition that America's society, through its government, took on a major new assignment when it began to address directly the backlog of poverty remaining despite economic growth, although that recognition is implicit in Blinder's analysis of the changes in the distribution of economic well-being and in Break's discussion of government transfer expenditures. Little is said, also, about the increasing concern with pollution and other aspects of the environment and the effort to do something about them, except in the discussions of adverse effects of detailed regulation. The book would have benefited by a survey chapter that brought together the main changes emerging from its present chapters. Neither the introduction by Feldstein nor the short concluding comment by Arthur Burns, which lists seven "remarkable postwar advances" and some trends that "many of us, perhaps all of us, would regard as unfortunate," fully serves that purpose. The principal deficiency of the book is that its different subjects are treated independently of one another. Most of the authors have described events or developments without making much effort to dig below the surface in search of underlying causes. But several others have made efforts to do so, and their essays are valuable not only for their own content but because their efforts to dig beneath the surface point the way for others who propose to analyze economic change. And even the recording of long-term change, to which all the essays contribute, is valuable as the first step in deeper analyses of causes.

Endnotes

1. I have discussed a number of specific ways in which the flexibility of the economy has been reduced by the increase in the importance of the nonmarket sector relative to the market sector of the economy in the appendix to "International Transmission of Inflation" in Lawrence B. Krause and Walter S. Salant (1977, pp. 219-21). See also Salant (1980, pp. 97-98).

2. Tibor Scitovsky makes this and related points in his Ely Lecture appraising capitalism's chance of survival. He sees individuals and firms as less responsive than formerly to price changes and tending increasingly to ignore the gains from adaptation and the losses from failure to adapt. He attributes this largely to growing affluence, the character of improved technology, the increased bureaucratization and expanding size of private firms, and the greater role of government. In addition, he notes that the price signals themselves are increasingly rigid. Because these signals work by redistributing income, yielding large profits to some and imposing losses on others, he says, they grate on our sense of distributive justice. For that reason and because the victims protest evermore vigorously and effectively, there is an increasing tendency to prevent these signals from operating (1980, pp. 1-9).

3. In view of the vast amount of statistical and other information in the book, it is not surprising that it also contains many editorial, proofreading, and typographical errors. I have noticed two or three dozen, some that are obvious and others that I have found only upon exploring the details of some statement. Readers who have become accustomed over the years to rely upon the accuracy of the National Bureau's books will share my hope that this does not signify a relaxation in the care with which its books are being prepared for publication.

41

The Multinational Corporation

NEIL H. JACOBY

I

Multinational Corporation Defined

A multinational corporation owns and manages businesses in two or more countries. It is an agency of *direct*, as opposed to *portfolio*, investment in foreign countries, holding and managing the underlying physical assets rather than securities based upon those assets.

Almost every large enterprise has foreign involvements of some kind. Whatever its home, it will probably send agents to other nations, establish representative offices abroad, import foreign materials, export some products, license foreign firms to use its patents or know-how, employ foreign nationals, have foreign stockholders, borrow money from foreign bankers and may even have a foreigner on its board of directors. None of these circumstances, however, would make an enterprise "multinational," because none would require a substantial *direct* investment in foreign

Neil H. Jacoby, "The Multinational Corporation," *The Center Magazine*, Vol. III, No. 1 (May 1970), pp. 21-52. Excerpted and reprinted with permission from *The Center Magazine*, a publication of the Robert Maynard Hutchins Center for the Study of Democratic Institutions in Santa Barbara, California.

countries' assets nor entail a responsibility for *managing* organizations of people in alien societies. Only when an enterprise confronts the problems of designing, producing, marketing, and financing its products within foreign nations does it become a true multinational.

Although we define the multinational corporation by ownership and management of businesses in several nations, in reality this is generally only one stage in a process of multinationalization. Characteristically, the expanding corporation traverses the following stages:

1. Exports its products to foreign countries.
2. Establishes sales organizations abroad.
3. Licenses use of its patents and know-how to foreign firms that make and sell its products.
4. Establishes foreign manufacturing facilities.
5. Multinationalizes management from top to bottom.
6. Multinationalizes ownership of corporate stock.

Upward of one hundred thousand U.S. business enterprises are stage one exporters; many fewer have reached stages two or three; only about forty-five hundred firms are stage four multinationals. A mere handful of giant firms are approaching stages five and six.

Legally, a domestic corporation may multinationalize by establishing foreign branches, by operating wholly or partially owned subsidiaries in other countries, or by entering into joint ventures with enterprises in other countries. Whatever the legal format, it becomes a working corporate citizen within many nations. This makes the word "multinational" accurately descriptive of its character. Although business transactions are typically transnational or international in nature, no company is international in a legal sense, because it must obtain its charter from a national government.

II

Rise of Corporate Multinationalism

Multinational operations by private business corporations are comparatively recent in man's history. The companies of merchant traders of medieval Venice and the great English, Dutch, and French trading companies of the seventeenth and eighteenth centuries were forerunners but not true prototypes of today's multinational corporation. They were essentially trading rather than manufacturing organizations, with comparatively little fixed investment. And they operated mainly within the colonial territories or spheres of influence of their own nations rather than under the jurisdiction of foreign sovereign states.

During the nineteenth century, foreign investment flowed extensively from Western Europe to the undeveloped areas of Asia, Africa, and the Americas, including the United States. In this age of empire-building, Victorian Britain was the great capital exporter, followed by France, the Netherlands, and Germany. Little of this capital flow was direct investment outside imperial boundaries. Although British firms made large investments in India, Canada, Australia, and South Africa, French companies deployed capital in Indochina, Algeria, and other French colonies, and Dutch firms helped to industrialize the East Indies, corporate investment was conducted mainly within the matrix of empire. When British and European capitalists helped to finance the railroads and canals of the United States, Argentina, and other countries outside of their imperial jurisdictions, they did it by purchasing the securities of American governments or corporations. Rare was the profit-seeking business corporation that ventured outside the imperial realm to make commitments in brick and mortar under an alien regime. Nevertheless, by the turn of this century American firms were producing in Britain such products as farm equipment, sewing machines, printing presses, and revolvers, and a book entitled *The American Invasion* was published in London in 1902.[1]

The earliest substantial multinational corporate investment came in the mining and petroleum industries during the initial years of the twentieth century. Nature decreed a wide geographical separation of great mineral deposits in less-developed regions from important markets in the United States and Western Europe. Hence large oil companies like British Petroleum and Standard Oil Company were among the first true multinationals, and hard-mineral corporations, such as International Nickel, Anaconda Copper, and Kennecott Copper, were other early entrants. Singer, Coca-Cola, and Woolworth were early American manufacturing and merchandising multinationals; Unilever, Phillips, and Imperial Chemicals entered the foreign arena from Britain and the Netherlands. Chemical and drug companies went abroad from Germany.

Multinational corporate investment spread further in the years after World War I, spurred by rising barriers to international trade, and led by the burgeoning automobile and associated industries. General Motors and Ford acquired ownership of auto-making companies in Britain, France, and Germany. American companies making tires and rubber, plate glass, and auto accessories followed. By 1940, some six hundred American firms had invested more than half a billion dollars in factories in Britain.[2] The worldwide economic depression of the nineteen thirties throttled this incipient movement, and foreign corporate investment languished until after World War II.

After the Second World War, the multinational corporation flowered as American firms heavily invested abroad in a wide variety of manufacturing and merchandising operations. At the end of 1950, direct foreign investment by U.S. corporations was 11.8 billion dollars, mostly committed to the petroleum and minerals industries of Canada, Latin America, and the Middle East. By the end of 1968, the figure had almost sextupled to sixty-five billion. Paralleling this explosive growth were shifts in the location and industrial structure of the investment. Two-thirds of the total, 40.6 billion, was invested in manufacturing, mercantile, and other *non*-extractive industries. Almost two-thirds, 39.1 billion, was invested in Western Europe, even though commitments in other parts of the world had also expanded greatly.

American corporations are by no means the only multinationals. Direct foreign corporate investment in the United States stood at nearly eleven billion dollars at the end of 1968, having risen by twenty-five percent during the preceding three years as more foreign businesses gained the financial means and the managerial confidence to enter the huge American market.[3] Most of this investment was made by enterprises of Britain (3.4 billion), Canada (2.6 billion), the Netherlands (1.7 billion), and Switzerland (1.2 billion), with smaller sums from France, Germany, and Japan. Long used to the presence of such firms as Shell, Lever, and Bowater, Americans became conscious of new corporate citizens like British Petroleum, Courtaulds, Pechiney, Aluminium, Massey-Ferguson, Bayer, and Toyota.

Foreign *direct* investment was only one-seventh of the total foreign investment in the United States of seventy-six billion dollars at the end of 1968. In contrast, more than half of the total U.S. investment abroad, sixty-four billion of a total of a hundred and thirty-three billion, was direct in form.[4] Increasing European and Japanese business intrusion into the American continent demonstrates, nevertheless, that throughout the industrialized world, corporate business is outgrowing national boundaries. A nineteenth-century political organization provides an archaic framework for a twentieth-century economy.

American corporations led the world trend toward business multinationalism because the great size and wealth of the U.S. economy had enabled them to utilize enormous amounts of savings and because they were attracted by the relatively higher foreign rates of return to investment. U.S. capital outflow took the form of corporate *direct* investment because of the superior organization of American capital markets and the larger capabilities of American managers. With its multitude of stockholders, its ready access to equity capital and credit from efficient financial markets, its experience in allocating capital and in coordinating business operations over a continental area, its growth-and-profit orientation, and its use of advanced techniques of management, the large American corporation was far better prepared for foreign investment than the typical European enterprise, with its much smaller size, narrower market, emphasis upon security and stability, and traditional mode of management. Also, European capital markets were small and public ownership of corporate securities was limited, making it expensive for a European company to acquire external funds.

American corporate investment abroad is concentrated in the hands of the largest firms. Of a total investment of sixty-five billion dollars at the end of 1968, the five hundred largest American industrial corporations had invested more than fifty billion. A score of these firms held a third or more of their total assets in other countries; an even larger number derived more than one-third of their incomes from foreign operations. For the great majority, however, foreign operations constituted a minor segment of their businesses.

American corporate investment has penetrated deeply into the economies of a few advanced nations, such as Canada and Britain, and into those of certain raw-material producing countries in Central and South America and the Middle East. Foreign firms—primarily American—owned thirty-five percent of all Canadian mining, manufacturing, transportation, and merchandising business in 1962.[5] In Australia, foreign firms owned about one-quarter of all business corporation assets in 1965.[6] They controlled about one-fourth of Brazil's rail and electrical industries and about eighteen percent of its manufacturing.[7] British subsidiaries and joint ventures of American corporations accounted for ten percent of the industrial output of the United Kingdom and for seventeen percent of that country's export in 1965, according to a recent study.[8] This investment was concentrated in high-technology industries (pharmaceuticals, computers) and in industries for whose products people spend a rising fraction of their incomes as their standard of living increases (autos, cosmetics, packaged foods). American companies also owned considerable parts of the industrial apparatus of Honduras, Chile, Panama, and the Arab oil countries.

In the European countries, American corporate investment forms less than five percent of total business investment. What concerns Europeans, however, is the deep penetration by American companies of the high-technology sectors of their economies. In France, American firms controlled two-thirds of the photographic film, papers, farm machinery, and telecommunications industries. In Europe as a whole, they produced eighty percent of the computers, ninety-five percent of the integrated circuits, fifty percent of the semi-conductors and fifteen percent of consumer electronic products.[9] Thoughtful Europeans have been haunted by the specter of domination of their most advanced industries by American firms, relegating native enterprises to conventional tasks.

When taken globally, it has been estimated that the value of the output of all foreign affiliates of U.S. corporations was a staggering one hundred and thirty billion dollars during 1968.[10] This was four times U.S. exports of thirty-three billion in that year, showing that the preponderant linkage of the United States to other markets is foreign production rather than foreign trade. Foreign affiliates accounted for fifteen percent of the total production of nine hundred billion dollars in the non-communist world outside the United States. Thus United States industry abroad had become the third largest economy in the world, outranked only by those of the domestic United States and the Soviet Union. Moreover, foreign production of American firms has grown about ten percent a year, twice as fast as domestic economies. Multinational corporations are rapidly increasing their shares of the world's business.

III

Motives to Multinationalize

Direct investment in foreign manufacturing facilities is usually an alternative to exporting homemade products. Why have manufacturers endured the harder tasks and larger risks of foreign operations instead of shipping their products? Evidently, direct investment appeared to be a relatively profitable use of corporate funds.

The most frequent reason for direct foreign investment is that entrepreneurs confront foreign barriers to their exports. Nationalistic sentiment leads most nations to try to build their own industrial capabilities. By raising barriers against imports of manufactured products, they induce foreign as well as domestic firms to establish domestic industries. Large numbers of American corporations became multinationals simply in order to maintain or expand markets in Canada or in the European Economic Community that could not be as profitably served by exports.

Business firms also multinationalize because their presence as a producer in a foreign nation enables them more effectively to adapt their products to local demands. For example, during the nineteen-twenties General Motors acquired Vauxhall in Britain and Opel in Germany and opened assembly plants in fifteen foreign countries. It sought to meet consumer demand for autos in those countries that had expanded to a point where local manufacturing was more profitable than exporting from the United States.[11]

The relative attractiveness of direct investment in foreign nations had many other causes. The creation of larger free-trading regions, such as the European Economic Community and the European Free Trade Association, created opportunities to capitalize upon economies of scale the American firms were prepared to seize more quickly than their European counterparts. The rapid postwar expansion of European markets, with a spreading wave of mass consumption, opened doors to profits from the introduction of mass manufacturing and marketing methods. Another reason was that the dynamic of American business is expansion, and anti-trust laws and keen competition at home channeled the attention of corporate executives to opportunites abroad.[12] An important factor was the development of management science. Together with striking advances in communications and computer facilities, it made the management of distant operations feasible. Growing confidence in the political stability and economic strength of the advanced nations appeared to reduce the risk of foreign commitments. Also, geographical diversification of a corporation's operations into many national markets offered a means of stabilizing the growth of total earnings and thereby reducing the risk/reward ratio.

By multinationalizing, a company also acquires certain competitive advantages. It can monitor technological developments in many countries. It can borrow at low interest rates in one country to finance working capital shortages in a high-interest-rate country. It is able to adjust intra-company transfer prices in ways that reduce total corporate tax liabilities. It can move surplus funds between its multiple bases to minimize the cost of borrowed funds or to take advantage of predicted changes in the exchange rates of national currencies. Entry by American firms into Europe, for example, was facilitated by the typically large amounts of credit supplied by European bankers on a limited equity base.[13]

Manifestly, the forces behind corporate multinationalism are so potent that there is a high probability that multinational business will continue to expand relative to domestic business long into the future.

IV

Management Patterns and Processes

A multinational business corporation may adopt one of two basic organizational forms: a *world corporation* format, in which the basic business functions of finance, marketing, manufacturing, and research and development are the primary pillars of organization and domestic and foreign operations are merged; or an *international division* format, in which all foreign operations are separated from domestic in an "international division."[14] There are strengths and weaknesses in each format, and both have been used by successful firms. As firms gain experience, a wider use of the world corporation plan of organization is likely because it achieves more complete integration of foreign and domestic management.

In both types of multinational organization, the head office normally makes strategic policy decisions, such as expansion of product lines or marketing territories or capital budgets, and delegates to the managers of its foreign affiliates broad authority to operate under those policies within their respective countries. Policy control of foreign affiliates is exercised, first, through the use of annual budgets that specify planned targets to be attained and, secondly, through affiliate managers' periodical reports of progress toward the specified goals.[15] Coordinated control of policy through central staff functions, and decentralized operating responsibility with clearly defined line authority—the management technique developed within General Motors—has been the key to successful multinational management.[16] Although companies differ in the extent of the authority they vest in the managers of their foreign affiliates, it is simply not feasible to handle a many-based enterprise with a tight rein.

An important issue is the necessary or desirable extent of ownership of a foreign affiliate. Up to the present time, the predominant vehicle of direct corporate investment abroad appears to be the wholly owned subsidiary. Thus seventy-seven percent of the net assets of American firms in the United Kingdom in 1965 were held by wholly owned subsidiaries, fourteen percent by subsidiaries more than fifty percent American-owned, and only nine percent by entities financed mainly by British firms.[17] Most American and European companies believe that sole ownership is necessary to enable them to base their operations upon objective economic factors, free from the influence of foreign partners.[18] Although one hundred percent ownership may facilitate the enforcement of corporate discipline and progress toward assigned goals, it goes against prevailing opinion in most host countries, which want a "piece of the action" for their own citizens. Host countries prefer an equity interest by local businessmen because it reduces the danger of foreign control of their economies. In addition, local partners can help to improve the affiliate's relations with the foreign government and its people. The example of Japan and Mexico, which have admitted foreign companies only as minority owners of joint ventures, demonstrates that successful foreign investment does not require majority ownership. Although joint ventures are not free of difficulties, it is desirable—and probable—that more multinational business will assume this format in the future, despite investors' preferences for one hundred percent control. Another route to joint ownership, of course, is multinational ownership of stock in the parent company, which is also desirable to minimize international frictions.

Studies of comparative management in different countries indicate that the similarities are far greater than the differences. With appropriate adaptations to local conditions, American management technique has proved to be a hardy transplant in foreign soils. As David Lilienthal has poignantly observed, the most important managerial problems of multi-national corporations are their relations with governments. The legal systems and social and economic controls of host countries often conflict with those of the home country. Interminable negotiations with government officials are the lot of the foreign manager.[19]

Managers of the foreign affiliates of multinational companies once had the reputation of being "second-stringers," sidetracked from the main line of advancement to top management. This has changed, as companies have learned the folly of entrusting markets with high profit potentials to men of less than topflight abilities. A foreign assignment now is part of the grooming process for leadership of the multinational company. Overseas placement is typically not a preconceived career goal but a step in broadening the young executive's experience.[20] Indeed, the methods of multinational companies in developing executive leadership are worthy of study by national governments desiring to reform their foreign services so that they may function effectively in an age of instantaneous communication and supersonic flight.[21]

V

Effects on Less Developed Host Countries

The economic, political, technological, and cultural effects of multinational corporate investment are most striking when the host country is less developed than when it is relatively advanced, for it is in the less developed lands that investment has made a strong impact on development. This conclusion emerges clearly from thirteen case studies made over a fifteen-year period by the National Planning Association, whose credentials as an objective observer are beyond question.[22] In all cases the American corporation played an innovating and catalytic role, founding new industries, transmitting technological and managerial skills as well as capital, and in many cases creating entire social infrastructures of schools, housing, health facilities, and transportation in order to conduct its business.

Sears, for example, pioneered the modern general supermarkets of Mexico, and established a large coterie of native manufacturing industries to stock its stores.[23] United Fruit Company, one of the earliest American multinationals, was the major force in developing the international trade in bananas, pioneering in every aspect of the industry, from plantation production through disease control techniques, land and ocean transport, and sales promotion.[24] It enormously expanded the real incomes and welfare of the peoples of the six Central American republics in which it operated, while earning a profit on its investment that averaged *less* than that realized by corporate business in the United States.

International Basic Economy Corporation, organized for profit by the Rockefeller family for the purpose of introducing new industries and business methods into less developed countries, had established one hundred and nineteen subsidiaries and affiliates in thirty-three countries by the end of 1968. Its efforts were focused upon agri-business. Its subsidiaries made many innovations in the production of food and low-cost housing and in the economical distribution of food through super-markets. Because of its heavy developmental and innovational costs, which broke the ground for later entry by local entrepreneurs, I.B.E.C's return on investment was subnormal.[25]

These cases illustrate the role played by the American corporation in the poor countries. Although the conduct of American business abroad has not been impeccable, the over-all record strongly encourages an extension of this mode of "foreign aid." Indeed, the constructive developmental re-sults of private business investment led the U.S. Agency for International Development (A.I.D.) to launch private enterprise support programs in 1958, and thereafter to rely increasingly upon enterprises in carrying out developmental tasks. Stimulation of private investment was the motive behind the 1968 proposal of the Nixon Administration to establish a new public corporation for this purpose.

In the face of a generally constructive record, how may one explain the widespread denunciation of American corporations abroad by foreign politicians as well as by American critics? Charges of "exploitation," "plundering," and "greed for profits" are often made, especially in the Latin-American countries. As the authors of the study of United Fruit Company have pointed out, there has been a "striking disparity between the reputation and the performance" of the company.[26] Ignorance of the realities of private enterprise, of the hard tasks to be performed and the high risks to be run, is surely one part of the answer. For those ventures that succeed, profits may appear to be inordinately high. Yet, as Professor Raymond Vernon has remarked, "the history of such investment is littered with the bleached bones of many enterprises; and taking the failures with the successes, it is not clear that the investment has been handsomely rewarded."[27] Many companies have been obliged to deal with a range of problems vastly wider than those confronted at home. They have had to create whole communities, with their appurtenant infrastructures, out of wilderness environments, usually in countries with unstable governments and politically immature populations. It is in the light of this imperative that their occasional interference with local governments should be interpreted. The foreign company is always a convenient "whipping boy" for local politicians.

American corporate investment abroad has been gradually shifting from an earlier emphasis upon the mining, extractive, and raw-material industries toward diversified manufacturing and merchandising operations. One important consequence has been a great increase in U.S. exports of technological and managerial skills and knowledge—values to the recipient country which are unrequited. This shift should serve to reduce the frequency of charges of "foreign exploitation."

The potential contribution of private corporations to the development of poor countries is large. It depends mainly on the development of stable governments in those countries and their actions to encourage private investment. Any less developed country that offers political stability, respect for contracts, financial responsibility, and equitable taxation will attract foreign investment—and domestic as well. The remarkable evolutions of such countries as Mexico, Malaysia, and Taiwan testify to this truth. If more low-income countries adhere to codes of foreign investment that reduce political risks, private firms will quickly expand their developmental roles.

The political risks of expropriation, civil war, and inconvertibility of currencies have risen in less developed lands as a result of changed world attitudes toward intervention by one nation into the domestic affairs of another. The era of "gunboat diplomacy" has passed. When an American corporation goes abroad today, it cannot expect the U.S. government to protect its foreign properties. Since the expropriation of U.S. business properties by the Soviet government in 1917, there have been major expropriations by the governments of Mexico, Cuba, Argentina, Peru, Indonesia, and Eastern European countries involving estimated losses of some 2.5 billion dollars.[28] "Prompt, adequate, and effective compensation," required by international law, has rarely been paid. The American company loses, but so does the expropriating country and the region in which it is located. Thus Cuba's expropriation in 1960 probably cost Latin America some five hundred million dollars of U.S. business investment in the following two years.[29]

The A.I.D offers insurance to American corporations against major political risks of investment in those less developed countries that receive American economic assistance. If the flow of private investment is to be expanded, this insurance should be extended to cover more risks and more countries. At the same time, the low-income countries should adopt and respect codes of foreign investment, and assure fair adjudication of disputes. The establishment of the International Center for the Settlement of Investment Disputes, in 1966, was a desirable move in this direction. By mid-1968 some fifty-seven nations had ratified the convention establishing the Center, thereby agreeing to submit to its panels of experts any disputes arising between their governments and foreign private investors.[30]

Private business investment is inherently superior to governmental aid as an instrument of development because it combines transfers of managerial and technical assistance with that of capital. General dissatisfaction with bilateral governmental aid makes it important to expand the flow of business investment.[31] While measures to limit or to insure against risks will help to enlarge this flow, they will not remove the root causes of international tensions. The foreign subsidiary of the U.S. corporation will still be charged with "exploitation" of local resources and with taking out too much profit. When it pays higher than prevailing wages and benefits to its employees, their higher living standards will provoke envy and resentment among other local citizens. Ways must be found to ameliorate this problem. . . .

VI

Effects on Developed Host Countries

In Europe, the impact of American multinational business was on politically mature societies, technologically advanced economies, and socially integrated peoples proud of their nations' long histories of achievement. Nevertheless, the physical presence in Europe of more than three thousand American corporations with forty thousand American employees could not help but be significant.[32]

Major economic results of the American "invasion" were to stimulate the growth of production, incomes, and living standards of Britons and Europeans. American corporate investment improved the efficiency of resource allocation. It also improved the balance of international payments of host countries, which benefited both from capital inflows and also from the exports generated by the foreign-owned affiliates.[33] More subtle and profound economic effects flowed from the new competition introduced by the Americans. "Hard sell" advertising, mass-marketing techniques, price competition, packaging and branding, and continental marketing strategies were some of these new concepts. Mass production of a host of new consumer products, such as fresh frozen foods, aluminum foil, and plastic containers, was both a response and a stimulus to the rising levels of European family income. The primary thrust of the American "assault" on the Continent was to accelerate the pace of a peaceful consumer revolution.

The newcomers were, of course, criticized for their "disruption of orderly marketing," "extravagant wages and salaries," and "reckless" financial practices, primarily by those in the old business establishments whose comfortable oligopolies were threatened by the new competition. American corporate managers did, on occasion, display insensitivity to local customs in their drive for lower costs and greater efficiency. General Electric was condemned for closing a computer plant and dismissing French engineers when it consolidated its foreign computer operations for greater efficiency. Goodyear and Goodrich were met with cries of protest from French tire-makers when they doubled the traditional discounts to dealers in order to make initial penetration of the French tire market. Effective competition inevitably disturbs the status quo. As Schumpeter said long ago, it is a "process of creative destruction." Available evidence indicates that affiliates of U.S corporations have generally earned higher rates of return on investment in both Britain and on the Continent than have local enterprises in the same industries.[34]

Although the American "invasion" was received calmly in most European countries, de Gaulle's France reacted sensitively. The French government changed its policy toward U.S. direct investment three times. After 1959, it encouraged the entry of U.S. corporations. As a result of popular disapproval of the actions of General Motors in laying off workers, of Chrysler's purchase of Simca, and of the sale to General Electric of the controlling interest in Machines Bull, American investment was severely restricted in 1963. When U.S firms reacted by switching their investments to other Common Market countries from which they could still penetrate the French market, Premier Pompidou once again relaxed the restrictions. Any Common Market country that restricts American investment only helps its rivals.[35]

The technological consequences of the American corporate invasion received much attention from European observers. U.S. investment was concentrated in the high-technology industries of computers, electronics, aerospace, and petrochemicals, and in such fast-growing industries as car manufacturing. American firms led or dominated those industries in many European countries. They excelled in the innovation of products and processes. American firms spent twice as much of their sales dollars on research and development as their European competitors. They were fast-footed in converting laboratory findings to commercial products. Many Europeans thought they saw a growing and insurmountable "technological gap" between Europe and America.

Europeans responded vigorously to the American challenge. Their governments fostered business mergers designed to create companies able to compete with the American giants. They expanded their research and development activities supporting industry. Basic European science has always been the equal of American science. Given adequate governmental and industrial support and an efficient scale of business operations, there is no reason why European industrial technology should fall behind, and, when taken overall, it is not clear that it is laggard. There is now general recognition that the real "gap" between European and American business is managerial rather than technological.[36] Europeans are now taking vigorous steps to close this gap by establishing graduate schools of administration and replacing nepotism with meritocracy in choosing industrial leadership. . . .

VII

Effects on Communist Countries

Multinational corporate business has begun to penetrate the socialist nations of Eastern Europe in novel ways, and with effects that may ultimately be even more momentous for the world than their operations within market economies. The novelty lies in cooperation between private firms and public corporations. These arrangements are called "industrial cooperation" in socialist countries, probably because "joint venture" has a capitalist ring. Typically, a Western private company agrees with an Eastern European public corporation to sell specialized machinery and equipment on instalment credit terms and to provide technical and managerial services necessary to produce certain products. The Eastern European country, in turn, agrees to provide land, buildings, and labor necessary to produce those products. The joint venture may market its output in the host country or in third countries. The Western company profits from the sale of equipment and products and is paid a fee for its technical and managerial services. The Eastern European enterprise gains valuable technological and managerial know-how, and title to specialized industrial equipment that it will later on operate by itself. While differing in legal form, the essential elements of multinational corporate investment are present—international transfers of capital, management, and technology.[37]

Such East-West industrial cooperation appears to have emerged initially in Yugoslavia during the nineteen-fifties. Now all socialist countries have industrial cooperation agreements with Western firms. Rumania had no less than nineteen in effect during 1969. For example, Renault of France had agreed with a Rumanian enterprise to build auto transmissions, partly for domestic use and partly for export. Fiat of Italy agreed during 1968 with the government of the Soviet Union to supply machinery, management, and technology to create a Russian industrial community capable of making six hundred thousand automobiles a year. Sharply rising East-West trade in capital equipment shows that the magnitude of such industrial cooperation increased during the nineteen-sixties. Mainland China has also purchased industrial plant and equipment from Western countries on long-term credit.

So far, East-West industrial cooperation has involved European and Japanese enterprises, because American firms have been barred by U.S. government rules from exporting "strategic" materials or technologies to communist countries. The result has been to divert exports from American firms to competitors in other Western countries, rather than to inhibit the development of communist countries. The Soviet Union is eager to deal with American companies able to give it access to advanced managerial and technological knowledge. The thawing of the Cold War and rising indications of U.S.-Soviet cooperation afford ground for hope that industrial cooperation between the superpowers will expand. Considering the great size of the economies, the potentialities of such economic intercourse are vast. The ultimate involvement of Mainland China in commercial intercourse with the United States is also a development holding great promise for lowering barriers to international understanding.

Socialist ideology, which precludes private ownership of fixed capital, has caused East-West industrial cooperation to take place on a basis of loans rather than equity capital. Yet cracks have appeared in this ideological barrier. The Foreign Investment Law of Yugoslavia was amended during 1967 to permit joint ventures of Yugoslavian and foreign companies to acquire ownership of domestic fixed assets.[38]

Expanding East-West industrial cooperation holds the promise of relaxing international tensions and creating an environment favorable to peace. It promotes travel and communication between the peoples of countries. It emphasizes the *common* economic goal of more efficient production and a better life for people, despite ideological and practical differences in economic systems. Technological and managerial knowledge is diffused more rapidly, accelerating gains in productivity, output, and standards of living. Because the peoples of *both* cooperating countries manifestly gain from such arrangements, there is no basis for feelings of "exploitation" of one country by the other.

VIII

Effects on Investing Countries

Multinational corporate investment has had important economic, political, and cultural impacts upon investing countries. Thus the United

States balance of payments was in substantial deficit during most of the nineteen-sixties, and foreign long-term investment is believed to have contributed to it. An Interest Equalization Tax was imposed in 1963 to deter Americans from making foreign loans or portfolio investments. Later, voluntary and then mandatory direct controls were imposed upon direct foreign investment by U.S. corporations in an effort to reduce capital outflow and to strengthen the U.S. dollar in the world's money markets.

Whether these foreign investment controls are achieving their aims and serving American interests is doubtful. Large American multinational firms are able to raise needed capital from foreign bankers or in the Eurodollar market. The heaviest impact of U.S. controls is on smaller enterprises unable to tap these financial sources. More fundamental is the argument that any improvement in the U.S. balance of payments resulting from the controls can be temporary at best. In the long run, controls have the perverse effect of enlarging the U.S. deficit by reducing the inflow of interest and dividends from foreign affiliates below the level to which it would otherwise have risen.[39]. . .

Endnotes

1. F. A. McKenzie, *The American Invasion* (London: Grant Richards, 1902). The "invasion" was primarily of American imports rather than of American products made in Britain.

2. John H. Dunning, *American Investment in British Manufacturing Industry* (London: Allen and Unwin, 1958).

3. U.S. Department of Commerce, *Survey of Current Business* (October 1969), p. 35.

4. *Ibid.*

5. Foreigners owned sixty-three percent of Canada's petroleum and mining industries. A. E. Safarian, *Foreign Ownership of Canadian Industry* (Toronto: McGraw-Hill, 1966).

6. D. J. Brash, *American Investment in Australian Industry* (Canberra: Australian National University Press, 1966).

7. McMillan, Gonzalez, and Erickson, *International Enterprise in a Developing Economy* (East Lansing: Michigan State University Press, 1964).

8. John H. Dunning, *The Role of American Investment in the British Economy*, Political and Economic Planning Broadsheet 507 (London: February, 1969), p. 119.

9. Jean-Jacques Servan-Schreiber, *The American Challenge* (New York: Atheneum, 1968).

10. Judd Polk, *The Internationalization of Production* (New York: U.S. Council of the International Chamber of Commerce, Inc., May 7, 1969).

11. See Frederic G. Donner, *The Worldwide Industrial Enterprise* (New York: McGraw-Hill, 1967).

12. J. N. Behrman, *Some Patterns in the Rise of the Multinational Enterprise* (Chapel Hill: University of North Carolina, Graduate School of Business Research Paper 18, 1969), pp. 6-8.

13. See Sanford Rose, "The Rewarding Strategies of Multinationalism," *Fortune*, September 15, 1968.

14. *Organizing for Worldwide Operations* (New York: Business International Corp., 1965).

15. See George A. Steiner and Warren M. Cannon, *Multinational Corporate Planning* (New York: Macmillan, 1966).

16. See Alfred P. Sloan, Jr., *My Years With General Motors* (New York: Duell, Sloan & Pearce, 1963), Chap. 4.

17. Dunning, *The Role of American Investment*, p. 126. See also J. C. Behrman, *Some Patterns*, pp. 58-60.

18. Donner, *Worldwide*, Chapter 4.

19. David Lilienthal, "The Multinational Corporation" in Melvin Anshen and George L. Bach, eds. *Management and Corporations* 1958 (New York: McGraw-Hill, 1960), Chap. 5.

20. Richard F. Gonzalez and Anant R. Neghandi, *The U.S. Overseas Executive: His Orientation and Career Patterns* (East Lansing: Michigan State University Press, 1967).

21. See E. Paul Imhof, "Selected Analogies Between the Foreign Service and the Multinational Corporation," Ms. 1969.

22. Publications in the program "United States Business Performance Abroad" since 1953 have analyzed the cases of Sears in Mexico, Grace in Peru, Creole Petroleum in Venezuela, Firestone in Liberia, Stancvac in Indonesia, United Fruit in Latin America, T.W.A. in Ethiopia, General Electric in Brazil, I.B.M. in France, Aluminium in India, U.S. Plywood in Congo, and International Basic Economy Corporation worldwide.

23. *Sears, Roebuck de Mexico*, S.A. (Washington: National Planning Association, 1953).

24. Stacy May and Galo Plaza, *The United Fruit Company in Latin America* (Washington: National Planning Association, 1958).

25. Wayne G. Broehl, Jr., *The International Basic Economy Corporation* (Washington: National Planning Association, 1968).

26. May and Plaza, *United Fruit*, p. 239.

27. Raymond Vernon, "The Role of U.S. Enterprise Abroad," *Daedalus* (Winter 1969), p. 1130.

28. Franklin Root, "The Expropriation Experience of American Companies," *Business Horizons* (April 1968).

29. *Ibid.*, p. 69.

30. See International Center for Settlement of Investment Disputes, Washington, D.C., *Convention on the Settlement of Investment Dispute, in force October*, 1966, *First Annual Report* 1966-67, *Second Annual Report* 1967-68.

31. Reasons for "de-politicizing" foreign aid, by replacing bilateral with multi-lateral assistance and private investment, are set forth by the author in *The Progress of Peoples*, Occasional Paper, II, No. 4 (June, 1969), of the Center for the Study of Democratic Institutions, Santa Barbara, California.

32. Estimates are from Edward A. McCreary, *The Americanization of Europe* (Garden City: Doubleday, 1964).

33. Evidence for Britain is given by Dunning, *American Investment*, pp. 142-45.

34. *Ibid.*, p. 130.

35. Servan-Schreiber, *American Challenge*, Chap. 2.

36. *Ibid.*, Chap. 7. See also *Gaps in Technology*, A General Report of the O.E.C.D. (Paris: 1968).

37. See "Note on Industrial Cooperation" in *Economic Survey of Europe in 1967* (New York: United Nations, 1968). pp. 79-86.

38. See *Joint Business Ventures of Jugoslav Enterprises and Foreign Firms* (New York: Columbia University Press, and Belgrade: Institute of International Politics and Economy, 1968).

39. See *U.S. Business Abroad*, an Economic Report of the Manufacturer's Hanover Trust Company (New York: March, 1969). The short-run effect of investment controls upon the U.S. balance of international payments depends upon the length of the recoupment period. See F. Michael Adler and G. C. Hufbaur, "Foreign Investment Controls: Object—Removal," *Columbia Journal of World Business*, III, No. 3 (May-June, 1969).

42

Thoughts on the Underground Economy

CHARLES J. HAULK

Unmeasured, untaxed economic activity may be growing faster than the "regular" economy. If so, and if it was as large as 15 percent of national GNP by 1978, this "underground economy" could be significantly distorting the economic models used for forecasting. As a result, fiscal and monetary policy makers run the risk of thinking they are restricting the economy when they may actually be overstimulating it.

Because of the fascination and infatuation of the public and the economics profession with official statistics about the economy, we have had our heads set spinning with the numbers released over the past several months. Productivity growth has come to a halt, consumers have virtually stopped saving, and we are faced with horrendous inflation at a time when the unemployment rate is high by historical standards. Real growth creeps along, and our potential for growth seems increasingly limited. And yet despite all the negative news and the predictions of recession, the economy

"Thoughts on the Underground Economy," by Charles J. Haulk is reprinted by permission from *Economic Review* of Federal Reserve Bank of Atlanta, March-April, 1980, pp. 23-27.

shows amazing resilience in the face of lower real incomes, high debt burdens, and rising taxes.

Why have so many highly skilled, well-intentioned students of the economy decided to modify their recession forecasts? Primarily because it is becoming increasingly obvious that the official statistics used in the economic analysis understate growth levels of output and income and overstate the degree of hardship due to unemployment. The reason for the distortion, many economists believe, is the existence of a large and evidently growing underground economy.

What Is the Underground Economy?

The "underground economy" is economic activity that avoids official detection or measurement. Income from this activity is unreported, unmeasured, and untaxed. Persons engaged in producing illegal goods or services, such as bookmaking, smuggling, prostitution, illegal drugs, etc., earn incomes which must be hidden in order to prevent detection of the illegal activity. Crimes, such as robbery, fraud, or embezzlement, are essentially redistributive and do not add to total output.

Persons engaged in otherwise legal production of goods and services but who can in some way cover up part or all of their income and thereby reduce their taxes are also part of the underground economy. Restaurant owners who don't ring up cash sales, the friends who help each other remodel their homes, the painter who paints for cash only and reports whatever income he thinks fit, and the mechanic who fixes his neighbor's car for cash are all examples of underground economic activities.

The underground economy which is accounted for by illegal activity is, by admission of law enforcement officials, a growing sector. Whether the sector is growing faster than the measured economy is not provable. However, much of the activity provided by this sector is services whose demands increase as incomes rise. In that regard, it seems reasonable to argue that income earned from these illicit activities is growing faster than the overall economy.

The underground economy which is accounted for by production of legal goods and services but is done so that income is hidden is probably due to the desire to increase after-tax income. There may be instances of a person hiding income so that a spouse or other interested party would not know the full extent of that person's income.

The income and product in the underground economy generated in the tax-avoiding sector are arguably growing faster than the overall economy. In the simplest economic terms, a person's willingness to participate in the underground economy and thereby engage in the illegal act of under-reporting income is based on his perceptions of the benefits and costs of such an act. When the benefits in terms of after-tax income gained from not reporting income are greater than the costs, then the temptation to underreport income becomes stronger.

The Benefits and Costs of Participating

The benefits are obvious—a higher standard of living with no increase in work effort or considerable gains in wealth can be achieved by more work effort when the tax rate is zero on the income thus earned. The benefits of underpaying taxes will grow relative to income as the tax rate increases. The cost of underpaying taxes is the probability of being caught and convicted multiplied by the punishment for violating the tax laws. Since much of the cost of being caught is the shame and embarrassment of the arrest and trial, that cost is virtually independent of the amount of tax underpayment. As a result, an increase in tax rates as income rises will increase benefits much faster than costs.

Another element that has contributed to an increase in the benefits of underpaying taxes relative to the costs has been a lowering of the public's assessment of the benefits it derives from government spending. This is particularly true in the area of transfer payments (subsidies, aid to the needy, etc.).

Government spending for national security, public safety, public health, and to a lesser degree, education is almost universally accepted. When a large share of tax dollars is used for transfer payments, the degree of taxpayer support dwindles. Because individuals perceive a smaller benefit from growing government spending, their willingness to pay taxes is further reduced.

Evidence of the growing incentive to cheat the tax collector is abundant. In 1950, 25 percent of personal income minus transfer payments went to pay income taxes, sales taxes, etc. By 1960, that figure was 33 percent; in 1970, 41 percent. As of 1979, taxes paid by individuals amounted to 45 percent of personal income minus transfer payments. Granted transfer payments recipients do pay some taxes, however, the rise from 25 percent to 45 percent has been borne mainly by persons who receive no financial assistance from the government. Although not as much as in Great Britain or Sweden, the U.S. taxpayer is increasingly saddled with higher tax rates.

Because it is nearly impossible to avoid property taxes and because not all citizens are property owners, most people who avoid taxes do so primarily by not reporting income. Sales taxes can be avoided, but probably to a much lesser extent, in terms of the total dollars involved, than income taxes.

How Do We Know It's There?

Economic theory very clearly suggests the existence of a growing underground economy. What evidence do we have to support the contention? The fact that participants in the underground are trying to escape detection means that measuring income and product will be extremely difficult and frustrating. Nonetheless, several attempts have been made and other work continues toward that end.

The IRS has made a "direct" estimation of unreported income in 1976 through the use of results obtained on the Taxpayer Compliance Audits, which are far more thorough than the normal audit.[1] Their results indicate that unreported income in 1976 was between $100 and $135 billion, or about 10 percent of measured personal income that year.

The IRS admits, however, that their more rigorous audit cannot track down income for which there are no records kept. Nor is there any good way to estimate the income of nonfilers. Their limited data also did not permit any strong conclusions about trends in noncompliance.

Several writers have tried to estimate the size of the underground economy through indirect means. The first widely publicized attempt by Peter Gutmann[2] was based on certain assumptions about the growth in the use of currency. Gutmann argues that the rapid increase in the amount of currency in circulation relative to the amount of money in checking accounts is indicative of increased use of underground transactions. Gutmann's estimate for 1976 put unmeasured output and income close to 11 percent of measured output.

Continued rapid growth of currency relative to demand deposits since 1976 would make the 1980 underground larger than 11 percent of the measured economy under Gutmann's assumptions. Edgar Feige[3] obtains estimates of total currency and checking account transactions in the economy and, by making certain assumptions regarding the growth in checking account transactions for purely financial purposes, estimates the size of the underground economy. Feige asserts that the unmeasured output in 1976 was as high as 19 percent of total output and, by 1978, was up to 27 percent of total output. His procedure would predict further growth in 1979.

Using a more conservative procedure than Feige, we have estimated that the underground economy grew from 9 percent of reported GNP in 1970 to at least 15 percent of GNP in 1978 (see Appendix). Our procedure assumes that all underground activities are done with cash; Feige does not. None of the estimates mentioned attempts to estimate the role of increased use of barter.

If the underground economy were an unchanging proportion of GNP, we would not need to be terribly concerned with it because it would not distort relationships between important aggregate economic variables (output, income, spending, etc.) over time.

Because our estimates and others show the underground economy to be growing relative to the regular or measured economy, we would expect changes in the measured variables (GNP, income, and employment) to be smaller than the true changes. The effects of the unmeasured forces, then, are expanding.

Effects of the Underground Economy on the Regular Economy

What important effects does the underground economy have on the regular economy, and what are the implications for economic policy?

First, a large and rapidly growing underground economy means that actual income and employment are larger than official statistics show and that resources are more fully utilized than unemployment rates indicate.

Second, because tax is avoided in the underground economy, initially, a lower price will be established for goods and services produced in the underground economy, drawing activity away from the regular economy, a shift unintended by policymakers and perhaps detrimental to long-run economic growth.

Third, those who produce in both the regular and underground economy are likely to be relatively more efficient in their underground pursuit because the after-tax reward is higher per hour of work effort. This would imply that productivity might be higher in an underground industry than in the same field in the regular economy.

Fourth, the fact that a much larger volume of final transactions is being carried out than the GNP figures show means that the estimates of money velocity and velocity increases are too low.[4]

Fifth, a disproportionate share of the tax burden is borne by those who are not engaged in the underground economy.

Sixth, if the share of unmeasured income going to investment or net exports is increasing, it would mean a rise in the savings rate in the unmeasured economy. In turn, this would be consistent with a decline in the measured savings rate while the true overall savings rate was unchanged or fell less than the published figure.

Seventh, because there is no price index for unmeasured activity, we cannot be sure what the inflation rate is in that sector. If the inflation rate is lower in the underground economy, then the rates of inflation reported for the measured economy would substantially overstate real earnings losses.

Finally, all of this suggests that the economic models used for forecasting may well be technically and theoretically deficient.

Policy Implications

These developments clearly have substantial implications for economic policy. To the extent that fiscal and monetary policy is expected to reduce unemployment and raise living standards in the long run, those policies could be massively overstimulative if measured income and employment are understating the true levels. If growth is measured low, in other words, economic policies are likely to be aimed too high—in pursuit of growth which is thought to be missing but is merely unmeasured. Stimulation of aggregate demand would then worsen inflation at a time when resources are, for all practical purposes, fully employed.

Monetary policy might also be deluded into maintaining an overstimulative stance. The setting of money growth rate targets is based on certain assumptions about the way money growth and nominal GNP growth are related. These assumptions are based largely on past performance. A rapid growth in the underground economy would mean that a given rate of money growth is supporting a much larger growth in activity than the monetary policymakers believe. In other words, money growth which policymakers would view as slow enough to restrain growth could, in fact, not be restrictive at all.

What can be done? In the absence of hard data for the underground economy, it would be difficult to try to take it into account precisely in policy formulation. It may be that monetary and fiscal policy will have to focus more on prices and interest rates directly, since data on income, output, and spending have become less reliable.

APPENDIX

In order to estimate the underground economic activity, we start with the assumption that all underground activity uses cash. We then obtain turnover rates for currency, using the Feige assumption that each unit of currency is used, on average, 125 times before it has to be destroyed because it is unfit for circulation. The annual turnover rate is estimated by dividing the average length of the life of currency into 125 to get the number of transactions per bill annually. We then multiply the turnover rate by the outstanding currency in each denomination to obtain the value of total currency transactions.

From 1950 to 1965, the ratio of currency to GNP fell at a rate of 2.9 percent per year. After 1965, the rate of decline was 0.9 percent per year. The decline in currency per dollar of GNP in the 1950s was due to several factors, including growth in the use of demand deposits by consumers. However, with the massive growth in charge cards and other technological advancements, one would expect that the need for currency would continue to decline relative to GNP, at least at the 1950-65 rate.

To estimate illicit transactions involving currency, we calculate the excess of currency in years after 1965 by assuming that without illicit demands for currency, the ratio of currency to GNP would have continued to fall at 2.9 percent annually. The transactions carried out through the use of the excess currency are assumed to be underground activity.

This procedure is very conservative in that it puts underground activities at zero in 1965, which is very doubtful. But our purpose in this article is to show the trend of underground economic growth, so we are not concerned with the absolute levels per se. Using more liberal assumptions, we would get higher levels and faster growth rates.

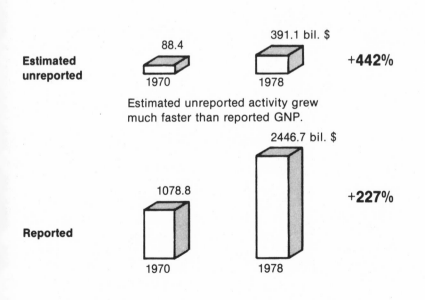

Estimated unreported

88.4
1970

391.1 bil. $
1978

+442%

Estimated unreported activity grew much faster than reported GNP.

2446.7 bil. $
1978

1078.8
1970

+227%

Reported

Endnotes

1. *Estimates of Income Unreported on Individual Tax Returns*, Department of the Treasury, Internal Revenue Service, Publication 1104 (9-79).

2. Peter Gutmann, "The Subterranean Economy," *Financial Analyst Journal* (November/ December 1977).

3. Edgar Feige, "The Irregular Economy: Its Size and Macroeconomic Implications," Working Paper 7916, Social Systems Research Institute.

4. Because money velocity (the average number of times a given monetary unit is spent during a given time period) is based partly on the total amount of spending activity.

43

Inflation
and the American Economy

MARTIN FELDSTEIN

Inflation has unquestionably become the primary economic concern of the American people. After a generation of virtually stable prices, the United States began in the late 1960's a process of gradually accelerating inflation. Between 1948 and 1968, the general price level (as measured by the GNP deflator) rose at an annual rate of only 2.2 percent. But between 1968 and 1980, the rate of price increase was 6.6 percent. And in the most recent two years it was 8.8 percent. It is no wonder therefore that many Americans have begun to fear that inflation is out of control and that the government cannot reduce the rate of inflation.

The increasing rate of inflation during the past 15 years has been accompanied by a declining rate of productivity increase. Output per man hour in the private nonfarm business sector increased between 1948 and 1968 at an average rate of 2.7 percent. In the next dozen years from 1969

Martin Feldstein, "Inflation and the American Economy," a lecture presented at the University of Vienna on March 12, 1981, to inaugurate the Schumpeter Guest Professor Lectureship. The lecture was published in its entirety in *Empirica; Zeitschrift des Österreichischen Institutes für Wirtshaftsforschung*, 2 '81, pp. 155-168. This excerpt is reprinted by the kind permission of the Österreichisches Institut für Wirtschaftsforschung.

through 1980, this measure of productivity declined to only 1.1 percent. And productivity growth has actually been negative in each of the last three years.

The causal relationship between inflation and productivity has not yet been satisfactorily examined. Is concurrent change in productivity merely a coincidence—as much economic theory would suggest—or does high inflation decrease productivity? My own view, as I shall explain in this lecture, is that inflation is far from neutral and has indeed contributed to our productivity decline.

The declining rate of productivity increase has of course been reflected in a slower rate of growth of real incomes and therefore a faltering rise in the standard of living of the typical American. This slowdown in the growth of real income has been exacerbated by the increased relative cost of the things that America imports. The most obvious example is petroleum and other energy prices. Since the United States now imports 6.5 million barrels of oil a day, the 60 percent increase in the real price of oil since 1973 represents a substantial loss of real income—approximately 31 bill. $ a year in aggregate or more than 500 $ for a family of four. More generally, since the weakness of the dollar in relation to the other major currencies has exceeded the relative change in domestic prices, the real cost for our imports has increased and the real value that we receive for our exports has declined. Although exports and imports are only about 12 percent of our GNP, this worsening in our terms of trade has further reduced our standard of living. . . .

1. *Sources of the current inflation*

For a monetarist, a search for the origins of inflation is a very uninteresting search. As Milton Friedman once said, "Inflation is always and everywhere a monetary phenomenon." In an important sense, this is both true and uninformative. It is true because a sustained increase in prices cannot occur without an increase in money. It is uninteresting because it is important to know why the monetary authorities allowed a sustained monetary increase. To prevent inflation it is not enough to lecture the monetary authority on the virtue of monetary restraint. When the central bank chooses, or is compelled by the political system, to respond to certain conditions by expanding money, it is important to know what those conditions are.

In considering these more basic causes of inflation, it is common to emphasize the series of particular events that were associated with spurts of inflation during the past two decades. There is no doubt that if these events had not occurred or had occurred differently, the path of inflation would also have evolved in a different way. Nevertheless, it would be wrong to put too much emphasis on these specific events. The more general tendency toward increasing inflation reflects a more fundamental set of beliefs about the economy and about macroeconomic policy that were shared by economists and policy officials during the past two decades. It is these fundamental beliefs that I want to emphasize after discussing briefly the series of events that catalyzed the accelerating inflation.

2. *The historical record*

From 1962 through 1965, the inflation rate (as measured by the GNP deflator) averaged only 1.8 percent a year. This period had begun with a relatively slack economy characterized by a low rate of capacity utilization and a relatively high rate of unemployment. The Kennedy administration had cut taxes and increased the rate of monetary expansion in 1962, but the substantial slack and the previous stability permitted the rapid expansion of output to occur with little upward pressure on prices.

In contrast, the second half of the 1960's saw an increasing pressure of demand and a rising rate of inflation. Lyndon Johnson was accelerating the war in Vietnam and was expanding rapidly the social welfare expenditures of his Great Society Program. Because the war was politically unpopular, Johnson rejected the advice of his economic counselors and refused to raise taxes. Instead, he permitted the deficit of the federal budget in 1967 to reach a new postwar high. Interest rates were already beginning to rise and, in an attempt to prevent a further rise in response to the increased supply of government debt, the money supply was increased substantially. The result of this was an overexpansion of demand, a fall in the unemployment rate of adult males to only 2 percent and a rise in the inflation rate to 5.2 percent in 1969.

The inflation rate began to subside in 1970 with a significant slump in economic activity in 1971 and 1972. Although the fall in inflation was welcome, the rise in unemployment was not. The government therefore ran a very large deficit and the money supply was increased at a rate that had not previously been seen in the postwar period. By 1973, the unemployment rate dropped to the lowest level since 1969, capacity utilization was again very high, and the inflation rate jumped to 5.7 percent. The sharp jump in energy prices between 1973 and 1974 after the OPEC countries curtailed oil production caused both higher inflation and a general contraction of economic activity. Although money growth was reduced in 1974, it jumped to even higher rates in 1975 and 1976. The government deficit and the unemployment rate also reached new postwar peaks. While other countries like Germany, Austria and Switzerland experienced only a mild and temporary increase in inflation, the U.S. inflation rate spurted to a new high and consumer prices rose more than 10 percent a year.

The Carter administration continued to expand aggregate demand and between 1976 and 1979 the adult male unemployment rate fell by nearly one-third. During these years there were sizable deficits and rapid money growth even though the inflation rate was climbing rapidly from 5.2 percent in 1976 to 8.5 percent in 1979.

The expansion lost momentum in late 1979 in response to the relative decline in the growth of the monetary aggregates (M1B declined 1.2 percent in real terms and the new M2 rose only 0.4 percent) and the surplus in government spending (the small federal deficit being outweighed by the larger surplus of the state and local governments). The recession began in January 1980 and the economy dropped sharply in the second quarter of the year but in June the Federal Reserve Bank reversed direction and the money supply began another period of very rapid growth. Between May and November, M1B grew at an annual rate of 15.5 percent and M2 grew at 14 percent. By the fourth quarter of the year, real GNP was rising very rapidly (an annual rate of increase of 5 percent) and the corresponding price index was increasing at more than 11 percent.

So much for the facts. Our experiences with and after the Vietnam War certainly bear out Schumpeter's warning that "it is of prime importance after a war so to adjust a country's economic process as to stop it from producing further inflation. But it is clear at the same time that this is an extremely difficult thing to do in a world where everybody is afraid of the short-run consequences of such a policy. . . ." But what were the fundamental characteristics of economic thinking during the past two decades that guided the policies that produced our unfortunate inflationary experience?

3. *Four misunderstandings*

In referring to the economic thinking that guided policies I do not mean to imply that the rising rate of inflation was chosen after a rational evaluation of the costs and benefits of alternative policies. I believe that the increasing rate of inflation, like the adverse consequences of a number of other government policies, was largely the unintended and unexpected by-product of well-meaning policies that were adopted without looking beyond their immediate purpose or understanding the magnitudes of their adverse long-run consequences. Expansionary monetary and fiscal policies were adopted throughout the past two decades in an attempt to reduce the unemployment rate but without anticipating the adverse effect on the inflation rate that eventually followed.

It is useful, I think, to distinguish four different kinds of misunderstandings that contributed to these inappropriate policies:

—the misunderstanding of unemployment,
—the misunderstanding of the Phillips curve,
—the misunderstanding of monetary policy and
—the misunderstanding of the cost of inflation.

It was easy enough to misunderstand the nature of unemployment.[1] The Keynesian tradition emphasized the involuntary nature of unemployment and the equivalence of unemployment to inadequate aggregate demand. The high unemployment rates of the early 1960's no doubt did reflect a lack of demand and unemployment did fall without any appreciable effect on inflation.

But by the mid-1960's, the economy had already reached a Keynesian full-employment level or what Friedman later called the natural rate of unemployment. At an unemployment rate of 4 percent, the unemployed were either voluntarily out-of-work or experiencing the kind of unemployment that was not very responsive to increases in aggregate demand. Some of the unemployed were merely in transition between jobs or had just entered or returned to the labor force. Unemployment insurance not only prolonged the period between jobs but also encouraged seasonal and temporary layoffs. More than half of the unemployed were teenagers, a group with relatively weak labor force attachment and weak incentives to find work. Even in the very much overheated economy of 1969, their unemployment rate remained over 12 percent.

The true character of unemployment was not appreciated at the time and monetary and fiscal policy was used to keep the unemployment rate below 4 percent in the second half of the 1960's. The misunderstanding of unemployment continued in the 1970's. The natural rate of unemployment increased in response to the changed demographic composition of the labor force, the more extensive unemployment benefits, the growth of welfare programs with work-registration requirements, and the like. Most experts now agree that an unemployment rate of less than 6.5 percent would currently induce an increasing rate of inflation. This was not recognized and the unemployment rate was driven by expansionary policies to 6.0 percent in 1978 and 5.8 percent in 1979, with the result that inflation accelerated from 5.8 percent in 1977 to 9.0 percent in 1980.

Closely related to the mistaken perception of unemployment was the misunderstanding about the Phillips curve. Soon after the British economist, A. W. Phillips published in 1958 his famous statistical relationship between inflation and unemployment, it was seized upon on both sides of the ocean as offering a stable menu of policy options. One could have low inflation and high unemployment or higher inflation and low unemployment. In 1960, two of the leading figures of American economics, Paul Samuelson and Robert Solow, presented an American version of the Phillips curve. Although they noted that it was neither as favorable nor as apparently stable as the British version, their presentation helped to make the Phillips curve a basic tool of policy analysis in the 1960's. Faced with the trade-off implied by the statistical Phillips curve, many economists and politicians concluded that it made good sense to accept a permanently higher inflation rate to get the benefits of a lower rate of unemployment.

We now recognize the deceptive nature of the Phillips curve, and understand that the apparent trade-off between unemployment and inflation is only a temporary or short-run relationship. Over a period of even a few years, it is not possible to lower unemployment by accepting a higher rate of inflation. Although unemployment can be *temporarily* reduced by accepting an *increase* in the rate of inflation, the higher rate of inflation soon gets built into the expectations of all market participants. Even when the excess demand is eliminated, the higher inflationary expectations keep the actual inflation rate at a higher level. Any further temporary reduction in unemployment requires a further increase in the built-in inflation rate. And reducing that established rate of inflation apparently requires a period of unemployment during which first the actual rate of inflation falls and then inflationary expectations are gradually reversed.

The attempt by governments during the 1960's and 1970's to move "up" the Phillips curve to lower unemployment and higher inflation was therefore repeatedly frustrated. Inflation rates rose while unemployment was only temporarily lowered. In the end, the misunderstanding of the Phillips curve has contributed to a much higher inflation rate. Moreover, by focusing employment policy on aggregate demand management instead of on removing distortions in the labor market, the Phillips curve also caused the unemployment rate to remain higher than necessary and than it might otherwise be.

The third misperception that has contributed to the inflationary policies has been the misunderstanding of the interaction between monetary policy and tax rules. I want to discuss this subject more fully and shall return to do so in a moment. Now I will just note that, because the monetary authorities and their critics ignored the taxation of interest income and the tax deduction of interest payments, they believed that the cost of credit was high and rising when it was in fact low and falling. The monetary authorities therefore expanded the money supply in an attempt to ease credit conditions when credit was already too cheap. The reasons for this misunderstanding and the consequences for the pattern of expenditures is the subject that I will address in a moment.

First, however, I want to comment on the fourth and final misunderstanding that caused macroeconomic policy to be too stimulative: the misunderstanding of the adverse consequences of inflation. The leading American economists of the 1960's and 1970's did not echo Joseph Schumpeter's warning that inflation would weaken the social framework or Friedrich Hayek's warning that inflation would create imbalances that could only be corrected by a major contraction. Far from it, the opponents of inflation like Milton Friedman pointed only to the resulting reduction in the use of non-interest-bearing money balances which James Tobin derisively dismissed as mere shoe-leather costs. This attitude that the costs of inflation were minimal no doubt contributed to the feeling that a reduction in unemployment was worth-while even if it raised the rate of inflation.

What in fact have been the costs of inflation in the United States? I have already mentioned the uncertainty and anxiety that the volatile inflation rate has caused. The inability to make long-term financial plans affected not only individuals but also businesses and no doubt caused both individuals and companies to make choices that promised short-run and relatively certain rewards instead of longer-term and potentially more productive options. For individuals, this meant a reduced rate of personal saving and the allocation of personal investment to gold and other potential "stores of value." For businesses, this meant forgoing long-lived projects in favor of short-term investments in equipment or in the acquisition of existing businesses. Special problems were also created for banks, thrift institutions and insurance companies that held large portfolios of nominal assets with fixed interest rates.

The most direct effect of inflation was to reduce the rate of return on investments in plant and equipment. The primary reason for this has been that the tax law and inflation interact to raise the effective tax rate on the profits earned on investments in plant and equipment and thereby to reduce the net-of-tax rate of return on such investments. This increase in the effective tax rate reflects the use by firms of the "historic cost" or "original cost" method of depreciating plant and equipment for tax purposes and the "first-in-first-out" method of calculating the value of inventories. Both of these accounting methods have the effect of understating the cost of production and therefore overstating the amount of profits on which tax must be paid. In 1977, the extra tax was 35 bill. $ and raised the total tax on the income of non-financial corporations by 50 percent.[2] By 1980 the effect was undoubtedly larger both absolutely and in relation to true economic profits.

More generally, inflation raised the total tax rate on the capital income of nonfinancial corporations that is paid by the corporations themselves, their shareholders and their creditors. In the mid-1960's, before the inflation rate began to accelerate, the individuals and institutions who provided capital to nonfinancial corporations received 45 percent of the pre-tax return to capital after all taxes had been paid. By 1979, this 45 percent had been reduced to less than 31 percent. This increase in the effective tax rate happened because of the interaction between inflation and the existing tax rules since the statutory tax rates on this investment income were actually reduced during these years.

The reduced rate of return on investments in plant and equipment had the predictable effect of reducing investment in those assets. The value of net investment in plant and equipment was about one-third lower in the second half of the 1970's than it had been in the previous 15 years. Although some part of this decline reflects the generally weak economy, statistical evidence indicates that the low after-tax rate of return was the primary reason.[3]

Experts on productivity agree that the reduced rate of growth of the capital stock was one of the reasons for the substantial slowdown in productivity growth to which I referred earlier. It thus seems quite likely that the high and uncertain rate of inflation, by reducing the rate of business investment and channelling a disproportionate share of that investment into short-lived assets did indeed contribute to the decline of productivity in recent years.

I do not believe that this exhausts the list of the adverse effects of our inflation or even that all such effects have become visible. If the inflation continues or accelerates, new consequences will emerge. But my main concern here is not to catalog or foretell all such consequences but only to emphasize that these costs of inflation have been misunderstood and underestimated and that this misperception contributed to the inflationary character of macroeconomic policies in the past two decades.

4. *Tax rules and the mismanagement of monetary policy*

This brings me back to the issue that I postponed for later discussion: the way in which ignoring the fiscal structure of the economy caused a misunderstanding and mismanagement of monetary policy.[4] As I noted a moment ago, I believe that the monetary authorities' failure to recognize the implications of the fiscal structure caused them to underestimate just how expansionary monetary policy has been. Moreover, because of our fiscal structure, attempts to encourage investment by an easy-money policy have actually had an adverse impact on investment in plant and equipment. The prescription of "easy money and a tight fiscal position" that has been the conventional wisdom of American economic policy for at least two decades has been an unfortunate guide for macroeconomic policy.

To understand the nature of this misperception, it is useful to recall that until 1951 there was an agreement between the Treasury and the Federal Reserve System to peg the short-term rate of interest at a low value. During the postwar period, when the agreement was in effect, the 3-month Treasury bill rate remained at less than 1.5 percent and the yield on long-term corporate BAA bonds remained at less than 4 percent. But even in the dozen years after this formal policy was abandoned, the yield on BAA bonds varied only in the narrow range between 3.5 percent and 5 percent. In contrast the 15 years that followed saw that rate rise from less than 5 percent in 1964 to more than 12 percent at the end of 1979. It is perhaps not surprising therefore that the monetary authorities, other government officials, and many private economists worried throughout this period that interest rates might be getting "too high." Critics of what was perceived as "tight money" argued that such high interest rates would reduce investment and therefore depress aggregate demand.

Against all this it could be argued, and was argued, that the *real* interest rate had obviously gone up much less. The correct measure of the real interest rate is of course the difference between the nominal interest rate and the rate of inflation that is *expected* over the life of the bond. A common rule of thumb approximates the expected future inflation by the average inflation rate experienced during the preceding three years. In 1964, when the BAA rate was 4.8 percent, this three-year rise in the GNP deflator averaged 1.6 percent; the implied real interest rate was thus 3.2 percent. By the end of 1979, when the BAA rate was 12.0 percent, the rise in the GNP deflator for the previous 3 years had increased to 7.8 percent, implying a real interest rate of 4.2 percent. Judged in this way, the cost of credit had also increased significantly over the 15-year period.

All of this ignores the role of taxes. Since interest expenses can be deducted by individuals and business in calculating taxable income, the net-of-tax interest cost is very much less than the interest rate itself. Indeed, since the *nominal* interest expense can be deducted, the real net-of-tax interest cost has actually varied inversely with the *nominal* rate of interest. *What appears to have been a rising interest rate over the past 25 years was actually a sharply falling real after-tax cost of funds.* The failure to recognize the role of taxes prevented the monetary authorities from seeing how expansionary monetary policy had become.

The implication of tax deductibility is seen most easily in the case of owner-occupied housing. A married couple with a 30,000 $ taxable income now has a marginal federal income tax rate of 37 percent. The 11.4 percent mortgage rate in effect in the last quarter of 1979 implied a net-of-tax cost of funds of 7.2 percent. Subtracting a 7.8 percent estimate of the rate of inflation (based on a three-year average increase in the GNP deflator) leaves a real net-of-tax cost of funds of *minus* 0.6 percent. By comparison, the 4.8 percent interest rate for 1964 translates into a 3.0 percent net-of-tax rate and a 1.4 percent real net-of-tax cost of funds. Thus, although the nominal interest rate had more than doubled and the real interest rate had also increased substantially, the relevant net-of-tax real cost of funds had actually fallen from 1.4 percent to a *negative* 0.6 percent.

As this example shows, taking the effects of taxation into account is particularly important because the tax rules are so non-neutral when there is inflation. If the tax rules were completely indexed, the effect of the tax system on the conduct of monetary policy would be much less significant. But with existing tax rules, the movements of the pre-tax real interest rate and of the after-tax real interest rate are completely different. Monetary policy in the last decade was so expansionary in large part because the monetary authorities and others believed that the cost of funds was rising or steady when in fact it was falling significantly.

The fall in the real after-tax interest rate has caused a rapid increase in the price of houses relative to the general price level and has sustained a high rate of new residential construction. There were, of course, times when the ceilings on the interest rates that financial institutions could pay caused disintermediation and limited the funds available for housing. To that extent, the high level of nominal interest rates restricted the supply of funds at the same time that the corresponding low real after-tax interest cost increased the demand for funds. More recently, the raising of certain interest rate ceilings and the development of mortgage-backed bonds that can short-circuit the disintermediation process have made the supply restrictions much less important and have therefore made any interest level more expansionary than it otherwise would have been.

The low real after-tax rate of interest has also encouraged the growth of consumer credit and the purchase of consumer durables. It is not surprising that, with a negative real net rate of interest, house mortgage borrowing has soared to over 90 bill. $ a year, more than double the rate in the early 1970's. More generally, even households that do not itemize their tax deductions are affected by the low real after-tax return that is available on savings. Because individuals pay tax on nominal interest income, the real after-tax rate of return on savings has become negative. It seems likely that this substantial fall in the real return on savings has contributed to the fall in the personal saving rate and the rise in consumer demand.

The analysis is more complex for corporations because inflation changes the effective tax rate on investments as well as the real net-of-tax interest rate. More specifically, because historic cost depreciation and inventory accounting rules reduce substantially the real after-tax return on corporate investments, an easy-money policy raises the demand for corporate capital only if the real net cost of funds falls by more than the return that firms can afford to pay. This balance between the lower real net interest cost and the lower real net return on investment depends on the corporation's debt-equity ratio and on the relation between the real yields that must be paid on debt and on equity funds. Although it is difficult to say just what has happened on balance, I believe expansionary monetary policy reduced the demand for business investment at the same time that it increased the demand for residential investment and for consumption goods.

It is useful to contrast the conclusion of this section with the conventional Keynesian analysis. According to the traditional view, monetary expansion lowers interest rates which reduces the cost of funds to investors and therefore encourages the accumulation of plant and equipment. In the context of the U.S. economy in recent years, this statement is wrong in three ways. First, a sustained monetary expansion raises nominal interest rates. Second, although the interest rate is higher, the real net-of-tax cost of funds is lower. And, third, the lower cost of funds produced in this way encourages investment in housing and consumer durables (as well as greater consumption in general) rather than more investment in plant and equipment. Indeed, because of the interaction of tax rules and inflation, a monetary expansion tends to discourage saving and reduce investment in plant and equipment. The low real net-of-tax rate of interest on mortgages and consumer credit is an indication of this misallocation of capital.

Perhaps the problems of misinterpretation and mismanagement might have been avoided completely if the monetary authorities and others in the financial community, as well as the Congress and the economics profession, had ignored interest rates completely and focused their attention on the money supply and the credit aggregates. Presumably, under current Federal Reserve procedures, there will be more of a tendency to do just that. But since the temptation to look at rates as well is very powerful, it is important to interpret the rates correctly. What matters for the household borrower or saver is the real net-of-tax interest rate. A very low or negative real net-of-tax rate is a clear signal of an incentive to overspend on housing and on other forms of consumption. What matters for the business firm is the difference between the real net-of-tax cost of funds (including both debt and equity) and the maximum return that, with existing tax laws, it can afford to pay. The difficulty of measuring this difference should be a warning against relying on any observed rates to judge the ease or tightness of credit for business investment.

5. *The mix of monetary and fiscal policies*

Since past policies have failed, what should be done? There is widespread agreement on the two central goals for macroeconomic policy: achieving a level of aggregate demand that avoids both unemployment and inflation, and increasing the share of national income that is devoted to business investment. Monetary and fiscal policies provide two instruments with which to achieve these two goals. The conventional Keynesian view of the economy has led to the prescription of easy money (to encourage investment) and a tight fiscal policy (to limit demand and prevent inflation). Our low rate of investment and high rate of inflation indicate that this approach has not worked. It is useful to review both the way such a policy is supposed to work and the reason why it fails.

Keynesian analysis, based on a theory developed during and for the depression, is designed for an economy with substantial slack and essentially fixed prices. This Keynesian perspective implies that real output can be expanded by increasing demand and that the policy mix determines how this increased output is divided between investment, consumption and government spending. An increase in the money supply favors investment while a fiscal expansion favors consumption or government spending. Whatever the validity of this analysis in an economy with vast excess capacity and fixed prices, it has not been appropriate for the U.S. economy in recent years.

There is a way in which a policy mix of easy money and fiscal tightness could in principle work in our relatively fully-employed economy. The key requirement would be a persistent government surplus. Such a surplus would permit the government to reduce the supply of outstanding government debt. This in turn would induce households and institutions to substitute additional private bonds and stocks for the government debt that was removed from their portfolios. The result would be an increased rate of private capital accumulation. Under likely conditions, this substitution of private capital for government debt would require a lower rate of interest and a relative increase in the stock of money.

Unfortunately, the traditional prescription of easy money and a tight fiscal position has failed in practice because of the political difficulty of achieving and maintaining a government surplus.[5] As a result, the pursuit of an easy-money policy has produced inflation. Although the inflationary increase in the money supply did reduce the real after-tax cost of funds, this only diverted the flow of capital away from investment in plant and equipment and into owner-occupied housing and consumer durables. By reducing the real net return to savers, the easy-money policy has probably also reduced the total amount of new saving.

The traditional policy mix reflects not only its optimistic view about the feasibility of government surpluses but also its overly narrow conception of the role of fiscal policy. In the current macroeconomic tradition, fiscal policy has been almost synonymous with variations in the net government surplus or deficit and has generally ignored the potentially powerful incentive effects of taxes that influence marginal prices.

An alternative policy mix for achieving the dual goals of balanced demand and increased business investment would combine a tight-money policy and fiscal incentives for investment and saving. A tight-money policy would prevent inflation and would raise the real net-of-tax rate of interest. Although the higher real rate of interest would tend to deter all forms of residential and nonresidential investment, specific incentives for investment in plant and equipment could more than offset the higher cost of funds. The combination of the higher real net interest rate and the targeted investment incentives would restrict housing construction and the purchase of consumer durables while increasing the flow of capital into new plant and equipment. Since housing and consumer durables now account for substantially more than half of the private capital stock, such a restructuring of the investment mix could have a substantial favorable effect on the stock of plant and equipment.

A rise in the overall saving rate would permit a greater increase in business investment. The higher real net rate of interest would in itself tend to induce such a higher rate of saving. This could be supplemented by explicit fiscal policies that reduced the tax rate on interest income and other income from saving.

In short, restructuring macroeconomic policy to recognize the importance of fiscal incentives and of the current interaction between tax rules and inflation provides a way of both reducing the rate of inflation and increasing the growth of the capital stock.

Endnotes

1. For a fuller description of this, see Feldstein, M., "Economics of the New Unemployment," *The Public Interest*, 1973.

2. See Feldstein, M., Summers, L., "Inflation and the Taxation of Capital Income in the Corporate Sector," *National Tax Journal*, 1979.

3. Feldstein, M., "Inflation, Tax Rules and Investment," *Econometrica*, 1982.

4. This section incorporates material previously discussed in a paper presented at the 1979 meeting of the American Economic Association and that was published in the May 1980 *American Economic Review*. See also my "Inflation, Capital Taxation and Monetary Policy," in Hall, R., (ed.), *Inflation* (University of Chicago Press, 1982).

5. It might be argued that the inflationary erosion of the real government debt means that the government has in fact had real surpluses even though nominal deficits. But such an inflation adjustment also implies an equal reduction in private saving, indicating that private saving has in fact been negative. The conventional government deficit should also be augmented by the off-budget borrowing and the growth of government unfunded obligations in the social security, and civil service and military service pension programs.

44

The Economics
of Women's Liberation

BARBARA R. BERGMANN

It will take a lot of changes if equal participation in the American economy for women is to become a reality. In the feminists' vision of a better future there would be, with few exceptions, no "men's occupation"; women would get equal pay for equal work; they would do less unpaid work at home, and men would do more. I want to consider two sets of issues concerning the postliberation world. First, I shall explore the nature and strength of the economic forces blocking the way to the development of a world in which women would have (and would take advantage of) equal opportunities for paid work. Second, I shall try to describe some of the changes in economic and social arrangements which a more equal participation of women in the economy and a more equal participation of men in the home would entail.

"The Economics of Women's Liberation," by Barbara R. Bergmann, *Challenge; The Magazine of Economic Affairs*, May-June, 1973, pp. 11-17, is reprinted with the permission of the publisher, M.E. Sharpe, Inc., Armonk, New York, 10504.

What's Blocking Women's Liberation?

Aside from inertia, there are four factors that have been alleged to be at work to keep things as they are: (1) discrimination against women in employment and promotion due to male prejudice or malevolence; (2) inferior job performance by women; (3) the disinclination of many women to enter into what they view as men's roles; and (4) the profits to be made by business from keeping women in their present roles. Not all of these factors are of equal importance, as we shall see.

When we speak of employer prejudice against women we generally do not mean feelings of hatred or a desire to refrain from association with them. After all, most men are very glad to have a woman secretary right outside their office door. The most important manifestation of employer prejudice against women is a desire to restrict them to spheres which are viewed as proper for them. Everybody knows which jobs are "fit" for women: domestic and light factory work for the least educated ones; clerical and retail sales work for the high-school graduates and even some of the college graduates; and teaching, nursing, and social work for those with professional inclinations. We must look to the future researches of psychologists and sociologists to tell us why human beings enjoy enforcing and conforming to occupational segregation along sex (and racial) lines, and how the occupations "belonging" to each group are selected. But the enjoyment is clearly there. In Aldous Huxley's *Brave New World*—a novel truly remarkable for the number of ominous tendencies to which it correctly called attention—each occupation is performed by genetically identical persons in identical uniforms. Huxley was satirizing not only the misuse of science and the inhumanity of the drive for efficiency but also the strong human liking for castes in economic life.

The economist Victor R. Fuchs of the National Bureau of Economic Research, who is one of the pioneers in research on women's role in the labor market, finds occupational segregation by sex to be far more extreme than occupational segregation by race. In a 1970 study he says, ". . . one of the most striking findings is how few occupations employ large numbers of both sexes. Most men work in occupations that employ very few women and a significant fraction of women work in occupations that employ very few men." Fuchs attributes occupational segregation and the low pay for women it entails largely to the conditioning of women by society to avoid certain fields. A later study, by Malcolm Cohen of the University of Michigan, attributes most of the pay differences between men and women to "barriers to the entry of women into employment in higher paying jobs."

Up to now, the relative importance of discrimination in filling these high paying jobs and the relative importance of women's failure to compete for them in explaining occupational segregation by sex have not really been carefully measured by anyone. In the end, it may prove statistically impossible to separate out the precise importance of the various factors. However, there is considerable evidence that discrimination is far from a negligible factor. Much of the evidence is anecdotal, but no less real for being so.

The economic results of occupational segregation for women are low wages. Women are relegated for the most part to those occupations in which experience adds very little to the status and productivity of the worker as she advances in age. After a year or two a secretary is about as good as she will ever be, while her junior executive boss, who may have the same formal education as she, continues to gain in confidence, knowledge and technical competence, and of course makes commensurate advances in pay.

Since the boundaries separating the men's occupational preserve from the women's are economically speaking artificial and not easily changed, the women's preserve may tend to get overcrowded, especially if the proportion of women in the labor force increases. This is exactly what has been occurring. Between 1950 and 1970, the number of men working increased by 15 percent, while the number of women working increased by 70 percent (see Table 1).

Into what kinds of jobs did these women go? Because of employer discrimination and their own limited horizons, millions of them went into the traditional women's preserve—clerical work. In that 20-year period, there was a very great increase in the number of women clerical workers: they more than doubled their numbers. About one quarter of women workers were in the clerical category in 1950, and by 1970 more than one in three working women were clerical workers. There was no change in the nature of the economy to require such a dramatic upsurge in clerical employment. On the contrary, computerization tends to reduce the demand for clerks. These extra women were absorbed through the classic mechanism of a flexible economy—clerks lost ground in pay, and took on lower-priority work. That clerical jobs of the type filled by women became relatively overcrowded is shown by the fact that, during this period, wage rates in this relatively poorly paid occupation lagged still farther behind all other occupational groups for men and women (see last column of Table 1).

Interestingly, some progress apparently was made in the professional and technical group and the service worker group during the fifties and sixties. Women increased their representation in these occupations substantially, yet enjoyed better than average increases in pay rates. I take this as evidence of expanding demand for women in these fields, possibly

(Continued on page 480)

Table 1: **Employed persons by major occupation group and sex, 1950 and 1970**

Major occupation group	Employed persons (thousands of persons) 1950	1970	Percent change, 1950-70	Percent of total, 1950	Percent of total, 1970
Men					
Professional and technical workers	2,696	6,890	+155.6	6.4	14.2
Managers, officials and proprietors	5,439	6,896	+ 26.8	12.9	14.2
Clerical workers	3,035	3,497	+ 15.2	7.2	7.2
Sales workers	2,379	2,724	+ 14.5	5.6	5.6
Craftsmen and foremen	7,482	9,737	+ 30.1	17.7	20.0
Operatives	8,810	9,539	+ 8.3	20.9	19.6
Nonfarm laborers	3,435	3,499	+ 1.9	8.1	7.2
Private household workers	125	26	− 79.2	0.3	0.1
Other service workers	2,560	3,185	+ 24.4	6.1	6.5
Farmworkers	6,196	2,692	− 56.6	14.7	5.5
Total men	42,156	48,686	+ 15.3	100.0	100.0
Women					
Professional and technical workers	1,794	4,431	+147.0	10.3	14.9
Managers, officials and proprietors	990	1,301	+ 31.4	5.7	4.4

Clerical workers	4,597	10,337	+124.9	26.3	34.8
Sales workers	1,443	1,990	+ 37.9	8.2	6.7
Craftsmen and foremen	188	290	+ 54.3	1.1	1.0
Operatives	3,336	4,272	+ 28.1	19.1	14.4
Nonfarm laborers	84	115	+ 36.9	0.5	0.4
Private household workers	1,758	1,559	– 11.3	10.0	5.2
Other service workers	2,092	4,954	+136.8	12.0	16.7
Farmworkers	1,212	472	– 61.1	6.9	1.6
Total women	17,493	29,722	+ 69.6	100.0	100.0

Source: U.S. Bureau of the Census, *Statistical Abstract of the United States, 1970* (91st ed.), Washington, D.C.: U.S. Government Printing Office, 1970, p. 225.

(Continued from page 477)

involving some desegregation of employment in the particular jobs which make up these two large occupational groups.

Allegations concerning women's inferior job performance center on the lower commitment of some women to the labor market. Many women do leave jobs for prolonged periods to give birth to and take care of babies, or to follow their husbands to another city. At any given age they have less work experience, on the average, than men of the same age. A great deal has been made of women's relative lack of experience, but the truth is that in the kinds of jobs women are mostly consigned to, experience counts for very little in terms of skill or pay.

Women have been quitting jobs at a higher rate than men (the latest figures, for 1968, show quit rates of 2.6 percent per month for women in manufacturing and 2.2 percent for men). But calculations by Professor Isabel Sawhill of Goucher College indicate that about half of the gap in quit rates is due to the fact that women are heavily employed in the kinds of occupations in which *men and women* tend to quit more often, whereas men are heavily employed in the kinds of jobs in which stability of employment is rewarded.

Unfortunately, the women dropouts give all women a bad name in the labor market. Unless the liberationists can succeed in making maternity leaves of more than three weeks unfashionable (as the bearing of three or more children has recently become unfashionable), the women who do want equality with men are going to continue to suffer guilt by association. There will also have to be a decrease in the propensity of men to accept a job in another city without consideration of the effect on their wives' careers.

We come finally to the allegation, usually made by radicals out to discredit capitalism, that women's subjection is all a capitalist plot. Who benefits financially from maintenance of the *status quo*? The most obvious beneficiaries of prejudice against women are male workers in those occupations in which women are not allowed to compete. This lack of competition raises pay and in certain circumstances may reduce unemployment in an occupation largely reserved for males. Of course, wives who have a stay-at-home ideology also gain when women are excluded from their husbands' occupations. This undoubtedly accounts for some of the social pressure against women's liberation.

It is not the male workers or their wives who do the discriminating, however. The employers of the male workers (almost entirely males themselves) are the ones who do the actual discriminating, although of course they are cheered on in their discriminatory ways by their male employees. The employers actually tend to lose financially, since profits are lowered when cheap female help is spurned in favor of high-priced male help. Thus, good strategy for the women's movement would be to fight against the exclusion of women from "men's jobs" and leave the equal-pay-for-equal-work battle until the former fight was won, by which time the pay issue might have solved itself. Whatever losses there are to discriminating employers are in all probability not very large. However, profits to discriminating employers from discriminating hiring cannot possibly be an important roadblock in the way of nondiscriminatory treatment for women.

Will capitalism collapse if women don't stay home and spend their time purchasing consumer goods? In fact, women who stay home are a poorer market for capitalist enterprise's products than women who go to work. Women who stay at home bake cakes and make dresses. Women who go to work patronize bakeries and dress shops more. A woman who leaves the home for a job will undoubtedly spend less time thinking about and seeking the detergent that will leave her clothes whiter than white, but she will probably buy the same amount of detergent, unless she starts patronizing a commercial laundry, in which case it will be the laundry that buys the detergent. Some nonworking women do make a career out of shopping and spend a great deal of money on items of doubtful utility, but the spending tendencies of most of these women would probably not be significantly reformed if they went to work. It is true that they would have to spend more dollars per hour, but they and their spendthrift male counterparts would have plenty of hours left, as we shall see.

To sum up, discrimination against women is an important factor in keeping women segregated by occupation and earning low pay. This discrimination does not by and large serve the economic ends of those who do the discriminating, although it does benefit male employees. The financial gains to those who do the discriminating are low or negative. The major cause served is psychological (it feels so good to have women in their "place"). The cavalier attitudes and low expectations of many women themselves concerning their paid work are also probably important, and may help to rationalize some employer taboos against hiring women for occupations (such as executive) in which a considerable investment in on-the-job training by the employer is called for. In short, for the postliberation world to arrive, women's attitudes must be liberated, employers' attitudes must be liberated; but we may be able to do without a revolution which overthrows capitalism.

What Would the Postliberation Economy Look Like?

The success of the women's liberation movement would mean a radical reduction in the division of labor by sex, both inside and outside the home. It is difficult to imagine a "women's liberation" which did not include greater participation and success for women in the economy. Some of the ideologues of the movement have emphasized that postliberation woman should not adopt the aggressive habits of preliberation man, but it is difficult to envision success for women in the economic spheres from which they have been hitherto excluded without at least some movement in that direction.

The economic consequences of those changes in habit of both women and men which would constitute "women's liberation" would be enormous. We can assume it would be customary for all women who are not students to do paid work outside the home and for all men to do as much unpaid work inside the home as women will do. Both in paid employment and in unpaid work at home there would be an end to the stereotyping of occupations and tasks as suited for men or for women only.

One obvious consequence would be a large increase in the size of the labor force in paid work. If women had participated in the labor force to the degree that men of their age group did in 1970, the labor force would have been 30 percent larger than it was. . . . Certainly, a rapid growth of the labor force by anything like that extent would create grave problems of digestion for the economy, but the change in habits and the growth of the labor force are both likely to be gradual.

Gradual or not, any important increase in the size of the labor supply tends to create downward pressures on wage rates, and to raise profits. I would expect, however, that the increase in the number of persons on the labor market would be at least partially balanced by a fall in the number of hours worked, so that the labor supply in terms of person-hours might increase a great deal less than 30 percent. If the fall in the workweek just balanced the increase in persons working, we would have a 31-hour workweek (for both men and women, of course). This might work out to five six-hour days per week or to four eight-hour days. Quite obviously, both working men and working women would have more time than they now do to enjoy the pleasures of domestic life; and those wives who changed over from full-time housewifery to "full-time work" would experience less of a wrench than they would have to under the present 40-hours-per-week regime in paid work.

One of the most dramatic effects of women's liberation would be the change in the size and pay of occupations from which women had been excluded or had excluded themselves. Assuming, for example, that the number of places in medical schools will in the future be responsive to the number of qualified applicants, the number of physicians might in time double, and the income of physicians would surely come down at least relatively. The benefits to nonphysicians in terms of better services and cheaper health care are quite obvious. The financial losses to the present members of the medical profession (and their stay-at-home wives) are also obvious, but even they might enjoy the shorter workweek and lower patient load.

After a discussion of women as physicians it is only fair to discuss women as streetcleaners. The Soviet Union is always held up as a horrible example of what happens when women's liberation is tried; we have all seen the pictures of elderly women, scarves tied around their heads, sweeping the streets in the Moscow winter. These pictures and their captions are supposed to make us feel sorry for these women in a way we would not feel sorry for male streetcleaners. But I don't think we should shrink from the notion of streetcleaning as an occupation appropriate to the physically fit of both sexes. Streetcleaning is probably healthier and more interesting than clerical work; and when these jobs are well paid, they are much sought after.

Professor Estelle James of Stony Brook made some calculations of the effect on wage rates that a relaxation of occupational segregation by sex would entail. She assumed that women would compete on an equal footing with men of the same educational achievement. Occupations having similar requirements in terms of education, intelligence, skill, and experience would not have different pay scales, as they now do, depending on whether they are in the men's or women's preserve. Occupations previously reserved for women, which currently command low pay, would shrink in size as the rate of pay in them rose. Women would shift to those occupations previously reserved for men, which would increase in size, and which would experience a fall in pay. For example, in jobs held by those with a high-school diploma or better, she estimates that previously male occupations would increase in size by almost 15 percent and that wage rates in these occupations would decrease by about 15 percent. Employment in previously female occupations would be cut about 35 percent, and the pay would increase about 55 percent. Let me hasten to add that the decreases in wage rates projected for men would in actuality be translated in most cases into low or zero rates of increase, because the transition would occur only gradually and would be mitigated by increases in productivity. Despite this fact, Professor James' calculations suggest that women's liberation would bring a radical change in the lineup of occupational wage rates.

One of the benefits of the achievement of women's liberation would be a reduction in the incidence of poverty. One-third of poverty families are those the Census Bureau defines as "headed by women." When a man leaves his family or dies, the family loses the worker who was discriminated against least. The low pay of most of the jobs open to women means that when the woman goes out to work she has a poor chance of earning an income above the poverty level. The boring nature of many of these jobs, plus the lack of incentive that the low pay entails, induces may women who have lost their husbands through separation or death to languish at home on welfare payments. Thus, in the United States, discrimination against women combined with a high incidence of marital instability has helped to increase the incidence of poverty. We have estimated that about two-thirds of the poverty among black and/or female-headed families in which the head of the family works is due to discrimination.

The achievement of women's liberation obviously involves changed distribution of work in the home. Arrangements may be made for outside paid help in cooking, dishwashing, shopping, child care, and cleaning chores, but family members are still going to have to do a considerable amount of unpaid domestic work. Norton Dodge's monumental study *Women in the Soviet Economy* shows that Soviet men have taken over some of the housework, but probably far from a fair share of it. Russian men who work an eight-hour day spend an average of one and a half hours a day on household chores, whereas women who work an eight-hour day spend three and seven-tenths hours a day on such chores.

In the United States, one effect of greater participation in paid employment for women might very well be an increase in the popularity of communal living arrangements. In addition to the virtue of broadening the companionship of the family circle, such arrangements take advantage of economies of scale in meal preparation and child care.

But all of this is, so far as I can see, grossly unlikely. If the current level of interest in women's liberation were to continue for decades, then the transformations I have been describing would occur. But that is a very big "if." In the meantime, individual women who want to do work other than full-time unpaid domestic labor will just have to go on bucking the prejudice of employers, fighting their own laziness and sense of insufficiency, and nagging their husbands to help them with the dishes.

45

The Female-Male Earnings Gap: A Review of Employment and Earnings Issues

JANET L. NORWOOD

In the last 20 years, a profound change has occurred in the labor force participation of women. The unprecedented entry of large numbers of women into the Nation's work force and the sustained commitment to gainful employment have brought about a revolution in male-female relationships in the workplace. In 1960, only a little more than 23 million women (38 percent of the population) were in the labor force. Today, that number is more than twice that level and the labor force participation rate has risen to 53 percent (Table 1).

Janet L. Norwood, *The Female-Male Earnings Gap: A Review of Employment and Earnings Issues*, U.S. Department of Labor, Bureau of Labor Statistics, Report #673 (September, 1982). Ms. Norwood, Commissioner of Labor Statistics, U.S. Department of Labor presented this statement at The Pay Equity Hearings before the Committee on Post Office and Civil Service, Subcommittee on Human Resources, Civil Service, and Compensation and Employee Benefits, U.S. House of Representatives, September 16, 1982. Ms. Norwood acknowledges the contribution of Elizabeth Waldman and B. K. Atrostic in the preparation of the report. Reprinted by permission of U.S. Department of Labor, Bureau of Labor Statistics.

Table 1: **Women in the population and labor force, annual averages, selected years, 1960-82**

(Numbers in thousands)

Year	Civilian noninstitutional population	Labor force Number	Labor force As percent of population (rate)
1960	61,582	23,240	37.7
1965	66,731	26,200	39.3
1970	72,782	31,543	43.3
1975	80,860	37,475	46.3
1980	88,348	45,487	51.5
1981	89,618	46,696	52.1
1982 (Second quarter)	90,621	47,707	52.6

Along with this increase in the number of working women have come far-reaching social changes, as well as structural changes in the very nature of work itself. Over the past two decades, the work force has become younger, marital patterns have changed, fertility rates have dropped, and women have increasingly sought higher education. In addition, landmark equal pay and antidiscrimination requirements have been enacted into law, tax legislation has provided for some deductions for child-care expenses, and the employment shift from goods-producing to service-producing industries has accelerated.

It is important to recognize that young women (25 to 34 years old) accounted for almost half (47 percent) of the increase in the number of female workers between 1970 and 1980. Today, 53 percent of the female work force is under age 35, compared with 38 percent in 1960.

Increasingly, women are obtaining the education to qualify them for a broader range of jobs, especially those requiring training past the high school level. In 1970, only 28 percent of working women ages 25 to 34—the most active group in the labor market in the last 10 years—had completed at least 1 year of college. By 1980, that figure had grown to 46 percent.

Family Status

The change in marital and family patterns has been an even greater departure from the past, when it was generally expected that young women would marry and devote most of their lives to raising a family. Many young people are postponing marriage, families have become smaller, and many young mothers are continuing to work. Thus a much larger proportion of young women are gaining more years of work experience than in the past, and fewer young women are interrupting their worklives.

Since 1960, the participation of wives in the labor force has increased dramatically. By March of this year, 51 percent of all wives were working or looking for work. This compares to 41 percent in 1970 and 31 percent in 1960 (Table 2). Contributing strongly to this trend has been the astounding growth in the labor force activity of mothers with young children. Nearly 8-1/2 million children under age 6 now have working mothers. Altogether, some 32 million children under age 18—55 percent of all children these ages—have mothers in the labor force.

As the number of wives in the labor force has increased, the multiearner family has become a prominent feature of American life. Approximately two-thirds of the wives in these dual-earner families work all or most of the year, and most of them work full-time. Median income for families in which both husband and wife were the only earners was $27,969 in 1981, nearly 30 percent greater than the income for families where the husband was the only earner.

In addition to these developments in married-couple families, the number of women maintaining families on their own—with no spouse present—has more than doubled over the past two decades (from 4.5 million in 1960 to 9.7 million in 1982). Today, 1 of every 6 of the 61.4 million families in the Nation is maintained by a woman. In fact, of every 8 women in the labor force, 1 is a woman who maintains her own family (Table 3).

Despite their increased labor force participation, the economic status of many families maintained by women falls far below that of other families. Their overall median family income in 1981 ($10,802) was only 43 percent of that for all married couples. And working did not bring their family incomes close to parity with other families. Even when female house-holders were employed, their families were nearly 4 times as likely as other families with employed householders to have annual incomes below the officially estimated poverty threshold. Consistently, about one-third of all families maintained by women have incomes below the poverty level.

Industry and Occupation

During the period of women's rapid labor force growth, the rising number of jobs in the service-producing sector has become increasingly important. By 1980, service-producing industries accounted for 7 out of 10 jobs in the American economy. Most of the job gains have occurred in

Table 2: Labor force participation rates of married women, husband present, by presence and age of own children, 1960-82

Year[1]	Total	With no children under 18 years	With children under 18 years Total	6 to 17 years, none younger	Under 6 years
1960	30.5	34.7	27.6	39.0	18.6
1961	32.7	37.3	29.6	41.7	20.0
1962	32.7	36.1	30.3	41.8	21.3
1963	33.7	37.4	31.2	41.5	22.5
1964	34.4	37.8	32.0	43.0	22.7
1965	34.7	38.3	32.2	42.7	23.3
1966	35.4	38.4	33.2	43.7	24.2
1967	36.8	38.9	35.3	45.0	26.5
1968	38.3	40.1	36.9	46.9	27.6
1969	39.6	41.0	38.6	48.6	28.5
1970	40.8	42.2	39.7	49.2	30.3
1971	40.8	42.1	39.7	49.4	29.6
1972	41.5	42.7	40.5	50.2	30.1
1973	42.2	42.8	41.7	50.1	32.7
1974	43.0	43.0	43.1	51.2	34.4
1975	44.4	43.9	44.9	52.3	36.6
1976	45.0	43.8	46.1	53.7	37.4
1977	46.6	44.9	48.2	55.6	39.3
1978	47.6	44.7	50.2	57.2	41.6
1979	49.4	46.7	51.9	59.1	43.2
1980	50.1	46.0	54.1	61.7	45.1
1981	51.0	46.3	55.7	62.5	47.8
1982	51.2	46.2	56.3	63.2	48.7

The participation rate is the percent of population in labor force.

[1]Data were collected in March of each year.

Note: Children are defined as "own" children of the women and include never-married sons and daughters, step children, and adopted children. Excluded are other related children such as grandchildren, nieces, nephews, and cousins, and unrelated children.

retail trade, State and local governments, and such other service industries as health, business, legal, social, protective, educational, and recreational services. These are, of course, the very industries which women have entered in large numbers. Of the 11.9-million increase in the number of women on nonagricultural payrolls between 1970 and 1980, three-quarters occurred in these industries.

While women have made some inroads into the semiskilled and skilled blue-collar jobs of the goods-producing industries, their employment in this sector has grown very slowly—by only 10 percent since 1970. And employment of women—as well as men—in many of these industries has been sharply reduced by the current economic recession. Since the prerecession employment peak in July of last year, the overall unemployment rates of both adult men and adult women have risen sharply—to 8.9 and 8.2 percent, respectively.

Table 3: **Families by type, selected years, 1940-82**

(Numbers in thousands)

| | | | | Other families[3] | |
| | | | | *Maintained by women* | |
Year[1]	All families	*Married couple families*[2]	*Maintained by men*[2]	Total	*As percent of all families*
1940	32,166	26,971	1,579	3,616	11.2
1947	35,794	31,211	1,186	3,397	9.5
1950	39,303	34,440	1,184	3,679	9.4
1955	41,951	36,378	1,339	4,234	10.1
1960	45,062	39,293	1,275	4,494	10.0
1965	47,836	41,649	1,181	5,006	10.5
1970	51,227	44,415	1,239	5,573	10.9
1971	51,947	44,735	1,262	5,950	11.5
1972	53,280	45,743	1,353	6,184	11.6
1973	54,361	46,308	1,453	6,600	12.1
1974	55,041	46,810	1,433	6,798	12.4
1975	55,699	47,069	1,400	7,230	13.0
1976	56,244	47,318	1,444	7,482	13.3
1977	56,709	47,497	1,499	7,713	13.6
1978	57,215	47,385	1,594	8,236	14.4
1979	57,804	47,692	1,654	8,458	14.6
1980	58,729	48,169	1,740	8,819	15.0
1981	60,702	49,316	1,969	9,416	15.5
1982	61,391	49,669	2,009	9,712	15.8

[1]Data were collected in April of 1940, 1947, and 1955 and March of all other years.

[2]Includes men in Armed Forces living off post or with their families on post.

[3]Never-married, widowed, divorced, or separated persons.

Most women continue to work in the country's lowest paying industries. A broad list of industries, ranked from high to low by the percentage of female employees, shows a high inverse relationship with a similar ranking of the same industries by level of average hourly earnings; that is, those industries with a high percentage of female employees tend to have low average hourly earnings.

A ranking of 52 industries from the July data in the BLS monthly establishment survey (Table 4) shows that the apparel and other textile products industry has the highest percentage of women employees (81.9). It ranks 1st in female employment but 50th in average hourly earnings. The bituminous coal and lignite mining industry, on the other hand, ranks 52nd in percentage of women employees (only 5.1 percent) but is 1st in average hourly earnings.

These data show the concentration of working women in particular industries. And women today, in spite of some changes in occupational distribution, continue to be concentrated in certain occupations. For example, over the last decade, the largest number of job increases in the professional occupations occurred among nurses, accountants, engineers, and computer specialists (Table 5). In 1981, women accounted for almost 97 percent of all registered nurses, little changed from 1970; 39 percent of all accountants, up from 25 percent; close to 5 percent of all engineers, up from 2 percent; and 27 percent of all computer specialists, up from 20 percent.

The nonprofessional occupations with the greatest job gains were white-collar secretaries and cashiers; service workers who were cooks; and, in the operative field, truckdrivers. Nearly all secretaries were women in 1981 (99 percent) just as they had been in 1970, and 86 percent of all cashiers were women, little different from 1970. The proportion of women who were cooks, however, declined from 63 percent in 1970 to 52 percent in 1981, while the proportion who were truckdrivers rose to 3 percent, almost double the 1970 figure.

Earnings

Some of the major changes just mentioned in the female labor force and in the concentration of women in particular occupations and industries have a profound effect upon the earnings they receive.

The most comprehensive data on earnings by sex comes from the *Current Population Survey* (CPS)—the monthly household survey. The CPS provides a rich body of data which can be used to evaluate overall pay equity. The CPS data today—as they have for many years—show a wide disparity in the median earnings of women and men, and a basic ratio of women's to men's earnings that has not changed much. In 1939, median earnings for women who worked year round, full-time in the experienced labor force were 58 percent of the median earnings for men. Similar figures for 1981, the latest period for which earnings over an entire year are available, show women's earnings at 59 percent of the median for men (Table 6). Over the long term, the ratio has remained relatively unchanged.

The CPS data on weekly earnings show a similar ratio. The most recent figures for the second quarter of this year show median weekly earnings for full-time wage and salary workers were $370 for men and $240 for women, or 65 percent of men's earnings. Comparable figures 10 years ago were $168 for men and $106 women, a 63-percent ratio (Table 7).

These aggregate data can be examined in more detail. For example, for women as well as men, more years of schooling usually translate to higher annual earnings. Median earnings for women college graduates who worked all year at full-time jobs were 45 percent more than for women whose formal education terminated with high school graduation and 80 percent more than for those who had not completed high school. For men, the proportions were similar. However, at every level of educational achievement, women's median earnings continued to lag far behind men's earnings. The $15,325 which women college graduates earned was only about 63 percent of the amount earned by male graduates. On average, therefore, whether college graduates or high school dropouts, women earned about 60 cents for every dollar their male counterparts were paid.

This 60-percent ratio in the national aggregate data shows a female-male wage gap or differential of about 40 percent. A more detailed analysis of the CPS underlying microdata can, however, provide greater insight into the reasons for this disparity. We can compare the contributions to the female-male gap made by a number of economic and demographic characteristics. We can use such other characteristics as occupation, marital status, education, work experience, family size, weekly hours worked—factors which affect productivity and wage determination—to get a better understanding of the earnings of women. This "human-capital" approach estimates the importance of each personal factor in explaining female-male wage differentials. For example, we know that the distribution of men and women differs among occupations, and that male and female workers frequently differ in education and job experience. Using the CPS microdata (appropriately masked so as to retain our pledge of confidentiality regarding survey responses), we can compare the female-male earnings differential based on aggregate data with differentials derived from the microdata for which many (although not usually all) of the important variables can be held constant. *(Continued on page 495)*

Table 4: Employment and average hourly earnings by industry, ranked by proportion of women workers from highest to lowest, July 1982

1972 SIC Code	Industry	All employees (in thousands)	Women workers (in thousands)	Percent of women workers	Rank of proportion of women workers	Average hourly earnings¹	Rank of average hourly earnings
23	Apparel and other textile products	1,095.9	897.9	81.9	1	$ 5.18	50
80	Health services	5,820.8	4,732.9	81.3	2	7.01	36
60	Banking	1,667.8	1,180.6	70.8	3	5.80	46
56	Apparel and accessory stores	948.9	664.1	70.0	4	4.85	51
61	Credit agencies other than banks	587.7	409.7	69.7	5	5.99	43
81	Legal services	583.6	404.7	69.3	6	8.75	21
53	General merchandise stores	2,193.8	1,447.9	66.0	7	5.40	47
63	Insurance carriers	1,230.5	745.9	60.6	8	7.70	30
31	Leather and leather products	195.7	117.8	60.2	9	5.31	49
58	Eating and drinking places	4,883.2	2,746.9	56.3	10	4.06	52
59	Miscellaneous retail	1,950.1	1,058.6	54.3	11	5.36	48
22	Textile mill products	727.0	349.0	48.0	12	5.81	45
39	Miscellaneous manufacturing industries	378.4	171.4	45.3	13	6.40	38
48	Communication	1,397.8	627.8	44.9	14	10.01	14
54	Food stores	2,463.2	1,072.7	43.5	15	7.25	34
73	Business services	3,304.1	1,436.7	43.5	16	7.03	35
36	Electric and electronic equipment	2,004.7	852.3	42.5	17	8.18	25
38	Instruments and related products	708.3	299.8	42.3	18	8.30	23
79	Amusement and recreation services	976.3	402.1	41.2	19	5.87	44
78	Motion pictures	227.6	92.5	40.6	20	8.22	24
27	Printing and publishing	1,262.4	511.2	40.5	21	8.72	22
21	Tobacco manufacturing	60.8	22.0	36.2	22	10.32	11
30	Rubber and miscellaneous plastic products	689.8	240.5	34.9	23	7.67	31
57	Furniture and home furnishing stores	586.5	200.3	34.2	24	6.20	41

Female-Male Earnings Gap / 493

89	Miscellaneous services	1,069.0	363.0	34.0	25	10.22	13
25	Furniture and fixtures	429.1	129.1	30.1	26	6.33	39
20	Food and kindred products	1,672.9	492.0	29.4	27	7.87	29
51	Wholesale trade—nondurable goods	2,188.0	625.0	28.6	28	8.17	26
28	Chemicals and allied products	1,075.0	280.7	26.1	29	10.01	15
52	Building materials and garden supplies	598.6	155.0	25.9	30	6.02	42
41	Local and interurban passenger transit	230.0	57.4	25.0	31	7.43	33
50	Wholesale trade—durable goods	3,126.0	766.0	24.5	32	7.99	28
26	Paper and allied products	659.4	149.1	22.6	33	9.40	16
35	Machinery, except electrical	2,262.3	476.0	21.0	34	9.31	17
34	Fabricated metal products	1,426.9	299.8	21.0	35	8.85	20
49	Electric, gas and sanitary services	881.3	174.7	19.8	36	10.70	8
76	Miscellaneous repair services	296.3	58.7	19.8	37	8.00	27
32	Stone, clay, and glass products	598.1	114.1	19.4	38	8.93	19
55	Automotive dealers and service stations	1,659.8	319.8	19.3	39	6.28	40
75	Auto repair, services and garages	582.0	100.6	17.3	40	6.68	37
37	Transportation equipment	1,738.6	285.5	16.4	41	11.26	7
13	Oil and gas extraction	710.6	112.7	15.9	42	10.43	9
29	Petroleum and coal products	209.3	32.0	15.3	43	12.40	2
24	Lumber and wood products	630.8	91.3	14.5	44	7.63	32
42	Trucking and warehousing	1,209.6	153.8	12.7	45	10.26	12
15	General building contractors	1,039.5	122.1	11.7	46	10.41	10
33	Primary metal industries	909.1	105.8	11.6	47	11.38	6
10	Metal mining	64.8	6.3	9.7	48	12.24	3
17	Special trade contractors	2,195.4	199.0	9.1	49	12.08	4
14	Nonmetallic minerals, except fuels	118.1	9.5	8.0	50	8.94	18
16	Heavy construction contracting	913.8	66.2	7.2	51	11.47	5
12	Bituminous coal and lignite mining	229.5	11.7	5.1	52	13.05	1

[1]Average hourly earnings are for all production and nonsupervisory workers.

Table 5: **Women employed in selected occupations, 1970 and 1981**

(Numbers in thousands)

Occupation	Number 1970	Number 1981	Women as percent of all workers in occupation 1970	Women as percent of all workers in occupation 1981
Professional—technical	4,576	7,173	40.0	44.7
Accountants	180	422	25.3	38.5
Computer specialists	52	170	19.6	27.1
Engineers	20	65	1.6	4.3
Lawyers—judges	13	80	4.7	14.0
Physicians—osteopaths	25	60	8.9	13.8
Registered nurses	814	1,271	97.4	96.8
Teachers, except college and university	1,937	2,219	70.4	70.6
Teachers, college and university	139	202	28.3	35.3
Managerial—administrative, except farm	1,061	3,098	16.6	27.4
Bank officials—financial managers	55	254	17.6	37.4
Buyers—purchasing agents	75	164	20.8	35.0
Food service workers	109	286	33.7	40.5
Sales managers—department heads; retail trade	51	136	24.1	40.4
Sales workers	2,143	2,856	39.4	45.4
Sales clerks, retail	1,465	1,696	64.8	71.3
Clerical	10,150	14,645	73.6	80.5
Bank tellers	216	523	86.1	93.7
Bookkeepers	1,274	1,752	82.1	91.2
Cashiers	692	1,400	84.0	86.4
Office machine operators	414	696	73.5	73.7
Secretaries—typists	3,686	4,788	96.6	98.6
Shipping—receiving clerks	59	116	14.3	22.5
Craft	518	786	4.9	6.3
Carpenters	11	20	1.3	1.9
Mechanics, including automotive	49	62	2.0	1.9
Printing	58	99	14.8	25.0

(Continued on next page)

(Table 5—continued)

(Numbers in thousands)

Occupation	Number 1970	Number 1981	Women as percent of all workers in occupation 1970	Women as percent of all workers in occupation 1981
Operatives, except transport	4,036	4,101	38.4	39.8
Assemblers	459	599	48.7	52.3
Laundry and dry cleaning operatives	105	125	62.9	66.1
Sewers and stitchers	816	749	93.8	96.0
Transport equipment operatives	134	304	4.5	8.9
Bus drivers	68	168	28.5	47.3
Truckdrivers	22	51	1.5	2.7
Service workers	5,944	8,184	60.5	62.2
Private household	1,132	988	96.9	96.5
Food service	1,913	3,044	68.8	66.5
Cooks	546	723	62.5	51.9
Health service	1,047	1,752	88.0	89.3
Personal service	778	1,314	66.5	76.1
Protective service	59	145	6.2	10.1

(Text continued from page 491)

A large body of "human-capital" research is available. Many of these studies focus on characteristics of individual workers such as age, years of schooling, labor force experiences, etc. A review of this research by a recent National Academy of Sciences panel shows that in the studies reviewed, worker characteristics account for at most 44 percent of the female-male earnings gap.[1]

These estimates are somewhat sensitive, of course, to the accuracy with which the characteristics are measured. In particular, years of labor force experience are usually approximated by calculating experience as the number of years since the completion of schooling. For persons with interruptions in their work experience—which includes more women than men—experience estimated in this way will be overstated. The measurement of this factor alone has been the subject of a number of studies (not all of which agree with each other) in the past 10 years.

My purpose here is not to resolve a research debate, but rather to demonstrate the complexity of the analytical task before us. For example, two BLS economists, Wesley Mellow and B. K. Atrostic, have found that, when a different measure more nearly approximating actual work

Table 6: **Median annual earnings of year-round full-time workers 14 years and over by sex 1960-81**

| Year | Annual earnings | | Women's earnings as percent of men's |
	Women	Men	
1960	$ 3,293	$ 5,417	60.8
1961	3,351	5,644	59.4
1962	3,446	5,794	59.5
1963	3,561	5,978	59.6
1964	3,690	6,195	59.6
1965	3,823	6,375	60.0
1966	3,973	6,848	58.0
1967	4,150	7,182	57.8
1968	4,457	7,664	58.2
1969	4,977	8,227	60.5
1970	5,323	8,966	59.4
1971	5,593	9,399	59.5
1972	5,903	10,202	57.9
1973	6,335	11,186	56.6
1974	6,970	11,889	58.6
1975	7,504	12,758	58.8
1976	8,099	13,455	60.2
1977	8,618	14,626	58.9
1978	9,350	15,730	59.4
1979	10,151	17,014	59.7
1980	11,197	18,612	60.2
1981	12,001	20,260	59.2

Note: Data for 1960 to 1966 are for wage and salary workers only and exclude self-employed workers. Data for 1979 to 1981 are for persons 15 years and over.

experience is used while holding unchanged other characteristics, the estimated female-male wage gap is reduced by about 7 percentage points.

A fairly consistent finding from any studies of microdata is that the estimated female gap is reduced—but not eliminated—as more economic and demographic factors are introduced into the analysis. Another recent study by Mellow,[2] for example, estimates the female-male wage gap at 27 percent when the following variables are held constant: Area, occupation, industry, union, part-time status, and estimated labor force experience.

In addition to the "human capital" that individual workers bring to their job situations, it is quite evident that earnings are highly correlated with the occupation and the industry in which a worker is employed. And we know that working women are more concentrated in generally low-paying occupations in low-paying industries. Here again, we can start with aggregate data on earnings by occupation from the household survey and then gain more insight by looking at some limited samples of data from BLS establishment surveys.

Recent CPS median earnings data (for the second quarter of 1982) show that in the female-intensive clerical field, women working full-time earned $236 a week, compared with $337 for men. At 70 percent, the current ratio of women's to men's median earnings was practically the same as it was 10 years ago. But women clerical workers are far more likely to be in lower paying groups of the occupations, such as secretaries, typists, cashiers, and bookkeepers.

The same sort of pattern emerges when we look at both ends of the pay spectrum for men and women. A recent study by BLS demographer Nancy Rytina examines wage and salary earnings in 250 occupations.[3] Seven of the twenty lowest paying occupation groups were the same for both men and women: Farm laborers, food service workers, cashiers, waiters and

Table 7: **Median usual weekly earnings of full-time wage and salary workers by sex, May, 1967-78, and Second Quarter, 1979-82**

Year	Usual weekly earnings (current dollars)		Women's earning's as percent of men's
	Women	Men	
May of:			
1967	$ 78	$ 125	62
1969	86	142	61
1970	94	151	62
1971	100	162	62
1972	106	168	63
1973	116	188	62
1974	124	204	61
1975	137	221	62
1976	145	234	62
1977	156	253	62
1978	166	272	61
Second quarter[1]			
1979	183	295	62
1980	200	317	63
1981	221	343	64
1982	240	370	65

[1]Data not strictly comparable with previous years.

waitresses, cooks, nurses' aides and orderlies, and bartenders. The female-male earnings ratios in these occupations ranged from a low 72 percent for waiters and waitresses to a high of 92 percent for cashiers. With the exception of farm laborers and bartenders, all of these occupations were both female intensive and relatively low paying. For example, 85 percent of cashiers were women, as were 85 percent of waiters and waitresses. Even among bartenders, nearly half (45 percent) were women.

When we compare median earnings for the high-paying wage and salary occupations which men and women hold in common, we find that median earnings of women are substantially less than for men. There are eight of these occupations: Lawyers, computer systems analysts, health administrators, engineers, physicians and dentists, elementary and secondary school administrators, personnel and labor relations workers, and operations and systems analysts. Unlike the low-paying occupations, however, these jobs are male intensive. Only about 22 percent of the wage and salary lawyers are women, as are 32 percent of elementary and secondary school administrators and only 5 percent of engineers.

The pay differences between men and women in these occupations tend to be somewhat greater than among men and women in the low-paying jobs. The median earnings ratios ranged from 64 percent for those who were personnel and labor relations workers (the greatest difference) to 82 percent among operations and systems analysts (the smallest difference).

Obviously, many factors may influence the female-male pay ratio within a specific occupation group. Seniority, level of responsibility, quality of performance, and geographic location are only a few of such factors. While it is true that some of these factors can be isolated at the microdata level, it is difficult to use household survey data to obtain a complete picture of pay situations in specific occupations and specific types of firms within specific industries.

Information from the BLS establishment wage surveys provides more area and industry detail than the CPS data discussed previously. On the other hand, the data are limited to only a few occupations and industries and, therefore, may not be representative of the total. In addition, the data are averages which include firms with different employment and pay structures. The averages, therefore, mask female-male differences in individual firms.

A sample of wage data for a limited number of occupations from BLS Area Wage Surveys for 1981 shows that women working as computer programmers, a relatively new and high-paying occupation, earn almost as much as men in that occupation. Data from recent *Industry Wage Surveys* show that in the men's footwear industry, the female-male wage gap is 15 percent for cement process sole attachers and 6 percent for fancy stitchers using automatic machines. In woodworking mills, the differential ranges from 31 percent for mortising-machine operators to 2 percent for hand sanders.

Although wage and employment data for men and women are available for only some occupations and industries, detailed information from *Industry Wage Surveys* shows that even those women employed as production workers in high-paying manufacturing industries typically receive wages below the average for that industry. For example, the glass container, motor vehicle parts, and prepared meat products industries all paid average earnings for production workers that exceed the all-manufacturing average earnings rate. In only one of these industries did as many as 30 percent of the women employed have earnings above the industry average, while in all three industries at least 48 percent of the men received earnings above the industry average.

The available data suggest that these differences in female-male earnings stem more from differences in occupational employment than from differences in earnings for the same job. Consider one of these high-paying manufacturing industries, motor vehicle parts, and two production occupations within it, assemblers (classes A-C) and machine tool operators (classes A-C). Within each class, female earnings are 74 to 92 percent of male earnings. However, women constitute only 4 percent of employment of class A assemblers (the highest paid) but 70 percent of employment of class C assemblers (the lowest paid). The respective numbers for machine-tool operators, 2 and 35 percent, are in the same vein (Table 8).

The Bureau of Labor Statistics is the national statistical agency with responsibility for the development and analysis of wage and earnings data. We have seen that aggregate as well as detailed data are available from BLS to study—in many different ways—the existence and the size of the earnings gap. It would, of course, be useful to have more industry and occupational detail covering all sectors of the economy and for individual jobs in individual establishments. But development of such data could result in increased respondent burden.

For more than half a century, the Bureau has conducted wage surveys by occupations with separate detail for men and women. The surveys—based on data gathered from establishment payrolls—rely heavily on voluntary cooperation from the Nation's business community. I am extremely pleased at the cooperation BLS receives from the business community—response rates on these wage surveys typically exceed 90 percent.

We have noticed, however, that in recent years it has become more difficult to collect separate wage information by sex. Increasingly, identification of the sex of employees has been eliminated from payroll records—perhaps as a result of interpretation of regulations under equal

Table 8: **Female-male earnings ratios and females and percentage of employment for selected occupations in the motor vehicle parts industry, 1973–74**

Occupation	Total employment	Percent of females in the occupation	Female-male earnings ratio
Assemblers:			
Class A	[1]1,626	4.4	0.77
Class B	[1]15,992	49.5	.74
Class C	23,134	70.0	.83
Machine-tool operators, production:			
Class A	10,424	1.6	.92
Class B	[1]14,575	4.1	.84
Class C	[1]12,212	34.7	.86

[1]Employment by sex was not reported by all establishments in the survey.

NOTE: The motor vehicle parts industry, last surveyed in 1973–74, is scheduled to be resurveyed in 1983.

pay laws or because employers now believe such information is not pertinent to pay-setting decisions. Since BLS wage surveys depend on company payroll records, the task of collecting pay data by sex has become more difficult.

Conclusion

This review of the earnings gap provides some evidence of the complexity of the Nation's wage structure, and I hope sheds some light on the issue of pay equity by sex. Use of median earnings data demonstrates that a sizable gap exists between the earnings of men and women. The use of "human-capital" variables helps to explain only a portion of the earnings gap. Even when detailed occupational and industry wage survey data are used, the differential is reduced but not eliminated. In short, every approach to analyzing differences in the earnings of men and women with which I am familiar agree on the same basic fact: Earnings of women are generally lower than earnings of men.

Some elements of structural change in the American economy have begun which, over the long run, could have some effect on the earnings gap. Several of the Nation's important high-wage, durable manufacturing industries which have "male-dominated" work forces have been going through an extensive period of dislocation. Some of the people previously employed in industries like steel and auto manufacturing may not be employed in these industries again even when recovery from the current recession is vigorously under way. At the same time, some of today's jobs requiring little training and skill at the low end of the pay scale are being displaced by new technology. The combination of these two developments at opposite ends of the pay scale could result in some reduction of the overall pay gap.

There are, of course, many alternative approaches to the pay equity issue that are important in understanding the female-male earnings disparity. We have seen from the data that are available that a substantial part of the earnings gap results from an employment distribution that is highly different by sex. We do not know exactly why women continue to work more in jobs that have traditionally been female intensive rather than in other jobs. We do not know how much of their occupational choice may result from the demands of family responsibilities; how much may still reflect discrimination in promotion, hiring, or recruiting practices; or how much may reflect other factors.

What we do know is that a great many factors, often interrelated, play different roles in occupational choice at different periods in women's lives, as well as in the history of our country. And we also know that women in general earn less than men today and that much of the difference is because the jobs that women hold are generally paid at lower rates than the jobs held by men.

Endnotes

1. *Women, Work, and Wages: Equal Pay for Jobs of Equal Value* (National Academy of Sciences, 1981).

2. Wesley Mellow, "Employer Size, Unionism and Wages," in *Research in Labor Economics* (JAI Press, forthcoming).

3. Nancy F. Rytina, "Earnings of Men and Women: A Look at Specific Occupations," *Monthly Labor Review*, April 1982.

46

Blacks in the American Economy: Review and Outlook

ANDREW F. BRIMMER

The beginning of a new decade is a good occasion to take stock of the economic status of the black community in the United States. It is also a good time to examine the trends which will shape opportunities for blacks in the future. These opportunities have been, and will continue to be, dependent on the behavior of the national economy. This dependence will increase as blacks are further integrated into the nation's marketplace during the 1980s.

Before looking ahead, however, it would be useful to review the economy's behavior over the last decade.

Overall Economic Performance

The American economy in the 1970s fell far short of the performance recorded during the preceding decade. Between 1969 and 1979, gross

Andrew. F. Brimmer, "Blacks in the American Economy: Review and Outlook," *Black Enterprise*, March, 1980, pp. 55-56 and "Facts and Figures," *ibid*., September, 1982, p. 32. Reprinted by permission of The Earl G. Graves Publishing Co., Inc., 295 Madison Avenue, New York, N. Y. 10017. Copyright 1980 and 1982. All rights reserved.

national product corrected for inflation (real GNP) rose at an average annual rate of 2.8 percent. The nation's work force increased by 28.4 percent, to 103.7 million. Employment rose by 24.3 percent, to 97.6 million, and the number of jobless workers more than doubled, to 6.0 million. These figures represent an average annual rate of increase of 2.5 percent for the labor force, 2.3 percent for jobs, and 7.9 percent for unemployment. Reflecting the latter, the overall unemployment rate rose from 3.5 percent to just under 6.0 percent.

This experience was in sharp contrast to the experience of the 1960s. In that period, the average annual rates of growth were 4.5 percent for real GNP, 1.7 percent for the labor force, and 6.0 percent for employment. The unemployment rate decreased from 6.7 percent in 1961 to 3.5 percent in 1969.

A number of reasons help to explain the poor performance of the American economy in the 1970s. These include a five-fold jump in the price of imported oil, which contributed to a deep recession and virulent inflation. The recession of 1974-75 was the worst since the end of World War II, and the subsequent recovery was mixed. The rate of inflation spurted from just over 5 percent in 1969 to 13 percent last year. The growth of output was held down—and inflation was aggravated—by a noticeable decrease in productivity, while labor compensation continued to rise at close to double-digit levels.

Lag in Black Employment

Developments in the national economy had a significant impact on the economic status of the black community. This is shown clearly in the trend of jobs.

Blacks did share in the expansion of employment over the last decade. However, job gains were relatively smaller than the growth of the black labor force. For instance, between 1969 and 1979, the black work force climbed by 38.4 percent, to 12.4 million. The corresponding figures for whites were 27.2 percent, to 91.3 million. Over the same decade, black employment rose by 31.9 percent, to 11.1 million. The increase for whites was 24.5 percent to 86.6 million.

Thus, the black labor force rose about 1 2/5 times as fast as its white counterpart. Yet, jobs held by blacks increased roughly 1 1/3 times as fast as white employment.

Additional insights into the deterioration of blacks' relative position in the labor market during the last decade are provided by tracing changes in their job "deficit." This measure is calculated by comparing blacks' employment and unemployment percentages with their share of the civilian labor force. For example, in 1969, blacks represented 11.1 percent of labor force; they held 10.8 percent of the jobs, and they accounted for 20.2 percent of total unemployment. Thus, in 1969, blacks had a "deficit" of 0.3 percent in their share of jobs and a "surplus" of 9.1 percent in their share of unemployment. Similar calculations were made for blacks by sex and age, and the exercise was repeated for 1979.

The results show that blacks' overall job deficit had risen in 0.6 percent by the end of last year. This figure translates into an actual short-fall of 659,000 jobs. The largest fraction of the job deficit (305,000) was borne by teenagers. For adult black males, the gap was 143,000 jobs, and for adult black females, the figure was 211,000.

Family income status—1979

	White	Black	Spanish origin
Total families	50,447,534	6,092,694	3,287,852
Less than $5,000	2,787,414	1,182,862	453,842
$5,000 to 7,499	2,766,012	673,230	315,817
7,500 to 9,999	3,290,715	608,119	306,156
10,000 to 14,999	7,223,147	1,020,274	600,469
20,000 to 24,999	7,515,791	612,596	399,284
35,000 to 49,999	5,723,598	343,550	186,435
50,000 or more	3,121,637	115,439	78,408
Median	20,840	12,618	14,711

Source: Bureau of the Census—1980, U.S. Department of Commerce

Long-term Economic Outlook

During the 1980s, the American economy will be plagued by a combination of energy shortages, slow expansion, and high rates of inflation. The recession that is currently under way will be followed by a moderate recovery, and the growth of output during the rest of the decade will also be restrained. Real GNP may expand at an average annual rate of roughly 3.0 percent. This figure is considerably below the 3.7 percent annual expansion of real GNP required to prevent the overall level of unemployment from increasing. (A higher rate—about 4.0 percent—is required in the case of blacks). Inflation may average close to 7 percent

(Continued on page 508)

Trends in money income in the United States, by race 1978 and 1979 and projections, 1980 (amounts in billions of dollars)

INCOME

*Money income
by race
1978-1980*

Reflecting job gains, the black share of total money income increased in 1979. Brimmer & Company estimates that the money income of black workers grew by 14.5 percent last year. The corresponding figure for whites was 11.9 percent. Total income rose by 12.0 percent. Total money income for 1979 is estimated at $1,545.9 billion—of which black workers received $112.9 billion or 7.2 percent. If they had received a share commensurate to their representation in the population (11.6 percent), they would have gotten $179.3 billion, or 66.5 percent more than they received.

Category	1978[a]	1979[e]	1980[p]
Money Income: Total	$ 1,380.6	$ 1,545.9	$ 1,699.6
Percent of Total	100.0	100.0	100.0
Black	98.6	112.9	125.8
Percent of Total	7.2	7.3	7.4
White	1,258.3	1,408.3	1,546.6
Percent of Total	91.1	91.1	91.0
Other Races	23.7	24.7	27.2
Percent of Total	1.7	1.6	1.6

a: Actual   e: Estimated   p: Projected

Source: U.S. Department of Commerce, Bureau of the Census (Money Income, 1978). Estimates and projections by BRIMMER & COMPANY, INC.

A statistical profile of black economic development

FACTS & FIGURES

Employment

Civilian Labor Force Employment and Unemployment, December 1979

The unemployment rate for blacks in December was 11.3 percent, up from 10.9 percent in November. In contrast, unemployment for whites in December, at 5.1 percent, was virtually unchanged from the previous month. The number of black workers unemployed rose by 61,000, the result of an increase of 41,000 in the black labor force coupled with a fall of 20,000 in the number of blacks employed. The number of unemployed whites rose by 14,000 as the white labor force increased by 337,000 and only 323,000 found jobs.

	Total		Blacks and Others[1]		Whites	
	Number (thousands)	Percent distribution by Race	Number (thousands)	Percent distribution by Race	Number (thousands)	Percent distribution by Race
Civilian labor force	100.0		100.0		100.0	
TOTAL	104,011		12,432	12.0	91,579	88.0
Employed	100.0		100.0			
TOTAL	97,918		11,024	11.3	86,894	88.7
Unemployed	100.0		100.0			
TOTAL	6,093		1,408	23.1	4,685	76.9
Unemployment Rate	5.9		11.3		5.1	

[1]Blacks constitute about 92 percent of this category.

Source: Bureau of Labor Statistics.

(Continued from page 505)

over the decade. Again, higher energy prices and the persistent rise in labor costs will be major contributors.

By 1990, total employment may expand to 114 million, an increase of 16.4 million from the level recorded last year. More than half of the expansion will occur in white-collar occupations. The spreading use of computers and other technological innovations will have a considerable impact. In every job category, the level of skills required will be raised, and the competition for jobs will be more intensive.

Outlook for Blacks

According to the Census Bureau, by 1990 the black population will have risen to 29.8 million. Blacks will represent about 12.2 percent of the total population, which is projected at 243.5 million.

By the end of the decade, the total civilian labor force may have expanded to 120.6 million workers. Of these, 15.8 million, 13.1 percent, will be black. Blacks may actually hold 14.5 million of the jobs, or 12.7 percent.

Consequently, blacks can look forward to some modest improvements in their labor market position over the present decade. Nevertheless, the actual job deficit for the black community would remain relatively large, perhaps in the neighborhood of 500,000. If blacks are to shave this deficit significantly, they will have to press vigorously for a large share of the new jobs that will be created in the private sector over the next ten years.

47

The Consumption of Sport

BARRY D. MCPHERSON

Introduction

Sport consumption in North America is not a recent phenomenon. For example, Voigt (1971: 34-37) noted that spectator sports were popular as early as 1860, while Betts (1953) described the impact that urbanization and the technological revolution had on the rise of sport, especially commercialized spectator sport. However, it is only in recent years that the age of high mass consumption (Rostow, 1971) has been attained. . . .

Degree of Direct Sport Consumption

Direct sport consumption appears to vary by sex, age, season, and sport. In the following, statistics first from empirical studies are presented; these are then followed by those released by sport organizations. Kenyon (1966) reported that only a small minority of adults actually attend sport events, and that the attendance varies by season. For example, he found that 29

Barry D. McPherson, "The Consumption of Sport," from Donald W. Ball and John W. Loy, eds., *Sport and Social Order: Contributions to the Sociology of Sport*, © 1975. Addison-Wesley, Reading, MA., pp. 244-275. Reprinted with permission.

percent of the men and 21 percent of the women attended events once per month or more often in the summer; 26 percent of the men and 15 percent of the women attended once per month or more often in the fall; while only 12 percent of the males and 12 percent of the females attended sport events once per month or more often in the winter.

In a cross-national study of adolescents, Kenyon (1968) found that two-thirds of the adolescents studied consumed sport directly once per month or more. Again, there was lower direct consumption in the winter compared to the summer and fall, and by females compared to males. Similar trends were noted by McPherson (1972) from a sample of urban-dwelling Canadian adolescents. In fact, only 4.8 percent of the males and 4.3 percent of the females reported that they never attended a sport event in a given year.

A study by Lowe and Harrold (1972) indicated that among college students direct attendance is declining. They found that the percentage of students purchasing season tickets for events dropped from 51 percent in 1962 to 13.8 percent in 1971. Thus, while direct attendance by adolescents in the high school system appears to be high (Kenyon, 1968; McPherson, 1972), there is a declining involvement after the high school years, even among college students (Lowe and Harrold, 1972). This results in relatively few adults consuming sport directly.

Despite the small percentages, the actual number who attend sport events is quite high compared to attendance at other forms of mass consumption. For example, in 1972, approximately 60 million North Americans spent more than $300 million for tickets to watch 95 major sport teams (Toronto *Globe and Mail* October 2, 1973: 34). More specifically, over 17 million attended professional baseball games, over 13.5 million attended professional football games, while approximately two million attended golf tournaments. Similar statistics are readily available from all organized sport leagues or associations. In addition to interest in attending regular season games, there is an even greater interest in special events such as the Super Bowl (80,000 plus), the World Series (350,000 plus), the Olympics, the Michigan-Ohio State football game (100,000), and the Bobby Riggs-Billy Jean King tennis match. For the most part, this direct attendance at professional sport events is restricted to the higher-income residents of large urban centers. Unfortunately, statistics are not readily available to indicate how many attend sport events below the college and professional level.

Degree of Indirect Sport Consumption

Although most consumption tends to be indirect, the data are less accurate since they are based on estimates rather than tickets sold or number of admissions. Therefore, the following statistics could be overinflated or underinflated because of sampling errors. As in the previous section, the results from empirical studies are presented first, followed by a brief presentation of statistics released by the media or survey agencies.

In his study of adults in a midwestern state, Kenyon (1966) found that over 50 percent of the sample listened to sport on the radio or watched it on television at least once a week. Again, there were sex differences, as 79 percent of the men and 59 percent of the women reported that they consumed sport at least once a week. In the cross-national study with adolescents, Kenyon (1968) found that four to five hours per week of watching sport on television was not unusual. As with direct consumption, males were more involved than females. It was also noted that 75 percent of the males and 50 percent of the females read the sport pages in the newspaper at least once per week. . . .

More specifically, consuming sport on television and talking about sport appeared to be the most frequent form of indirect consumption for both sexes. Lowe and Harrold (1972) also indicated that there was considerably more indirect than direct consumption. They reported that almost 80 percent of the college students watched sport on television at least occasionally, 50 percent read a sport magazine occasionally, while 40 percent read the sport page in the campus newspaper.

In the studies cited above most indirect consumption occurred via television. In view of this it is not surprising that detailed statistics are recorded concerning the consumption habits of North American viewers by both the networks and by independent rating services. Again, since statistics become dated, the following are presented only to indicate variations by sport and season. The most popular viewing times are Saturday and Sunday afternoons and between 7:30 p.m. and 11:00 p.m. each weekday. However, even when special events (e.g. Olympics) are telecast early on a weekday morning or after midnight during the week, it is not unusual to find that four to five million consume the event. In recent years it has been estimated that over 100 million watch the entire World Series, that an average of five million view a regular season National Basketball Association game, that 7.5 million consumed each Olympic telecast from Munich, that 60 million viewed the Riggs-King tennis match, and that over 80 million consume the Super Bowl each year. In fact, whereas 64 million viewed Super Bowl V, three weeks later at the same time only 55 million watched the launch of the Apollo 14 spacecraft. In short, sport consumption via television is a pervasive facet of contemporary lifestyles.

In addition to television, the growth of specialized sport magazines and sport journals has increased the opportunity to consume sport. Thus, not only are there daily, weekly, biweekly, and monthly newspapers or magazines which report news about all sports, but also many specialized publications covering such sports as yachting, skiing, tennis, auto racing, snowmobiling, fishing, and roller derby. In fact, one of the indicators that a new sport has become institutionalized is the appearance of a periodical which describes the rules, outcomes, personalities, strategies, and techniques of the sport; and advertises the fashions, equipment, and accessories necessary for playing or consuming the sport. In summary, North Americans are insatiable sport consumers, especially via television, publications and discussion.

Background Factors Influencing the Rate of Consumption

Before an individual can participate in or consume sport, an opportunity set must be created. For the sport consumer, the opportunity to directly attend a sport event is facilitated by the length of sport schedules and by the amount of overlap between sport seasons. For example, the elapsed time from preseason games until the final championship game in 1968-69 was 173 days for professional football, 214 days for basketball, 226 days for baseball, and 239 days for hockey (*The New York Times*, April 13, 1969: 45). As the number of teams and games increases each year due to expansion the seasons become longer and the overlap between sports increases to the point that there are very few weeks in the year when at least three of the major sports are not being offered to the consumer. For those who consume indirectly there are daily newspapers and either live or delayed sport telecasts every weekend of the year. The opportunity to consume is also influenced by the economic situation of the consumer in that the admission to events ranges from no cost for some amateur events to as high as $100 per ticket for championship boxing matches. As indicated earlier, there do appear to be sex differences in the type of sport which is consumed directly or indirectly. A report by Nielsen (1971) indicated that the 1970-71 average for sport consumption via television was 5.8 million male adults, 3.4 million female adults, and 2.6 million non-adults (i.e., under 18 years of age) per broadcast. The rate of consumption by females tends to be higher for special events (e.g., Super Bowl, World Series) than for regularly scheduled contests.

Marital status may also be related to sport consumption in that those who are single may have higher rates of direct consumption than the married because there are fewer constraints as to how and where they spend their incomes. Similarly, the married may be more involved in indirect consumption since it is a home-centered activity. Finally, it might be hypothesized that more single women than married women would consume sport directly since the dating patterns of high school and college students often include attendance at sporting events. To date, however, there are no data to support the hypotheses concerning marital differences.

Another background factor which influences consumption is age. Nielsen (1971) noted that males under 35 years are the highest consumers, followed in order by those over 50 years and those 35-49 years of age. The decrease in television consumption across all sports for males between 35 and 49 years of age may possibly occur because of career and family commitments. The increase in the later years may be accounted for by those who need to fill time as they approach or enter retirement.

Education and occupation also influence the pattern of consumption. Kenyon (1966) found that those from the lower socioeconomic strata did not attend sport events as frequently as others, but that there was no relationship between socioeconomic background and the indirect consumption of sport. Similar results for adolescents were reported by McPherson (1972). Thus, it appears that while direct consumption may be related to socioeconomic background, indirect consumption is not. . . .

The Economics of Sport Consumerism

Introduction

With the arrival of the age of high mass consumption (Rostow, 1971), it is not surprising that the consumption of sport should also increase. Concomitant with this increased consumption, there has been an increased expenditure of money by spectators to consume sport and by local governments, team owners, and the media, to produce sport. As a result of this exchange, sport has had a profound influence on the economy and has become a source of income for athletes, coaches, officials, writers, television and radio broadcasters, concession operators, manufacturers, and many others who directly or indirectly produce sporting events. For example, the manufacture of sporting goods is a billion dollar industry (Snyder, 1972: 438-442) while clothing manufacturers have found a lucrative market in manufacturing practical, attractive attire to be worn while playing or consuming sport. Similarly, building contractors and architects have become wealthy by building (at a cost of up to $700.00 per seat) or remodeling stadia, games sites, or ski resorts. For example, the recently constructed stadium and arena in Kansas City cost $71 million and $18 million respectively (*Sports Illustrated*, 40, February 4, 1974:11). . . .

The Consumer

The income necessary to operate sport organizations is derived from ticket sales, television and radio network rights, concessions and parking. According to Noll (1971), ticket prices for baseball average $3.10; for football, $6.80; for basketball, $4.17; and for hockey, $4.00. More specifically, Noll reported that the revenue from tickets varies from $1 million to 4.5 million in hockey, all of which goes to the home team. In all cases these averages have increased annually since 1971. In addition to the admission price, spectators must often pay for parking and usually make a purchase at concession stands (40 cents by the average fan per game: Noll, 1971). These two expenditures alone have led to the growth of million dollar enterprises, with most of the profits being retained by the owners or agents to whom they sublet the contract. As reported earlier, over 16.5 million attend professional baseball games each year, while over 10 million pay admission to professional football games. In addition to the money paid for admissions, parking, and refreshments, sport consumers wager as much as an estimated $15 billion a year on sport events (*Time*, January 14, 1974: 47). While none of this money accrues to owners or athletes, it is but another example of the investment consumers are willing to make in organized sport.

The Media

Televised sport has become an integral facet of contemporary life-styles now that over 95 percent of the homes in North America have a television set. Each year television networks in the United States produce over 1,200 hours of sport, or approximately 15 percent of all programs (Nielsen, 1971). Not only does this medium provide the consumer with low-cost entertainment, but it also provides sport organizations with a sizeable and predictable revenue; and it provides sponsors with a known audience at which to direct their promotional efforts. With respect to this latter situation, broadcast media serve as middlemen by collecting revenues from sponsors, deducting their expenses, retaining a profit, and returning the remainder to sport leagues or individual sport teams. In effect, the process works in reverse as the media buys the right to broadcast games from sport organizations, and then sells advertising time slots to sponsors willing to pay the price.

The selling of broadcasting rights is therefore an increasingly important source of revenue for organized sport. In major league baseball, for instance, the range of regular season rights-payments in 1972 was $800,000 to $2.2 million, and for football the range was $1.7 to $1.9 million (Horowitz, 1971). The rights for the 1974 Super Bowl were sold to CBS for $2.75 million which in turn made an estimated $1.2 million in profit by selling commercial time at a rate of $240,000 per minute (Lalli, 1974). The wide interclub differences are accounted for largely by the number of telecasts and the size of the broadcast market. Most recently, the American

Broadcasting Corporation won the bid to televise the 1976 Olympic Games, in the United States only, by offering to pay $25 million for the rights. Additional revenue will be derived by the Canadian Olympic Committee from the sale of European and Canadian rights. Because the sale of broadcast rights has become a major source of revenue, sport organizations have become heavily dependent on them and franchises have been shifted primarily to take advantage of a more lucrative television market. In fact, Horowitz (1971) noted that not a single major league baseball team would have earned a profit in either 1952 or 1970 if broadcast receipts were not available as revenue. Although many have argued that gate receipts would increase if games were not broadcast on television or radio this has proved difficult to verify. Furthermore, sport may be dependent on the media as an interest-generating source to promote attendance at the events. . . .

In most cases, network television rights far outweigh local rights in importance. The size of national rights is influenced by a sponsor's interest in gaining a monopoly for the league and thereby utilizing an attractive game, either regionally or nationally, to promote its products. Thus, the price the sponsor will pay is greater. From the perspective of the team, each club receives an equal share of the revenue through collective bargaining so that the economic power in the league is more equitably distributed. As a result of this policy, the most successful and powerful teams have lost power. Finally, the size of the national rights continues to increase because of the insatiable demand for sport telecasts on holidays, "prime-time" telecasts, and football double-headers, all of which generate greater revenue for the owners (Horowitz, 1971).

In summary, the local and national sale of television and radio rights benefit both the sport organizations and the sponsors. The rights enable the financially weak and less successful teams to survive and, because the network agreements are frequently long-term, the league gains some financial stability since revenues are independent of team performance. Furthermore, the rights have been instrumental in the promotion and formation of new leagues and the expansion of established leagues, often into smaller cities. For the sponsors, the economic advantage of securing rights is that they gain a monopoly of the audience to which they can direct their advertising. Since the composition of this audience is well known they thereby insure a greater likelihood of reaching the "right" clientele. It is no accident that breweries, gasoline refineries, insurance companies, automobile[1] and cigarette manufacturers are the major sponsors of sport telecasts. In order to gain this right a sponsor would normally pay between $32,000 and $75,000 for one commercial minute, depending on the time and event. However, the cost per reaching a household ($0.00521) is relatively low since the average audience size for all sport broadcasts is approximately 5,380,000 (Horowitz, 1971). Horowitz also noted that the practice of selling rights has implications for the public in that fewer competitive broadcasts are available and they have fewer viewing choices because of local blackouts.

The Entrepreneur

With few exceptions, the owner of a professional sport organization is an entrepreneur whose ultimate goal is to maximize profits either directly from the sport franchise, or indirectly by using financial losses in the sport domain as a tax deduction for other interests. Although a large amount of capital is required to purchase a franchise, profits are realized by those who have been owners for a number of years. For example, in 1910 the Montreal Canadian Hockey Club was purchased for $7,500. Eleven years later it was sold for $11,000 and in 1935, it was sold again for $165,000. This same organization was purchased in 1957 for an estimated $2.7 million and in 1971, 58 percent of the shares were sold for an estimated $15 million (Kidd and Macfarlane, 1972: 120). This later exchange represents a 14-year profit of $13.5 million plus annual dividends approaching three million dollars. It is not only the major owners who have profited from professional sport, but also those who purchased stock in this industry. Kidd and Macfarlane (1972: 120-121) reported that 100 shares of Maple Leaf Garden Stock purchased at $100 in 1936 would be worth $18,750 today.

In this era of team and league expansion, original owners are reaping vast profits by new franchises. For example, an original franchise in the World Hockey Association cost $25,000, yet three years later the cost increased to $200,000. Thus, those who paid out $25,000 now share $200,000 each time a new team is admitted to the league. Yet, this is still a bargain in that the latest National Hockey League franchise cost $6 million. Furthermore, when the New York Islanders entered the league in 1972 they were required to pay an additional $4 million to compensate their cross-town rivals, The New York Rangers. These prices are again modest compared to the minimum entry fee into the National Football League, which is $15 million. This sum is divided equally among the existing teams and is intended to pay for the thirty to forty players received from existing teams. In effect, this means that a second string tackle making $20,000 a year is suddenly worth $400,000 (*Sports Illustrated*, 37, October 23, 1972: 83). (More will be said about the effect of expansion on the players in the next section.)

The amount of profits realized by a professional sport organization is difficult to identify or substantiate. Most of the evidence is based on a combination of ticket prices, attendance concessions, broadcast revenues, salaries paid, and rental payments. To date, the only comprehensive analysis of team profits has been completed by Noll (1971) in a report given at the Brookings Conference on professional sport. He estimated that total revenues (broadcast rights, total sales) probably range from $2 million to $6.5 million per team. From this revenue, he indicated that basketball and baseball teams realize an annual profit of approximately $200,000 and $500,000 respectively, while professional hockey and football teams may accumulate almost one million dollars per team each year.

In an attempt to determine the factors which influence team profits Noll (1971) employed regression analyses for baseball attendance between 1969 and 1971. He found that the most important factors included winning a pennant, the presence of superstars, the demand for tickets, and the population of the community. More specifically, he noted that winning a pennant has an influence up to two years later if the team stays close to the top of the league standings. He suggested that league attendance is higher, and, so too, profits, if several teams alternate in winning league championships.

With respect to the presence of superstars in baseball, Noll predicted that in a city of 3.5 million, a superstar may add 90,000 fans per season. Finally, an examination of community size indicated that to draw one million fans per year, an average team would have to be located in a metropolitan area of at least two million residents. Similarly, a last-place team would have to be in one of the five largest urban areas to draw one million spectators.

In his conclusion, Noll (1971) stated that, based on the financial data gathered for his study, after-tax profits total about $56 million for all teams in professional baseball, basketball, hockey, and football. Furthermore, he reported that in cities where the demand for sport is great, team profits are between 25 and 50 percent of revenue. Thus, he concluded that most teams could cut ticket prices in half and still realize a profit, that the larger cities could support more sport franchises, and that all sports could expand to smaller cities if gate and broadcast revenues were shared as they are in football.

To this point it has been seen that professional sport is a profitable enterprise. On the surface this appears surprising if one examines the revenue-expense breakdown. It appears that revenue is generated from the sale of tickets and broadcast rights. On the other hand, the major expenses include salaries, travel costs, rental of facilities, equipment, and publicity. If these revenues and expenses were balances, most teams would find it difficult to show a profit. However, a detailed study by Okner (1971) revealed that professional sport organizations receive subsidies from local and federal governments in the form of tax concessions and low rentals of stadiums.

At the local level, Okner (1971) found that of the 77 different stadiums being used by professional sport teams, 54 were publicly owned. Thus, the public actually owns more than 70 percent of all professional sport facilities and rents the facility to the owners, often at a rate below that which a similar nonsport facility would cost. In this way the owners are able to improve their financial position. Okner cites the following reasons as to why communities give this rental break to sport organizations:

1. to enhance the prestige of the community and thereby stimulate economic activity in non-sport enterprises,

2. to generate employment, consumer sales and tax collections from sporting events,

3. to provide recreational opportunities for community residents,

4. to improve the morale of the citizens,

In addition to direct subsidies at the local level there are also indirect subsidies in the form of reduced taxes. For example, Okner (1971) estimated that for 44 of the 54 publicly owned facilities, the property taxes forgone amounted to about $9 million to $12 million. Thus, while the community loses this tax, the subsidy assists in keeping admission prices lower, provides the athletes with higher salaries, and enables the owners to increase their profits.

Professional sport organizations also receive subsidies at the federal level in the form of tax breaks and tax exemptions. In the late 1960s and early 1970s the construction of most new sport facilities was financed by stadium or arena construction bonds which were tax exempt. Okner indicated that if the interest on stadium construction bonds were taxable, federal government revenues would be increased by about $10.2 million annually. Furthermore, he noted that interest on these bonds is usually exempt from state and local taxes, thereby resulting in a further loss of revenue to government agencies. In addition to tax exemptions or construction bonds, the income derived from the sale of players, franchises, or equipment is not taxed as capital gain. Furthermore, team owners are permitted to account for depreciation in player contracts, equipment and facilities when filing tax returns.

By way of summary, Okner estimated that the subsidies to professional sport owners [are] approximately $40 million per year, of which $18 million (45 percent) resulted from publicly owned facilities that are rented at less than full cost and from local property taxes forgone. The remaining $22 million (55 percent) was secured via tax provisions. Further, based on the findings of this study, Okner (1971) concluded that, because of subsidies, needed public services are not undertaken; that the benefits from publicly owned facilities do not accrue to the poor; that the major benefactors of subsidies are the owners; that owners realize profits because they can depreciate player contracts for accounting and tax purposes; that league expansions produce millions in capital gains for existing franchises, yet are not taxed as such; and, that the subsidies have the effect of raising net profits before depreciation from 17 to 30 percent of gross revenue.

In short, professional sport owners are engaged in a profitable enterprise, especially if they are the original owners of a franchise, and do very little to pass the benefits of these subsidies on to the consumer via lower admission prices, or to athletes via higher salaries. . . .

The Laborer

Although the occupational organization of sport is discussed elsewhere in this volume, this section briefly discusses the economic effects of consumerism for contemporary professional athletes. Until recently the salaries paid to professional athletes were relatively low considering the profits maximized by the owners. This situation held because there was no competition for their services (i.e., a second league), there was little intraleague movement because of the "reserve clause" and "waiver rule" (only in football was it possible to "play out one's option"); because television revenues were small; and because player associations were nonexistent. Nevertheless, although underpaid in comparison to present salaries, at certain stages in their career the salaries of athletes exceeded other males of comparable age and education in the civilian labor force.

Using 1960 Census data, Scoville (1971) found that the average income of active male athletes was higher than for all males in the labor force, and peaked at least a decade ahead of the whole group. He also noted that between 1950 and 1960 the median income of male athletes rose 131 percent compared with 77 percent for the rest of the male labor force. During this same period personal consumption expenditures on spectator sports rose 31 percent. In the late 1960s and early 1970s the average salary in football ranged from $18,600 to $31,300; in baseball from $12,007 to $29,470; and in basketball from $30,000 to $83,000. Scoville found significantly lower salaries in the newer and less established franchises since many of the employees were castoffs or unproven draftees. Furthermore, employing a regression analysis, he noted that the age of the franchise and the won-loss percentage were the principal factors influencing the salary levels for a football team.

More recently, as a result of competition for services because of expansion and increased television revenues, salaries have risen. That is, the law of supply and demand is now closer to being totally functional in professional sport since there are relatively few highly qualified employees available for the over 95 professional teams representing most professional sports. Eagleson (*The Globe and Mail*, October 2, 1973: 34) reported that the average salary of hockey players has increased from about $30,000 in 1971 to $55,000 in 1973; that those in basketball have risen from an average of $12,000 to $85,000 since the ABA-NBA player war began; and that the average salary in football has dropped from $40,000 to $30,000 since the merger of the two rival leagues.

At the upper end of the wage scale, there are now athletes in the four major professional team sports and in golf, tennis, and boxing whose salary or earnings exceed $200,000 per year (Pietschmann, 1973).

Not only are athletes accruing larger salaries, but those who are highly successful or who exhibit some element of charisma are able to generate endorsements far exceeding their salary. For example, it has been estimated that while Péle earns $218,000 per year playing soccer, he earns over $250,000 per year on promotions and outside investments. Similarly, Bobby Orr Enterprises includes a $300,000 summer hockey camp, a car wash, apartment projects, stocks, a farm, and a condominium (Kidd and Macfarlane, 1972: 128). In summary, professional athletes, especially the stars, are extremely well-paid laborers at the present time.

Despite the high salaries, a recurrent theme throughout sport has been that blacks are discriminated against with respect to salary (Ball, 1974). An article in *Time* (April 6, 1970; 79) reported that black athletes, at least those who are highly successful, do not lag behind in salary. They noted that in the 1970 season four of the six baseball players earning over $100,000 were black. An empirical study by Pascal and Rapping (1972) also supports this finding. They found that contrary to popular belief there was no salary discrimination (1968-1969), regardless of position, against black baseball players who had achieved major league status. This conclusion was based on a linear regression model in which the player's salary for the coming season was regressed on his expected ability (based on lifetime batting average, batting average for the previous year, and number of years of experience in the major leagues) and the alternative salary that the player could earn outside baseball. In addition, they reported that, on the average, black salaries were higher than white salaries in the major leagues. They suggested that this occurs for two reasons: (1) major league executives tend to pay players as a function of their demonstrated ability, and (2) baseball may restrict major league opportunities to those blacks who are superior to their white counterparts. Thus, they noted "that there seems to occur equal pay for equal work but unequal opportunity for equal ability" (Pascal and Rapping, 1972: 149).

Scully (1971) also examined this question. Employing the salary data from the Pascal and Rapping study, he found that blacks earn more, position by position, than whites. However, he also noted that whites earn significantly more than blacks for improving their hitting performance, while blacks gain larger salary increments over their playing careers than do white players. He indicated that the salary differentials favoring blacks are due to the "equal pay for superior performance" theme. Thus, based on regression analyses, he stated that to earn $30,000 black outfielders must out-perform whites by about 65 points in their slugging average. In summary, by holding performance levels constant, Scully found that there was salary discrimination against blacks since they earn less for equivalent performance. A more recent study by Mogull (1973), based on 96 questionnaires returned by professional football players, found no significant differences in salaries between blacks and whites among either rookies or veterans.

Similar to contemporary white athletes, the black athlete seeks to pursue entrepreneurial gains while he is an active player and can capitalize on his achieved prestige from the role of professional athlete. Two additional sources of income include a bonus for signing the initial contract with a team, and remuneration received for endorsing or promoting commercial products. Again it has been claimed that access to these benefits is highly dependent on the race of the athlete. For example, Boyle (1963: 129-30) reported that black major league baseball players complained about the lack of commercial endorsements, and about receiving lower bonuses than whites when they signed their initial contract.

It has been additionally charged that only the few black athletes who are potential "stars," and who therefore are highly visible, will receive a bonus comparable to that which a white player might receive. Pascal and Rapping (1972: 135-36) found that the difference in the percent of whites and blacks who received large bonuses was substantial and statistically significant prior to 1958 in professional baseball. However, this difference decreased so that by 1965-1967 it was almost totally eliminated. They interpreted the initial differential to be the result of a "combination of information lag and monopolistic practice rather than bigotry per se" (Pascal and Rapping, 1972: 137). This study should be replicated for other professional sports.

Similarly, it has been argued that only a minority of black athletes are associated with commercial product endorsements, and that those offers they do receive are less lucrative than those received by their white teammates. For example, Pascal and Rapping (1972: 148), citing the Equal

Employment Opportunity Commission report of 1968, reported that black athletes appeared in only five percent of 351 television commercials associated with New York sport events in the fall of 1966. In a similar analysis, Yetman and Eitzen (1972) found that of the starting players on one professional football team in 1971, eight of eleven whites and only two of thirteen blacks appeared in advertising and media program slots. They hypothesized that this difference may be related to the fact that blacks are relegated to nonglamor positions. For example, for the 17 professional football teams which returned data to the investigators in 1971, 75 percent of all advertising opportunities (television, radio, newspapers) were given to football players who occupied glamorous positions.

A final impact of the rise of consumerism on the players' affluence has been the growth of player associations which demand fringe benefits for the sport employees. For example, expense money during spring training and removal expenses when traded, are now part of professional baseball contracts, while pension plans have been initiated, such that a 15-year veteran in the NFL receives an annual pension of $13,020 at age 55. However, very few athletes are employed in a league for more than five years and thus postcareer opportunities must be available for ex-athletes who enter the civilian labor force in their thirties or forties. Recognizing that many have failed to make the transfer, a group of ex-professional athletes recently instituted an organization entitled the United Athletes Coalition of America (UACA) to help ex-athletes initiate a second career.

To *summarize*, this final section has indicated that while player salaries and benefits have increased greatly, the employees of professional sport organizations still consider themselves underpaid if they are part of a cartel where competition for their services is restricted by contractual arrangements. Furthermore, only the established "stars" or those with unique charisma derive the benefits of outside endorsements. Finally, within the labor force a number of ex-athletes are attempting to create organizations and conditions whereby the former professional athlete can be resocialized into a second career.

Summary and Conclusions

In this chapter the phenomenon of sport consumption has been examined as a social problem. More specifically, this review of literature has considered the degree of direct and indirect consumption; the background factors influencing consumption; the functions, causes and effects of consumption; the process whereby individuals become socialized into the role of sport consumer; and the economics of consumerism from the perspective of the consumer, the media, the entrepreneur, and the athlete.

Endnote

1. Lalli (1974) reported that the Ford Motor Company annually spends $10 million for advertising during professional football games.

References

Betts, J. R. 1953. "The Technological Revolution and the Rise of Sport, 1850-1900." *Mississippi Valley Historical Review*, 40: 231-256.

El-Hodiri, M., and J. Quirk. 1971. "An Economic Model of A Professional Sports League." *Journal of Political Economy*, 79 (November-December): 1302-1319.

—1972. "On The Economic Theory of A Professional Sports League." Social Science Working Paper Number 1 (January), California Institute of Technology, Pasadena, California.

Horowitz, I. 1971. "Professional Sports Broadcasting and the Promotion of Sequential Oligopoly." Presented at the Brookings Conference on Government and Sport. Washington, D.C., December 6-7.

Jones, J. C. H. 1969. "The Economics of the National Hockey League." *Canadian Journal of Economics*, II (February): 1-20.

Kenyon, G. S. 1966. "The Significance of Physical Activity as a Function of Age, Sex, Education and Socio-Economic Status of Northern United States Adults." *International Review of Sport Sociology*, 1: 41-54.

—1968. "Values Held for Physical Activity by Selected Urban Secondary School Students in Canada, Australia, England and the United States." Report of U.S Office of Education, Contract S-276. Washington: Educational Resources Information Center.

Kenyon, G. S., and B. D. McPherson. 1973. "Becoming Involved in Physical Activity and Sport: A Process of Socialization." Chapter 12 in *Physical Activity: Human Growth and Development*, G. L. Rarick (ed.). New York: Academic Press.

Kidd, B., and J. Macfarlane. 1972. *The Death of Hockey*. Toronto: New Press.

Lalli, F. 1974. "And Now For the Pre-Game Scores." *Rolling Stone*, 115, February 28: 40-41.

Lowe, B., and R. D. Harrold. 1972. "The Student as Sport Consumer." Paper presented at the 75th Annual Meeting of the National College Physical Education for Men, New Orleans (January).

McPherson, B. D. 1972. "Socialization into the Role of Sport Consumer: A Theory and Causal Model." Ph.D. Dissertation, University of Wisconsin.

Mogull, R. 1973. "Football Salaries and Race: Some Empirical Evidence." *Industrial Relations*, 12 (February): 109-112.

Nielsen, A. C. 1971. *A Look At Sports*. Chicago: Media Research Division, A. C. Nielsen Company.

—1972. *A Look At Sports*. Chicago: Media Research Division, A. C. Nielsen Company.

Noll, R. G. 1971. "Attendance, Prices and Profits in Professional Sports." Paper presented at the Brookings Conference on Government and Sport. Washington, D.C. December 6-7.

Okner, B. A. 1971. "Direct and Indirect Subsidies To Professional Sports." Presented at the Brookings Conference on Government and Sport. Washington, D.C. December 6-7.

Pascal, A. H., and L. A. Rapping. 1972. "The Economics of Racial Discrimination In Organized Baseball." In *Racial Discrimination in Economic Life*, A. H. Pascal (ed.). Lexington, Massachusetts: D. C. Heath and Company. 119-156.

Rostow, W. W. 1971. *The Stages of Economic Growth*. London: Cambridge University Press.

Schecter, L. 1969. *The Jocks*. New York: Paperback Library.

Scoville, J. G. 1971. "Labour Aspects of Professional Sport." Paper presented at the Brookings Conference on Government and Sport. Washington, D.C. December 6-7.

Scully, G. W. 1971. "The Economics of Discrimination in Professional Sports: The Case of Baseball." Paper presented at the Brookings Conference on Government and Sport. Washington, D.C. December 6-7.

Snyder, R. 1972. "The Sporting Goods Market at the Threshold of the Seventies." In *Sport In The Socio-Cultural Process*, M. Hart (ed.). Dubuque, Iowa: W. C. Brown Company. 438-442.

Voigt, D. Q. 1971. "America's Leisure Revolution." In *America's Leisure Revolution*, D. Q. Voigt (ed.). Reading, Pennsylvania: Albright College Book Store. 20-40.

48

A View from Abroad

ANDREW W. J. THOMSON

Introduction

The purpose of this chapter is to evaluate the American industrial relations system between 1950 and the present day in the context of developments in other systems, primarily those in Western Europe. The perspectives are those of a Briton who has spent some years in the States. . . . Some important dimensions, such as those in labor economics and the behavioral sciences, will be either omitted or treated in cursory fashion. Moreover, comparative analysis in industrial relations has not been notably successful:[1] statistics are notoriously difficult to match, cultural diversity cannot be explored adequately, and so on, but the greatest danger in the present chapter is perhaps in portraying European industrial relations systems as much more homogeneous than is in fact the case for the purpose of contrast with the United States. There is a further issue of the appropriate criteria of comparison: this chapter proposes to use the

Andrew W.J. Thomson, "A View from Abroad," in *U.S. Industrial Relations, 1950-1980: A Critical Assessment*, Madison, Wisconsin: Industrial Relations Research Association, 1981, pp. 297-342. Excerpted and reprinted by permission of the Industrial Relations Research Association.

strength and vitality of the pluralist institutions of industrial relations, together with a crude estimate of their appropriateness within their national context.

The primary topic of the chapter will be the ostensible relative stability or, some would argue, stagnancy of the U.S. industrial relations system as compared with flux and change in Europe over the last 30 years, viewed largely in terms of two interrelated themes, namely, the structure of collective bargaining and the relative political roles of the labor movements. . . . In the very recent past the . . . view has tended to dominate . . . that the role and legitimacy of unions, and hence collective bargaining as an institution, are being seriously challenged by a combination of interrelated factors—changing industrial structure, public hostility, loss of political power, and a new managerial aggressiveness.[2]

In contrast, the position in Europe is one where unions have everywhere gained social, economic, and political power over the last 30 years, where collective bargaining has frequently moved into a central position in macroeconomic decision making and where indeed the democratic state itself seems under challenge from the activities of the unruly industrial parties.[3] Almost everywhere there has been legislative change and experimentation with new modes of industrial relations going beyond collective bargaining, such as codetermination, social contracts, and corporatism. Moreover this has taken place in the framework of an intensifying ideological debate about the industrial system and class relations, in which union-management relations are at the core.[4] It can be argued that some of the changes are more of form than substance, and that much of the debate is empty rhetoric, but there can be no gainsaying the enhanced importance of industrial relations as an issue in Europe.

Thirty years ago these relative positions were far from true. In 1950 the industrial relations system in the United States played a highly important part in political debate, in the economic policies, and in the shifts in social structure. In spite of the Taft-Hartley Act, the unions were seen as rampant, exerting power over the whole economy and polity. . . . In Europe in 1950, by contrast, although there were challenges by the unions both in their political and economic guises, these were muted for the most part by a general consensus within the European economies that the primary objective was to redevelop the economy after the years of war. Unions shared these objectives. . . .

There are, of course, many common features in the development of the industrial relations systems of the United States and Europe over the past 30 years, especially in consequence of similar changes in industrial and labor market structures, and in the encroaching role of the state, especially in its regulatory guise. Nevertheless, the reversal of the relative positions of the industrial relations systems . . . is striking, and furthermore, broadly speaking, developments elsewhere in the world outside these two areas have been closer to the European model than to the American one. . . .

There are very considerable strengths in the American system, but they are largely at the lower day-to-day levels, reflecting the strength of institutional structure, the comprehensiveness and codification of the system at the local levels, the professionalism of the actors, the relatively closely defined links between levels and organizations on both sides. These are very important benefits and they continue and have been built upon. But, it will be argued, they do not make up for the weaknesses of the system at the higher levels, such as the lack of any coherent philosophy within the union movement, the apparent complacency about questions of union structure and level of organization, the loss of political power and credibility of unions within American society, and consequentially the fact that there are few issues of social significance being channeled through the industrial relations system. Thus, from a European social democratic, never mind Marxist, perspective, the system is not carrying out its primary function of social change agent. Instead it remains a means of setting the terms and conditions of employment for an increasingly narrow group of American workers, creating no social dynamic as it does so and posing no challenge to the established order. The net result is that European unions have had the range of activities to be able to adapt to and, indeed, to promote changes in economic structure and decision making, whereas American unions have not been able to adjust to change outside industrial relations, with stagnating results for the industrial relations system as a whole. . . .

The outline of the chapter from this point is to present the basic hypothesis of difference in bargaining structure, and follow this by an examination of structure in practice, the roles of the industrial parties, and a look at the operation of collective bargaining. Thereafter we will look at the role of law in the systems, the extent of conflict, and industrial democracy before returning to evaluate the relative efficiencies of the American and European systems. Penultimately, it is proposed to examine the important political context within which the industrial system operates before proceeding to the conclusions.

The Hypothesis

The underlying hypothesis builds on that of Clegg,[5] who saw the structure of bargaining as an important determinant of union roles and behavior. Clegg argued *inter alia* the following propositions:

1. Union government is relatively centralized where agreements are made at an industry or national level and relatively decentralized where they are made at regional or plant level.

2. Factionalism in unions is linked with decentralization in union government and hence with the level of bargaining.

3. Where the scope for plant bargaining is narrow, or where its independence is limited by the law or by the joint action of the parties, workplace organization plays a minor part in union government. Conversely, where plant bargaining is important, it will affect the extent and nature of union organization at this level.

4. Strikes are expected to be few where collective bargaining is conducted at higher levels, and numerous where there is plant bargaining.

5. Where bargaining is at a high level, there has been a development of schemes of worker-directors and consultative arrangements to supplement collective bargaining, but these are not felt to be so necessary by unions where there is decentralized bargaining.

Clegg was dealing with aspects of union organization and behavior under collective bargaining, but it is possible to extend his approach to other aspects of industrial relations.

6. Bargaining, and therefore organization, at a national or centralized level is likely to give much better access to the political and macroeconomic decision making processes than in a decentralized bargaining structure. This is both because the industrial parties are more capable of delivering results for the policymakers than in a decentralized system and also because the industrial relations system tends to become meshed into the economic and political systems.

7. From this it follows that national labor policies are easier to carry out under a centralized than a decentralized system and that there is more likely to be co-option of the industrial parties in some form of shared decision making. . . .

8. It also follows that centralized bargaining is more compatible with the direct participation of the industrial parties, and especially unions, in politics. Moreover it leads to what Barbash has called economic policy unionism, which in his terms is characterized by "a union undertaking to relate its protective demands in collective bargaining and legislation to specified national policy goals."[6]

9. Under centralized bargaining, recognition of unions as a prerequisite for collective bargaining is only of limited significance once a certain threshold density has been achieved. This is because the reach of collective bargaining is more determined by the extent of employer association membership than by the unionization of any one plant or firm. . . . Under a decentralized structure, on the other hand, recognition is a vital issue at every plant in an industry. Even allowing for pattern-setting, there will be

differences in terms and conditions between plants, and if the nonunion sector is or becomes sizable, it may significantly affect union bargaining power in the organized plants.

10. Centralized bargaining is likely to be less intensive or detailed than decentralized bargaining, which can be geared much more easily to the needs of particular workplaces. In this sense, decentralized bargaining may be intrinsically more satisfying to the workers and managers who have to live under the agreement.

11. Centralized bargaining is likely to be associated with rather different forms of law than is decentralized bargaining. . . .

The above propositions are intended as a starting point for discussing differences in American and European trends, but of course political, economic, and social factors not directly related to the industrial relations system have also had a considerable impact.[7]

Bargaining Structure

It is well accepted, in spite of the difficulties of definition, that the North American systems of collective bargaining are the most decentralized in the world. . . . According to the Bureau of Labor Statistics in 1974, the United States has some 194,000 collective agreements, and this is up from some 150,000 a few years earlier.[8] By comparison, the numbers of agreements in Europe range from a few hundreds to the lower thousands, although the process of supplementation makes the counting of separate agreements very difficult. Nevertheless, the coverage of collective bargaining is very much greater in the more centralized European systems, where it is only distantly related to union membership. Although accurate figures are not available, coverage probably ranges from 70 percent to well over 90 percent, as compared to the 27 percent of the United States and 31 percent in Canada.[9] Inevitably, this very large discrepancy between the two sides of the Atlantic makes for a very different significance of collective bargaining in the economy.

The considerable differences between bargaining structures have been best characterized by Ulman,[10] who postulated two distinctive models: (A) reflecting the system generally in the U.S. manufacturing sector, and (B) reflecting the model found in much of Europe. Model (A) involves the negotiating of wages, fringes, and some working conditions between the company and one or more national unions, the latter connecting the company-wide wage settlements in the industry via pattern bargaining. Working conditions and, to a lesser degree, some pay questions are also negotiated at the plant level with local unions, and local and national unions are sequentially involved in grievance handling. Ulman saw this model as giving management "an arrangement designed to connect the wage setting and productivity determining activities as closely as possible" and as permitting the national union, for its part, "to perform vital and highly visible services for local officers and members alike in processing their grievances and policing the contract."[11] Model (B) on the other hand

> is characterized by wider separation of the centres of decision making and more overlap in the determination of pay. Pay is determined by formal industry-wide bargaining and again, less formally at plant level by management activity either unilaterally or under pressure from shop stewards or local shop committees; the company-wide level tends to drop out as a visible locus of wage determination. The role of the national union in the determination of non-pecuniary conditions and in the disposition of grievances is minimal; these functions tend to be discharged by management and/or local work groups, as in the determination of local wage supplements, and also by legislative en-actment and labour courts.[12] . . .

The continued relevance of Ulman's models should not, however, conceal the extent of structural change. That in the American system over recent years has been relatively small, and its origins have been largely economic in nature, with such factors as the widening of product or labor markets, the growing size of companies, and coalition bargaining being important influences. There has also been a certain amount of governmental pressure to increase the size of units in areas where whipsawing has been frequent, as in some parts of the construction industry.[13] But, on the whole, the configuration of bargaining structure in the United States in 1980 is not vastly different from that in 1950, although there are of course significant changes in the balance of individual sectors, most notably the public sector. By comparison, changes in European systems have been more substantial, usually less planned or even intended, and not always embodied in formal institutional structures. . . .

Employers

Compared with Western Europe, where employer cooperation has a history which often predated unionism, American employers have never organized to the same extent for any purposes, and there are no significant signs of change. There is, of course, a considerable amount of multi-employer bargaining in the U.S., although very little at industry level, and there are powerful employer lobbies in Washington, as the labor movement has discovered in recent years. But the differences between

America and Europe are arguably much more significant on the employer side than on the union side. . . .

The sheer size of America has something to do with the difference, but two other factors are probably much more important. One is the rapid emergence of large companies under American industrialization, which did not need to be serviced by employer associations; this was particularly true given that the extensive unionization of American manufacturing was not until the 1930s. By contrast, European employers at a relatively early stage of economic development saw an advantage in taking costs out of the sphere of competition and of forming associations to respond to the growth of unions. The other factor, which partly results from the preceding one, is the antitrust ethos which has always been strong in America, and which resulted in large part from populist reaction to the growth of the large companies. But once American industrial relations had taken on its special characteristics of decentralized organization, there was no real reason for employers' associations to form. European employer organizations essentially exist to protect the marginal firm; large firms increasingly act outside of or even leave their associations in order to pay higher rates for higher performance and to co-ordinate and professionalize their industrial relations. There was no need to protect the marginal firm in America because in some cases the unions have never been powerful enough to threaten it by imposing unacceptable standards,[14] in others because pattern bargaining performed some of the same functions. There has, of course, been a good deal of informal cooperation even in large-scale industry, and in small-scale industries employer associations have been the norm. The implications of employer structure in America are twofold. One is that there has never been a central focus for employer dealings with government on macroeconomic issues, and this has been one important missing factor in the possible development of corporatist tendencies.[15] The other is that there was a necessity for professionalism in industrial relations at the plant and company levels, and for all the perceived ambiguities of the personnel function in the U.S.,[16] it was and is better trained and possesses a more clear-cut role and higher status than in Europe. We now look more explicitly at how companies handle labor relations in the U.S.

Most large American employers have been able to develop well-organized routines for industrial relations and, as a Conference Board report has put it,[17] to "manage" coexistence. Labor relations has become highly centralized within the company, with control of bargaining at the corporate level even where bargaining is ostensibly at plant level. In three-fifths of the Conference Board companies, the chief executive officer has final authority over the labor-cost terms of bargaining, but beyond this there are a wide number of activities primarily carried out by specialized staff functions. The survey interestingly reports that on wage and benefit targets, one-quarter of the companies achieved their target, one-quarter negotiated a package below the target cost, and the other half settled above their target. Even in this latter instance, however, the extent of overshoot was less than 1 percent for more than half the companies. With some caveat about the target-setting process, this indicates not only a capacity to plan, but also power to achieve targets; it is also significant that 88 percent thought that agreements, when reached, would stick. . . .

The overall picture is therefore one in which American employers feel that their labor relations are manageable, predictable, and stable and that this will continue into the future. Often the union performs useful quasi-managerial functions for them and even if most would rather do without unions and resist organization at new plants, from this picture it is only at the margin that there is a threat to established relationships as a result of employer withdrawal. This margin is important, however, because it must be seen in conjunction with what Kochan has called "the growth of aggressive, sophisticated, and generally successful attempts to avoid unions,"[18] while Raskin has also warned that many companies are questioning whether their investment in union good will pays dividends.[19] Such developments are especially connected with the geographical changes in American industry, as Rosow has noted:

> Expansion of plants to the Sunbelt and other areas with little unionization is usually preceded by plans to build a non-union fence around the new facilities. This includes offering attractive wages, benefits and working conditions, as well as establishing selection procedures and training to ensure a union-free organization. These employer efforts are not consistent or failsafe, yet the willingness to anticipate employee needs and to offer as much or more than the unions before they can get in is stronger than ever.[20]

Another reason for the growth of antiunion activities has undoubtedly been the economic pressures of the last decade, of inflation, low profitability, greatly increased foreign competition, and the consequent desire on the part of management to have as free a hand as possible. Decentralization has been a disadvantage to the unions here because of the competitive posturing required and the implication that union recognition is a comment on managerial human relations skills.

Management and employer associations in Europe have developed along very different lines than those in the United States. There has until recently been far less professionalism at the company and plant, and indeed a 1954 study by Harbison and Burgess of France, Italy, and Belgium found an attitude of autocratic paternalism, with an undermanned but highly centralized management structure.[21] Communication was from the top down with little or nothing in the reverse direction. Most industrial relations issues in this period were in any case left to the employers associations.

Management has now changed a great deal in Europe, both in terms of increased professionalism, and especially in the extent to which they have been forced to accept unions as an integral part of the socioeconomic system. . . .

. . . Reynaud reports that employers are one of the groups that has altered most in French society,[22] with the CNPF taking initiatives in . . . areas such as redundancy, consultation, and working conditions. In Germany there has always been a high degree of sophistication in the BDA, but after their immediate postwar lack of popular trust, the employers have become more aggressive, as the constitutional challenge to the new Codetermination Act indicates; nevertheless, they felt the need for consensus by Germany employers has always been strong. In Britain there has been a decline in the significance of industry associations as bargaining has become increasingly decentralized, but to counter this there has been the creation in 1965 and rise to a position of major significance (but still less than the TUC) of the Confederation of British Industry.[23]

Large European companies have also generally been forced to consider the overall policy of their enterprises apart from their association membership.[24] Since the employer association is geared to the marginal firm, the large firms have been under pressure to pay more and to seek higher standards and efficiencies. Some firms have resigned from their associations, but more have developed supplementary policies or agreements over and above the industry agreement. These trends are somewhat toward the American model, but in terms of their changing relative position vis-a-vis the unions European employers stand in very considerable contrast to the picture of American employers outlined above. It is true that in many European countries the strike record is much better than in the U.S, but the foundations of the whole system have been much less stable both in relation to the immediate challenges of the unions and the underlying political system. There has been no equivalent study in Europe to the Conference Board survey from which attitudes can be gauged, but employers everywhere have seen institutional and legislative advances by the unions and a growing challenge from the political system, with unions playing a leading role, to the principles of the capitalist system. It is paradoxically in those countries with the most outwardly stable systems of industrial relations that the challenge has been most coherently pressed through proposals such as the Meidner Plan in Sweden and the union proposals for the extension of codetermination in West Germany.[25] In other countries the challenge for employers has been that of more immediate firefighting resulting from the decentralization of bargaining, but ideological issues are not far from the surface. Moreover, unlike

American employers escaping to the Sunbelt, European employers have nowhere in their own countries to hide, and it is an interesting comment that at least some of the European capital which has recently flowed into the U.S. is reported to have done so to avoid unions.

Unions

There is no space available to do justice to the diversity of characteristics both within and between the labor movements in the United States and Europe; this is especially so of the very important organizational, coverage, and ideological differences to be found within Europe.[26] It is therefore proposed to review the three main common characteristics of European unionism and use these as a base with which to compare the American situation.

First, the European unions have the benefit of a wide coverage of collective bargaining based on employer association coverage, and even beyond that in many countries there are legislative means for extending the operation of collective agreements. This means that union membership is not the crucial factor that it is in the United States, although, of course, it is far from unimportant.[27] Union memberships in the period under review have generally grown, if not dramatically, but more importantly they have managed to respond to changing industrial and labor force structures, especially in the white-collar field. . . .

Second, European unions have been centralized in structure, at least until recently. Their focal point of operation was generally industry-wide bargaining, which meant that there was no strong reason for an organizational presence at plant level. Indeed, in several countries this was effectively precluded by the legislative provision of works councils. However, over the period under review there has been a considerable move on the part of the unions, and often backed by legislation, to establish themselves at the plant level as various aspects of bargaining have appeared at this level. . . .

Third, European unions are political,[28] often in the sense of being associated with a political party, but also in the sense of having ideological objectives of more or less radical change in society. Over the period this ideological dimension has become more pronounced in most European unions, although very few have gone to the lengths of defining their alternative society in any rigorous way.[29]

. . . The first striking feature of contrast between the American and other industrial relations systems has been the diminishing proportion of union membership in the United States, which has fallen from approximately one-third of nonagricultural workers in 1950 to less than a quarter at the present time.[30] But the overall figures hide the major structural differences between America and other countries. American unionism is entrenched in the areas of the economy which are declining or likely to grow, at best, slowly, namely, in white, male, private-sector, manufacturing, northern, urban, large-scale industry. Almost all these are areas of decline within the context of the total labor force. Only in the public sector has there been union vitality and growth over the last couple of decades, but from an extremely low base, and even here there seems to be a leveling off now.[31] By comparison, European countries do not have the massive gaps that are apparent in American union coverage, or the big differences even within categories. It must also be remembered that most of Western Europe, with the major exception of Britain and Denmark, has no union security provisions to enforce union membership.[32]

Moreover, the loss of American union membership has not only been a function of the massive structural changes in the labor force from manufacturing to nonmanufacturing, significant though these have been. There has also been a considerable drop in the percentage organized both within manufacturing and within nonmanufactruing separately. The losses are not large and they are by no means irreversible, but they illustrate a worrying momentum for labor. . . . Unions are not only winning smaller and, indeed, less than half the numbers of certification elections, but are now beginning to lose very significant numbers of decertification elections.[33] The growth of antiunion consultancy has been a feature of the last decade, and a 250 percent growth in illegal discharge for union activity between 1961 and 1976 has been reported.[34]

The reasons for American union growth have tended to be more dependent upon external factors than in almost any other country;[35] by external is meant the pressures of war, inflation, the business cycle, or the impact of favorable legislation, rather than personal motivation because the cultural drives which encourage collectivist and group action in other countries seem in the United States to be replaced by a pervasive individualism. There are no external events such as produced the periods of growth of unionism in the past which are at all discernible on the horizon today. Recent attempts to use political power to gain a better legislative mechanism for organization have merely led to a public exposure of union lack of power, and hence an enhanced loss of credibility. Recent legislation may in fact have had the paradoxical effect that the expansion in legislated job rights may have diminished the grievance-handling protective function which was always a major appeal of American unionism. The only economic pressure which seems favorable is the world recession, but this by itself would seem to be an unlikely source of union growth without some other trigger such as governmental action; indeed, the recession both internationally and nationally may have increased the union wage differential and increased the likelihood of nonunion substitution.[36] This appears to have happened in construction. We therefore turn to look within the union movement for sources of growth.

The organizational structure of the union movement itself has several possible dimensions relating to membership growth. One is the absence of any strategy for developing a structure which might facilitate growth in the key white-collar sector. There is no union which appears likely to be able to organize white-collar workers in the private sector; the jealousy of the unions within the AFL-CIO makes it unlikely that such a union can be chartered, and it is also unlikely that the predominantly manual unions will have sufficient attraction for white-collar workers to be able to encompass them within the existing structure. Moreover, American legislation has proved to be of little use to white-collar workers; supervisors and those in authority are excluded, while the need for a majority in an election has proved too much for most other white-collar groups.

Second, the AFL-CIO as the central confederation is less able than its counterparts elsewhere to bargain nationally as the acknowledged representative of the total labor force or, more importantly for membership purposes, to give strong central leadership to the labor movement. This is in part due to low coverage and a fissiparous labor force, in part to political forces, but also because its affiliates are unwilling to delegate power to it. This lack of delegation follows in turn from the degree of decentralization of bargaining, and it is indeed arguable that the single central federation is weaker than either of its components were separately, since each separate labor movement required a strong center for defensive purposes, but now the national unions can be more self-sufficient. In an international survey,[37] Windmuller concluded that the AFL-CIO was among the weakest of the national centers on the basis of three criteria: the confederation's share of total income; the degree of interaction in affiliate union affairs; and participation in setting the terms of employment.[38] The only criterion on which the AFL-CIO was given less than the lowest marking in Windmuller's categorization was intervention in the affairs of affiliates, and this on the basis of its disciplining and expelling of unions for corruption. . . . The other reasons for the weakness of the AFL-CIO are essentially to do with the fact that Washington is relatively less important in the economic process than the capitals of other countries, that legislation is relatively less central to American labor's interests, and that labor does not exert much influence there anyway.

Third, a strategy for growth would require considerable investment. But a good deal of research has shown that American union members view their unions in a fairly narrow instrumental way,[39] and this does not include using union funds for organizational purposes. Members want services directly related to themselves, and unless new organization is likely to add to the existing members' bargaining power, the existing members see no reason why it should be carried out. . . . Many of the pressures to join unions in Europe and Japan result from collectivist or class-based pressures. By contrast, American workers tend to view unions as means of achieving their job-related objectives. A union is therefore not taken as part of a total social philosophy, but rather in order to achieve improved terms and conditions of employment. In the most thorough recent study,[40] Kochan has however noted that there are relatively few distinctions between categories of workers with respect of their propensity to join unions, although nonwhite workers were much more willing to organize than whites. Even among southern and white-collar workers there appeared to be no uniform antiunion orientation except in the managerial and administrative areas. This suggests that the problem is one of tapping instrumental objectives in competition with management, rather than facing an ideological barrier. But one further interesting feature of Kochan's study was that there was less orientation to join unions in very large establishments than there was in medium-sized ones; he suggests that this may be due to the ability of larger employers to offer sufficiently high wages and other benefits to reduce the incentive to join the unions. This illustrates the dilemma for unions of high organizing costs per member gained, since there are high fixed costs and low variable costs in any organizing situation.

Nevertheless, within the framework of what they see as their role, American unions appear to do a good job for their members. They always have been, and still are, relatively professional by world standards, and their nonwage contribution is probably at least as important as the economic contribution. Their structure maintains a reasonable balance of power between the various levels within unions and internal communications seem generally to be better than in Europe. There seems to be no evidence that the membership wants any different kind of representation, or that the leadership believes that there are radical new directions to pursue. . . . At the day-to-day level of industrial relations, American unions must be judged as successful.

Collective Bargaining

Many of the trends in collective bargaining in the United States and Europe over the past 30 years have been in the same direction. In both there has been a widening of the scope of bargaining, although this has paradoxically been associated with a wider range of state regulations covering aspects of the employment relationship as well. The widening scope of bargaining has been much more marked in Europe than the U.S., largely because Europe started from a lower base. The period has also seen a major development of bargaining at the plant and company level in Europe, thus creating the basis for the type of detailed agreements which have been the hallmark of American bargaining. But the collective agreement still remains the cornerstone of the American relationship in a way which it has not yet generally achieved in Europe where there is still more informality, more vagueness. However, the widening of scope in the United States has predominantly taken the form of fringe benefits, procedures, seniority, and job and union security, whereas that in Europe, while encompassing some of these items and obtaining others via legislative means, has tended to make more challenges to management rights, in keeping with the broader philosophy of antimanagerialism which suffuses European unionism. Nevertheless, it is probably still true that the net effect of collective bargaining in America is to give a greater degree of immediate job control than in Europe, although the total impact of collective bargaining in Europe is certainly greater at the level of the economy, and there are some cases in Europe, such as instances of resistance to layoffs or changes in technology, where European unions have exerted more control of a negative kind. One noticeable development in the U.S. which has had no real parallel in Europe has been the shift to the longer term contract since 1950, such that the great majority of contracts last three years. This has given an additional amount of predictability to the employer. This has held up remarkably well during inflation, although the widespread COLA clause does help here.

There are also much greater differences in Europe between establishments in relation to the scope of bargaining; industry-wide agreements cannot be as detailed as plant agreements, and there are wide variations within Europe as to the effectiveness of collective agreement coverage depending on whether the employer accepts his association's agreement, engages in supplementary bargaining, or has certain aspects of the industry agreement extended to him. In many instances in Europe, collective bargaining still has little relation to what actually happens at the plant, especially if there is no union presence at this level. In this sense, the impact of collective bargaining is much more uniform in the United States.

A second common development has been the rise of problems in public-sector bargaining. Although many of the American difficulties in this area in the last two decades have been about union organizational issues, others have been about the political dimensions of much public-sector bargaining, the ambiguities of structure on the employer side, and problems of setting criteria for the supply, demand, productivity, and financing of services.[41] All these latter issues have been at least equally important in Europe, and in fact with a larger and more densely unionized public sector in a period where a reaction to increasing public expenditure is setting in, these problems have brought the public sector into the forefront of concern about the impact of collective bargaining on the economy.

A third dimension of collective bargaining common to both continents has been the growing complexity, formality, and multiplicity of grievance and negotiating procedures. Europe has tended to have more parallel procedures,[42] given the general supplementation of grievance procedures with a system of labor courts, and these latter have tended to become more influential as new regulatory legislation has accumulated. The internal grievance procedure has, however, tended to become more significant as well, especially where the decentralization of bargaining has taken place. In Britain in particular the grievance procedure has moved much closer to the American model. . . . But even so, nowhere in Europe is the grievance procedure as important as in America, not least because the concept of contract administration through the procedure is not as well developed and there is not the same differentiation between rights and interests issues. Voluntary grievance arbitration is also far better developed in America and is indeed the ultimate guarantee of impartiality which makes the grievance system acceptable. However, the grievance process in the U.S. is not without problems. One aspect is that it has become much more formal over the period, much more concerned with the narrow interpretation of the language of the contract, much less with extending its scope. This has been inevitable as the parties themselves have become more sophisticated and as the contract itself has been fleshed out to codify most areas of uncertainty. But at the arbitration level the use of other cases as precedent, the almost court-room style of presenting evidence, and the increasing use of lawyers have made the process more rigid and remote than hitherto.[43] A second aspect for concern is that the traditional dominance of the internal grievance procedure has been challenged by external legal procedures permitting individuals or sometimes parties to bring cases under the agreement. . . . On the negotiating procedure front, there has been more development in America than in Europe in the search for new negotiating procedures to diminish the likelihood of damaging strikes, with proposals such as continuous negotiations, no-strike strikes, the experimental negotiation agreement in steel, and so on, but although imaginative, these have done little to change traditional patterns of bargaining.

Another area where there has been some growth of interest on both sides of the Atlantic is in the development of consultation and the creation of joint committees for specific purposes. In part this reflects growing economic problems, and a joint recognition of the need to face up to them.

But again there is probably some difference in emphasis, with the American approach being to concentrate on the problem without it having any significant effect on the wider relationship, while the European approach on the union side at least is to see it as a contribution to joint decision-making. *Work in America* began,[44] or at least signalled, an impetus to move beyond traditional collective bargaining to new types of programs. . . . Dyer, Lipsky, and Kochan found that there was indeed some willingness among unionists to consider joint programs in the quality-of-working-life area, some limited willingness in the productivity area, and very little in the traditional areas of collective bargaining.[45] . . .

Industrial Democracy

The possibility of a greater involvement of employees and their union representatives in decision-making over and above that obtained in collective bargaining is one of the clearest distinctions between the United States and Europe since it has evinced an immense amount of interest and a fair amount of implementation in Europe, but very little indeed of either in the U.S.[46] . . . Part of the European interest is happen-stance. West Germany wanted some institutional bulwark against the power of Hitler-tainted big business in the immediate postwar period, and codetermination fitted well with this goal. Thereafter codetermination became Germany's contribution to the Common Market, and it was incorporated into EEC policy in 1972.[47] The other big European countries, Britain, France, and Italy, only then began to respond.[48] But industrial democracy also satisfied the growing feeling that collective bargaining was not enough to enable unions to come to terms with many other corporate decisions which affected the labor force, or to provide unions with an ideological rationale as organizations rather than as part of a wider political movement. This was the genesis of some of the most developed thinking in the area . . . and it has been pursued by many left-wing groups distrustful of the centralized state and seeing unions as the most available vehicle for radical social change. The political dimension of industrial democracy is undoubtedly of the greatest significance. No union has or is likely to achieve industrial democracy in the sense of power-sharing over a wide range of company decisions purely by its economic power, but the political route to compulsory industrial democracy is a very real challenge to existing systems of industrial relations and one taken very seriously by employers.[49]

But underlying these two threads of development is the structural point articulated by Clegg, namely, that the pressure for industrial democracy is a function of the structure of bargaining. In those countries with centralized bargaining systems, there is little access to managerial decision-making at company and to a lesser extent at plant level, and industrial democracy is a logical means of achieving such success.[50] . . . In the now widely quoted words to Thomas Donahue of the AFL-CIO: "We do not seek to be a partner in management—to be most likely the junior partner in success and the senior partner in failure. We do not want to blur in any way the distinctions between the respective roles of management and labor in the plant."[51] . . .

The Role of Law

Before assessing the role of law in the industrial relations systems of America and Europe, it is perhaps best to try to distinguish various different kinds of law in the industrial relations system. . . .

The best rationale for American labor law has been provided by Bok,[52] who argued that the law was derived from the preexisting industrial relations system and also from the wider culture. A permissive auxiliary law was eventually required because American society, with its highly individualistic slant, was not disposed to grant easy recognition to collective bodies such as unions. But the already decentralized nature of the system at the time of the passage of the Wagner Act also contributed to some of the unique features of American labor law. Exclusive representation was made necessary by the existing degree of interunion competition, but it also made more difficult the development of larger bargaining units, as evidenced by the great length of time that it has taken for coalition bargaining to develop in the United States. Again, the very detailed provisions for recognition, including the issues of unit determination and the unfair labor practice of failure to bargain in good faith, were made necessary by the unwillingness of employers to have any truck with unionism. These provisions further cemented the decentralization of the system. . . . Once the laws were created, there was a process of judicial development: "An early articulation of simple standards is typically followed by a constant embellishment of exceptions, qualifications, complex reformulations and ad hoc decision-making."[53]

In Europe the law played a less significant role in the development of industrial relations. Much of the early recognition of unions took place outside any legal framework in France, Germany, Sweden, and Britain, and the common-law-based clashes between the law and the unions over bargaining behavior were as fierce in Britain as in the U.S., but they were ended by legislation in 1906. . . . Changes in European law over the last two decades have been aimed at primarily three sets of objectives: first, the expansion of union rights, especially at the plant level; second, the expansion of union rights in respect of sharing in management decision-making; and third, the expansion of individual rights in respect of job security and welfare provisions.[54] . . .

In the postwar period, American law has moved in two rather separate directions. On the one hand the auxiliary and restrictive aspects of law are still essentially geared to achieving a satisfactory implementation of the 1935 principles. The arguments have become much more detailed, but in essence the debate has not moved forward from 1935 at a time when European issues are now much more concerned with the nature of control in industrial society.

. . . There has been enormous expansion of regulation in the United States. Between 1960 and 1975 the number of regulatory programs administered by the Department of Labor tripled from 43 to 134, and Kochan has therefore argued that the basic premise underlying the National Labor Relations Act, the promotion and regulation of the process of collective bargaining but neutrality with respect to its substantive outcome, should be viewed as "mere historical rhetoric" rather than as an accurate description of present day reality.[55] . . . Unlike European unions, moreover, American unions have not strongly pursued legislation. As Barbash has noted: "The union in America employs law and its administration mainly as an auxiliary strategy. It is subordinate to collective bargaining because, by comparison (a) its effects on the terms of the employment relation are less clearly perceived by union people, (b) it is not necessarily as responsive to union influence and (c) it is not as adaptable to *particular* union interests."[56]

Many of the pieces of regulatory legislation which have been introduced in recent years create much more difficulty than earlier legislation in setting standards and need a great deal of judgment with which to operate them; this is the case with the equal employment legislation, the Occupational Health and Safety Act, and the various pieces of employment and training legislation. . . .

Not only is the welter of legislation causing problems in its own right, but it is causing a major impact upon existing voluntary institutions, especially grievance and arbitration procedures. . . . A further important result has been the growth of multiple remedies offered by overlapping jurisdictions in the industrial relations area. . . . Certainly choice of jurisdiction is now an important issue in deciding where the best chance of success lies in an American industrial relations suit. . . . This growth of regulation has not unnaturally led to considerable dissatisfaction and also to concern for the bargaining system. Thus Dunlop has argued that regulatory legislation does many types of damage to the existing system, such as offering over-simplistic remedies to complex problems, being too rigid to apply to diverse settings, being extremely slow in adjudication, producing unintended consequences, creating side-effects which are as severe as the problems they are intended to cure, discouraging mutual accommodation and compromise, encouraging legalistic gamesmanship, creating a mass bureaucracy, and inevitably producing regulatory over-lap.[57]

It can thus be argued that law in the United States is encroaching upon collective bargaining, with a net impact detrimental to the unions, both because it carries out labor's protective job for it, and also because many aspects of law are aimed at controlling unions as well as employers in their relations with individuals. At the same time American labor's strength depends upon the law, lacking sufficient inherent economic or political power, and although a policy set up in 1935 can sustain the industrial relations system for so long, eventually it requires further backing from the political system. However, this backing seems unlikely to be forth-coming. . . .

Toward a Comparison of Relative Efficiencies

. . . Ulman has argued that the decentralized system of bargaining as found in the American manufacturing sector is presumptively more efficient than the centralized system found in Europe.[58] We now look at three criteria for testing this proposition, namely, wage inflation, pro-ductivity, and conflict, although Ulman was primarily interested only in the inflationary consequences. There are considerable dangers beyond shortage of space in trying to be too definitive about the results of such an examination, because not only are many potentially relevant variables omitted even within the industrial relations system, but factors external to the system may have a major impact on it. Nevertheless, Table 1 provides the most comprehensive set of comparative economic data over the period, covering the wage and productivity aspects for 11 countries in manufactur-ing industry. Data for the period 1950-1960 are unfortunately not available in directly comparable form; however, for the broad purposes of this essay, the patterns during that decade were sufficiently similar to those of the period 1960-1973 for the points made to be extended to the earlier decade also.

Wage Inflation

Table 1 suggests that the contribution of wages alone to inflation has been less in the United States than elsewhere, in that hourly compensation

(Continued on page 546)

Table 1: Annual percentage change in manufacturing 1960-1979: selected indicators for eleven countries

	Output			Output per hour			Hourly compensation		
	1960-79	1960-73	1973-79	1960-79	1960-73	1973-79	1960-79	1960-73	1973-79
U.S.	3.8	4.7	2.0	2.6	3.1	1.4	6.3	5.0	9.4
Canada	5.1	6.4	2.2	3.8	4.6	2.2	8.1	6.2	12.4
Japan	10.4	12.8	5.3	9.2	10.3	6.9	14.4	15.1	12.8
France	5.4	6.7	2.6	5.5	5.8	4.8	11.7	9.8	15.8
Germany	4.2	5.2	1.9	5.4	5.5	5.3	10.1	10.2	10.0
Italy	5.8	7.0	3.2	6.1	7.2	3.7	16.0	13.6	21.2
U.K.	1.8	3.0	-0.7	2.9	4.0	0.5	11.8	8.6	19.2
Belgium	5.0	6.7	1.4	6.7	7.0	6.0	11.7	10.9	13.5
Denmark	4.8	6.1	2.0	6.1	7.0	4.4	12.2	11.5	13.5
Netherlands	4.6	6.0	1.6	6.7	7.4	5.3	12.6	13.1	11.5
Sweden	3.8	5.5	0.3	5.3	6.7	2.4	11.8	10.4	15.0
Eight European countries	4.3	5.5	1.8	5.2	5.8	4.0	11.6	10.4	14.1
Ten foreign countries	5.7	7.0	2.9	6.0	6.5	4.8	11.6	10.6	13.7

Source: Arthur Neef and Patricia Capdevielle "International Comparisons of Productivity and Labor Costs," Monthly Labor Review (December 1980), pp. 32-38.

Table 1—Continued

	Unit labor costs			Unit labor costs in U.S.$		
	1960-79	1960-73	1973-79	1960-79	1960-73	1973-79
U.S.	3.7	1.8	7.9	3.7	1.8	7.9
Canada	4.1	1.5	10.0	3.1	1.3	7.1
Japan	4.7	4.4	5.5	7.5	6.7	9.4
France	5.9	3.8	10.5	6.7	4.6	11.3
Germany	4.4	4.4	4.5	9.0	8.1	11.1
Italy	9.3	5.9	16.9	7.6	6.5	10.1
U.K.	8.7	4.4	18.6	7.1	3.3	15.7
Belgium	11.7	10.9	13.5	7.7	5.8	12.2
Denmark	12.2	11.5	13.5	7.2	5.4	11.3
Netherlands	12.6	13.1	11.5	9.0	7.8	11.7
Sweden	11.8	10.4	15.0	7.2	4.8	12.5
Eight European countries	11.6	10.4	14.1	8.0	6.4	11.6
Ten foreign countries	11.6	10.6	14.1	7.3	5.8	10.6

Source: Arthur Neef and Patricia Capdevielle "International Comparisons of Productivity and Labor Costs," Monthly Labor Review (December 1980), pp. 32-38.

(Continued from page 543)

increased less than in any other country over all the three time periods recorded. American rates of inflation have themselves been well below the European average over the period, and American average wages, from being vastly higher than anywhere else in the world in 1950, have now been caught by several European countries such as Germany, Sweden, Denmark, and the Netherlands.[59] Although part of this catching-up process is due to exchange rate changes, most of it is real. In fact, if the various social welfare costs directly tied to employment are added to wages, American labor costs per hour become lower than the countries mentioned.[60]

Some considerable part of this lower rate of wage increase must be attributed to the collective bargaining system, thus endorsing Ulman's contention that a decentralized system of bargaining need not be more inflationary than a centralized one. In spite of pattern bargaining, the American system produces a good deal of competitive cost-consciousness on the part of individual firms, whereas in Europe, firms must accept a base wage and due to lack of detailed information about earnings, often allow supplemental bargaining to increase this. In neither aspect of bargaining does the firm exercise the degree of control that is true in the U.S. Two potential caveats, however, require to be made on this issue. One is that the very limited coverage of American collective bargaining is a strong deterrent to wage inflation in the covered sector. Second, U.S. real wage rates have actually declined since the early 1970s, which may be a function of the weakness of the unions as much as a comment on the structure of the system.

Productivity

All industrialized countries have become worried by falling productivity, but nowhere has this concern been more strongly expressed than in the U.S., even though GDP per employee is still higher than anywhere else in the world. As can be seen, American productivity growth over the whole period has been lower than in any other country. Such a trend runs counter to the concept of a more efficient bargaining system, and in particular to Ulman's argument that a higher rate of productivity growth due to more detailed bargaining would offset a tendency to higher wage increases. In fact, as we see, the reverse is the case: the U.S. has lower wage increases and lower productivity increases. Productivity, of course, includes many factors other than labor input, including the rate of technological change, which in turn is associated with investment and profitability. The fact remains that American productivity levels are very poor by international standards, and, in fact, dropped under 1 percent over the 1977-1979 period. It is debatable, however, to what extent this can be attributed to industrial relations. Brown and Medoff found that unions were associated with a positive productivity effect of the same order of magnitude as the wage effect.[61] Moreover, American unions have been on the whole cooperative in achieving technological change,[62] while managements have certainly used the bargaining process to achieve objectives of their own, as opposed to providing higher wages with little in return, as has tended to be the case with industry-wide bargaining in Europe.

Taking productivity and wages together in unit labor costs, the United States again comes out very well, with the lowest rate of increase over the whole period, even if not since 1973, although it still remains below the overall average. Moreover, the key statistic is the exchange rate adjusted figure rather than the absolute increase, and the decline of the value of the dollar in relation to strong currencies such as the mark and the yen has maintained the American advantage after 1973 vis-à-vis all overseas countries. By these standards, therefore, the American industrial relations system has certainly not significantly reduced American competitiveness.

Conflict

North America and Europe differ very considerably in patterns of strikes, and a good deal of attention has been given to these.[63] Although groups of variables have been used, such as political, structural-institutional, and economic, there is considerable agreement that the bargaining structure is significant. The strike plays a very important part in the American bargaining process; it tends to be economic, professional, and calculated in nature, and its conduct is usually within the rules of the industrial relations game. By contrast, strikes in Europe are relatively rare at a formal level of industry bargaining, but when they do occur can have an economy-wide impact. But strikes do not last as long and are often intended as much to be a protest, sometimes a political protest, as to inflict economic damage on management. The European system also tends to generate more wildcat strikes, although these are of course far from unknown in the U.S. . . .

. . . All European nations are aware of the potential challenge of the strike to existing social and political institutions, in a way which does not seem remotely likely of the U.S. with its decentralized system. In other words, if there is a price to pay for the decentralized type of bargaining in terms of higher strike activity,[64] it is not a price which includes the potential social challenge of more centralized bargaining.

The implications to be drawn from this brief review of relative efficiencies must be inconclusive; but even if Ulman's thesis is not substantiated, there is nothing to suggest that the United States suffers any significant economic disadvantage from its industrial relations system on the basis of the data provided. Efficiency, however, may not only be a statistical concept. It might be suggested that a decentralized system of bargaining tends to breed an adversarial relationship, and that there seems to be a growing recognition of the economic advantages of consensus at several levels in the industrial relations system.[65] But whatever the balance of advantage at the lower levels, account must also be taken of the higher levels. In particular, the industrial relations system interacts with and depends on the political system for its development and maintenance, and it would be unrealistic to attempt any final conclusions without setting it in its sociopolitical context.

The Political Context

Of all the differences between the European and American systems of industrial relations, perhaps the most immediately noticeable is the political and cultural context in which they operate.[66] Almost all European unions are ideological in the sense that they see their representational role as extending beyond the workplace into the political system for the purpose of radically changing the social and economic structure. All European countries have unions which are associated with, often very closely, political parties of a socialist or communist persuasion, and politics can generally be seen on a left-right ideological spectrum in which economic philosophy and social class play a very important role.

By contrast, the United States has never had a close connection between unionism and the political parties, nor have the parties themselves been formulated along the ideological spectrum which is general in Europe. The reasons for the absence of a labor party in the United States have often been examined: the absence of class structures, the small industrial labor force when the vote was obtained, the problem of organizing new parties within the complex federal structure, and, most importantly of all, the political attitudes of individualism, or pragmatism, almost of antiphilosophy which has permeated American political thought have all been put forward as partial explanations.[67] Bargaining structure has also played a not insignificant part, since it has not only contributed to the particularism of business unionism and its lack of claim to represent interests outside work, but also to weak central institutions. We are, however, here less concerned with the reasons than the implications of this situation. . . .

. . . It is the contention put forward here that the political system has changed and that labor, as an old political bloc, has been able to do relatively little about it, although its own lack of cohesiveness, its inability to organize much beyond the traditional manual working class, and its continued taint of excessive power and corruption as far as the general public is concerned have certainly not helped. . . .

In short, American unions are losing political significance not only because of their own deficiencies but because centrifugal forces have tended to prevail in the American political scene, whereas, with strong central institutions to start with, centripetal forces have been dominant in Europe, and this has added to the power of the economic parties.

Conclusions

The great advantage of the American system of industrial relations for the worker covered by collective bargaining is that he is provided with a highly professionalized system of industrial self-regulation; for the unionized employer there is a high degree of predictability that he is getting what he pays for; and for the society at large the system provides an excellent, if limited, example of competitive pluralism whilst keeping well within the fundamental philosophical tenets of capitalism. But the system is limited in a number of ways—in coverage, scope of interaction, flexibility in response to changing industrial and occupational patterns, popular acceptance, and political significance—and moreover the limitations look more obvious from the perspective of 1980 than they did from that of 1950. Since that time the system has become assimilated and institutionalized, progressively reducing the status of unions as major actors on the economic and social scene. It can be argued that it is precisely because "unions in America have been unswerving in their affirmation of private property, the capitalist system, and the prevailing system of government,"[68] that they can be taken for granted by politicians and outflanked by managements, since they offer no alternatives and pose no threats. Their social role is being pre-empted by other institutions and they appear to have become increasingly instrumental agencies to their members. In spite of this, they are still viewed as contrary to the American ethos and have provided a convenient scapegoat for America's doubts about itself and its role.

It is, of course, true that: "Reports of organized labor's death are, as were those of Twain's, greatly exaggerated,"[69] and even on a pessimistic prognosis there is no indication that the basic functions of unionism are under challenge. But the situation in the United States does contrast with that in Europe, where many of the philosophical, social, and economic changes in the societies are being channeled through the industrial relations system, and where the unions pose perhaps the major threat to the stability of governments. Much depends on what a society expects from its industrial relations system—a limited but stable institution or a social change agent and challenge to the existing order. . . .

Endnotes

1. Michael Shalev, "Industrial Relations Theory and the Comparative Study of Industrial Relations and Industrial Conflict," *British Journal of Industrial Relations* 18 (March 1980), p. 26. For the best approaches to comparative analysis, see *Collective Bargaining in the Industrialised Market Economies* (Geneva: International Labor Office, 1973), Part I, by John P. Windmuller; and John T. Dunlop, *Industrial Relations Systems* (Carbondale: Southern Illinois University Press, 1958).

2. Books and articles have recently begun to appear highlighting this decline: Hervey A. Juris and Myron Roomkin, *The Shrinking Perimeter: Unionism and Labor Relations in the Manufacturing Sector* (Lexington, MA: D.C. Heath, 1980), and R. Schlank, "Are Unions an Anachronism?" *Harvard Business Review* (September/October 1979).

3. B. Peper, "Tradeoffs and Politicization," in *Collective Bargaining and Government Policies* (Paris: OECD, 1979), and Solomon Barkin, ed., *Worker Militancy and its Consequences* (New York: Praeger, 1975).

4. C. Crouch and A. Pizzorno, eds., *The Resurgence of Class Conflict in Western Europe Since 1968* (London: Macmillan, 1978), 2 vols.

5. H. A. Clegg, *Trade Unionism Under Collective Bargaining* (Oxford: Blackwell, 1976).

6. Jack Barbash, *Trade Unions and National Economic Policy* (Baltimore: Johns Hopkins University Press, 1972), p. 161.

7. Some writers have stressed these factors rather than the internal structural aspects espoused by Clegg. Thus Shalev: "I would argue that collective bargaining arrangements are reflections of the distribution of power and the outcome of conflicts between labour movements, employers and the state at the time these arrangements came into being. In so far as they subsequently acquire a degree of 'functional autonomy,' the institutions of industrial relations should still occupy no more than the position of intervening variables in comparative theories, the task of causal explanation being reserved for factors in the social, political and economic environment" (Shalev, p. 29).

8. Quoted in Thomas A. Kochan, *Collective Bargaining and Industrial Relations* (Homewood, IL: Richard D. Irwin, 1980), p., 85.

9. OECD, *Collective Bargaining and Government Policies in Ten OECD Countries*. It will be noticed that there is some difference in union membership and collective bargaining coverage in the U.S. as well as Europe, although nothing like as much. See Kochan, Table 5-2, p. 129.

10. Lloyd Ulman, "Connective Bargaining and Competitive Bargaining," *Scottish Journal of Political Economy* 21 (June 1974).

11. *Ibid.,* pp. 99-100.

12. *Ibid.,* pp. 100-101.

13. Lewin notes that John T. Dunlop resigned as Secretary of Labor when the picketing bill for the construction industry was vetoed, because he felt that this would have helped reduce the degree of decentralization in the industry (David Lewin, "The Impact of Unionism on

American Business: Evidence for an Assessment," *Columbia Journal of World Business* [Winter 1978], p. 103).

14. Even beyond the reach of employers' associations, many European countries have a capacity for legal extension of industry-wide collective agreements.

15. But cf. Robert J. Flanagan, "The National Accord as a Social Contract," *Industrial and Labor Relations Review* 34 (October 1980).

16. G. Ritzer and H. Trice, *An Occupation in Conflict: A Study of the Personnel Manager* (Ithaca: New York State School of Industrial and Labor Relations, Cornell University, 1969).

17. Audrey Freedman, *Managing Labor Relations* (New York: The Conference Board, 1979).

18. Thomas A. Kochan, "An American Perspective on the Integration of the Behavioural Sciences into Industrial Relations," in *The Behavioural Sciences and Industrial Relations: Some Problems of Integration*, ed. A. Thomson and M. Warner (Farnborough: Gower Press, 1981), p. 8.

19. A. H. Raskin, "Management Comes Out Swinging," *Proceedings of the 31st Annual Meeting, Industrial Relations Research Association*, 1978, p. 228.

20. Jerome Rosow, Industrial Relations Research Association Newsletter, 1979, p. 1.

21. Frederick Harbison and G. Burgess, "Management in Post War Europe," *American Journal of Sociology* 60 (September 1954).

22. Reynaud, p. 56.

23. This was a classic case of an institution being created for corporatist purposes, since the Labor Government of that period badly needed an employer organization with which to negotiate its ill-fated National Plan.

24. W. Brown and M. Terry, "The Changing Nature of National Wage Agreements," *Scottish Journal of Political Economy* 25 (June 1978).

25. R. Meidner, *Employer Investment Funds* (London: George Allen and Unwin, 1978): *Mitbestimmung in Unternchuen* (Bundestags-Drucksache VI 334—The Biedenkopf Report, 1970); B. Wilpert, "Research on Industrial Democracy: The German Case," *Industrial Relations* 6 (Spring 1975).

26. W. Kendall, *The Labour Movement in Europe* (London: Allen Lane 1975).

27. No comparative union membership statistics are provided because statistics for key countries such as France and Italy are considered unreliable to the point of meaninglessness, and, of course, American statistics are provided elsewhere in this volume. The most comprehensive discussion of comparative union statistics is in G. S. Bain and R. Price, *Profiles of Union Growth: A Comparative Statistical Portrait of Eight Countries* (Oxford: Basil Blackwell, 1980).

28. See the symposium on European unions and politics in *Industrial and Labor Relations Review* 28, Nos. 1 and 2 (October 1974 and January 1975).

29. But see the series of major publications by the Swedish LO, including T. L. Johnston, ed. and trans., *Economic Expansion and Structural Change: A Trade Union Manifesto* (London: Allen and Unwin, 1963); and Meidner.

30. Kochan, *Collective Bargaining*, Tables 5-1 and 5-2, and for the most detailed analysis, Richard B. Freeman and James L. Medoff, "New Estimates of Private Sector Unionism in the United States," *Industrial and Labor Relations Review* 32 (January 1979).

31. Thus Cohen argues that there has been a public reaction against public-sector unions and denies the argument that they are inherently powerful (Sanford Cohen, "Does Public Sector

Unionism Diminish Democracy?" *Industrial and Labor Relations Review* 32 [January 1979]).

32. It is a moot point as to the effect of union security provisions. Some have argued that the right-to-work laws in some 20 states have had little effect (Frederic Meyers, *Right-to-Work in Practice* [New York: Fund for the Republic, 1959]). But this is rather different from estimating the effect had there never been any union security clause in the Wagner Act. It is also to be noted that a case has been brought before the European Human Rights Court to decide whether the union shop is an infringement of personal liberty and a preliminary hearing has decided that it is (*Industrial Relations Europe* 11 [March 1981], p. 1).

33. The numbers of decertification elections rose from 234 in 1967 to 849 in 1977, and the percentage lost by unions rose from 70.5 percent to 76.0 percent (Kochan, *Collective Bargaining*, p. 140).

34. W. Tillery, "Conventions," *Monthly Labor Review* 101 (March 1978), p. 36.

35. G. S. Bain and F. Elsheikh, *Union Growth and the Business Cycle* (Oxford: Blackwell, 1976); Woodrow L. Ginsburg, "Union Growth, Government, and Structure," in *A Review of Industrial Relations Research*, Vol. 1 (Madison, WI: Industrial Relations Research Association, 1970).

36. The widening of the union differential in periods of recession is a well-observed phenomenon (H. Gregg Lewis, *Unionism and Relative Wages in the United States* [Chicago: University of Chicago Press, 1963]). This result would also follow from union pushfulness (Kochan, *Collective Bargaining*, p. 139).

37. John P. Windmuller, "The Authority of National Trade Union Confederations: A Comparative Analysis," in *Union Power and Public Policy*, David B. Lipsky, ed. (Ithaca: New York State School of Industrial and Labor Relations, Cornell University, 1975).

38. Some of the centers which also ranked low on Windmuller's scale may well have increased their relative ranking since he wrote, in line with the general argument about the increased politicization of industrial relations in recent years. One such example would be the increased involvement of the British TUC in national-level bargaining over wages under the Wilson and Callaghan Labor Governments. (A. W. J. Thomson, "Trade Unions and the Corporate State in Britain," *Industrial and Labor Relations Review* 33 [October 1979], p. 51.)

39. Thomas A. Kochan, "How American Workers View Labor Unions," *Monthly Labor Review* 102 (April 1979); T.V. Purcell, *The Worker Speaks His Mind on Company and Union* (Cambridge, MA: Harvard University Press, 1956).

40. Kochan, *ibid.*

41. The American literature on public-sector bargaining is too voluminous and too well known to require citing. The European literature is much less extensive. See Charles M. Rehmus, ed., *Public Employment Labor Relations: An Overview of Eleven Nations* (Ann Arbor: Institute of Labor and Industrial Relations, University of Michigan-Wayne State University, 1975); J. Schregle, "Labour Relations in the Public Sector," *International Labour Review* (November 1974); A. W. J. Thomson and P. B. Beaumont, *Public Sector Bargaining* (Farnborough: Saxon House, 1978).

42. Benjamin Aaron, ed., *Labor Courts and Grievance Settlement in Western Europe* (Berkeley: University of California Press, 1971).

43. R. W. Fleming, *The Labor Arbitration Process* (Urbana: University of Illinois Press, 1965).

44. *Work in America: Task Force Report for the Secretary of Health, Education, and Welfare* (Cambridge, MA: MIT Press, 1971).

45. Lee Dyer, David Lipsky, and Thomas Kochan, "Union Attitudes to Management Cooperation," *Industrial Relations* 16 (May 1977).

46. Perhaps the most comprehensive review is "Industrial Democracy in International Perspective," *Annals of the American Academy of Political and Social Science* 431 (May 1977). Important American works are P. Blumberg, *Industrial Democracy* (London: Constable, 1968); G. Hunnius, G. Carson, and J. Case, eds., *Workers Control* (New York: Vintage Books, 1973).

47. Proposal for a Fifth Directive on the Structure of Limited Liability Companies (EEC Doc. COM 172/887 fin, 1972).

48. *Report of the Committee of Inquiry on Industrial Democracy*, Chairman Lord Bullock (London: HMSO Cmnd 6706, 1977); Rapport du Comite d'Etude pour la Reforme de l'Enterprise, Chairman Pierre Sudreau (Paris: La Documentation Francaise, 1975).

49. H. G. Myrdal, "The Swedish Model—Will It Survive?" *British Journal of Industrial Relations* 18 (March 1980).

50. Clegg, p. 83.

51. Quoted in John T. Dunlop, "Past and Future Tendencies in American Labor Organizations," *Daedalus* 107 (Winter 1978), p. 91.

52. Derek Bok, "Reflections on the Distinctive Character of American Labor Law," *Harvard Law Review* 84 (April 1971).

53. *Ibid.*, p. 1462.

54. ILO, *Collective Bargaining*. In some respects individual rights and union rights merge in that the expression of individual rights can sometimes be vested in unions (M. Moran, "Citizens and Workers," *Political Quarterly* 50 [January-March 1979]). Moran has also argued that the expansion of industrial rights has been such as to place them on a par with the individual's political, civil, and social rights. It should also be noted that in Europe the changing balance between legal regulation and collective bargaining has not all been in the direction of the former; the gain for collective bargaining has been particularly true of France (Reynaud, p. 70).

55. Kochan, *Collective Bargaining*, p. 478.

56. Barbash, p. 193.

57. Quoted in Kochan, *Collective Bargaining*, p. 430.

58. See the section on "Bargaining Structure," above.

59. Institute of the German Economy, *Wage Costs in Manufacturing Industry*, 1979.

60. *Ibid.*

61. C. Brown and J. Medoff, "Trade Unions in the Production Process," *Journal of Political Economy* 86 (June 1978).

62. Sumner Slichter, James Healy, and E. Robert Livernash, *The Impact of Collective Bargaining on Management* (Washington: The Brookings Institution, 1960).

63. A. Ross and P. Hartman, *Changing Patterns of Industrial Conflict* (New York: Wiley, 1960); D. Hibbs, "Industrial Conflict in Advanced Societies," *American Political Science Review* 70 (December 1976); D. Snyder, "Institutional Setting and Industrial Conflict," *American Sociological Review* 40 (June 1975); Shalev.

64. For the costs, see Neil W. Chamberlain, "Strikes in Contemporary Context," *Industrial and Labor Relations Review* 20 (July 1967).

65. See, for example, *Business Week*, June 30, 1980.

66. *Industrial and Labor Relations Review* Symposium (note 41); for the United States, the most recent book on the political role of unions is G. K. Wilson, *Unions in American National Politics* (London: Macmillan, 1979).

67. Wilson, *ibid*.

68. Bok and Dunlop, p. 485.

69. Peter J. Pestillo, "Learning to Live Without the Union," in *Proceedings of the 31st Annual Meeting, Industrial Relations Research Association*, 1978, p. 233.

49

The Coming Scientific Society

MICHEL PONIATOWSKI

The thesis of my book is that all the certainties of the industrial society in which we live are disintegrating. We are witnessing an erosion of ideologies, economic theories, and traditional culture. That is because all our assumptions, all our theories and religions come from the 19th century, from an industrial period that is approaching its end. Marxism and capitalism, for example, are 19th-century doctrines, each intended as the driving force of a system that no longer corresponds to the prevailing economy or to the scientific age now being ushered in.

Why this change?

Two hundred years ago we moved from an agricultural to an industrial era. The industrial society was achieved by maximizing human and animal might through the use of machines powered by fossil fuels. Today we are

---

Michel Poniatowski, Minister of the Interior under former French President Valéry Giscard d'Estaing, a member of the European Parliament and author of *History Is Free* (1982), interviewed by Jacques Wiame for the newsmagazine *Pourquoi Pas?* of Brussels and translated in *World Press Review* (October, 1982), pp. 23-25. Reprinted by permission of *World Press Review*.

moving from an industrial to a scientific society marked by computerized information and telecommunications and by a technology ranging from the laser to nuclear power and robotics.

The computer has a capacity for analysis, synthesis, and memory that expands man's intellectual capacity. Today's more sophisticated computers provide some answers that we do not yet understand, because specialized scientists—such as chemists and physicists—live in compartmentalized worlds. It is now possible to feed into a computer a whole range of basic knowledge, whereas the individual scholar has only a sectoral grasp of a problem. The answers the computer gives him take into account all the data, while he is knowledgeable only in his particular field of competence.

All the technological discoveries of the scientific era, from nuclear power to robotics, derive from the insights of Albert Einstein—from the theory of relativity and the quantum physics of 1930-35. Today's major strides in nonlogical physics take the theory of relativity a step further. Einstein defined the relativity of time and space; nonlogical physics defines the relativity of objects. Everything becomes relative, not only time and space but the object contemplated in relation to time and space. That means that two plus two no longer equal four but always more than four, something more than the truth.

Another aspect of the change is speed. In an industrial society the results and applications of a discovery evolve slowly. Photography was discovered in the 19th century; it took many decades to improve upon the discovery, and we are still at it today. It took 160 years to advance from the early railroads to the high-speed train.

Is the time for applying a discovery shrinking?

Yes. The first computer was developed by an IBM team in 1944; we are already working on fifth-generation (Japanese) computers. The first workable rockets, Wernher Von Braun's V-1 and V-2, were launched in 1942: we reached the moon in 1969, only twenty-seven years later. The first nuclear fission was produced in 1942; today we are approaching the final stage of nuclear fusion, which will come in a few years. In the relatively new field of biogenetics we have already begun mixing genes from living animal and vegetable species. All this acceleration has happened thanks to computerized information, the great accelerator in a scientific society.

I wonder to what degree the human community in rapid succession can continue to assimilate these shocks, each of which is a challenge to the mind. We must adapt to advances in science and technology. In the industrial age the shocks were slow and adapting to them meant hardships, rejections, crises, and revolutions. Revolutions were characteristic of societies lagging in technology and industry.

Industrial society was mass-oriented: mass production, mass consumption, mass services, mass housing, mass transfers. In the scientific age that trend is being reversed. Companies are being virtually emptied of their working people, who are replaced by robots and machines. I have observed robotization in Japan, and it is now on Europe's threshold. Management uses sophisticated equipment and investments geared to specialized goals.

Even consumption is becoming individualized. The manufacture of suits, for instance, can be personalized through computers. Similarly, medical care is becoming increasingly personal. Research under way on DNA will make it possible to receive preventive care tailored to genetic makeup.

Another example is the fifth-generation computers now being developed. The fourth type, the Large Scale International System (LSI), has a great capacity for storing the full range of basic knowledge—which can be tapped through your own computer, endowing it with an extraordinary access to data and processing capacity. The fifth-generation computer does something different. It is linked to microphones and installed in your home. It will then perform myriad tasks, from drawing up your shopping list to booking your airline tickets, because it can reason by analogy.

How will it work?

The computer will record everything you say to your family or friends in telephone conversations. It will file away all these words and phrases, and you will be able to consult it on any problem you may have. It will answer in terms of everything it knows about you, including your personal feelings. You will be able to ask questions bordering on the intimate—about your health and your subconscious, for example. This is likely to come by 1990. The Americans and the Japanese are racing to see who will have this gadget first. It may seem unthinkable, but so did the fourth generation of computers ten years ago.

Will the scientific era bring profound changes in society as we know it?

In the industrial age power stemmed from privileged information—company secrets or state secrets. From now on things will be different. Computerized knowledge will become public knowledge. There will be such extensive ways of checking on those in power that, in my opinion, decision-making will have to be broadened. In *History Is Free* I say, "The state will have to slim down or die." Computerized information will place decision-making under intense scrutiny, and will be decentralized.

Could some accident of history, such as a third world war, interrupt this trend?

I do not believe that one country can master the world. The super-powers, with their combined population of 480 million, cannot control a world of 7 billion. And they have no stake in trying, because that would disperse their strength. Imagine a country trying to take charge of Pakistan or Bangladesh; it would sap its resources.

The superpowers are trying to get strategic footholds and strike a balance in their relations. At this point the game consists of destabilizing the other side by acquiring influence or using terrorism. Even the Soviet Union would pay with its soul for trying to occupy Western Europe.

What will be the legacy of the industrial era?

The moving forces behind industrial civilization—Marxism and capitalism—are completely outdated on the eve of the scientific era. A totally different kind of thinking is emerging. The legacy of the industrial era has no place either in our reasoning or in our way of perceiving political life.

There is another problem in store. Societies and countries that refuse to adapt to technology will become increasingly disaffected. But man is a biological being; we came from a cell that appeared on earth billions of years ago. We went through stages of evolution until we became a species. All of those stages are inscribed in the structure of our spines and brains.

It is fascinating that each human, from conception to birth, repeats the whole history of the species: the single cell, the reptilian structure, the mammalian structure, the hominid structure, and on reaching the human stage he is born. That is why we are so biological, so animal. And in our animal nature there is a vital force that compels us to live, to defend life, to multiply, to extend life.

At some point man grew aware of his aspiration to a supernatural life, a spiritual force that accompanies the life force. I think there is a danger in divorcing the life force from our spiritual aspirations. Some great religions have made the mistake of trying to subordinate the life force to the spiritual. What comes naturally to us is a balance, a harmony between the two. The danger is great because human nature rests on this balance between body and soul.

Another danger arises when the spiritual force loses touch with its origins. Biological man was essentially in his element in agricultural society. Man's physical world, his systems, his body, even his religions were harmonious parts of that agricultural way of life. Industrial life plunged man into a semi-artificial world, and there is a question whether he is happy in it.

The religions that have remained vigorous are agricultural religions. Islam is strong because it is a religion of the agriculture era, and because it is still living and growing in countries where agriculture predominates. Traditional religions placed in an industrial setting have withered. In the scientific era the danger will lie in our moving even farther from our roots.

Will the scientific era have its have-nots?

Experts who study that issue say that in a scientific society some 20 percent of the people will be left out of the mainstream because they will be unable to adapt. In that society man will be both lonelier and part of a much larger crowd. His crowd will be his village—and all the technological instruments driving home the fact that he lives on a single, small planet.